Behavior Disorders
of Children
and Adolescents

third edition

Behavior Disorders of Children and Adolescents

Assessment, Etiology, and Intervention

Marilyn T. Erickson

Virginia Commonwealth University

PRENTICE HALL, Upper Saddle River, New Jersey 07458

Library of Congress Cataloging-in-Publication Data

ERICKSON, MARILYN T.
    Behavior disorders of children and adolescents : assessment,
etiology, and intervention / Marilyn T. Erickson.
        p.   cm.
    Includes bibliographical references and index.
    ISBN 0-13-649187-1
    1. Behavior disorders in children.   2. Developmental disabilities.
3. Child psychiatry.   4. Adolescent psychiatry.   I. Title.
    [DNLM: 1. Child Behavior Disorders.   2. Adolescent Behavior.
3. Child Development Disorders, Pervasive.   4. Risk Factors.
5. Psychotherapy—in infancy & childhood.   WS 350.6 E686   1997]
RJ506.B44E75 1997
618.92'89—dc21
DNLM/DLC
for Library of Congress   97-19787
                                                            CIP

Editor-in-Chief: Nancy Roberts
Acquisitions Editor: Bill Webber
Director of Production and Manufacturing: Barbara Kittle
Senior Managing Editor: Bonnie Biller
Production Editor: Randy Pettit
Manufacturing Manager: Nick Sklitsis
Prepress and Manufacturing Buyer: Tricia Kenny
Director of Marketing: Gina Sluss
Marketing Manager: Michael Alread
Cover Design: Bruce Kenselaar

This book was set in 10/12 Baskerville by DM Cradle Associates
and printed and bound by R.R. Donnelley & Sons Company.
The cover was printed by Phoenix Color Corp.

© 1998 by Prentice Hall, Inc.
Upper Saddle River, NJ 07458

Printed in the United States of America
10 9 8 7 6 5 4 3

ISBN   0-13-649187-1

Prentice-Hall International (UK) Limited, *London*
Prentice-Hall of Australia Pty. Limited, *Sydney*
Prentice-Hall of Canada, Inc., *Toronto*
Prentice-Hall Hispanoamericana, S. A., *Mexico*
Prentice-Hall of India Private Limited, *New Delhi*
Prentice-Hall of Japan, Inc., *Tokyo*
Pearson Education Asia Pte. Ltd., *Singapore*
Editora Prentice-Hall do Brasil, Ltda., *Rio de Janeiro*

To my sons
Lars, Nils, and **David**
who continue to enrich my life

Contents

Preface

The purpose of this book is to introduce undergraduate and beginning graduate students to the developmental and behavior problems of children and adolescents, as well as to the clinical methods for assessing and treating these problems. The primary goal is to present an overview that relates past and present trends to future directions; thus the book contains a variety of theoretical and clinical approaches to children's psychological problems. Another goal is to discuss the methods used to obtain information about children's development and behavior problems and also the difficulties of evaluating and interpreting this information. The final goal is to familiarize students with the major types of children's psychological problems as related to their assessment, etiology, and treatment.

The first half of the book contains general information about assessment methods, theories and research on etiology, and approaches to treatment. The second half contains comparable specific information that has been obtained about children and adolescents with specific types of behavior problems. The student should be aware that the population of children and adolescents with behavior disorders may be subdivided in a variety of ways; the diagnostic system used in this book is based primarily on the fourth edition of the *Diagnostic and Statistical Manual of Mental Disorders*.

For this third edition, several of my current and former doctoral students agreed to join me in revising and updating the book. I am especially appreciative of their significant and timely contributions: chapters 2 and 3—Teresa Parr, M.S., Clinical Psychology Intern, University of North Carolina School of Medicine; and Barry Rand, M.S., Clinical Psychology Intern, Hall Institute, University of South Carolina School of Medicine; chapters 6 and 7—Lyn Vinnick, Ph.D., Assistant Professor of Clinical Psychology in Psychiatry, Columbia University College of Medicine; chapter 8—Beth Wildman, Ph.D., Associate Professor, Psychology Department, Kent State University; chapter 9—Andrew Bondy, Ph.D., Director,

Delaware Autism Program & President, Pyramid Educational Consultants; chapter 10—Sharon Carmanico, Ph.D., Staff Psychologist, Virginia Learning Centers; chapter 11—Cassandra Stanton, M.S., Clinical Child Psychology doctoral student, Virginia Commonwealth University; chapter 13—Joni McKeeman, Ph.D., Clinical Assistant Professor, Pediatrics Department, University of North Carolina School of Medicine; chapter 14—Anthony Spirito, Ph.D., Associate Professor, Psychiatry Department, Brown University School of Medicine; and Emily Smith Rappold, Ph.D., Coordinator of Training, Mental Health Center, Gallaudet University.

Most books require an extended period of devotion by the author, and this one is no exception, having been written in parallel with the many other activities of academic life. In a larger perspective, however, an author's work is the result of a much longer history of contact with the research literature and interactions with specific individuals. I am particularly indebted to Lewis Lipsitt, Judy Rosenblith, Harrie Chamberlin, and the late John Hill for their lasting influences as mentors and colleagues.

—Marilyn T. Erickson

Behavior Disorders
of Children
and Adolescents

1

Introduction

The study of children's behavior disorders is largely a twentieth-century phenomenon. Descriptions of children's abnormal behavior did appear sporadically in the writings of the eighteenth and nineteenth centuries, but disordered behavior was viewed as primarily reflecting some inherent evil in the afflicted person. The role of early childhood experience in the etiology of behavior problems was not formally recognized until the advent of psychoanalytic theory. With the exception of mentally retarded children, concentrated study of children with behavior disorders did not occur until the 1930s. Many changes in society contributed to the new focus on children's problems: greatly decreased childhood mortality rates, the introduction of educational opportunities for all children, the development of psychological treatment for adult problems, the development of methods for measuring human behavior, and the accumulation of data describing children's growth and behavior.

Knowledge of the behavioral repertoires of children at different ages was a crucial prerequisite to the study of child psychopathology. The child development researchers of the 1920s and 1930s initiated the first large-scale studies of behavior using both longitudinal and cross-sectional approaches. The longitudinal approach involved the periodic observation of the same children from infancy throughout their developmental period. The cross-sectional approach utilized different groups of children at each age level. Both approaches have provided a critical foundation for judging the normality or abnormality of children's behavior.

Reliance on the norms of behavior has not been universally accepted by professionals who deal with children's problems. Some clinicians prefer to use personal standards for judging whether or not a behavior is abnormal, and some rely almost exclusively on the judgments of the adults who complain about the child's behavior. Lack of reference to norms, however, can result in a child's behavior being diagnosed as abnormal when it, in fact, is not significantly different from that of same-aged children.

THE CLINICAL PROFESSIONS

Several professional disciplines have been involved in the assessment and treatment of children's behavior problems. In the early child guidance clinics, three professionals, the child psychiatrist, the clinical child psychologist, and the social worker, provided the services for the child and the parents. Initially, their activities were complementary. The psychologist administered and interpreted tests; the psychiatrist interviewed the family members and later treated the child; and the social worker counseled the parents. Through the years, changes in the training programs created an overlap in the clinical skills of these professions. Clinical psychologists, for example, are now trained to conduct the diagnostic interview as well as to administer and interpret a broad spectrum of tests and much of the psychologists' training also focuses on treatment techniques. Thus, to a large extent, the skills of clinical psychologists and psychiatrists in assessment and treatment are comparable. The principal differences between psychiatrists and clinical psychologists lie in the medical training of the former, which prepares the psychiatrist to diagnose physical problems and to use medication in treatment.

In this section, we describe the characteristics of training programs and educational requirements for clinical psychologists, psychiatrists, and other professionals involved in the assessment and treatment of children's behavior problems.

Clinical Psychology

Clinical psychologists are trained primarily in university departments of psychology and receive the Ph.D. or Psy.D. degree upon completion of the program, which usually takes about five years. During this time the graduate student takes courses in the theoretical and applied aspects of psychological principles and receives supervised experience in assessment and treatment. Most clinical psychology doctoral programs prepare students both to do research and to provide clinical services.[1] Research training is considered to be necessary for several

---

[1]Doctor of Psychology (Psy.D.) programs emphasize the practitioner role and deemphasize training in research.

reasons: (1) to provide the clinician with the skills to evaluate the research literature, (2) to emphasize the importance of research in the advancement of the field, and (3) to encourage and provide the background for conducting research on clinical problems. A large number of Ph.D. clinical psychologists are employed in positions in community clinics, institutions, and private practice that involve the delivery of assessment and treatment services to clients. Other clinical psychologists join the faculties of university psychology departments or medical schools where they teach courses, supervise students, and conduct research.

Training programs in clinical psychology emphasize clinical work with adults and vary greatly in their training resources for students who plan to work with children and their parents. Only a few programs specialize in the training of clinical child psychologists or have close relationships with child development programs whereby the student can acquire a comprehensive understanding of children. Efforts are continually being made to establish guidelines for the training of professional psychologists who deliver services to children (Roberts, Erickson, & Tuma, 1985; Roberts et al. 1997). Such guidelines are very important to assure the public that professional child psychologists are at least minimally qualified to provide clinical services to children. The December issues of the *American Psychologist* provide annual listings of APA-accredited doctoral programs and internships.

Doctoral training programs in clinical psychology may be accredited by the American Psychological Association (APA). APA accreditation indicates that the training programs meet certain requirements. During the period of graduate study, one year is devoted to a clinical internship. APA accreditation is also available for internship training that takes place in settings such as community mental health clinics, university medical centers, and institutions.

Doctoral level clinical psychologists are not the only professional psychologists offering clinical services. Counseling and school psychologists, whose training programs (also eligible for APA accreditation) may be in either departments of psychology or in schools of education, also provide assessment and therapeutic services for children and adolescents. In addition, a large number of master's degree level professionals in clinical, school, and counseling psychology are employed by agencies, clinics, and schools. The APA does not grant full membership to master's level psychologists or accredit master's degree programs.

Psychiatry

Psychiatry is one of the medical specialties; intensive training in psychiatry begins only after the student completes undergraduate and medical school programs, each of which takes about four years. In medical school the student is given a curriculum in the basic sciences and small amounts of supervised clinical experience in many of the medical specialties, including psychiatry. Intensive training in a medical specialty is called a *residency* and is usually based in the appropriate clinical department of a medical school. Many residency training programs affiliate with community facilities, such as clinics, hospitals, and institutions, and these settings are thereby also available for the training of residents.

Residency training programs in psychiatry require two years of supervised experience working primarily with adults after the one year internship. Residents who are interested in focusing on the problems of children spend an additional two years as Child Psychiatry fellows gaining supervised experience with children and their parents. Departments of psychiatry typically employ clinical psychologists and social workers who also contribute to the training of residents.

The goal of the residency in psychiatry is to train the student to provide diagnostic and treatment services for a broad spectrum of behavioral problems. The goal is achieved through seminars and direct experience with a variety of patients. Supervision of the resident's activities with patients usually involves the trainee's describing the interactions during a session or playing a tape recording of portions of the session while the experienced clinician (supervisor) makes suggestions about the resident-patient interactions. Occasionally, the resident may have the opportunity to observe experienced clinicians conducting interviews or providing treatment or doing both. Supervision may be conducted on a one-to-one basis, or several residents may meet weekly with a supervisor to share their training and experiences.

A small number of psychiatrists supplement their therapeutic skills by enrolling in a psychoanalytic institute. Completion of the course of study, which is usually pursued part-time over a number of years, allows the therapist to be called a *psychoanalyst.* The training includes seminars, the psychoanalysis of several patients under the supervision of an experienced psychoanalyst, and a personal pyschoanalysis. Psychoanalytic institutes may accept candidates who do not have medical training. A person without an M.D. degree who has completed training in psychoanalysis is called a *lay analyst.*

Other Professions

In addition to psychology and psychiatry, members of other professional disciplines provide services for children with behavior problems. Social workers, for example, have a long history of helping parents to cope with children's problems. The master's degree in social work is the principal academic degree and is awarded after two years of coursework and supervised clinical experience. A few universities offer the Ph.D. in social work, but the recipients of the doctoral degree usually go into teaching, research, and administrative positions.

Other specialists in medicine (pediatricians, neurologists, and general practitioners, for example) are often called upon to evaluate and recommend treatment for children with behavior disorders. Physicians are trained primarily in the physical aspects of children's problems but are also expected by parents to provide advice on a wide variety of behavior problems. Medical school and residency training programs vary greatly in the emphasis placed on normal and abnormal child behaviors, and many physicians must rely heavily on their own clinical experience with children to provide advice to parents on behavioral problems.

Most of the remaining professions providing services for children with developmental and learning problems require at least master's degree level training. Other professionals currently involved in some aspect of assessment and/or treatment of children's behavior disorders include special educators, physical therapists, occupational therapists, nursing specialists, nutritionists, speech pathologists, and rehabilitation counselors.

RESEARCH APPROACHES TO UNDERSTANDING CHILDREN'S BEHAVIOR PROBLEMS

It is generally agreed that the goal of behavioral science is to acquire knowledge that will enable us to predict and control behavior. In the specific case of children's behavior disorders, the ultimate goals are to develop effective treatment procedures and to prevent problems through a complete understanding of the factors that cause these problems. As you will learn in the remaining chapters of this book, our knowledge falls far short of these goals, although significant progress in some areas has been made.

The quality of scientific knowledge depends on both the creativity of the investigator and the research strategy employed in the collection of data. The creative component of this equation is not well understood but basically consists of ideas or hypotheses about relationships among variables. The sources of these hypotheses may be determined by previously acquired knowledge in one area or in more than one related area of study and direct observation of phenomena. The highest level of scientific creativity is reflected by theory that states general principles about relationships among variables and provides testable hypotheses. Although relatively few scientific investigators have created theories, most of them work within a theoretical system and design their research to test specific hypotheses. Creativity is often also a significant component in research methodology (for example, in choosing measuring instruments, apparatus, and specific procedures). It is through the continuous interweaving of creativity and research strategy that new knowledge is acquired.

Our understanding of children's behavior disorders has come from a variety of sources ranging from descriptive studies to experimental research. Each of the research strategies has made unique contributions to our knowledge, but each also has certain disadvantages or problems associated with it. In addition, the history of psychology suggests that the various research strategies are mutually dependent and that no single one can provide all of the necessary information.

Descriptive Studies

Fundamental to the acquisition of scientific knowledge is description of the phenomenon of interest. Descriptions of behavior, normal and abnormal, may take many forms. For example, the earliest sources of information about the developmental progression of young children may be found in the "baby biographies," which are narrative descriptions of individual children's behaviors, in most instances recorded by their psychologist-parents (Kessen, Haith, & Salapatek, 1970, p. 299). Biographical accounts of behavior offer a richness of description not attained by other methods of study and have provided a fund of information for investigators who have subsequently applied more systematic research methods in the collection of data. For instance, the early baby biographies depicted the regularity and timing of developmental changes and most probably contributed to later studies on the development of large groups of children. The biographical approach, however, does present serious problems for the researcher seeking general principles of behavior. The reliability of the biography is questionable in that the parent-biographers might have biases that distort the data. Moreover, the biographers vary their organization of the data and attention given to specific behaviors and therefore preclude any direct comparisons among the biographies. These particular problems have been solved to a large extent by the development of standardized procedures in the collection of behavioral data.

The studies that have provided us with normative data on the developing child (behavioral abilities of children of different ages) have used several variations of the descriptive approach, including narrative accounts by parents during interviews, description based on observed behavior, ratings of behavior by parents, teachers, and researchers, and scores on specific tasks or tests. Statistical analysis of narrative descriptions requires the intervening step of someone rating the written description on a psychological dimension, such as aggression.

In order for investigators to make statements with reference to groups of children and to compare individual children to other children of the same age, all data have to be classified or quantified (reduced to numbers), or both. A variety of methods, therefore, have been developed for translating narrative description into numerical description. At the simplest level, a child might be scored on whether a particular behavior is present or absent. Because observers do not necessarily agree on the definitions of specific behaviors or concepts encompassing multiple behaviors, investigators began to use *operational definitions*, which are exact descriptions of the behavior or characteristic being assessed. Operational definitions of behavior are exemplified in psychological testing in which the behavioral criteria for passing or failing are clearly designated in the test manual. Operational definitions ensure that each child is being rated or scored on the basis of the same criteria.

Describing the performance of groups of children usually involves two statistical measures: a measure of central tendency, which represents all of the scores in the group; and a measure of variability within a set of scores. The most frequently used measure of central tendency is the *mean*, the arithmetic average of the scores. Among the available measures of variability, the *standard deviation* is most often reported in psychological research studies. The standard deviation is particularly useful because it provides an objective method for determining whether an individual score is unusually high or low by showing how far it is from the mean.

In general, descriptive studies have focused on the assessment and comparison of behaviors as a function of the child's age, gender, or socioeconomic level. These demographic variables, of course, cannot be designated as having caused differences in behavior and are better conceptualized as correlates of behavior differences. Behavioral differences between males and females, for example, may be the result of differences in child-rearing patterns *or* of genetic and other biological differences *or* of varying combinations of biological and environmental differences.

Although descriptive studies of behavior rarely provide direct evidence of cause-effect relationships, they have been invaluable for providing hypotheses and theories regarding factors that may cause differences in behavior. In many ways, the clinical assessment of a child with behavior problems parallels descriptive research. The clinician accumulates a large amount of information about the child and subsequently forms hypotheses about the factors that may be responsible for the child's problems. The clinician has no way of knowing with certainty what the critical factors have been and, therefore, relies on a combination of previous clinical experience, knowledge of the research literature, and descriptive information about the child to derive hypotheses about the nature of the problem and the treatment methods that might be effective.

Correlational Studies

Correlational studies represent a second approach to the understanding of behavior. In comparison with descriptive studies in which behavior is simply described or presented as a function of demographic variables, correlational studies measure the extent to which two or more variables may be related to one another. In the typical correlational study, data on at least two characteristics or variables are collected from or about each individual within a group. Examples might be test scores on two types of tests: parents' attitudes on child rearing and children's social behavior; ratings of problems during pregnancy and child behavior ratings at three years of age. The sets of scores are subjected to statistical analysis, which summarizes the relationship of these scores in a correlation coefficient that may range from +1.0 through 0 to −1.0. A +1.0 correlation indicates a perfect positive relationship between the two sets of scores—a high score on one variable is invariably related to a high score on the other variable. A −1.0 correlation indicates a perfect negative relationship between the two sets of scores—a high score on one variable is invariably related to a low score on the other variable. In both of these instances, knowledge of a person's score on one variable permits optimal prediction of that person's score on the second variable. A correlation coefficient of zero indicates that there is no relationship between the variables. In practice, it is rare to find either perfect positive or negative correlations between psychological variables. Rather, the majority of correlational studies report values that are less than perfect but that are different from zero. The size of the correlation is evaluated in terms of the probability that it could have been obtained by chance. The statistical significance of a correlation is substantially influenced by the number of individuals from whom the data were obtained; that is, relatively low correlations (closer to zero) may reach statistical significance when large numbers of participants (several hundred or more) are involved in the study.

Unfortunately, correlational studies frequently lend themselves to misinterpretation. The greatest misinterpretation is that a high correlational relationship necessarily implies a cause-effect relationship between the variables. It is important to remember that correlational studies only reflect the extent to which two variables are related; they *may* indeed be causally related, but there is always the possibility that a third (unmeasured) variable is causing the changes in the two measured variables. In many psychological studies, no decision with respect to these alternatives can be made without further investigation.

Correlational studies have provided us with a substantial amount of our knowledge about children's behavior disorders. They have been particularly valuable in providing hypotheses regarding the variables that may be implicated in the etiology of behavior problems. In addition, correlational research provides the foundation for many of our assessment methods. For example, the reliability of psychological tests may be measured by correlating the scores obtained on the first administration of a test with scores obtained on a second administration (test-retest reliability) or correlating scores on one half of a test with scores on the other half of the test (split-half reliability). Since tests must be reliable to be useful, high correlations (.8 to .9) are required for a test to be considered reliable. Another example of the use of correlation in evaluating assessment methods is the determination of the amount of agreement between ratings of behavior by two observers. Just as in the case of psychological tests, behavioral ratings must be demonstrated to be reliable by high correlations; that is, the independent ratings of two observers must be in agreement before that method of assessing the behavior is considered to be reliable.

Experimental Studies

Experimental studies also examine the relationships among variables, but they possess the asset of giving us better information about cause-effect relationships. In the simplest case, an experimental study evaluates the relationship between an independent variable and a dependent variable. The *independent* variable is usually some aspect of the participants' environment (e.g., type of treatment) that the researcher varies or manipulates, and it includes several experimental conditions. Participants are randomly assigned to the different experimental conditions to control for individual differences among the participants due to biological factors and prior history. That is, random assignment tends to make the groups more similar or comparable to one another at the beginning of the study. After the participants have experienced their respective experimental conditions, the researcher obtains data on the *dependent* variable, a measure of the participants' response or behavior.

Let us consider an example in which a researcher wishes to evaluate the effect of two forms of treatment on children with a specific type of behavior disorder. In this example, the researcher would probably include what is called a *control group*, that is, a group that did not receive either of the two forms of treatment. The independent variable, then, would be type of treatment and would be applied to three groups of children: two groups receiving different forms of treatment and one control group. Individual children with the behavior disorder would be randomly assigned to one of the three groups. After the treatment phase had been completed, the same behavioral measure of the dependent variable would be obtained for each child in each group. The dependent variable in this case could be a direct evaluation of behavior through observation or ratings of the child's behavior by parents or teachers. The scores or ratings for the children within each group would be combined and described in terms of means and standard deviations. Statistical analysis of these data would determine the extent to which any differences among the groups were due to chance or random variability. In psychological research, differences among groups that might occur by chance five or fewer times out of one hundred are considered to be statistically significant. That is, when the probability is very low (5 percent or less) that the differences among groups occurred by chance, there is general consensus that the differences in group scores were most likely due to the different experimental conditions.

There are many possible variations of the basic experimental design. For example, more than one independent and/or dependent variable may be included. In addition, experimental designs are not confined to groups but may be used with individuals. Chapter 6 provides a description of the experimental designs currently being used to evaluate the treatment of individuals.

Experimental studies require a number of safeguards or precautions to prevent the validity of the data from being jeopardized. Expectations or hypotheses on the part of experimenters or observers may, for example, influence the accuracy of the data. It is often necessary, therefore, for the person collecting the data not to know the group to which the subject has been assigned because such knowledge may bias the behavior ratings in favor of one group or another.

Because experimental studies involve doing something to or for subjects, they lend themselves to greater concerns about ethical issues than do descriptive or correlational studies. Much experimental research on the causes of children's behavior problems, for example, cannot be conducted because injury or potential harm to the subjects might occur. In some instances, similar experimental research might be conducted with animals, but in other instances our information is necessarily confined to the findings of observational and correlational studies. Both alternatives often result in knowledge that is incomplete.

Most experimental research cannot be clearly divided into "harmful" and "beneficial" categories. Although the researcher may believe that a particular treatment could be of benefit to clients, it may not be so. For this and other reasons, researchers usually submit their research plans to ethics committees for appraisal and then obtain "informed consent" from research participants. Informed consent includes the participant's signing a paper that designates that the participant has been informed about the procedures and goals of the study. In the case of children, informed consent must be obtained from the parents or guardians.

CONCLUSIONS

A variety of professional disciplines provide services and conduct research on children's behavior disorders. Although there is some overlap in their clinical skills, professionals in the various disciplines tend to complement one another in their capacities to assess and treat children with behavior problems.

Our knowledge about children's behavior disorders has been derived primarily from descriptive, correlational, and experimental research studies. Descriptive and correlational studies have been invaluable in providing hypotheses about cause-effect relationships with respect to the etiology and treatment of children's behavior disorders. Experimental studies provide the direct tests of these hypotheses and are our best source of understanding causal relationships.

2

Diagnostic and Assessment Methods

Part I

Assessment refers to the collection of information about a child's behavior problem and the evaluation of that information to determine the possible relevant factors with respect to its cause or maintenance, or both aspects of the problem. In addition, assessment information is used in the designing of the treatment/intervention program.

A variety of methods have been devised to assess the behavior problems of children. The range of available techniques reflects the fact that professionals from several disciplines have been responsible for the assessment of children's behavior problems. The professionals most often called upon to assess these problems are physicians (particularly psychiatrists, pediatricians, and neurologists), psychologists, and educators. Members of some disciplines are more competent than those of other disciplines in the use of specific assessment procedures. Although most

This chapter was revised by Teresa Parr and Barry Rand.

children with behavior problems are examined and diagnosed by a single professional, there has been a strong movement toward interdisciplinary diagnosis, a procedure involving the combination of information derived from the assessment methods of two or more disciplines. The typical child guidance clinic, for example, usually has a child psychiatrist, clinical psychologist, and social worker on each diagnostic team. A number of federally funded training programs affiliated with universities have as many as a dozen or more disciplines represented on a diagnostic team. These larger diagnostic teams are able to assess in greater depth the child's physical, neurological, developmental, and psychological status as well as the effects of past and current environmental factors.

There is considerable controversy regarding the efficiency of assessment methods and the problems resulting from the labeling of children. The principal goal of assessment and diagnosis is to determine what form of treatment should be initiated to alleviate the problem. Unfortunately, a system that accomplishes that goal has not yet been developed for children's behavior problems. Clinicians have not been able to agree on the diagnostic labels that are appropriate for children's problems or the exact criteria for the use of particular labels. Much of the difficulty resides in the inconsistency of labels; some describe an assumed internal psychological state, others describe current behaviors, and still others describe etiological factors. In recent years, several attempts have been made to improve the diagnostic criteria used in the labeling of children's behavior problems.

You may ask why labeling or formal diagnosis is necessary. Your question is heard by a growing number of psychologists who feel that the labels currently used, such as mental retardation and neurosis, do not facilitate the choice of treatment and may, in fact, result in psychological harm to children because of the reactions of other people, such as relatives, teachers, and friends, to the labels. On the other hand, clinicians need labels for purposes of communication, a kind of shorthand in lieu of extended descriptions of behavior and etiological factors. These abbreviated descriptions have been used as a way of grouping children with behavior disorders and of separating children whose problems are believed to be of different origins.

Most clinicians agree that the primary purpose of classification is to improve communication among clinicians rather than to facilitate the understanding of a particular child's problems. Clinicians are aware that no label can adequately describe all the nuances of a particular child's behavior or environment. Although labels are meant to group children according to common characteristics, they are sometimes used incorrectly to draw inferences about other characteristics. That is, the usefulness of labels has tended to be undermined by those who make inferences about children's characteristics that are less than perfectly correlated with the particular diagnostic label. For example, a diagnosis of mental retardation could be inferred to mean that the child is incapable of learning to read, and reading instruction may be denied to the child. The inference would probably be drawn from the observation that the percentage of children who did not learn to read with conventional instruction is higher for retarded than normal groups. Such an inference is clearly incorrect. Many retarded children do, in fact, learn to read. Also, the technology of teaching is continually improving and will no doubt result in greater numbers of retarded children learning to read in the future. Inferences focusing on lack of performance tend only to ensure that the performance will continue to be lacking (this is the self-fulfilling prophecy).

The available diagnostic or classification systems used by clinicians tend to delimit the available choices. Although it is possible to defer diagnosis or to conclude that none of the labels is appropriate, clinicians tend to choose the one label in the system that best fits the child's problem. This situation deserves careful consideration because some children may be labeled inaccurately if no adequate label is available in the system.

This chapter and the next one review the procedures typically used by clinicians in the assessment of children's behavior disorders: the interview, standardized psychological tests, rating scales, and behavioral observation. The principal classification system in use today is discussed throughout these two chapters; therefore, a description of this system is included before turning to specific assessment procedures.

CURRENT CLASSIFICATION SYSTEM

The classification and labeling of children's behavior problems have a long history with origins in both education and medicine, particularly psychiatry. The principal classification system in use today is contained in the *Diagnostic and Statistical Manual of Mental Disorders: Fourth Edition* (DSM-IV; American Psychiatric Association, 1994). The DSM-IV specifies that each client be evaluated on the basis of five axes:

Axis I	Clinical Syndromes and Other Conditions That May Be a Focus of Clinical Attention
Axis II	Personality Disorders and Mental Retardation
Axis III	Physical Disorders and Conditions
Axis IV	Psychosocial and Environmental Problems
Axis V	Global Assessment of Functioning

The major categories of Axis I that are likely to apply to children and adolescents are:

Disorders Usually First Evident in Infancy, Childhood, or Adolescence
Substance-Related Disorders
Schizophrenia and Other Psychotic Disorders
Mood Disorders
Anxiety Disorders
Eating Disorders
Sleep Disorders
Adjustment Disorders

The Disorders Usually First Evident in Infancy, Childhood, or Adolescence include:

Learning Disorders
Motor Skills Disorders
Communication Disorders
Pervasive Developmental Disorders
Attention-Deficit and Disruptive Behavior Disorders
Feeding and Eating Disorders of Infancy or Early Childhood
Tic Disorders
Elimination Disorders
Other Disorders of Infancy, Childhood, or Adolescence (e.g., Separation Anxiety, Selective Mutism, Reactive Attachment Disorder, Stereotypic Movement Disorder)

Axis II includes Mental Retardation and Personality Disorders. The Personality Disorders are labeled: Paranoid, Schizoid, Schizotypal, Antisocial, Borderline, Histrionic, Narcissistic, Avoidant, Dependent, Obsessive-Compulsive, and Passive Aggressive. Historically, clinicians were reluctant to diagnose personality disorders in children and adolescents because their personality traits were considered to be unstable. However, at present, all of the diagnoses, except Antisocial Personality Disorder, may be made for children and adolescents when the criteria are met.

Axis III is used to indicate any physical problem that may be relevant to the understanding or management of the client. The classification system used for Axis III is the *International Statistical Classification of Diseases, Injuries, and Causes of Death* published by the World Health Organization.

Axis IV is used to indicate any psychosocial and environmental problems that may be relevant to the understanding or management of the client. Problems which have not been present during the year prior to an evaluation are included only if they appear to be clearly related to current difficulties. The Psychosocial and Environmental problems most likely to apply to children and adolescents are:

Problems with primary support group
Problems related to the social environment
Educational problems
Economic problems

Axis V is a scale ranging from 0 to 100 that assesses psychological, social, and occupational functioning on a hypothetical continuum of mental illness versus health. For example, a score of 80 would indicate that if symptoms are present, they are transient and expectable reactions to psychosocial stressors; a score of 50 would indicate serious symptoms or any serious impairment in social or school functioning. A score of 10 or less would indicate that a person is in persistent danger of severely hurting self or others, shows a persistent inability to maintain minimal personal hygiene, or has committed a serious suicidal act with clear expectation of death.

Interrater agreement for the diagnostic categories of the DSM-III ranged from 20 to 100 percent with a mean of 54 percent for child referrals (Mattison, Cantwell, Russell, & Will, 1979). The higher levels of agreement were found for mental retardation, psychosis, conduct disorder, and hyperactivity, while the lowest levels were obtained for anxiety disorders and the subtypes of depression. Validity was examined by comparing the classifications of referred children with those of "experts" (Cantwell, Russell, Mattison, & Will, 1979). The average agreement between the experts and the raters was less than 50 percent; the highest agreements were for mental retardation, psychosis, hyperactivity, and conduct disorder. Although the authors of these studies found these results to be supportive of DSM-III, the levels of reliability and validity are far short of those expected for psychological instruments. A more recent study of interrater reliability for 195 child inpatients indicated that only the major categories, Attention Deficit Disorder with Hyperactivity, a combination of Conduct Disorder and Oppositional Disorder, Anxiety Disorder, Eating Disorder, and Schizophrenia, met the minimal acceptable criteria (Werry, Methven, Fitzpatrick, & Dixon, 1983).

Studies have suggested that reliability has improved with successive editions of the DSM; however, reliability remains below optimal levels (Kirk & Kutchins, 1992). In constructing the DSM-IV, extensive literature reviews were conducted, and this information was used to improve the reliability and validity of the diagnoses (APA, 1994). Diagnoses which showed poor reliability or validity in their DSM-III-R form were revised or eliminated. It is, therefore, thought that reliability studies utilizing DSM-IV diagnoses will indicate further improved reliability and validity.

REFERRAL INFORMATION

The assessment process usually begins before the child is seen. Children are typically referred to clinicians or community clinics by other professionals or by parents who have recognized the possibility of a behavior disorder. During the preschool years general practitioners or pediatricians have frequent contact with children and may observe problem behavior in the context of routine physical care of the child. If parents are concerned about a behavior problem during this period, they often bring it to the attention of the child's physician. Thus, physicians are likely to be responsible for most referrals to clinicians during the preschool years.

After the child enters school, teachers become an important source of referrals, although physicians continue to refer their patients (who are seen less frequently for routine physical care). Most of the less severe childhood behavior disorders either occur after the age of school entry or are recognized only in the context of a large peer group. The teacher, then, may become aware that a particular child's behavior is atypical or inappropriate in comparison with the behavior of other children. The child's teacher, by describing the behavior problem in the school setting, also contributes relevant referral information.

The clinician attempts to secure relevant information from other professionals familiar with the child. Permission to obtain such information from other professionals must be given by the parents in writing. Occasionally, parents withhold permission or do not inform the clinician about earlier contacts with other professionals. In these instances, it is often discovered that the parents have been unable to accept the previous diagnosis and are "shopping" for another opinion. Discovering that their child has a serious behavior disorder with a poor prognosis is difficult for most parents to accept readily, and unfortunately, these parents may be willing to invest themselves and their financial resources in any program that promises a cure or complete rehabilitation.

Information from the professionals who are familiar with the child may help the clinician to conceptualize the problem and to design a more efficient assessment procedure. The interview will more quickly focus on the problem, and the selection of standardized tests to be administered can be more efficiently determined.

THE INTERVIEW

Interviewing is the assessment technique used most often by professionals. Interviewing consists of talking with the parents and the child with the goal of determining the nature of the problem, its possible causes, and the situations in which it occurs. Clinicians of various theoretical persuasions differ in the amount of information they seek in any one area of inquiry. In general, diagnostic interviews are structured carefully so that the clinician is actively seeking information and has delineated those areas in which information is needed. This section on the interview describes the primary aspects of the clinical interview as conducted by most professionals.

In most cases, the clinician must depend primarily on information obtained from parents through interviewing. Children often do not possess the verbal skills to provide the necessary information or are reluctant to discuss their problem with the clinician. They may be reluctant to speak freely about matters such as hostility toward their parents because they are afraid that the clinician will share this information with the parents. Interviews with parents also present problems for the clinician because parents may feel guilty or may be afraid that they will be blamed for the child's problem; thus, they distort the information given to the interviewer.

In a child guidance clinic, the initial interview with the parents is usually conducted by a social worker or a child psychiatrist, although it may also be conducted by a psychologist. The interview usually begins with the clinician's request that the parents describe the problem that caused them to seek help. It should be kept in mind that parents do not always initiate the diagnostic process. While most parents are earnestly seeking help for their child, some of them have been "forced" to obtain professional aid and may not be optimally motivated. Often, for example, a community agency, such as the school or juvenile court advises parents to seek help for their child when the child is presenting a problem behavior outside of the home environment. It is understandable, therefore, why some parents feel ambivalent and helpless under these conditions, particularly if they are not having any problems with the child at home.

After the parents describe the problem for which they are seeking help, the clinician explores with them the circumstances under which the problem occurs, the frequency with which it occurs, and the length of time it has occurred. They are also asked what they have done and currently do when the problem occurs. The parents are asked to recall when the problem was first brought to their attention and what the circumstances were at that time. The clinician may then inquire about other problems that might have occurred in the child's history.

Early in the interview many clinicians attempt to secure a developmental history on the child. The parents are asked about the pregnancy, labor, and delivery of the child to determine whether physical factors might have been involved. The possibility of physical factors is also explored by inquiring about illnesses and accidents occurring during infancy and childhood. If the clinician has a psychodynamic (Freudian) orientation, the parents will be asked to recall experiences involving feeding and toilet training. The clinician in this instance is seeking evidence for unusual or traumatic circumstances surrounding these psychologically important events. An attempt is also made to describe developmental milestones, which include the ages at which the child sat alone, took the first step alone, said the first word, and combined two words when talking. Guidelines exist for a number of developmental milestones. These milestones give the clinician a general impression of the child's early rate of developmental progress. Although there is considerable variation among children, variations of 30 percent above or below normal are noted. It is difficult for parents to remember when these milestones occurred, particularly if they have had more than one child. If parents have kept a baby book or other records of the child's developmental achievements, they are requested to bring them to the interview.

In addition to the review of the child's developmental progress, information is sought regarding the child's social behavior. The clinician is interested in the child's social interactions with peers, siblings, and parents. During the interview the clinician is attempting to assess the parents' attitudes toward the child and their possible role in the development of the behavior problem. Parents are questioned about their own histories, including physical, developmental, learning, and psychological problems. The rationale for this inquiry is that behavior problems are sometimes repeated in successive generations, and this repetition of occurrence may alter a parent's perception of the problem. For example, a father may report that he also had great difficulty learning to read when he was in school and was able to overcome the problem (that is, he has a job that requires only minimal reading ability); in this instance, the father may not perceive his child's inability to read as a significant problem. If the clinician suspects a hereditary factor, the parents will also be asked if other blood relatives have had the same problem or one similar to it.

Depending on the nature of the problem and the age of the child, some clinicians find it useful to conduct the interview in whole or in part with the parents and child together. With this arrangement the clinician is seeking to assess the family interaction patterns and their possible role in the development of the behavior problem. The clinician observes which members of the family do most of the talking and who looks at whom during the interview; some clinicians draw inferences from these behaviors. For example, if the mother speaks most of the time during the interview and tends to answer questions directed toward the husband or child, the clinician may infer that she is the dominant parent and is presenting an inappropriate model for the child. (As can be seen in this example, inherent in some inferences is the assumption that the clinician knows what the correct interaction pattern should be.)

Although cognizant of the difficulties, many clinicians attempt to interview the child alone in the hope that the child's behavior will reveal information that will enable the clinician to understand more thoroughly the nature of the problem. Initially, the clinician asks questions that require relatively brief answers, such as the child's name, age, and the school attended. The interviewer gradually moves into areas that are related to the problem behavior, simultaneously attempting to secure the child's confidence and ease in the situation. The clinician often asks child clients why they were brought for the interview; the answer to this question frequently reveals information regarding the child's perception of the problem as well as the source of knowledge leading to the perception. Sometimes, parents do not openly discuss the problem with the child and do not prepare the child for the interview. In other instances, the parents may present the visit to the clinician as a negative experience, as punishment for the problem behavior. Lack of preparation or presentation of the interview as punishment may result in a child who is unresponsive or hostile, or both, to the interviewer. It is then the clinician's task to communicate to the child the reasons for the visit and to assure the child that help will be forthcoming.

As the child's confidence develops, the clinician begins to inquire about relationships among family members. Such relationships are considered by many clinicians as important causal factors and are explored in considerable depth. The child's behavior during the interview is often interpreted by the clinician as being characteristic of the child's behavior in general. Given the unique qualities of the conditions surrounding the clinical interview, it may not be correct to generalize to other situations; however, the behaviors presented during the interview may well provide hypotheses about the variables controlling the child's behavior.

When the child to be interviewed is young, below the age of six or seven years, some clinicians utilize doll play as a substitute for the direct verbal interaction between the interviewer and the child. That is, a doll is introduced into the situation and serves as a mediator between the clinician and the child. In the doll play interview, the clinician asks questions about the doll, and the child answers for the doll. In using this technique, it is assumed that the child, in answering for the doll, is answering for himself or herself. With the doll as mediator, the child is presumed to be less anxious about revealing feelings and thoughts.

The clinician may add other dolls, which are presented as members of a family, and ask questions about these dolls. Again, the clinician is attempting to secure information about the child's perception of interactions among family members. The play interview may also include a wide variety of other toys with which the children are permitted to play as they wish. The play interview technique is frequently used by psychodynamically oriented clinicians who believe that children act out unconscious conflicts, defenses, and wishes in a symbolic manner during play. The clinician may view play behavior in the child as analogous to free association in the adult.

During the play interview the clinician asks questions about the child's behavior with the dolls or other toys and observes which toys the child chooses to play with and which toys the child chooses to exclude. The clinician is also interested in the child's emotional responses to the various toys—particularly responses indicating distress. Many clinicians believe that these emotional responses and the toys that evoke them may provide valuable insights regarding the source of the child's problems.

In summary, the aims of the clinical interview are to identify the type of psychological problem presented by the child and to determine the source of the underlying conflict. In pursuit of these goals the clinician collects information from the child and parents through verbal interaction, occasionally using the play interview to facilitate the interaction with young or fearful children.

Structured Interviews

Structured interviews were designed in response to concern about the reliability of unstructured interviews. Their use has increased among researchers and clinicians due to several advantages, including improvements in reliability. For example, several factors which decrease reliability, such as variations in amount of information, content, and phrasing by different interviewers, are improved by using structured interviews (Groth-Marnet, 1990). Other advantages to structured interviews are that they typically provide more detailed information than behavior rating scales and allow the interviewer to derive the most commonly used diagnoses (i.e., DSM-IV diagnoses).

The primary purpose of a structured interview is to ascertain appropriate diagnoses according to a particular classification system, usually the *Diagnostic and Statistical Manual* (APA, 1994). Questions are designed to help the clinician evaluate whether a particular individual meets the criteria for one or more disorders included in the classification system. Structured interviews generally use a branching structure in which every interviewee is asked a few questions relevant to every disorder or major group of disorders with more detailed questions being asked in areas where affirmative answers are given to the initial questions. These follow-up questions are used to obtain information about all criteria for relevant disorders, including duration, severity, frequency, and level of impairment. This procedure decreases the length of the interview while still allowing for an optimal level of depth. For example, initial questions may ask whether the person experiences frequent sadness or irritability and other primary symptoms of depressive disorders. Follow-up questions would include questions which would help determine the particular depressive disorder(s) involved, for example, Major Depression versus Dysthymia or Bipolar Disorder. Once a particular disorder(s) is determined, further questions are asked to determine additional details about course, severity, impairment, frequency, and duration. Structured interviews are generally comprehensive in their coverage of diagnostic criteria; however, there is less coverage of other areas of potential interest such as developmental history.

Structured interviews contain a list of specific questions which the interviewer always asks every interviewee. While questioning may branch, as described above, this procedure is different from unstructured interviews in which the interviewer asks questions based solely on clinical judgment about what is most relevant to a particular problem.

Structured interviews contain detailed instructions for training, scoring, and conducting standardized administration (including instructions for clarifying responses). While interviewing as a clinical skill requires training, relatively less training is required as interviews become more structured. Some structured interviews can be administered by trained lay interviewers while others require administration by a mental health professional with formal training in assessment. Just as more training is needed with less structure, reliability tends to decrease with less structure. In addition to varying in degree of structure and training, structured interviews also differ in response type (e.g., yes/no versus rating scales) and time period covered by the questions (e.g., lifetime, present, 6–12 months; Kamphaus & Frick, 1996). Different interviews cover different numbers of disorders (e.g., only anxiety disorders, only Axis I disorders, all DSM diagnoses). Most interviews provide equivalent forms for questioning the child and parents or other informants.

There are several disadvantages to using structured interviews. One, structured interviews can take a long time to administer, especially when the child has multiple presenting problems. Two, if the initial questions are not worded carefully, the branching system can result in missing particular problems because the initial questions were answered negatively. Three, due to their reliance on the categorical DSM classification system, the same criticisms apply to structured interviews as apply to the DSM (e.g., reliance on categorical versus dimensional classification, questionable construct validity). Four, structured interviews often fail to assess all important areas of functioning for children (e.g., no form for teachers to assess classroom behavior).

There are five major structured interviews for children and adolescents: Interview Schedule for Children (Kovacs, 1985), Schedule for Affective Disorders and Schizophrenia for School-aged Children (Puig-Antich & Chambers, 1978), Child Assessment Schedule (Hodges, Klein, Stern, Cytryn, & McKnew, 1982), Diagnostic Interview for Children and Adolescents (Reich, Herjanic, Welner, & Gandhy, 1982; Herjanic & Reich, 1982), and the Diagnostic Interview Schedule for Children (DISC-2.3) (Fisher, Wicks, Shaffer, Piacentini, & Lapkin, 1992). For illustrative purposes, the DISC-2.3 will be discussed in more detail.

The DISC is a highly structured interview. It was originally created for research purposes to be administered by lay interviewers. The DISC was designed to assess child and adolescent psychopathology according to the DSM; however, the appropriateness of using this instrument with children aged 9 to 11 years has been questioned due to difficulties they may have understanding both question content and time concepts (Brenton, Lise, Valla, & Lepine, 1995; Schwab-Stone, 1995).

There are several advantages to the DISC-2.3. One advantage is that the authors have designed an experimental teacher version (Frick et al., 1994). This version allows the interviewer to gain information comparable to that obtained from the parent and the child from another important area of children's functioning from a direct source. Another advantage of the DISC-2.3 is that the interview can be administered by lay interviewers after a 3-4 day training program; therefore, training and administration are less expensive. In addition, a computerized version exists to assist the interviewer with administration and scoring.

The DISC-2.3 consists of six modules representing six major classes of disorders: Anxiety Disorders, Mood Disorders, Psychosis, Disruptive Behavior Disorders, Alcohol and Substance Use Disorders, and Miscellaneous Disorders such as Bulimia/Anorexia Nervosa and Elimination Disorders.

Proper administration of the DISC-2.3 requires the interviewer to read the questions exactly as written. Unlike some of the other interviews, interviewers are not permitted to reword the questions or ask for additional information not requested by the interview itself. The short-term test-retest reliabilities for diagnoses were generally moderately high. With one exception (children's report of Oppositional Defiant Disorder; kappa = .16), test-retest kappa statistics ranged from .55 to .88 (Schwab-Stone et al., 1993; Piacentini et al., 1993; Shaffer et al., 1993). Validity studies have shown inconsistent results. For example, better results were found when comparing the parent data to diagnoses made by clinicians than with the child data (average kappa for parent version = .50; for child version = .34) (Piacentini et al., 1993). However, many of the disagreements were reported to be close (e.g., a difference of one symptom).

The reliability and validity of structured interviews are mediated by the reliability and validity of the classification system upon which they are based, in this case the DSM. Validity studies of structured interviews are especially difficult because the standard to which they are compared, namely, diagnoses rendered by experienced clinicians, has its own problems. For example, Groth-Marnet (1990) noted that "diagnoses by trained psychiatrists still cannot be said to be an ultimate, objective, and completely accurate standard" (p. 75). While the reliability estimates for this instrument are quite reasonable, the validity estimates render the DISC-2.3 best used in conjunction with other measures.

Special Areas of Focus by Behavioral Clinicians

The behavioral clinician is generally less interested in historical factors than is the traditional clinician and tends not to interview the parents in depth about the child's early developmental history. Although the behavior problem is recognized to have originated at some point in the child's history, the behavioral clinician is more concerned with discovering the environmental factors currently maintaining the behavior than with determining the circumstances under which the behavior originated.

One problem faced by the behavioral clinician in the interview is that adults are accustomed to using vague terms in describing children's problems. Adults often use such labels as "nervous," "lazy," or "bad" to describe adults' traits, and they also use these labels to describe children's. The behavioral clinician must attempt to determine exactly what behaviors have been occurring to warrant the trait label. The clinician cannot readily make a translation from the trait label to specific behaviors because people tend to use trait labels to refer to a wide variety of behaviors. The label "nervous," for example, could refer to sweaty hands, faltering voice, overactivity, temper outbursts, or any combination of symptoms and behaviors. Furthermore, the same label might be used whether the behavior occurs in one or many settings.

The behavioral clinician directs inquiry during the interview toward a description of the behaviors that are the basis for the complaints from people in the child's environment. The clinician also inquires as to which behaviors the parent wishes to have as replacements for the problem behaviors. The parent is asked to describe more precisely the situations in which the problem behavior occurs; the situations are considered to be the antecedents of the problem behavior. *Antecedents* include all stimulus factors present immediately before and during the occurrence of the problem behavior. For example, a preschool child may be described as having temper tantrums only in the home and only when the mother is present. The antecedents then would include the presence of the mother and the home environment.

The behavioral clinician asks the parent what usually happens immediately after the behavior occurs; these occurrences are called consequences. *Consequences* include all stimulus factors present immediately after the occurrence of the problem behavior. For example, a mother might say that when her son has a temper tantrum she ordinarily approaches him and tries to calm the child by talking to him. In this instance, the consequences for the temper tantrums include the mother approaching and talking to her son. Parents usually try several methods for changing the problem behavior prior to consulting a clinician, and clinicians inquire about what methods were used and the consistency with which they were used.

The behavioral interview also includes asking the parents what objects and experiences the child enjoys. In securing this information, the clinician is seeking stimuli that may serve as reinforcers for the acquisition of appropriate behavior. Even though certain types of food almost always serve as reinforcers, other reinforcers are preferable in terms of ease of administration. The clinician will ask how the child spends free time to determine the relative reinforcement potential for various activities. Children vary greatly in terms of what environmental stimuli may serve as reinforcers. Adults sometimes make mistakes when they designate potential reinforcers for children. Giving an article of clothing to a child who has no interest in his appearance, for example, is not likely to serve as a reinforcer. On the other hand, presenting the same item to a child who spends time looking at clothing in stores may well be an effective reinforcer. Asking children what objects they would like to have or what activities they enjoy is one efficient way of determining potential reinforcers.

The interview also serves the purpose of permitting the clinician to evaluate the parents' and other adults' potential for optimal involvement in a behavioral intervention program. Consideration must be given to a variety of reality factors, such as the amount of time the parent has available or is willing to make available for the child's treatment. Similarly, this evaluation must include an assessment of the parents' receptivity to behavioral approaches to treatment. Since most behavioral intervention programs take place in the child's natural environment rather than in the clinic, the responsibility placed on parents and teachers for direct implementation is considerably greater than that imposed by traditional treatment programs. Many parents may not be prepared to make major commitments of time and effort. The behavioral clinician has the added task of convincing parents and teachers that their direct and continued involvement is crucial to the success of the intervention program.

The behavioral clinician often includes an interview with the child as part of the assessment procedures. Although beset with difficulties, children's interviews can contribute useful information with respect to the child's understanding of the problem and the factors implicated in the maintenance of the problem behaviors. At the very least, an interview with the child can provide the child's perception of the reasons for the referral and identification of reinforcers that may contribute to the intervention program's effectiveness. Although the child's views may not match those of the mediators, they are likely to exert a significant influence on the child's behavior. For example, if a boy reports hating his father, the father's effectiveness as a social reinforcer may be questionable, whether or not the father "deserves" the child's hatred.

BEHAVIOR PROBLEM CHECKLISTS AND RATING SCALES

The development of behavior problem checklists and rating scales began in the 1920s and 1930s when researchers became interested in describing both normal and abnormal characteristics of children at different ages. Several of these early investigators developed lists of behaviors, which other researchers subsequently modified and used as the bases for collecting normative data on the incidence of behavior problems in normal children. The most well-known study is that by Macfarlane, Allen, and Honzik (1954). Both early and more recent investigators have obtained items for their checklists by examining clinical case files describing referred children's behavioral histories and symptoms.

The development of behavior problem checklists has also led to an interest in the relationships among behavior problems. In some instances, items have been grouped together because they have common features or seem to occur together in individual children. One statistical method for grouping items is called *factor analysis*, which determines the correlations among all of the items and permits groupings of items that appear to be measuring the same factor. A factor, then, is composed of several items that measure the same entity. The label given to a factor is assigned by the investigator on the basis of what the items appear to be measuring. A more recently applied statistical technique, *cluster analysis*, holds considerable promise for identifying diagnostic categories because it groups children on the basis of their responses to items, that is, it groups children who respond alike.

A number of behavior problem checklists and rating scales have been designed to facilitate the assessment process. A typical list enumerates behaviors or characteristics to be checked if they occur or have occurred in the referred child. Certain behaviors must be judged and designated in terms of their frequency, such as "sometimes," "less than average," "frequently." Some checklists have also been developed into scales in which the scores from particular items are added together.

The available checklists and scales vary on several dimensions: number and kinds of problems covered, specificity of behavior, specificity of the setting in which the behavior occurs, the age range of children for which the checklist applies, and the person(s) designated to complete the checklist. Some checklists contain items related to one kind of behavior problem, such as hyperactivity, while others are considerably more comprehensive in their coverage. The comprehensive checklists are particularly advantageous in clinical or institutional settings where they may be used as the initial assessment or screening devices prior to having interviews with the child's parents. While the checklists clearly emphasize observable behaviors, the items within the checklists vary in their level of abstraction ("hits other children" or "aggressive") and to the extent to which items require judgment by the responder, the person completing the list.

Some items are relatively straightforward in that the response involves only presence or absence of the behavior, while other items require judgments that are considerably more difficult. For example, items such as "too few friends" and "excessively late" rely heavily on the personal experiences and value system of the responder. Having three friends might be an adequate number in the judgment of one teacher but too few to another teacher.

Specificity of the setting for the behavior may also affect the ease or difficulty of judgment. Items without reference to setting may be interpreted in various ways. For example, "overactive" may be checked by one mother only if her child is overactive in most settings, while another mother might mark that label although her child is overactive only on shopping expeditions and in church.

These characteristics of behavior problem checklists affect their reliability, but extensive research in this area has not been conducted. The available research suggests that items specifying behavior and setting are more likely to be reliable than the more abstract items.

Current research is beginning to examine the relationships among behavior ratings by various persons such as parents, teachers, peers, and the children themselves. In general, persons who observe the child in the same setting (e.g., teachers and peers or mothers and fathers) show more agreement than observers and the children themselves show. Among the people most frequently in the child's presence, teachers and peers tend to show the highest agreement (Shoemaker, Erickson, & Finch, 1986), whereas parents and teachers show the lowest (Touliatos & Lindholm, 1981). The disagreements between raters, however, may also reflect the fact that children can behave differently in the company of different people.

Children also tend to rate themselves as less behaviorally problematic than others who rate them, and parents endorse more problem behaviors than do teachers (Touliatos & Lindholm, 1981). Agreement between parents is only moderate and probably reflects differences in the two parents' involvement and exposure to children.

Assessing the validity of behavior checklists and rating scales poses at least one serious problem, namely, deciding on the validity criterion. Behavior ratings and their statistical analyses are currently viewed as being a reasonable alternative to other diagnostic systems (Achenbach & Edelbrock, 1984). Behavior ratings may thus be considered as validity criteria against which other assessment techniques are validated.

Ratings by Parents, Teachers, and Others

Achenbach and Edelbrock (1983) developed the *Child Behavior Checklist* (CBCL) as a comprehensive checklist for children between the ages of 4 and 16 years. Its most recent version (Achenbach, 1991) extends the upper age limit to 18 and contains 113 items that parents or other caretakers rate on a three-point scale. It takes about 20 minutes to complete, and the ratings are supposed to be based on behavior during the last six months.

Factor analyses of the CBCL were conducted for 2,300 children referred to 42 mental health settings (Achenbach & Edelbrock, 1989). Because the frequency and patterning of the behaviors varied with age, separate analyses were conducted for each gender for ages 4–5, 6–11, and 12–16. Eight or more factors or syndromes were found for each group. The 1991 version includes only the eight syndromes which were common across all age groups. Factor analyses revealed two major groups labeled Internalizing and Externalizing; the Internalizing scale includes Withdrawn, Somatic Complaints, and Anxious/Depressed, whereas the Externalizing scale includes both Delinquent and Aggressive Behavior. Social Problems, Thought Problems, and Attention Problems are not included in the two major groups.

The test-retest reliability of the CBCL is quite high over short periods of time (.89 for one-week test-retest). Validity has been demonstrated by large differences in CBCL scores found between the clinic and normal groups of children as well as significant correlations between the CBCL and other empirically derived measures (Achenbach, 1991, p. 72).

The CBCL has also been modified to make it suitable for use by teachers in school settings. The *Teacher's Report Form* (TRF) (Achenbach, 1991) has been factor-analyzed for referred children, and the syndromes on the CBCL were identified. A computer program and manual were designed to help compare forms from different informants (Achenbach, 1991).

The *Behavior Assessment Scale for Children* (BASC) (Reynolds & Kamphaus, 1992) has three different forms for three different age groups (4–5, 6–11, and 12–18). The BASC was designed to measure both behavioral excesses and behavioral deficits. Behavioral excesses are measured by clinical scales which are very similar to those of the CBCL. Behavioral deficits are measured by four adaptive behavior scales such as Social Skills, Leadership, and Adaptability.

The BASC was developed in much the same way as the CBCL, offering several sets of norms for comparison purposes. Factor analysis revealed three factors: Internalizing, Externalizing, and Adaptive. Since the BASC is fairly new, reliability and validity studies are limited. The parent version had a median reliability estimate of .80. Criterion-related validity studies indicate a clear and reasonable relationship between the BASC and other behavior rating scales. Like the CBCL, the BASC offers versions for parents, teachers, and youth self-assessment; however, the BASC does not offer the extensive research support provided by the CBCL, nor are the different versions as directly comparable. The chief advantage of the BASC is its inclusion of adaptive behavior scales.

Ratings by Self

A number of behavior problem scales have been designed to be completed by the children and adolescents themselves. Because reading ability is a necessary prerequisite, the scales are useful only for older children and adolescents (fourth- or fifth-grade reading ability or greater). Interestingly, self-rating scales can be much less behavioral because items can reflect private events, such as emotions and thoughts, that may or may not be correlated with observable behavior.

Achenbach's CBCL was modified to create the *Youth Self-Report* (YSR) for 11–18 year olds. The factor analyses of the original version of the YSR revealed syndromes similar to those found for parent-completed CBCLs. The 1991 version includes syndromes which were present across informants. The Withdrawn scale was not identified clearly in factor analyses of the YSR; however, it was included because of its presence for all other informants (Achenbach, 1991). As with the CBCL and the TRF, the YSR has the advantage of having a larger base of research from which to draw than other behavior checklists.

Use of Behavior Problem Rating Scales.   Checklists and rating scales are particularly useful in the preliminary assessment of referred children. They may also make a major contribution in screening programs for early identification of behavior problems. Because these scales take relatively little time to complete, teachers and parents are more likely to be willing to cooperate in their use.

Most adult complaints about children's behaviors revolve around *undercontrolled* behaviors, that is, behaviors that occur too often. If viewed from a normative perspective, it is also apparent that *overcontrolled* behaviors or behavioral deficiencies should be of equal concern. Such deficiencies could certainly be as detrimental to the child's future functioning as undercontrolled behaviors. The development of comprehensive behavioral checklists that include both types of behavior problems as well as positive behaviors would likely result in assessment that clearly delineates which behaviors should be increased and/or decreased during the treatment or intervention program. These newer checklists would have to be designed with reference to behavioral norms and evaluated in terms of their reliability and validity, just as contemporary intelligence and achievement tests are.

STANDARDIZED TESTS

A wide variety of tests have been designed to assess the psychological characteristics of children. A standardized test is one for which data from a large number of children have been collected and information is provided regarding the average performance of children at different ages. The test results obtained from a particular child are then compared with those of the standardization group with the same chronological age. A standardized test also provides information about the reliability and validity of the test. The most important measurement of this *reliability* is the amount of agreement in the test results when the test is administered on two occasions separated by an interval of time. A reliable test is one that yields similar results on both occasions; an unreliable test is not an acceptable assessment tool. *Validity* refers to the test's ability to measure what it purports to measure. In the case of intelligence tests, the validity of a new intelligence test is measured by the extent to which its results agree with the results of other intelligence tests administered to the same individuals. The American Psychological Association (1985) has published standards for educational and psychological testing.

Multicultural issues in testing have come to the forefront in recent years. Contemporary training programs in clinical psychology are required to present didactic material that address the complexities of multicultural assessment. The American Psychological Association has recently released the *Guidelines for Providers of Psychological Services to Ethnic, Linguistic, and Culturally Diverse Populations* (APA, 1993). This document provides specific and helpful advice to the clinician regarding assessment issues with culturally diverse clients.

Standardized tests are administered primarily by clinical and school psychologists who have been trained in graduate programs and during internship in their proper use. In the administration of a test the psychologist is seeking an optimal performance from the child while following precisely the instructions developed for the test. To ensure getting the most accurate results on a test, the examiner must take certain precautions, which include being assured that the child is not physically ill, that the child's principal language is English, and that the child is not excessively anxious or fearful. Many psychologists request that the child receive a general physical examination and vision and hearing tests prior to the administration of psychological tests. Physical problems and sensory defects can seriously impair performance on psychological tests and could, therefore, lead to inaccurate interpretations of a child's behavioral functioning.

Anxiety or fear in the testing situation can also result in depressed performance on a test. Young children are particularly susceptible to anxiety in strange situations. To decrease the possibility of reactions based on fear, it is usually advisable for a parent to accompany a preschool child during test administration, although exceptions may be made when there is reason to believe that the presence of the parent may interfere with the child's performance. Young children are often reluctant to talk spontaneously or to respond verbally in novel situations, and examiners, therefore, tend to begin testing sessions with tasks not requiring verbal responses, such as drawing a picture. A useful technique is to engage the parent in conversation for the first 10 minutes or so of the session and make no demands on the child. Having very young children seated in the lap of the parent during testing frequently prevents them from reacting strongly in fear, although the examiner must instruct the parent not to participate in the testing (that is, not to help the child by repeating the instructions or manipulating the test objects).

Many different types of tests are available to the clinician. The clinician's choice of specific tests is determined by the information obtained from the referral source, interviews, and observation of the child's behavior during the interviews. Because many behavior disorders reflect or are accompanied by problems in development, intellectual functioning, or learning, intelligence and achievement tests are usually administered during the assessment procedure. Personality tests are also frequently administered to determine the type and possible causes of certain behavior problems (which may or may not be accompanied by intellectual problems). Tests for special functions (e.g., language, visual perception, visual-motor integration) may also be administered, particularly when the clinician suspects that specific deficits may be hindering a child's performance on the more general tests or in learning at school. Some of these tests for special functions will be described in later chapters dealing with specific behavior disorders.

Assessment of Intelligence

The first intelligence test was developed in 1905 by Alfred Binet to identify French schoolchildren whose abilities would prevent them from progressing adequately in the regular public school program. Since that time, the original Binet scales have been revised periodically, and other intelligence tests have been developed.[1]

The principal intelligence tests are administered individually by master's or doctoral level psychologists. Intelligence tests that are given to groups of children have also been developed, and they may be administered by school teachers and other professionals with less training in test administration and interpretation.

The success of Binet's original test prompted two American psychologists at Stanford University, Lewis Terman and Maud Merrill, to develop an English-language edition of the test for use with schoolchildren in the United States. This American edition of the test is called the *Stanford-Binet Intelligence Test*. The Stanford-Binet has been revised several times to update some of the items and to improve the sample of children upon which the norms are based.

The most recent version, the *Stanford-Binet Intelligence Scale: Fourth Edition* (SB-4) (Thorndike, Hagen, & Sattler, 1986a), was standardized for use with persons from 2 through 23 years and has 15 subtests. The standardization sample included 5,013 persons who were representative of the U.S. population as depicted in the 1980 census data. A special effort was made to include items that were culture-fair; a group of ethnic minority reviewers evaluated items for culturally biased content. The 15 subtests are distributed among four areas as follows:

Area		Subtest
A.	Verbal Reasoning	Vocabulary
		Comprehension
		Absurdities
		Verbal Relations

---

[1]The concept of intelligence and the use of intelligence tests have stimulated much debate among psychologists, educators, and the public. For a review of these issues, see Cronbach (1975), Wechsler (1975), Jensen (1980), and Weinberg (1989).

B.	Abstract/Visual Reasoning	Pattern Analysis
		Copying
		Matrices
		Paper Folding and Cutting
C.	Quantitative Reasoning	Quantitative
		Number Series
		Equation Building
D.	Short-Term Memory	Bead Memory
		Memory for Sentences
		Memory for Digits
		Memory for Objects

All 15 subtests are not used with children of all ages. Some are given beginning at 2 years, others beginning at 7 years, and still others beginning at 12 years. Only six subtests are useful throughout the age range—Vocabulary, Comprehension, Pattern Analysis, Quantitative, Bead Memory, and Memory for Sentences. Raw scores for the subtests are converted into three standard scores: subtest (mean = 50, SD = 8), area (mean = 100, SD = 16), and composite (mean = 100, SD = 16), which summarize performance across all areas and subtests.

The composite score has excellent internal consistency reliability ranging from .95 to .99 over the different age groups; the reliabilities of the individual subtests ranged from a low of .73 for Memory for Objects to a high of .94 for Paper Folding and Cutting. The test-retest reliability or stability results indicated that the composite score has excellent reliability; however, the individual subtests were not reliable enough to use as measures of ability (Thorndike, Hagen, & Sattler, 1986b).

The SB-4's *Technical Manual* reports a number of studies that examine validity, the relationship among SB-4 composite scores, and comparable scores on other intelligence tests. In general, particularly for children who were neither retarded nor gifted, validity was high. In most studies, the average SB-4 score was lower than that of the comparison test, but usually the difference was five points or less. For both gifted and retarded samples, however, the average SB-4 scores were nine or more points lower than those of the comparison test.

One of the major weaknesses of this version of the Stanford-Binet is that the factor analytic studies do not support the use of the four area scores; Sattler (1988, p. 289) recommends the use of factor scores rather than area scores. Other problems include a lack of a comparable set of subtests throughout the age range of the test and a long administration time. In addition, the range of possible scores varies depending on the age of the child or adolescent being tested.

The *Wechsler Intelligence Scale for Children: Third Edition* (WISC-III) (Wechsler, 1991) is an individually administered test designed for children 6 through 16 years of age and is a revision of the WISC-R (Wechsler, 1974). The WISC-III was standardized on 2,200 children who were representative of the population as depicted in the 1988 U.S. Bureau of the Census report. Like the Stanford-Binet: Fourth Edition, the WISC-III arranges items according to subtests, with the items within each subtest arranged according to difficulty. There are 13 subtests, 10 of which are used to compute the IQ scores, with 3 as Supplementary tests. The 10 required subtests are equally divided into verbal and performance categories. Verbal and Performance IQ scores are calculated in addition to the Full Scale IQ score, which is based on the sum of the scores from the Verbal and Performance subtests.

The primary advantage of the separate IQ scores is that the children with specific deficits may be more readily identified. Children with certain motor or visual perception problems, for example, are likely to obtain considerably lower Performance IQ scores than Verbal IQ scores, and an overall IQ score could, in some cases, mask important diagnostic information. In general, differences between the Verbal and Performance IQ scores that are 15 points or greater are considered to be significant and call for further investigation. The construction of the WISC-III therefore permits the examiner to identify strengths and weaknesses of intellectual functioning.

A score is obtained for each of the subtests using the scoring criteria in the manual. This raw score is then converted to a standard score,[2] where the mean has been set at 10 with a standard deviation of 3. The conversions from raw scores to standard scores are given in the manual for the various chronological ages. The standard scores are then added and converted into Verbal, Performance, and Full Scale IQ scores where the mean has been set at 100 with a standard deviation of 15.

The WISC-III contains six verbal and seven performance subtests that are administered in alternating order. The examiner has the option of administering four or five subtests of each type to derive IQ scores. A short description of each subtest is presented below.

WISC Verbal subtests

1. *Information.* This subtest consists of questions that cover general information that the child acquires at home and school.
2. *Comprehension.* In this subtest the examiner orally presents the child with situational problems. The aim of this subtest is to measure practical judgment.
3. *Arithmetic.* In this subtest the examiner presents the child with arithmetic problems that must be solved within a certain time limit without the use of pencil and paper.
4. *Similarities.* This subtest requires the child to explain how pairs of objects or concepts are alike and measures the child's conceptual skills or abilities to perceive relationships.
5. *Vocabulary.* The child is asked to define a series of words that vary in difficulty.
6. *Digit Span.* The examiner presents increasingly long lists of digits, and the child must repeat them forwards and backwards. This subtest measures short-term memory.

---

[2]A standard score, or z-score, is a unit of measurement that allows the results of tests of different lengths to be compared by converting their raw scores to a common scale. A standard score is computed by the following formula:

$$\frac{\text{raw score} - \text{mean score}}{\text{standard deviation (SD)}}$$

WISC Performance subtests

1. *Picture Completion.* In this subtest a series of pictures with line drawings of objects is presented to the child who must identify the missing part.
2. *Picture Arrangement.* Sets of pictures are presented to the child who must arrange them from left to right in an order that reflects a sensible story. This subtest measures the child's ability to put visual stimuli in a sequence to reflect temporal relationships.
3. *Block Design.* Cards with geometric patterns are presented to the child who must reproduce the patterns with colored blocks. The child obtains extra points for reproducing the design faster than the allotted time. This subtest measures visual discrimination and the ability to perceive spatial relationships.
4. *Object Assembly.* Pieces of increasingly more difficult puzzles are presented to the child who must assemble them within a certain time limit. Extra points are given when the child assembles the puzzle in shorter time periods. This subtest measures object recognition, the ability to perceive spatial relationships, and perceptual-motor skills.
5. *Coding.* The child is required to draw symbols that correspond to other symbols as quickly as possible. The score is determined by the number of correctly drawn symbols completed within a certain time limit. This subtest measures perceptual-motor abilities.
6. *Mazes.* In this subtest a series of line-drawing mazes is presented to the child through which a continuous, unobstructed path must be drawn. The Mazes subtest measures spatial perception and concentration.
7. *Symbol Search.* In this subtest a series of paired groups of symbols, each pair consisting of a target group and a search group, is presented. The child scans the two groups and indicates whether or not a target symbol appears in the search group. The Symbol Search subtest measures perceptual speed.

Within a subtest, the examiner presents items in order of difficulty until the child fails a certain number of consecutive items. The criterion for reaching the ceiling varies for each subtest. When this ceiling is reached, the examiner discontinues the presentation of items for the subtest and begins presenting the easier items on the next subtest.

The WISC-III manual reports average split-half reliability coefficients of .96 for the Full Scale IQ, .95 for the Verbal IQ, and .91 for the Performance IQ. The average split-half reliability coefficients for the individual subtests range from .70 to .87. The test-retest coefficients are also high. Based on results from several age groups, the results were .90 to .95 for the Full Scale IQ, .90 to .94 for the Verbal Scale IQ, and .86 to .88 for the Performance Scale IQ, and a range of .54 to .93 for the individual subtests.

The validity of the WISC-III has been evaluated by examining its relationship to the Stanford-Binet and a variety of other measures. The average correlation between IQ scores on the Stanford-Binet (1988 norms) and the WISC-III Full Scale IQ was .82, the Verbal IQ .75, and the Performance IQ .68. Other instruments measuring *g*, or a general abilities construct, against which the WISC-III has also been examined include the *Differential Abilities Scales* (DAS; Elliot, 1990), the *Kaufman Assessment Battery for Children* (K-ABC; Kaufman & Kaufman, 1983), and the *Wechsler Adult Intelligence Scale–Revised* (WAIS-R; Wechsler, 1981). The WISC-III Full Scale IQ has been found to have correlations ranging from .70 to .96 with these instruments. It should be noted that the WISC-III has been found to produce Full Scale IQ scores that are 4 to 7 points lower than the WISC-R. The principal criticism of the WISC-R is that the IQ range (40 to 160) is not adequate for severely retarded and extremely gifted children.

The *Wechsler Preschool and Primary Scale of Intelligence–Revised* (WPPSI-R) was designed for use with children ranging in age from 3 to 7 years, 3 months old (Wechsler, 1989). The basic format of the WPPSI-R is similar to that of the WISC-III and provides Full Scale, Verbal, and Performance IQ scores. The verbal subtests of the WPPSI-R include Information, Vocabulary, Arithmetic, Similarities, Comprehension, and Sentences. The performance subtests include Animal House, Object Assembly, Picture Completion, Mazes, Geometric Design, and Block Design. Some WPPSI-R items overlap with WISC-III items, which presents a disadvantage for retesting. Basically, familiarity with the items may influence future scores (Sattler, 1992).

The reliability coefficients (correlations between odd and even items) for the Full Scale, Verbal, and Performance scales are .96, .95, and .92, suggesting that the reliability of these scales is excellent. The reliability coefficients of the individual subtests, however, are lower and range from .63 to .86. Validity studies indicate that the WPPSI-R has high correlations with the Stanford-Binet: Fourth Edition. The usefulness of the WPPSI-R is hampered by its restricted age range and long administration time. As with the WISC-III, the WPPSI-R is not suitable for children who are likely to be severely retarded or extremely gifted.

The *Bayley Scales of Infant Development: Second Edition* is appropriate for children from 1 month to 42 months (Bayley, 1993). The standardization procedure for the Bayley provided the most representative sample achieved for infant scales to date. Three standard scores are provided: the Mental Developmental Index, the Psychomotor Developmental Index, and the Behavior Rating Index.

The items on the Mental Scale evaluate the infant's social responsiveness, vocal and verbal behavior, simple problem-solving abilities, and reactions to environmental changes. The Psychomotor Scale items evaluate the child's gross motor and sensory-motor development. The Behavior Rating Index items compare the child's behavior to normative standards. The child's performance on each of the scales is calculated by adding up the number of passed items and converting these numbers to standard scores that are based on the distribution of scores for children of the same age. These scores are converted to developmental quotients of which the mean is 100.

The Bayley Scales are particularly useful in clinical diagnosis because of the larger number of items at each age level, the separate evaluation of mental and motor functioning, and their superior standardization. The administration time for the Bayley tends to be lengthy (over one hour) and is probably fatiguing for many infants. The examiner must be well-trained and practiced with the instrument to be able to maintain the infant's optimal attention and to minimize the amount of administration time.

Due to the desire to identify children with behavioral and developmental problems as soon as possible, the Behavior Rating Index was added to the original Bayley Scale (Bayley, 1969). Interest remains strong in infant tests and early behaviors that might be predictive of later problems. In general, sensory-motor functioning appears not to predict later intellectual abilities, except perhaps for children who perform very poorly. Vocal and verbal abilities, on the other hand, may well be the best available predictors of later intellectual functioning.

The *Kaufman Brief Intelligence Test* (K-BIT) (Kaufman & Kaufman, 1990) is a brief, individually administered, measure of verbal and nonverbal intelligence. It can be used to assess persons ranging in age from 4 to 90 and takes approximately 15 to 25 minutes to administer, with younger children taking the least time. To facilitate comparisons with other standardized intelligence tests, the K-BIT provides age-based standardized scores, called "IQ standard scores" with a mean of 100 and a standard deviation of 15. The K-BIT consists of two subtests: Vocabulary (including Part A, Expressive Vocabulary and Part B, Definitions) and Matrices. The manual reports that Vocabulary measures verbal, school-related skills and Matrices measures nonverbal skills and the ability to solve new problems.

The K-BIT is not designed to replace a multisubtest, comprehensive test battery. The manual recommends using the K-BIT when professional examiners are not available, for large-scale screenings, and for situations where time and resources are limited.

The K-BIT was normed on a nationwide sample of 2,022 children and adults, age 4 to 90 years, that was stratified according to the most recent U.S. Census figures on four variables: race or ethnic group, age, gender, and SES. Test-retest reliability coefficients are reported to range, based on age, from .86 to .97 for the Vocabulary subtests and from .80 to .92 for the Matrices test. Validation studies have compared the K-BIT with many other major intelligence tests. Most studies have reported validity coefficients in the moderate range, indicating acceptable levels of comparisons with other tests. In many cases, the K-BIT is the brief intelligence test of choice because it includes verbal, nonverbal, and composite scores and can be administered by nonprofessionals in a time-efficient manner.

The *Peabody Picture Vocabulary Test Revised* (PPVT-R) was designed to provide an IQ score that is based on receptive language skills (Dunn & Dunn, 1981). The test consists of a graded series of plates, each of which includes four pictures. The examiner presents a word, and the child is requested to indicate which picture depicts the word. The test covers an age range from $2^{1}/_{2}$ years through adult. Administration time is about 15 minutes. A new version was scheduled for publication in 1997.

The manual presents alternate form reliabilities ranging from .67 to .88, with the highest reliabilities being obtained for the oldest children and the lowest reliabilities for the preschool children. The validity of the PPVT-R with the WISC-R ranges from .16 to .86 with a median correlation of .68 (Sattler, 1992, p. 350). For ethnic minority children, scores on the PPVT-R tend to be lower than WISC-R scores.

The PPVT-R should not be used as a substitute for the Stanford-Binet or the WISC-III. It may be useful as a screening test for children with expressive language problems.

The tests described in this section are only a sample of the available individually administered intelligence tests that are used for screening purposes or for assessing children who are referred for psychological problems. The reader is advised to consult *Mental Measurement Yearbook* (Buros, published yearly) for additional information about these or other tests.

Group-administered intelligence tests have been developed for administration to groups of children in school settings. These tests enable school personnel to assess large numbers of children for the purpose of describing the general level of intellectual functioning of a group (e.g., class, grade, school). Group tests are also sometimes used to identify children who should receive individual assessments. The administration and scoring of group tests do not require trained professionals, as do most of the individually administered intelligence tests. They are usually administered by teachers who follow the instructions in the booklet.

Group intelligence tests have certain disadvantages in comparison with the individually administered intelligence tests. The greatest disadvantage is that the examiner is not able to observe the behaviors of the children taking the test. Group tests, therefore, result in scores and nothing more. The scores that are derived from group tests can be misused or misinterpreted. Scores on group intelligence tests have sometimes been used erroneously to make decisions about individual children. Some of these decisions, such as placement in special educational programs, have profound influences on the child's future and should be based on the more reliable and valid data derived from individually administered tests. In addition, group intelligence tests, relying heavily on reading and pencil-and-paper skills, may greatly penalize children with specific reading disabilities by giving IQ scores that are considerably below those that would be obtained on the individually administered tests that sample a broader spectrum of skills.

· *Use of Intelligence Tests in Diagnosis.* Psychologists administer intelligence tests to the majority of children referred for the assessment and diagnosis of behavior problems. The frequent use of intelligence tests in the diagnostic process reflects the important role that level of intellectual functioning plays in the complex array of behaviors manifested by children. Mischel (1968) has suggested that intelligence may well be the only characteristic or trait of individuals to remain stable over relatively long periods of time.

Securing an IQ score is rarely the only goal of the psychologist administering an IQ test. The assessor observes very closely the child's responses to each item and records the child's answer to each question. The content of children's answers often provides hypotheses regarding specific problem areas. Bizarre or very unusual responses, for example, would have a different meaning from vague or imprecise responses. A child's answers could also suggest the presence of a hearing deficit or a lack of understanding of the meaning of certain words. The assessor is also particularly interested in describing the child's strengths and weaknesses in the various areas of intellectual functioning. In many cases, knowledge of strengths and weaknesses provides a beginning point for the development of a therapeutic program.

The assessor also seeks an understanding of the child's approach to problem situations. For example, is the child concerned about the correctness of his or her answer? Some children seem not to care about whether they are right or wrong in answering questions, while others ask the examiner about their performance quite often during the administration of the test. Does the child answer the questions or approach task items impulsively without adequate reflection? For some children, tasks that are timed are performed more poorly than items without the imposition of time limits. The examiner notes the child's response to complex tasks. Is the task approached in a systematic or disorganized way? In puzzle tasks, for example, the child may move several pieces around at a time in a random fashion or move one piece at a time.

The examiner also observes how the child responds to the increasingly difficult items. Some children will simply state that they do not know the answer, while others will present elaborate rationalizations. Perseveration, or giving the same answer without regard to the question, is also a possible response when the correct answer is not known. Does the child give up easily or become upset when the items become difficult? The behaviors of children while taking tests should not be freely generalized to other situations, but they do aid the examiner in understanding the relationships among the behaviors being observed. They may further provide hypotheses regarding variables that control the child's behavior in other settings, particularly the contingencies that have been used in the past for problem-solving behaviors.

3

Diagnostic and Assessment Methods

Part II

STANDARDIZED TESTS

Assessment of School Achievement

Like intelligence tests, achievement tests may be administered either to individual children or groups of children. School systems frequently administer group achievement tests to all pupils on a regular basis, such as once a year or every two

This chapter was revised by Teresa Parr and Barry Rand.

years. Individually administered achievement tests are given by professionals who have received specific training in testing methods and the diagnosis of learning problems. Children who are given individual achievement tests have usually been identified on the basis of poor performance on the group tests or have been referred by their teachers on the basis of poor classroom performance.

Achievement tests are oriented toward performance in school subjects such as reading and arithmetic. The scores obtained on achievement tests are given in terms of grade equivalent; for example, a score of 3.5 on a reading achievement test indicates that the child's reading performance is equivalent to that of the average child in the fifth month of the third grade.

The assessor chooses an achievement test on the basis of the problem presented by the child. In some instances, a child may be referred for a behavior problem, but the clinician may want to determine whether the child's academic achievement may be a factor in the development of the behavior problem. In cases for which the clinician wants a global measure of achievement in the basic school subjects, Part Two of the Woodcock-Johnson or the Peabody Individual Achievement Test–Revised would be used.

The *Woodcock-Johnson–Revised Tests of Achievement* (WJ-R) (Woodcock & Mather, 1989) consists of nine individually administered tests: Letter-Word Identification, Passage Comprehension, Calculation, Applied Problems, Dictation, Writing Samples, Science, Social Studies, and Humanities; five supplementary tests on Word Attack, Reading Vocabulary, Quantitative Concepts, Proofing, and Writing Fluency are also included. Scores from the nine tests of the standard battery are combined to provide five cluster scores: Broad Reading, Broad Mathematics, Broad Written Language, Broad Knowledge, and Skills. The median reliabilities for school-aged children ranged between .91 and .96 for the five clusters. The WJ-R was nationally standardized on 6,359 subjects between 2 and 95 years of age and includes norms for college students. The WJ-R Tests of Achievement takes about 30 minutes to administer. It appears to be well standardized, reliable, and valid and is probably one of the best achievement tests in use.

The *Peabody Individual Achievement Test–Revised* (PIAT-R) (Markwardt, 1989) is individually administered and provides screening tests in Mathematics, Reading Recognition, Reading Comprehension, Spelling, Written Expression, and General Information from preschool through post-high school. It takes about 30 to 40 minutes to administer. The PIAT-R norms were based on a representative sample of 1,563 students in kindergarten through high school. The PIAT-R has good test-retest reliability ranging from a median low correlation of .84 for Mathematics to a median high correlation of .96 for Reading Recognition.

Group-administered achievement tests have been developed for administration in school settings. These tests are used to assess academic achievement for groups of children and sometimes to identify children who should receive individual assessment of school achievement. Group-administered achievement test scores are highly related to reading skills and may be low compared with scores from individually administered tests for children with specific reading disabilities.

Assessment of Neuropsychological and Other Special Functions

The psychological assessment of brain dysfunction is conducted with neuropsychological tests. Such assessment is usually a joint venture between a neurologist (a physician with specialized training in brain functions) and an appropriately trained psychologist. In addition to the examination procedures, the neurological examination may include one or more laboratory procedures such as the CT (computerized tomography) scan, EEG (electroencephalogram) or "brain wave test," skull X-rays, spinal tap, and cerebral angiogram. In general, the neurological examination focuses on the lower-level brain functions, such as the reflexes and motor abilities, while the neuropsychological examination focuses on higher-level brain processes, such as language and memory (Selz & Reitan, 1979).

Neuropsychological assessment can be used to assess functioning after a brain injury or brain dysfunction which may be related to behavioral or emotional problems. In either case, clinicians often use one of the published test batteries; however, they may also develop their own screening battery for specific neurological deficits, adding other tests depending on initial findings. Neuropsychological assessment for children and adolescents is a relatively young science, especially in the case of assessment of behavioral and emotional problems from a neuropsychological perspective. When published studies or appropriate specific norms are not available, clinicians must rely on their own internal norms until they or other researchers conduct relevant studies.

Two test batteries are particularly useful for assessing children suspected of brain dysfunction: the *Halstead-Reitan Neuropsychological Test Battery for Older Children*, designed for children between the ages of 9 and 15, and the *Reitan-Indiana Neuropsychological Test Battery for Children*, designed for children between the ages of 5 and 9 years (Reitan & Davison, 1974; Selz, 1981; Reitan & Wolfson, 1985). The Halstead battery also includes the administration of an intelligence test. There is relatively little information regarding the reliability, validity, and norms for these two tests. Selz and Reitan (1979) reported that the *Battery for Older Children* and some additional tests were able to classify children into normal, learning-disabled, or brain damaged groups with 73 percent accuracy.

Each battery consists of a large number of tests and takes several hours to administer. The principal methods used to interpret the results of neuropsychological evaluation are: level of performance, pattern of performance, specific abnormal responses, and comparison of the two sides of the body. Brain damage may decrease the overall level of performance relative to an earlier level; it may also significantly decrease level of performance in specific areas, thus providing a pattern of strengths and weaknesses that is otherwise unlikely to occur. Some of the abnormal responses that may be suggestive of brain dysfunction are hyperactivity, short attention span, lability of mood, perseveration, and memory difficulty. Significant weakness of verbal and analytic skills in comparison with perceptual and nonverbal skills may be suggestive of damage to the left hemisphere of the brain.

There are a large number of specialized tests available that enable the clinician to assess specific functions when screening or psychoeducational testing suggests potential dysfunction or deficiencies. Tests that evaluate visual-motor integration and speech and language abilities are frequently used as supplemental assessment instruments.

Assessment of Personality

Most clinical psychologists have been trained in the administration and interpretation of personality tests. A number of assumptions are implicit in the use of personality tests; the foremost is that individuals have traits that are fairly stable across situations. The goal in personality testing is to assess these traits and to determine their role in the development of the client's problem(s). Two types of tests have been devised to assess personality characteristics in children and adolescents: inventories and projective techniques. The inventory consists of series of items or questions to which clients or their parents respond. Clients or their parents may rate a series of attributes or answer questions regarding the client's feelings, attitudes, and interests. Inventories have some features in common with behavior rating scales in that some of the items are based on observable behavior; however, other items are highly inferential and therefore not acceptable as rating scale material. As research on the usefulness of various testing methods progresses, we can expect a merger of inventories and rating scales. Projective tests consist of series of pictures, inkblots, or statements upon which clients must impose meaning, such as describing what is happening to the people depicted in a particular picture.

Inventories. The *Personality Inventory for Youth* (PIY) (Lachar & Gruber, 1995) is based on the *Personality Inventory for Children* (Wirt, Lachar, Klinedinst, & Seat, 1984). The PIY is a multidimensional, objective, self-report measure for use in the evaluation of children and adolescents ages 9 to 18 years. The PIY has 270 true-false items, written at a low- to mid-third-grade reading level. Full administration of the PIY averages approximately 45 minutes. The first 80 items of the PIY can provide a brief screening assessment using the standard administration materials. The manual provides evidence of the PIY's reliability and validity.

Completion of the 270-item format provides scores for three basic kinds of scales: response validity, clinical scales, and the subscales. The four measures of response validity identify those profiles that are likely to generate inaccurate interpretations. The four validity scales are Validity, Inconsistency, Dissimulation, and Defensiveness. The Validity scale measures infrequent responses. The Inconsistency scale assesses test-taking behaviors that include inattention to inventory item content and difficulties in item comprehension. Elevation on the Dissimulation scale suggests either an extreme pattern of maladjustment or the intentional exaggeration of current problems, and the Defensiveness scale measures the tendency to deny or minimize problems.

The nine clinical scales depict several domains. Among these domains, "externalizing symptoms" are assessed with three scales: Impulsivity and Distractibility,

Delinquency, and Family Dysfunction. "Internalizing symptoms" are evaluated with three scales: Reality Distortion, Somatic Concern, and Psychological Discomfort. The clinical scales also measure self-report of cognitive limitations and poor school performance with the Cognitive Impairment scale as well as social alienation and conflict with peers in the Social Withdrawal and Social Skill Deficits scales. Each clinical scale consists of PIY items that appear on only one of these scales

Each scale includes two or three subscales. Examination of subscale scores provides the detailed assessment material. For example, the Psychological Discomfort scale includes subscales that target Fear and Worry, Depression, and Sleep Disturbance, respectively. The PIY can also be administered in conjunction with the *Personality Inventory for Children–Revised* (PIC-R; Wirt, Lachar, Klinedinst, & Seat, 1984), a parent report form that measures similar constructs as the PIY. Through the use of parent and child report forms, case conceptualization can be developed from a wider perspective.

Traditionally, most personality inventories were designed primarily for adult clients, and only a few of them provided norms for children. One adult inventory, the *Minnesota Multiphasic Personality Inventory* (MMPI), has norms for adolescents (13 years and older). The MMPI, devised by Hathaway and McKinley, was first published in 1943 and revised in 1951 and 1989 (Dahlstrom, Butcher, Graham, Tellegen, & Kaemmer, 1989). Although the MMPI was used extensively with adolescents and adolescent norms were developed in the 1970s, in 1989 a committee was appointed to determine the feasibility of developing an adolescent form of the MMPI. After several years of research, the MMPI Adolescent version (MMPI-A; Butcher, Williams, Graham, Archer, Tellegen, Ben-Porath, & Kaemmer, 1992) was published.

The MMPI-A was developed for use with adolescents ranging from ages 14 to 18. It contains 478 statements covering many areas of life experience to which the youth responds "true," "false," or "cannot say." Administration time is usually one to two hours. Responses are counted and yield scores on 4 validity scales, 10 clinical scales, 15 content scales, and 6 supplementary scales. The validity scales assess the youth's test-taking attitudes. Scores on the validity scales are taken into consideration in the scoring and interpretation of the clinical scales. Archer (1992) has published a book that describes the clinical use of the MMPI-A.

The 10 clinical scales of the MMPI were designed to discriminate among various types of patients receiving diagnostic labels from psychiatrists. The names of the scales reflect psychiatric diagnostic labels, some of which are rarely used today. Each of the 10 clinical scales of the MMPI-A is described briefly:

1. *Hypochondriasis.* A measure indicating abnormal concern about bodily functions.
2. *Depression.* A measure of the feelings and behaviors associated with depression.
3. *Hysteria.* A measure of symptoms related to the loss of sensory and motor functions of psychogenic origin.
4. *Psychopathic Deviate.* A measure of the client's inability to experience deep emotional responses, to profit from experience, and to conform to social mores.

5. *Masculinity-Femininity.* A measure of the tendency toward traditionally masculine or feminine interests.
6. *Paranoia.* A measure of suspiciousness, oversensitivity, delusions of persecution.
7. *Psychasthenia.* A measure of phobias and compulsive behaviors.
8. *Schizophrenia.* A measure of bizarre and unusual thoughts and behaviors.
9. *Hypomania Scale.* A measure of excessive productivity of thoughts and actions.
10. *Social Introversion.* A measure of social withdrawal.

The test-retest reliability of the MMPI-A has been acceptable with one-week test-retest correlations averaging in the .70 to .80 range for individual scales. Use of the MMPI-A emphasizes the pattern or profile of the scores on the various clinical scales along with the supplementary information provided by the content and supplementary scales. Some of the more common abnormal profiles are correlated with traditional diagnostic labels.

Projective Tests. Projective tests are frequently used by clinical psychologists in their assessment of children with behavior problems. Many of the projective tests can be used with both adults and children, and a few of them have been designed primarily for children.

The most widely used projective test is the *Rorschach Inkblot Test* (Rorschach, 1942). The Rorschach consists of 10 inkblots printed on individual cards that are presented to the client one at a time. The client is asked to look at the card and tell what is seen or represented on the card. No time limit is given. When the client has responded to all 10 inkblots, the examiner inquires about each response in order. In this inquiry the examiner is attempting to determine what part of the inkblot elicited the response and what perceptual cues were involved. The Rorschach is administered to clients of all ages, although it is more commonly used with adolescents and adults.

Each Rorschach response is scored for location, determinants, and content. Location designates whether the client's response refers to the whole blot or specific parts of it; determinants include all references to form, color, shading, and movement; content refers to the type of object depicted by the response, such as humans, inanimate objects, or plants. A variety of scoring procedures have been devised for the Rorschach, but the one described by Exner and Weiner (1982) has become the most widely used. The interpretation of the Rorschach is based on the absolute as well as relative scores in the various categories and subcategories. Norms for the *Exner Comprehensive System,* for use with children and adolescents, have been published by Exner (1991). Long-term test-retest reliability on Rorschach responses for children has not shown the same degree of stability as with adults. This lack of long-term stability has been attributed to children's lower attention span, varying motivation, and changing personality. One-week test-retest reliability has been shown to be acceptable with 8 and 9 year olds (Exner, 1986). Long-term stability was found to occur when children reach the age of 14 or older.

Several thousand articles and books have been written about the Rorschach, but the validity of the test has not been historically demonstrated to the satisfaction of many research psychologists. The research studies that have reported high Rorschach validity have been strongly criticized as having major flaws (Eysenck, 1950). The widespread use of the Exner System has done much to establish the Rorschach as an empirically valid instrument. Clinicians maintain that the interpretation of patterns of scores on the Rorschach is based on substantial experience with clients and is, therefore, clinically valid.

The *Thematic Apperception Test* (TAT) is also a frequently used projective test. The TAT was developed by Murray and his coworkers at Harvard University (Murray, 1943) to assess the drives, emotions, and conflicts of personality. The test consists of 30 pictures, some of which are primarily for men, women, girls, or boys; others are for everyone. The client is instructed to make up a story for each picture the examiner shows. The client is asked to tell what led up to the event in the picture, what is happening in the picture, what the people in the picture are feeling and thinking, and what the outcome will be.

The basic assumption underlying the TAT is that the stories created by the client will reveal inhibited tendencies that the client will not or cannot describe. Interpretation is based on the central figure in the story who is assumed to represent the client. The examiner attempts to characterize the central figure in each story, noting similarities in characteristics across stories. The examiner then determines the general nature of the situations confronting the central figure, again attending particularly to those features that recur. The examiner lists the traits recurring among the people with whom the central figures interact. Murray has developed a list of types of environmental situations that are classified according to the effect they have on the central figure, and the examiner uses this list as the framework for the interpretation of the test results. Examples of these kinds of environmental situations are Affiliation (the central figure having close personal relationships with others), Dominance (other persons trying to force or prevent the central figure from doing something), and Physical Danger (the central figure being exposed to danger from nonhuman sources). In analyzing the reactions of the central figure, the examiner usually uses Murray's list of needs or drives to assess the client's motivational patterns. Murray's list includes Achievement, Nurturance, and Destruction.

The reliability of scoring of an interpretation of TAT protocols appears to be quite satisfactory. Research studies on the validity of the TAT have yielded contradictory findings.

One of the more recent apperception tests designed specifically for use with children is the *Roberts Apperception Test for Children* (RATC; McArthur & Roberts, 1982). The RATC is one of the few thematic techniques that includes an explicit scoring system. The RATC is intended for use with children between the ages of 6 and 15. The RATC has 11 card parallel versions for males and females, and there is also a supplementary set of cards featuring African-American children. Although the adoption of an explicit scoring system is reported to have increased interrater reliability, split-half reliabilities in the acceptable range ($r > .70$) are reported for only 6 of the 13 scales.

Human Figure Drawings are another projective approach to personality assessment. A typical projective drawing task is the *Kinetic Family Drawing* (KFD) (Burns &

Kaufman, 1970, 1972). Given a plain white sheet of paper and a pencil, the child is asked to "Draw a picture of everyone in your family, including you, DOING something. Try to draw whole people, not cartoons or stick people. Remember, make everyone DOING something—some kind of actions" (Burns & Kaufman, 1972, p. 5). No time limit is imposed. After the drawing is completed, the examiner asks a series of questions about the figures in the drawing. The answers to the questions as well as the characteristics (actions, styles, and symbols) of the drawing are used to make inferences about the child's psychological status.

The KFD manual does not include information about reliability and validity. Subsequent research provides only limited support for the clinical usefulness of the KFD. Scores based on children's drawings tend not to be very stable over a 2 to 4 week period. This instability tends to undermine attempts to demonstrate reliability and validity.

BEHAVIORAL ASSESSMENT

Bijou and Peterson (1971, pp. 63–64) have stated that the basic reason for assessment is to secure information that can be used to plan a treatment program. Behavioral assessment is composed of two parts: (1) delineation of the problem that caused the child to be referred and (2) an evaluation of the child's behavioral repertoire. In general, delineation of the child's problem involves referral information, completion of a behavior problem checklist by the parents or teacher, interviews with relevant adults and the child, and, occasionally, testing with standardized instruments. Evaluating the child's behavioral repertoire requires direct behavioral observation either in a clinic or in the child's natural environment, where the behavior problem occurs, whether in the home or school.

Behavioral approaches to assessment have some features in common with the more traditional approaches. For example, both approaches usually include the collection of referral information and interviews with relevant adults. The behavioral clinician typically emphasizes the collection of data about current behaviors and events and gives relatively little attention to searching for the origin of the problem or to documenting the past history of the child. Standardized test results are not usually an integral part of behavioral assessment. The primary reasons for this omission appear to be related to the behaviorists' rejection of traditional clinical methods and past misuses and misinterpretations of test data. The "medical model" of mental illness has historically emphasized the importance of underlying psychic conflict and the identification of "personality" characteristics in the assessment procedure. Behavioral clinicians have seriously questioned the utility of the medical model and have rejected personality tests on the basis of their poor reliability, validity, and utility with respect to facilitating the planning of treatment programs. Behaviorists maintain that behavior is situation-specific and, therefore, that trait labels cannot accurately describe people. Mischel (1968, 1979) has suggested that apparent consistencies in behavior reflect similarities in stimulus environments rather than internal personality traits.

The rejection of personality tests by behavioral clinicians has perhaps been overgeneralized to other types of standardized tests. Mischel (1968) has presented a strong case for the use of intelligence tests on the basis of their reliability, validity, and utility. Nevertheless, these tests are probably underused by behaviorists because in some instances the use of scores on these tests has had negative consequences for children. For example, low scores have sometimes resulted in inferior or no treatment. The stability of IQ test scores over time has unfortunately been misinterpreted by some professionals to mean that treatment programs can have no effect on later test performance when, in actuality, the stability may reflect that children's general environments tend to remain similar over time.

From a behavioral point of view, intelligence tests may be conceptualized as a sample of tasks for which norms have been developed. A low score suggests that the child's rate of learning these tasks is lower than for other children of the same age. Knowledge of a child's status relative to that of peers can aid in the decision as to whether the child's behavioral repertoire is indeed deficient. Low scores on intelligence tests do not indicate, however, the reasons for the behavioral deficiencies. Intelligence tests can also be utilized as assessment tools in the evaluation of treatment programs that aim for comprehensive skill development through a comparison of scores obtained before treatment with scores obtained after treatment.

Achievement tests are more often used by behavioral clinicians because they assess more clearly defined skill areas. They include only a sample of the possible specific behaviors comprising the skill area and provide an estimate of the child's performance relative to that of peers. If a child is referred for learning problems in school, an achievement test would be used to assess the current level of skills in the various school subjects. Behavioral clinicians also use achievement tests to assess the effectiveness of remedial programs by comparing pretreatment and posttreatment scores and determining whether the rate of learning the academic skills was significantly higher during the treatment phase.

It should be kept in mind that a number of the training programs for behavioral clinicians, particularly those for master's level psychologists, do not provide courses or supervised experience in the administration and interpretation of standardized intelligence and achievement tests. Nevertheless, many research studies on behavioral treatment programs include scores on standardized tests in their descriptions of the subjects. In some of these cases, the tests were administered by traditional clinicians for other purposes, and the extent to which behavioral clinicians utilized the information derived from testing is unknown.

For several reasons, it is likely that standardized tests will be utilized more frequently in the future. First, behavioral clinicians will increasingly have to make decisions about whether children's behavioral repertoires are abnormal, and these tests provide norms for the behaviors that are assessed. Second, standardized test results can often save the clinician time during the behavioral assessment process by pinpointing the developmental or mental age level for a broad range of behaviors; that is, they may reduce the total number of behaviors to be assessed more thoroughly.

Self-Observation

A number of studies have examined procedures whereby children assess the quality and quantity of their own behavior. Although many children can be trained to collect accurate data about themselves, self-assessment procedures have inherent problems that reduce their reliability and validity. Namely, requesting children to record their own behaviors may lead to changes in those behaviors. Reports of these reactive effects have led to the use of self-assessment as a treatment procedure by some behavioral clinicians. Several studies have suggested that self-assessment of appropriate behaviors is associated with an increase in their frequency, while self-assessment of inappropriate behaviors leads to decreases in the frequencies of these behaviors.

Observation by Others

Direct behavioral observation is the principal assessment procedure used by behaviorally oriented clinicians. Behavioral observation is the method of choice because the data are considered to be more valid than data obtained by the traditional assessment methods. That is, because behavioral clinicians regard psychological problems as behavior problems (and, therefore, subject to the laws of learning), the direct observation of the behavior problem has been assumed to be more valid than the other, particularly the traditional psychometric assessment methods. Since abnormal behavior is believed to be developed and maintained by environmental stimuli, the direct observation of the relationship between the behavior problem and the environmental factors should provide the most valid hypotheses about changes that would lead to improved behavior.

The behavioral clinician's first task in behavioral observation is to identify and delineate the target behaviors to be observed. The choice of behaviors is based on the information obtained from referral sources, behavior checklists, and the interviews with the mediators and the child. The second task is to determine the frequency with which these target behaviors occur and the environmental factors that are associated with the occurrence of the behaviors.

The initial period of observation is called the *baseline* observation period and focuses on the behavior as it normally or naturally occurs. The data obtained during the baseline observation period is later used in the evaluation of the intervention or treatment program. One of the important advantages of direct behavioral observation is that it permits a continuous assessment of behavior, thereby allowing the clinician to know the child's status with respect to the target behavior at any point in time during the assessment and treatment phases.

Settings.   Behavioral observations are usually conducted in the setting in which the problem behavior occurs. Thus, if the problem occurs in the home, direct observation of the child would take place in the home. Research investigators have reported the recording of behavior in a wide variety of settings, such as schools, homes, and institutions. Studies have also been conducted in which behavioral observation takes place in a setting that is not part of the child's natural environment, such as a clinic office or a research laboratory.

The diversity of settings in which behavior problems occur presents difficulties for the behavioral clinician. Permission for observation must be obtained, and observers who can work in that setting must be secured. For example, not all teachers are receptive to observers in the classroom, and few schools have personnel whose specific duties include the type of behavioral observation we are discussing here.

Behavior Codes. Many different types of behaviors have been observed and recorded. In general, the kinds of behaviors to be recorded are determined by the child's particular clinical needs. A number of behavior codes have been developed, however, for use in particular settings, such as the school, and these codes have been used frequently in the research literature. The clinician or researcher who designs a behavior code attempts to describe each behavior as precisely as possible, including examples of both its occurrence and instances that would *not* be considered part of the response class. This description of positive and negative instances of the response class is called an *operational definition.* While the same label may appear on several behavior codes (e.g., playing), the operational definitions of each may, in fact, vary. Let us now examine an example of a behavior code.

In 1970, O'Leary, Kaufman, Kass, and Drabman reported a study on the effects of loud and soft reprimands on the behavior of disruptive students. Two children from each of five classrooms had been selected as subjects because of their high rate of disruptive behavior. In this study, college undergraduates were the observers. Each child was observed daily for 20 minutes each day during the arithmetic lesson. A time-sampling technique was employed in which the child was observed for 20 seconds followed by 10 seconds for recording the disruptive behaviors that occurred during the observation period. Disruptive behaviors were categorized into nine classes as follows:

1. *Out-of-chair*: movement of the child from the chair when not permitted or requested by teacher.
2. *Modified-out-of-chair*: movement of the child from the chair with some part of the body still touching the chair (exclude sitting on feet).
3. *Touching others' property*: child comes into contact with another's property without permission to do so. Includes grabbing, rearranging, destroying the property of another, and touching the desk of another.
4. *Vocalization*: any unpermitted audible behavior emanating from the mouth.
5. *Playing*: child uses hands to play with own property so that such behavior is incompatible with learning.
6. *Orienting*: the turning or orienting response is not rated unless the child is seated, and turn must be more than 90 degrees, using the desk as a reference point.
7. *Noise*: child creating any audible noise other than vocalization without permission.

8. *Aggression*: child makes movement toward another person to come into physical contact (exclude brushing against another).
9. *Time-off task*: child does not do assigned work for entire 20-second interval. For example, child does not write or read when so assigned.

The investigators used as their primary behavior measure the mean frequency of disruptive behavior. The mean frequency was calculated by dividing the total number of disruptive behaviors by the number of intervals. They might have used the frequency of disruptive behavior each day, but unavoidable circumstances, such as assemblies, occasionally prevented them from observing the children exactly 20 minutes each day.

Other studies have focused on a broader range of behaviors. For example, Werry and Quay (1969) were concerned with three general categories of behaviors: inappropriate pupil behaviors, pupil attending behaviors, and teacher-pupil interactions. Each of these categories has various subcategories for which operational definitions similar to those in the previous example were developed. Commercially available coding systems such as the Behavioral Assessment System for Children–Student Observation System (BASC-SOS; Reynolds & Kamphaus, 1992) also tend to focus on a broad range of behaviors, including both desirable and undesirable behavior. The BASC-SOS has 13 categories of behavior used to group 65 operationally defined behaviors. Nine of the categories cover problem behavior; four cover adaptive/desirable behavior.

Methods of Assessing Observed Target Behavior. There are several types of objective methods for observing and recording behavior. Since behaviors are observed in a variety of settings and under a variety of circumstances, specific methods of observation are usually designed for individual situations. Observations may be recorded every day or only on certain days when the child is in a particular situation. On the days of observation, the behavior may be observed for a relatively brief period, such as 15 minutes, or for all of the hours that the child is awake. The important feature to note is that the observation period (the time of initiation and length) remains constant throughout the baseline and treatment phases. The specific period chosen should include the time when it is most probable that the behavior problem will occur.

The most common methods for quantifying behavioral observations are counting the number of times the behavior occurs, counting the number of time intervals during which the behavior occurs, or measuring the duration or the amount of time the behavior occurs. These methods are used both by commercially available coding systems designed for use across a wide range of children and by those designed by clinicians or researchers for individual children.

FREQUENCY. Frequency measures involve counting the number of times that the behavior occurs within a specific period of time. Response rate is determined by dividing the frequency of the behavior by time. Response rate is a particularly useful measure when the behavior can be clearly delineated, and each occurrence of the behavior takes about the same amount of time. Examples of behaviors that lend themselves to counting are number of words spoken, number of classroom assignments completed, and number of times the child hits another child. A mechanical counter or a tally sheet on a clipboard is the only necessary equipment.

INTERVAL RECORDING.   With interval recording, each observation session is subdivided into small time units, such as 15 or 20 seconds, and the observer indicates on a data sheet those units or intervals during which the behavior was observed. This method is also called *time sampling* when the observer takes time away from observing the child to record behaviors occurring during the previous interval. A typical time-sampling procedure, for example, would involve the clinician's observing the child's behavior for 20 seconds and then recording the behaviors that occurred during the 20-second interval during the next 10 seconds. Behaviors occurring during the 10-second recording period would not be recorded. The sequence of 20-second observe and 10-second record is then repeated throughout the session; if the sessions are lengthy, observers are given brief (predetermined) rest periods during which they neither formally observe nor record the child's behavior. Interval recording would appear to have the disadvantage of not providing an accurate measure in that only the presence or absence of the target behavior during each interval is indicated on the data sheet. Having the precise frequency of the behavior appears not to have great utility for many behavior clinicians because their programs focus on the direction and relative amount of change in the behavior as a function of intervention rather than on the specific number of behaviors occurring before and after treatment. When a serious, but infrequent, behavior problem is being assessed, a frequency, rather than an interval recording, method would probably be used.

The interval recording method has gained favor because of its usefulness in situations where the clinician wishes to observe a number of behaviors during the session. In these cases, the observer records the presence or absence of each form of behavior at the end of each interval. It would be very difficult to record the frequencies of more than a few behaviors simultaneously.

DURATION.   Response duration involves measuring the interval of time between the onset and termination of the behavior. This assessment method is particularly useful when the amount of time spent engaging in the behavior is the criterion upon which appropriateness or inappropriateness is based. The difficulties involved with this method are that the onset and termination of the behavior must be defined so that observers can readily agree on when the behavior began and ended. Either a stopwatch or access to a clock is required for the duration method.

Assessing Antecedents, Consequences, and Setting Events

In addition to determining the frequency or duration of the target behavior, the behavioral clinician must secure additional information regarding the stimuli that might be involved in the maintenance of the behavior. Some of this information has been derived from the interview and will be used to determine those aspects of the environment that will be included for assessment during the baseline phase.

Antecedent stimuli are those events that take place immediately before the behavior occurs and may serve the function of signaling to the child that reinforcement will be forthcoming if the behavior occurs. For example, mother's coming into a room may be a signal that attention will be forthcoming if a temper tantrum occurs. During the baseline phase, then, the observer records any change in environmental stimuli that precedes the occurrence of the behavior.

Consequences are those events that occur immediately after the behavior occurs and may serve as reinforcers that strengthen the behavior. The observer also records the stimulus events that follow the behavior. The recording of both antecedent and consequent stimuli will provide information to guide the clinician in the selection of an intervention program because these stimuli have a high likelihood of having a role in the maintenance of the behavior.

Setting events are those stimuli that appear to alter the effectiveness of reinforcement. For example, a mother's reprimand may serve to punish a given behavior in one setting and to reinforce it in another. The role of setting events has not been adequately explored in the research literature on abnormal behavior, but its importance in certain instances may be considerable. When clinicians are aware of the role of setting events in behavioral control, they are able to design more effective intervention programs. If the period of behavior observation includes setting changes (e.g., home, park, grocery store), the observer may be able to detect differences in the effectiveness of reinforcers in the various settings.

Formal procedures for assessing the role of stimulus events are not as well developed as those for assessing target behaviors. Often, the assessment of stimulus factors is conducted in a casual fashion, rather than recorded and quantified. Preliminary behavioral observations during which setting events, antecedent stimuli, and consequent stimuli, as well as the target behavior, are recorded are usually helpful. In addition, the inclusion of written descriptions about stimulus events during the recording portions of an interval procedure also provides descriptions of functional relationships.

A frequently used method for assessing the role of stimulus events is an ABC diary. A diary can be kept by parents, teachers, an outside observer such as an undergraduate, and/or the child. The basic procedure involves operationally defining the behaviors ("B") and recording the environmental conditions before and after the behavior occurs in a three-column table. Antecedents and setting events are recorded under the "A" column. Consequences are recorded under the "C" column. The parameters for keeping the diary are determined by a number of factors such as availability of observers, frequency of the behavior, and constraints of the setting. For example, it would be relatively easy to make an entry every time a behavior occurred in some cases but unrealistic in other cases (e.g., once an hour versus once every few seconds).

Observers. Since behavioral observation requires substantial amounts of time, use of professionals for this purpose is usually precluded. Fortunately, research studies have demonstrated that a wide variety of people, including parents, teachers, undergraduates, and peers, can be taught to observe behavior. Most of the research studies utilize independent observers, paid observers, or undergraduates who are earning course credit for participation in the research. Many clinical practitioners do not have access to such resources and have to rely more heavily on "volunteers" from the child's environment. To a large extent, the design of the behavioral observation procedure is determined by the availability and skills of the observers available to the clinician.

Ideally, the data collected are not influenced by the observers. Independent observers collecting data in natural environments are instructed not to interact with the children, since such interactions would not be part of the children's typical experiences and would interfere with the observers' attention to the observation and recording tasks. Observers are told to be as inconspicuous as possible while maintaining a position that permits them to see and hear. In the classroom, for example, observers usually position themselves in the back of the room. After a few days of observation, children in classroom settings cease to give more than minimal attention to the observers. Turning around and looking at the observer is handled effectively by the observer's avoiding eye contact with the child.

A behavioral assessment procedure for an individual child usually involves two or more observers, with the number depending on the amount of time required and the availability of observers. If one person is able to observe during all of the sessions, that person becomes the primary observer whose data are used. A second observer participating in some of the sessions is necessary for establishing interobserver agreement.

Interobserver Agreement. Because behavioral observation data may be influenced by a number of factors, notably the observer's interpretation of the behavior categories and the demands of the observation task, certain procedures are carried out to make possible the replicability of studies using human observers. One such procedure involves measuring the extent to which two or more observers agree that certain behaviors have occurred. Before the initiation of the baseline phase, the observers are trained in the behavior code and practice observing and recording the behaviors simultaneously but independently of one another. The observers then compare their ratings to determine the amount of agreement. The most commonly used formula to compute interobserver agreement is number of agreements divided by the sum of the number of agreements and the number of disagreements, and the ratio is expressed in terms of percent agreement. Instances of agreement that a particular behavior did *not* occur are usually not included in the computation of interobserver agreement.

During the practice sessions, the observers compute their agreement and discuss each instance of disagreement, arriving at a mutual decision about how that behavior should be rated in the future. Training and practice sessions are continued until the observers achieve an agreement level of 80 to 85 percent or greater. Interobserver agreement continues to be monitored throughout the study to ensure continued agreement on the definitions of the response classes and the instances of occurrences of the response classes.

A formal assessment of interobserver agreement is generally not possible when the rater is chosen from the child's normal environment. Ratings from different settings (e.g., school versus home) are not useful for this purpose because differences could represent differences in the child's behavior across settings.

There are a few commercially available observation systems for which interobserver reliability studies have been conducted (e.g., CBCL-Direct Observation Form; Achenbach, 1986). In these cases, interobserver reliability and the conditions under which it was tested are reported in the manual. If the clinician assures that the observations are conducted under the same conditions (e.g., same type of rater with same amount of training), it is not necessary for the clinicians to conduct such tests themselves.

The Baseline Observation Period. Ideally, the baseline phase should be continued until the behavior becomes stabilized. In practice, it is difficult to determine when the baseline phase should end because children's baselines rarely reach the stable levels found in the animal research literature. The greater variability in children's session-to-session behavior is no doubt due to the greater variety of environmental changes experienced by children. Thus, behavioral clinicians and researchers either decide that the baseline period will be of a particular length prior to the initiation of behavioral observations or arbitrarily terminate the baseline phase when it is apparent that the data reflect reliable high and low points. The general consensus is that a minimal baseline period should include one week (or five days in school settings) of data collection.

Figure 3-1 (page 52) presents three examples of baseline data. In Example 1 the child engaged in an inappropriate behavior during either seven or eight intervals out of a possible eight intervals. The data reflect a high and fairly stable rate. The data in Example 2 reflect more variability, showing that on some days the child's rate of inappropriate behavior is very high, while on others the rate is moderate. The data in Example 3 would be considered unstable in that they show a strong directional trend, the limits of which are more ambiguous than those in Examples 1 and 2.

Reliability and Validity. Attention has been directed to the reliability (as separate from interobserver reliability or agreement) and validity of data obtained through direct behavioral observation. In one perspective, session-to-session variability in behavior may be viewed as an indication of reliability when the measuring instrument, setting, condition, and observer training level are held constant. Perhaps statistical methods will eventually be used to measure this reliability and provide guidelines for determining the appropriate number of baseline sessions for individual clients.

The validity of behavioral data poses greater problems because there has been no agreement about adequate validity criteria. One view is that the criterion is the data collected on a continuous time basis for the same sessions in which time sampling was utilized (e.g., Powell & Rockinson, 1978). Another view is that behavioral data are samples from a behavioral domain or class of behaviors; therefore, behavioral assessment methods should be examined for their content validity, namely, the extent to which a particular assessment procedure measures the class of behaviors

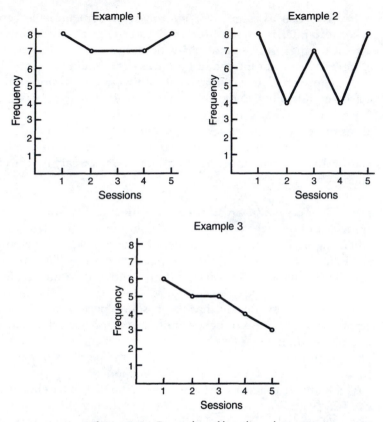

Figure 3-1   Examples of baseline data

it was designed to sample (Linehan, 1980). A study by Cosper and Erickson (1984) indicated that three-week samples of behavior observations were not significantly related to teachers' ratings of children's behavior. The results suggested that teachers' ratings are global in nature and perhaps reflect the teachers' entire history with the children, while behavioral observations reflect behavior that is much more circumscribed to the particular time and setting.

SCORING, INTERPRETATION, AND DIAGNOSIS

After the tests are administered, they are scored and interpreted by the clinician. A detailed report based on all of the assessment data is then written. This report usually includes information obtained from the referral source, the interviews, and the test results. The later portions of the report provide the clinician's diagnosis of the problem, probable etiological factors, and suggestions for types of treatment or specific treatment plans. Diagnosis refers to the labeling of a child's behavior problem after the formal assessment procedures have been completed. Diagnostic labels are sometimes changed after the initiation of treatment, when additional information suggests that they are not accurate. That is, most clinicians do not consider assessment to terminate with the choice of a diagnostic label but rather to continue throughout the course of treatment.

If the assessment procedures have been conducted by a team of professionals, each writes a report on his or her individual findings, but the formal diagnosis and treatment plan are deferred until the team has a conference and members exchange information. The combined reports and clinical opinions are then used as the basis for a group determination of diagnosis and treatment plan.

CONCLUSIONS

Most clinical child psychologists utilize the interview and standardized tests in their assessment of children's behavior disorders. The clinician must be aware that adults do not always remember historical events or report current events accurately. The parental interview is of paramount importance because children's behavior problems occur in the context of children's interaction with parents and other relevant persons. Standardized intelligence and achievement tests are particularly useful in comparing an individual child's performance with that of same-aged peers and may be useful in determining the type of treatment needed by the child. Many clinicians also find that data from personality tests are useful in planning treatment programs, but other clinicians challenge their utility for a number of reasons, including low or unavailable reliability or validity, or both.

The most salient feature of behavioral assessment is its reliance on observable behavior and environmental events. This approach reflects the major assumption that behavior is largely controlled by environmental stimuli. The collection of behavioral data is subject to many of the same types of methodological problems found for the more traditional assessment techniques, namely, problems of reliability and validity.

The diagnostic and classification system most frequently used (DSM-IV) is evolving from an originally clinical basis toward an empirical basis. Increasing attention has been given to its reliability and validity. Although the DSM system has been improved, the sections related to children and adolescents continue to present significant difficulties in usefulness, reliability, and validity.

RECOMMENDED READINGS

Achenbach, T.M., & McConaughy, S.H. (1996). *Empirically based assessment of child and adolescent psychopathology: Practical applications* (2nd ed.). New York: Plenum.

Buros, O.C. (published yearly). *Mental Measurements Yearbook.* Highland Park, NJ: Gryphon Press.

Johnson, J.H., & Goldman, J. (Eds.). (1990). *Developmental assessment in clinical child psychology: A handbook.* Elmsford, NY: Pergamon.

Kamphaus, R.W., & Frick, P.J. (1996). *Clinical assessment of child and adolescent personality and behavior.* Boston: Allyn and Bacon.

Mash, E.J., & Terdal, L.G. (Eds.). (1997) *Behavioral assessment of childhood disorders* (3rd ed.). New York: Guilford.

Rourke, B., Fiske, J., & Strang, J. (1986). *Neuropsychological assessment of children: Treatment oriented approach.* New York: Guilford.

Sattler, J.M. (1992). *Assessment of children* (Revised and Updated 3rd ed.). San Diego: Author.

4

Etiology: Genetic, Prenatal, and Perinatal Risk Factors

This chapter describes some of the genetic, prenatal, and perinatal factors that are believed to increase the risk for developmental and behavior disorders. Later chapters describe the roles of these and other factors in the etiology of specific behavior disorders.

GENETIC RISK FACTORS

Our earlier understanding of the role of genetic factors was derived from studies focusing on pedigree descriptions (that is, incidence of abnormalities in generations of families). Historically, Gregor Mendel is responsible for the postulation and demonstration of hereditary factors through his hybridization experiments with plants. Identification of the physical basis of inheritance, the chromosome, was the next most salient discovery. The contemporary phase began with the direct visual examination of chromosomes and biochemical analyses of genetic material.

Until 1956, it was generally thought that the human cell had 48 chromosomes. Improved techniques for human tissue culture and for promoting and arresting cell division made possible Tijo and Levan's (1956) finding that the human cell has only 46 chromosomes (22 pairs of autosomes and one pair of sex chromosomes). The better visualization of the chromosomes also made it possible to observe their size and morphology (that is, form and structure) and to arrange them in a particular order. Being able to count the number of chromosomes and to examine their gross morphology has led to the discovery of a number of chromosome abnormalities.

Great progress has been made in the knowledge of chromosomes because newer methods for laboratory staining of the chromosomes (called "banding techniques") and other chromosome mapping methods have permitted parts of the chromosomes and the locations of these parts to be clearly identified. Applications based on the mapping of chromosomes include the possibility of prenatal identification of individuals who will not manifest serious hereditary disorders until later in life. In 1989 molecular biologists embarked on a 15-year project to identify the exact sequence of all three billion nucleotide pairs that together encode all inherited human traits. Watson and Crick's (1953) description of the structure and replication of DNA initiated the science of molecular biology and thus the possibility of understanding genetic processes at their most fundamental levels.

Chromosome Abnormalities

The clinical syndrome first found to be associated with an abnormal number of chromosomes was Down syndrome or "mongolism." Lejeune, Gautier, and Turpin (1959) discovered that chromosome 21 was represented in triplicate (trisomy) instead of in duplicate, thus increasing the chromosome count in each cell to 47 instead of 46. Trisomies of other autosomal chromosomes (for example, 13, 15, 17, and 18) have subsequently been described in the research literature. Many of the possible chromosomal abnormalities have been found only in spontaneously aborted fetuses, suggesting that certain abnormalities in the number of chromosomes are incompatible with life.

Engel (1977) noted that at least 10 percent of pregnancies begin with some chromosomal abnormality, but most of these pregnancies end in spontaneous abortion. Chromosomal defects can be identified in about 2.5 percent of newborn infants (Willis & Walker, 1989). Some chromosomal errors are not inherited but are caused by environmental agents (e.g., radiation).

In the normal human, sex chromosome constitutions are XY in the male and XX in the female. Considerable research on the sex chromosomes has become possible through the relatively inexpensive sex chromatin test that identifies the number of X chromosomes. In an early large-scale survey of newborn infants, 11 out of 4,400 were found to have abnormalities in the number of sex chromosomes (Leonard, Landy, Ruddle, & Lubs, 1974). Prospective studies of children diagnosed at birth as having sex chromosome abnormalities have found higher than expected rates of developmental, learning, and behavior problems (e.g., Robinson, Bender, Borelli, Puck, & Salenblatt, 1983).

A large number of inherited metabolic disorders have been discovered, and some of them have been found to be associated with behavioral disorders. These conditions are almost always autosomal recessive or sex-linked and due to one defective gene. The abnormalities are detected by means of urine and blood tests that evaluate amino acid levels. A number of the metabolic disorders can be treated by restricting or providing particular foods, chemicals, or drugs.

Psychological Studies of Genetic Factors

The area of behavior genetics encompasses a variety of approaches for determining the hereditary basis of behavior. Animal studies, which utilize selective breeding techniques, have yielded the most direct measures of the influence of heredity. Studies with humans, necessarily correlational in design, have measured the contribution of heredity indirectly as a function of the genetic relationships among the persons examined.

Pedigree Analysis. One of the earliest techniques for evaluating the hereditary contributions to behavior involved the initial identification of an individual (proband) who had the behavior (or trait) and the tracing of the incidence of this trait in the proband's ancestors, siblings, and children. Galton (1869) used this method in his study of the families of eminent men. Pedigree studies have a number of methodological shortcomings, not the least of which is the confounding of hereditary and environmental influences. Galton's eminent men, whose abilities he believed were due to hereditary factors, were also raised in intellectually stimulating environments. In addition, reliable descriptions of family members beyond a few generations are seldom possible. The chances of locating hereditary abnormalities are more likely, however, when families with more than one defective person are studied.

Twin Studies. The most popular research approach in behavior genetics involves the comparison of identical twins, whose genetic endowment is identical because they result from the splitting of the same fertilized egg, and same-sex fraternal twins, whose genetic relationship is essentially the same as that of nontwin, same-sex siblings. Specification of identical and fraternal twin status is not a simple matter; obstetricians and parents are incorrect in their designation about 10 to 15 percent of the time (Lykken, 1978). All of the earlier twin studies contain some error in the designation of identical and fraternal twin status. The most recent twin studies have tended to employ a series of 20 or more blood tests to discriminate the types of twins. When the results of every blood test are the same for a set of twins, they are considered identical; if the results of any one or more of these blood tests differ, the twins are considered fraternal.

The results of several dozen twin studies have suggested that heredity is the primary factor in determining the differences among people with respect to intellectual functioning, accounting for between 50 and 70 percent of the variance among the persons studied (Plomin, 1989). Such findings have often been misunderstood to mean that intelligence is fixed or predetermined, when, in fact, they only describe the contribution of heredity under the environmental conditions experienced by that particular group of subjects. There is nothing inherent in the attribution of heritability that precludes a specially designed environment from increasing intellectual abilities. Theoretically, if all people lived under environmental conditions that best used their potential, then all remaining individual differences would be attributable to heredity. Scarr-Salapatek (1971) found that heritability of intelligence was considerably higher for children in the upper socioeconomic groups than for children from lower socioeconomic environments.

Twin studies have been proposed as significant contributors to our understanding of etiological factors (LaBuda, Gottesman, & Pauls, 1993). More recent research has utilized structural equation modeling to examine heritability of behavior problems in large samples of twins; for example, Silberg, Erickson, Meyer, Eaves, Rutter, & Hewitt (1994) found significant heritability for maternal ratings of both internalizing and externalizing behavior problems in 8–16-year-old twins as well as significant contributions of shared and unshared environments. Plomin (1994a) has argued that because genetic influence on developmental psychopathology has only rarely accounted for more than half the variance, genetic research provides the best evidence for the importance of environmental influences.

. One objection to the twin method has questioned the assumption that the environments of identical and fraternal twins are similar. In a sense, this argument is not a very strong one, since (1) the environment of twins raised together is likely to be as similar as could be found in nonexperimental situations, and (2) differences in the environments of twins reared together have a higher probability of being related to behaviors resulting from genetic factors than of being due to random environmental variations. That is, environmental differences are more likely to be dependent on the idiosyncratic responses of each twin than on differences in the environment per se.

In twin studies, all concordance is attributed to heredity while discordance is considered to reflect the influences of environment. It is possible that not all concordance is due to the direct influence of the genetic constitution. For example, a particular complication during pregnancy could affect identical twins similarly and fraternal twins differentially, since fraternal twins are more likely to be at different embryologic stages at the time of the complication. In these instances, the prenatal factors may be of primary importance in terms of prevention. Some of the discordance found in identical twins may also be due to prenatal and perinatal events that affect only one of the twins (for example, lack of oxygen during a difficult delivery). Since heredity and environment are confounded beginning with conception, and perhaps prior to conception (Erickson, 1967), heritability figures should be carefully interpreted.

Generalizations to other populations from the data of twin studies have also been criticized on the basis that twins differ from these populations. Twins tend to weigh less at birth, to have older mothers, and to show small but consistently higher levels of both externalizing and internalizing behavior problems (Gau, Silberg, Erickson, & Hewitt, 1992).

Problems in the criteria used for diagnosis have also been mentioned in the criticisms of twin studies. That is, the criteria for diagnosis are neither consistent nor always precisely defined. Twin studies also have not always used some of the controls now deemed necessary in research. For example, some investigators have utilized observer-interviewers who were familiar with the hypotheses of the studies, possibly biasing the results in favor of the investigators.

Experimental Studies with Animals. Experimental behavior genetics utilizes the selective breeding of insects and higher animals to examine the effect of heredity on behavior. In addition, the environments in which the animals are raised are controlled. Behavioral differences among breeds of domestic animals have long been recognized. Studies have shown, for example, some breeds of dog to be more independent than others, some to be more excitable, and others to be more easily taught.

Tryon (1940) and Heron (1941) used an experimental procedure that is considered to be a classical approach in animal behavior genetics. A group of laboratory animals is observed and measured for a particular behavior or trait. Animals that have the highest scores are interbred, and the animals with the lowest scores are interbred. The offspring of these matings are measured for the trait; again the highest scorers are selected for interbreeding, and the lowest scorers are selected for interbreeding. This procedure is continued for a number of generations. The studies of Tryon and Heron demonstrated that this method could be used to breed selectively for maze-learning ability in rats. Their maze-bright animals, however, were not necessarily superior in other learning tasks.

Inbred strains have been shown to differ in a wide variety of characteristics, such as alcohol preference, activity level, hoarding, emotionality, and social behaviors. Animal studies have lent support to the thesis that a variety of behaviors may be governed to a significant extent by genetic constitution.

PRENATAL RISK FACTORS

A number of prenatal factors have been implicated in the etiology of behavioral disorders, but it should be stressed that much of our knowledge comes from correlational research that permits only hypotheses regarding cause-effect relationships.

Although experimental studies have been conducted with animals, generalizations to humans must be made with extreme caution. For ethical reasons, experimental studies with humans are rarely done.

A primary source of correlational information has been the determination of those prenatal factors that have been associated with an increased infant mortality rate. The factors that cause death in some infants are also likely to cause other infants physical damage that may be manifested in learning and behavioral problems.

Most of the available information in this area has been derived from retrospective studies. Children with particular physical or behavioral characteristics are identified, and their prenatal histories examined for evidence of detrimental conditions. There are a number of possible weaknesses in this approach, especially the reliance on poorly documented medical and hospital records. The errors involved in the poor recordkeeping are often those of omission, which reduces the chances of identifying a significant factor. When retrospective studies are carefully designed, however, they do add substantially to our statistical understanding of the role of prenatal factors in the etiology of developmental and behavioral problems. It should be emphasized that such knowledge does not permit the specification of etiology in the individual case. When a prenatal event known to be detrimental on a statistical basis has occurred, its causal role cannot be assured because very few complications of pregnancy, labor, and delivery affect all children in the same way. While certain pregnancy complications may increase the mortality rate of the infants who experience them, most of the infants survive and most of the survivors show little or no adverse effects.

Prospective longitudinal studies have contributed to our understanding of prenatal etiological factors, but they are relatively rare due to their expense and the great lengths of time involved. One substantial study, the Collaborative Perinatal Project (Hellmuth, 1967), involved 14 institutions of higher learning and 20,000 children whose mothers were studied during pregnancy. The children received physical and psychological examinations at regular intervals from infancy through eight years of age. This project has provided significant information regarding the impact of prenatal events.

As will be seen later, the child is most vulnerable during the first trimester (three months) of gestation. During some of this period the mother is frequently not sure that she is pregnant. Many women are not even under a physician's care until near the end of the first trimester. Prevention of adverse conditions during this period would, therefore, necessitate a comprehensive public education program.

Nutrition

The mother's nutritional status has long been recognized as one of the most important determinants of the infant's status. The condition of the child at birth depends not only on the mother's nutrition during pregnancy, but also on her whole nutritional history. If the mother has been poorly nourished during her development, her physical condition during pregnancy will be less than optimal and increase the probability of adverse conditions for the child *in utero*. Even optimal nutrition during pregnancy will not counteract the deficiencies of a malfunctioning mother.

Next to genetic factors, nutritional history most strongly determines differences in height, weight, physical development, and morbidity rates. In the United States, an adolescent girl is likely to be the most poorly nourished member of the family. This problem is at least partly due to the culture's emphasis on slimness and the preponderance of easily available but relatively nonnutritious foods. Unfortunately, poor dietary habits developed in adolescence may continue into adulthood. Since approximately 25 percent of mothers having their first child are less than 20 years old, adolescent nutrition is an important factor. Loss of body fat from dieting or exercise can cause fertility problems; fat tissue appears to exert a regulatory effect on the reproductive ability of women (Frisch, 1988).

Experimental studies with lower animals have shown that nutritional deficiencies are capable of producing serious disturbances in the growth and development of the embryo and fetus. Experimental research involving the deprivation of particular nutritional substances prior to conception and during pregnancy has demonstrated an increased rate of fetal death and congenital abnormalities (absence of eyes, small eyes, harelip, cleft palate, underdevelopment of lungs and kidneys). The timing of the nutritional deficiency during pregnancy is also important in determining whether or not a specific congenital defect will result. Genetic factors are also involved, however, because these studies show that different strains of the same species will respond differently given the same nutritional deficiency.

One of the earliest studies with humans to demonstrate the substantive effect of maternal diet on the health of the infant was that of Ebbs, Tisdall, and Scott (1942). These investigators studied a group of women who were all originally poorly nourished. Nearly half of the original group was given a diet that increased their intake of protein, calcium, iron, and calories to a desirable level. The women on the supplemental diet and their infants did better on all criteria than the subjects who remained on their usual diet. The poor diet was significantly associated with poor prenatal status, prolonged labor and convalescence, and a three- to fourfold greater incidence in illness of the infants during the first six months of life. Nearly 12 percent of the poor-diet infants were lost through miscarriage, stillbirth, or later death, while all of the supplemented-diet infants survived.

Similarly, studies of women living under wartime conditions with very strict rationing of food have shown that about half of them stopped menstruating and the other half experienced irregular menstrual periods. For the women who did conceive, the rate of premature births, stillbirths, and congenital malformations of the infants was increased considerably (Smith, 1947). Children who were malnourished *in utero* have also been found to have poorer verbal comprehension and expressive language skills (Walther & Ramaekers, 1982).

Maternal nutrition has also been found to influence the intelligence of children. Harrell, Woodyard, and Gates (1955) conducted a study that examined the influence of vitamin supplementation of pregnant and lactating women's diet on the intelligence of their children. The study involved 2,400 women from Kentucky and Virginia. Four kinds of vitamin supplements and a placebo that contained no supplements were administered in such a way that no participant knew the contents of the tablets. When tested at four years of age, the children of the Virginia mothers who were given the supplements surpassed the placebo group by an average of 5.2 Stanford-Binet IQ points. The average for the B-complex groups exceeded that of the placebo group by 8.1 points. There were no significant differences among the Kentucky groups, a finding that was attributed to the Kentucky groups' regularly good diet. High caloric supplementation from birth to two years predicted higher levels of social involvement, both happy and angry affect, and moderate activity level at school age, whereas low supplementation was associated with passivity, dependency, and anxious behavior (Barrett, Radke-Yarrow, & Klein, 1982).

Maternal Age

Difficulties during pregnancy and birth, as well as the frequency of developmental abnormalities, have been shown to be highly correlated with the age of the mother. The available evidence indicates ages 23 to 28 years as being optimal for pregnancy, since this age span is associated with the highest survival rates for mother and child and the lowest abortion, miscarriage, stillbirth, prematurity, and malformation rates.

The higher incidence of problems at younger ages has been attributed in part to the immaturity of the reproductive system; the pelvic organs are not fully developed until at least 10 years after the beginning of menstruation. It has been estimated that over one third of all females between 15 and 20 years of age in the United States have at least one unwanted pregnancy. Although many choose abortions, large numbers of teenagers subject their infants to both physical and psychological risks (see Chapter 5). Furthermore, these young mothers endanger their own physical and psychological welfare by curtailing their education and in many instances, guaranteeing themselves and their child a life of poverty. Prematurity and child abuse are significant correlates of teenage parenting.

After the age of 28 years, a gradual increase in the rate of problems associated with pregnancy begins, and this rate accelerates after the age of 35, when the reproductive system begins to lose efficiency. Evidence for the loss of efficiency is apparent in the increased rate of two-egg twins (due to the release of two ova instead of the usual one) in the older mother. Statistically higher rates of mental retardation and other behavior disorders have also been found to be correlated with the increased age of the mother.

Viral and Bacterial Infections of the Mother

At one time it was believed that the mother's diseases could not affect the fetus. As the number of investigations has increased, evidence has accumulated that both viruses and bacteria can be transmitted from mother to child. A number of these infections are capable of seriously affecting the development of the fetus. We have also learned that when the mother is immunized during pregnancy the fetus will receive maternal antibodies and will be immune for several months after birth.

The idea that viruses could affect the embryo or fetus was strongly resisted at one time. This position was understandable in view of the fact that most of the common viral diseases, such as mumps, measles, and chicken pox, usually occur in childhood, giving the potential mother immunity that lasts through the childbearing years. Because few pregnant women would develop these diseases, data were incomplete. One exception is rubella (German measles), which is likely to occur in young adulthood. A relatively mild communicable disease, rubella can be very damaging to the fetus during the first trimester of pregnancy.

The effects of viral diseases on the fetus have usually been discovered retrospectively. That is, the condition of the child is noted first, and the history of the mother during pregnancy is obtained later. This method is likely to lead to an overestimate of the risk, since normal children of mothers who had the infection during pregnancy are not taken into consideration. Prospective studies begin with the identification of mothers experiencing an infection and then assess the effect of the infection on the child. Several prospective studies have indicated that the risk of a major defect is 50 percent if the mother is infected with rubella in the first month of pregnancy, 25 percent in the second month of pregnancy, 17 percent in the third month, 11 percent in the fourth, 6 percent in the fifth, and essentially no risk in later months. Bell (1959), in a study of 712 women who had rubella during the first half of pregnancy, found that 62 percent of the children were deaf, 50 percent had congenital heart disease, and 35 percent had cataracts. Milder forms of defects also occur, but they are frequently not detected in the first few years of life.

Since the risk of defects is so high, most physicians advise terminating the pregnancy if the mother has rubella during the first four months of pregnancy. Prevention has been greatly emphasized by advising parents to immunize their children to rubella. Pregnant women should take special precautions to avoid being exposed, since it is possible for the fetus to be affected by the virus without the mother's showing any clinical symptoms. The live virus vaccine for rubella should not be given to pregnant women. Gamma globulin is considered to be effective in preventing the disease if it is administered within eight days of exposure to rubella.

A number of other formerly common childhood diseases, such as measles and mumps, can lead to spontaneous abortions and possibly to congenital defects. The live vaccines for these diseases also cannot be given to pregnant women because they may harm the fetus. Prevention of these problems would be largely accomplished if all parents were careful about getting their children immunized early in life and maintaining the recommended immunization schedule.

Influenza was initially associated only with a high rate of abortion. Coffey and Jessop (1959), taking advantage of a predicted flu epidemic in Ireland, studied women for whom influenza virus A was isolated during pregnancy and a group of pregnant women who had not had flu, both groups being matched for age, parity, and blood groups. They found that 3.6 percent of the babies born to the flu-exposed mothers had malformations, while malformed infants accounted for only 1.5 percent of the children of the mothers who had not had influenza. The risk of malformation was highest for the first trimester of pregnancy. While the risk of defect is relatively low, the numbers of children involved may be considerably greater because flu epidemics are fairly frequent and affect large numbers of people.

Our most recent concern about viruses involves pediatric AIDS or *human immunodeficiency virus* (HIV) infection (Task Force on Pediatric AIDS, 1989). While the number of child cases of AIDS is a small percent of the total reported AIDS cases in the United States, they have been increasing. About 19 percent of reported child AIDS cases are the result of transfusions of HIV-contaminated blood, but this proportion is expected to decrease with improved screening of the blood supply. The majority of cases involve transmission from the mother to child either prenatally or during delivery. The mother's infection can usually be traced to her own or her sexual partner's use of intravenous drugs.

Prenatal and perinatal infection increases the risk for the development of HIV symptoms. In addition to frequent illnesses, the children are also likely to show failure to thrive and delayed development.

As a group, bacterial infections of the pregnant woman have not been associated with congenital deformities of the child, but many of these infections are transmitted to the child from the mother. In the case of tuberculosis, for example, the mother may not know that she has the disease and gives birth to a child with congenital tuberculosis who will very likely die without treatment. Treatment of tuberculosis became quite effective following the introduction of antibiotics.

Syphilis, a bacterial disease transmitted by sexual intercourse, can also be transmitted from the mother to the child. Congenital syphilis is not as common as it once was because infected mothers can be successfully treated with penicillin. If the mothers are untreated, up to 80 percent of fetuses will contract the disease, but when treatment is begun before the fifth month of pregnancy, the rate will be less than 2 percent. Congenital syphilis has been associated with fetal abortion, death, and extensive damage to many organs.

Toxoplasmosis is a protozoan disease that is essentially symptomless in the adult but has serious consequences for the child *in utero*. Congenital toxoplasmosis is related to hydrocephalus (large head associated with an excessive amount of fluid in the cranium), serious damage to the eyes, convulsions, and calcification (hardening) of small areas of the brain. Hydrocephalus occurs in about 80 percent of the cases. Mental retardation is almost always present, varying from mild to profound. Many of the infants die soon after birth. Since toxoplasmosis is a relatively common disease, it is advisable for all women to be given a skin test prior to pregnancy and for those with negative reactions to be reexamined at intervals during pregnancy. Prevention programs include avoiding cats (who may transmit the disease through their stools) and eating only well-cooked meat.

Maternal Dysfunction

In this section we deal with those physical conditions of the mother, other than infections, that bear on the subsequent status of the child.

Obesity is associated with an increased mortality rate for both mother and child. Obese women also have high risk for a variety of other physical problems.

Because of these relationships, physicians have exerted considerable pressure on pregnant women to gain only moderate amounts of weight. More recently, there have been concerns that physicians have been too stringent in their standards for weight gain, and that some mothers and infants have thereby been subjected to possible nutritional deficiencies. Obstetricians are currently advising the average pregnant woman that a weight gain of 25 pounds is optimal.

In some cases, weight gain per se may not be a cause of complications during pregnancy. That is, unusual patterns of weight gain during pregnancy may be the result of a metabolic disturbance that is also causing the complications (Erickson, 1971).

The *toxemias* (presence of toxic substances in the blood) of pregnancy, preeclampsia and eclampsia, whose causes are currently unknown, affect about 5 percent of pregnant women. The symptoms of preeclampsia include excessive weight gain because of fluid retention in the tissues, a rise in blood pressure, and the detection of albumin in the urine. Eclampsia includes these symptoms with the addition of maternal convulsions. Toxemia is the principal cause of maternal death, although the majority of cases can now be prevented. There is evidence that the brain of the toxemic woman's child can be adversely affected.

Pregnant women who have high blood pressure, or *hypertension*, also have higher rates of fetal and maternal mortality, especially when the mother was also hypertensive in her nonpregnant condition. Hypertension often alters the development of the placenta such that oxygen deficiency occurs, which results in a slower growth rate of the fetus.

Sickle cell anemia is a genetically determined blood disorder primarily affecting black people. This condition, when present in pregnant women, increases the rate of abortions, stillbirths, and abnormalities; there is also a tendency for the children to have low birth weight. Those who survive either are carriers of the trait or manifest the condition themselves.

Diabetes is characterized by deficiency in the supply of insulin, which controls the metabolism of carbohydrates. The principal symptoms are excessive urination, sugar in the urine, high blood sugar, excessive thirst and hunger, weakness, and loss of weight. Diabetes during pregnancy may create significant risks for both mother and child. Probably because of the hyperactivity of its pancreas, the fetus grows at a greater than usual rate, reaching the weight of an average newborn several weeks before the end of gestation. If permitted to go to term, many are injured during the birth process. Early diagnosis and treatment have greatly improved the originally poor prognosis. Dietary treatment and early delivery of the child can save the lives of virtually all infants of diabetic mothers. Special precautions after birth must be maintained. Even though quite large, the newborn of the diabetic mother is very much like a premature infant and must be handled as such in the hospital after delivery.

Maternal hormonal disorders may have both transient and permanent effects on the child. *Hyperthyroidism* in the mother is related to unusually high abortion and stillbirth rates. Some infants will manifest hypothyroidism, which usually subsides within a few weeks after birth. Several types of hypothyroidism are related to cretinism which, if untreated, results in mental retardation.

Blood group incompatibilities present still another problem to the developing child; the most well-known of them is the Rh factor. Second- and subsequent-born children of an Rh negative mother and an Rh positive father have an increased risk of dying *in utero* or soon after birth from a blood disorder called *erythroblastosis*. The baby suffers from anemia caused by the destruction of the blood cells by maternal Rh antibodies that are stimulated by fetal antigens passing through the placenta into the mother's blood. Infants born with this condition have a high probability of being brain damaged by a substance called bilirubin.

Infants who present high bilirubin levels are given exchange transfusions. Rh negative blood is used in the exchange transfusion because the mother's antibodies would continue to destroy Rh positive blood. The baby's damaged blood is removed at the same time he or she is given the transfusion of intact red blood cells. Prevention of this problem is now possible by the administration of a vaccine, Rh immune globulin, within 72 hours after the mother's first delivery, abortion, or miscarriage and subsequent ones as well.

Medications and Addictive Substances

The thalidomide tragedy during the 1960s increased our awareness of the effects of medication on the developing fetus. Thalidomide was prescribed as a mild tranquilizer in Europe, primarily in Germany. When taken early in pregnancy, it caused the absence or shortening of the infant's limbs. Thousands of physically handicapped children were born before thalidomide was identified as the cause and taken off the market.

Medication, drugs, and other chemicals are being manufactured and consumed in great quantities. For example, many of the foods we eat contain additives and preservatives. Although there are laws that govern the testing of drugs and other substances consumed by humans, much of this testing research has not been adequate. While it is true that medications that are to be administered to adults must be tested on adults, these drugs may not be tested for their effects on the unborn child. There is ample evidence that the adult's reaction to a particular drug in no way adequately predicts its effect on the fetus. Drugs taken by a pregnant woman may affect the fetus, but this effect depends on the particular drug, the period of pregnancy, the amount taken, and the genetic constitutions of mother and child.

Moreover, adverse effects may not become apparent for a number of years after the pregnant woman has been given the medication. For example, in the early 1970s, it was discovered that the synthetic estrogen DES, used for threatened miscarriage during the 1950s and 1960s, increased the rate of vaginal cancer beginning in the early adulthood of the female offspring. This group of women may also have a higher risk of spontaneous abortions and lowered fertility rates, which are probably due to uterine structural abnormalities.

A number of case studies in medical literature link the ingestion of particular medications to fetal abnormalities. Because many medications have not yet been evaluated with respect to their risk of causing developmental abnormalities, physicians are being extremely cautious in prescribing medication to pregnant women and are advising them against taking any drugs, even over-the-counter preparations, without consultation. Evidence is beginning to accumulate that a variety of substances ingested by the male may affect his reproductive system as well and thus may contribute to birth defects in the child.

Although much recent attention has been given to the relationship between drugs ingested during pregnancy (particularly the first trimester) and *physical* defects in the child, concern is developing about possible relationships between drugs and *behavioral* defects in the child, such as lower intelligence, shorter attention span, or higher activity levels. Animal studies (e.g., Kellogg, Tervo, Ison, Parisi, & Miller, 1980) have found that drugs given to pregnant females can affect the subsequent behavior of their offspring.

It has become common practice to administer drugs and anesthesia during delivery. Drugs given during labor and delivery may present hazards to the infant. Most anesthetics, analgesics, and sedatives produce depressed physiological functioning of the mother and, as a result, may alter the oxygen supply to the fetus. Premature infants are especially vulnerable to the adverse effects of anesthetics. For these reasons, obstetric drugs are used judiciously (Finster, Petersen, & Morishima, 1983).

A woman who is addicted to narcotics during pregnancy will produce a child who is physiologically a drug addict. The baby appears normal at birth but within a day or two begins to show marked agitation, sleeplessness, tremors, convulsions, breathing difficulties, and feeding problems. The severity of the symptoms is directly related to the drug dosage taken by the mother. If the mother is deprived of drugs during pregnancy, the fetus manifests the withdrawal symptoms by excessive kicking. It is current practice not to have the mother go through withdrawal therapy during pregnancy because of the risk of harming the baby *in utero*. Narcotics-addicted pregnant women have a high rate of complications; their infants have perinatal medical problems, impaired interactive and physiological state control behavior during early infancy, and cognitive and psychomotor deficits (Householder, Hatcher, Burns, & Chasnoff, 1982). The mother who is a drug addict can also transmit narcotics to her infant through her breast milk. The infants of mothers maintained on methadone during pregnancy seem to be at less risk; their psychological status at four months of age was found to be primarily determined by their mothers' psychosocial resources (Jeremy & Bernstein, 1984).

With the increasing number of persons using illicit drugs has come an increase in the number of women who use illicit drugs during pregnancy. Recent surveys indicate that up to 18 percent of newborn infants have been exposed to substance abuse prenatally. A high proportion of these infants have been exposed to cocaine. The results of research on prenatal cocaine exposure have been equivocal; a recent study suggests that earlier negative effects may have been due primarily to low SES rather than cocaine per se (Hurt, Brodsky, Betancourt, Braitman, Malmud, & Giannetta, 1995).

Evidence has been accumulating that lysergic acid diethylamide (LSD) taken by the mother during pregnancy may be a hazard to the child. In a study of 148 pregnancies in which one or both parents were LSD users, Jacobson and Berlin (1972) found a high spontaneous abortion rate. Of the children born alive, nearly 10 percent had major congenital defects; the normal incidence of such defects is below 1 percent. Again, a definitive relationship between LSD and reproductive risk could not be established in this study because many of the women had infectious diseases and probably nutritional deficiencies during pregnancy that may have contributed to the increased rates.

A link between marijuana use and birth defects in animals has been established. Adult male mice given oral administration of cannabinoids showed both reductions in fertility and an increased incidence of chromosomal abnormalities in their offspring (Dalterio, Bader, Bartke, & Mayfield, 1982). Another animal study (Dalterio & Bartke, 1979) has indicated that the male offspring of mothers given cannabinoids orally during late pregnancy and early lactation later exhibited inferior copulating behavior.

Virtually all gases can pass through the placenta to the fetus. Carbon monoxide poisoning, less than fatal to the mother, can cause multiple congenital abnormalities in the fetus as well as brain damage. In addition, excessive amounts of oxygen administered to the premature infants have been found to be related to subsequent blindness in the infant.

Until the last few decades, the intake of alcoholic beverages was not believed to have direct deleterious effects on the fetus. The higher mortality rate for the children of alcoholic women had been attributed to their poorer nutritional status. A study by Jones, Smith, Ulleland, and Streissguth (1973), however, described a pattern of physical defects and behavioral problems found in children of chronic alcoholic mothers. The pattern, called *fetal alcohol syndrome*, includes physical growth deficiency, abnormal development of the heart, defects of the joints, and facial abnormalities, especially the eyes. The children of chronically alcoholic women have a high death rate during infancy, and close to half of the survivors may be retarded, even if they are raised in good foster homes. Behavioral and cognitive problems are also common (Steinhauser, Williams, & Spohr, 1994). Heavy drinking (four to five drinks per day) or binge drinking (multiple drinks during a 1–3 day period in the first trimester of pregnancy) can result in fetal alcohol syndrome, low birth weight, and infants with physical problems and/or developmental delays (Willis & Walker, 1989). At one year of age, a higher percentage of infants whose mothers reported greater consumption of alcohol prior to, during, and following pregnancy were insecurely attached than infants whose mothers reported abstinence or light drinking (O'Connor, Sigman, & Brill, 1987).

The effects of maternal tobacco smoking on the fetus have also been examined. As early as 1935, Sontag and Wallace showed that smoking one cigarette resulted in heart rate changes of fetuses in the last few months of gestation. Usually the pregnant mother's smoking caused a transient fetal heart rate increase, while occasionally the smoking was followed by a fetal heart rate decrease.

Smoking mothers give birth to children who weigh less than the children of nonsmoking mothers. Experimental studies with animals have also shown that the offspring of rats and rabbits exposed to tobacco smoke during pregnancy weigh less at birth than do the offspring of control subjects. Furthermore, prematurity rates rise as a direct function of the number of cigarettes smoked per day (Cardozo, Gibb, Studd, & Cooper, 1982). Cigarette smoking in pregnant women is related to decreases in placental blood flow, fetal activity, and fetal breathing movements.

Psychological Factors

Considerable folklore and speculation exist about the impact of *maternal emotions* on the developing fetus. For some time, scientists rejected the possibility of the mother's communicating her feelings to the child. It was also during this period that physicians believed in the existence of a placental barrier that prevented all detrimental substances from reaching the blood supply of the infant.

Thompson (1957) reported experimental research with rats that examined the impact of emotional trauma during pregnancy on the emotional characteristics of the offspring. The stress procedure involved exposing pregnant rats three times a day to a buzzer sound that had previously been associated with shock in an avoidance situation, but avoidance was now prevented. The results indicated that there were striking differences between the offspring of the mothers who were under stress during pregnancy and the offspring of mothers not under stress (the control group). The control group was found to be more active in an open field test and left their cages more quickly to secure food at 30 to 40 days of age. Several measures of emotionality still discriminated between the two groups at 130 to 140 days of age.

More recent animal studies have suggested that prenatal stress may produce a variety of more long lasting effects. Herrenkohl (1979) found that female rats whose mothers were under stress during pregnancy subsequently experienced more spontaneous abortions, longer pregnancies, and fewer live-born young than rats not under stress; the offspring weighed less and were less likely to survive the neonatal period. It was hypothesized that prenatal stress influences the balance of hormones in the fetus and thereby produces reproductive dysfunction in adulthood. Further, an experimental study with squirrel monkeys demonstrated impairment of neuromotor development when mothers were socially stressed repeatedly during pregnancy; a short period of stress during the middle of gestation did not result in adverse effects, however (Schneider & Coe, 1993).

At the human level, pregnant women's attitudes and feelings have been found to be correlated with the later incidence of complications of pregnancy, labor, and delivery in the prospective studies. Davids, DeVault, and Talmadge (1961) noted that anxiety was higher for a group of women who later gave birth to children with developmental problems than for a control group. Erickson (1965), in a study of middle-class patients, found that multigravidae (women having their second or subsequent children) who later experienced one or more complications expressed more fears for self and baby, irritability, and depression than did multigravidae who were to have no complications. The psychological variables did not discriminate between primigravidae (women having their first child) who were to have complications and those who were to have no complications. Erickson postulated that anxiety symptoms may be determined by many causes. Although investigators have tended to emphasize anxiety as the result of psychological conflict, the possibility exists that anxiety may be an early indicator of biological stress in the organism.

The psychological aspects of human pregnancy are complex and not yet well understood. A pregnancy that has been planned has a different impact from one that has not been planned. An unplanned pregnancy can create considerable stress in a family that depends on the mother's continued employment, as it can for a woman in graduate school who is preparing for a career. Physicians and psychologists have tended to attribute all emotional changes and most symptoms associated with pregnancy to psychological factors, particularly unconscious rejection of the pregnancy. Not enough research effort has been expended on the reality aspects of pregnancy or the psychological aspects of hormonal changes that accompany pregnancy. Research has shown that psychological variables, such as anxiety and depression, are correlated closely with the hormonal changes that take place during the menstrual cycle. The psychological impact of the hormonal changes during pregnancy is very likely to be of equal importance, although little is currently known about these relationships.

Research findings on the psychological aspects of pregnancy have frequently been misinterpreted through incomplete analysis of the possible reasons for correlational relationships. For example, in one study the authors found a positive correlation between rejection of the pregnancy and nausea during the early prenatal period and interpreted the results as indicating that the rejection of the pregnancy was responsible for the nausea. Among the possible alternative explanations, a plausible one is that three months of nausea could create bad feelings toward the pregnant state. Another investigator could find no relationship between nausea and rejection of pregnancy but did find one between nausea and disturbed sexual functioning, both of which were interpreted as being due to unconscious rejection of the pregnancy. Again, an alternative hypothesis is that nausea itself could cause a disruption of sexual activity.

PERINATAL RISK FACTORS

The dividing line between prenatal and perinatal factors in the etiology of childhood disorders is difficult to specify, since the child's condition at birth is a product of the total intrauterine period. The perinatal factors to be discussed in this section will thus be a combination of those variables that seem to be relevant during labor and delivery and other variables that begin to be relevant earlier in pregnancy but which manifest themselves primarily during and immediately after the birth process. Mothers' self-reports of perinatal complications have been associated with poorer school achievement in children with learning problems (Gray, David, McCoy, & Dean, 1992).

Anoxia

Oxygen lack is most likely to occur immediately before, during, and immediately after the child is born. It is estimated that difficulty in the initiation and maintenance of respiration occurs in 5 to 10 percent of newborn infants. Anoxia can occur if the placenta detaches too soon (placenta previa), if the umbilical cord becomes knotted, or if the cord gets wrapped tightly around the baby's neck, as sometimes happens during the course of delivery.

Even though anoxia has received considerable research attention, its effects are not clearly understood. The primary reason for our inability to interpret the findings is the confounding of anoxia with other complications of pregnancy. Indeed, the possibility exists that some other physical malfunction prevents the infant from withstanding the effects of anoxia. Many of the early studies used different criteria for the definition of anoxia and did not use control groups. One of the best studies with human subjects found that anoxia at birth was associated with mild impairments of intelligence, neurological status, and personality functioning. Graham, Ernhart, Thurston, and Craft (1962) and Thurston, Graham, Ernhart, Eichman, and Craft (1960) did not include in their anoxic group children who had experienced other complications, and all examinations were conducted without the examiner's knowledge of the child's birth status.

No discussion of the effects of anoxia is complete without a reference to Windle's (1958) classic studies on monkeys. He deprived full-term infant monkeys of oxygen for specific periods of time after he had delivered them by Caesarean section. He found that anoxia at birth resulted in impaired motor functioning; longer periods of oxygen deprivation were associated with more profound motor problems. In humans, anoxia is frequently a correlate of both very rapid labors (less than one or two hours) and very long labors (more than 24 hours).

Although the fetus and newborn infant are quite resistant to the adverse effects of oxygen deprivation, the brain is the first organ to be affected when the minimum oxygen needs are not met. The brain requires more oxygen and has a more active metabolism than any other organ of the body. Within the central nervous system, the different parts vary in their vulnerability to oxygen deprivation, with the higher levels, such as the cortex and cerebellum, being least resistant, and the spinal cord and sympathetic ganglia being most resistant, to anoxia.

Prematurity and Postmaturity

An infant is designated as premature when its birth weight is $5^1/2$ pounds (2,500 grams) or less. The average birth weight in the United States is about $7^1/2$ pounds. About 5 to 10 percent of births are premature, and the neonatal mortality rate for the premature infant is 11 times that of the mature infant. Prematurity occurs more often under conditions of poor nutrition and inadequate medical care and is correlated with many of the complications of pregnancy; low socioeconomic status may exacerbate the negative effects of low birth weight (Liaw & Brooks-Gunn, 1994). Prematurity is so confounded with other variables that there is no agreement among researchers on the effects of prematurity per se on the infant. A premature birth in a healthy woman without other complications is relatively infrequent.

Without the technology of modern medicine many more premature infants would succumb. Most infants weighing over three pounds at birth can now be expected to survive; infants weighing between 500 and 999 grams (about 1.1 to 2.2 pounds) have survival rates ranging between 13 and 65 percent. In one study of 89

(25.4 percent) out of 351 infants with birth weights between 500 and 999 grams who survived to the age of 2 years, 72 percent had no functional handicap at the age of 5 years, 19 percent had severe handicaps, 5 percent had moderate handicaps, and 4 percent had mild handicaps (Kitchen, Orgill, Lissenden, Yu, & Campbell, 1987). Of particular interest in this study was the finding that the two-year evaluation of these extremely low birth-weight children was considerably more negative.

In one recent study, Hack, Taylor, Klein, Eiben, Schatschneider, and Mercuri-Minich (1994) matched a surviving group of children with birth weights under 750 grams with a group weighing between 750 and 1,499 grams at birth and a group born at term. At school age, the rates of mental retardation (IQ less than 70) in the three groups were 21, 8, and 2 percent, and the rates of cerebral palsy were 9, 6, and 0 percent, respectively; the lowest birth-weight children had poorer psychomotor and social skills, poorer academic achievement, and more behavior and attention problems.

Current research suggests that environmental factors beginning at birth contribute significantly to the premature infant's future cognitive and behavioral status (Cohen, 1995). Thompson, Goldstein, Oehler, Gustafson, Catlett, and Brazy (1994) identified maternal stress as one such environmental "marker." Lee and Barratt (1993) maintained that environmental influences eventually overshadowed the biological influences in their longitudinal study of 5- to 8-year-old low-birth-weight children.

The premature infant whose gestational age is less than full term has a decreased risk for later problems in comparison to the infant who is born underweight at term, a condition suggesting chronic problems *in utero*. Highly improved technology and a greater medical/social concern for the quality of the child's life have increased the number of premature infants who subsequently show normal development.

There is some possibility that the hospital procedures designed to ensure the life of the child may be otherwise detrimental to later optimal functioning. Immediately after birth the premature infant is placed in an isolette crib in which oxygen supply and temperature are carefully controlled. The child is handled minimally and is often fed in the isolette and remains there until a sufficient amount of weight has been gained. In the isolette, sensory stimulation is quite different from that received when *in utero* or in the natural environment after birth. The basic question is whether the alterations of sensory stimulation during the hospital stay have any adverse effects on the premature infant. Several studies have increased the amount of tactile, vestibular, and visual stimulation provided to premature infants in the hospital and have found increases in the rate of weight gain and better performance on tests of developmental status.

Postmaturity is the term used when infants are born several weeks or more beyond the expected date of delivery. As with prematurity, designation of postmaturity on the basis of gestational age may involve considerable error. The expected date of delivery is usually based on the date of the last menstrual period, but menstrual periods in some women may continue for one or several months after conception. Other women do not keep records of their menstrual periods and cannot accurately remember the dates. Usually, when obstetricians have to make decisions regarding the date for induction of labor or Caesarean section, they use additional criteria for determining the age of the fetus, such as the date the mother first felt the fetus move (quickening). About 12 percent of births occur two or more weeks after the due date, while 4 percent are delayed by as much as three weeks. The mortality rate of the postmature baby is about three times that of the term infant. The average postmature infant weighs a little more than the term baby, but a number of postmature babies weigh less, suggesting a bimodal distribution within this group. The small infants do less well than the heavy ones, presumably because they have experienced placental dysfunction over a period of time. Most of the deaths of postmature infants occur during labor, being secondary to anoxia and cerebral hemorrhage.

Birth Injury

During the birth process the fetus must be removed through the pelvic opening and vaginal canal. The strong muscular contractions that occur during labor serve to effect this movement. Usually the mother's pelvic opening is of adequate size such that, if the baby's head position is right, the delivery proceeds smoothly. Babies are usually born head first with face downward and tilted slightly to the left or right. The head is pliable and usually undergoes some change in shape (molding) in the process of delivery, but it readily assumes its normal shape within a day or two after birth. The placenta usually remains attached during the passage of the baby through the canal.

There are several situations that may cause a difficult delivery and thus increase the risk to the child. Sometimes the infant presents itself feet first or in some other position; such deliveries are much more difficult mechanically, and the risk of anoxia or injury is increased. If aware of the abnormal position of the baby early enough, the physician may try to change the baby's position manually. Once a significant portion of the baby has descended into the birth canal, such manipulations are not possible. If the physician is concerned about the baby's status, forceps (high, mid, or low) may be used to deliver the head more quickly. Mid and high forceps are used with caution because of the damage they might do to the head. The use of low forceps ranges widely; some hospitals report that physicians use them for the majority of deliveries, while others report their use only infrequently.

Generally, obstetrical procedures are designed to prevent death and injury to mother and child. There are instances in which some obstetrical procedures are used solely for convenience, however, and it is imperative that research be done to determine whether or not subtle injuries are the by-products of such elective procedures. For example, induction of labor through the use of pitocin has been used to correct an irregular labor when all indications suggest that the child and mother are physiologically ready for delivery. Pitocin has sometimes been used for convenience, however, and in certain of those cases may have resulted in a premature child or a child whose head is pushed against an unready cervix. Normally, the cervix gradually dilates as the birth contractions get stronger and more frequent. Pitocin, unless used very carefully, can create very strong contractions before the cervix is adequately dilated. Rupture of the membranes holding the amniotic fluid is also occasionally performed to hasten the delivery process, but the child has a high risk of infection if delivery is not completed within 24 hours after the membranes have been ruptured.

CONCLUSIONS

It is generally accepted that genetic factors and a wide range of physical factors occurring during the prenatal and perinatal periods greatly influence the risk of developing behavioral disorders during childhood. Our knowledge with respect to these factors is far from complete. For many children with severe behavior disorders, the etiology is unknown, suggesting that important factors remain to be discovered. Limitations in our knowledge of etiological factors are also created by the fact that most of the data on humans is based on correlational studies and that most of the known physical factors do not affect children's behavior in a uniform manner. It is highly probable that the risk of behavior disorders is governed by a combination of genetic factors, physical factors, and the timing (stage of prenatal or postnatal development) of the physical factors.

RECOMMENDED READINGS

Loehlin, J.C. (1992). *Genes and environment in personality development.* Newbury Park, CA: Sage.
Plomin, R., DeFries, J.C., & McClearn, G.E. (1990). *Behavioral genetics: A primer.* San Francisco: W.H. Freeman.
Rutter, M., & Casaer, P. (Eds.). (1991). *Biological risk factors for psychosocial disorders.* Cambridge, UK: Cambridge University Press.
Steissguth, A. (1997). *Fetal alcohol syndrome.* Baltimore, MD: Brookes.

5

Etiology: Demographic, Postnatal

Physical, and Social-Psychological

Risk Factors

This chapter continues the review of factors associated with an increased risk for developmental and behavior problems. It should be recognized that many prenatal and postnatal factors may be interactive; that is, the effect of a postnatal event may be governed to a significant extent by the child's genetic constitution and prenatal events. Demographic variables are not, strictly speaking, causal factors, but they are useful for subdividing the population and, thus, facilitating the investigation of etiological factors. Certain demographic factors, such as the gender of the child, influence the child's development from the time of conception and should, therefore, be recognized as factors that span the entire period of life. Physical factors, such as abuse, may increase the probability of behavior disorders through brain damage or indirectly through their psychological effects, or both. Among the social-psychological factors, greatest attention has been given to parents as causes of their children's behavior problems.

DEMOGRAPHIC RISK FACTORS

Gender

The human male is more biologically vulnerable in general than the female, beginning at conception and continuing through old age. Between 130 and 150 males are conceived for every 100 females, but only 105 boys are born for every 100 girls. Reproductive wastage in the form of abortions and miscarriages affects males more often than females. Since such a large percentage of spontaneously aborted fetuses show chromosomal abnormalities, and since a large number of chromosomal abnormalities involve the sex chromosomes, it is possible to hypothesize that the male is more vulnerable genetically. This explanation is more plausible when it is remembered that males express recessive genes that are on the sex chromosomes because there is no opportunity for a counteracting gene on the other sex chromosome.

The male dies more often during the neonatal period and through childhood until the sex ratio of live persons approaches 100 males to 100 females during adolescence. Males continue to succumb to a variety of illnesses more often than females throughout the life span, resulting in proportionally fewer males during middle and old age.

Proctor, Vosler, and Murty (1992) examined the demographic characteristics of children referred to an outpatient child guidance clinic and found that boys, minorities, and low-income children were more likely to receive a serious psychiatric diagnosis.

Although many studies of children report gender differences in a variety of characteristics, very few of these characteristics demonstrate consistent gender differences (Maccoby & Jacklin, 1974). During childhood, consistent findings include girls showing greater verbal ability than boys and boys showing more aggression than girls (Maccoby & Jacklin, 1980). Research on sex-steroid hormones with adolescents indicates that the *variability* of a person's hormone levels may be more predictive of behavior than the *absolute amounts* of circulating hormones. For example, both boys and girls whose circulating levels of testosterone varied widely from day to day were more likely to show anger (Inoff-Germain, Arnold, Nottelmann, & Susman, 1988).

It is becoming apparent that many, if not most, of the behaviors considered to be typically masculine or feminine are learned rather than primarily biologically determined. Even gender differences that occur early in infancy may be confounded with environmental variables. Research data (Korner, 1974) suggest that mothers may interact with their male and female infants in different ways; for example, boys are more likely to receive proximal stimulation (holding) and girls distal stimulation (talking, looking) from their mothers. These maternal behaviors can, of course, be the result of initial behavioral differences in the infants, but they could also be due to the mother's expectations and therefore differential reactions to particular infant behaviors. In a study of parental discipline techniques used by the mothers of fifth graders, Zussman (1978) found that boys received more power assertion and love withdrawal and less reasoning than did girls.

Anthropological studies suggest that some gender differences may be explained by the descriptor: "We are the company we keep" (Jacklin, 1989); that is, individuals you interact with elicit particular behaviors from you. If you spend time with an infant, the infant elicits nurturing behavior from you and, in effect, teaches you to become a nurturer. Research on males who are given infant care roles may help us to understand the extent to which gender differences in nurturing are acquired through life experiences.

Age

The number and types of behavior problems reported for children vary with age. Many children with developmental and cognitive problems are not diagnosed until after they have started school. The peaks for referrals to clinics occur within a few years after school entry and again within a few years after the onset of adolescence. A significant number of problems are recognizable during the preschool years, but there has been a strong tendency to delay referral of the preschool child and hope that the child will "grow out of it." Some abnormal conditions, especially those associated with congenital physical abnormalities, can be recognized at birth, while others, whose principal symptoms involve forms of behavior that develop at a later age, can only be diagnosed later.

Just as the normal behaviors of children change as a function of age or developmental status, so do abnormal behaviors change. Indeed, genetic factors could be expected to influence behaviors differently at different ages; in addition, pre- and perinatal factors may affect behaviors at some ages and not others. Although behavior patterns have traditionally been viewed as relatively unstable during childhood, recent research suggests substantial stability for general types of behavior problems, such as externalizing behavior disorders, but that specific characteristics may vary with age (Campbell, 1990; Cohen, Cohen, & Brook, 1993).

POSTNATAL PHYSICAL RISK FACTORS

Accidents

Minor injuries to the head are quite common in infancy and childhood, but little is known about the effects of these everyday occurrences. Physically, the skull does not offer as much protection to the brain during the first six months of life as it does later in the child's life. Accidents, especially those involving automobiles, and abuse are responsible for many cases of brain damage. Laws requiring the use of seatbelts and compliance with this requirement contribute significantly to reductions in head injury cases. Traumatic brain injury is one of the largest contributors to death and disability among children and adolescents. About one million children per year sustain closed head injuries, and a large majority of these children will have physical, cognitive, and/or behavioral problems as a result (Telzrow, 1987). Both the families in particular and society in general will pay enormous costs, economically and psychologically, in their attempts to rehabilitate children with traumatic brain injury.

Malnutrition

It has been estimated that 40 to 60 percent of the world's children are mildly or moderately undernourished; the exact prevalence of undernourishment in the United States continues to be debated (Lozoff, 1989). Nutrition is an important factor in determining physical and behavioral status throughout postnatal life. Severe nutritional deficiencies during infancy and later preschool years have been associated with detrimental alterations in brain development, which in turn retard physical growth and behavioral development (Winick, 1979; Stoch, Smythe, Moodie, & Bradshaw, 1982).

Galler (1984) reported a study conducted in Barbados comparing a group of children severely undernourished only in the first year of life with similar children who had no history of undernourishment. The undernourished children eventually caught up in physical growth, but they continued to show deficits in cognitive and behavioral functioning. The undernourished children had IQ scores that were 12 points lower, and 60 percent of them displayed the symptoms associated with attention deficit disorder. These symptoms persisted throughout the school years.

Undernourished children tend to come from the most disadvantaged families—the ones that have low incomes, poor housing and medical care, and mothers with low intelligence. Children who are undernourished become less active and demand even less from environments that are already poorly equipped to give them attention and stimulation. Grantham-McGregor, Schofield, and Powell (1987) found that their psychosocial stimulation program in the home was able to remediate the psychological deficits of severely malnourished children.

Children from low-income families who participate in school breakfast programs have been shown to score higher on achievement tests in the elementary school grades; the participating children also have lower rates of school absence and tardiness (Meyers, Sampson, Weitzman, Rogers, & Kayna, 1989).

Neglect

Neglect refers to parents' not providing or withholding adequate resources for the child's physical well-being. Child neglect may include inadequate food, shelter, clothing, or caring. In some instances, parents do not provide these necessities for the child due to poverty and/or ignorance, while in other instances, parents choose to deprive their children of these basic necessities.

Obviously, neglect occurs on a continuum. Extreme neglect inevitably leads to the child's death, while intermediate levels may be associated with chronic malnutrition and illnesses that increase the risk for developmental and behavioral problems.

Abuse

Child abuse has begun to receive considerable professional and public attention. In earlier times, children were considered the property of their parents, and parents could abuse and/or neglect them, but strong counterpressures were also present in the form of wanting healthy children who were able to contribute to the family's economic welfare. In modern times, children do not usually contribute significantly to the family's income, and the economic consequences of child abuse and neglect may be more greatly felt by society than by the individual family. All states now have laws that require professionals to report suspected and known instances of child neglect and abuse to local social service authorities, who investigate the case to determine whether court action, therapy, or other services are needed by the family. Clinicians are frequently confronted with the dilemma of whether a child's injury has occurred accidentally or is the result of abuse. Although some of the same factors are precursors to both accidents and abuse, research has identified particular factors that appear to separate the families of children with inflicted and noninflicted injuries. Dubowitz, Hampton, Bethoney, and Newberger (1987) reported that the occurrence of abuse as compared with accidental injury was more likely with the presence of poverty, single parenthood, father unemployment, a history of the parent's having been abused as a child, the infancy (versus older) period, and limited access of parent(s) to recreation.

Reports of child abuse have doubled over the last decade, and a large body of research has focused on both the short- and long-term psychological consequences of child maltreatment (Cicchetti, 1994). This research suggests that early maltreatment is associated with poor social relationships, poor self-perceptions, and depression. As adults, people who have been abused appear to have a higher risk for aggressive and violent acts as well as self-injurious and suicidal behavior. A history of physical abuse has also been associated with adult psychological problems such as anxiety and depression (Malinosky-Rummell & Hansen, 1993). Belsky (1993) has proposed a developmental-etiological analysis of child maltreatment that analyzes community, cultural, and evolutionary contexts.

A review of 45 studies by Kendall-Tackett, Williams, and Finkelhor (1993) demonstrated that sexually abused children had more psychological symptoms than nonabused children, with abuse accounting for between 15 and 45 percent of the variance; the most frequently occurring symptoms were fears, posttraumatic stress disorder, behavior problems, sexualized behaviors, and poor self-esteem. However, no specific behavioral syndrome was found for children who had been sexually abused. Degree of symptomatology was affected by penetration, duration and frequency of abuse, force, relationship of perpetrator to the child, and maternal support. Another review of the long-term correlates of child sexual abuse revealed that child sexual abuse survivors reported higher rates of substance abuse, binge eating, somatization, and suicidal behavior (Polusny & Follette, 1995).

Environmental Hazards

What children ingest and breathe may be harmful to their development. For example, lead is capable of producing severe inflammation of the brain with resulting hemorrhage and lesions. Lead poisoning is becoming a more common problem. A few decades ago, children became ill by chewing on furniture covered with paint containing lead, but laws were passed designating that articles used by children be covered with lead-free paint. Children, mostly in slum areas, are still exposed to the toxic substances in peeling paint from walls and windowsills. Lead may also enter the body by breathing air that is polluted with lead particles. Of children hospitalized with lead poisoning, more than one-fourth die, and an equal number become permanently brain damaged. Several studies have demonstrated that less-than-toxic levels of lead may also be detrimental. Their results show a continuous inverse relationship between intelligence and relatively low levels of lead in the body; higher levels of cognitive functioning appear to be affected before any signs of motor impairment are seen (e.g., Thatcher, Lester, McAlaster, Horst, & Ignatius, 1983). Classroom behavior, particularly the ability to attend, to inhibit distracting stimuli, and to follow directions, seems to be sensitive to lead's effects (Needleman & Bellinger, 1984; Fergusson, Fergusson, Horwood, and Kinzett, 1988). Other air pollutants may also affect children's health. Children living with parents who smoke appear to be at increased risk for respiratory problems (Pedreira, Guandolo, Feroli, Melba, & Weiss, 1985).

Poisoning is more likely to occur when parents are neglectful or do not anticipate the development of children's locomotion skills. Young children are prone to ingest substances that resemble food or drinks and may be especially attracted to colorful containers. Childproof caps and other devices no doubt prevent some poisonings.

Disease and Illness

Several diseases are known to cause brain damage in children. *Meningitis* involves an inflammation of the meninges, the covering of the brain. It is usually a bacterial infection and can be treated with antibiotics, thereby offering the possibility of preventing the adverse effects, if the disease is diagnosed early enough. Usually the child who develops meningitis has had normal physical and mental development up to the time of the illness. The onset of the illness is indicated by a rise in temperature, vomiting, and signs of neurological involvement. Likely to be accompanying the high fever are stupor, coma, or restless delirium; headaches, paralysis, rigidity of the neck, and convulsions are often present. Treatment with antibiotics later in the course of the disease keeps many children alive who would die without treatment; many of these children are likely to be significantly impaired. In almost all such cases, complete recovery is never achieved. Intellectual functioning may be grossly impaired, and behavioral changes can be profound.

Encephalitis is usually a viral infection that involves inflammation of the brain itself. There is often no medical treatment available, and the risk of serious consequences is always present. Encephalitis is known to occur as a complication following the common childhood diseases, especially measles, but also chicken pox, scarlet fever, and whooping cough. Immunization programs for measles will significantly reduce the incidence of encephalitis in the future. The clinical signs of encephalitis are extremely varied; sometimes they are sudden and cause death, other times they are in such a mild form initially that they resemble the symptoms of the common cold. In the case of epidemic encephalitis, or sleeping sickness, about one-third of the patients die; of the two-thirds who recover, half become physically or mentally disabled.

Infections in young children are sometimes accompanied by high fevers. Parents are usually advised by their physicians to use procedures such as cool baths and medications to reduce high fevers because they may result in damage to the brain. Middle ear infections are among the most common infections during the first three years of life; chronic ear infections may cause partial or temporary deafness that is associated with later language problems (Secord, Erickson, & Bush, 1988).

Children who suffer from chronic physical illness, especially during the preschool years, may be at risk for later developmental and psychological problems because their pain and medical interventions may prevent them from learning what other children their age are learning and from having age-appropriate life experiences (see Chapter 15).

Brain Tumors

Brain tumors rarely occur in children; the incidence is 2.4 per 100,000 children under the age of 15 years with between 1,000 and 1,500 new cases being identified each year. The most common early symptoms are those associated with intracranial pressure, such as convulsions, headache, dizziness, and vomiting. Additional symptoms vary with the size and place of the tumor and are likely to be due to damage at the site of the growth or the pressure on the adjacent areas. Tumors of the cerebellum, the part of the brain involved in motor behavior, occur twice as often in children as tumors of the cerebral cortex, the area that is primarily involved with cognitive behavior. The behavioral symptoms associated with tumors are often too diffuse to be useful in the localization of the tumors. Skull films, neurological tests, and brain scans are used in the diagnosis and location of brain tumors.

SOCIAL AND PSYCHOLOGICAL RISK FACTORS

Children's behavior problems have been attributed to a wide range of social and psychological factors. Social and political environments, including social institutions, sometimes create conditions that place children at risk. The most attention by far, however, has been given to parents as the primary cause of their children's behavior problems.

Social Conditions

Societies vary in their definitions of behavior disorders; a behavior that is condoned and reinforced in one culture may be disapproved or punished in another. The well-adjusted person, then, may be conceptualized as one whose behaviors are compatible with the prevailing norms of the dominant culture in the society. Almost any country has a variety of subcultures within it (e.g., tribes or religious sects), but the United States is unique in its collection of people whose ancestors came from all over the earth. Children may perhaps be expected to encounter greater problems when they are subjected to cultural demands that may differ markedly from those of their subculture.

Group rivalries and prejudice occur in all nations, but they have received particular attention in the United States, perhaps because the population is uniquely complex. As far as can be determined after the fact, rivalry among groups of immigrants began with the arrival of the *Mayflower*. High social status, for example, is still attributed to those who are descended from the earliest settlers. Early arrival seems to be the most relevant variable, since relatively few of the early settlers had high status in their countries of origin. Many were rejected in their own countries for religious or political reasons, and more than a few came as an alternative to prison.

As each succeeding wave of immigrants arrived, they were assigned to the lowest rung of the social ladder. Many individuals were eventually able to better their situation; in most cases, their success was correlated with their adoption of the dominant cultural standards. Being white, Anglo-Saxon, and Protestant has been a significant advantage throughout our history.

Success in our society is also correlated with (and defined by) certain behaviors. For adults, those behaviors include being achievement-oriented, intelligent, and nonemotional and having a job that is dependent on mental, rather than manual, activity. Children who are raised by parents displaying these characteristics have a higher probability of acquiring these characteristics than children whose parents are poor, undereducated, blue-collar workers. Equal opportunity for learning has become a major goal for our educational institutions only in the last few decades.

Low socioeconomic status (SES) has been associated with a higher prevalence of behavior disorders. Low SES, however, is also related to other etiological factors. For example, low SES mothers are apt to have had poor nutrition during their own development; during pregnancy, they have a higher incidence of almost all complications, including nutritional deficiencies. Their children are more likely to be born prematurely and to experience problems during the perinatal period.

Family Conditions

Adoption. Being adopted is a risk factor for behavior problems during childhood and adolescence (Goldberg & Wolkind, 1992). The basis for this risk appears to include prenatal factors, such as young age, substance abuse, and chronic psychological stress of the mother and perinatal factors, such as prematurity and other complications of labor and delivery. If the infant is not placed in a stable home environment within the first few months of life, then attachment processes may not be optimal.

Family Composition. Increased mobility has been a primary factor creating change in the composition of families. A few generations ago, the average person was raised in a small town where most of the individual's relatives also resided. The person was trained to do a job that would in some way benefit the community, usually married a person from the community, and spent the rest of his or her life there. In these small towns everyone knew everyone else, and parents were soon informed when their children's behavior did not measure up to the expectations of the community. In a sense, the whole community participated in child rearing. Many of the old neighborhoods in more populated areas also demonstrated community rearing of children. But now, the transient quality of contemporary living precludes such participation. On the other hand, mobility has created certain advantages that facilitate the development of individuality. Children no longer have to choose the occupation of their parent or one that is useful in a restricted geographical area. Their education need not be determined by local facilities, nor must a son's status as head of the household be postponed until the death of his father. The price for individuality has not yet been deemed too high.

Older models of parenting seem, at least retrospectively, to have been correlated with fewer behavior problems in children. The extended (inclusion of other relatives) family, now relatively uncommon in our society, appears to have been a situation in which children were likely to receive more individual attention from adults, and parents were less likely to be overwhelmed by child-rearing responsibilities. That is, all adults in the family shared in the child-rearing activities. Multiple "parents" are fairly common in so-called primitive societies. Among the Murngin, for example, children call their paternal uncles "father," and their relationships with the uncles are no different from their relationships with their biological fathers.

Contemporary clinicians have indicated that optimally the family should be composed of a mother, a father, and their children. Deviations from that pattern have been felt to be detrimental to all members of the family, especially the children. The emphasis on having both a mother and a father in the home has been related to the appropriate gender role development of the children. That is, children are assumed to need strong and continuous models of both genders in order to become adequate men and women. And yet, research comparing children in lesbian and single-parent households has found no differences between the groups in terms of their gender identity, gender role behavior, sexual orientation, or other psychological characteristics.

The major problem for single parents would seem to be that the responsibility and work of two parents are largely shifted to one parent. In comparison to two-parent families, single parents are more socially isolated, work longer hours, receive less emotional and parental support, have less stable social networks, and experience more potentially stressful life events (Weintraub & Wolf, 1983). Kallam, Ensminger, and Turner (1977) have reported that a higher risk of problem behavior in children is associated with mother alone and mother/stepfather family structures; in their poor, urban, black sample, mother/grandmother family structures were nearly as effective as mother/father structures.

In two-parent households, there is a continuum of parental availability to children, whether the mother and father are married to each other or not. In some marriages, one parent is away from home for long periods due to military service, imprisonment, employment, or choice. In most marriages, the mother is more available to children than the father, but that pattern is reversed in some families. In some cases of divorce, the children have considerable access to both parents, but divorce usually means that one parent is only occasionally available to the child. Research findings on the effects of divorce or other types of parental separation are frequently difficult to interpret because they are confounded with the effects of other variables.

Separation and Divorce. Half of the children born during the 1980s are likely to experience their parents' divorce; the majority of these children will also experience the remarriage of their parents (Hetherington, Stanley-Hagan, & Anderson, 1989). Although most children initially experience their parents' divorce as stressful, their responses are diverse. The long-term effects of parental divorce are related to the child's age, gender, and temperament; the qualities of the home environment; and the social and economic support systems available to the family.

When a marital relationship is terminated, it has been customary for the mother to assume custody of the children, with the father providing all or some of the financial support. Whether or not she has worked prior to the separation, the probability is high that the mother will have to be employed in addition to having the major responsibility of child rearing. Although the father is required to contribute to the support of the family, the total amount of available income may still be considerably less than what the family had to live on before the separation. Mothers' working may mean that preschool children will have inadequate caregivers and that schoolchildren will be unsupervised in the afternoon. When the mother arrives home from work, she may be confronted with all of the household duties. The point to be emphasized is that the remaining parent and children may be faced with considerable change in their circumstances, and this change is likely to be the key factor in determining child behavior. The implications are that gross changes in the child's environment may increase the probability of behavior problems.

Research suggests that it is parental conflict, not family constitution, that is predictive of children's behavior disorders (Long & Forehand, 1987; Kurdek & Sinclair, 1988). Parental conflict is more likely to occur during the separation and divorce processes and often continues long after divorce.

In a three-year longitudinal study, Katz and Gottman (1993) found that husbands' angry and withdrawn pattern predicted teachers' ratings of children's internalizing behavior problems, while a mutually hostile pattern predicted teachers' ratings of children's subsequent externalizing behavior problems. Interparental verbal and physical conflict placed 3–6 year-old children from low-income families at high risk for both conduct and emotional problems, the latter of which were worse when the mothers and children resided in a shelter; the authors hypothesized that shelter placement deprived the children of coping mechanisms available in their natural environment, leaving them less protected from stress (Fantuzzo, DePaola, Lambert, Martino, Anderson, & Sutton, 1991).

Number of Children. The number of children in the family has also been assumed to influence the incidence of behavior problems. Both only children and children from large families have been considered to be at a disadvantage. Although only children tend to be referred to clinics disproportionately, there is no evidence suggesting that presence of a sibling would have affected the referral. Many parents have decided to have a second child to prevent the "psychological problems" assumed to be associated with being an only child.

Some behavior problems have appeared to be more prevalent in families with a large number of children. The obvious explanation is that parents cannot adequately care for and train more than a few children, but the findings on large families reveal that there are important additional aspects to be considered. In many cases, large families are acquired "involuntarily" because the parents have not been educated about birth control. Many children have been born to parents who do not have adequate resources for their support. In such instances, both the physical and psychological environments are likely to be less than optimal.

In the recent past, middle-class parents believed that it was all right to have as many children as they could afford. Ecologists have attempted to counter this attitude by demonstrating that people with high standards of living consume far more of the world's resources per person than do people with lower standards of living.

The decreasing birth rate during recent decades, however, is due in large part to two interrelated factors: successful birth control methods and large numbers of women joining the work force. Couples now have considerably more choice in their economic status and the number of children that they will have.

Adolescent Parenthood.   It is well known that many adolescents in our society are sexually active, but we have not been able to agree on how to decrease the sexual activity or how to prevent the pregnancies that occur as a result. Many sexually active teenagers do not use reliable birth control methods and do not have an accurate understanding of reproduction.

Having a child during adolescence not only increases the child's physical risk (see Chapter 4), but increases the psychological risks to both mother and child. Children born to teenage mothers show poorer social and intellectual competence than children born to older mothers (Roosa, Fitzgerald, & Carlson, 1982). Current attention on the mental health problems of adolescent mothers suggests that depression and/or drug abuse may be important factors in determining which mothers and children will have poor outcomes (Zuckerman, Amaro, & Beardslee, 1987). The responsibility of rearing a child may force the parents to curtail their education and thereafter be confined to a poverty level of existence. Moreover, few adolescents are prepared for the demands of parenthood, and their inadequate parenting skills may have a negative impact on the developing child (Sugar, 1984) and increase the risk of their becoming abusive parents.

Family Stressors

Family stressors are life events that affect the family unit. Some life events affect one or both parents directly and the child indirectly, other events affect the child directly, and still others directly affect all members of the family unit. There is a growing body of research suggesting that short-term (up to one year) accumulations of stressors have small but significant negative effects on children's behavior (Johnson & Bradlyn, 1988). The effects of accumulated life events on children's behavior have not yet been adequately studied, although we are beginning to understand the effects of particular life events over the course of development.

Particular life events may vary in the amount of stress they cause particular families. For example, the death of a grandparent who had minimal involvement with the family is likely to be less stressful than that of a grandparent with strong ties to the family. The negative impact of a life event may be conceptualized as a deprivation of a previous positive condition or the addition of a negative condition; sometimes, a particular life event contains both elements. In addition, some life events have both positive and negative features. For example, the birth of a new sibling may have been planned and viewed as a positive family experience, but all new infants require time and effort from parents that may have been spent on older children or other pleasant activities.

The adverse effects of life events may be decreased when social support systems are available. In contrast, they may be increased when such systems are deficient or unavailable. When mothers are depressed, for example, they may not be psychologically available to buffer their children's stressors. Fergusson, Horwood, and Shannon (1989) reported that life events mediated by maternal depression were correlated with maternal reports of child-rearing problems. Interpretation of these results is unclear, however, because the mothers were the only source of information and may not have given accurate information; mothers' depression may have altered the way the children were perceived rather than the way the children behaved.

Child Care

At one time, orphanages for young children were much more common than they are today. The primary reason for their demise was the increasing awareness that children who were placed into institutional settings at an early age had high mortality and behavior problem rates. Goldfarb (1944), Spitz (1945), and Bowlby (1952) have described the conditions in which many of the orphans lived. The basic needs of the children were adequately met; that is, they were fed, kept clean, and protected against contagious diseases. In spite of these efforts, between 30 and 75 percent of the children were dying within two years of being placed in the institutions and were found to be extremely susceptible to disease and illness. Each child was typically placed in a cot whose sides were draped in sheets, thus effectively preventing the infants from seeing the other children and the rest of the room. Unless the infant could stand up in the crib, he or she was confined to a world almost totally lacking in visual stimulation. Social contact between caretakers and infants was extremely brief, and the children were usually not held, even for feeding.

The observers of these conditions interpreted the high mortality rate, poor development, and emotional apathy (depression) as being due to the child's having been separated from his or her mother. Bowlby (1952) proposed that normal mental health requires a continuous relationship with a mother or mother substitute during infancy. Casler (1961) and Yarrow (1964), however, have suggested that the devastating effects of institutions on infants and young children may not be caused by the infant's separation from the mother per se, but by the deprivation of the stimulation that she provides and mediates. Infants apparently need a minimal amount of stimulation in order to develop normally. Children who are adequately stimulated, whether by one or several caretakers, do not present the symptoms of institutionalization.

Many people have been convinced that any care, other than that given by the mother or a comparable caregiver, is detrimental to the children's emotional development. This belief might account for the inadequate development of day-care programs for children and the refusal of many people to recognize in a concrete way that a substantial portion of working people are women, many of whom are mothers of preschool and school-aged children (Stipek & McCroskey, 1989).

Research evidence is beginning to demonstrate that group care for infants and young children can be designed to be as effective as, and sometimes better than, that given by some mothers. A review by Belsky and Steinberg (1978) concluded that high-quality day care does not negatively affect IQ scores, is not disruptive to the emotional bond between mother and child, and increases both positive and negative peer interactions. More recent research suggests that children in day care may be more likely to avoid their mother after a brief separation as one year olds and to be more aggressive with their peers a few years later; Clarke-Stewart (1989) presents several possible interpretations of these data and recommends that future research focus on factors that may moderate or mediate the effects of infant day care.

Until relatively recently, women with children were actively discouraged from working outside the home. Some women had to work for economic reasons, and they and their children were deprecated or pitied. Women's educational backgrounds and economic conditions have led to steady increases in the percentage of mothers in the work force during the last several decades. Increasingly more women have been entering the work force by choice rather than by economic necessity.

Over half of mothers with infants under 12 months of age are working outside the home—a rate that is comparable to that of mothers with children under six years (Belsky, 1988). Interestingly, less than 15 percent of these children are in day-care centers; about a third are taken care of in their own homes by relatives or non-relatives, and the remaining children are taken care of in the homes of relatives or sitters.

It is clearly extremely important that infants and children receive the care and stimulation that will optimize their physical and psychological development. While it has not yet given exact specifications, research has at least provided some information about the most salient variables. In general, infants and children need adults to care for their physical needs (food, water, shelter, protection from harm, temperature control, cleanliness) and to give them experiences (visual, language, and tactile stimulation) that will facilitate their learning about people and the environment. Included in this care from adults should be the message that adults care about them and that they should care for others. Unfortunately, many of the world's children arrive unwanted, and the adults in their lives sometimes do not protect them from experiences that are harmful physically and/or psychologically.

Parental Characteristics

It is generally acknowledged that parental psychological characteristics have considerable potential for influencing children's behavior. Many of the behaviors learned by children, particularly those learned early in life, are learned from parents.

Among the individual difference variables that may be important is the mother's mental health status. Parents' psychological health may have a large impact on their everyday behavior toward the child. It has been assumed that mental illness and certain personality characteristics may lead the parent to behave in ways that deprive the child of needed interpersonal relationships and/or that create pain and anxiety in the child.

In examining the relationship between parental psychological status and child behavior disorders, two subject selection procedures have been utilized by investigators. One procedure involves examining the children of parents who have been clinically diagnosed as abnormal. In general, children of parents with psychological problems have a higher risk for psychological problems than children of parents without diagnosed psychological problems. However, the children's problems may not be the same as the parents' problems. Such relationships have been found for most types of parental psychopathology. For example, one study (Orvaschel, Walsh-Allis, & Ye, 1988) found that 41 percent of the children of parents with recurrent depression met criteria for at least one psychological disorder compared with 15 percent of the control children. The high-risk children had significantly greater rates of affective and attentional disorders. A review of 34 studies indicated that the children of depressed parents were at greater risk for both internalizing and externalizing behavior problems (Forehand, McCombs, & Brody, 1987). A few prospective, longitudinal studies are in progress, but we do not yet know what the psychological contribution of parental psychopathology is. We also do not understand what makes many children resistant to the adverse effects of parental psychopathology.

The second procedure for examining the relationship between parent and child psychological status is to assess the parents of children who have been clinically diagnosed as abnormal. Huschka (1941), for example, using clinical records of children with behavior disorders, found that 42 percent of the mothers had neurotic symptoms, depression, suicidal impulses, or paranoid tendencies; he concluded that the mother's psychological status greatly affected children at all stages of development. A number of studies using objective personality tests for assessing the adjustment of parents of children with behavior problems have also been conducted. Wolking, Quast, and Lawton (1966) administered the Minnesota Multiphasic Personality Inventory (MMPI) to parents of six diagnostic groupings of children. They found elevations of several MMPI clinical scales for all groups of parents with behavior-problem children in comparison to control parents, but no relationship between parental profile types and specific child disorders could be determined.

These earlier correlational findings were typically interpreted as reflecting that the parental characteristics caused the children's behavior problems and were rarely interpreted as suggesting the possibility that behavior problems in children could adversely affect the parents or that some other variable could be responsible for both the parent and child findings (Erickson, 1968a).

We are only beginning to understand what aspects of parenting behavior may be affected by parental mental illness; one possibility is that parental mental illness may increase the rate of physical and psychological abuse. A substantial number of articles and books have documented the correlates of physical and sexual abuse on children's psychological functioning. In addition to the physical consequences of abuse, a number of short- and long-term psychological correlates for the children have been found: aggression, social skills deficits, relationship problems, and affect disturbances (Wolfe, 1987). Parental depression may be associated with neglect and/or increases in negative interactions as the parents are more focused on their own psychological discomfort (Gotlib & Avison, 1993).

Parental alcohol and substance abuse has been implicated as another risk factor for child psychopathology, including an increased rate of alcohol and substance abuse in the children (Phares & Compas, 1992). A review of studies on children of alcoholic parents revealed a higher incidence of psychological symptoms in the children; however, the authors (West & Prinz, 1987) cautioned that "neither all nor a major portion of the population of children from alcoholic homes are inevitably doomed to childhood psychological disorder" (p. 204). A large-scale study of adults who experienced childhood exposure to parental problem drinking found an increased incidence of psychological symptoms and marital instability but not in occupational functioning (Greenfield, Swartz, Landerman, & George, 1993).

Much has been written that blames parents for children's psychological problems and infers parental psychopathology as the reason for poor parenting. In many instances, however, parents probably behave inappropriately toward their children due to the modeling of important adults in their own past and out of ignorance of the long-term consequences of their behavior. For example, only recently has physical punishment been questioned as an effective child management technique. Most adults living today were probably hit by their parents during their childhood, and some of them are simply following the modeled example of their parents. In addition, many parents today do not believe that there is potential harm in physical interventions. They are impressed with the quick results that such interventions sometimes effect. The line between physical punishment and child abuse is not always easy to draw. Parents may begin by spanking a child for *specific* serious infractions, then to reduce *any* unwanted behavior, and finally whenever the child reminds them of something unpleasant (e.g., the child resembles a disliked relative or the child is perceived as too much of a responsibility). Improved education for parenting and psychological support of parents would likely reduce at least some ineffective and damaging parental practices.

Child Characteristics

Just as parents vary in their personal characteristics, so do children, even from birth. For a long period, individual differences among infants and young children did not receive very much attention from clinicians because it was assumed that behavioral variability in children was due to variations in parenting. Beginning in the 1960s, a longitudinal study of infants by Chess and Thomas (Thomas, Chess, & Birch, 1968; Thomas & Chess, 1977) began to demonstrate the implications of infants' behavioral characteristics.

Thomas and Chess (1977) identified three constellations of temperament: easy, slow-to-warm-up, and difficult. Easy children were high in rhythmicity and adaptability and not extreme in any other dimension. Slow-to-warm-up children showed slower adaptability with mildly intense and negative responsivity, but adapted positively over time. Difficult children were irregular in their biological functioning, resisted changes in their environment, and cried a lot. Thomas and Chess hypothesized that particular temperament styles would be associated with later psychopathology; their research stimulated a change in professionals' perceptions of infants. Infants began to be perceived as having their own style or temperament virtually from birth.

In an ongoing longitudinal study, Kagan and his colleagues have reported a relationship between social inhibition in the second and third years of life and numbers of fears several years later; similarly, the laboratory index of inhibition in the second year of life had a .52 correlation with an aggregate index of behavioral inhibition at $5^1/2$ years. Although early dispositions of children tended to be preserved through $7^1/2$ years of age, environmental events appeared to modify these characteristics (Kagan, Reznick, and Snidman, 1990).

There has been evidence that infant temperament is somewhat stable during the preschool years, but that stability gradually erodes over time (Garrison & Earls, 1987, p. 48). Moderate heritability has been found for the temperamental traits of sociability, emotionality, and activity (Plomin & Rowe, 1977). Although it would be interesting to consider temperament as a primarily hereditary characteristic, we cannot avoid acknowledging that pre-, peri-, and postnatal physical factors will affect behaviors based on temperament as well as other behaviors. As soon as the child is born, its behavior begins to produce responses from parents who communicate their acceptance, rejection, or neutrality. Cameron (1977) reported that negative changes in temperament were associated with parental intolerance, inconsistency, and conflict.

Parent-Child Interactions: Theoretical Views

It probably makes more sense to discuss parent-child interactions as predictors of behavior problems rather than parent or child characteristics alone. One way of conceptualizing the parent-child relationship is through the notion of "goodness of fit." In the broadest sense, we would anticipate the optimal relationship as one in which both parent and child receive what they need and/or expect. There are probably only a few adults who would be perfect parents regardless of the child's behavior, just as there are relatively few adults who would be bad parents regardless of the child's behavior. Parents and children can be placed on a continuum of compatibility, but the relative placement may vary with the child's age or stage of development. Some parents are able to meet the needs of infants optimally, but when the child shows signs of independence, their good care diminishes; other parents find that infants and young children are not to their liking, but they do very well with their children when they reach school age.

This section will focus on parent-child interactions in the context of contemporary theory.

Psychodynamic Theory. Sigmund Freud was a highly respected physician throughout his long career. Among his many referrals, there were a significant number of patients for whom he could find no organic abnormality. On the basis of interviews with these patients, Freud began to develop a theory to account for their symptoms. His theory was based on the assumption that these patients' problems were psychological and had their origin in childhood, particularly during the preschool years. The information derived from interviews convinced Freud (1953, originally 1905) that young children experienced sexual thoughts and feelings—an idea that was not well received by his contemporaries in Victorian society.

According to Freud, there are a number of potential situations during the preschool years in which the various parts of the child's mind can be placed in conflict, the most common of which include feeding, toilet training, and masturbation. One of the principal effects of intrapsychic conflict is *anxiety*, a central concept in psychoanalytic theory and the basis for the formation of psychological problems. Anxiety is considered to originate as an inborn response to excessive stimulation. That is, humans are biologically designed to react with fears or anxiety to particular events. Psychoanalytic theory (Freud, 1959, originally 1926) postulated that anxiety also results from mental representations of these events, such as thoughts of forbidden behaviors and memories of traumatic occurrences.

The developing child is viewed as being confronted with a series of "normal" crises or conflicts, such as weaning and separation from the mother. The parents' handling of these crises is considered to have profound effects on the child's later personality. Satisfaction of the child's early needs by the mother is viewed as not only facilitating the child's early needs by the mother but also as developing the child's capacity for relating to other people in general. Anna Freud (1971) added that when early bodily needs are not met the involved organ systems remain vulnerable in the future.

Parents can alter the timing and progress of the psychosexual stages in various ways and thus determine the child's later personality characteristics. The child may be deprived of an adequate amount of stimulation, such as being prevented from sucking long enough, or the child may be severely punished for obtaining sexual pleasure. These situations are viewed as creating excessive anxiety and the development of defense mechanisms to avoid the experience of anxiety.

Among the people who studied with Sigmund Freud, several came to disagree with some of the basic tenets of psychoanalytic theory and developed alternative hypotheses. One of the fundamental aspects of the theory, the psychosexual stages of development, was greatly deemphasized by several followers who preferred to acknowledge a broader variety of etiological factors, namely, environmental impediments to optimal personality development.

Erik E. H. Erikson (1963) is prominent among the theorist-clinicians who gave greater emphasis to the role of the ego in the development of personality. He proposed that a person's resolutions of a sequence of developmentally determined stages have specific implications for later personal-social behavior. Erikson's developmental stages are clearly derived from Freud's psychosexual stages, but Erikson specifies in greater detail the role of the parents during each stage.

The resolution of the first stage, which he calls *basic trust versus mistrust*, lays the foundation for all later development. The development of trust is based on the infant's feeling comfortable physically and experiencing a minimum of fear or uncertainty. To the extent that these conditions are met, the infant will expect new experiences to produce positive outcomes. The quality of interpersonal contacts while the child's needs (primarily oral) are being satisfied becomes the principal determinant of early social development. Children are considered to be capable of sensing both the conscious and unconscious thoughts of their parents. The child's social perception is based more on the feelings of the parents than on their specific caretaking skills. The infant who develops mistrust would be expected to have problems developing and maintaining intimate or close relationships.

The second stage, called *autonomy versus doubt and shame,* coincides with Freud's anal stage. The child's greater ability in motor skills stimulates a strong interest to explore the environment and to accomplish new tasks. At the same time, the child experiences doubt about abandoning the previously enjoyed dependency. This conflict is most apparent during toilet training but is involved in all aspects of the child's behavior. Erikson specifies that the parents' allowing the child freedom in some areas while maintaining firm limits in others facilitates the development of autonomy. Doubt is likely to be the result of parents' lack of control. Excessive punishment from the parents or the child's failure to meet the parental standards produces shame in the child.

The third stage, called *initiative versus guilt,* coincides with Freud's phallic stage and the period of the Oedipus complex. Initiative results from the child's being challenged by the social environment to be active and to master new skills. Again, the parents' role is primarily that of support and control. If the child's initiative either receives no limits from the parents or is excessively punished, then a feeling of guilt is likely to result. It is during this period that the child begins to identify with the parent of the same sex and parental values become incorporated.

Erikson's fourth stage, which is called *industry versus inferiority,* coincides with Freud's latency stage. During this period, the child's principal tasks are to learn the basic skills necessary for progressing toward the adult role. Peers become increasingly significant, and children continuously compare their accomplishments with those of their peers. Failure to develop the culturally or parentally prescribed skills can lead to lasting feelings of inferiority.

The fifth stage, *identity versus role confusion,* denotes the end of childhood and the beginning of adolescence. The feeling of identity represents a mastery of the earlier conflicts and a readiness to meet the problems of the adult world as well as the successful integration of psychosexual drives. During this period, the parent-child relationship continues to be important, but the adolescent relies more on relationships outside of the family.

Erikson also described three stages that occur during adulthood: *intimacy versus isolation, generativity versus stagnation,* and *ego identity versus despair.* These adult stages are hypothesized to be influenced by the earlier childhood and adolescent stages. Erikson's view of the developing person may be characterized as a continuous process of balancing internal needs and the requirements of the social environment. Parents are expected to transmit the values of society to their children while remaining sensitive to the needs, abilities, and limitations of the growing child. Lack of adequate support, unrealistic expectations, and excessive punishment of the child can lead to less-than-optimal psychological development.

Psychodynamic theory and its variations, greatly emphasizing the impact of experiences during the preschool years, easily lent themselves to the extrapolation that parents are primarily responsible for the development of behavior problems.

Behavior Theory. In general, behaviorists have not concerned themselves greatly with the origins of behavior problems in children, and thus their interest in historical events has been considerably less than that of psychoanalytically oriented clinicians. Behaviorists' interest in etiology is usually confined to a search for the environmental stimuli that are currently maintaining the problem behavior. This search is based on the assumption that behavior is continuous in time; that is, regardless of its origin, behavior that is occurring is largely controlled by contemporary environmental stimuli rather than events that are remote in time. In some situations, the behavioral clinician does not even search for these controlling stimuli because other environmental stimuli can be used to change the behavior.

The basic assumptions of the behavioral theorists are that most behavior is learned and that both normal and abnormal behaviors are learned on the basis of the same principles. Only during the past few decades have these principles of learning been used to account for the behavioral problems of adults and children. The application of these principles is based on some 50 years of research with animals and humans. Much of the evidence supporting a behavioral account of etiology, however, comes to us indirectly through assessment and treatment programs, rather than through retrospective or longitudinal studies.

Although behavioral clinicians recognize the important role of parents in the development of their children, a wide variety of other persons, including peers, have been credited with having a primary role in the etiology of behavior problems. Similarly, a wide range of nonhuman stimulus events have been suggested as having significant etiological functions. Thus, the behavioral clinician considers the child's total environment (Wahler, House, & Stembaugh, 1976) rather than a narrow spectrum to have the potential for increasing the probability of behavior problems.

Several types of learning have been described in the psychological literature: operant conditioning, modeling, and respondent conditioning. These types of learning are distinguished on the basis of relationships between stimuli and responses. Responses include any activity, such as smiling, complaining, or crying, that can be counted or otherwise measured. Stimuli include all situations, objects, or events that have an effect on behavior. Stimuli may control responses in a variety of ways.

Operant conditioning refers to an increase in the occurrence of a response when it is followed by a reinforcing stimulus. The responses that are likely to be operantly conditioned are what we would call *voluntary* behaviors. It is assumed that humans are biologically designed to emit a certain spectrum of behaviors, but that the future occurrence of these behaviors depends greatly on the consequences of these behaviors.

Operant conditioning appears to have a significant role in the development of children's behavior problems. That is, a number of studies have shown that behavior problems were being maintained by certain reinforcers. This control was demonstrated when the reinforcers were omitted and the behavior decreased. For example, in an early study Williams (1959) described a case study in which a 21-month-old boy presented severe temper tantrums, particularly at bedtime. A parent was spending one to two hours per night in the child's bedroom; if the parent tried to leave the room before the child was asleep, temper tantrums occurred. That is, temper tantrums were consistently followed by the parent's remaining in the room with the child. The intervention procedure consisted of the parent putting the child to bed and then leaving the bedroom. On the first night the child screamed for 45 minutes. During the following nights, however, the tantrums were markedly reduced, and they were absent by the seventh bedtime. This study strongly suggests that the child's temper tantrums were being maintained by the parent's remaining in the room.

While it can be assumed that many behavior problems are being maintained by reinforcement, it is not always possible to identify the reinforcers in the available time. In some of these cases, an intervention program in which all possible sources of reinforcement are controlled through a brief period of social isolation each time the behavior occurs may be successful. In these instances, one cannot determine whether the behavioral change is due to the omission of reinforcement or other factors.

The baseline data from many studies suggest that adults in the child's environment may be responsible for supplying the reinforcement that maintains the problem behavior. In the majority of cases, the adults do not realize that they are maintaining the behavior; in fact, they are usually the ones who are complaining about the behavior and are trying to "help" the child. In other words, it is often appropriate to conclude that these adults are inadvertently reinforcing the behavior. Most adults are not aware that giving social attention to inappropriate behavior may strengthen that behavior.

Some behavior problems may best be described as deficits in the behavioral repertoire. In many of these cases, the child will not have had the opportunity to learn the necessary behaviors, while in others, effective reinforcers have not been employed. Few parents or teachers have been adequately trained to develop children's behavioral repertoires to their best levels.

Behavioral deficits could also be the result of negative consequences or punishment. That is, low rates of behavior could be due to the behavior's having been followed by an aversive stimulus (e.g., scolding, spanking) or the withdrawal of a positive reinforcer (e.g., TV privileges). The behavioral research literature does not, however, contain adequate evidence that these factors were involved in the maintenance of deficits in appropriate behavior.

Although we often do not know the factors that are responsible for the origin of a behavior problem, it can be demonstrated that many new responses are added to the child's behavioral repertoire through *observational learning,* or *modeling.* Observational learning is demonstrated when the child imitates a behavior after having observed it in another person. That is, simply observing another person engaging in a behavior may increase the probability of a child's producing that behavior. One of the early demonstrations of modeling in children was reported in a study by Bandura, Ross, and Ross (1961). In this study, preschool children observed either aggressive adult models, nonaggressive adult models, or no models. When tested in a similar situation in the absence of the model, the children exposed to the aggressive model engaged in more aggressive behaviors than did the children in the other groups. These results were subsequently replicated in studies in which the modeled behaviors were presented on film rather than live (Bandura, Ross, & Ross, 1963). An interesting finding was that children who imitated the aggressive behaviors often spoke disapprovingly of the behaviors.

It may be hypothesized that persons in the child's environment serve as models for children and that children acquire many behaviors by imitating others. During the preschool years, parents are the most available models, while at older ages, teachers, peers, and others provide behaviors which the child may imitate. Although modeling may affect the initial occurrences of these behaviors, subsequent consequences also affect their continuation.

Another type of learning that may be involved in the etiology of children's behavior problems is *respondent*, or *classical, conditioning*. Respondent conditioning involves one stimulus taking on the function of another stimulus in eliciting a particular response through a pairing of the two stimuli. Respondent conditioning is best demonstrated with involuntary behavior, such as eyelid closure to a puff of air. If another stimulus (one that initially does not cause eyelid closure) is paired with the puff of air several times, this stimulus may then become capable of eliciting eye closure when it is later presented without the puff of air.

A very early study (Watson & Rayner, 1920) demonstrated that fear of a white rat was learned through respondent conditioning by a young child who was previously not afraid of the rat. The investigators paired the presentation of the white rat with a very loud sound and found that the child later continued to express fear when the rat was presented without the accompanying loud sound. Respondent conditioning has been invoked as the process by which behavior problems associated with anxiety are learned. Certain environmental stimuli (for example, loud, sudden sounds) cause involuntary fear or anxiety responses; these stimulus-response relationships are biologically determined. On occasion, these stimuli are "accidentally" paired with other "neutral" stimuli that may then elicit the anxiety responses. These fears are often maintained for long periods because the feared stimulus poses no real threat. That is, according to the principles of respondent conditioning, repeated presentations of the feared stimulus, in the absence of the stimulus with which it was originally paired, should lead to a decrease in the conditioned response; avoidance of the feared stimulus therefore tends to maintain the anxiety response.

Accidental pairings may well account for a number of behavior problems, and more than a few of them are mediated, probably inadvertently, by people in the child's environment. For example, the goal of the teacher who suddenly yells at a child is usually to stop an inappropriate behavior, but one of the by-products of the teacher's yelling may be that the child learns to be fearful in the classroom.

Without knowing the principles of learning, parents and teachers may unintentionally foster the development of children's behavior problems. They may reinforce the very behaviors they consider to be inappropriate, or they may ignore appropriate behaviors that should be strengthened through reinforcement. Without knowledge of the effects of modeling, they may model behavior that, when imitated by the child, will be considered a behavior problem. Likewise, parents and teachers sometimes expose children to situations that foster the development of fears and anxiety. In these instances, the adults are not intending to create a behavior problem but are unaware of the relationship between their behavior and that of the child.

CONCLUSIONS

Demographic studies suggest that male children have an increased probability of developing behavior problems. Postnatal physical factors, such as disease, head injury, and the ingestion of poisons, cause brain damage that results in a variety of behavioral abnormalities. Certain environmental conditions, particularly those related to stimulus deprivation and abuse can have a detrimental effect on both physical and psychological development. Psychoanalytic theory suggests that psychological disturbances, particularly neurotic problems, are caused by faulty parent-child relationships during the preschool years. Behavior theory, on the other hand, either focuses on the identification of stimuli currently maintaining the behavior problem or omits consideration of etiological factors. The available evidence suggests that significant persons in the children's environment (including parents) may inadvertently strengthen and maintain problem behavior.

RECOMMENDED READINGS

Brodzinsky, D.M., & Schechter, D. (Eds.). (1990). *The psychology of adoption.* New York: Oxford University Press.

Cummings, E.M., & Davies, P. (1994). *Children and marital conflict.* New York: Guilford.

Emery, R.E. (1994). *Renegotiating family relationships.* New York: Guilford.

Plomin, R. (1994). *Genetics and experience: The interplay between nature and nurture.* Newbury Park, CA: Sage.

Silverman, W.K., & Ollendick, T.H. (Eds.). (1997). *Developmental issues in clinical treatment of children.* Needham, MA: Allyn & Bacon.

Chapter 20: Grych, J.H., & Fincham, F. D. *Children of single parents and divorce.*

Chapter 21: Anderson, E., & Greene, S. *Children of stepparents and divorce.*

Chapter 22: Finley, G.E., *Children of adoptive families.*

Chapter 23: Azar, S.T., & Bober, S.L. *Children of abuse.*

Chapter 24: Windle, M., & Tubman, J. *Children of alcoholics.*

Chapter 25: Gotlib, I.H., & Goodman, S.H. *Children of parents with chronic depression.*

Chapter 26: Finney, J. *Children of parents with chronic medical conditions.*

6

Therapeutic Interventions

Part I

The earliest approaches to the treatment of children's behavior problems included a variety of therapies that were either based directly on psychodynamic theory or variations of psychodynamic theory. These therapies may be described as adhering to a medical model of mental illness in that the symptoms, or behavior, were not believed to be the "real" problem, but rather reflected underlying defects in personality. These earlier treatments focused on a search for underlying defects, the motives behind the behavior problem that were largely unconscious and not readily available to the client.

    Virtually none of the treatment procedures currently being used to alleviate children's behavior problems existed before this century. In fact, the need for treat-

This chapter was revised by Lyn Vinnick, Ph.D.

ment (outside institutional settings) of children's behavior problems did not become formalized in this country until the 1920s. Through the ensuing years, psychodynamic theory came to dominate the treatment programs conducted by psychiatrists, psychologists, and social workers. Subsequently, considerable effort has gone into the development of theoretical systems, professional training programs, and facilities for the provision of services. Until about 20 years ago, the research literature consisted primarily of a collection of treatment technique descriptions and a large number of case studies that purported to demonstrate the effectiveness of these techniques.

Some evaluation of therapeutic effectiveness through the use of well-designed research studies has been done since the 1970s, but the early research failed to show that psychotherapy with children was effective (Levitt, 1971, p. 474). In a review of child psychotherapy research, Barrett, Hampe, and Miller (1978) reached the following conclusions: (1) child psychotherapists did not assume an appropriate responsibility for evaluating therapeutic effectiveness; (2) child psychotherapy research did not provide adequate attention to important variables such as the developmental stage and diagnostic category; and (3) child psychotherapy research lacked a model that took into account the larger context (e.g., family and school) in which psychotherapy occurs. Although faced with largely negative results from child psychotherapy research, clinicians continued to use these treatment methods because they personally believed them to be effective in their own clinical work.

In recent years, training programs for psychologists and psychiatrists have begun to include in-depth exposure to a broader spectrum of theoretical orientations and treatment methods. This change in training is producing more professionals who adhere to an eclectic approach to the treatment of children and reflects the increasing recognition that no single treatment approach is likely to be effective for all children.

SETTINGS FOR CHILD THERAPY

Settings for therapy have traditionally been designated as either outpatient or inpatient. *Outpatient settings* are those that the client visits for specific therapeutic sessions while living at home. Child guidance clinics, offices of professionals in private practice, and therapeutic day treatment centers are examples of outpatient facilities. Most psychotherapy with children is conducted in outpatient facilities with psychiatrists, psychologists, and social workers who are in private practice or employed by community or university-affiliated clinics. There is a growing trend, however, for those professionals to leave their offices and provide therapeutic intervention for children indirectly through consultation with other persons in the child's environment. For example, a psychologist employed by a mental health clinic might go to a school and consult with a teacher who is having a problem with a child in the classroom. School systems are increasingly hiring psychologists to provide both direct and indirect services to children.

Sometimes, the severity of a child's problem, the condition of the home environment, or both, leads to a recommendation that the child live away from home. An *inpatient facility* is one in which the child resides most of the time. The child may require hospitalization for a short time, and then may need further treatment away from home. One such option is the *residential treatment center* that attempts to provide an optimal therapeutic environment to facilitate the child's recovery. Residential treatment centers may be public or private, and the quality of both varies greatly. Financial resources determine, in large measure, the number of professional and nonprofessional staff employed, but the centers with the highest per capita costs are not necessarily the most effective. Some centers are so poorly supported that they have become nothing more than warehouses for children, while other centers are focused almost solely on treatment and prevention of future psychiatric problems.

Communities sometimes provide *foster homes* and *group homes* supported by public agencies, which are less restrictive than residential care or institutionalization for a child who must be removed from the home. Foster homes provide a family environment for children who would otherwise be institutionalized or receive no help at all. They offer care for children who are awaiting adoption, for handicapped children who are presumed to be "unadoptable," for children whose parents are temporarily unable to care for them (if, for example, both parents are badly injured in an accident), for children whose parents are judged to be abusive and/or neglectful, and for children whose parents cannot currently cope with their children's behavior problems at home.

Foster homes are licensed by the states and must be approved by social service agencies that control assignment of children. Foster parents tend to be older couples whose children have grown up and left home or younger couples who have no or few children. The number of foster children cared for by one family is usually limited to about five children, although the family can choose to have only one or two children at a time. A monthly stipend for each child is paid to the foster parents for living expenses, and the agency also pays for other necessary expenses, such as medical and dental treatment. Some agencies provide financial support for psychotherapy when it is indicated.

In the last several decades, there has been an effort to decentralize large state institutions in favor of keeping patients in their own communities. One alternative to the large regional institutions has been the development of community-based group homes. A group home is usually supported by a public agency or community group that employs one or more adults to be house parents and counselors. The counselors have usually received formal training that prepares them for their therapeutic role. Group homes are used in various ways in different communities, sometimes as a holding facility for children awaiting court proceedings or in lieu of sending delinquent children to training schools. They are also used as halfway homes for persons who have recently been discharged from mental hospitals or institutions for the retarded. The group home offers much potential for the improvement of treatment and rehabilitation of children with problems—a potential that is only slowly being realized.

PSYCHOANALYSIS

Psychoanalysis attempts to comprehend and explain the normal and abnormal functioning of the mind. It is generally recognized that Freud carried out the first systematic treatment of a child. Freud himself did not conduct the treatment, but he advised the child's father, who conducted the treatment program in the home. Freud had been particularly interested in the development of infantile sexuality and emotional conflict and had been collecting observations of young children from several sources. The child's father was supplying Freud with observations of his son's behavior for two years prior to the onset of the problem. When nearly five years old, the boy, called Little Hans, developed a fear, or phobia, that a horse would bite him.

Although Freud published his famous case study of Little Hans in 1909, it was not until 1926 that the next significant event in the history of child psychotherapy occurred. During that year Anna Freud, Sigmund Freud's daughter, presented a series of lectures to the Vienna Institute of Psychoanalysis entitled "Introduction to the Technique of the Psycho-Analysis of Children." The publication of these lectures aroused great interest, and a group of psychoanalysts began to hold regular meetings with Anna Freud in Vienna to discuss the technique of analysis with children and to report on their case material. Both a wide age range (two years old through adolescence) and a broad spectrum of behavior problems were characteristic of the children whose cases were presented at these meetings.

The principal impediment to the use of psychoanalysis with children is their lack of skill in free association. Free association is a technique enabling the patient to say anything that comes to mind. It is one of the most important techniques of psychoanalysis with adults, allowing the analyst access to the patient's mental life. The early analysts therefore needed a substitute for free association and finally settled on children's play. As early as 1919, Hug-Hellmuth proposed that children's play be utilized as a way of understanding their unconscious processes during therapy. Melanie Klein elaborated the idea, hypothesizing that children's play is equivalent to adults' free associations, and she began to interpret the unconscious meaning of her clients' play during therapy.

The writings of Anna Freud (1946a, 1946b, 1965) were considered primary sources of information regarding psychoanalysis with children (Scharfman, 1978). She described the motivational differences between adult and child patients—the child's tendency to externalize and "act out" when anxiety is experienced, thus presenting a problem to others in the environment, in contrast to adults, who present themselves for analysis to alleviate internal suffering. Children are greatly dependent on their parents; the therapist must determine to what extent parents are protecting the child from experiencing anxiety and to what extent they are obtaining secondary gain from bringing their child for therapy.

In child psychoanalysis the patient may be seen by the therapist several times a week, thus encouraging an intense patient-analyst relationship and a continuity of therapeutic activity. The frequent visits aid the child in tolerating the anxiety engendered by the treatment, because the therapist is more available for support. As with adults, psychoanalysis with children is a lengthy treatment procedure, usually lasting several years or more. The expense involved, more often than not, currently precludes its use for other than the most well-to-do families.

Although psychoanalytic treatment is clearly focused on the child, the therapist will find it necessary to meet with one or both parents during the course of the child's analysis. Parents are the primary source of information about the child's development, symptomatology, and personal interrelationships. In addition, since young children are not always accurate reporters, the analyst must rely on parents to obtain information about the child's status outside of the therapeutic sessions. During the early phase of analysis many therapists see the parents once every week or two to obtain information about events in the child's life. As the child becomes a better reporter, sessions with the parents are gradually reduced and eventually terminated.

One major assumption of psychoanalytic treatment is that healthy functioning comes about when children recognize and manage their feelings and defensive styles. The primary goal of psychoanalysis is therefore to help children to achieve insight—to recognize their feelings and defenses and to deal with them in a direct manner. The analyst hopes "to undo the various repressions, distortions, displacements, condensations, etc., which had been brought about by the neurotic defense mechanisms, until, with the active help of the child, the unconscious content of the material is laid bare" (A. Freud, 1946a, p. 49). Child analysis therefore involves the investigation and examination of past emotional experiences by the analyst and the child, particularly those emotional experiences of which the child is only dimly aware or not at all aware (unconscious). The course of the child's development is assumed to have been inhibited or retarded through the by-products of past emotional trauma; the analyst attempts to show the child the relationships between present and past feelings. The analyst focuses on fantasy, emotion, and behavior to understand how the child expresses conflict, motivation, and impulses (Lesser, 1972). The designation of such relationships is an aspect of psychoanalytic technique called interpretation, which also includes delineating for the child the relationships between defenses and feelings and between fantasies and feelings (Kessler, 1966, pp. 379–380).

Another major assumption in psychoanalytic treatment is that children experience a normal progression of growth and development unless the environment interferes. Implicit in this theoretical context is that some aspect of the environment (i.e., a parent) is inhibiting the child's natural, and perhaps optimal, development and causes the child to fear or distrust close relationships. The analyst is interested in determining the present purpose served by the child's disorder. The analyst and child work together to examine the child's behavior and the context in which it occurs with the goal of redressing the imbalances uncovered. To that end, analysts must learn the child's language, rather than impose their own, provide warmth and support, and communicate a commitment to the analysis. The child may then become free to progress toward individuation and independence.

PSYCHOTHERAPY

While psychoanalysis was becoming the treatment of choice for clinicians who had access to Freud's teaching and writings, changes were taking place in society that would pave the way for the provision of other forms of treatment for children's behavior problems. Before the twentieth century, children and their problems received little public or professional attention. One of the reasons for this neglect might have been the high death rates of infants and preschool children from diseases such as diphtheria and smallpox—diseases that have been essentially eradicated through mass immunization. Parents had to have a large number of children in order to have some who would live long enough to make an economic contribution to the household. Children, then, were seen as economic assets rather than as persons in their own right. Indeed, they were put to work as soon as possible, often as young as six or seven years of age, originally on family farms and later in factories. Abuse of children in factories led to the enactment of child labor laws that put limits on children's ability to work. Later, of course, compulsory public education kept young children out of factories altogether.

The development of children's rights has taken an interesting course. As long as children were raised and worked within the context of the family, few rights were accrued to them. As society moved toward urbanization and children were employed outside of the family, concern about their status gradually began to develop. Remnants of the compromise made between the early rural family model and society's recognition of children's needs for education may be seen in the nine-month school year. Children were needed to work on the farm during the summer months, and the school year was designed to accommodate the needs of the rural community. A few public school systems have recognized that children are rarely needed to work on farms today, and the school year has been extended.

Compulsory education began to have the positive by-product of alerting others to the problems of children—a function that it continues to have today. With larger numbers of children coming together in groups, similarities and differences among children began to become more dramatically apparent, and children whose behavior differed markedly from that of their peers were viewed as needing help. Of course, some of the problems identified in school settings were no doubt created in that environment. In fact, the first clinic for children, developed by Witmer in 1896 at the University of Pennsylvania, focused on the adjustment of children to the school environment.

Beginning in the 1920s, a movement was also initiated to provide help for disturbed children and their families. This movement grew out of an increasing recognition that many of the emotional problems of adulthood originated during the years of childhood. The first few decades of this century saw the development of a number of clinics for children that were affiliated with mental hospitals, schools, colleges, and social agencies. At the same time there was a growing interest in all aspects of children's behavior that culminated in the founding of a series of child development institutes at universities. The period of the 1920s and 1930s saw a tremendous increase in the amount of research activity directed toward an under-standing of children's growth and development.

The establishment of child guidance clinics, begun in 1922 by the National Committee for Mental Hygiene and the Commonwealth Fund, was a major mile-stone in the development of services for children with behavior disorders. These clinics were unique in their emphasis on a multidisciplinary team approach to the diagnosis and treatment of children's problems. The team usually included a psy-chologist who administered and interpreted the diagnostic tests, a social worker who counseled the families, and a psychiatrist who provided therapy for the child.

Given the growing demand for treatment services, several changes in the orig-inal team format evolved over time. One change included psychologists' and social workers' becoming directly involved in providing child therapy. In addition, a num-ber of different treatment approaches were developed to suit the broader range of children's problems being brought to practitioners and clinics. That is, although psychiatrists were being trained primarily in psychoanalytic theory, psychoanalysis was neither suited to many of the problems presented at the clinics nor feasible in terms of professional and financial resources. These practical considerations were to be responsible for a number of the treatment techniques that later evolved.

Psychodynamically Oriented Psychotherapy

Much of the therapy currently conducted with children in clinics and in pri-vate practice would be labeled by its practitioners as psychodynamic psychotherapy because the training received by a great majority of psychiatrists, psychologists, and social workers practicing today was heavily imbued with psychodynamic theory. Although relatively few practitioners have had training in psychoanalysis per se, they do attempt to use the theoretical system evolved by Freud and his followers and the techniques that are feasible within their professional settings. During the 1940s and 1950s, training programs for all three disciplines involved in the treat-ment of children's behavior problems emphasized very similar theory and practice. Gradually, other theoretical orientations and treatment techniques have been introduced into training programs so that substantial changes both within and among the disciplines are taking place. Among younger members of the profes-sions there is already a strong tendency toward eclectic approaches in which treat-ment techniques are chosen to fit the problem, rather than toward a strict adherence to a unitary theoretical model.

Psychodynamic psychotherapy was developed and refined after World War II in response to a vast majority of patients who were not suitable candidates for psy-choanalysis proper. A primary goal of psychodynamic psychotherapy is the relief of symptoms that precipitated the child's being brought to a therapist or clinic. That is, the therapist concentrates primarily on behavioral manifestations of the under-lying problem. On a practical level this concentration means that the therapist more actively guides the activities during therapy and is more selective about responses to the child's behavior than would be a psychoanalyst. The therapist is more active in identifying the child's feelings and defenses but at the same time does so only when the feelings and defenses appear to be related to the manifested problem. In contrast to long-term psychoanalysis, psychodynamic psychotherapy requires that children be seen only once or twice a week over a period of months, although some problems require a year or more of treatment. Treatment of the child is almost always accompanied by treatment of one or both parents by another therapist. The parent is usually seen once a week throughout the course of the child's treatment. The two therapists communicate at regular intervals regarding the child's progress in therapy.

Brief Psychodynamic Psychotherapy

Certain theoreticians have advocated briefer, more active, and more focused psychodynamic psychotherapies. Brief dynamic psychotherapy is indicated when a specific emotional problem can be identified and when the patient can explore it in a brief time frame. The goals of therapy are more focused and narrowly defined as opposed to more thorough and diffuse goals in longer dynamic therapy. Brief therapy is limited to a fixed number of sessions (usually 12 to 20) and it is practical—treatment is cost effective and accessible to a broader segment of the population (Marmar, 1988). Brief dynamic psychotherapists include Rank, Balint and his coworkers, Malan at the Tavistock Clinic in London, and Sifneos in Boston. Their therapeutic principles include resolution of a specific problem, facilitating a rapidly established therapeutic relationship that is empathic and nonjudgmental, and carefully considering the meaning of termination of therapy for the patient.

Relationship therapy is a form of brief dynamic therapy evolved from Rank's view that therapy should focus on the meanings of separation. His interest was focused on the physical separation of the infant from the mother at the moment of birth and later psychological separation of the child from the mother (Marmar, 1988). Rank believed that the benefits resulting from therapy were best when the therapist understood and utilized the patient's reactions to the therapeutic relationship. This idea was later expanded and had a substantial influence on the therapeutic procedures used by social workers and other child guidance professionals. In writing the first two books on psychotherapy of children published in the United States, Taft (1933) and Allen (1942) emphasized the importance of the patient's active participation in the therapeutic process. The patient's past history and unconscious are deemphasized in favor of attention being focused on the present situation. The relationship between the patient and the therapist is viewed as a unique experience rather than a recapitulation of the parent-child relationship. The technique of interpretation is not used, but the therapist does reflect what the child seems to be feeling. Some of the early proponents of relationship therapy advocated setting a time limit for therapy, an arbitrary date agreed upon by both patient and therapist. The reason behind the setting of a time limit is apparently its role in helping the patient to accept reality.

Although not all of the original aspects of relationship therapy are strongly supported now, several components have greatly influenced contemporary therapists. Therapists now recognize the need to actively develop a positive relationship with their patients in order to establish themselves as significant persons in the therapeutic interaction. This active participation on the part of the therapist may take a number of forms, ranging from warm acceptance of the child's verbalizations and activities to providing sweets during the therapy session. Relationship therapy does not imply indiscriminate acceptance of the child's behavior but rather a human response that is appropriate to the situation.

BEHAVIOR THERAPY

Behavior therapy is a more recently developed form of treatment for children, and is based on the principles of learning which date back to the early part of this century. Behavior therapy is the application of learning principles to behaviors that are inappropriate, inadequate, or stressful to the person doing them or to significant people in that person's environment.

Classical and Operant Conditioning

The emphasis on behavior, rather than on mental processes, has been an important aspect of behavior theory since its proposal by Ivan Pavlov and John B. Watson in the first decade of this century. Advocates of behaviorism focus on observable behavior and emphasize learned rather than unlearned behavior. They proceeded to investigate those variables that affected learned behavior. Through carefully controlled laboratory research with both animals and humans, experimental psychologists attempted to discover the conditions under which learning takes place. They then formulated principles concerning the prediction and control of behavior, and these principles of learning are the foundation upon which behavior therapy is based.

In his experiments on learned and unlearned (conditioned and unconditioned) behavior, Ivan Pavlov (1849–1936) trained dogs to salivate to the sound of a bell by repeatedly pairing the bell with food powder (which naturally causes salivation). Similarly, Watson and Rayner (1920) were the first to demonstrate that an infant could learn a fear. At about nine months of age, a child named Albert was tested and showed no fear to a number of live animals, such as a rat, a rabbit, and a dog, and to various inanimate objects, such as cotton and human masks. He did show fear, however, when a steel bar was unexpectedly struck with a hammer just behind him. Two months later, this loud sound was presented when Albert touched a white rat placed before him; seven pairings of the rat and the loud sound occurred in two sessions one week apart. Albert subsequently reacted with crying and avoidance when the rat was presented without the loud sound. Five days later, Albert reacted in fear not only to the rat but also to a rabbit, a dog, and a sealskin coat. He showed a moderately fearful response to a bearded Santa Claus mask and Watson's hair, and had a mild response to a package of white cotton. Albert's negative responses to stimuli other than the rat were interpreted as evidence that a learned fear could be transferred to other objects.

Jones (1924), a student of Watson's, showed that a young child could both learn and unlearn a fear response. On this occasion fear of a white rabbit was learned in a manner similar to that in the Watson and Rayner study. To bring about the unlearning of the fear response, Jones arranged for the child to observe other children playing with the rabbit. She gradually brought the rabbit closer and closer to the child and simultaneously gave the child food each time he made approach movements toward the rabbit. The child was eventually able to approach the rabbit without a fear response.

For their research using *classical conditioning,* Pavlov and Watson are credited with beginning the systematic study of the effects of the environment on behavior (Levenson & Pope, 1988). Although Watson became famous for his books on child rearing, psychological theory was not yet developed well enough for application of his behavior theory. These early studies, although important in retrospect, did not appear to have an impact on the clinical practitioners of the time. Moreover, the early learning psychologists were concerned about the development of psychology as a science and were not yet ready to develop practical applications. These factors may have encouraged the early clinical psychologists to adopt the psychodynamic approach to treatment being used by their psychiatrist colleagues, rather than adopt a behaviorally oriented approach.

In 1949, Fuller reported the first clinical study of a behavioral technique called *operant conditioning.* He worked with a young man considered by physicians to be a "vegetative idiot" and incapable of learning. Fuller used a warm sugar-mild solution as a reinforcer for successively greater movements of the young man's right arm, thereby demonstrating in four sessions that the man was capable of learning.

Another significant step taken toward the application of learning principles in clinical practice is represented in a series of studies conducted by Lindsley and Skinner at Metropolitan State Hospital in Massachusetts during the 1950s. In one study they used patients who averaged 17 years of hospitalization. They compared the effects of two schedules of intermittent reinforcement for lever pulling and found that the patients' lever-pulling behavior was stable and predictable, mirroring the results found earlier with lower organisms. Lindsley (1960) reported the interesting finding that the hospitalized patients had very slow rates of response in comparison to normal adults.

The early 1960s saw the beginning of applied behavioral research with children's problems by Donald Baer and Sidney Bijou at the University of Washington. Working with them were Ivar Lovaas, Robert Orlando, Jay Birnbrauer, Robert Wahler, Montrose Wolf, Todd Risley, and James Sherman, who have subsequently contributed significantly to the applied research literature.

Behavioral vs. Earlier Therapy Models

The behavior therapy approach has come to be contrasted with earlier models of psychotherapy in several important ways. Traditional approaches, for example, psychoanalysis and psychodynamic psychotherapy, emphasize a medical model of disease. The premise is that child behavior disorders are manifestations or symptoms of underlying pathology. Therefore, the goals of traditional psychotherapy are to extirpate the underlying pathology and thereby remove the symptoms. In contrast, behavior therapy conceptualizes a symptom as an abnormal behavior that has been learned in the same way that other behaviors are learned. Traditional psychotherapists believe that removal of the symptom alone, that is, *only* addressing the behavior or symptom, will result in symptom substitution and would, therefore, be of very little therapeutic benefit. In contrast, behavior therapists view the removal of the symptom as the primary goal of therapy and cite follow-up studies that have found no evidence of symptom substitution for persons who have had behavior therapy. Behavior therapists emphasize the importance of the current environment in maintaining abnormal behavior, while traditional psychotherapists view abnormal behavior as a direct result of an historical antecedent.

From a behavioral point of view, therapy consists of establishing, increasing, and maintaining appropriate or desirable responses and decreasing or eliminating inappropriate or undesirable responses. Each child who is referred for behavior therapy is recognized as having a unique pattern of responses and environmental stimuli, and therapy programs are therefore individually designed. Because the principles of learning are relatively easily understood, many people are under the impression that behavior therapy is easy to learn and simple to perform. Most behavior therapists, however, realize that knowledge of learning principles alone is not adequate for the treatment of children. Learning principles describe the lawful relationships between stimulus events and responses, but they do not tell the therapist what stimulus events are controlling the behavior of a particular child. The therapist must determine that information correctly—success of the therapeutic program depends on it. Securing this information requires considerable knowledge about children's environments in general and the client's environment in particular.

The behavior therapist must also be knowledgeable about normal developmental sequences of behavior. Therapists who are naive about normal child development and learning might expend much wasted energy working on types of behavior that have no precursors in the child's repertoire. Behavior therapists should know the research literature, both basic research that serves as the foundation for behavior therapy and applied research that describes the applications of learning principles for a variety of children's problems in a variety of environmental situations.

Behavior therapy brought together a group of professionals with a broad range of backgrounds. Some child behavior therapists were trained in traditional clinical programs in psychology and later became advocates of the behavioral approach. Some of the most productive researchers in behavior therapy with children were originally trained in experimental child or developmental psychology. Clinical psychology training programs added behavior therapists to their faculties, thus increasing the number of graduate students being trained in behavioral theory and techniques.

Treatment Designs and Evaluation

One of the most important characteristics of behavior therapy is the continuous collection of data throughout the course of treatment—data that will be used to evaluate the effectiveness of the intervention plan. Data obtained during the baseline phase (the period before treatment has begun) are later compared with data obtained during the treatment phase. Since the goal of behavior therapy is to effect changes in behavior, either increases of appropriate behavior or decreases of inappropriate behavior, a comparison of the behavior's frequency during the baseline and treatment phases is conducted. Effectiveness is measured by the amount of increase or decrease in appropriate or inappropriate behaviors, respectively.

In designing behavioral intervention programs, behavior therapists must take precautions against five major threats to internal validity. These threats are factors that systematically bias or confound treatment effects; they may be mistaken for treatment effects or mask true treatment effects (Gelfand & Hartmann, 1984, pp. 60–61). The first factor involves coincidental occurrences that happen to the child, such as a change of teacher or a mother's returning to work, that produce behavior change mistakenly attributed to the treatment program. The second factor is the effect of maturation and experience with the environment; for example, as children get older, their general competence improves, and some fears and concerns tend to fade away.

Testing experience is a third factor; improvement in performance may occur only because the child has had practice on the test. A fourth factor involves observers' changing their criteria for performance. That is, the child's behavior may appear to improve only because the observer has lowered his or her standards. The fifth factor has to do with chance or statistical occurrences. For example, a child may be selected for treatment on the basis of an erroneous high score and may then appear to improve when the cause of the measurement error is not noticed in a subsequent administration.

Operant Conditioning Methods for Increasing Appropriate Behaviors

Many children are referred for therapy because one or more of their appropiate behaviors is occurring too infrequently. That is, adults in the child's environment are concerned about behavioral deficiencies in the child's repertoire. Various methods have been developed based on learning principles to increase or establish behaviors that are considered to be necessary or desirable. In this section we describe the principal methods for increasing appropriate behaviors: contingent presentation of positive reinforcement, prompting, shaping, and contingent removal of negative reinforcement.

Contingent Presentation of Positive Reinforcement. It is a well-known learning principle that the probability a specific behavior will occur is increased when the behavior is followed by certain pleasurable consequences (reinforcers). The most frequently used method for increasing the rate of an appropriate behavior is to present a positive reinforcer immediately after the appropriate behavior occurs. This method is appropriate for children who have the behavior in their repertoire, but its rate is lower than what is considered optimal.

One example of an undesirably low rate of behavior might be that of a child who only rarely interacts with people at nursery school. The label of "socially withdrawn" would be used by some clinicians to describe that child, but the behavior therapist describes such a child as having a low rate of social responses. In this example, the behavior therapist's first step might be to delineate the behavior with the help of the child's teacher and to observe its occurrence in the school setting. The therapist would probably at the same time record what occurred both when the child was being social and when the child was not being social (the baseline phase). Therapy begins with the presentation of a stimulus, which the therapist has judged to have high potential for reinforcer effectiveness, following each occurrence of a social response.

REINFORCERS.   Choosing the reinforcer is an important component of operant conditioning procedures. The therapist looks for a reinforcer that is likely to be effective with the child and easily available in the setting in which the behavior occurs. One such reinforcer in the nursery school might be teacher attention. If teacher attention is the therapist's choice, the therapist would ask the teacher to go over to the child and make positive statements, such as "I'm really glad to see that you and David are having a good time together," each time that the teacher observes the child interacting with a peer. It should be stressed that the teacher's attention should coincide immediately with the occurrence of the desired behavior.

There are several ways of determining which stimuli have a high probability of being reinforcers for a particular child. During the assessment procedure the therapist could ask the child, parents, and/or teacher what things the child likes to have or which activities the child particularly enjoys, or the therapist could ask the child to complete one of several reinforcement survey schedules (see, for example, Keat, 1974). Still another way is to observe the child in the setting in which the change in behavior is desired and apply the Premack Principle (Premack, 1965), which states that a high-frequency activity can be used as a reinforcer for a low-frequency behavior. The general idea is to determine how the child prefers to spend time when free to choose activities, and use that preferred activity as the reinforcer for a desired behavior. This principle is particularly useful for identifying reinforcers in the preschool and home environments.

In choosing a reinforcer, the therapist must take into account the child's motivational status with respect to the stimulus. Reinforcers that are freely available or that the child receives frequently may not be effective. Stimuli, such as food, are usually effective after a period of deprivation, but they are relatively ineffective immediately after the child has had a meal. The effectiveness of social stimuli, too, might be increased with deprivation and decreased under conditions of satiation. Thus, a teacher's very frequent use of positive statements could decrease the effectiveness of that kind of attention as a reinforcer.

Although behavior therapists have become associated with using M & M candies as reinforcers, sweets and other foods are not used or even preferred in most settings. Food sometimes has to be used because no other reinforcers can be found for particular clients; researchers in laboratory settings have often used food as a matter of convenience. In most natural settings, however, behavior therapists tend to avoid the use of candy and other snack foods for dietary and dental reasons, unless, of course, no other reinforcers are available.

Some adults express concern when a behavior therapist suggests the use of a tangible reinforcer, such as stickers, trinkets, or money, in an intervention program. One of these concerns is that the therapist is "bribing" the child. Two statements can be made in response to this concern. First, the correct use of the word "bribe" refers to payment for an illegal activity, while the therapist's goal is to increase *appropriate* behavior. Second, adults receive tangible reinforcers for much of their life's work—how many adults would continue going to work everyday if their salaries were cut off? In other words, there are situations in which tangible reinforcers are necessary to develop and maintain behavior.

The use of tangible reinforcers does present some problems to the therapist, however. The long-range goal of therapy is to increase the appropriate behavior and to have "natural" contingencies take over its maintenance. A natural contingency is a response-reinforcer relationship that exists in the child's environment prior to intervention by a behavior therapist. An example of natural contingency is a teacher's occasional verbal praise of a child for good work. If the teacher's praise is not naturally effective as a reinforcer for the child, however, the therapist might design a program that temporarily uses tangible reinforcement. The therapist in this situation would introduce a reward to be given by the teacher each time a selected behavior occurs. The teacher would also be instructed to praise the child at the same time the tangible reinforcer is given. The therapist's aim is that with a large number of such pairings stimulus substitution will occur through classical conditioning; that is, the teacher's praise will acquire reinforcing properties. After the desired rate of appropriate behavior is achieved, then a program is initiated in which the tangible reinforcer is carefully faded out while teacher praise is maintained. Teacher praise will later be gradually decreased until it approximates the natural contingencies available to all children in the classroom.

EVALUATION OF TREATMENT EFFECTIVENESS. While the target behavior is being reinforced, the therapist arranges that observation records of the behavior's occurrence be collected at regular intervals, usually by the same person who collected the baseline data. Comparison of the behavior with baseline data will quickly reveal the effect of the intervention program designed by the therapist. Most behaviors begin to change rather rapidly, and it would be unusual for a therapist to continue a program that has not produced change within a few days or weeks.

If the behavior remains unchanged and continues at a low rate, then the therapist would assume that there is something wrong with the plan and would take steps to correct it. The therapist first has to determine whether the plan has been implemented correctly. Sometimes instructions are misunderstood, and the mediator may omit a crucial component of the program or add some factor to the situation that would decrease the program's effectiveness. If the therapist is satisfied that the program has been carried out as intended, then the fault may reside in the choice of the stimulus to serve as the reinforcer. In this event, the therapist would seek a more effective reinforcer. For example, teacher's praise is not a reinforcer for some children, but the same children will work very hard for points that will give them a free choice of activities later in the day.

When a particular stimulus does not have the intended effect on changing a behavior, it is incorrect to say that reinforcement does not work. The definition of reinforcement stipulates that a stimulus is properly called a reinforcer only after it has been demonstrated to affect behavior with its contingent use. Reinforcement always works, but therapists and other adults are not always accurate in their choice of stimuli to serve as reinforcers for particular children.

THE TOKEN ECONOMY. In settings such as institutions and group homes, the token economy has been demonstrated to be an effective means for increasing appropriate behaviors. The token economy is a system by which children earn tokens for performing certain behaviors and exchange the tokens later for a variety of items, such as special clothing, trips, or videos. In designing a token economy, the behavior therapist must identify those behaviors that will earn tokens; such behaviors might include self-care and household work as well as academic accomplishments. Then each behavior must be assigned a value in tokens, and finally a set of rules must be developed to effect the exchange of tokens and the token values of the desired items.

Token economies have been most effective in increasing a wide variety of appropriate behaviors of children who had not responded to other forms of therapeutic intervention before, but several of the problems related to the token economy have not yet been solved. For example, since the token economy is very different from the contingencies in the natural environment, the behavior therapist is confronted with the problem of maintaining the behavior after the child is removed from the token economy setting. Researchers continue to work on procedures, one of which is similar to that described for fading tangible reinforcers, to ensure a successful transition from the token economy setting to the natural environment.

CONTINGENCY CONTRACT. A contingency contract may be one aspect of a token program or may be used as a treatment plan by itself. A written contract is drawn up stating what behaviors are expected from the child and what reinforcement the child will receive for performing the desired behavior. The contents of the contract are agreed upon in one or several joint meetings with the child, the therapist, and the parents. Daily records are kept on a chart at home and brought to the therapist periodically for evaluation. If the contract is not being kept by either party, the therapist in a joint meeting with parents and child attempts to determine the source of the failure, setting the stage for the renegotiation of the contract. Parents can easily be taught the principles behind the use of the contingency contract and often continue to devise successful contracts without the help of the therapist.

Prompting. Prompting includes several procedures that have been found to facilitate increases in the qualitative aspects of behaviors. Prompting procedures include instructions, modeling, and physical guidance. These procedures essentially make it easier for the client to perform the response and thereby obtain reinforcement. After the behavior reaches a desirable level, the prompts can be removed (faded).

INSTRUCTIONS. A large number of behaviors may be generated by someone describing the behaviors and requesting that they be performed. Being able to follow instructions, of course, requires having learned the words used in the instructions and the behaviors represented by the words. To be most productive, then, instructions must be compatible with the level of the child's verbal competence.

MODELING. Modeling refers to instances of behavior change after observing that behavior performed by another person. Modeling or observational learning is probably responsible for the initial occurrence of most of the responses in our repertoire. The development of language, for example, is highly dependent on the models heard during childhood.

Bandura (1969) has been a major investigator of modeling in children and the application of modeling to children's problems. Bandura and others have engaged in theoretical arguments about whether reinforcement is a necessary condition for modeling. Bandura does not view reinforcement as being necessary for the initial acquisition of modeled behavior but recognizes that reinforcement can increase the rate of the modeled response after its initial acquisition. Baer and Sherman (1964), on the other hand, view modeling as an instance of generalized imitation. They demonstrated that children will imitate new responses that are never reinforced after they have had experience getting reinforced for imitating other responses.

Theoretical differences such as these do not alter the fact that modeling is a powerful method for creating new responses. Modeling has been demonstrated to occur in young children following the observation of both live and filmed models. Various studies have shown, for example, that after the behaviors were modeled, children previously afraid of dogs increased their approach responses to dogs, and that children who observed aggressive behavior on film emitted larger numbers of aggressive responses. One topic that has been receiving nationwide attention is the effect of televised violence on children. From what we know about modeling, the effect would, at least in part, depend on what happens to the models. In one study, children who observed others receiving punishment for aggressive behavior were less likely to model it than were children who observed the aggressive behavior followed either by reward or no consequences (Bandura, 1965).

PHYSICAL GUIDANCE. When instructions and modeling are not effective, the behavior may be facilitated by the therapist's physically guiding the child through the behavior. Teaching children to respond to instructions, for example, may be helped through physical guidance. A child who is unresponsive to the request "stand up" may be gently lifted to the standing position immediately after the request and then reinforced. After a succession of trials the therapist may gradually reduce the amount of physical guidance proportional to the child's participation in the response until the response is finally made to the verbal instruction alone.

In treatment programs, therapists may use instructions, modeling, physical guidance, or varying combinations of these methods. Even though the child may require considerable assistance with prompts, each response can be reinforced on a continuous schedule until it is reliably performed. Only after the behavior has reached a level that is qualitatively and quantitatively acceptable is reinforcement gradually shifted to an intermittent schedule.

Shaping.   Shaping is a technique that is frequently implemented when the desired behavior is not in the client's repertoire. It consists of reinforcing successive approximations of the desired behavior. Because it is often a very difficult and time-consuming procedure, shaping would be used only if the response could not be obtained through instruction, modeling, or physical guidance.

For shaping to occur, the behavior therapist first determines what the final response should be and then, on the basis of observation, chooses the response that is most similar to the final response for reinforcement. The therapist continues to reinforce that approximation to the final response until another response, which more closely approximates the final response, appears. Then that response gets reinforced and thereby strengthened. As responses closer to the final response become strengthened, the therapist gradually stops reinforcing those responses strengthened earlier. This process continues until the final response is obtained and strengthened. A study by Lovaas, Berberich, Perloff, and Schaeffer (1966) on teaching speech to severely disturbed children vividly demonstrated the application of shaping procedures for children who formerly had no functional language.

Contingent Removal of a Negative Stimulus.   Responses can also be increased by the contingent removal of an aversive stimulus. For a number of reasons, very few examples of the use of this method have appeared in the applied research literature. First, the method requires the use of aversive stimuli, and behavior therapists prefer not to use such stimuli when other methods can accomplish the same behavioral results. Second, except under well-controlled laboratory conditions, the method may generate negative side effects. For example, the onset of the aversive stimulus might coincide with an appropriate behavior, although not the appropriate behavior that the therapist plans to increase. This coincidence would serve to decrease the appropriate behavior (one of the methods to be described later), a result that is not particularly desirable. The importance of the behavior that is increased by the termination of the aversive stimulus may, however, outweigh the loss of the appropriate behavior.

It is apparent that much human behavior is controlled by the removal of a negative stimulus outside of therapy situations. Many children have had the experience of their mothers continuously nagging at them until the desired chore was accomplished, at which point the nagging stops. This method is even built into seatbelts that produce a noxious sound until they are fastened.

We have just reviewed the many ways behavior therapists can go about increasing appropriate behavior in children. In the next chapter we will begin with a discussion of how behavior therapists help to eliminate inappropriate behaviors in children through the use of other techniques.

7

Therapeutic Interventions

Part II

This chapter was revised by Lyn Vinnick, Ph.D.

BEHAVIOR THERAPY, CONTINUED

Operant Conditioning Methods for Decreasing Inappropriate Behaviors

In the previous chapter we discussed a variety of ways that behavior therapists can help to increase appropriate behaviors in children. However, more often than not, children referred for therapy have behaviors that adults in their environment consider to be excessive, inappropriate, or even harmful. The therapeutic goal in these situations is to decrease or eliminate such behaviors. Several methods, based on the principles of learning, have been devised to decrease or eliminate inappropriate behaviors. In this section, we will describe the methods that have been used with children, including extinction and punishment (timeout, response cost, application of aversive consequences).

Extinction: Contingent Omission of Positive Reinforcement. When the therapist is able to identify and control a reinforcer that has been maintaining a high rate of an inappropriate behavior, extinction is likely to be an effective method for decreasing that response. Extinction refers to a procedure whereby a reinforcer that is responsible for the maintenance of a response is omitted, thus resulting in a decrease in the rate of that response.

The rapidity with which a response is extinguished after the initiation of the reinforcement omission depends considerably on the schedule of reinforcement during maintenance. If the behavior has been reinforced on a continuous schedule, extinction takes place quite rapidly. Since most behaviors in natural environments appear to be maintained on intermittent schedules of reinforcement, they may be expected to extinguish more slowly.

Before coming to a therapist, parents frequently try different ways of changing the behavior themselves. Their approaches to the problem sometimes include the omission of reinforcement. When the therapist describes the procedure for extinction, parents may have occasion to remark that they have already tried that method, and that it only made the behavior worse. Psychologists have known for a long time that omission of reinforcement after a history of reinforcement for a particular response results initially in a temporary increase of the behavior followed by the more permanent decrease phase. In other words, things may get worse before they get better. Parents are not aware of these relationships; thus, their efforts toward "extinguishing" a behavior are usually prematurely terminated. The behavior therapist is particularly careful to describe expected changes in behavior to prevent parents from giving up. With extinction it is also extremely important that the withholding of reinforcement be consistent, because a few "accidental" reinforcers may well result in the reinstatement of a high rate of response of the undesired behavior.

Use of extinction procedures for decreasing inappropriate behaviors in children has often been reported in the applied research literature. Extinction is useful when the behavior problem could potentially be allowed to occur without consequences, that is, it isn't inherently dangerous or disruptive to others. This qualification depends very much on the setting and the characteristics of the behavior itself. In some group settings, for example, a behavior may be disruptive to the point at which extinction or ignoring the behavior could not be tolerated. Similarly, extinction may not be the method of choice if the behavior involves self-injury or injury to others.

Extinction, or the omission of reinforcement, may be accompanied by emotional responses by the child, such as anger, frustration, and aggression. Although these reactions have not been studied extensively, they appear to be transient and diminish as the response being extinguished decreases. It is likely that they would decrease more rapidly if, during extinction, reinforcement is given for an alternate, appropriate response. In this manner, the level of reinforcement for the child would be maintained but would be provided contingently for an appropriate behavior. When using extinction to decrease an inappropriate behavior, behavioral clinicians often include a program for reinforcing an incompatible behavior (e.g., extinguish social withdrawal while reinforcing social contact).

Punishment. "Punishment" has had varied meanings in its everyday usage; therefore, psychologists have attempted to define it to facilitate communication among themselves. In general, punishment involves a procedure whereby a specific behavior is followed by a noxious stimulus. Punishment is most effective when it is combined with a reinforcer given for desired behavior. Azrin and Holz (1966) described punishment as any procedure using "any consequence of behavior that reduces the future probability of that behavior" (p. 381). Aversive procedures such as punishment are useful clinically in two main sets of circumstances: when dysfunctional or inappropriate behavior is naturally reinforcing to the individual (addictions, deviant sexual behavior), or when the behavior is self-destructive and dangerous and needs to be brought under control quickly.

The term *punishment* may evoke a wide range of emotions and attitudes, among both professionals and nonprofessionals. Some people feel that punishment, particularly corporal punishment, is necessary to control children's behavior, while others believe that any form of punishment is not at all necessary, and, in fact, may be harmful. As you will learn, punishment procedures themselves vary in their effectiveness in reducing inappropriate behavior, their intrusiveness, and their potential for unwanted effects.

Three aversive procedures that fit within this definition will be described: timeout, response cost, and the application of aversive consequences.

Timeout. *Timeout* is a procedure that involves a child's being removed from all sources of reinforcement for a brief period immediately upon the occurrence of an inappropriate response. It is a brief period without the availability of reinforcers and should not be construed as a method to frighten children. For example, in a home the child might be taken to a room without television or toys, and in school, the child might be seated in the corridor. Timeout is a useful procedure when the reinforcers maintaining the behavior problem cannot be identified or controlled. Short timeout periods of two to five minutes are usually effective.

The timeout method is not easy to implement in many natural environments because positive reinforcers, such as social attention from peers in the corridor, are too readily available. Portable timeout booths have been designed for such settings, and a few of the newer schools contain timeout rooms. The place for timeout is always fully lighted; children in the setting have had the opportunity to examine it and have been told which inappropriate behaviors will be followed by timeout.

Timeout is not the same as isolation, a method that is sometimes used in institutions and other settings. Isolation usually involves longer time periods, such as 24 hours, and is not necessarily initiated immediately after the inappropriate behavior. The effectiveness of isolation in reducing future occurrences of the behavior has not been fully demonstrated. On the other hand, isolation may be reinforcing for the staff in that the necessity for coping with the problem behavior is eliminated for the duration of the isolation period.

Response Cost.   Another method for decreasing the rate of a response involves removing a positive reinforcer immediately after the occurrence of the inappropriate behavior. This is called *response cost.* An example might be removing a favorite toy for a period of time after a child is involved in an incident of fighting.

Behavior therapists use contingent removal of positive reinforcement to decrease responses in situations in which the reinforcer for the inappropriate behavior cannot be identified or in situations that call for a more rapid decrease than would be obtained using extinction. One of the problems posed by this method is that the therapist may encounter difficulty in finding a positive reinforcer that can be taken away. Potential reinforcers for middle-class children, for example, might include a wide variety of privileges, such as going bowling or to a movie, riding a bicycle, and swimming. Lower-class children tend to have fewer privileges that may be controlled by parents.

Finding positive reinforcers that can be taken away is also difficult in many school settings. Certain activities that might be considered as privileges, such as recess, are felt to be necessary for the child's well-being and are not to be used as positive reinforcers. In general, environments that provide either no reinforcers or primarily free (noncontingent) reinforcers present great difficulties to the behavior therapist. Several creative researchers, however, have found that there are substantial behavioral improvements in school settings permitting the introduction of positive reinforcers that could be used both to increase appropriate behaviors by their contingent presentation and to decrease inappropriate behaviors by their contingent withdrawal.

Token economies provide an excellent example of using withdrawal of reinforcement to decrease behaviors. As described earlier, token economies are designed to provide positive reinforcement for appropriate behaviors. Since inappropriate behaviors have a high probability of occurring in the populations selected for the token economy programs, methods for decreasing inappropriate behaviors must be included. One effective method is to withdraw a certain number of tokens from the child for each occurrence of particular inappropriate behaviors. Before the program is initiated, the response cost (e.g., the number of tokens withdrawn) is determined for each unacceptable behavior and is communicated to the child.

Application of Aversive Consequences.   Presenting an aversive stimulus immediately after the occurrence of an inappropriate behavior also has the effect of decreasing the rate of that behavior. In comparison to other methods, it tends to decrease behavior faster and sometimes more effectively in the short-term, but its effect in reducing behavior may not last over time. The rapidity and relative power of an aversive stimulus usually depend on its strength—the stronger the stimulus, the longer the decrease in responding may last. The stronger aversive stimuli tend to be those associated with pain and other physical discomforts; reprimands by parents and teachers, however, also serve as aversive stimuli for many children.

This method of decreasing behavior has presented the most controversy (Repp & Singh, 1990) among both professionals and nonprofessionals and has been used less frequently than other methods by behavior therapists. The use of aversive stimuli is itself aversive to therapists and tends to create ethical issues that are not easily resolved. For example, some institutionalized children would engage in self-injurious behaviors to the point of seriously harming themselves if their arms and legs were not restrained by tying them to a bed. Several investigators have found that a few administrations of electric shock to the skin contingent to self-injurious behavior may be effective in eliminating these behaviors, thus making it possible for such children to acquire repertoires of appropriate behavior. Ethical issues, however, have been raised regarding the use of electric shock for such therapeutic procedures, and strong attempts have been made (with some success) to prevent the use of such techniques in institutional settings. This issue may be posed as a question of whether it is more ethical to leave such children tied to their beds indefinitely than to administer electric shock to eliminate the self-injurious behavior more rapidly.

Use of contingent aversive stimuli has also been avoided by behavior therapists because earlier research with animals (with painful stimuli) suggested that there may be certain negative by-products, such as emotional behavior, associated with the method. When an aversive stimulus is presented, the decrease in the inappropriate behavior may also be accompanied by a strong emotional response, characterized by fear or anger. The problem for the therapist is that the child may learn to associate one or more aspects of the environmental stimuli, including the therapist or parent, with the emotional response elicited by the aversive stimulus. That is, the child may learn through respondent conditioning to become fearful of the therapist or parent, or the child could become fearful of the place in which the punishment is administered.

A problem that has been increasingly studied is the long-range effect of the modeling of punishment on children's behavior. Clinical reports have suggested that many parents who have been found to physically abuse their children were themselves subjected to considerable physical or corporal punishment. The question, then, is whether the administration of punishment to a child unduly affects the child's use of punishment in the future.

COGNITIVE-BEHAVIORAL THERAPY

Although there are many types of behavioral and cognitive therapies, they share common elements and are frequently combined into a single therapeutic modality called *cognitive-behavioral therapy*. Cognitive-behavioral therapy focuses on the behavior problem or symptom which is observed or noted by the child or others in the environment. Goals of therapy focus on specific behaviors and an evaluation is made regarding conditions in the environment that trigger or maintain the undesired behaviors. By altering the behavior, the environment, or both, the target behaviors are changed. Therapy is often directive, structured, and time-limited, focusing on the here and now rather than on past events.

In cognitive-behavioral therapy, children and adolescents change their own behavior with guidance from the therapist through the use of self-instructions, self-monitoring of behavior, self-reinforcement, self-punishment, or a combination of these methods. These methods have been increasingly explored for both increasing appropriate behaviors and decreasing inappropriate behaviors. All of these techniques involve self-control in that the client is free to behave or not behave. Society greatly values the learning of self-control because less effort then has to be expended to arrange external contingencies. Until the 1970s, children had seldom participated in studies of self-control, although a substantial number of studies had been conducted with adults. The primary reason for this lack may have been an assumption that children were not capable of implementing self-control procedures.

The research literature suggests that the teaching of self-control to children holds considerable promise for increasing appropriate behaviors. Broden, Hall, and Mitts (1971) found that an eighth-grade girl's method of studying was improved simply by asking her to record her own study behavior. Other children have been successfully taught to control their own behaviors by making statements to themselves covertly and prompting themselves to behave appropriately. Cognitive-behavior therapy is particularly useful for phobias and fears, obsessive-compulsive and other anxiety disorders, adjustment disorders, impulse control problems, and social skills deficits.

Research suggests that self-control procedures produce effects that are comparable to external control procedures and may be superior for maintaining therapeutic goals (O'Leary & Dubey, 1979). Meichenbaum and Goodman's (1971) initial work with impulsive children has stimulated the development of a variety of self-instruction programs. In training children to instruct themselves (by saying, for example, "take your time"), the therapist models the verbal statements and then asks the child to repeat the statements first aloud, then in a whisper, and finally covertly. The children are also taught to reinforce themselves for completing the task. Kendall (1993) and others have developed effective treatment programs for impulsive, emotionally disturbed children; self-control methods appear to be particularly effective for children who are hyperactive, disruptive in class, and aggressive.

SYSTEMATIC DESENSITIZATION

Desensitization refers to the complex of techniques that has proven to be effective in reducing extreme anxiety responses in adults. The goal of desensitization is to substitute a relaxed or nonanxious state for the anxiety responses to a particular stimulus situation. The learning model is generally believed to be that of respondent conditioning but has components of operant conditioning as well; both positive reinforcement and aversive procedure are used. The procedure of desensitization with adults focuses on creating a state that is incompatible with anxiety, fear, or tension and then gradually introducing the feared stimulus. It includes the teaching of muscle relaxation, the construction of a fear hierarchy, and the gradual movement through the steps of the hierarchy while in a relaxed state. Each step of the hierarchy represents an actual situation that evokes a certain amount of fear as assessed by the client. The desensitization process itself begins by having the client either experience or imagine the scene, previously given the lowest fear rating while in a relaxed state. Each scene is successively experienced by a client who attempts to maintain the relaxed state. If the client experiences anxiety, the therapist returns to the previous scene. The patient is eventually "desensitized" to the feared stimulus.

The procedure designed for adults, which uses a hierarchy of imagined scenes, has not been rigorously examined for its effectiveness with children. In general, it does not appear to be useful for children under nine years of age. Factors other than age that might contribute to the effectiveness of systematic desensitization therapy are the child's level of visual imagery, ability to relax, ability to follow instructions, level of acquiescence, and threshold for fatigue.

Emotive imagery has been used to counteract anxiety in children (Lazarus & Abramovitz, 1962). In emotive imagery the client is asked to imagine a specific pleasant scene into which the therapist gradually introduces anxiety-arousing stimuli. Other variations have also been used. For example, Lazarus, Davison, and Polefka (1965) successfully treated a child with school phobia by gradually exposing the child to the school environment (*in vivo* desensitization) and using positive reinforcement to strengthen going-to-school behaviors.

GROUP THERAPY

Group therapy involves the assembly of a number of children or adolescents and one or several therapists. Although group therapy is conducted by therapists who have a wide variety of theoretical orientations, group therapists often emphasize the importance of interpersonal and social factors in the facilitation of the treatment process. The composition of the group is considered to be an important factor for success; some groups are focused on treating one type of problem (e.g., support groups for children of divorce or for bereaved children), while other groups may consist of children with various types of problems (e.g., teenagers in an inpatient hospital unit) (Farmer & Galaris, 1993).

Group treatment of children began in the 1930s with Slavson (1943) acknowl-edged as the innovator (Johnson, Rasbury, & Siegel, 1986, p. 266). Group therapy aims at reducing the symptomatology and improving interpersonal relations through controlled group experiences. On a practical level, group therapy is eco-nomical in that the members of the group share the cost of the therapist's time. While group therapy is not usually recommended as the sole therapy for serious dis-orders, it does seem to have a distinct advantage for children with problems relat-ed to social functioning (e.g., children who lack or have weak social skills). Most group therapy is time-limited and includes core objectives (e.g., improving com-munication in a group for shy children). Interventions often consist of empathic lis-tening, enactments and behavioral rehearsal, and problem solving.

Three basic approaches to group therapy with children have been described: activity group therapy, activity-interview group psychotherapy, and behavioral group therapy. *Activity group therapy* (Slavson & Schiffer, 1975) is used for groups of four to eight elementary school children and consists of providing materials for arts and crafts and a setting for free acting out. The two basic crite-ria for including children in activity group therapy are a capacity to relate to oth-ers (the child's history should reveal at least one moderately positive relationship with a family member, a peer, or a teacher) and a capacity to change attitudes and behavior through corrective experiences. Behavior problems considered to be optimal for activity group therapy are conduct disorders, bed-wetting and thumb-sucking, mild anxiety disorders, and situational anxiety. Children with severe dis-orders, such as psychoses, mental retardation, and excessive generalized aggressiveness, and those with physical handicaps are not considered to benefit from activity group therapy.

Activity group therapy members are usually selected to achieve a balance between aggressive, active children and socially withdrawn children and are usual-ly homogeneous with respect to gender. The therapeutic effect is derived from the group activity that serves to attenuate the aggression of some children and increase the social responsiveness of the previously withdrawn children. A two-hour session is scheduled weekly, with the average child terminating therapy at the end of two years. The therapist is totally accepting of the children, remains relatively passive, and gives no attention to the children's hostility and aggression except, of course, to prevent physical harm. The therapist occasionally gives words of praise and, in general, serves as a model of self-control for the children.

Activity-interview group psychotherapy is a combination of activity group psy-chotherapy and individual psychotherapy. The children meet in activity groups that are structured and include limit setting and guidance by the therapist. The thera-pist interprets their behavior and encourages them to communicate their problems and anxieties to one another and to the therapist. The goal of activity-interview group psychotherapy is to provide the children with insight into the reasons for their behavior and to help them develop more appropriate social responses. Activity-interview groups can be homogeneous or mixed with respect to gender and usually include four to six mid- to late latency-aged children. Materials used for the group are chosen to facilitate expression of certain emotional conflicts.

Behavioral group therapy includes the systematic observation of both individual and group behaviors. The therapist utilizes learning principles to change behaviors that occur in the group. There is sometimes a clear advantage for the group members to be homogeneous with regard to referral problem, particularly when instructions and modeling are provided (e.g., for social skills deficits). Compared to the other types of groups, behavioral groups are more structured, and the therapist monitors the group more carefully. The initial phase of treatment is characterized by high levels of control and reinforcement by the therapist who gradually shifts the responsibility to the group members and who must plan for generalization of new skills or behaviors to the children's natural environment. During the 1970s and 1980s, a large number of studies on group treatment with children were published. In general, the research was methodologically unsound, and therefore meaningful conclusions could not be drawn.

FAMILY THERAPY

Clinicians have long believed that the family is the primary influence on the development and/or maintenance of most childhood behavior problems. It is somewhat surprising, then, to find that psychotherapy with families has had such a relatively brief history. A few therapists began to interview families together during the 1940s, but not until the 1950s and 1960s did the theoretical formulations and clinical presentations begin to have a significant impact on clinical practice.

Family therapy evolved from investigations of severely disturbed young adults with schizophrenia, and their parents. It was hypothesized that schizophrenia was caused by communication failure among family members. Ackerman (1958) presented a flexible model of family therapy that included various combinations of family members in individual and group psychotherapy; he is usually given credit for providing the impetus for family intervention in instances of childhood behavior disorders.

The common definition of family therapy as treatment of all or most members of a family at the same time is not strictly accurate. Most family therapists work chiefly with the parents and children; others work with extended families or only with the parents. A few work with only one family member. Most family therapists tend to vary the attendance requirements during different phases of therapy, according to the issues at hand (Shapiro, 1988). A fundamental assumption common to all family therapies is that the disturbance or "problem" does not reside in a single individual per se but rather reflects disturbed interactions between and among people who have significant relationships with each other.

Goldenberg and Goldenberg (1991) describe six major approaches to family therapy: family systems, psychodynamic, experiential/humanistic, structural, strategic, and behavioral. *Family systems theory* dates back to Murray Bowen's work in the 1950s when he proposed that there was a direct relationship between excessive emotional bonding and family dysfunction. He conceptualized the family as an emotional relationship system, and described a set of eight interlocking concepts that explain the emotional processes that take place in nuclear and extended families (Bowen, 1978). Bowen emphasizes the differentiation of self as a primary goal. He theorized that a married couple under stress has a tendency to triangulate with a third person, and that person, usually a vulnerable child, becomes fused with the couple and is thereby denied adequate autonomy. The family systems approach examines the roles of the adult family members in *their* families of origin (multigenerational model) and assists individuals to maintain appropriate connectedness with other family members while maximum self-differentiation is maintained.

Psychodynamic therapists attempt to lead the family toward an understanding of its problems and to optimize communication among family members. A general assumption of psychodynamic family therapy is that treatment must uncover or identify historical events that have been repressed. Family symptoms, and the child's symptoms in particular, are expected to disappear if family members are able to relive and react emotionally to these events. Therapists with this orientation tend to focus on providing an atmosphere that encourages open and free communication. Their assumption is that family members' interactions in the therapy setting will reflect their relationships in the home, thereby permitting the therapist to determine the ways in which the family system may be supporting the child's problem. The therapist carefully observes which members of the family dominate the conversation and which ones are submissive or salient and notes the relative frequency with which various members of the family speak and to whom their communication is directed. The therapist also attempts to ascertain the degree of marital conflict and the child's role in this conflict.

Experiential/humanistic family therapy focuses attention on the present and assists family members to realize their potential for growth. Virginia Satir, until her death in 1988, was at the forefront of the humanistically oriented family therapy movement. Marital therapy is a large component of Satir's family therapy in that she viewed children's problems as a by-product of current marital conflict. Parents are usually seen together for a few sessions before children are included in the family group. Satir's therapy may be characterized as active, direct, and authoritarian in the sense that the therapist generally talks more than any family member during the session. Family members are taught to acknowledge and accept individual differences, to realize that disagreements and differences should not be viewed with alarm, and to communicate their perceptions and feelings clearly (Satir & Baldwin, 1983).

Structural family therapy (Minuchin, 1974) deemphasizes the typical focus on the referred child by considering the family itself as a social system. This approach assumes that the child's problem serves an important role in maintaining family homeostasis. According to this theory, if the child's problem were to disappear, new symptoms within the family would appear or the family unit would disintegrate. Structural family therapy attempts to change the family structure so that the child's problem is no longer "needed."

According to Minuchin, normal families are supposed to have specific boundaries. For example, parents have boundaries between themselves and the children that protect their marital relationship. Children's boundaries are derived on the basis of age. If the father and son are acting like siblings, then the father would be instructed to change this relationship by taking paternal responsibility for the son.

Strategic family therapy (Haley, 1963) emphasizes the designing of interventions to solve a specific problem; the problem, rather than the family, is the focus of attention. Strategic family therapists believe that the curative agent in family therapy is the paradoxical manipulation of power. One technique, called paradox, involves the therapist's requesting that family members continue or retain the problem they want to change. The therapist agrees with family members' inappropriate feelings, attitudes, and behaviors and encourages the family to practice them. Apparently, simply prescribing a symptom has the effect of decreasing or eliminating it. Another technique, reframing, may be used in which a perceived negative attribute is positively restated. For example, hostility may be reframed as concerned interest.

Behavioral family therapy has been the most recent addition to the array of family therapy approaches. All of the principles of learning, based on both classical and operant conditioning, including cognitive-behavioral techniques, are utilized to increase positive interactions among family members. The most successful programs focus on teaching parents behavioral skills that optimize the management of their children (Patterson, 1971; Dishion & Patterson, 1992). This may occur within the context of a family session, or parents may be invited to join a parent skills training group as an adjunct treatment to the behavioral family therapy. Parent skills groups are generally didactic, psychoeducational, and time-limited. In parent training programs, characteristics such as parental stress and depression were found to cause treatment relapse for children. Therefore, many parent training programs are now being enhanced by adjunct treatment of adult skills to manage distress and interpersonal problems (Webster-Stratton, 1994). Behavioral family therapy generally includes the use of a thorough clinical assessment, observation and recording of behaviors, devising family intervention procedures, training parents in child management techniques, and tracking generalization and maintenance of behavior change. It may also include work on the parents' marital relationship (Sanders & Dadds, 1993).

Because family therapists assume that problems of children indicate family dysfunction, individual therapy would leave the family's problems unprobed; individual treatment success would be short-lived without treating the family problems. Family therapy is therefore often indicated for children's problems that arise from failure of performance by parents in crisis situations, for families in which there is excessive emotional involvement or a rigid coping mechanism, and for adolescent behavior problems. Often, family therapy offered in clinics is relatively brief and focused on reality factors in child rearing, such as discipline practices. This brevity of treatment is not necessarily a characteristic of the therapy itself but rather a consequence of the selection of patients and the practical problems associated with both parents' attending sessions, which are usually held once a week.

Gurman, Kniskern, and Pinsof (1986) found family therapy to be more effective than various types of individual therapy. They advised that: (1) as yet, the relative superiority of behavioral or nonbehavioral approaches has not been empirically demonstrated; (2) there is no evidence that conducting cotherapy is more effective than single-therapist interventions; (3) structural family therapy appears to be particularly helpful for certain psychosomatic symptoms; and (4) behavioral child management training with parents produces more positive results with acting-out children than nonbehavioral approaches. Finally, in a comprehensive research study of family therapy, the average client was found to be better off at termination than 70 percent of untreated clients. Behavioral family therapy tended to outperform nonbehavioral family therapies in overall effectiveness. In general, controlled treatment research strongly supports the efficacy of family therapy (Shadish, Montgomery, Wilson, Wilson, Bright, & Okwumabua, 1993).

PHARMACOTHERAPY

The relationship between physical status and behavior is not well understood. Behavioral and emotional problems have been related to a variety of chronic physical problems, such as malnutrition and abnormal hormonal levels, and neurological problems. Because of the possibility that a behavior disorder may be caused or exacerbated by a current physical malfunction, which may be best treated medically, therapists request that the child receive a physical examination, including tests of sensory functioning, prior to diagnostic examination. Sometimes, during the psychological examination, the clinician observes certain behaviors such as involuntary movements, or developmental abnormalities such as retarded physical growth that are closely tied to physical malfunctioning and refers the child to a medical specialist prior to psychological intervention. In a few instances, medical treatment will eliminate the need for psychological intervention; however, psychological help is often required as an adjunct to medical intervention.

Physicians, particularly pediatricians and psychiatrists, have used a variety of physical methods to treat children's behavior problems. For example, electroconvulsive shock, chemical agents, and prefrontal lobotomies have been used with severely disturbed children. Bender (1955) conducted much of the pioneer research with these methods, which were believed to be effective in alleviating adult psychological problems. Bender maintained that the severe disorders (psychoses) of children were the result of organic pathology and would, therefore, be optimally treated with physical methods. Although Bender claimed some of them to be effective, these methods have not been generally adopted by physicians. The physical treatment methods now in use consist almost exclusively of interventions with medication.

The use of psychoactive medication with children has become increasingly more common since the 1950s, when research began to demonstrate its usefulness with adult clients. Research on the effectiveness of medication therapy with children, however, has been greatly hampered by inadequate criteria for diagnostic classifications of children's behavior problems in the past, and by a lack of well-designed research studies. Earlier diagnostic categories frequently included children with widely heterogeneous behaviors, and this behavioral variability probably contributed to the lack of findings in some studies. Later drug studies have attempted to group children on the basis of more specific behavioral characteristics. Improvements in diagnostic criteria in DSM-III-R (1987) and DSM-IV (1994) have greatly improved opportunities for productive research.

Studies using group designs must take several precautions to ensure the reliability and validity of the research findings: (1) research participants must be randomly assigned to groups or carefully matched across groups on the basis of relevant pretest measures; (2) a placebo control group should usually be included to control for nonspecific factors, such as increased attention to the child, and (3) the study should have a double-blind research design in which group assignment is not known by the child, significant adults in the child's environment, or the person arranging the drug therapy with the family. These precautions must be taken because reports of improved behavior are frequently given when the client and other persons in the environment believe that treatment is taking place (even when sugar pills or placebos are given instead of medication).

Evaluation of drug therapy can also be done within the context of a single subject design. In a single subject design, periods of medication would be alternated with placebo periods. Ideally, no one in regular contact with the child should know whether the child is taking the medication or a placebo, particularly the person evaluating the child's behavior each day. Use of the single subject design also lends itself to establishing the optimal dosage of medication because dosage levels may be varied among the medication periods.

Many physicians appear to be reluctant to prescribe medication for children with behavior problems. Some older physicians do not use the newer medications because they do not have the time to keep up with the research literature, or because they are satisfied with their previous practices. In addition, physicians vary in their methods of placing children on medication; some start with the dosage level recommended by the manufacturer, while others begin with a lower dosage level and systematically increase it, depending on its effects. Psychoactive drugs prescribed for children are often inadequately evaluated, and many children are either prematurely taken off medication that would be effective at another dosage level or left on medication that is ineffective. Psychologists, with their special training in behavioral observation and research design, often work effectively with physicians to reduce this problem.

The medications currently being used for children presenting behavior problems may be classified into five principal categories: stimulants, neuroleptics, antidepressants, lithium carbonate, and benzodiazepines In the remainder of this section, each category is described in terms of the drugs' effects on behavior.

Stimulants

Stimulants are the most frequently prescribed psychiatric drugs during childhood (Green, 1991). Several medications that stimulate the central nervous system have been found to be helpful in about 75 percent of children with hyperactivity, inattentiveness, and short attention span. Recent studies suggest that some stimulant medications may decrease aggression that coincides with inattention and hyperactivity (Murphy, Pelham, & Lang, 1992). Until recently, it was believed that these medications had "paradoxical" effects on hyperactive behavior in that they apparently reduced the activity levels. The current view is that stimulants affect attentional processes and that the improved behavior is secondary to the child's being able to concentrate and focus attention appropriately. Both normal and abnormal children with attention deficits and/or hyperactivity respond to stimulants differently from young adults, reporting dysphoric feelings rather than euphoria. This finding cannot be explained pharmacokinetically, and the reason for this effect is as yet unknown (Teicher & Baldessarini, 1987).

The most commonly used stimulants have been dextroamphetamine (Dexadrine) and methylphenidate (Ritalin); magnesium pemoline (Cylert) is a more recently studied stimulant considered to be effective. As in the case with virtually all medications, stimulants produce a variety of side effects. About one-third of children taking moderately high doses of dextroamphetamine or methylphenidate have a loss or reduction of appetite and difficulty falling asleep. A small percentage of children show an increase of sad mood. These side effects are most pronounced when treatment begins and usually subside within several weeks. Side effects can also sometimes be reduced by using a slow-release form of Ritalin. There are some data suggesting that dextroamphetamine may have an inhibiting effect on physical growth when it is taken for long periods of time, such as several years. It is generally recommended that a growth chart be kept for children treated with stimulants to alert the physician to possible growth problems. As opposed to Ritalin and Dexadrine, which require multiple dosing throughout the day, Cylert is longer acting and can be administered in a single morning dose. Cylert is, however, contraindicated for children with impaired liver function. Some physicians may suggest that medication "holidays" be scheduled both to counteract growth inhibition and to provide an opportunity for monitoring the medication's effectiveness. Stimulants are contraindicated for children with psychoses.

Neuroleptics

In adults, neuroleptics are used primarily for the treatment of schizophrenia and other psychoses, but in children they have been prescribed for a greater range of disorders. A trial of neuroleptic treatment has been advised for the following conditions: schizophrenic disorders, tic disorders, autism, Tourette's syndrome, conduct disorder with severe aggression, mental retardation with behavioral symptoms, and attention deficit hyperactivity disorder with severe hyperactivity (Green, 1991). Neuroleptics appear to produce primarily a sedative effect; the symptoms that respond optimally to these medications include hyperactivity, aggression, tics, tantrums, withdrawal, hallucinations, and delusions. The most commonly used neuroleptics are chlorpromazine (Thorazine), thioridazine (Mellaril), haloperiodol (Haldol), thiothixene (Navane), and trifluoperazine (Stelazine).

Side effects are particularly problematic with neuroleptics. Thorazine and Mellaril appear to be associated with impairment of cognitive functioning and may interfere with both learning and performance. This side effect is more serious for children and adolescents who are developing cognitive and academic skills. Neuroleptics are also associated with involuntary motor movements, the worsening of preexisting symptoms, irritability, dramatic increases or decreases in activity level, apathy, and daze-like behavior. In these instances, lowering the dose is recommended. In almost all cases, neuroleptics would be used only after behavioral interventions and other medications with fewer side effects had been unsuccessful.

Antidepressants

At the present time tricyclics are the antidepressants of foremost importance in treating children and younger adolescents. Although other types of antidepressants are approved for treating older adolescents diagnosed with depression, their use is essentially for adults and will not be reviewed here. The principal tricyclic antidepressant, imipramine (Tofranil), has been used successfully with adult depressives. This medication is useful for prepubertal children who meet the criteria for major depressive disorder; older adolescent depressives are less responsive, however. The primary use for imipramine with young children has been for enuresis (bed-wetting). Clinical studies have also described improvement of hyperactivity, attention deficits, aggressiveness, school phobia, and some sleep disorders (Green, 1991). This medication is contraindicated for children with heart problems, seizures, and psychoses.

Lithium Carbonate

In adults, lithium carbonate is effective specifically for the manic episodes in manic-depressive disorders. These disorders are rare in prepubertal children. Lithium carbonate has been reported as successful in a few clinical studies of children with severe, impulsive aggression toward others and self-aggression. It is contraindicated for persons with kidney, heart, or thyroid problems and females at risk for pregnancy. Blood levels of the medication are monitored closely because there is a narrow margin between the therapeutic and toxic levels.

Benzodiazapines

The benzodiazapines are central nervous system depressants prescribed primarily for relief of anxiety, sleep problems, and convulsions. In children they are used primarily for sleep and seizure disorders and much less commonly for their muscle relaxant qualities. A few clinical studies suggest that benzodiazepines may also be useful for helping children with anticipatory anxiety related to school phobia and for short-term relief of other anxiety.

MULTIMODAL THERAPY

Lazarus (1976), recognizing that adult clients rarely present a single problem for treatment, designed a multimodal system for ensuring that all aspects of the client's psychological life are examined and treated, where necessary. Keat (1979, 1990) subsequently adapted Lazarus's system for use with children. The acronym BASIC ID is used to help the therapist to remember seven interactive modalities: *B*ehavior, *A*ffect (feelings, emotions), *S*ensation, *I*magery, *C*ognition, *I*nterpersonal relations, and *D*rugs (physical factors). For children, school factors are added to the sensation modality, and the interpersonal relations modality is expanded to include significant adults in the child's life. A treatment plan is designed by the clinician for each of the problems identified. Although Keat's therapy model is primarily seven-behavioral, his repertoire of treatments is extensive and reflects what he refers to as "pragmatic technical eclecticism."

More recently, multimodal treatments have been expanded and developed to address multiple systems that influence development of behavior problems in children. Multisystemic therapy includes treatment with the individual child, close relations in the child's life such as parents and peers, social settings such as school, and societal influences such as the community (Tolan, Guerra, & Kendall, 1995). At times, provision of services may occur in the child's natural environment (home, school, neighborhood) itself, providing the advantage of a decrease in the rate of missed therapy appointments. There is a general philosophical shift from traditional psychotherapy in that families are viewed as collaborators in treatment rather than as recipients. In addition, assessment and treatment are focused on strength and competency, treatment plans are linked to the reality of the family's own life circumstances, and there is a very strong sense of involvement with and support for the family. Multisystemic treatment is likely to be the most effective and promising treatment for children with severe acting-out behavior problems, such as children and adolescents with conduct disorder and those who are delinquent (Henggeler, Melton, & Smith, 1992; Vinnick, Fleiss, LaPadula, & Gonzales, 1996).

CONCLUSIONS

During the 1940s and 1950s psychotherapeutic methods for children's behavior problems were dominated by psychoanalytic theory and its variations. The most frequently used model involved a therapist's conducting one or two treatment sessions with the child each week and a second therapist treating the parents during one session each week. Treatment lasted from several months to several years. Both the demands for psychotherapeutic services and the development of theoretical variations created an increased emphasis on current environmental intervention in individual, group, and family therapies.

Beginning in the early 1960s, an increasing number of studies demonstrated that the learning principles derived from earlier experimental research with animals and adults could be used to increase appropriate behaviors and decrease inappropriate behaviors in children.

A meta-analysis of 108 outcome studies with 4- to 18-year-old youngsters showed that the average treated youngster was better adjusted than 79 percent of those not treated (Weisz, Weiss, Alicke, & Klotz, 1987). Professional therapists were particularly effective for internalized problems (e.g., anxiety, depression) but were *not* more effective than paraprofessionals for externalized problems (e.g., aggression, impulsivity). Behavioral treatments were more effective than nonbehavioral treatments regardless of the client's age, the therapist's experience, or the type of behavior problem. Newer multimodal treatments that incorporate a variety of factors affecting children's behavior are considered to be the most promising treatments at this time.

RECOMMENDED READINGS

Brown, D.T., & Prout, H.T. (Eds.). (1989). *Counseling and psychotherapy with children and adolescents* (2nd ed.). Brandon, VT: CPPC.

Kazdin, A.E. (1988). *Child psychotherapy: Developing and identifying effective treatments.* Elmsford, NY: Pergamon.

Kendall, P.C. (Ed.). (1991). *Child and adolescent therapy: Cognitive-behavioral procedures.* New York: Guilford.

Kratochwill, T.R., & Morris, R.J. (Eds.). (1990). *The practice of child therapy* (2nd ed.). Elmsford, NY: Pergamon.

Mash, E.J., & Barkley, R.A. (Eds.). (1989). *Treatment of childhood disorders.* New York: Guilford.

Reineke, M.A., Dattilio, F.M., & Freeman, A. (Eds.). (1996). *Cognitive therapy with children and adolescents.* New York: Guilford.

Sanders, M.R., & Dadds, M.R. (1993). *Behavioral family intervention.* Needham, MA: Allyn & Bacon.

Schiffer, M. (1984). *Children's group therapy.* New York: Free Press.

Waters, D.B., & Lawrence, E.C. (1993). *Competence, courage, and change: An approach to family therapy.* New York: W.W. Norton.

8

Mental Retardation

This chapter was revised by Beth Wildman, Ph.D.

Jamie, a five-year-old girl, was referred by her preschool teacher because she appeared to lack many of the skills achieved by her peers. Her interactions with her classmates have tended to decrease over the past several months, her closest companion being the youngest child in the group of four- and five-year-old children.

Jamie was the first child of 18-year-old parents and was conceived out of wedlock. Her mother attempted to abort herself with an unknown substance early in the pregnancy. The mother experienced intermittent bleeding during the first half of pregnancy before she was under a doctor's care. Both parents dropped out of high school and married when the mother was five months' pregnant. Although Jamie was born at term, she weighed only five pounds. The doctor had difficulty initiating breathing at birth, and Jamie had several episodes of respiratory distress while in the hospital nursery. She was discharged from the hospital at three weeks of age.

Jamie's infancy was unremarkable except for two illnesses of unknown origin accompanied by very high fevers. The parents were not particularly concerned about Jamie's development, although they remembered that she did not walk alone or say her first word until two years of age. Neither parent had had experience with young children before Jamie, but their observation of the children in the preschool and their discussions with Jamie's teacher have led them to wonder whether Jamie is "slow."

In comparison with the other types of behavior disorders described in this book, perhaps the greatest amount of information has been acquired about mental retardation. One reason for the interest in mental retardation may be that approximately 9.1 out of every 1,000 children under the age of 8 years has mental retardation (Katusic, Colligan, Beard, O'Fallon, Bergstralh, Jacobsen, & Kurland, 1995). Half of these children are classified with milder mental retardation, and the other half with more severe mental retardation.

There is at present a general consensus on the assessment procedures and the criteria for diagnosis of mental retardation. The most recent classification system of mental retardation has shifted the basis for assessment and classification of mental retardation from a description of deficiencies to a description of the amount of support an individual with mental retardation requires (Luckasson, Coulter, Polloway, Reiss, Schalock, Snell, Spitalnik, & Stark, 1992). A wide variety of etiological factors have been investigated, and a great amount of research effort has been devoted to treatment and development of remedial programs for individuals with mental retardation.

Our greater understanding of mental retardation is no doubt due to a long history of theoretical speculation and empirical attempts to investigate the nature of intelligence and its individual variations. The beginning of the modern conceptualizations of intelligence may be placed at the turn of the twentieth century with the work of Binet and Simon in 1905. Although many definitions of intelligence have been proposed and strongly debated (Cronbach, 1975), most of the earlier definitions were global and included as common elements the ability to learn, the amount of acquired knowledge, and the ability to adapt to the environment. Other definitions emphasized the possibility that intelligence is made up of several independent components. For example, Spearman (1904) proposed a two-factor theory in which one factor (the general, or *g*, factor) was reflected in all cognitive functions and a second factor (the specific, or *s*, factor) comprised a variety of elements reflecting different abilities. Using factor analysis on many different specific test items, Thurstone (1938) later identified a series of factors, some of which were labeled general reasoning, verbal comprehension, associative memory, numerical reasoning, and word fluency.

The most complex and comprehensive view of intelligence has been presented by Guilford (1959), who proposed a three-dimensional model consisting of *contents, operations,* and *products* (Anastasi, 1988, pp. 385–387). Contents refers to four types of information to be processed. Operations include five processes for handling information. Products refers to six types of results from processing information. This three-dimensional model produces 120 hypothesized primary intellectual abilities; Guilford and his coworkers have identified or developed tests for about one hundred of these abilities.

Contemporary intelligence tests reflect some of the diversity of thought about the nature of intelligence. Some of them are global measures of intelligence; others evaluate specific aspects of intellectual functioning, and still others combine the two approaches in a single test. Practical considerations (such as time limitations), however, have precluded the use of tests or combinations of tests that measure more than a dozen or so different aspects of intelligence.

ASSESSMENT AND DIAGNOSIS

Referral

Referral for assessment of mental retardation may occur at any age beginning in earliest infancy. Even at birth, some physical abnormalities that are highly correlated with mental retardation may be observed. Children suspected of being mentally retarded early in infancy tend to be those who are more severely affected and who show abnormalities on physical examination. Most children with mental retardation, however, are not referred for diagnosis until the late preschool or early school years. Later referrals are associated with fewer physical abnormalities and less severe mental retardation. It is usually an adult in the child's natural environment (home or school) who first suspects a problem. This suspicion is usually based on the behavior of the child, who is typically described as being slow in development or learning. Parents often have a difficult time persuading their family physician to refer their child for testing because in many instances the physician has not had an opportunity to observe a sample of the child's behavior that is adequate for making a judgment. Relatively few physicians keep a record of the ages at which their child patients achieve the important developmental milestones, and still fewer incorporate developmental screening tests into their routine practice. Records kept by the parents, teachers, and physicians, as well as the information obtained during interviews, greatly assist the clinician in the choice of additional assessment techniques. Parents currently take a more active role in the referral process, although professionals such as teachers and physicians continue to play an important part in alerting parents to potential developmental problems.

In the past, no one took explicit responsibility for the identification of children at risk for serious mental handicaps, particularly during the preschool period. As it became increasingly apparent that the cost to society could be greatly reduced if these children were identified and provided with intervention and prevention services early in life, Public Law 94-142, the Education for All Handicapped Children Act, and Public Law 99-457 (Part H), Services for Infants and Toddlers with Handicapping Conditions, were enacted to place responsibility for identification with the community, primarily with the public school systems. These laws mandate interdisciplinary and parental involvement (Gallagher, 1989).

Definition and Assessment Methods

Definitions of mental retardation have been numerous and have tended to be influenced by the predominant conceptualization of intelligence at the time (Landesman & Ramey, 1989). Over the years, definitions that have relied on vague terminology, etiological factors, and prognosis have given way to definitions that describe current behavior or behavioral deficits relative to other persons in the population of the same chronological age. That is, mental retardation is defined as a slower rate of learning or as a collection of behavior deficits in relation to the rates of learning and behavioral repertoires of the average child of the same age.

The American Association on Mental Retardation's (AAMR) manual on classification of mental retardation (Luckasson et al., 1992) revised the paradigm for classifying mental retardation. The latest classification system focuses on the amount of support required from the environment by an individual with mental retardation rather than the deficits that the individual has. These revised standards emphasize the relationship between the individual and the environment, rather than focusing almost exclusively on the individual. The current standards do not classify individuals with mental retardation based upon the severity of their deficits, as was the standard prior to the latest revision. Classification is based on individual support requirements: intermittent, limited, extensive, or pervasive in each of the following four areas: intellectual functioning and adaptive skills, psychological/emotional functioning, physical/health, and environment (Coulter, 1996).

The new standards adopted by the AAMR are a significant departure from the previous approach to the classification of mental retardation. As a result, these new standards have yet to become part of routine practice. The new definition focuses on interventions for individuals with mental retardation and is considered by some authors as more compatible than the previous deficit model with laws (e.g., Part H of Public Law 99-457, Services for Infants and Toddlers with Handicapping Conditions) which mandates the use of multidisciplinary teams to develop Individualized Family Service Plans for qualified preschool children (Vig & Jedrysek, 1996). The new AAMR standards emphasize needed services, rather than a description of deficits.

The overwhelming majority of the research in the area of mental retardation is based upon the previous AAMR classification system (Grossman, 1983). In addition, some investigators and service agencies have opted to use the classification system for mental retardation adopted by the American Psychiatric Association in the fourth edition of its *Diagnostic and Statistic Manual of Mental Disorders* (DSM-IV; APA, 1994). The DSM-IV defines mental retardation similarly to the current AAMR standards (Luckasson et al., 1992), but maintains the classification system found in the previous AAMR standards (Grossman, 1983).

The AAMR definition of mental retardation is:

Mental Retardation refers to substantial limitations in present functioning. It is characterized by significantly subaverage intellectual functioning, existing concurrently with related limitations in two or more of the following applicable adaptive skill areas: communication, self-care, home living, social skills, community use, self-direction, health and safety, functional academics, leisure, and work. Mental retardation manifests before age 18. (p. 5)

Mental retardation as defined denotes a level of behavioral performance without reference to etiology. Thus, it does not distinguish, for example, between retardation associated with psychosocial influences and retardation associated with biological deficit. Mental retardation is descriptive of current behavior and does not necessarily imply prognosis. Prognosis is related more to such factors as associated conditions, motivation, treatment, and training opportunities than to mental retardation itself.

General intellectual functioning is operationally defined as the results obtained by assessment with one or more of the individually administered standardized general intelligence tests developed for that purpose.

Significantly subaverage is defined as IQ of 70 or below on standardized measures of intelligence. This upper limit is intended as a guideline; it could be extended upward through IQ 75 or more, depending on the reliability of the intelligence test used. This particularly applies in schools and similar settings if behavior is impaired and clinically determined to be due to deficits in reasoning and judgment.

Impairments in adaptive behavior are defined as significant limitations in an individual's effectiveness in meeting the standards of maturation, learning, personal independence, and/or social responsibility that are expected for his or her age level and cultural group, as determined by clinical assessment and, usually, standardized scales.

Developmental period is defined as the period of time between conception and the eighteenth birthday. Developmental deficits may be manifested by slow, arrested, or incomplete development resulting from brain damage, degenerative processes in the central nervous system, or regression from previously normal states due to psychosocial factors. (p. 11)

This definition describes mental retardation on the basis of scores on standardized intelligence tests, evaluation of adaptive behavior, and the age at which the problem was manifested. Although a large number of intelligence tests have been devised, the Stanford-Binet and the Wechsler scales are by far the most frequently used when a child is referred with a question of mental retardation. Group intelligence tests and shorter versions of individual intelligence tests, such as the Slosson Intelligence Test, may be used for screening purposes, but they are not considered adequate for making a diagnosis.

Until relatively recently, infant tests were not considered to be useful for diagnosing mental retardation because they were not good predictors of later intelligence scores for samples of normal children. However, several studies (see, for example, Erickson, 1968b; Bernheimer & Keogh, 1988; Goldstein & Sheaffer, 1988) have presented evidence that children who obtain scores in the range of mental retardation on infant tests during the first few years of life have a high probability of receiving scores in the range of mental retardation at later ages. Although *all* children diagnosed with mental retardation should be retested at frequent intervals, such as yearly, to check on the reliability of the original test results, follow-up testing is extremely important in the case of infants and young preschool children whose test performance is considerably more unreliable than that of older children.

Classification

Based upon the current AAMR (Luckasson et al., 1992) classification system for mental retardation, a diagnosis of mental retardation must be based upon a score on a standardized intelligence test and an assessment of adaptive behavior across a variety of areas. In order to receive a diagnosis of mental retardation, an individual must score approximately two standard deviations below the average IQ score (100) or less. Based upon the AAMR (1992) system, individuals may be classified with mental retardation if they meet the following three criteria: (1) IQ score below 70–75 on a standardized IQ test, (2) significant limitation in two or more of the adaptive skill areas, and (3) onset of these delays at or before 18 years of age. Once diagnosed, a description of the individual's strengths and weaknesses in each of the following four dimensions must follow: intellectual functioning and adaptive skills, psychological and emotional well-being, health and physical well-being, and life activity environments. Finally, a profile of the intensities of needed supports is developed for each of the four dimensions. Supports may include teaching, befriending, financial assistance, behavioral support, in-home living assistance, community and school access, and health assistance. The intensity of these supports can be intermittent, limited, extensive, or pervasive.

The DSM-IV system of classification of individuals with mental retardation (APA, 1994) maintains the four levels of classification that have been accepted for many years and were found in the previous AAMR standards of classification (Grossman, 1983). These levels and their corresponding IQ score ranges are as follows:

Level	IQ Range
Mild mental retardation	50–55 to approximately 70
Moderate mental retardation	35–40 to 50–55
Severe mental retardation	20–25 to 35–40
Profound mental retardation	Below 20 or 25

Each successively lower level is one standard deviation below the level above it. Thus, children who obtain IQ scores in the range of profound mental retardation have scores that are more than five standard deviations below the mean.

When comparisons are made between the *actual prevalence* of mental retardation in the U.S. population and the number *expected* on the basis of a normal distribution curve (the bell-shaped curve), it has been found that there are nearly two thousand times as many individuals with profound mental retardation and a little over twice as many individuals with moderate and severe mental retardation than would be expected if the distribution of IQ scores were normal. The prevalence of individuals with mild mental retardation closely approximates the expected frequency.

In California, the use of intelligence tests with African-American pupils was banned on the basis of apparent bias because African-American children were overrepresented in special education classes. The same issue was raised in Chicago, but the court decided that intelligence tests were not biased and not responsible for the overrepresentation of African-American children in special education classes. Considerable research has examined this issue, and the consensus is that IQ scores are not biased because they predict school achievement scores equally well for majority and minority groups. Meanwhile, there are some African-American children in California who might have been helped by special education services but who have been denied these services (Taylor, 1990).

During the 12-year period from 1976/1977 through 1988/1989, the number of children who received special education services because of mental retardation in the United States decreased by more than 45 percent (Frankenberger & Fronzaglio, 1991; U.S. Department of Education, 1990). During this same time period, the number of children who received special education services who were classified with learning disabilities increased by 152 percent (Frankenberger & Fronzaglio, 1991). This decrease in the number of children classified with mild mental retardation is likely to be due to several factors: (1) changes in the definitions and procedures used by states in identifying mental retardation, (2) a decline in the number of minority children identified with mild mental retardation, (3) improved medical diagnosis and treatment of conditions that can result in mental retardation, (4) an emphasis by schools on mainstreaming students with special needs into nonspecialized educational settings, and (5) a general preference by parents and school personnel for the label of "learning disability" rather than "mental retardation" (Frankenberger & Fronzaglio, 1991).

Assessment of Adaptive Behavior

The measurement of adaptive behavior presents greater problems to the clinician because few objective tests have been developed for this purpose. Before the publication of the Adaptive Behavior Scale, clinicians had to rely primarily on information derived from interviews with significant adults and observation of the child in the clinic setting or on tests which evaluated relatively narrow ranges of the child's behavioral repertoire.

The revision of the AAMD Adaptive Behavior Scale (Nihara, Foster, Shellhaas, & Leland, 1975) is a comprehensive approach to the evaluation of adaptive behavior and uses the interview approach for data collection. Because the items on the scale are based on observed behavior, and the scale can be administered by persons without special training in psychological testing, information should be obtained from the person who spends the greatest amount of time with the child. The scale consists of two parts. The first part includes 10 behavior areas and 21 subareas:

I. Independent Functioning
   A. Eating
   B. Toilet Use
   C. Cleanliness
   D. Appearance
   F. Dressing and Undressing
   G. Travel
   H. General Independent Functioning
II. Physical Development
   A. Sensory Development
   B. Motor Development
III. Economic Activity
   A. Money Handling and Budgeting
   B. Shopping Skills
IV. Language Development
   A. Expression
   B. Comprehension
   C. Social Language Development
V. Numbers and Time
VI. Domestic Activity
   A. Cleaning
   B. Kitchen Duties
   C. Other Domestic Activities
VII. Vocational Activity
VIII. Self-Direction
   A. Initiative
   B. Perseverance
   C. Leisure Time
IX. Responsibility
X. Socialization

Within each area or subarea items are arranged developmentally, that is, in the order that the behaviors tend to occur in the average person. Each item is scored on the basis of the client's most advanced performance.

The second part of the scale consists of 13 areas of maladaptive behavior and one variable evaluating the use of medications:

    I. Violent and Destructive Behavior
    II. Antisocial Behavior
    III. Rebellious Behavior
    IV. Untrustworthy Behavior
    V. Withdrawal
    VI. Stereotyped Behavior and Odd Mannerisms
    VII. Inappropriate Interpersonal Manners
    VIII. Unacceptable Vocal Habits
    IX. Unacceptable or Eccentric Habits
    X. Self-Abusive Behavior
    XI. Hyperactive Tendencies
    XII. Sexually Aberrant Behavior
    XIII. Psychological Disturbances
    XIV. Use of Medications

Within each of these 14 areas are varying numbers of subareas and specific behaviors that are scored on the basis of whether they never occur (zero), occur occasionally (1), or occur frequently (2). Scores for the specific behaviors are combined to give subarea scores that are, in turn, combined to give one score for each of the maladaptive behavior areas with higher scores reflecting greater amounts of maladaptive behavior.

One major problem with the scale is that norms for a representative sample of normal children have not been reported. Rather, data for a group of institutionalized children with mental retardation and adults (on the basis of IQ scores) are presented in the scale manual as a standard against which to compare individuals. While the norm group of individuals with mental retardation may be useful for comparing the profiles of individual children from institutional settings, it is not adequate for assessing the adaptive behavior of children from home settings referred for possible mental retardation. Lambert, Windmiller, Tharinger, and Cole (1981) and Lambert, Leland, and Nihira (1992) have published a public school version of the AAM Adaptive Behavior Scale that has been examined for reliability (Mayfield, Forman, & Nagle, 1984); teachers' and parents' ratings for 22 children with mental retardation did not differ on the three factors: Personal Self-Sufficiency, Community Self-Sufficiency, and Personal-Social Responsibilities (Foster-Gaitskell & Pratt, 1989).

The Vineland Adaptive Behavior Scale (Sparrow, Balla, & Cicchetti, 1984) provides norms from birth to 18 years, 11 months and is based on information obtained during an interview with an adult who knows the client well, such as a parent or other caregiver. It contains four major domains: Motor Skills, Communication, Socialization, and Daily Living Skills; these four domains have 14 subscales. Research by Middleton, Keene, and Brown (1990) has corroborated its validity.

In general, there is a correlation between level of intellectual functioning and level of adaptive behavior. Such a relationship should be expected in view of the fact that intelligence is involved in the acquisition of most behaviors. The AAMR standards specify, however, that individuals whose adaptive behaviors are within normal limits are *not* to be diagnosed with mentally retardion even when their IQ scores are within the range of mental retardation. That is, there is recognition that some children and adolescents with subaverage IQ scores cope adequately with environmental demands and do not require special services; labeling such persons with mental retardation would serve no useful function. Although labels have generally been assumed to have detrimental effects on children, very little research evidence has been presented to support that assumption (MacMillan, Jones, & Aloia, 1974).

Medical Classification

The AAMR publication also contains a medical classification system in which known or suspected etiological factors and associated physical or environmental conditions may be coded and added to the description of mental retardation. The major headings are

1. Infections and intoxications
2. Trauma or physical agent
3. Metabolism or nutrition
4. Gross brain disease (postnatal)
5. Unknown prenatal influence
6. Chromosomal anomalies
7. Other conditions originating in the perinatal period
8. Following psychiatric disorder
9. Environmental influences
10. Other conditions

These major medical headings include up to nine subheadings that vary from specific medical syndromes to general types of disorders. Some of these medical conditions are described in the chapters on etiology. The medical classification system presented in the AAMR publication closely follows those in the *International Classification of Diseases* and the *Diagnostic and Statistical Manual of Mental Disorders*.

Behavioral Assessment

Behavioral clinicians have worked extensively with children with mental retardation, but their involvement has typically begun after the diagnosis has been made. From a behavioral point of view, "a retarded individual is one who has a limited repertory of behavior shaped by events that constitute his history" (Bijou, 1966, p. 2). This view, in general, rejects notions of defective intelligence and of mental retardation being a symptom of underlying pathology. Rather, the behaviorist focuses on the child's current behavior as being a product of past antecedent and consequent stimuli. Although children with mental retardation engage in inappropriate forms of behavior, by far the greater problem resides in their behavioral deficits. Behavioral assessment typically includes an inventory of the child's behavioral repertoire through the use of rating scales or a behavior checklist and direct observation of the child in the natural environment. In addition, one or more interviews are conducted with the child's principal caregivers to determine the methods currently being used to manage the child's behavior and to evaluate the environment's potential for identifying, reinforcing, and shaping appropriate behavior.

Characteristics of Children with Mental Retardation

It is sometimes believed that children with mental retardation tend to resemble one another more closely than do nondisabled children. In actuality, the individual differences in behavioral characteristics among children with mental retardation are substantial, even within groups having the same mental age or level of retardation, just as they are for normal children. For most developmental characteristics and learned behaviors, children with mental retardation greatly resemble normal children of the same mental age. For example, Siperstein and Bak (1989) found that special education classes for adolescents with moderate mental retardation contained social structures similar to those found in regular classrooms; the students with mental retardation were selective in choosing friends, experienced reciprocity in their friendship choices, and frequently chose as friends members of the opposite gender, peers from other classes, and adults in the school and community. However, children with mental retardation have more behavior problems than their same-aged nondisabled peers (Gully & Hosch, 1979). Hyperactivity has been reported as the most common problem behavior occurring during preadolescence in children with mental retardation (Koller, Richardson, Katz, & McLaren, 1983).

Perhaps more variability may be demonstrated for physical characteristics. Children with IQ scores below 50 have a higher probability (which increases with the severity of mental retardation) of physical abnormalities that are apparent to the casual observer. These physical abnormalities range from relatively mild defects to severe distortions of the body, such as an unusually large or small head or limb deformities.

ETIOLOGY

Many factors have been identified as increasing the risk of mental retardation. In some instances, the presence of a particular risk factor makes it a virtual certainty that the child will have mental retardation, while in many more instances, risk factors are associated with small increases in the probability that the child will have mental retardation. Even though a large number of etiological factors have been identified, specification of etiology for *individual* children with mental retardation is not possible for many because either none of the known etiological factors has been found in the child's history or more than one factor has been reported in the history, and there is no way of determining which single factor or combination of factors caused the mental retardation. Keep in mind that there are etiological factors that have not yet been identified. The causes of 30 to 50 percent of severe mental retardation are undetermined (McLaren & Bryson, 1987).

Genetic Risk Factors

An increasing number of chromosomal abnormalities are being identified in persons with mental retardation (Lubs & Walnowska, 1977). Chromosomal abnormalities are implicated in 10 to 20 percent of the cases in which there is a known cause for the mental retardation (Payne & Patton, 1981, p. 64). Among the various conditions involving abnormal numbers of chromosomes is Down syndrome, which accounts for about 10 percent of persons with moderate to severe mental retardation. Because individuals with this condition share a number of physical features, they have been identified and studied since the middle of the last century, but it was not until 1959 that Lejuene, Gautier, and Turpin discovered that Down syndrome involved an extra chromosome 21; that is, instead of the usual two chromosome 21s (one from the father and one from the mother), three are present, bringing the total number of chromosomes in each cell to 47.

As more research has been conducted, three types of Down syndrome have been described. The first type, called *nondisjunction*, accounts for 95 percent of Down syndrome cases and involves either an error during the egg or sperm development, in which the mother or father contributes two instead of one chromosome 21, or an error during the first cell division after fertilization. The probability of nondisjunction increases greatly with the age of the mother, ranging from one in 1,500 for mothers under 30 years of age to one in 65 for mothers 45 years of age and older (Mikkelsen & Stene, 1970).

The second type of chromosomal abnormality resulting in Down syndrome is *mosaicism*, which accounts for less than 5 percent of the cases. In this type, the complement of chromosomes is normal when the egg is fertilized. During the second or subsequent cell division, an error produces one cell with 47 chromosomes (three chromosome 21s) and one cell with 45 chromosomes (one chromosome 21). The cell with 45 chromosomes dies, and the cell with 47 chromosomes continues to reproduce itself as do the remaining normal cells with 46 chromosomes. The result is an individual whose body contains a mixture of normal and abnormal cells. The physical signs and the mental retardation are less severe in persons with mosaicism and probably depend on which organs of the body are affected by the abnormal cells.

Both nondisjunction and mosaicism involve errors in cell division and are *not* hereditary in the sense that the parents have the condition or are carriers and pass the condition to their children. A third type of Down syndrome, *translocation*, may, however, be traced directly to abnormal chromosomes in one of the parents in about one-third of the cases (the remaining two-thirds being due to an error in the development of the egg or sperm or in the first cell division). In these cases, the parent is normal physically and mentally and has the genetic material of 46 chromosomes. Two of the chromosomes (usually chromosomes 14 and 21) are attached to one another, however, giving the parent 45 chromosomes (44 normal chromosomes and one translocation chromosome). When these chromosomes divide to form the egg or sperm, an extra chromosome 21 may result, giving the fetus 46 chromosomes (45 normal chromosomes and one translocation chromosome) but the genetic material for 47 chromosomes with chromosome 21 represented in triplicate. Individuals with the translocation type of Down syndrome are similar in characteristics to those with the nondisjunction type.

Having an extra chromosome 21 (trisomy 21) affects many aspects of development, the most salient of which is a decreased rate of intellectual development. Physical abnormalities, such as heart and intestinal defects, cause an increased mortality rate (20 to 30 percent) during the first few years of life, and about 1 percent of children with Down syndrome develop leukemia. Improved cardiac surgical techniques have extended the life span of many individuals with Down syndrome. Among the other physical abnormalities associated with Down syndrome are a small skull; a small nose with a flattened nasal bridge; eyes that tend to slant upward; small ears; small mouth with a normal-sized tongue which often protrudes; a short, broad neck; small hands with short fingers and abnormalities of the palm and fingerprints; and short stature. Sexual development is usually delayed or incomplete, although a few women have reproduced. In general, Down syndrome individuals seem to age at a more rapid rate and display signs of Alzheimer's disease at earlier ages than individuals without Down syndrome. Mental retardation is almost always present in affected persons, although the level varies widely from profound to mild.

Syndromes involving trisomies of other chromosomes have been reported, but most of them are associated with early death. Trisomy 18, for example, has an incidence of one per 3,000 newborn infants, but only 10 percent survive the first year. The survivors are severely mentally retarded (Weber, 1967) and have a number of physical abnormalities such as an abnormally shaped head, a weak cry, low birth weight, and heart defects. Trisomy 13 occurs once in 5,000 births, and 18 percent survive the first year. The survivors are severely retarded and have seizures. Physical abnormalities include defects of the eyes, nose, lips, and heart; extra fingers; and poor growth.

Absence of only a portion of a chromosome can be incompatible with life or result in severely handicapped individuals. A partial absence of the short arm of chromosome 5, for example, results in severe mental retardation, poor growth, and a number of physical abnormalities, one of which causes the characteristic high-pitched catlike cry during infancy. A partial absence of the long arm of chromosome 18 has been found to be associated with moderate and severe mental retardation, a small skull, visual and hearing defects, and a variety of other physical abnormalities.

In comparison with the autosomal chromosomes, abnormalities in the sex chromosomes appear to be more compatible with life. That is, a greater proportion of individuals with abnormal sex chromosomes survive. Fragile-X, or Martin-Bell, syndrome is currently believed to be the second most common chromosomal cause of mental retardation (after Down syndrome) (Ho, Glahn, & Ho, 1988; Spitz, 1994). It is considered to be an X-linked trait in that females are usually the carriers and males usually manifest the problems associated with it. About 80 percent of the males with the genetic abnormality have mental retardation (usually moderate, but varying from mild to severe); some of the males with normal intelligence have specific learning disabilities. The clinical features include speech delay and behavior problems, including hyperactivity, self-mutilation, violent outbursts, and some autistic-like behaviors, as well as craniofacial and other physical abnormalities.

In *Turner syndrome*, the female has one, instead of two, X chromosomes, giving a total of 45 chromosomes. Turner syndrome results in higher rates (about 20 percent) of mild retardation and is strongly associated with substantial space-form perceptual deficiencies. In one study with 18 Turner syndrome women, the mean Verbal IQ on the Wechsler Adult Intelligence Scale (WAIS) was 118, while the Performance IQ on the WAIS was 88 (Alexander, Ehrhardt, & Money, 1966). Many individuals with Turner syndrome are not diagnosed until adolescence, when sexual development fails to occur and short stature is noted. Others are diagnosed at birth when certain physical abnormalities, such as webbing of the neck, are present. Although women with Turner syndrome are sterile because they lack functional ovaries, development of the secondary sexual characteristics is possible with the administration of female hormones.

Klinefelter syndrome is a genetic abnormality in which males have more than one X chromosome in addition to the Y chromosome. Individuals with up to four X chromosomes have been identified. Mental retardation occurs in 25 to 50 percent of cases but is usually mild with no outstanding deficits. Cognitive and physical defects are usually proportional to the number of extra X chromosomes present. In addition to their decreased rate of growth and sexual development, Klinefelter individuals have been described as socially unskilled and likely to drop out of school (Nielsen, 1969).

Conditions associated with mental retardation that are inherited on the basis of a specific dominant gene are relatively infrequent in comparison to those inherited on the basis of recessive genes. A dominant genetic condition is usually one in which a parent has the condition. In some instances, the presence of the condition in the child is indicative of a new mutation and has not been inherited. Dominant gene syndromes associated with mental retardation in children are probably relatively infrequent because individuals with mental retardation procreate at greatly reduced rates and therefore do not pass on these dominant genes.

Many disorders due to specific recessive genes have been identified. Carrier parents can be identified through biochemical tests in some instances, but testing of adults is usually confined to high-risk persons or groups because the incidence of any particular recessive condition in the population is quite low. Since most of the recessive conditions do not begin to manifest their adverse effects until after birth, considerable effort has gone into the development and implementation of mass screening programs for newborn infants for conditions amenable to treatment programs.

Phenylketonuria (PKU) is a recessive condition occurring once in approximately every 17,000 births and is related to a high incidence of mental retardation that is a by-product of an inactive liver enzyme. PKU individuals also manifest a high rate of behavior problems such as hyperactivity, anxiety, and temper tantrums. Inexpensive screening methods for PKU have been developed; some states have mandatory screening programs for newborn infants, while others rely on voluntary screening programs. An effective dietary treatment program has been developed and will be discussed in the treatment section of this chapter.

Another recessive condition, although more rare than PKU, is *galactosemia*, a disorder involving the metabolism of galactose, which is derived from foods containing lactose. This disorder results in malnutrition, cataracts, and mental retardation, but it may be effectively treated with a special diet. *Microcephaly* (small head) may also be inherited as a recessive condition and usually results in severe mental retardation.

Prenatal, Perinatal, and Postnatal Physical Risk Factors

Most of the prenatal, perinatal, and postnatal factors described in the earlier chapters on etiology have been implicated as causes of mental retardation. Again, most of the research studies are correlational and retrospective, and some of the findings must, therefore, be considered tentative, requiring further research for their corroboration. In addition, the etiological factors for some syndromes related to mental retardation have yet to be identified.

Experimental studies with animals have clearly demonstrated that severe malnutrition of the mother during pregnancy adversely affects the growth and development of the offspring. Protein restriction in pregnant rats, for example, has been shown to reduce the number of brain cells in their offspring (Winick & Rosso, 1973). In humans, it is generally accepted that severe malnutrition reduces the infant's birth weight and the number of cells in the placenta and increases the rate of spontaneous abortions and premature births. Research suggests, however, that malnutrition of the mother only during pregnancy does not lead to an increased rate of mental retardation (Stein, Susser, Saenger, & Marolla, 1972). It may well be that the fetus is able to draw from the mother whatever resources are necessary for brain development.

Postnatal malnutrition, especially during the first few years after birth, does appear to retard intellectual development, but unfortunately the research with humans is almost always confounded by socioeconomic factors, prenatal and perinatal obstetrical complications, and postnatal infections. In addition to the obvious physical effects, hunger very likely also reduces the child's attention to the environment and thereby the opportunity to learn (Birch & Gussow, 1970).

A number of chronic viral and bacterial infections in pregnant women are known to increase the risk of mental retardation in the offspring. Of the infants who survive a prenatal case of *toxoplasmosis*, 85 percent will be mentally retarded and manifest various severe physical abnormalities, such as hardened areas of the brain, microcephaly, and seizures. Untreated maternal *syphilis* greatly increases the rate of death, mental retardation, blindness, and deafness in the child. Other viruses, such as a certain type of *herpes* virus and one that causes *cytomegalic inclusion dis-*

ease, have mild or no effects on the mother but may adversely affect the developing brain of the child.

HIV (human immunodeficiency virus) infection is expected to become the largest infectious cause of mental retardation, with estimates of 20,000 infants infected with HIV in the United States (Gray, 1989; Cohen, 1992; Novello, Wise, Willoughby, & Pizzo, 1989). Of infants born with the HIV infection, nearly all will become disabled through central nervous system involvement, usually during the first five years of life. Larger numbers of these children with intellectual and other developmental problems are expected to survive longer in the future because of the effective use of medical therapies (Diamond, 1989); they and their families will need psychological assessment and intervention services.

Among the acute maternal infections that increase the abortion and stillbirth rate (Sever, 1970), *rubella* has the most profound effects in terms of congenital defects and mental retardation. Chess, Korn, and Fernandez (1971) reported that one-fourth of a group of children who contracted rubella prenatally were found to be mildly to profoundly retarded.

Of the maternal dysfunctions known to increase the mortality rates of infants, knowledge is still inadequate to determine their effect on the rate of mental retardation. In the case of maternal *diabetes*, however, it has been found that children are more likely to have intellectual deficits when the diabetes is not well controlled. Medicine has clearly decreased the risk to the diabetic mother and her child, but not all cases of diabetes are easily controlled. Since hypertensive disorders affect between 5 and 10 percent of pregnant women and are implicated in a sizable percentage of maternal and fetal deaths, research on the surviving infants is greatly needed to assess the possibility of their being at high risk for mental retardation.

Deficits in intellectual functioning may also be the result of maternal sensitization, such as *Rh incompatibility*. An effective intervention for the effects of Rh incompatibility is vaccination of the mother with Rh immunoglobulin within 72 hours after the termination of the first pregnancy (birth, miscarriage, or abortion) and of each subsequent Rh positive pregnancy. The immunoglobulin destroys the Rh positive cells that may have passed from the infant's to the mother's circulatory system, thus inhibiting the development of antibodies that would otherwise damage the next fetus.

Our understanding of the effects of drugs and addictive substances on later physical and cognitive functioning is only beginning to develop. Although several hundred drugs are known to produce physical defects in animals, only a few dozen are known to produce defects in the human fetus; the effects of most of the remaining drugs on the unborn child are unknown. In a few instances, widely used drugs have been demonstrated to have adverse effects when ingested by the mother early in pregnancy. For example, Milkovich and Van den Berg (1974) found that anxious women who took meprobamate or Librium during pregnancy had more children with physical defects and mental retardation than did an equally anxious group of women who did not receive either of these two drugs. The absolute number of cases, however, was quite small.

The administration of sedatives and anesthesia during labor and delivery is highly variable among physicians. General anesthetics are usually avoided because it has long been known that they may depress the newborn's respiratory functioning. The long-term consequences of various drugs and drug dosages on the cognitive development of children remain to be explored.

Research on the effect of maternal *alcoholism* during pregnancy has revealed a significant incidence of mental and physical retardation in addition to a syndrome of congenital physical defects (Jones, Smith, Ulleland, & Streissguth, 1973). Future research may delineate the effects of the amount of alcohol and the period during pregnancy when it was ingested. Jones (1986) reported that alcohol ingestion is the third most common recognizable cause of mental retardation in the United States. Fetal alcohol syndrome occurs in approximately 1 in 750 births (Menke, McClead, & Hansen, 1991).

Although a relationship between maternal anxiety and complications during pregnancy and delivery has been demonstrated in several studies, very little follow-up research on the children of anxious and nonanxious mothers has been conducted. One such study (Stott, 1973) has shown that long-term, chronic stress, such as severe marital problems, are related to higher incidences of physical and intellectual disabilities.

Prematurity, or low birth weight, has been linked with higher rates of mental retardation. Niswander and Gordon (1972) found that premature children were three times as likely to show neurological abnormalities at the age of one year as nonpremature children. A study of six- and seven-year-old children reported higher incidents of intellectual deficiencies for those with low birth weights, even after children with IQ scores below 60 and those with obvious physical or emotional handicaps were excluded from the study (Wiener, Rider, Oppel, Fischer, & Harper, 1965). In a study with nine pairs of identical twins in which one twin's birth weight was significantly less than that of the other, the twin of lower birth weight had the lower rate of physical growth and intellectual development into adulthood (Babson & Phillips, 1973). At one time, a number of premature infants were given high concentrations of oxygen as part of their postnatal care in the hospital. It has subsequently been discovered that premature infants may become blind (retrolental fibroplasia) and sometimes become mentally retarded when they are subjected to high concentrations of oxygen. Use of hexachlorophene soap for bathing newborn infants has been discontinued since it was found to cause brain damage in premature infants and sometimes led to death that appeared to be due to oxygen deprivation. Thus, it appears that the premature infant may be especially vulnerable to certain environmental conditions.

Anoxia may also produce long-lasting cognitive deficits, although the problems are not severe in most cases. One of the most thorough examinations of anoxia effects involved over 300 preschool children who were divided into groups, those who had normal full-term births, those who were full term but anoxic at birth, and those who had other complications at the time of birth (Graham, Ernhart, Craft, & Berman, 1963). The children judged to be oxygen-deprived at birth were found to have lower scores on a variety of cognitive measures and a greater number of neurological abnormalities than the children who had normal births.

In comparison with anoxia, the occurrence of perinatal head injury is considerably less frequent. Head injury is usually the result of head compression during birth. Head compression may be caused by a number of factors, such as size of the pelvic opening, head position during birth, and length of labor. A few studies with large numbers of children have examined some of the relevant variables; the findings typically reveal small differences in IQ scores in favor of the group with normal delivery.

Postnatal head injury appears to be occurring with a high frequency due to car accidents and child abuse, as well as the usual accidental falls, and the resulting brain damage can permanently impair the child's intellectual functioning. Several studies of persons with mental retardation have indicated that postnatal head injury has occurred in about 1 percent of the cases.

Animal research has led us to believe that injury to the brain of the young organism has less severe consequences than the same injury to the older organism. Teuber (1970) has suggested, however, that the situation with humans might be different in that early injury may lead to even greater deficits in particular behavioral functioning—probably the more complex, higher-level behaviors—not usually tested in animal studies, while the lower-level behaviors may be relatively more often "spared" for younger human organisms, as they are for younger infrahuman animals. Marlowe, Errera, and Jacobs (1983) reported higher lead levels in the bodies of mildly retarded and borderline intelligence children and suggested that continuous exposure to presumably safe levels of lead may in fact be related etiologically to mental retardation.

Among the diseases of childhood, encephalitis probably carries one of the highest risks for mental retardation. The viruses that cause encephalitis are often those involved in common childhood diseases, such as measles and chicken pox. Of the children who survive, half are severely mentally or physically impaired. Lead and mercury poisoning, now more commonly caused by air, water, and food pollution, are capable of causing brain damage that may manifest itself in mental retardation. There are, no doubt, other physical factors, most of them probably artificial, that increase the risk of mental retardation. Our efforts to identify these factors have only begun.

Demographic Risk Factors

Age of the mother is related to the risk of having a child with mental retardation, with teenage mothers and women over 35 having the higher risks. Older mothers are more likely to have children with chromosomal abnormalities and to have multiple births (e.g., twins). Young mothers tend to have unfavorable backgrounds involving nutrition, medical care, and psychological history. In addition to their increased risks for complications during pregnancy, labor, and delivery, both young and older mothers may provide postnatal environments for their children that are different from those of other children.

Socioeconomic status also affects the child's risk for mental retardation, with children from the lower socioeconomic groups having the higher risk. This factor is, of course, related to many of the physical factors mentioned earlier; lower socio-economic groups tend to have poorer nutrition, medical care, and general physical status. Moreover, socioeconomic status continues to affect the child through both postnatal physical and environmental-psychological factors, which are discussed in the next section.

Sex of the child is related to the risk of mental retardation; most studies have found a higher proportion of males than females, usually a ratio of two or three males with mental retardation to one female with mental retardation (Mumpower, 1970). Genetic factors no doubt contribute to these differences in view of the more numerous chromosomal abnormalities affecting males, but consideration must also be given to the possible effects of differential societal expectations for the two sexes. Perhaps more males have been referred, and therefore diagnosed, because parents have been more concerned about the implications of slow development for males than for females. In addition, males may manifest other behavioral characteristics that may increase the probability of their being referred.

Environmental and Psychological Risk Factors

Theoretically, a child with optimal genetic material and physical background who is deprived of environmental stimulation postnatally would become mentally retarded. Occasional case studies of children who have been confined to one room or an attic have reported severe behavioral consequences of extreme reduction in environmental stimuli, although, in these instances, we cannot determine the child's initial status. Similarly, studies conducted in certain institutional settings in which infants were greatly deprived of environmental stimulation also demonstrated that mental retardation was a frequent occurrence. It appears, then, that children require a certain amount of interaction with the environment to develop a behavioral repertoire that is within normal limits. The only problem remaining is to describe the necessary quantity and quality of environmental stimulation. On the basis of animal studies and research with infants, there is a strong indication that the infant's sensory capacities are well developed at birth and that early sensory stimulation is necessary for development. Although speculative, it is reasonable to assume that virtually all home environments have the potential for providing the minimal stimulation required for development of the infant. Even the poorest of homes can provide a wide variety of visual, auditory, and tactile experiences.

Mental retardation, however, may also be found in infants whose environments are chaotic or extremely variable. Case studies of children who have been abandoned and who have had a succession of caregivers (e.g., multiple foster homes) suggest that there are limits to the infants' capacities to adjust to changes in environmental stimulation. When these limits have been exceeded, the child fails to develop at a normal rate.

The importance of environmental factors to the developing child has led to their implication in the etiology of mild mental retardation, which accounts for over 70 percent of the population with mental retardation. In examining the relationship between level of mental retardation and five socioeconomic groups, Birch and his colleagues (1970) found that children with mental retardation with IQ scores below 60 were equally represented among the socioeconomic groups, while children with IQs of 60 or higher were greatly overrepresented in the lower socioeconomic groups, suggesting that the etiological factors were different for the higher- and lower-IQ children. Organic conditions were present for most of the low-IQ children, while two-thirds of the higher-IQ children presented no evidence of organic conditions relating to etiology. Compared with nondisabled children from the same lower socioeconomic groups, the children with mental retardation were more likely to come from large families and live in poorer housing (more people in each room). Half of the siblings of these children with mental retardation had IQ scores below 75. Other investigators have found similar familial and environmental factors for large percentages of mildly retarded children and have coined the term *cultural-familial* to describe the etiological factors.

At various times, greater or lesser emphases have been given to specific aspects of the obviously confounded variables involved in the etiology of cultural-familial retardation. Many researchers have proposed the view that mild mental retardation simply represents the lower end of the normal IQ distribution and is not reflective of pathological conditions; they support this view by pointing out that mildly retarded persons are not overrepresented in the population. On the other hand, there is reason to believe that mildly retarded children are primarily the products of less-than-optimal environmental and psychological conditions, such as the lack of opportunity to learn (inadequate models and antecedent stimuli) and the lack of reinforcement for learning cognitive skills. Evidence for this belief comes from intervention studies that are discussed in the next section.

In general, research permits us to conclude that mild mental retardation, like other levels of intellectual functioning, is a product of both genetic and environmental influences (Plomin, 1989; Weinberg, 1989). Correlations between children's and biological parents' IQ scores are generally higher than those between the children and their adoptive parents (Scarr, 1981). The absolute IQ score, however, may be determined by environmental factors. Children with mild mental retardation have received particular attention in recent years because it has become increasingly apparent that they have more problems adapting to contemporary society. This attention also raises the issue of the extent to which all children, both those with and without mental retardation, might benefit from improved environmental and psychological conditions.

Certain behavioral patterns formerly attributed to mental retardation per se have been shown to be determined by environmental conditions. Zigler (1973), for example, concluded that perseveration (e.g., repetition of a task) was more likely to be due to the effects of social reinforcement (after a history of social deprivation in an institutional setting) than to mental retardation. In a similar vein, the history of experiencing failures by children with mental retardation has been invoked as the basis for the research results showing that, in comparison with nondisabled children of the same mental age, the children with mental retardation set low goals for themselves and are content with minimal success on tasks on which they could do better.

THERAPEUTIC INTERVENTIONS

Physicians, educators, and psychologists have long been involved in the treatment of individuals with mental retardation. At the beginning of the nineteenth century, Itard, a physician, spent five years attempting to train a boy who had been captured in the forest of Aveyron, France. Although Itard was far from successful in "curing" the boy, his program, with its emphasis on sensory training, contained much that is still used in contemporary education. Seguin, a student of Itard's, who arrived in the United States in the middle of the nineteenth century and became the superintendent of the Pennsylvania Training School for Idiots, designed programs that involved both sensory and motor training and emphasized the necessity of individualized teaching as well as a good relationship between child and teacher. Montessori, a student of Seguin working in Rome, was successful in teaching a number of children with mental retardation to read and write. Although she used Seguin's methods, her successes were also due to her unique contributions, namely, an emphasis on early education, practical life experiences, and self-teaching, a method whereby the child chooses materials from an available array. Montessori's innovations have subsequently become popular in preschool programs for middle-class children.

Although institutions for individuals with mental retardation have a long history, the training of teachers and the establishment of programs for persons with mental retardation did not begin until after the turn of the twentieth century. The slow increase in the number of college training programs for teachers and special classes in public schools between 1915 and 1930 was suddenly terminated, probably because of a combination of the financial problems associated with the Depression and changes in educational philosophy. After World War II, public support of special classes for individuals with mental retardation was reinstated and was substantially influenced by pressures from the parents of children with mental retardation, most of whom had previously received no special services in school or had been excluded from school altogether.

Historically, treatment of persons with mental retardation has not generally had a high priority among mental health professionals. Before the 1950s and 1960s very few clinical psychologists and psychiatrists had used psychotherapy with persons with mental retardation, the principal "reasons" for this neglect being that mental retardation was not curable and that the characteristics of individuals with mental retardation (such as poor verbal ability and low motivation) precluded the successful use of psychotherapy. During the last few decades, beginning with the Kennedy presidency, the availability of financial resources for professional training programs, research, and direct services to persons with mental retardation has encouraged the exploration of both traditional and newer forms of therapy.

The 1960s through the 1980s was a period of considerable gains for persons with mental retardation. In addition to the increases in funds for education and treatment, a number of changes in the law have benefited persons with mental retardation. Public Law 94–142, the Education for All Handicapped Children Act, and Public Law 99–457, Services for Infants and Toddler with Handicapping

Conditions, require the schools to provide education for children with mental retardation beginning at birth. In addition, Public Law 95–602, the Rehabilitation Comprehensive Services and Developmental Disabilities Amendment of 1978, specifies the right of individuals with mental retardation to services in the least restrictive environment. In effect, these laws guarantee all children with mental retardation the right to education. Public Law 99–457 also mandates family service plans to focus intervention within the context of the family (Mahoney & O'Sullivan, 1990).

Family Support

It has gradually been acknowledged that parents are rarely able to understand and accept a diagnosis of mental retardation when it is first presented (Fajardo, 1987). Initial reactions frequently include denial and a search for another professional opinion. In some cases, treatment programs may be postponed or ineffective treatment programs initiated on the basis of the parents' denial of mental retardation. Under the best circumstances, most parents need a continuing interpretation of the child's problem, concrete suggestions for child rearing, and psychological support (Magrab & Johnson, 1980). Practical problems such as daily care, cost of medical interventions, inability to find a babysitter, and so on, significantly affect the psychological lives of the family members both within the family structure and in relationship to persons outside the family. Mothers who have to spend a disproportionate amount of time with a child with mental retardation necessarily spend less time with their spouses and normal children as well as less time outside the home. Similarly, older siblings who have increased child-care responsibilities have decreased opportunities for peer contacts and out-of-home activities (Stoneman, Brody, Davis, & Crapps, 1988).

Earlier research (Farber, 1959, 1960) suggested that the presence of a child with severe mental retardation was often detrimental to marital adjustment and to normal female siblings who were expected to provide care and help with the housework. A review of the research literature by Benson and Gross (1989) indicates that the presence of a congenitally handicapped child may have both positive and negative effects on the marital dyad. Various factors in the family may affect the impact of a child with mental retardation on the marital dyad. For example, Willoughby and Glidden (1995) reported that when fathers participated in the care of their children, both parents reported greater satisfaction with their marriage than when fathers did not participate in child care.

Cultural background may also affect coping processes; for example, Mary (1990) found that Hispanic mothers espoused an attitude of self-sacrifice toward the child and reported greater denial of the disability by their husbands compared with black and white mothers. Another study of 9- to 13-year-old children with younger siblings with severe handicaps concluded that these children appeared to be faring better than their earlier counterparts who were studied before schooling for children with handicaps was mandated (Wilson, Blacher, & Baker, 1989). (See the November 1989 issue of the *American Journal of Mental Retardation*, Volume *94*, for additional research findings on the families of children with mental retardation.) Unfortunately, community services for the families of children with mental retardation are not easily available. Respite care, when available, tends to be used by families that are larger, have children who are more handicapped, and have more serious behavior problems (Marc & MacDonald, 1988). Physicians and community clinics may offer supportive services and advice to parents, but pediatricians may express lower expectations for the children than other professionals caring for children with mental retardation (Wolraich, Siperstein, & O'Keefe, 1987). The National Association for Retarded Citizens (NARC), consisting primarily of local parents' groups, has been an important source of psychological support for many families and has been responsible for the development of many programs that provide services for children with mental retardation.

Institutionalization

One of the more difficult decisions that some parents have to make is whether to institutionalize the child. Such a decision is based on many factors. In the past, for example, physicians strongly urged parents to institutionalize children with Down syndrome at an early age because the burden of their care was considered to be excessive and parental rewards minimal. Institutionalization during infancy and the preschool period is relatively uncommon now and is determined more by family circumstances and the behavioral characteristics of the child. Rousey, Blacher, and Hanneman (1990) reported that choice of out-of-home placement of children with severe and profound mental retardation was increased as the child became older and had more behavioral deficits, more maladaptive behaviors, and multiple handicaps.

In spite of the many problems posed by the child with mental retardation in the home, only about 4 percent of children with mental retardation are institutionalized. Most parents choose to keep their child with mental retardation at home. To the extent that families can be helped with their overwhelming problems, the necessity for institutionalization will be decreased. Improvements in community services might also facilitate the release of children and adults for whom institutionalization was deemed necessary. For example, the development of foster home placement and group homes offers considerable promise for an early release from institutions as well as an alternative to initial institutionalization. Even the most severely handicapped child with mental retardation might benefit more from an inpatient facility that is located in the home community than a regional institution located at some distance from the family's residence, since the family might be more likely to visit the child and take an active interest in the child's care and treatment program.

Educational Programs

Educational programs for children with mental retardation have changed dramatically since the 1970s. In earlier times, children with mental retardation may have been excluded from school, given no special services, or received services in a special education classroom restricted to students with handicapping conditions. Currently, there is a broad range of programs and settings for providing services to students with mental retardation.

For children with mild mental retardation, the possibilities include regular class-based programs, special materials, equipment, consultation, itinerant services, resource rooms with special education teachers, and diagnostic-prescriptive teaching centers. Regular class placement meets the goal of the least restrictive environment; it is the most beneficial when the teacher has the time for individualizing instruction, available supportive resources, and the opportunity for consultation if the need arises. Itinerant programs provide regular classroom teachers with ongoing consultative and instructional services for children with mental retardation. Resource rooms with special education teachers supplement regular classroom teaching; the resource room is less restrictive than the special education classroom because the children go there only for specific academic subjects. Diagnostic-prescriptive teaching centers provide assessment of the child and design individualized educational plans.

Children with mild or moderate mental retardation have available to them special class-based programs, special education classes, part-time in regular classes, and full-time in special classes, while children with severe retardation may optimally be served with special school-based programs, special day schools, or special residential schools. The children with the most severe and profound mental retardation may benefit from non-school-based programs, homebound instruction, or hospital instruction.

Special class programs provide self-contained educational environments for children who cannot fully profit from regular classroom programs. These classes are usually half the size of regular classes and often have an aide to assist the teacher, but they contain children with a wider age range.

Although some educators feel that all children with mental retardation, no matter how severe their handicap, should be placed in regular schools, others believe that other facilities offer more potential for optimizing the child's performance. In extreme cases, when the child's handicaps preclude travel to an instructional facility, instruction in the hospital setting or at home may be available.

Special education programs have traditionally involved the assignment of children with mental retardation to separate classrooms or schools. Most public school systems divide children with mental retardation into two groups on the basis of IQ scores: educable mentally retarded (EMR) and trainable mentally retarded (TMR). Although there is some variability with respect to the exact IQ score limits, EMR children usually have IQ scores within the mildly retarded range and TMR children within the moderately to severely retarded range.

The EMR elementary primary class is for children between the ages of 6 and 10 years. The focus of this class is on readiness skills that are compatible with their mental ages of 3 to 6 years. In the EMR elementary intermediate class for children from 9 to 13 with mental ages of 6 to 9 years, emphasis is placed on the learning of basic school subjects: reading, writing, and arithmetic. The EMR secondary class for children of junior and senior high school ages continues to emphasize basic school subjects with a significant addition of practical skills and occupational training.

In recent years, there has been a strong movement away from self-contained classes for EMR children. The impetus for change comes from several sources or assumptions, some having meager or no research support. Research comparing the achievement of children with mental retardation in special education and regular classrooms has presented equivocal results. This failure to establish the academic effectiveness of special education has also led to the idea that EMR children might enjoy greater social adjustment in regular classrooms. Research suggests, however, that children with mental retardation in regular classes are more often rejected by peers and have poorer adjustment than their peers with mental retardation in special education classes (Goldstein, Moss, & Jordan, 1965).

Current educational programs tend to fall between the regular class and self-contained special education class in structure. EMR children are assigned to regular classrooms with similar-age peers and participate in many of the regular activities. For specific academic subjects, however, they leave the classroom and receive special training in small groups from resource teachers. Evaluation of this newer model has not yet been conducted, and there may well be serious roadblocks to its success, such as less-than-enthusiastic regular classroom teachers (MacMillan, Jones, & Meyers, 1976).

Although it is reasonable to assume that most special education teachers are conscientious and competent, there tend to be few incentives for excellence. School systems have been more lax about evaluating the progress of children with mental retardation and, in the past, were prone to assign the less-qualified (in training and experience) teachers to special education classes. Unfortunately, negative attitudes about individuals with mental retardation and poor expectations for their future still prevail in our society and adversely affect the quality of education and social experiences. The development of special training programs, particularly at the master's degree level, has no doubt had a positive influence on the quality of teacher education; the goal now is to use this improvement in teacher education to increase expectations for individuals with mental retardation.

Because of their relatively small numbers and greater diversity of physical problems, education of *trainable* mentally retarded children poses greater challenges. Professionals have increasingly noted the importance of providing children with severe retardation with skills that will maximize their independence as adults (Wehman & Bates, 1978). The teaching of self-care skills such as self-feeding, toilet use, and dressing, as well as vocational skills, may well be a better long-range investment than the teaching of academic subjects.

Special education programs are offered within institutional settings for individuals with mental retardation. Although children at all levels of mental retardation may be found in institutions, proportionately more persons with severe and profound mental retardation are admitted. Institutions would seem to offer more potential for the training and education of individuals with severe handicaps because the facilities, trained personnel, and clients are relatively easily brought together. Research, however, suggests that institutionalization is more often followed by slower rates of progress. Decreases in the rate of progress found for institutionalized children with mental retardation have been attributed to a lack of opportunity to learn; that, in turn, has presumably been caused by a shortage of personnel. Institutions, like schools, have been lax in the evaluation of their programs and in the qualifications of persons who have daily contact with the residents with mental retardation.

Educational programs for the preschool child with mental retardation have been receiving the most research attention during the past 20 years. Most of this attention has been focused on disadvantaged children who are at high risk for mild mental retardation. The earlier studies in this area concentrated on relatively brief intervention programs with older preschool children and were able to demonstrate small gains in cognitive functioning that were subsequently lost. The more recent studies have concentrated on training programs with children beginning in the first or second year of life (Odom & Karnes, 1988).

One of the most intensive studies (Heber & Garber, 1975; Garber, 1988) selected children from a poverty population in which the mothers had IQ scores below 75. The program was begun when the children were between three and six months of age and continued through the preschool years. The full-day stimulation program emphasized language skills, a structured environment, and maternal training. Differences between the experimental and control groups were apparent at 18 months of age; at 72 months of age the average Stanford-Binet IQ score of the experimental group was 121 and that of the control group 87. Subsequent comparisons revealed some declines for both groups after the intervention ceased and the children entered regular schools. There has, however, been a consistent 20 or more IQ (WISC) point difference between the groups through age nine (Garber & Heber, 1977).

A review of seven infant and preschool programs for low-income children conducted in the 1960s revealed that they were successful in helping the children to meet regular school requirements and in preventing special education placement and grade retention (Darlington, Royce, Snipper, Murray, & Lazar, 1980). While IQ scores showed some increases for several years after preschool, these increases were not maintained; these results replicate those found in other studies. Zigler and Trickett (1978) have recommended that evaluations of early childhood intervention programs include multiple measures of social competence, such as physical health status, school achievement, motivational and emotional variables, school attendance, and incidence of juvenile delinquency, rather than be based only on IQ scores that are, at best, indirect measures of school performance.

Early intervention programs may offer an opportunity for attenuating mental retardation, particularly in children who are reared in disadvantaged or impoverished environments. The available research does indicate that successful programs must be intensive and therefore costly. Cost-effectiveness analysis may, however, reveal that the price represents a bargain when it is compared with the price of nonintervention.

Behavioral Intervention

Although the application of behavior principles with children with mental retardation has had a relatively short history, the results have been impressive. Behavioral clinicians have effected changes in a wide variety of behaviors in both

institutional and school settings. Much of the pioneering research has been conducted with institutionalized children with severe and profound mental retardation
who were considered incapable of learning and who lived under custodial care conditions.

Self-Care. Self-care skills were notably lacking in institutionalized persons
with mental retardation prior to the 1970s. The application of behavior principles
has resulted in many children with moderate and severe retardation learning to
feed themselves with utensils, to dress and groom themselves, and to perform
household tasks such as sweeping floors, hanging and folding clothes, and making
beds. Perhaps the most significant behavior principle in teaching self-care skills has
been *backward chaining,* in which the children are taught the last step in a training
sequence first and the first step last. For example, the sequence of steps in teaching
a child to take his pants off might be as follows: (1) removes pants from one foot,
(2) removes pants from both feet, (3) pushes pants down from knee, (4) pushes
pants down from groin, (5) pushes pants down from waist. Similarly, in teaching
children to put their pants on, the first step would be to pull the pants from the
groin to the waist, and the last step would be placing the feet into the pant leg open-
ings. Each trial of a step that is completed correctly is reinforced with verbal praise,
a hug or pat, and, if necessary, food or tokens. Watson and Uzell (1981) have developed a comprehensive program for training staff to train clients with mental retardation in a wide variety of self-care skills.

Some skills are equally or more easily taught using a *forward chaining* technique. Again, the task is broken down into steps. Then the steps are taught in order.
For example, the order of steps in teaching the use of roll-on deodorant might be:
(1) pick up the deodorant, (2) shake the container, (3) remove the cap, (4) rub the
deodorant on one underarm, (5) put the deodorant in the other hand, (6) rub the
deodorant on the other underarm, (7) put the cap on the container. After the first
step is learned, each subsequent step is added to it; the client thus accumulates relatively greater practice with the earlier steps in the chain.

Physical guidance is usually added to the forward and backward chaining techniques. Physical guidance ensures that the client does not make errors. Applied
researchers (e.g., Azrin & Armstrong, 1973) have found that a combination of backward chaining and physical guidance is an effective method for teaching self-feeding. In this procedure, the child's hand is physically guided through the sequence
of picking up the spoon, putting food on the spoon, and bringing food to the
mouth; the hand is released immediately before the spoon enters the mouth, thus
allowing the child to complete the behavioral chain that is followed by reinforcement. This physical guidance is gradually decreased to allow the child to complete
greater portions of the behavioral chain, with the last step of physical guidance
involving picking up the spoon. Training in correct self-feeding, however, does not
automatically eliminate the quicker method of eating with the hands or food stealing. These inappropriate behaviors have been successfully decreased by short-term
(e.g., 15 seconds) removal of the plate for inappropriate feeding behaviors and
removal from the dining hall for stealing (Barton, Guess, Garcia, & Baer, 1970).

Toilet training of institutionalized individuals with mental retardation has also received considerable research attention because, like self-feeding, successful use of the toilet decreases the aversive chores of attendants, contributes to better social interactions between attendants and residents, and provides time for attendants to teach other constructive behaviors. Improved use of the toilet has been reported with the use of methods commonly used by parents of nondisabled children: placing the child on the toilet at intervals when the child is likely to urinate or defecate; rewarding the child for successes; and either ignoring or punishing "accidents." These methods typically lead to gradual decreases in accidents over a period of weeks or months. Azrin and Foxx (1974), however, devised a method whereby accidents were reduced by 80 percent after 1 to 14 days of intensive training. Their training procedure was carried out for 8 hours each day during which placement on the toilet was scheduled every 30 minutes, lasting for 20 minutes or until urination occurred, and fluids were given every 30 minutes. Special toilets were designed to signal urination or defecation immediately, as were moisture-sensitive pants that signaled accidents. Both social and edible reinforcers were given every five minutes if the resident was dry and after toilet successes. Azrin and Foxx's "package" also includes the procedures for establishing and maintaining self-initiated use of the toilet.

Another approach to toilet training has been proposed by Van Wagenen, Meyerson, Kerr, and Mahoney (1969). The child wears moisture-sensitive pants, and when the tone sounds, the trainer shouts "no," which has the effect of stopping urination briefly but long enough to get the child to the toilet where it can be resumed. Success at the toilet is then reinforced. All eight children with profound mental retardation in the training program for three to four hours each day responded to the tone by going to the toilet and voiding, within 45 hours or 15 days of training. These examples represent only a few research approaches to toilet training institutionalized children with mental retardation—approaches that opened up the possibility of toilet training to a large proportion of children previously believed to be untrainable (McCartney & Holden, 1981).

Language Acquisition. Language deficiencies are hallmark problems in persons with mental retardation. Many children with severe and profound mental retardation do not acquire even minimal language skills in their natural environments. During the past 20 years, behavioral researchers have been developing language programs that provide useful language repertoires for these children (McCoy & Buckholt, 1981). The principal language acquisition programs use operant conditioning procedures including positive reinforcement, aversive consequences, correction procedures, prompting, physical guidance, modeling, imitation, fading, shading, and chaining in teaching their curricula. To a greater or lesser degree, they also rely on normative and psycholinguistic data for structuring and sequencing the stages of the program. Guess, Sailor, and Keogh (1977) have reviewed the basic components of 12 different training models. One of the greatest problems with the current programs is that they are conducted in clinical or laboratory settings, and the language acquired there may not be generalized to the home setting.

Professionals are being encouraged to seek solutions to this problem by

1. Making the locus of language intervention the home and other places where the child spends much time, instead of the clinic or laboratory. Making the parents the primary language interventionists, with language therapists and other professionals serving as consultants.
2. Making better use of the linguistic knowledge the parent already possesses as a native speaker of the language. Also, to the extent possible, making the content and methods of intervention as close as possible to the "natural" methods and content of language acquisition, so that parents feel more comfortable.
3. Diagnosing and remedying difficulties in communication between parents and child, attending first to interactions taking place before the child begins to speak, including verbal and nonverbal interactions. Teaching parents to be sensitive to the child's attempts at communications, which may differ from those of a nondisabled child. Teaching effective forms of responsiveness and reciprocal communication.
4. Concentrating on giving parents simple, rather than complex, instructional guidelines and relying on their knowledge of the child and of the language to shape the specific course of intervention. (McCoy & Buckholt, 1981, p. 323)

Classroom Behavior. Behavior principles have also been utilized to improve both academic and nonacademic behaviors in classroom settings. Birnbrauer, Wolf, Kidder, and Tague (1965) designed a token economy in conjunction with social reinforcement for appropriate behaviors and timeout for inappropriate behaviors for two programmed classes for children with mental retardation and found that most of the children performed better when the token system was in effect. The behaviors observed in the classroom studies have typically been attending behaviors and specific inappropriate behaviors. Reinforcers such as tokens and free time have been shown to increase attending behaviors, while response cost (loss of tokens or free time) and timeout have been effective in decreasing inappropriate behaviors. Unfortunately, increases in attending behaviors and decreases in inappropriate behaviors do not necessarily lead to gains in the learning of academic material; such gains are optimally demonstrated when specific contingencies are arranged for correct strategies or answers, or both.

One of the most impressive behavioral projects is a curriculum for EMR children from 5 to 10 years of age (Ross & Ross, 1974) that is based on a series of experimental studies. The experimentally based training areas included in the curriculum are: (1) basic academic skills (reading, vocabulary, verbal expression, and arithmetic), (2) general learning skills (listening and following directions, planning, and problem solving), (3) social behavior, (4) gross and fine motor skills (physical education), and (5) fine arts (painting and music). In their studies, Ross and Ross used a combination of modeling the correct behavior, requiring the children to respond, and reinforcing the correctly modeled behavior with tokens that could be exchanged for prizes. The unique aspect of these studies is their successful attempt to teach children with mental retardation cognitive strategies that transfer to new situations.

A number of problem areas in applied behavioral research with children with mental retardation still remain. Although positive reinforcement and punishment have been quite effective in changing behavior, the improvements tend not to be maintained when the specific contingencies are removed and are rarely transferred to other behaviors or settings. Generalization and maintenance of behavioral gains are, therefore, important problem areas for future research. In addition, more attention needs to be focused on the selection and training of behaviors with long-term positive consequences, such as social behaviors required in everyday interactions and the asking of questions (Bondy & Erickson, 1976).

Aggressive, Self-Injurious, and Self-Stimulatory Behaviors. Children with mental retardation, particularly those who are institutionalized, are at an increased risk for serious behavior problems. Positive procedures, such as differential reinforcement of nonaggressive behaviors or a low rate of aggressive behavior, can be very effective, although time-consuming, and should be tried first. Neutral methods, such as extinction, may be effective after a prolonged period; however, some behaviors are too dangerous to be ignored. Negative or aversive procedures such as contingent electric shock, verbal reprimands, timeout, and overcorrection (excessively restoring the environment to its original condition) (Foxx & Azrin, 1972) have also been found to be effective, but they should not be considered for use unless attempts at reducing the aggressive behavior through positive and neutral procedures have been unsuccessful (Repp & Brulle, 1981).

The self-injurious behaviors observed in some persons with mental retardation can be severe and cause permanent injury or maiming (e.g., blindness from a detached retina due to head injury). In institutional settings, self-injurious behavior is often prevented by restraining (tying) such clients to the bed; restrained clients are, of course, not able to benefit from any programs that might improve their mental or physical status. According to Schroeder, Schroeder, Rojahn, and Mulick (1981), behavioral intervention for self-injurious behavior requires careful consideration of the behavior's topography, the setting, and the contingencies that maintain it. Gedye (1989) has presented data suggesting that extreme self-injury may be due to frontal lobe seizures and is not primarily voluntary. Other studies have suggested that some self-injurious behavior may be related to insufficient amounts of dopamine or interference in neurotransmitter function. If substantiated, these studies may suggest that certain pharmocological interventions may be helpful for treating and preventing certain types of self-injurious behavior (Schroeder, 1991).

Self-stimulatory behaviors are repetitive motor behaviors, such as hand waving, hand rubbing, and rocking in a stereotypic manner, that do not appear to produce positive environmental consequences or physical injury. It is assumed that persons with mental retardation and other developmental disabilities perform these behaviors to increase stimulation for themselves. The negative aspect of these behaviors is that they preclude other activities or learning. It is important that intervention programs to decrease self-stimulatory behavior also include components for teaching and reinforcing adaptive behavior (O'Brien, 1981). Attempts to decrease self-stimulatory behavior by reinforcing other behaviors have not been consistently successful. However, significant decreases have been reported when consequences, such as electric shock, timeout, verbal reprimands, overcorrection, and interruption of the behavior, are applied. A review of research by LaGrow and Repp (1984) indicated that contingent electric shock was the most effective procedure, and that there were no significant differences in effectiveness among the remaining aversive and positive procedures.

Some people feel very strongly that aversive stimulation should never be used with persons with mental retardation; the issue reduces to the ethics of leaving the person with the behavior problem versus presenting some discomfort in order to give the person the opportunity to live without the problem (Schroeder & Schroeder, 1989). This controversy seems to have led to a decrease in research that examines the effectiveness of aversive interventions (Butterfield, 1989). At the same time, attempts are being made to design programs that can be conducted without the deliberate use of aversive procedures (McGee, Menolascino, Hobbs, & Menousek, 1987; Walker, 1989).

Psychotherapy

The indications for psychotherapy with children with mental retardation are essentially the same as those for nondisabled children, namely, maladaptive behaviors. Emotional and behavioral problems are two to three times more common in children and adolescents with mental retardation than in the general population (Tonge, Einfeld, Krupinski, Mackenzie, McLaughlin, Florio, & Nunn, 1996). Einfeld and Tonge (1996) reported that 40.7 percent of 4- to 18-year-olds with mental retardation could be classified with a severe emotional or behavioral disorder or as being psychiatrically disordered. Several types of psychotherapy have been utilized with children with mental retardation. Play therapy has perhaps been used most frequently with younger children with mental retardation because of their less-developed verbal skills. Newcomer and Morrison (1974) reported a study in which 5- to 20-year-old institutionalized children with mild and moderate mental retardation were given individual play therapy, group play therapy, or no therapy. The results indicated that the no-therapy group showed no progress, but both play therapy groups improved on the Gross Motor, Fine Motor, Language, and Personal-Social scales of the Denver Developmental Screening Test (Frankenburg & Dodds, 1970) over 30 sessions (18 weeks) of therapy. The therapy techniques used in this study were based on the earlier writings of Axline (1947) and Leland and Smith (1965). In a second study Morrison and Newcomer (1975) found no differences in improvement between children with mental retardation given directive play therapy and those given nondirective play therapy.

Group psychotherapy has been reported most often with older children with mental retardation, particularly adolescents, and is usually conducted in institutional settings in which groups may be easily formed. Group therapy is viewed as having particular advantages for individuals with mental retardation: increasing the residents' awareness of the problems of others, reducing social withdrawal, and orienting the residents toward the immediate environment.

Very few well-designed studies on the effectiveness of psychotherapy with older children with mental retardation are available; of these studies, several report increases in IQ scores and improvement of behavioral problems, while the remaining ones report no differences between treatment and no-treatment groups. These results, however, are similar to those of studies with nondisabled children.

Physical Interventions

Until relatively recently, physical treatment of mental retardation had been either not feasible or unsuccessful. One type of physical intervention that is now often used with individuals with mental retardation is medication. Various types of medication are employed primarily to control seizures and to aid in behavior management. Drug therapy is effective for controlling seizures in approximately 70 to 85 percent of patients. In a small-scale study, Varley and Trupin (1982) reported that 5 out of 10 children with mental retardation and who met the DSM-III diagnostic criteria for attention deficit disorder showed significant behavioral improvement in their school and home environments with the administration of methylphenidate (Ritalin).

In the treatment of seizures, phenobarbital is a commonly used medication because it has been effective for a broad range of seizure disorders. Dilantin is also frequently used to control certain types of seizures, particularly grand mal seizures, which are characterized by total loss of consciousness and repetitive motor movements. For optimal seizure control and to counteract various drug side effects, combinations of medications may be employed. Seizures in some children with mental retardation cannot, however, be eliminated with our current medications. Concern has also been raised about inappropriate use of anticonvulsant medication for institutionalized persons with mental retardation (Kaufman & Katz-Garris, 1979).

Use of psychoactive drugs with persons with mental retardation is widespread, especially in institutional settings. There have been complaints that these drugs are used excessively as substitutes for behavioral training programs. A study by Lipman (1970), for example, surveyed over 100 institutions with nearly 150,000 residents with mental retardation and found that 37 percent were being administered major tranquilizers, 8 percent minor tranquilizers, and 4 percent antidepressants. More recent surveys (Aman & Singh, 1991) indicate that this practice is still widespread, with 30 percent to 50 percent of institutionalized individuals with mental retardation receiving psychotropic medication. In contrast, children with mental retardation who live in the community are much less likely to receive psychotropic medication. Approximately 3 percent to 7 percent of school-age children with mental retardation are prescribed psychotropic medications.

Unless carefully monitored, one could expect to find large percentages of residents of institutions being given psychotropic medications because the resulting changes in behavior are very likely to reduce the amount of work required by attendants, who, in many instances, are responsible for 20 or more residents. Thus, the combined shortage of personnel and the unavailability of programs for behavior management make drugs an attractive alternative. Findholt and Emmett (1990) reported significant reductions in the use of psychotropic medications when an institution initiated interdisciplinary review of each resident's medication every six months.

One of the most dramatic breakthroughs in treatment and prevention has been the development of special diets for children with some of the hereditary disorders. In the case of galactosemia, for example, the omission of milk and other foods containing lactose from the child's diet prevents most of the mental retardation. When the diet is initiated soon after birth, the effect on intelligence test scores is greatest (Kalakar, Konoshita, & Donnell, 1973); however, some improvement occurs even when the diet is begun later in the infancy period. The diet is usually continued through the preschool years, although deprivation of milk and milk products may continue for longer periods. A number of the treated children do seem to have learning problems in school and visual-motor difficulties. Two of the problems associated with the evaluation of dietary treatment programs are that (1) the child may obtain and ingest the forbidden foods without the parents' knowledge, and (2) the deprivation of these foods may have negative effects on other areas of functioning.

Perhaps the most well-known diet is that used for children with phenylketonuria (PKU). This diet restricts the intake of foods containing phenylalanine, the substance that cannot be metabolized and is responsible for the ensuing brain damage. Most of the children placed on the diet very early in life do not develop mental retardation, although a large study in England found that treated PKU children had some behavior problems such as hyperactivity, anxiety, and social withdrawal (Smith, Beasley, Wolff, & Ades, 1988). Later initiation of the diet, although ineffective in reversing the brain damage already present, has been found to improve behavior problems and to facilitate the effectiveness of drugs for seizure control. The diet is difficult to administer in that extreme restriction of phenylalanine leads to protein loss in the body and growth retardation. New advances in dietary control offer the promise of complete prevention of mental retardation in children with PKU. Commercially prepared milk substitutes are available. Most children are taken off the diet between the ages of six and nine years, but Fishler et al. (1987) recommend its continuance to age 10 based on their psychoeducational findings. Women with PKU have a very high probability of having children with mental retardation. It is possible that strict adherence to the diet immediately before and during pregnancy could prevent mental retardation in their offspring (Rohn et al., 1987).

Facial plastic surgery has been proposed as one way to improve the quality of life of Down syndrome persons whose physical appearance may accentuate their mental retardation. This surgery often involves reduction of tongue size, implants to the bridge of the nose, chin, cheeks, and jawbone, and plastic surgery to the eyelids. Use of this surgery is controversial among plastic surgeons (May & Turnbull, 1992). The great majority of parents whose Down syndrome children have had plastic surgery express satisfaction with it and would recommend it to others, but very few changes in the children's behaviors have been demonstrated (Katz & Kravetz, 1989).

CONCLUSIONS

Mental retardation refers to a subaverage rate in the development of cognitive and adaptive behaviors detectable before the age of 18. The criteria for diagnosis have been established by the American Association on Mental Retardation and are generally accepted by clinicians and researchers. The current diagnostic standards of the American Association on Mental Retardation have eliminated references to severity of mental retardation and have moved to a functional model of description. The diagnostic standards of the American Psychiatric Association have maintained classification of mental retardation using a deficit model. The causes of mental retardation include genetic, pre-, peri-, and postnatal physical factors as well as environmental and psychological factors. The cause or causes of mental retardation in *individual* children cannot, however, be specified in the majority of cases.

Although cures for mental retardation are rare, several intervention approaches have reduced or prevented mental retardation in high-risk children—namely, special diets for children with certain genetic abnormalities and stimulation or education programs, or both, for disadvantaged children. Behavioral approaches to the treatment of children with mental retardation have been successful in the teaching of a variety of self-care and cognitive skills.

RECOMMENDED READINGS

Baroff, G.S. (1991). *Developmental disabilities: Psychosocial aspects.* Austin, TX: Pro-ed.

Garber, H. (1988). *The Milwaukee Project: Preventing mental retardation in children at risk.* Washington, DC: American Association on Mental Retardation.

Jacobson, J.W., & Mulick, J.A. (Eds.). (1996). *Manual of diagnosis and professional practice in mental retardation.* Washington, DC: American Psychological Association.

MacLean, W.E. Jr. (Ed.). (1996). *Handbook of mental deficiency, psychological theory and research.* Mahwah, NJ: Lawrence Erlbaum.

Matson, J.L., & Mulick, J.A. (Eds.). (1991). *Handbook of mental retardation* (2nd ed.). New York: Pergamon Press.

Odom, S.L., & Karnes, M.B. (Eds.). (1988). *Early intervention for infants and children with handicaps: An empirical base.* Baltimore: Paul H. Brookes.

Rowitz, L. (Ed.). (1992). *Mental retardation in the year 2000.* New York: Springer-Verlag.

Schroeder, S. (Ed.). (1987). *Toxic substances and mental retardation.* Washington, DC: American Association on Mental Retardation.

9

Pervasive Developmental Disorders and Schizophrenia

Tim, a three-year-old boy, was referred by his family physician because he exhibited unusual behaviors and lacked a number of behaviors, particularly social and verbal skills. The physician had seen Tim only a few times, and only when he was physically ill, during the past two years.

This chapter was revised by Andrew Bondy, Ph.D.

Tim was the second son of a young couple in their 20s. He was conceived four months after the birth of their first child when the mother believed that she could not get pregnant while breast-feeding the older child. She went to her physician complaining that she had not yet had a period, and he gave her a shot which was supposed to bring it on. The mother reported that she became extremely ill after the shot; she experienced severe nausea, vomiting, and dizziness for a week and had to remain in bed.

The pregnancy was later confirmed and proceeded uneventfully. The birth was normal, with Tim weighing a little over eight pounds. The mother reported that there were some difficulties caring for two infants, but that Tim was a very good baby and gave her no trouble at all. In fact, he seemed happier when left alone. The mother recalled that Tim didn't smile and didn't seem to recognize her as a young infant. He learned to walk early, at nine months, and from the beginning was especially adept at motor skills, never falling or hurting himself.

The parents first became concerned about Tim's development during his second year when he did not begin to talk. They were advised that he was probably a "late bloomer" and perhaps did not need to talk because his needs were being anticipated by his parents. Their concern increased, however, as they gradually realized that Tim was not responding to them, and they insisted on a hearing test, the results of which indicated no hearing loss. The continued lack of speech and responsiveness to people and an increase in unusual behaviors, such as turning the wheels of his toy cars and rocking his body for long periods, finally led to his referral.

Children such as Tim display perhaps the most severe of the behavior disorders because most of the child's behavioral repertoire is affected. Although they occur rarely in comparison with other types of behavior disorders, these children have received a great amount of attention from psychiatrists and psychologists. This attention has been reflected in the substantial body of clinical research on assessment, etiology, and treatment.

ASSESSMENT AND DIAGNOSIS

Over the past several decades, there has been a great deal of professional discussion about the appropriate terms used to describe children with complex behavioral characteristics like Tim's. As for children with other disorders, the family physician is usually the first professional from whom the family seeks assistance. If a serious behavior disorder is suspected, the physician will probably refer the family to a child psychiatrist. Often, however, the child's behaviors may suggest other possible problems, and referral to a mental health professional may be delayed for months or even years. Diagnosis by the psychiatrist is based primarily on the interview with the parents and observation of the child in the office. The psychiatrist frequently requests psychological testing and sometimes a complete physical examination to aid in the diagnosis.

A proliferation of labels referring to the type of severe behavior disorder noted in the previous example has appeared in the research and diagnostic literature. Unfortunately, even the same label does not always have the same meaning for different investigators. The reader should be aware that some clinicians and researchers have used the terms *childhood psychosis, childhood schizophrenia, atypical child,* and *autism* interchangeably. Recently, there is increasing convergence toward the term *pervasive developmental disorder* as reflective of the broad impact this type of disorder has upon all aspects of a child's development. Within DSM-IV, there are several specific types of pervasive developmental disorder (PDD), including Autism, Rett's Disorder, Disintegrative Disorder, and Asperger's Disorder, and PDD not otherwise specified.

Autism

In 1943, Leo Kanner made the first attempt to describe a particular type of childhood psychosis when he published a paper entitled "Autistic Disturbances of Affective Contact." His original description of *early infantile autism* included the following features that were considered to be characteristic of the condition: (1) severe withdrawal of contact with other people, (2) an intense need to preserve sameness, (3) an inability to deal with people, (4) particular skills in motor functioning, (5) apparently good intellectual potential as reflected by average or better performance on some tasks and by an intelligent facial expression, and (6) severe disturbance of language functioning.

During his career Kanner examined several thousand psychotic children referred by other clinicians; he diagnosed fewer than 200 of them as having early infantile autism. Kanner's criterion that the child have at least one area of normal functioning was probably the basis for separating children with early infantile autism from the many other children who also manifested other autistic behaviors. In other words, there were perhaps a substantial number of children referred to Kanner who showed most of the features of autism, but only a relatively small percentage who gave evidence of having a particular ability that was age-appropriate or above. This evidence for normal functioning in at least one area of development has been inferred by many clinicians to reflect the child's potential in all areas, potential that was somehow being masked by the autism. If no evidence of normality was present, the child was probably considered to be mentally retarded.

The relationship between mental retardation and autism has been a subject of controversy among clinicians. For theoretical reasons that will be discussed later the earlier clinicians did not consider the mental retardation that was observed in the majority of autistic children to be severe or irreversible. It was viewed more as an artifact of the test situation and the child's inability to relate to others (including the tester). The assumption was that the autistic child was in fact quite intelligent but "chose" not to demonstrate intelligence.

In the past, it seemed particularly important to decide whether a child was autistic or retarded, probably because retardation implied a more permanent condition, and autism was inferred to be a problem that could receive remedial aid. More contemporary clinicians are deemphasizing this aspect of differential diagnosis and are increasingly recognizing that the retardation observed in autistic children represents true deficits.

DSM-IV (1994) describes three major areas of concern regarding autism. The first area involves impairments regarding social interactions. Individuals with autism have impairment in their social interactions with other adults and children. Social interactions are regulated and modified through several means. Children with autism demonstrate particular difficulty in their use of nonverbal behaviors to initiate and respond to social interactions. For example, many of these children rarely display appropriate eye contact either to look at someone who is speaking or to get others to look at them when they speak. Similarly, these children display difficulty acquiring the use of facial expressions or related body language (i.e., posture, proximity, gestures, etc.) to produce more effective social interactions, and have comparable difficulty in understanding the use of such social cues by other people.

Autistic children typically fail to develop friendships and similar social roles that correspond to their developmental age. They often fail to initiate demonstrations of sharing their interests or pointing out important aspects or changes in the environment, such as pointing to items that spill or break, or sharing news about their own accomplishments. Young children with autism are often noted for the infrequency with which they imitate their peers, either in action, play themes, or speech. Individuals with autism often fail to show empathy for the emotional reactions of other people, such as not seeking to comfort someone in pain or distress, not smiling or laughing in response to someone else's joy, or not spontaneously helping someone who appears frustrated.

The second major area addressed within DSM-IV involves impairments associated with the development of language. Children with autism demonstrate a significant delay, or total lack of, the development of spoken language. Furthermore, this delay or absence of speech is not accompanied by the development of other forms of communication, such as the use of systematic gestures or mime. About 80 percent of preschoolers entering intervention programs show no use of functional communication. When some children with autism do repeat things they have heard, it is often without meaning. For those children who can talk, there generally is a marked limitation of initiated speech (i.e., speech in the absence of prior direct questions or models). Furthermore, when other people attempt to engage a person with autism in a meaningful conversation, that person often exhibits marked impairment in his or her ability to sustain the dialogue.

When autistic children acquire speech, it is often characterized by unusual repetitive and stereotypic patterns. For example, a child may use the same tone of voice for all statements (whether declarative statements or questions), or appear to have virtually no tone at all (i.e., a flat affect). Other ritualistic uses of language may include perseveration on a particular phrase or topic. Some children seem to have fairly complex language but manage to turn every conversation into their favorite topic, whether it is cars, dates, animals, etc. Other children with relatively strong language skills may have difficulty in engaging in make-believe play routines or in being able to act out a social role commensurate with their developmental level.

For these children, playing with dolls as representative of people in different roles (i.e., teachers, nurses, doctors, etc.) remains remarkably difficult.

The third broad area of concern within DSM-IV involves a host of repetitive and stereotyped patterns of behaviors. Some of these children engage in particular forms of self-stimulation that involve flicking fingers or hands, spinning themselves or objects, or holding or moving the extremities in a peculiar fashion. These actions are of great concern because these children often seem to focus their attention on these stereotypic actions to the exclusion of attending to important events within the environment. While some children engage in these routines with a part of their body, other children use particular objects around them, such as pulling thread out of their socks, spinning small objects, lining up objects in a set pattern, or repeatedly writing the same letters.

Another behavior pattern that can be difficult to address involves a child's extreme resistance to changes in the physical environment or the temporal sequence of events. For example, a child with autism may display an intense tantrum after the furniture in a room has been rearranged. Another child with autism may become aggressive when library class is substituted for the usual cooking class. Furthermore, when a child's ritualistic pattern is interrupted or blocked, that child may become distraught for extended periods of time.

Within the DSM-IV guidelines, autism can be identified when a person displays at least six total features, including two features within social orientation and one within each of the other areas. Furthermore, delays or abnormal functioning in the areas of social interaction, language as used in social communication, or symbolic or imaginative play must be noted prior to age three years. Although the disorder is formally diagnosed only infrequently prior to age two years, one recent review of birthday party videotapes of children at one year of age was able to predict subsequent diagnosis in over 90 percent of cases (Osterling & Dawson, 1994). The most distinguishing features at that age included not orienting to one's name, not pointing to interesting things or events, and not looking at someone else's face.

Kanner's papers on early infantile autism greatly influenced research and clinical work in the area. His original descriptions of the characteristics of autistic children continued to be widely used until the 1980s. The incidence of Kanner-type autistic children has been estimated at 5 per 100,000 (Rimland, 1964, p. 139). Epidemiological studies, however, reveal that the incidence is 4.5 per 10,000 when DSM-III criteria are used—a rate 10 times that found when Kanner's requirement of at least one area of normal functioning is included. In other words, only about 10 percent of children diagnosed as autistic on the basis of DSM-III criteria have at least one area of normal functioning.

Infantile autism typically originates very early in the child's life. Short and Schopler (1988) found that 76 percent of autistic children were identified by their parents by 24 months, and 94 percent by 36 months. Unfortunately, delays of several years between parental observations and placement into intervention programs are common (Siegel, Pliner, Eschler, & Elliott, 1988). Parents frequently report that their autistic children did not tense their bodies in anticipation of being picked up and were not responsive in social situations during the first year. During this period the parents often become concerned about possible deafness because the infant's responses to sound seem to be inconsistent. Hearing tests usually reveal that the child's ability to hear is normal. Parents also report that the infant seems happiest when left alone. Excessive repetitive body movements, such as rocking and head banging, are very common.

During the second year, the child's lack of social responsiveness becomes more apparent. In contrast to younger normal children, autistic children do not make eye contact (look at another person's eyes) and only infrequently turn toward the sound of a person's voice. The absence or severe delay of speech begins to be recognized during this period when most children are beginning to acquire labels for common objects. Some parents have reported the use of a few words, which were later "lost."

Many clinicians believe that the autistic features are most pronounced around the age of three or four years, an age when many autistic children are referred and diagnosed. Eye contact and speech development continue to be absent or minimal. If speech has begun to develop, certain abnormalities are likely to be present. The voice quality may be unusual and intonation exaggerated. *Echolalia*, a repetition of a speaker's words, is often a characteristic of autistic children with speech. For example, if asked "Do you want a cookie?" the echolalic child responds "Do you want a cookie?" Some echolalic children display remarkable memory for phrases and television commercials, which may be repeated long after they were originally heard. If they do learn functional speech, autistic children tend to use minimal speech; that is, one word may convey the meaning of several sentences. The meaning conveyed in their speech continues to be literal and concrete; abstract, subtle, or symbolic meanings are seldom utilized.

The motor development of autistic children may be normal, retarded, or superior, but it is usually the child's most advanced area of functioning. Some autistic children show remarkable skills in visual-motor tasks, such as completing puzzles, and tasks involving visual discrimination (for example, rapid learning to discriminate among printed words). Both hyperactivity and hypoactivity are considered to be characteristic of autistic children. Peculiar repetitive movements, such as arm flapping, hand twisting, spinning, facial grimacing, and walking on tiptoe, are also frequently reported. Their play behavior with toy vehicles, for example, may consist solely of a repetitive spinning of the wheels.

Although relatively unresponsive to auditory stimuli, certain sounds appear to generate greater than normal responses in autistic children. Music, for example, may be particularly enjoyed; some autistic children learn to sing before learning to talk and can reproduce complex tunes. Some sounds, such as loud noises and speech, appear to be aversive in that the child will move away, cover his or her ears, or become distressed in their presence.

Responses to other sensory experiences may also be unusual in the autistic child. For example, some autistic children are described as being insensitive to pain in that they do not cry or complain when they are obviously physically hurt. Autistic children sometimes spend long periods of time feeling materials of certain textures and repeatedly scratching surfaces. Vigorous physical play, including tickling and swinging, is particularly enjoyed and often the only occasion when the child laughs or appears happy.

Although they are typically described as being remote, aloof, or distant, autistic children react with temper outbursts on occasion. The temper tantrums may be the result of a frustration, but they also seem to occur randomly. Laughing and giggling are also likely to occur and stop suddenly for no apparent reason. Autistic children seem to lack the normal fears of real dangers, but they often exhibit fear of harmless objects and events.

Infantile autism is considered to be a chronic disorder and is about three times more common in boys than girls. About 90 percent of autistic children have IQ scores in the mentally retarded range (DeMyer et al., 1974). Most of them remain severely handicapped and are unable to function independently at maturity. The most important prognostic factor for status at ages 16–23 years are IQ at diagnosis and communicative speech development before the age of six years (Gillberg & Steffenburg, 1987). Some autistic children with higher IQ scores and better language skills do eventually lead independent lives, but poor social skills frequently persist. A very small number of the parents of autistic children appear to meet the criteria for autism (Ritvo, Brothers, Freeman, & Pingree, 1988), suggesting that marriage and parenting are possible for some autistic persons.

Rett's Disorder

Another, very rare (estimated incidence is 1 in 15,000 births), pervasive developmental disorder identified within DSM-IV, and only noted in females, is Rett's disorder. The disorder is characterized by persistent and ritualistic-like hand movements resembling hand wringing. These children apparently have normal motor development for the first five months of life. There follows a loss of typically developed intentional hand motions over the course of the next two years. Other significant problems include diminished social interest, as well as severe impairments in language skills (both expressive and receptive). Children with Rett's disorder may display emotional signs of joy and sadness within a few seconds of each other without a corresponding significant change in their surroundings. Most of these children function in the severe or profound range of mental retardation.

One significant physiological characteristic is a marked deceleration of head growth, following five months of normal head circumference development, during the first four years after birth. Virtually all of these children develop seizures. Children with Rett's syndrome also appear to have poorly coordinated fine (i.e., use of their hands and fingers) and gross motor skills, including walking or other whole-body actions. Difficulties with walking often persist and a high proportion of adolescents and adults must use wheelchairs. Thus far, the reported prognosis for this disorder is very poor.

Childhood Disintegrative Disorder

Another form of pervasive developmental disorder has a markedly distinct developmental course when compared to autism. In childhood disintegrative disorder (also known as Heller's syndrome or disintegrative psychosis), the child displays apparent normal development for the first two years of life. After this time (usually between ages 3 and 4 years but prior to age 10 years), the child displays a significant loss in acquired skills associated with language use and understanding, social interactions and play, as well as various motor skills. There is a concomitant increase in stereotypic and repetitive nonfunctional actions. Although specific prevalence figures are limited, the condition appears to be very rare.

Asperger's Disorder

Some children display behavioral difficulties related to social interactions and stereotypic areas of interest and behavior similar to that observed in autism. However, these children, who are identified as having Asperger's disorder, are not observed to have delays in early language development and adaptive or self-help skills, unlike children identified as autistic. Although these children often acquire age-appropriate language skills, they display marked impairments in the use of speech and nonverbal behaviors, including eye contact, facial expressions, and body posture to govern typical social interactions. These limitations significantly interfere with the development of friendships. Their rituals frequently revolve around routines (i.e., when particular TV shows air, the order of school topics reviewed, etc.) or body actions (i.e., complex whole-body movements, particular finger play, etc.). These children typically display age-appropriate cognitive skills and thus often achieve grade-appropriate academic skills. However, their limitations associated with social interactions may decrease their school or vocational success (or even opportunities). These children usually require specific social skill training to be able to utilize their academic and other cognitive competencies within mainstream community settings. A 4:1 male-female ratio has been noted, with a prevalence rate of 3–4 per 1,000 (Ehlers & Gillberg, 1993).

Pervasive Developmental Disorder Not Otherwise Specified

Some children display persistent and significant impairment in their social interactions, use of functional communication, or degree of stereotypic actions and interests as noted in autism but not of sufficient degree to warrant a specific PDD diagnosis. In such cases, a diagnosis of PDD not otherwise specified (PDD-NOS) or *atypical autism* may be noted. In most cases of PDD-NOS, this diagnosis is used when a child displays some of the critical features of autism but not the number, severity, or pattern of the full syndrome can be identified. For example, a young boy might display unusual language development (such as echolalia) and have limited social skills (such as not developing friendships) but no bizarre, ritualistic play or behavioral patterns have been observed. This boy may not warrant a diagnosis of autism because he does not display problems in each of the three primary areas previously noted. For this category to be used, the clinician must be certain that no other diagnosis, such as schizophrenia, would more appropriately describe the condition.

Schizophrenia

Schizophrenia is diagnosed in approximately 1 percent of the adult population. However, only a small percentage (approximately 4 percent) of adult schizophrenics became psychotic during childhood; onset is usually during adolescence or early adulthood. The majority of schizophrenic children continue to be considered schizophrenic throughout adulthood, with the remaining individuals being relabeled mentally retarded (Bennett & Klein, 1966).

The DSM-IV criteria for schizophrenia involve several distinct features. The first concerns symptoms involving at least two of the following features: delusions, hallucinations, disorganized speech, grossly disorganized or catatonic behavior, and negative symptoms, such as a flat affect or displaying little volition. These features must be displayed for at least one month. Furthermore, the presence of these symptoms must have a significant negative impact upon routine social behaviors (including personal care, blunted or inappropriate affect, the expression of odd beliefs or magical thinking) or vocational functioning (significant impairment in maintaining a job). The duration of these disturbances of functioning must be at least six months.

Schizophrenia can be diagnosed only if other disorders have been ruled out, such as affective or mood disorders (including major depression with psychotic features), disturbance due to substance abuse (or medication) or known medical condition, and pervasive developmental disorder. If pervasive developmental disorder has been previously established, then the diagnosis of schizophrenia is made only if significant delusions or hallucinations have been identified lasting at least a month. It is rare for an individual to be diagnosed as autistic and then later to be diagnosed as schizophrenic. The median age for the first psychotic episode for schizophrenics is in the mid-20s (with the first episodes tending to appear earlier in males than in females), while autism is identified prior to 30 months of age. The prognosis for psychosocial adjustment for schizophrenics diagnosed as adolescents as opposed to young adults is poor (Cawthron, James, Dell & Seagroatt, 1994; Gillberg, Hellgren, & Gillberg, 1993).

The distinction between autism and childhood schizophrenia has not yet been clearly made, except perhaps for age of onset. Using a retrospective approach, Watkins, Asarnow, and Tanguay (1988) examined symptom development from birth in a group of 18 children who met the criteria for schizophrenia before 10 years of age; they found that 72 percent of the children had language deficits and motor development problems and 39 percent had symptoms of autism prior to 6 years of age, but none met the criteria for schizophrenia before 6 years of age. The onset of schizophrenia occurred at an earlier age for the children who had histories of autistic symptoms during infancy.

In a comparison of nonretarded autistic, schizophrenic, and normal children between the ages of 8 and 14 years on a number of psychological tests, Schneider and Asarnow (1987) concluded that autistic and schizophrenic children had different cognitive impairments—namely, a core deficit in momentary processing capacity in schizophrenia and a core cognitive deficit in the ability to use language to regulate and control ongoing behavior in autism.

Mental retardation is not considered to be a cardinal feature of childhood schizophrenics, but between one-third and one-half have IQ scores in the mentally retarded range. Psychotic children are difficult to assess with standardized tests. With autistic children, the examiner must frequently use infant tests in order to obtain a basal mental age for language items. Testing tends to be prolonged both because the autistic child's behavior is rarely under social control and because the range between the basal mental age and ceiling mental age is much wider than average.

Schizophrenic children's test behavior is likely to be very erratic; they may successfully complete complex tasks and then fail simpler ones. The persistent examiner often finds the schizophrenic child's IQ score to be within normal limits and achievement scores to be low. Both autistic and schizophrenic children present severe educational problems and require special education programs.

For the present, behavioral assessment appears to offer the most relevant data for planning remedial programs. Although many of the psychotic child's behavioral excesses and deficits are obvious during the initial interview process, formal observations are usually scheduled in addition to the behavioral interview and standardized test administration.

Certain diagnostic problems could be solved with further research. We need to learn more about the developmental norms of psychotic children, that is, to design longitudinal studies in which standard behavioral assessments are conducted at specific ages over a period of years. This behavioral assessment could ideally include all aspects of the children's behavioral repertoire rather than just the presence or absence of psychotic characteristics. Analyses could then be performed on the behavioral data collected at each age level to determine the extent to which behaviors are related. The results would provide some guidance about the possible types of psychoses and the behaviors associated with each type as the children get older.

ETIOLOGY

Historically, the lack of common criteria for the diagnosis of childhood psychoses has posed a substantial impediment to our understanding of etiological factors. Some of the investigators examining etiological factors in childhood psychoses have selected a specific type of psychosis, while others have used heterogeneous groups of psychotic children. Unfortunately, adequate descriptive characteristics of individual children are not available in most of the research articles.

Autism

Genetic Factors. The only abnormal morphology of the chromosomes associated with autism has been the Fragile X syndrome (a specific marker on the male's only X chromosome); it has been found in 10 to 12 percent of persons diagnosed with autism. There is some evidence (Sudhalter, Cohen, Silverman, & Wolf-Schein, 1990) that mentally retarded males with Fragile X syndrome can be discriminated from non-Fragile X autistic as well as Down syndrome persons on the basis of language behavior; the autistic Fragile X males produced significantly more perseverative deviant language but less deviant language when answering questions and imitating communication as well as less echolalia than the autistic males without Fragile X.

Probably because autism is relatively rare, only a few behavior genetic twin studies have been reported. Judd and Mandell (1968) reported that concordance was close to 100 percent in a small sample of identical twins for which zygosity had been adequately established. Folstein and Rutter (1977) found that none of 10 fraternal pairs was concordant for autism, but 4 of 11 identical pairs were concordant. In a survey of Scandinavian autistic twins, Steffenburg et al. (1989) found a concordance of 91 percent for "monozygotic twins and zero percent for 10 dizygotic twins." The latter two studies also reported that in most of the discordant pairs, the autistic twin had more perinatal stress. Rutter and Bartak (1971) have proposed the presence of some small, but significant, genetic contribution based on the finding that the rate of autism in siblings (approximately 2 percent) is considerably above the population rate of 4 or 5 per 10,000.

A statewide study in Utah failed to confirm the results of studies showing that siblings of autistic children had higher than expected levels of cognitive dysfunction (Freeman et al., 1989). Folstein and Rutter (1988) maintain that the research literature suggests that genetic factors play an important role in the etiology of autism; they proposed that "it is not autism itself that is inherited but an abnormality of language or sociality that interacts with other factors to produce autism" (p. 3). The data reported on the heritability of autism could be interpreted as supporting a physical, rather than a genetic, basis for autism. The higher concordance rates for identical twins might be, at least in part, due to an interactive effect of physical insult occurring during the prenatal or perinatal period when identical twins are more equally vulnerable (are in comparable embryological stages of development) than are fraternal twins.

Rimland (1964) proposed an interesting theory that includes both genetic and biological factors. He hypothesized that Kanner-type autistic children inherit genes for high intelligence and that high intelligence requires a higher level of oxygen supply to the brain. Thus, children with the genes for high intelligence would be more vulnerable to pre-, peri-, and postnatal factors that affect the brain's oxygen supply.

Physical Factors. In his original paper, Kanner (1943) clearly specified his assumption that autism was due to some biological defect, but the role of biological factors in the etiology of autism was not seriously examined until the later 1960s.

A number of studies have found higher than normal rates of prenatal and perinatal complications in autistic children (e.g., Gillberg & Gillberg, 1983; Levy, Zoltak, & Saelens, 1988). Larger-scale studies of autistic children confirm higher incidences of bleeding during pregnancy, fetal anoxia, and forceps deliveries. DeMyer (1979) found possible biological etiological factors in about 88 percent of autistic children during the first three years of life. Chess (1971) reported an increased incidence of autism (using Kanner's criteria) in children infected with rubella during the prenatal period, suggesting a possible role of prenatal physical factors.

High rates of neurological abnormalities have also been reported for autistic children (Gillberg, 1988). Rutter, Bartak, and Newman (1971) found that 29 percent of the autistic children they followed over a 12- to 24-year period developed seizures during adolescence or adulthood.

A variety of neurological studies have revealed that autistic children have more signs of malfunctioning central nervous systems than normal children, but the rates of neurological signs in autistic children are comparable to those of retarded children. Higher rates of abnormality have been found in neurological examinations, fingerprint patterns, hand dominance, right-left orientation, EEG, brain scans, and tissue and fluid analyses (DeMyer, Hingtgen, & Jackson, 1981). For example, using brain scans, Gillberg and Svendsen (1983) found gross abnormalities in 26 percent of the autism cases. Attempts to identify specific types or sites of the brain damage have not been successful, but various neurological models have been presented (Prior, 1987) now that there is more confidence in the presence of neurological disorder (Gillberg, Steffenburg, & Jakobsson, 1987).

Psychological Factors. Until fairly recently, the dominant view among clinicians has been that childhood psychosis is a functional disorder, that is, one caused by adverse psychological conditions. These adverse conditions have been described primarily in terms of parent-child interactions by proponents of both psychodynamic and behavior theory. Most of what has been learned about the parents of psychotic children has been derived from the clinical assessment of parents during or after diagnosis and interpretation of the child's condition. In this context, a number of studies have reported that the parents of psychotic children are themselves clinically deviant. Virtually all of these studies, which are basically correlational in design, assumed that the parents' problems originated before the child's problem and that the parents' psychological problems in some way caused the child's psychosis.

Attention to the parental role was initiated by Kanner's (1954) description of the parental characteristics of his first 100 autistic children. As a group, these parents were highly intelligent, and the majority of fathers were employed as professionals. Although Kanner noted that there was very little mental illness in the families of the autistic children, the parents were described as very obsessive, unemotional, and lacking in warmth ("refrigerator parents"). Bettelheim (1967) took a more extreme position, arguing that autism was the child's defense against the hostility of parents who had emotionally rejected the child.

Ferster (1961) used behavior principles to account for the development of autistic behavior and thereby implicated parent-child relationships in the etiology of autism. He suggested that the behavior of autistic children is quantitatively, not qualitatively, different from that of normal children, that is, characterized by very low response rates. Ferster hypothesized that these very low response rates may be the result of the parents' failure to provide adequate reinforcement for the development of a normal response repertoire. Yates (1970, p. 257) has pointed out the similarity between Ferster's description of the parental role and Kanner's "refrigerator parent" concept.

After a long period of assuming that parents had a primary role in causing their children's autism, clinicians have begun to acknowledge that indeed there are no data to support that assumption. A number of studies have shown that, although the parents of autistic children show more evidence of psychological problems than the parents of normal children, they show no more evidence of these problems than do the parents of children with other types of handicaps, such as mental retardation, brain damage, and dysphasia (Erickson, 1968a; DeMyer et al., 1972; Cantwell, Baker, & Rutter, 1979).

These studies also indicate that the parents do not have unusual personality characteristics such as coldness, obsessiveness, rage, or social anxiety, nor do they show particular deficits in caring for infants and young children. A 1988 study by Burd et al. showed, for example, that the breast-feeding rate for children with pervasive developmental disorder was not different from that of a control group matched for age, sex, and IQ. Perhaps the higher rate of parental psychological problems is due at least partly to the stress of having a handicapped child (Erickson, 1968a).

Schizophrenia

Genetic Factors. No chromosomal abnormalities have been found consistently in schizophrenic children. Our knowledge of genetic factors in childhood schizophrenia has come primarily from a few twin and family studies. A large body of twin and family research indicates that heredity is a significant etiological factor in adult schizophrenia (Gottesman, 1978); twin studies with adult probands have found higher concordance rates in identical than fraternal twins, and family studies have indicated that the risk for schizophrenia increases proportionally with the closeness of blood relationship to a family member with schizophrenia.

One twin study (Kallman & Roth, 1956) focused on the role of heredity in childhood schizophrenia. In a sample of 52 preadolescent twin pairs, the concordance rates for identical and fraternal twins were found to be quite similar to those found for adult schizophrenics, supporting a significant role for heritability in childhood schizophrenia and the idea that child and adult forms of schizophrenia may be the same condition.

Several studies have examined the risk of schizophrenia for children born to schizophrenic mothers but reared by foster or adoptive parents. Heston (1966) located 47 adults who had been born to schizophrenic women in mental institutions and raised by foster parents. Control subjects who were from the same foundling homes were matched to the experimental subjects on the basis of gender, length of time in child-care institutions, and type of foster home placement. Evaluations of the subjects were made without knowledge of experimental or control group placement. The data collected were based on personal interviews by psychiatrists, IQ and personality tests, and agency records. The results of this study showed significantly greater amounts of psychopathology in the group born of schizophrenic mothers. Five of the subjects in the experimental groups were diagnosed as schizophrenic and four as retarded, while none of the control group members received either diagnosis. Of the experimental group, 23.4 percent had spent more than one year in psychiatric or penal institutions, compared with 4 percent of the control group. A subsequent study by Heston and Denny (1968) compared experimental and control subjects raised either in foster homes or primarily in child-care institutions. The experimental subjects with both foster home and institutional histories had higher rates of psychopathology than the control subjects. No differences were found between foster home and institution-reared subjects, however, suggesting that these environments did not have differential effects on the incidence of schizophrenia and other psychological problems. Other adoption studies (Rosenthal, Wender, Kety, Welner, & Schulsinger, 1971; Rosenthal, 1972) have demonstrated higher rates of schizophrenia in persons whose biological ancestors were schizophrenic whether or not schizophrenia was present in the adoptive families.

At present, several ongoing longitudinal studies are examining children who are at high risk for schizophrenia because one or both of their parents are diagnosed as schizophrenic. Children of parents who have no diagnosed psychological disorder and children of parents with another type of psychological disorder are typically compared to the high-risk children. Data are collected on all the children at particular ages; the groups may then be continuously compared as they get older. Also, as particular subjects in the high-risk group become schizophrenic, their data can be compared to that of the remaining sample. Early adulthood is the most common time of onset for schizophrenia, but onset could occur earlier or later.

An example of such a longitudinal study is that initiated by Erlenmeyer-Kimling with children between ages 7 and 12 years at the time of the first examination. The children were assessed with a broad range of cognitive, psychophysiological, psychological, and behavioral measures initially as well as two and five years later. One consistent difference that was found is that the high-risk children are more unstable emotionally and more likely to be withdrawn or aggressive or both (Glish, Erlenmeyer-Kimling, & Watt, 1982).

Physical Factors. With the exception of Bender, who began to study the neurological and physical correlates of childhood schizophrenia in the 1930s, serious interest in biological factors as etiological agents did not appear until the early 1960s. Bender continuously maintained that schizophrenia is the result of a faulty nervous system that is genetically vulnerable, that is, subject to both organic and psychological stresses that may precipitate the onset of schizophrenia.

Goldfarb (1961) conducted an intensive study of 26 psychotic children (a mixture of schizophrenic and autistic types) and found that 17 of them showed evidence of neurological abnormalities. Goldfarb hypothesized that childhood psychoses could be the result of either organic or psychological stresses, that is, that there are two types of childhood psychosis: organic and nonorganic. On nearly all of the neurological and psychological test measures in his study, the organics performed more poorly than the nonorganics, who, in turn, performed more poorly than the normal control group matched for age and gender. For example, the average IQ for the organics was 62 as compared with 92 for the nonorganics. His measure of family adequacy, however, based on a three-hour observation session in the home, revealed the families of organics to be more adequate than the families of nonorganics.

Creak (1963) reported that about one-half of her 100 schizophrenic children had selective or overall retardation in developmental milestones. Several studies have found higher rates of EEG abnormality in schizophrenic children.

Prenatal and perinatal complications have been examined in a number of studies. After reviewing the literature, Pollack and Woerner (1966) concluded that these complications occurred more frequently in the histories of psychotic children. This higher rate of incidence is comparable to those for mentally retarded and nonpsychotic behaviorally disturbed children (Fish, Shapiro, Campbell, & Wile, 1968). Postnatal head trauma has also been found to have occurred more often in the histories of adult schizophrenics when compared with those of manics, depressives, and surgical controls (Wilcox & Nasrallah, 1987). Walker and Emory (1983) argued that the offspring of schizophrenic parents may be constitutionally vulnerable, that is, more likely to sustain damage when complications do occur. Goodman (1988) also suggested that complications may well be an effect, rather than a cause, of schizophrenia.

The role of prenatal, perinatal, and postnatal physical factors was amplified in a study of 11 sets of adolescent and adult identical twins who were *discordant* for schizophrenia (Pollin, Stabenau, Mosher, & Tupin, 1966). In all cases, the schizophrenic twin weighed less at birth than the nonschizophrenic twin. In addition, the schizophrenic twins had more physical illness and injuries and showed more signs of subtle neurological dysfunction. A subsequent biochemical study (Pollin, 1971) revealed that both members of the pairs had higher levels of neurotransmitters active in brain metabolism (dopamine, norepinephrine, epinephrine) than a normal control group but that the schizophrenic twins had significantly higher levels of 17-hydroxysteroids than either the nonschizophrenic twins or the normal control group.

Psychological Factors. As early as 1938 Despert reported that the mothers of 19 out of 29 schizophrenic children were "aggressive, over-anxious, and over-solicitous," while the fathers displayed a "subdued role." During the 1940s and 1950s theorists writing in the clinical literature tended to blame childhood psychosis on mothers who were characterized as narcissistic and incapable of mature emotional relationships. The term, *schizophrenogenic mother* was coined during this period and frequently used as an explanatory concept with respect to the etiology of childhood psychosis. Variations on the theme of the "schizophrenogenic" mother have included mothers who reject their children emotionally and whose responses to their children reflect hostile feelings in the husband-wife relationship. A study by Ricks and Berry (1970), however, suggested that this maternal description may not be valid. They examined the child guidance clinic records of individuals who later developed schizophrenia or other psychiatric disorders, or who were evaluated as adequately adjusted. "Schizophrenogenic mothers" were found in all three groups but *least* often in the group that subsequently became schizophrenic. A more recent study (Asarnow, Goldstein, & Ben-Meir, 1988) found that the rates of parental communication deviance were higher in the parents of schizophrenic children than in those of children with major depression.

In his depiction of organic and nonorganic types of childhood schizophrenia, Goldfarb implicated faulty parent-child interactions as a primary etiologic factor in nonorganic childhood schizophrenia. His conclusions were based on observational studies of mothers and their schizophrenic children and the assumption that the observed interactions were characteristic of interactions throughout the child's life. Meyers and Goldfarb (1961) described mothers of schizophrenic children as reacting to their children with greater uncertainty and indecisiveness, with less spontaneity and empathy, and with a lack of control and authority. In comparison with the mothers of normal children, the mothers of schizophrenic children gave less evidence of guiding, instructing, reinforcing, and inhibiting their children. Goldfarb (1970) summarized maternal communication deficiencies as follows:

> (1) failure to stimulate the child's interest in active communication; (2) failure to maintain the continuous flow of communication with the child; (3) failure to reinforce normal and acceptable speech and communication in the child; (4) active confounding of the child in regard to his construction of reality; (5) missing or not responding to the child's cues; (6) failure to cope with the child's unusual deviancies in communication. (p. 812)

Goldfarb (1961) also found behavioral and familial variables that discriminated between organic and nonorganic schizophrenic children. The nonorganic children had higher IQ scores and were also superior in the areas of perception, body orientation, and psychomotor functioning. In contrast, the families of nonorganic schizophrenic children were lower in interactional adequacy; schizophrenia had been diagnosed in 44 percent of the mothers of nonorganic schizophrenic children in comparison with 21 percent of the mothers of organic schizophrenic children. These data were interpreted as supporting a psychological etiology for schizophrenia in the nonorganic children.

The distinction between organic and nonorganic schizophrenic children may present problems of validity. In Goldfarb's study the distinction was based on findings from the neurological examination and an implicit assumption, namely, that abnormal brain function is always detectable by neurological examination. There is ample evidence that neurological tests do not provide an exact determination of an organic problem but rather are capable of detecting only some types of brain dysfunction. For example, although the rate of abnormal neurological findings increases with the severity of mental retardation, many severely retarded children do not manifest neurological abnormalities other than developmental delays. Thus, in the case of psychosis, it is possible that all schizophrenic children may have an organic impairment that is not detectable by the neurological examination and that the neurological abnormalities detected for some schizophrenic children are either secondary etiological factors or represent by-products of the original cause of the schizophrenia.

This alternative explanation of Goldfarb's study is made in the context of subsequent research and is not intended to diminish the study's historical importance. Following two decades of clinicians' being convinced that childhood psychosis was determined primarily by pathological parent-child relationships, Goldfarb's study made a strong impact on subsequent research by presenting an intermediate view, namely, that psychoses might have either an organic or a nonorganic basis, and thus prepared the way for further research on biological factors that had not previously been investigated.

This section may be summarized by stating that there is no evidence that faulty child rearing is the primary basis of childhood schizophrenia, although parent-child interactions may affect the course of the disorder, as has been found for adult schizophrenics.

TREATMENT: AUTISM AND SCHIZOPHRENIA

Clinicians' theoretical orientations with regard to the etiology of childhood psychoses have greatly affected their approaches to treatment. The types of therapies that have been used with psychotic children have represented a broad spectrum, including psychoanalytic, behavioral, and physical treatments. In general, clinicians who have considered childhood psychoses to be caused by faulty parent-child relationships have tended to use psychotherapies with a psychoanalytic orientation, while those with strong persuasions toward an organic etiology have focused on physical treatments. In addition, a number of clinicians, particularly those espousing a behavioral approach to treatment, have developed therapy programs relatively independently of etiological considerations. Since precise diagnostic criteria for autism and childhood schizophrenia were not used prior to the 1980s, many treatment studies contain heterogeneous samples of psychotic children; therefore, we will consider both disorders together.

Psychotherapy

Until the 1970s, psychoanalytic psychotherapy was the primary form of treatment for psychotic children. One of the initial goals of psychoanalytic psychotherapy with psychotic children is to engender a close relationship with a permissive and loving mother figure—a relationship that the child's own mother presumedly failed to provide. This relationship, which may take years to develop in therapy, is believed to be the foundation from which all other progress in treatment will be made. Rank (1955) described two phases of psychotherapy with psychotic children. During the first phase, the therapist provides the maximum amount of support possible, offering gratification in large amounts and avoiding frustration of the child. The therapist attempts to be more understanding and emotionally consistent than the real parents are assumed to have been. The second phase focuses on the development of socialization skills, including the postponement of gratification.

Most of the psychotherapeutic programs for psychotic children described in the clinical research literature have taken place in inpatient settings. Inpatient facilities have been viewed as offering the potential for constructing an emotionally healthy environment for the child. The term *milieu therapy* refers to programs in inpatient settings that emphasize full-time socialization of the child by the encouragement and teaching of interpersonal and educational skills. Milieu therapy also frequently includes varying amounts of psychotherapy. Several studies have evaluated the effectiveness of milieu therapy with psychotic children. Goldfarb, Goldfarb, and Pollack (1966) compared the effects of full-time milieu therapy and a similar day-treatment program in which children spent the remaining time at home. These findings indicated that the most severely psychotic children did not benefit from either program. No differences in improvement for the "organic" schizophrenic children in the two programs were found; the "nonorganic" schizophrenic children in the full-time program showed greater improvement than did those in the day-treatment group, however, suggesting to these researchers that the residential program may have been serving the function of protecting the "nonorganic" children from emotionally unhealthy home environments.

Apparently different results were obtained in a study that compared the effectiveness of full-time treatment and day treatment for psychotic children (Wenar, Ruttenberg, Dratman, & Wolf, 1967). At the end of one year, improvement was greater for children in the day-treatment program than for those in either of two full-time residential facilities. Children were not randomly assigned to the various programs, however, and the full-time programs had a greater staff turnover, poorer staff-to-child ratios, and older children, who would probably have been more difficult to treat.

Perhaps, from a psychodynamic point of view, the epitome of a program that includes both milieu therapy and psychotherapy is Bettelheim's Orthogenic School in Chicago. Because his program is privately supported and requires at least several years of treatment, most of the psychotic children referred to it have parents who are highly educated and wealthy. Bettelheim's program is based on the assumption that the primary cause of psychosis is emotional rejection of the child by the parents; during the course of treatment parent visitation and home visits are restricted. In the earlier phases of treatment, the staff provides a totally accepting environment for the child regardless of the individual's behavior. The psychotic child is encouraged to regress (become more infantile) in order to relive earlier experiences in the more optimal emotional environment. Emphasis is put on the child's need to derive pleasure from bodily functions (e.g., eating and defecating) in an atmosphere of warm acceptance to replace the earlier experiences of faulty care by the mother. It would not be unusual, for example, to observe an older child being held on the lap of a caretaker and being fed from a bottle as one would feed an infant. By experiencing adults (caretakers and therapists) as positive agents, the children are expected to be able to begin interacting with people in human, rather than mechanical, ways.

Bettelheim wrote several books describing the treatment of individual psychotic children in his program. In one of them (Bettelheim, 1967, p. 414), he reviewed the outcome of 40 children discharged from the Orthogenic School. He described 17 or 42 percent as "good" or "cured," 15 or 38 percent as "fair," and 8 or 20 percent as "poor." Bettelheim indicated that the treatment outcome for his children was greatly superior because it was based on intensive institutional treatment carried out over a period of years. It should be noted that these improvement figures have not been independently confirmed or replicated by other investigators.

Several studies have suggested that psychoanalytic psychotherapy may not be effective for psychotic children. Brown (1960) compared 20 children who made the most progress with 20 children who made the least progress during several years of outpatient treatment. No differences between the groups were found for length of treatment, number of therapists, or experience of the therapists. Brown found that children who initially presented the most severe symptoms had the worst outcome. A later study by Brown (1963), comparing children who had either individual, small group, or no treatment, also failed to find significant differences due to treatment. A study by other investigators (Kaufman, Frank, Friend, Heims, & Weiss, 1962) found that length of treatment was inversely related to improvement, suggesting that longer treatment periods were associated with poorer outcomes.

Although many psychotic children have received and probably continue to receive psychotherapy on either an inpatient or outpatient basis, its effectiveness has not been demonstrated. In fact, there has been very little outcome research during the last two decades, but case histories continue to be reported (Kestenbaum, 1978). A few experimental studies comparing psychotherapy with behavior therapy (Ney, Palvesky, & Markely, 1971) and with structured special education (Rutter & Bartak, 1973) have found either no improvement or significantly less improvement for psychotic children given psychotherapy.

Physical Treatment

Bender was the principal advocate for the physical treatment of psychotic children and has conducted a significant portion of the pioneer research on physical treatments. She was a particularly strong proponent of electroshock therapy. Her follow-up study (Bender, 1960) of children receiving electroshock therapy during the 1940s and 1950s revealed that over 50 percent of the children improved socially. Moreover, no adverse effects such as impaired cognitive functioning were discovered, leading Bender to conclude that shock therapy was more effective with children than adults. Unfortunately, Bender's research design did not include control group conditions. Electroshock therapy is rarely used today in the treatment of psychotic children.

Use of medication for treating psychotic children greatly increased during the 1960s, probably as a result of successes in treating psychotic adults with medication. Most clinicians consider medication as an adjunct to therapy rather than as a primary form of treatment.

The neuroleptics are the drugs most widely used with psychotic children. Their effectiveness appears to be related to the child's age and level of functioning. Side effects have been reported for psychotic children and adolescents treated with the neuroleptics, thus necessitating careful monitoring to ensure that the minimally effective dosage is being given. Joshi, Capozzoli, and Coyle (1988) reported significant reductions in hyperactivity and aggressive symptoms and significant improvement in peer relations for 7- to 11-year-old childhood onset psychotic children given very low doses of neuroleptics with minimal side effects. A review of research on fenfluramine indicated that it reduced hyperactivity and stereotypic behaviors in 33 percent of autistic children; children with the highest IQs were the best responders (du Verglas, Banks, & Guyer, 1988).

Behavior Therapy

During the 1960s, investigators began to apply learning principles in treatment programs for psychotic children. The early studies focused on the reduction of a specific behavior problem, such as temper tantrums, or self-injurious behavior, through the use of extinction, timeout, punishment, and reinforcement of incompatible responses. Punishment in the form of contingent presentation of an adverse stimulus has been used infrequently and essentially only for problems that were severe and not efficiently treated through the use of other behavior principles. For example, some psychotic children engage in high rates of forms of behavior that can result in serious physical damage to themselves, such as head banging and biting their own bodies. To prevent these self-injurious actions, such children are often tied down to their beds in institutional settings. Several studies (see, for example, Risley, 1968) have demonstrated rapid decreases in self-injurious behavior through the use of brief contingent electric shock. Moreover, no negative effects of this procedure were observed; in fact, the elimination of these behaviors appeared to increase the occurrence of appropriate behaviors and facilitated the further development of appropriate behaviors during treatment.

The initial therapeutic attention to abnormal or inappropriate behaviors has seemed to be necessary because the rate of such behaviors for psychotic children is very high and greatly hampers programs for increasing appropriate behaviors. Subsequent research has increasingly focused on the development of behaviors not previously present in the psychotic child's repertoire and comprehensive therapeutic programs that dealt with multiple aspects of the child's behavioral repertoire. For example, considerable effort on the part of behavioral researchers has been invested in programs to develop speech and language skills in psychotic children who lacked verbal repertoires or whose speech was echolalic. Early in these programs it was discovered that autistic children had either deficient or absent imitative skills and, furthermore, did not attend to stimulus patterns that would facilitate imitation and the learning of other behaviors. Therefore, several research studies were directed toward the development of imitative skills and their relevant attending behaviors. This research has shown that the application of behavior principles has been successful in establishing eye contact, social interactions with adults, imitative repertoires, and expressive and receptive speech. Identifying reinforcers for psychotic children often presents problems for the researcher and clinician; therefore, many of the behavioral programs rely on food, at least initially, and may pair social stimuli with the presentation of food reinforcement in an effort to increase the effectiveness of social stimuli as reinforcers.

The work of Lovaas and his colleagues at the University of California at Los Angeles has epitomized the behavioral approach to the treatment of psychotic children (Lovaas, Koegel, Simmons, & Stevens-Long, 1973; Stevens-Long & Lovaas, 1974). In the initial study, 20 children, labeled as autistic by at least one other agency not associated with the research project, were treated intensively for about one year. Two groups of children were treated as inpatients eight hours each day, six to seven days a week, for about one year. The parents of the first group were not involved in treatment, but the parents of the second group were taught the treatment procedures. The remaining children were outpatients and essentially treated by the parents, while the project staff provided training and consultation to the parents about two to three hours per week.

From this project has come a series of studies indicating that behavior principles may be effectively applied to modify psychotic children's behavior. Therapy typically begins with training the child to respond appropriately to simple commands, such as "sit down" and "look." At the same time, inappropriate behaviors, such as tantrums and those forms of behavior that are aggressive, self-injurious, and repetitive are put on extinction or punished.

Although a significant amount of effort went into the reduction of the inappropriate behaviors, by far the greatest amount of attention was devoted to the development of imitative and language skills. The imitative language program consisted of four phases: (1) increasing the rate of all vocalizations, (2) teaching the child to vocalize immediately after the adult vocalized, (3) increasing the similarity of the child's vocalization to the adult's vocalization, and (4) teaching the child to discriminate between new and less recently learned imitative sounds. The training program included the use of contingent reinforcement and shaping, prompting, and fading. Subsequent language programs focused on the development of receptive speech (e.g., pointing to the object labeled), verbal labels for common objects and activities, and language abstractions (such as pronouns, prepositions, and words for temporal relationships).

The major findings of the project were that all of the children in the intensive program improved; that is, inappropriate behaviors were decreased, and appropriate behaviors increased. Characteristic of the various program results was the very substantial variability in the rate of progress among the children. Given the same programs and comparable amounts of professional time, dramatic improvements were achieved for some children, while other children made relatively little progress. Follow-up studies indicated that the initial four children who were institutionalized after their treatment in the project failed to make additional gains, while children who remained at home with parents, trained by the project staff, continued to show improvement. Although the majority of children could not be tested at the beginning of treatment, all of them could be tested at the end of the treatment period, with most of the children functioning in the mild to moderate range of mental retardation. The average social quotients on the Vineland Social Maturity Scale were 48 before treatment and 71 after treatment.

Because improvement seems to be greatly dependent on a treatment program conducted in the child's natural environment, the role of parents as therapists for their own children has received increased attention. In their second major project that focused on autistic children younger than four years, Lovaas and his staff train the parent, usually the mother, to become the child's primary therapist. Most of the training is done in the home environment with assistance from undergraduate students (10 to 20 hours a week), siblings, and neighbors (Lovaas, Young, & Newsom, 1978). After about six to eight months of treatment, placement in a normal preschool is carefully staged; the child is gradually added to the group, and the teacher is given both special training and aides.

Lovaas (1987), reporting on this intensive, long-term experimental project with 19 children with autism, found that 9 children achieved normal intellectual and educational functioning and successful first grade performance in public schools; 8 children were mildly retarded and assigned to special education classes; and 2 children were profoundly retarded. In contrast, of the 40 control group children, only 1 achieved normal intellectual and educational functioning, 18 were mildly retarded, and 21 were severely retarded and placed in special education classes. Long-term follow-up of the children in the experimental group indicated that the positive changes were maintained throughout grade school, although one child in the best achievement group did show some signs of regression (McEachin, Smith, & Lovaas, 1993).

A cornerstone to this intensive approach is the rapid development of vocal imitation and ensuing speech. However, a significant portion of children with autism (with estimates ranging from 30 to 50 percent) have difficulty acquiring speech even with intensive training. Recently, alternative approaches to communication training have been successfully used. For example, Carr (1982) reported on the use of sign language with children with autism and notes the potential advantages of using nonvocal cues for the child to attend to. However, most approaches to teaching sign language require the child to be able to imitate the hand actions of the teacher, a skill that many children with autism have difficulty acquiring.

Another approach to functional communication training with children with autism and related developmental disabilities is the Picture Exchange Communication System (PECS). The primary advantage of this approach is that the child needs very few prerequisite skills prior to beginning training (Bondy & Frost, 1994). For example, the child does not need to have good face-to-face orientation, or be able to imitate skills, or follow a set of simple commands. Children are quickly taught to give a teacher (or parent) a picture of something that they want in exchange for receiving the desired item. Rather than teaching via a series of verbal commands (i.e., "Give me the picture," "What do you want?") the child is taught through physical assistance from a second teacher to initiate the request. This assistance is quickly faded so that the child initiates the request without prompts from other people, thus avoiding having the child become prompt-dependent.

The PECS goes on to teach more complex communication skills, including the use of sentence structure, commenting, and various attributes. Descriptive reports suggest that about two-thirds of children who have used PECS as preschoolers for more than one year develop speech as their primary mode of communication, with another subset of children who speak while using the picture system (Bondy & Frost, 1994). Research continues on how the use of nonverbal strategies may enhance the development of speech. For those children who never acquire speech, the use of PECS has been beneficial in fostering their social approach and communication with other people while helping to ameliorate many of their behavior management difficulties. Refinements of the language programs for nonverbal children are made continuously (Koegel, O'Dell, & Koegel, 1987).

One complex issue involves the integration of intensive behavioral strategies with these children into school settings, both private and public. During the past decade, a number of successful intervention approaches have been designed (see Harris & Handleman, 1994, for a description of several such preschool programs). Although public schools are mandated to provide educational services for preschool developmentally disabled children beginning at the time of diagnosis, they have only recently focused attention on how to design effective programs (Bondy, 1995). The challenge for the future remains how to help these children achieve successful outcomes within academic, community, and residential settings.

Greater research attention is beginning to be given to adolescents and adults with autism (Schopler & Mesibov, 1983). Several studies have demonstrated the improvement of psychotic adolescents' social skills (Plienis et al., 1987) and increases in autistic adolescents' social interactions (Groden & Cautela, 1988).

CONCLUSIONS

While no single cause of pervasive developmental disorders and schizophrenia has been identified, research data strongly suggest that the primary etiological factors are physical in nature. Genetic factors and physical insults during the pre-, peri-, and postnatal periods have been associated with both autism and childhood schizophrenia. A variety of treatment approaches have been used with psychotic children. Behavioral studies have offered perhaps the most convincing evidence of therapeutic effectiveness. It appears that comprehensive programs begun very early in life result in the greatest effectiveness.

RECOMMENDED READINGS

Berkell, D.E. (Ed.). (1992). *Autism: Identification, education, and treatment.* Hillsdale, NJ: Erlbaum.

Cantor, S., (1988). *Childhood schizophrenia.* New York: Guilford.

Cohen, D.J., Donnellan, A.M., & Paul, R. (Eds.). (1987). *Handbook of autism and pervasive developmental disorders.* New York: Wiley.

Harris, S., & Handleman, J. (Eds.). (1994). *Preschool education programs for children with autism.* Austin, TX: Pro-ed.

Lovaas, O.I., & Smith, T. (1988). Intensive behavioral treatment for young autistic children. In B.B. Lahey & A.E. Kazdin (Eds.), *Advances in clinical child psychology* (Vol. 11, pp. 285–324). New York: Plenum Press.

Schopler, E., & Mesibov, G.B. (Eds.). (1988). *Diagnosis and assessment in autism.* New York: Plenum Press.

Schopler, E., & Mesibov, G. (Eds.). (1995). *Learning and cognition in autism.* New York: Plenum Press.

Walker, E.F. (Ed.). (1991). *Schizophrenia: A life course developmental perspective.* New York: Academic Press.

10

Attention-Deficit/Hyperactivity Disorder, Learning Disorders, Communication Disorders

Jeff, a nine-year-old boy, was referred by his third grade teacher because of poor achievement in reading and spelling. His teacher reported that he was in her lowest reading group and seemed to lack even the most basic word-attack skills. Jeff's first and second grade teachers had emphasized a phonics approach to reading. Jeff, a very active child, refused to participate in his reading group and had torn up his spelling papers several times. His teacher felt that his intelligence was at least above average based on his participation in class discussions.

Jeff's mother was eager to have an evaluation to find out what could be done about his problem. She was an avid reader and attended college for two years, dropping out to get married. She was considering a return to college when her youngest child entered first grade but was somewhat ambivalent because of its possible effect on her husband, who had not attended college. Jeff's father was less concerned about his son's problem. He reported that he and several members of his family had reading problems in school. He disliked school and remained in school only to please his mother. His job as an auto mechanic was not particularly fulfilling, but he was proud of his ability to support his family in reasonable comfort. He didn't think that reading was "as important as people say it is."

Jeff was the first of two sons born after three pregnancies had ended in two spontaneous abortions and a stillbirth. The pregnancy with Jeff was normal except for a very long labor and a difficult delivery. His development during the preschool period was normal, but his parents reported that he was "on the go" much of the time. Jeff's reading problem had not previously been brought to the parents' attention.

ATTENTION-DEFICIT/HYPERACTIVITY DISORDER

Attention-deficit/hyperactivity disorder (ADHD) has had a long history of clinical and research focus, although labels for the disorder have varied through the years. Originally, the syndrome was associated with mental retardation because it was observed more frequently in retarded children. Its etiology was linked to brain damage because the condition appeared to occur more frequently in retarded children with known brain damage. The disorder was separated from mental retardation when clinical evidence identified a population of children with the behavior symptoms who were not mentally retarded. Several decades ago, the diagnostic label for these children was "minimal brain damage" or "minimal brain dysfunction."

Because evidence of brain damage in the nonretarded children often could not be verified, the diagnostic label was eventually changed to "Hyperkinetic Reaction of Childhood" in DSM-III (APA, 1968). However, this label was not satisfactory because *attentional difficulty*, rather than hyperactivity, became increasingly recognized as the core problem. DSM-III (APA, 1980) changed the diagnostic label to "Attention-Deficit Disorder" (ADD) which could occur with hyperactivity (ADHD), or without hyperactivity (ADD). DSM-III-R (APA, 1987) changed the focus to hyperactivity again. The most recent revision, DSM-IV (APA, 1994) recognizes three subtypes of Attention-Deficit/Hyperactivity Disorder.

Assessment

The primary diagnostic symptoms of ADHD as described in DSM-IV (APA, 1994) are developmentally inappropriate degrees of inattention, impulsivity, and motor activity. For diagnosis of the disorder, the child must have six symptoms from one or two lists each of which contains nine symptoms. One list focuses on inattention, and the other list focuses on hyperactivity and impulsivity. Thus, three diagnostic labels may be applied: ADHD, Combined Type; ADHD, Predominantly Inattentive Type; ADHD, Predominantly Hyperactive-Impulsive Type.

Four additional criteria must also be met for diagnosis. The first is that the symptoms were present before the age of seven years. Second, the symptoms must be present in two or more settings. Third, the symptoms must be associated with impairment in social or academic functioning, and, fourth, the symptoms are not better accounted for by another mental disorder.

Clinical diagnosis of ADHD relies primarily on parental report during the interview process, although important information can be obtained from interviews with some children and input from teachers. Although clinicians rely on interviews for diagnosis, researchers have utilized other assessment methods. For example, in laboratory settings, attention may be evaluated with a continuous performance test (CPT) in which the child is instructed to push a button when a particular stimulus, such as a letter of the alphabet, is seen. Two kinds of errors can be detected: errors of omission when the child fails to detect the stimulus and errors of comission when the child reacts to the wrong stimulus. Children with ADHD make more of both kinds of errors (Barkley, 1990).

Objective assessment of activity level can be made with both direct observation and movement devices, such as pedometers. Researchers have associated impulsivity with the Matching Familiar Figures Test (Kagan, Rosman, Day, Albert, & Philips, 1964), which requires the child to select a matching picture from an array of similar pictures. Fast selection with matching errors is indicative of impulsivity.

Referral for ADHD problems usually occurs during the preschool years when hyperactivity may be prominent or during the early school years when problems in learning become apparent. The salient features of ADHD, namely, overactivity, short attention span, and impulsivity, can be expected to interfere with the child's learning in school. A child whose attention is removed from the teacher or the classroom task at hand is less likely to learn what the teacher is attempting to teach and less likely to perform according to the teacher's expectations.

It should come as no surprise, then, that ADHD has been associated with poorer academic achievement and that children with ADHD have higher rates of learning disorders (Robins, 1992). It is not yet known whether there are causal links between these two disorders and/or whether a third factor, such as a biological insult, may be responsible for both. ADHD is associated with a variety of other clinical problems, particularly oppositional defiant disorder and conduct disorder. Indeed, the prognosis for children with ADHD who also have oppositional/conduct problems is considerably worse than for ADHD children without these problems (McArdle, O'Brien, & Kolvin, 1995).

ADHD is estimated to affect 3 to 5 percent of school-age children (APA, 1994). Boys are consistently diagnosed with ADHD more frequently than girls, with the ratio being four to nine boys to one girl. Lower socioeconomic class may also be associated with ADHD.

Etiology

The risk factors for ADHD appear to be primarily biological, but environmental/psychological factors are apparent in many cases. Historically, brain damage has been linked to ADHD, but few ADHD children display neurological abnormalities. The abnormal EEG patterns found in the minority of ADHD children are indicative of underarousal of the nervous system; overactivity by the child may have the effect of "correcting" the underarousal. The newer imaging techniques will hopefully increase our knowledge of brain functioning in ADHD children and adolescents.

Genetic Factors. Family pedigree studies suggest that hyperactivity runs in families. Parents of children with ADHD show more psychopathology, as well as hyperactivity, than parents without ADHD children. Twin studies also support a genetic contribution with greater concordance found for identical than fraternal twins. Inheritance also plays a role in the co-occurrence of ADHD and learning disorders (Gillis, Gilger, Pennington, & DeFries, 1992).

Prenatal, Perinatal, and Postnatal Physical Factors. Complications of pregnancy, labor, and delivery appear to be at least weakly linked to ADHD (Sprich-Buckminster, Biederman, Milberger, Faraone, & Lehman, 1993). Maternal alcohol consumption during pregnancy has been associated with increased activity levels and attention problems that persist through the childhood years (Steinhausen, Williams, & Spohr, 1993). Children with ADHD show a higher than average rate of minor physical abnormalities whose origins have been placed in the first trimester of pregnancy. These minor physical abnormalities also occur at a higher rate in other disorders, such as mental retardation and autism. Exposure to lead during the preschool period has been associated with higher levels of activity and inattention (Fergusson, Horwood, & Lynskey, 1993).

Psychosocial Factors. Psychosocial factors are clearly involved and important considerations for children with ADHD, but they are probably not important as *causal* agents. A number of studies have shown ADHD to be related to marital discord, family dysfunction, and criticism of the child. More severe ADHD symptoms have been associated with increased family problems. It is reasonable to expect that the typical ADHD behaviors could create significant challenges to most parents. If the family unit has other risk factors, such as a single parent and low socioeconomic status, the child's behavior may present even greater stressors.

Treatment

It is no longer believed that hyperactivity disappears with the passage of time. We now understand that many ADHD children show signs of the disorder prior to school age when most of them are identified, and many of them continue to have problems during adolescence and adulthood. Fischer, Barkley, Fletcher, & Smallish (1993) reported that 50 to 80 percent of children with ADHD continue to be at risk for academic problems, conduct problems, substance abuse, and emotional problems during adolescence. Longitudinal studies of ADHD children into adulthood indicate that as adults they are at increased risk for poor social relationships, substance abuse, depression, and educational and occupational underachievement. Given this information, it would seem important to identify children with ADHD as early as possible and initiate intervention as soon as possible.

A variety of interventions have been examined for their effectiveness for ADHD: medications, behavioral methods, and cognitive behavioral methods. Stimulant medication is the most common treatment for ADHD with the most prescribed stimulants being methylphenidate (Ritalin), dextroamphetamine (Dexedrine), and pemoline (Cylert). Numerous studies have found that stimulants improve attention and decrease both activity and impulsivity for the majority of ADHD children.

Although used primarily to improve academic behavior, Ritalin has been found to improve ADHD children's compliance with parental requests and social interactions (Barkley, 1989) and to reduce hyperactive boys' aggression to a level comparable to that of nonpsychiatric controls (Hinshaw et al., 1989). When it became evident that ADHD is not "outgrown," stimulants began to be prescribed for adolescents and adults as well. Different areas of psychosocial functioning are more or less responsive to Ritalin effects. Stimulant-treated hyperactive young adults performed significantly worse than normal controls but similar to untreated hyperactives in areas involving school, work, and personality disorders; however, the treated hyperactives did significantly better than untreated hyperactives on measures related to car accidents, childhood perceptions, delinquency, and social skills (Hechtman, Weiss, & Perlman, 1984).

Despite the positive effects of stimulant medication on academic and psychosocial functioning, the limited action and negative side effects associated with stimulants may complicate treatment. Although medication often gives "immediate relief" from excessive activity, it does not correct learning disabilities or social deficits developed during earlier years of hyperactivity. Reduced appetite and weight loss frequently occur soon after stimulant medication is introduced; these effects are diminished when the medication is administered at mealtimes. Children may experience stomachaches, headaches, irritability, or sad feelings, which can sometimes be relieved by reducing the dosage. Long-term use of "high-normal" doses of stimulants may result in a decreased rate of physical growth (Roche et al., 1979). Discontinuation of Ritalin over the summer months may decrease the risk of suppressed growth.

Psychological and behavioral side effects of stimulant medications have also been identified. A double-blind pharmaceutical study indicated that side effects of stimulant medication may mimic ADHD symptoms, potentially masking therapeutic effects and exacerbating problem behaviors (Fine & Johnston, 1993). In a placebo-controlled study of stimulant treatment for hyperactive boys, prosocial behaviors remained unchanged, social engagement *decreased,* and feelings of dysphoria *increased* for treated boys, in comparison with untreated and placebo controls (Buhrmester, Whalen, Henker, & MacDonald, 1992). These findings suggest the importance of continued research to identify mediating and moderating variables that influence the efficacy and appropriateness of a stimulant medication intervention for ADHD.

The research history on the effects of behavior therapy is much shorter than that for medication; behavioral studies demonstrating significant changes in the behavior of hyperactive children first began appearing in the 1970s (Ayllon & Rosenbaum, 1977; O'Leary & O'Leary, 1977). Operant approaches using rewards have been popular, and response cost had some success. Cognitive-behavioral approaches attempt to optimize the match between the problem and the treatment by focusing on enhancing children's ability to monitor and regulate their own behavior (Henker & Whalen, 1989). A behavioral training program for parents of children with ADHD demonstrated significant and robust gains in child and parent functioning, with parents reporting less stress, improved self-esteem, and fewer child behavior problems following the nine-session program (Anastopoulos, Shelton, DuPaul, & Guevremont, 1993).

Cognitive-behavioral intervention focuses on self-control or self-regulation, and therefore the child or adolescent is the primary client. Through self-monitoring, children learn to observe and record their own behaviors and are instructed to reward themselves for appropriate behaviors. Through self-instruction, ADHD children are trained to make specific statements to themselves that may help to guide their behavior in particular situations or settings. One example might be to instruct themselves to "slow down" when answering questions from the teacher or on an exam. Cognitive-behavioral interventions appear to be most effective for decreasing impulsivity (Kendall & Panichelli-Mindel, 1995). There is currently a strong interest in examining the effectiveness of combining medication and behavioral treatments.

Integrated treatment approaches combining pharmacologic and behavioral interventions to suit the individual needs of each child are now being developed (e.g., DuPaul & Barkley, 1993). Several studies utilized a combination of behavior therapy and medication and found that medication facilitated the improvement of behavior initially but could be phased out later without affecting treatment efficacy (Ayllon, Layman, & Kandel, 1975; O'Leary & Pelham, 1978). Methylphenidate was as effective as behavior therapy in improving ADHD boys' classroom behavior, but more effective in increasing academic productivity and accuracy (Carlson, Pelham, Milich, & Dixon, 1992).

Integration of physical and psychosocial interventions in the treatment of ADHD may allow for a more specialized treatment regime adapted to meet individual needs and strengths. Because hyperactive children present multiple problems, most of them also need individualized educational programs and social training opportunities; in addition, their parents and teachers need guidance and support in their management of these children. The enhanced risk for conduct disorders and delinquency among ADHD children warrants further investigation of causal factors and treatment implications.

LEARNING DISORDERS

The terms *learning disorders* and *learning disabilities* refer to deficits in specific academic skills in relation to expected levels of performance. The deficient skill areas involve basic academic subjects taught in elementary school, such as reading, arithmetic, and writing (DSM-IV, 1994).

Learning disorders (LD) were originally described by physicians who emphasized organic etiological factors, an emphasis that has continued to the present. From the earlier literature, there evolved a series of medical diagnostic labels, such as "dyslexia," "dyscalculia," and "dysgraphia," which had fairly precise clinical definitions. For example, dyslexia originally referred to a person's inability to derive meaning from the written word. The medical labels have subsequently lost much of their precision of meaning. Contemporary use of the term *dyslexia* tends to make it equivalent to almost any problem related to reading. The writings of professionals working in the area of learning disabilities have frequently interchanged the terms *learning disability* and *minimal brain dysfunction.*

Increasing criticism has been focused on the use of "brain-damage" labels for children for whom the primary assessment and treatment techniques are behavioral or educational. Such labels may be detrimental to the child, particularly if the average teacher or parent perceives the child's condition to be untreatable; these labels are poorly defined and sometimes used when there is no direct evidence of brain damage; and, finally, the labels are not useful in assessing the child's educational needs. Proponents of the medical labels have expressed concerns about decreasing interest in etiology and about the risk of children with learning disabilities receiving inadequate medical attention.

Although important work in the area of learning disorders has been ongoing since at least the 1930s, the clinical descriptions and research findings were not incorporated into professional training programs until relatively recently; the average physician, teacher, and psychologist has not been trained to diagnose or provide remedial care for learning disabilities. In the 1970s and 1980s, clinical and educational training programs began to add courses and lectures in this area at an accelerated rate, and during that time perhaps the greatest attention to learning disorders has been given in school settings.

As has been true in the area of mental retardation, parents' groups have been greatly responsible for the acceleration in services for children with learning disorders. During the 1960s, parents' associations, such as the California Association for Neurologically Handicapped Children, facilitated the passage of legislation to support special programs for educationally handicapped children. Researchers similarly began to respond to the needs of children with learning disabilities by adding to our knowledge of etiology, assessment, and treatment. The initiation of the *Journal of Learning Disabilities* in 1968 was a major indication that professional interest in the area had begun to grow.

Before "learning disability" was recognized as a valid diagnosis, children with learning disabilities who also exhibited behavior problems tended to be diagnosed as emotionally disturbed, and the "emotional disturbance" was designated as the cause of the learning problem in school. Learning-disabled children without significant behavior problems were often considered to be mentally retarded.

During recent years, a movement has been evolving to deemphasize or "declassify" learning disorders. This movement seems, in part, to be due to increases in the numbers of children being diagnosed (about 4 percent nationally) and increases in the percentages of learning-disabled children in special education programs (the prevalence ranges from 26 percent to 64 percent of special education populations) (Chalfant, 1989). The Regular Education Initiative recommends that children with learning problems receive services from the regular classroom teacher within the context of the regular classroom (May 1987 issue of the *Journal of Learning Disabilities*). Vigorous debate and recommendations for national solutions have occurred (Hallahan, Keller, McKinney, Lloyd, & Bryan, 1988; Kauffman, Gerber, & Semmel, 1988; Chalfant, 1989).

Assessment

This section focuses on reading disorder (RD) because it accounts for the great majority of the learning problems related to school subjects. Relatively little research has been focused on specific disabilities in arithmetic, writing, and spelling. The primary difficulty in describing reading disorder is that our knowledge has been derived from the clinical experiences and research of professionals representing a variety of disciplines, and this knowledge has not been well integrated.

In the past, clinicians tended to agree with Eisenberg's (1966) definition of specific reading disability: "Operationally, specific reading disability may be defined as the failure to learn to read with normal proficiency despite conventional instruction, a culturally adequate home, proper motivation, intact senses, normal intelligence, and freedom from gross neurological defect" (p. 14). It is immediately apparent that this definition is more a description of what a reading disability is not than of what it is. Although we do have adequate operational definitions of "intact senses," "normal intelligence," "proper nutrition," and, perhaps,

"gross neurological defect," specification of "normal proficiency," "culturally adequate home," and "conventional instruction" has not been forthcoming.
Currently, most clinicians focus on chronological age, grade placement, and mental age as predictors of expected reading achievement and compare the expected
achievement with measures of actual achievement to determine whether a child
has a specific reading disability.

Many RD children are not referred in a timely manner for assessment because
most schools do not have screening programs that are adequate for initial identification. Although classroom teachers are usually the best informed persons in the
child's environment with regard to the child's status in reading, they do not often
have the background knowledge or access to information that is necessary to identify the RD child. The RD child with a behavior problem is probably more likely to
be referred for a diagnostic examination than an RD child who presents no behavior problem to the teacher. Thus, many children may be referred primarily for
behavior problems and are later discovered to have specific learning disabilities.

When a child is having learning problems in school, it is important to determine whether physical factors are involved. For this reason, many clinicians suggest
that the child receive a general physical examination as well as tests for vision and
hearing prior to undergoing psychological and educational testing procedures.
Most schools have periodic screening programs for vision and hearing, and the
results of these tests may be used if they have been obtained within six months to a
year of the referral. The clinician also requests a copy of the child's school grades
and standardized group test scores for background information.

Interview. When the child is referred, an interview is usually conducted with
the parents and sometimes with the child. During the interview with the parents,
the clinician obtains a history of both learning and behavior problems in school in
an attempt to determine whether the problems have been evident throughout the
child's school years or have developed recently.

While the behavioral clinician focuses on the child's present and recent past
academic problems, the traditional clinician is more likely to inquire at some
length about the parents' own school experiences, the assumption being that parents who have had adverse school experiences can unconsciously transmit their attitudes to the child. The traditional clinician may be particularly interested in
determining whether the affected academic subject has a special symbolic meaning
for the child or the parent-child unit. Doing poorly in reading may, for example,
represent the avoidance of seeing or reading about forbidden (sexual) material.

Parents are sometimes not well informed about the child's actual progress in
school and report that the child's grades did not reflect a problem in the early
years. In some cases, parents have received no oral or written indication of learning
problems before the recommendation that they arrange for a diagnostic evaluation. The lack of psychological preparation in such cases often contributes to
greater defensiveness and complaints about the school during the interview.

The interview with the child attempts to secure the child's perception of the
school problems. The clinician inquires about the child's favorite and disliked

school subjects as well as the quality of interactions with teachers. Occasionally, a strong antagonism has developed between the child and a particular teacher, and the teacher may or may not be aware of such feelings. Children vary considerably in their responsiveness during interviews; they range from extreme withdrawal to complete candor about the problem. At least some of their variability is due to what has previously been told to them about their referral for diagnostic evaluation. In spite of these difficulties, the child's contributions are generally believed to be a meaningful component of the diagnostic process.

Another important source of information is the child's teacher. If the clinician is employed by the school system, an interview with the teacher is usually part of the assessment process. Because of the time and expense, clinicians outside of the school system are seldom able to conduct a personal interview with the teacher, although a telephone interview or a request for written comments by the teacher, or both, are becoming increasingly common.

The teacher interview focuses on the child's behavior and learning in the classroom. The teacher is asked to describe the child's behavior under various conditions, such as during different instructional periods. Is the child having difficulty only with reading and reading-related school subjects, or are there problems in several areas? The teacher is asked about the methods used to try to help the child and the relative successes of these approaches.

Identification. Group intelligence and reading test scores are readily available from most schools; it is unfortunate that they have not been demonstrated to be valid with respect to the identification of RD children. Because most group tests are highly dependent on reading skills, they tend to penalize children with specific reading disabilities. Thus, an RD child is very likely to obtain a considerably lower IQ score on a group test than on an individual test (Muzyczka & Erickson, 1976). This likelihood precludes the use of group intelligence and achievement tests for identifying RD children.

The minimum testing requirements for identifying an RD child are an individually administered intelligence test and a reading achievement test. There are three basic approaches to the identification of RD children by educators and psychologists: the Years Below Grade Level Method, the Discrepancy Method, and the Regression Method. These approaches have usually excluded children with IQ scores below 90, although a case can be made that a child at any IQ level can manifest a reading disorder. In addition, most clinicians agree that a diagnosis of RD should not be made until the child has been in school one year.

The Years Below Grade Level Method designates a child as RD if the child's reading score is significantly below the actual grade placement. The difference between the grade placement necessary to be "significant" is somewhat arbitrary, although general guidelines are followed. For example, a child in the second grade who is more than six months behind grade placement and a child in the fifth grade who is more than one year behind grade placement would both be considered to have reading disorders. The difference required becomes larger as the child's school grade increases.

The Discrepancy Method involves computing an expected reading level on the basis of the child's IQ score and subtracting from it the child's actual reading level. Children with reading levels that are significantly lower than expected on the basis of their IQ score are considered to be RD. Again, the absolute difference between the two levels required for diagnosis has not been generally agreed upon, but a difference of one-and-a-half years at the fifth or sixth grade level, for example, would usually be considered adequate for diagnosis of RD.

The Discrepancy Method seems to have considerable advantage over the Years Below Grade Level Method for identifying children with reading disabilities. It has long been known that the IQ score is the best available predictor of reading achievement. This relationship is logical in view of the fact that both scores are measures of rate of learning. Thus, rate of learning to read could be expected to approximate the rate of learning a wide variety of cognitive skills. The Years Below Method would identify the poorest readers in a group of children without regard to IQ score. The resulting sample of RD children identified by the Years Below Method would consist primarily of the children with the lowest IQ scores in the group. Children with high IQ scores who are reading only at grade level would not be identified.

The Discrepancy Method has been criticized for not taking into account the "regression effect," which would result in an overestimation of reading disability in highly intelligent children and an underestimation in less intelligent children (McLeod, 1979). The regression effect refers to the tendency of extreme scores to regress toward the population mean when the same tests are readministered; this phenomenon occurs also for different tests that are highly correlated with one another. To correct this problem, the Regression Method formula utilizes the reliability correlations of the IQ and achievement test scores and the intercorrelation of the two tests. The various methods of identification are currently being actively evaluated.

After a child has been identified as RD, the clinician begins to focus on identifying psychological processes that might be responsible for the learning deficit. Hypotheses regarding deficient areas are derived from the child's responses on a variety of individual diagnostic tests.

Testing and Observation.   The list of test instruments that may be used in the assessment of learning disorders is lengthy. A basic test battery usually includes the Wechsler Intelligence Scale for Children and a comprehensive achievement test; additional diagnostic achievement tests and tests of special functions that are selected on the basis of earlier test findings may be administered subsequently. In spite of all the attention given to the use of objective tests in the diagnosis of learning disabilities, school systems may not be relying optimally on test results. A study by Vance, Bahr, Huberty, and Ewer-Jones (1988) indicated that test data accounted for only 33 percent of the variance in decisions to place referred children in special education learning disability programs. Rivers and Smith (1988) reported that for two hundred learning-disabled children from one school district, many had below-average intelligence and did not have severe discrepancies between achievement and ability.

Observation of behavior frequently begins during the test administration phase of the diagnostic process. Rather than simply designating whether a response to a test item is correct or incorrect, the clinician records the response itself. The types of errors seen on a test protocol give valuable information with respect to the deficiencies in reading behavior. Types of errors may include, for example, lack of letter discrimination within words, lack of discrimination between similar words, omissions of letters or words within sentences, and mispronunciation of words.

Although clinicians have utilized the informal reports of classroom behavior by teachers for some time, behavioral clinicians have been responsible for introducing the use of systematic observations to the classroom. Whenever a child has been referred for a problem in school, the behavioral clinician attempts to arrange observation sessions in the school setting. Much of the behavioral research in classroom settings has been directed toward disruptive children, but academic behaviors are beginning to receive increased study.

In some situations, the teacher is asked to observe the child's behavior, but research is beginning to suggest that using teachers as observers may present methodological problems that could obscure assessment findings. It has been proposed that teachers' observation of behavior may lead to change in both teachers' and pupils' behaviors before the initiation of an intervention program. The mechanisms for these changes are not yet fully understood, but teachers themselves report that their perception of the child changes as a result of recording the frequency of specific behavior. It is interesting to note that their subjective reports tend to reflect an increasingly favorable attitude toward the child.

The forms of behavior, the observer, and the classroom schedule determine the timing of the behavioral observations and the recording methods. If the child is having reading problems, for example, behavioral observations are conducted during the reading period. A teacher observing the child's behavior could keep account of only one or two behaviors. An outside observer could monitor a greater number of behaviors using a time-sampling technique. In the case of children with specific learning disabilities, it is particularly important to monitor both academic and nonacademic behaviors because the probability of problems in both areas appears to be high and tends to increase with children's age.

Medical Assessment.   Professionals who link a diagnosis of learning disorder to neurological dysfunction recommend that physical and specifically neurological examinations be included among the basic diagnostic procedures. The physical and neurological examinations are conducted as part of the current evaluation of the child; medical examinations obtained earlier for other purposes, such as a routine annual checkup, are not considered adequate.

The general physical examination is conducted to determine whether abnormal physical or organic factors are present and contributing to the child's problem. In the neurological examination, the physician also includes an assessment of the developmental aspects of neurologic integration. Children with learning disorders tend to present abnormalities of integrated motor behaviors rather than abnormal reflexes. The medical examination also includes an evaluation of visual acuity and auditory discrimination as well as the physical aspects of the visual and auditory systems. Routine blood and urine laboratory tests are usually included. The special laboratory tests, such as the EEG, X-rays, and biochemical analyses, are conducted only when indicated by findings from other portions of the medical examination.

A medical history of the child is obtained through one or more interviews before the medical examination is given. This history includes information related to the pre-, peri-, and postnatal periods. The physician obtains descriptions of the child's illnesses, paying particular attention to their severity, the age of the child, and the symptoms. Often included in the history is the parents' description of the child's motor and language development and information regarding the family constellation as well as events that might be related to psychological stress.

The Psychological Report.   After all of the assessment procedures have been completed, the clinician writes a report in which the behavioral characteristics of the child are described. The most important aspect of the test report is that it describes the child's strengths and weaknesses in the various areas such that a treatment program can be derived from the information. It is also important to remember that assessment does not terminate with the diagnostic report but should be a continuing process that is interwoven with the treatment program. In this manner, the child's status relative to the behavioral goals of treatment is continuously available.

General Description of Children with Learning Disorders.   The typical child with learning disorder is in an early elementary grade when referred. The child's IQ score is within the average or above-average range, but performance on the IQ test and tests of special function is more variable than average; that is, some abilities are adequate or excellent, while others are extremely poor. Achievement in some subjects may be average, but achievement in others may be well below what would be expected on the basis of grade level and IQ score. For many of these children, teachers and parents are likely to report behavior problems, such as poor memory and attention, poor organization, impulsivity, task incompletion, overactivity, and disruptive behavior. Learning-disabled children tend to have poor self-esteem and to refer to themselves as stupid. The adaptive behavior of learning-disabled children was found to be poorer than that of normal children but better than that of retarded children (Leigh, 1987).

Increasing evidence suggests that LD children are at higher risk for a variety of psychological problems (DSM-IV, 1994). Children with learning disabilities have been found to have more anxiety (Stein & Hoover, 1989) and higher levels of depression (Hall & Haws, 1989). Rourke (1988) in a review of research suggested that socioemotional disturbances should be examined in separate, more homogeneous, groups of LD children. Rourke, Young, and Leenaars (1989) reported that a particular subtype, nonverbal learning disability may predispose those afflicted to adolescent and adult depression and suicide risk.

Etiology

Because reading disorders have been diagnosed on the basis of many different criteria, our knowledge with regard to etiological factors continues to be incomplete. Very few studies have been conducted in which RD children were selected from large populations on the basis of objective criteria and then compared with appropriate control groups on variables related to possible etiological factors. The available studies typically include RD children referred by teachers or diagnosed in clinic settings, or both. It is, of course, unknown to what extent these RD children are representative of RD children in the population. The children in these studies may have been referred primarily because they presented behavior problems in addition to their academic problems, while RD children without behavior problems may not have been referred for diagnosis. Brain dysfunction has been strongly implicated as the primary etiological factor because a substantial number of RD children exhibit behaviors that are similar to those of persons known to have experienced brain damage. These behaviors include hyperactivity, short attention span, impulsivity, and distractibility. In addition, perceptual and short-term memory problems are frequently present and manifested, for example, by left-right confusion and inability to remember recently learned auditory information (Cohen & Netley, 1978).

Genetic Risk Factors. The evidence that implicates genetic factors in the etiology of RD has been derived primarily from family studies. In 1950 Hallgren reported that reading disabilities were found among the relatives of 103 out of 116 RD cases. Finucci, Guthrie, Childs, Abbey, and Childs (1976) found that 45 percent of the first-degree relatives of 20 RD children had reading disabilities. Because family studies confound genetic and environmental factors, no conclusions regarding heredity can be derived from them. Several studies involving small numbers of twins have found that monozygotic twins were 100 percent concordant and about one-third of the dizygotic sets of twins were concordant for reading disabilities. Smith, Kimberling, Pennington, and Lubs (1982) presented evidence for an autosomal recessive cause of at least some specific reading disabilities, and a more recent study on one family has suggested the possibility of an autosomal dominant etiology (Elbert & Seale, 1988). (Remember that extremely high concordance rates in identical twins may also be the result of a physical complication during the pregnancy or the birth process.)

Additional indirect evidence supporting a genetic basis is the consistently higher proportion of males identified as RD; reports of ratios ranging from two males to each female up to 10 males for each female have been made. Variability among these ratios may be due to differences in diagnostic criteria across studies (DeFries, 1989).

Prenatal, Perinatal, and Postnatal Physical Risk Factors. Most of the physical factors implicated in the etiology of mental retardation have also been suggested as causes of learning disabilities. Again, the available studies are few and tend to be inconclusive because the criteria for diagnosis are not adequately specified. Kawi and Pasamanick (1959) recorded data from the obstetrical records of retarded readers with IQ scores above 84 and found a greater frequency of pregnancy complications and premature infants in their RD group in comparison to the control group. Jayasekara and Street (1978) found that older mothers and fathers had a higher risk of having a dyslexic boy.

Considerably more research is needed before we can begin to identify the prenatal and perinatal physical risk factors that may be related to learning disabilities. Although retrospective studies are not an optimal approach, clearer hypotheses may be derived with respect to etiology if more precise diagnostic criteria were used.

Neurological dysfunction has repeatedly been presented as a significant cause of children's learning disorders; neurological dysfunction itself could be the result of genetic abnormalities and/or pre-, peri-, and postnatal physical insults to the brain. Rourke (1978) in a review of the research on the neuropsychological aspects of reading problems concluded that the evidence suggests a "significant, positive correlation between severity of reading retardation and severity of impairment on a large number of brain-related variables" (p. 170). One study (Arffa, Fitzhugh-Bell, & Black, 1989) attempted to identify clusters or subtypes of children with learning disabilities and documented brain damage using a comprehensive battery of neuropsychological tests. Five clusters were determined, but no single cluster was composed exclusively of learning-disabled or brain-damaged children. This result suggests that these tests do not discriminate between the two groups of children and that brain damage may be an underlying factor in learning disabilities.

Problems of Attention. (See previous section on Attention-Deficit/ Hyperactivity Disorder.) Difficulties in learning may be caused by the child's inability to attend to the relevant stimuli for a sufficient amount of time. Children with short attention spans have more learning problems in the regular classroom environment. Their learning can be improved by environmental changes such as one-on-one teaching and reduction of distracting stimuli in the learning environment.

Kinsbourne and Caplan (1979) proposed that the underlying bases of learning disabilities are either *cognitive power disorders* or *cognitive style disorders*. Cognitive power disorders refer to selective developmental lags, namely, immaturity of certain brain functions. Cognitive style disorders are of two types: (1) the overfocused or compulsive and (2) the underfocused or impulsive-distractible. Overfocused children tend to maintain their attention on one thing too long, while underfocused children shift their attention from one thing to another too quickly. Underfocused children are also the children considered to be hyperactive. Cognitive power disorders tend to affect specific learning tasks, while cognitive style disorders have more generalized effects on school performance and social relationships.

Psychological Risk Factors. Psychological factors have been considered important by many traditional clinicians who observed a high incidence of behavior problems in children with learning disabilities. For those children whose behavior problems are viewed as the cause of learning problems, one of the traditional forms of psychotherapy is usually recommended.

Kessler (1966, p. 201) suggested that poor school performance may be viewed as a neurotic solution to an underlying conflict. Learning requires psychic energy; if much of the psychic energy is being utilized by intense feelings and motivations, then learning will be impaired. Among the etiological factors that have been related to learning disabilities within a psychodynamic framework are poor parent-child relationships, inadequate self-concept, excessive failure, and inadequate early stimulation.

Perhaps the greatest amount of attention has been given to the role of parents in the genesis of children's learning problems. The parents have been the child's teachers prior to school entry and thereby determine much of the child's behavior in the school environment. If the child resents the authority of the parent at home, then that child is likely to resent the authority of the teacher at school. Interactions between parent and child around developmental tasks during the early years are believed to influence the quality of the teacher-child interaction and, therefore, learning. For example, if the parent plays a prominent role in encouraging and rewarding the child during toilet training, this positive experience predisposes the child to react favorably to learning later academic skills. Repression of curiosity about sexual matters in the home is also felt by some clinicians to contribute to the child's lack of involvement in school learning.

Clinicians are increasingly coming to believe that most of the psychological problems shown by *younger* learning-disabled children are either caused by the same factors that cause the learning disabilities or are secondary to stresses in the home and/or school from poor academic performance. Success in the remediation of academic and psychological problems during the earlier school years would, it is hoped, reduce the risk of personality and conduct disorders during adolescence.

Treatment

Children with specific reading disabilities receive a wide variety of treatment programs. Often several types of treatment are conducted simultaneously. The treatment program designed for a particular child depends on many factors, such as the theoretical orientation of the diagnostician, the services available in the school and community, and the socioeconomic status of the family. Most professionals are beginning to agree that educational remediation should be the primary form of treatment, although other types of treatment are frequently indicated and recommended.

Educational Remediation. Some children with reading disabilities, particularly those in the early elementary school years, present no outstanding behavioral problems and thus would benefit optimally from an educational remediation program. Children with behavior problems require other forms of intervention in addition to educational remediation.

Educational remediation is usually conducted by a teacher who has been trained to provide services to children with special educational needs. Teachers without the formal credentials have sometimes served in the same capacity, and many have provided excellent remediation programs. Most teachers who provide special education services are employed by school systems and work with children in schools; special education teachers are being included on the professional staffs of clinics, however, and some teachers provide tutorial services on a private basis.

As is the case in all learning disabilities, children with reading disabilities differ from one another to such a great extent that remedial instruction must be highly individualized. Information obtained from the diagnostic procedures provides the basis for designing each child's remedial program. The most important information is related to the child's level of functioning in the various aspects of the reading process: word recognition, comprehension, and word-attack skills or phonics. The program is designed on the basis of the child's strengths and weaknesses in reading performance, and reading materials are chosen to be compatible with the child's level of functioning. That is, the materials chosen initially for the remediation program should ensure a high level of success to develop optimal motivation on the part of the child.

A substantial number of studies indicate that reading remediation is effective (e.g., Gittelman & Feingold, 1983). There has been an ongoing debate about whether the deficient academic skill itself or the "underlying" deficit, or component deficit, such as visual perception or perceptual motor skills, should be emphasized in remedial programs. A series of studies suggested that component deficit remediation was not as efficient as direct teaching of the deficient academic skill (e.g., Vellutino, Steger, Meyer, Harding, & Niles, 1979). Wade and Kass (1987) subsequently presented evidence that a combination of the two approaches results in higher reading scores than does the teaching of only the deficient academic skill.

It appears that a remedial approach that utilizes behavioral principles with careful attention to the antecedent stimuli (materials) and consequent stimuli (reinforcers) had the highest degree of success. Because many children with reading problems have not adequately learned the most fundamental behaviors required for progress in reading, behavioral analysis of the child's repertoire is a necessary first step. Following this assessment, the teacher designates behavioral goals and chooses from the large selection of materials those that are appropriate for the specific behavioral goals. Reinforcers are also carefully chosen for each child. Children with histories of poor academic achievement have very likely experienced considerable negative feedback for their attempts or, at best, have been ignored in the classroom; as a result, their motivation is usually extremely low. A great deal of reinforcement may be necessary to get these children to respond to academic materials at normal levels.

Learning theory has made a substantial contribution to our understanding of children's academic progress. Behavioral clinicians have given little research attention to the unique problems that may be encountered by children with learning disorders, but a number of studies have examined the effect of certain stimulus variables on the behavior of children with deficiencies in specific academic subjects.

From learning theory, the idea of individualized instruction was developed and is manifested in teaching machines and programmed texts.

Programmed instruction may be described as a method of presenting academic material in small, sequential steps. Each step presents information, and the child is required to respond to the information. Feedback is given to the child's response before the next step is taken. The principal advantage of programmed instruction is that individual children can proceed at their own rates, in contrast to traditional classroom teaching in which the slower child may be left behind and the brighter child may become bored. Being allowed to proceed at their own pace, children with learning problems may be spared much of the negative feedback that accompanies performance that is below average. Another advantage of programmed instruction is that it frees the teacher to provide assistance to children when they need it.

Many programmed-instruction materials have been developed and marketed. Although research has not yet substantiated the superiority of programmed instruction over regular classroom instruction, only a few disadvantages of the former have become apparent. Perhaps the greatest problem associated with programmed instruction is that materials are often published before there is any evidence that they accomplish the goals they were intended to reach. Not having been trained to evaluate the quality of materials, teachers may be unduly swayed in their choices by possibly irrelevant factors, such as descriptions in advertising brochures. In addition, very few studies have directly compared the achievement levels of children taught with programmed materials and those taught by conventional methods. A second problem is that programmed-instruction materials may be more expensive than comparable traditional textbooks; their extra cost cannot be justified if they are not demonstrably effective. A third problem is that some of the programmed workbooks are designed so that cheating is much too easy; such materials may require that the children be monitored closely. In summary, the basic principles of educational remediation are essentially those of any sound educational program: know the child's level of performance, individualize instruction, and use antecedent and consequent stimuli appropriately to produce the best possible learning and performance.

Teachers are being trained to respond to the special problems posed by children with learning disorders in the classroom. Modifications in the usual classroom practices are clearly indicated in many instances. For example, if students have problems in reading, they may benefit by hearing the information, having visual material explained orally, or by being encouraged to read aloud to another person or a tape recorder. If students have problems in writing, they may be helped by learning to type, presenting their answers to exam questions orally, and by being allowed to dictate essays or substitute tape recordings for written assignments.

Psychotherapy and Behavior Therapy. Some children with learning disorders have problems that may be helped with psychotherapy. These problems may include feelings of anxiety or depression and poor self-image. Many LD children have had an accumulation of negative experiences at home and school that could account for these disturbances. Such feelings are not easily overcome, but many clinicians believe that psychotherapy has been moderately successful in helping to alleviate them. Family therapy has also been recommended to improve LD children's self-esteem, self-control, and frustration tolerance (Ziegler & Holden, 1988).

COMMUNICATION DISORDERS

Normal Language Development

Communication disorders are among the more common of the childhood behavior disorders. The acquisition of an expressive and receptive speech repertoire is an extremely complex learning task that may be disrupted by a variety of events throughout the life span. Normal speech development requires an unimpaired auditory sensory and perceptual system, memory functions, intact expressive speech motor functions, and adequate speech and language stimulation. The receptive and expressive speech acquisition processes are so strongly intertwined that distinctions between expressive and receptive speech problems cannot always be made. To a large extent, expressive speech is dependent on receptive speech or language comprehension; if expressive speech is faulty, the problem may be due to a dysfunction of receptive speech or primarily to the expressive speech functions themselves.

The professional most frequently involved with the diagnosis and treatment of speech and language problems is the speech pathologist who has been trained in a master's level graduate program. Doctoral level speech pathologists also provide services, but they usually spend most of their time teaching and doing research in college and university settings.

Speech and language skills develop in an orderly manner during the early years, and normative data allow us to determine whether a child's speech productions are within normal limits. From these norms we may begin to understand the stages of speech development and the significance of the language development sequence.

Infants are born with the capacity to vocalize; during the first month of life crying is the dominant vocal response and seems to occur primarily when the baby is uncomfortable (e.g., hungry, wet, or cold). Beginning in the second month, crying becomes differentiated in that different cries may signal different states of need. In addition, other vocalizations begin to emerge and are correlated with more positive states. During the second and third months of life a variety of vocal sounds, such as "oh," "uh," and "ooh," begin to emerge. Although their responses to sound are apparent at birth, not until three or four months of age do infants consistently turn toward the source of a sound or interrupt their own vocalizations to search for sounds.

Between three and six months of age, most infants spend considerable amounts of time vocalizing. Toward the end of this period a number of consonant-vowel combinations are added to their repertoire. Some of the combinations appear in repetitive form (e.g., "ba-ba," "ga-ga") and are described as babbling. The babbling stage is considered to be particularly important, since at this time the vocalizations of deaf and hearing infants can be discriminated and environmental contingencies begin to have a significant influence on the quality and quantity of sound production. Optimal hearing may be critical for language development because research indicates that infants are able to discriminate all the possible phonetic contrasts only during the first year of life (Werker, 1989).

At about eight or nine months of age, infants begin their attempts to imitate the speech sounds of others. This is the time when many infants learn to wave and say "bye-bye" in imitation. Their comprehension of language is also becoming more readily apparent in that they respond appropriately to specific words or phrases. For example, an infant may reach for or look at a ball when hearing the word *ball.*

Between 12 and 18 months of age, most children begin to say their first words. While parents tend to count some of the earlier utterances, such as "ma-ma" and "da-da," as words, they usually do not meet the criterion for true words. The criterion requires the child to produce the word spontaneously in the context of the appropriate stimulus (e.g., the child says "ball" while reaching for a ball). During the second year the child acquires up to 50 single words, which designate common objects, familiar persons, and requests. Sometimes, the single-word utterances stand for more complex communications; for example, the child says "up" to indicate a desire to leave the playpen or crib. At about two years of age, children begin to combine words into two-word phrases or sentences. During the third year these phrases and sentences are expanded and modified to be compatible with the grammatical structure of the English language.

While children are acquiring single words, they also appear to be learning the language system. Soon after children begin to combine words, combinations of words that have never been presented or taught to them begin to appear in their verbal repertoire. That is, children at this stage of development begin to demonstrate some knowledge of syntax and word order. They are also intent on communicating with others and show frustration when adults do not respond or indicate that they do not understand what the child is saying.

Between the ages of two and three years, the rate of vocabulary growth is probably higher than at any other period in a child's life. In addition, average sentence length is expanded to three and four words, including prepositions, conjunctions, and articles. By the age of three years the child is typically able to use the pronouns "I," "me," and "you" correctly. The three-year-old can understand several thousand words and has an active vocabulary of about one thousand words. Between the ages of three and seven years a child's speech productions increasingly approximate those of adults. By about eight years of age, a child's use of syntax closely matches that of adults and lacks only the nuances of complex sentence productions.

Speech Delay

While the norms for the onset and development of speech provide a general outline of expected progress, variability among children is substantial. For many physicians it has been difficult to determine whether a particular child's delayed speech development is within normal limits or indicative of some abnormality. Because most physicians know at least one instance of severe speech delay in which a child later developed normal speech, they are often reluctant to refer children younger than two or three years of age who are using minimal or no speech. On the other hand, research has indicated a very close relationship between speech development and general intellectual functioning. Fortunately, early speech development is beginning to be recognized as crucial to a child's later intellectual status, and many professionals are now emphasizing early identification and intervention for children whose speech is delayed.

Assessment. Until the past few decades, very few professionals from any discipline were trained to assess speech and language development in children younger than three years. Typically, psychologists would administer a developmental or intelligence test and clinically estimate children's levels of speech development from the relevant items on the test. More often than not, these estimates were valid, but they certainly did not reflect the child's total behavioral repertoire in the area of speech and language development.

With the increasing availability of norms and standardized tests for assessing speech and language in preschool children, more speech pathologists have been trained to assess young children's speech behaviors. An interview is also conducted in which parents are asked to relate their child's history of speech development and to describe the child's current speech repertoire. During the evaluation session, the child's spontaneous speech productions and responses to the speech of others are recorded. The speech pathologist also presents materials to the child that are designed to evoke speech responses.

Assessment of speech development in children under three years of age presents special problems for the evaluator. Young children typically react to strange environments by becoming nonverbal. Since speech pathologists need an optimal response from the child, they must arrange the situation to bring about maximal verbal behavior.

In addition to the formal and informal speech assessment, children referred for possible speech delay problems usually receive a hearing test; a general physical examination and a psychological evaluation are also recommended. Often, the hearing test is conducted by an audiologist who is a member of the speech clinic staff. Auditory testing includes evaluation of hearing sensitivity, speech discrimination, and middle ear functioning.

Since speech delay can occur alone or in conjunction with other behavior disorders, differential diagnosis becomes particularly important. The assessment procedure should include an attempt to determine possible etiological factors, since such information may be useful in treatment.

Etiology. A delay in speech may occur as a result of several factors, some physical and others environmental. As is true with other behavior disorders, determining etiology for individual children is not always possible. Occasionally, the assessment procedure does not identify any possible etiological factors, but more often it identifies several possible causes of the problem.

Perhaps the single greatest cause of speech delay is hearing loss. The speech-delayed child may be deaf or have varying amounts of hearing loss, particularly in the speech range of frequencies. Recent research is also suggesting that temporary hearing losses during the first few years of life may also be correlated with slow speech development. Children with frequent or untreated ear infections, or both, during infancy are particularly prone to speech delays. Low-birth-weight infants are also at risk for delayed language development (Vohr, Coll, & Oh, 1988).

Speech delay is often associated with other behavior disorders, such as mental retardation and autism, problems whose causes appear to be largely physical. Most clinicians feel that it is important to label these disorders differently, although the children in the different groups may have some problems in common. Having a behavioral deficit in common, however, does not mean that they share the same etiological factors or that optimal therapy will be identical.

Environmental causes of speech delay have also been proposed. Children whose language environments are grossly deficient can present speech delays and slow speech development of the magnitude observed in some children with organic impairment. Children need speech models in order to acquire speech themselves. Although extreme cases in which children have been totally deprived of language stimulation are rare, instances in which the quality and quantity of language stimulation are minimal are frequently documented. Such instances are almost always correlated with other forms of deprivation, making it difficult to ascertain the specific role of language deprivation. These other forms of deprivation may include malnutrition, poor medical care, and general parental neglect—conditions known to retard development.

Language delay is known to be more common in children from the lower socioeconomic classes (Silva, Williams, & McGee, 1987). Some of this delay is no doubt accounted for by differences between middle-class and other models available to children. Living conditions such as crowding and noise could alter some of the contingencies usually available for the young child's vocalizations and speech attempts. For example, the busy parent with many children vying for attention may ignore the vocalizations of the infant, or the noise level in the household could often be great enough to prevent others from hearing the infant's babbling and reinforcing it.

Even in families for which environmental deprivation is not a factor, otherwise normal children fail to develop appropriate speech. Many clinicians are convinced that speech delay can result from parents' being overprotective and anticipating the child's needs. That is, some children don't talk because they have no need to talk; their every wish is fulfilled without the necessity for speaking. Many of these situations are initiated by an episode of illness during which the parents devote a great deal of attention to the child. The child, in effect, trains the parents to continue their high rate of attention even after the illness has subsided.

In the past, some speech pathologists viewed these etiological factors in psychoanalytic terms. Since the demands for speech production usually coincide with initiation of toilet training, delayed speech may represent an anal conflict; that is, the child who is resisting toilet training also tends to resist other demands, such as parental pressures to speak. Although we cannot be sure how toilet training and learning to speak affect each other, clinicians tend to agree that most children go through a period, later in the second year of life, when they strongly resist requests and demands of all kinds.

Treatment. The treatment of speech delay depends greatly on the etiological factors known or hypothesized to have affected the child's speech development. If hearing is found to be impaired and correctable causes identified, medical or surgical treatment is indicated. Some types of hearing loss, not correctable by medical treatment, can be alleviated by fitting the child with one or two hearing aids. Correcting the hearing problems medically or with a hearing aid, however, does not often completely eliminate the need for speech therapy. Corrective therapy is indicated if the child has acquired speech patterns based on faulty hearing or if the child needs intensive experience with speech models to make speech acquisition possible.

When the child's speech delay is considered to be due to environmental deprivation (lack of appropriate models and inefficient contingencies), treatment is designed to overcome those deficiencies. Project Head Start and subsequent experimental preschool programs have provided important data on the early speech and language development in disadvantaged children, clearly substantiating deficits in those areas.

Several research projects conducted in the home and in preschool settings have also demonstrated that these language problems can be ameliorated by remedial training. One of the most successful of these projects was that conducted by Bereiter and Engelmann (1966). The Bereiter-Engelmann technique of teaching includes the following 18 procedures:

1. Work at different levels of difficulty at different times.
2. Adhere to a rigid, repetitive presentation pattern.
3. Use unison responses whenever possible.
4. Never work with a child individually in a study group for more than about 30 seconds.
5. Phrase statements rhythmically.
6. Require children to speak in a loud, clear voice.
7. Do not hurry children or encourage them to talk fast.
8. Clap to accent basic language patterns and conventions.
9. Use questions liberally.
10. Use repetition.
11. Be aware of the cues the child is receiving.
12. Use short explanations.
13. Tailor the explanations and rules to what the child knows.

14. Use lots of examples.
15. Prevent incorrect responses whenever possible.
16. Be completely unambiguous in letting the child know when his response is correct and when it is incorrect.
17. Dramatize the use value of learning whenever possible.
18. Encourage thinking behavior. (pp. 110–120)

Bereiter (1972) has reported that programs that teach a specific series of tasks (from the simple to the complex) and have specific behavioral goals facilitate achievement more than do traditional, child-centered preschool programs.

If the child's speech delay is considered to be the result of parental overprotection or of parent-child conflict, then psychotherapy or behavior therapy for the parents may be recommended. The goal of therapy is to communicate the relationship of the child's speech delay to parental behavior and to suggest ways that changes in their behavior may facilitate the child's speech development. Either direct observation of the parent-child interaction or information derived from the interview provides the hypotheses regarding which parent and child behaviors should be changed.

Therapy with parents is not always successful. A few parents have difficulty accepting their role in the problem and deny the possibility of such a relationship. Other parents acknowledge the possibility but cannot change their own behavior in response to the child. Such cases challenge even the most experienced and talented clinicians.

Expressive and Receptive Language Disorders

Expressive and receptive language disorders are communication disorders related to the production and understanding of oral language. Successful communication requires that individuals be able to decode the oral productions of others and to encode their own messages with all the participants sharing the same linguistic system or set of rules. Language consists of four major dimensions: the sound system (phonology), the system of meanings (semantics), the rules of word formation (morphology), and the rules of sentence formation (grammar) (Rice, 1989). Language disorders may reflect a disuse or misuse of these four factors. Diagnosis of a particular language disorder necessitates a comprehensive assessment of language functioning and related abilities.

Assessment. A diagnosis of an expressive or receptive language disorder requires the ruling out of certain other diagnoses and factors, particularly infantile autism, mental retardation, and general hearing loss. Formal assessment includes auditory, psychological, and language testing as well as interviews and medical evaluations.

Assessment of general intellectual functioning for children with language disorders poses special problems in that both expressive and receptive language are important components of cognitive functioning. Since the major intelligence tests, such as the Stanford-Binet and the Wechsler scales, rely heavily on both expressive and receptive language, children with these disorders would be penalized on these tests. If the child's handicap is not severe, that is, the child has some language skills, these tests might be administered and used for assessing strengths and weaknesses.

The clinician may also want to administer one of the intelligence tests that are not dependent on expressive or receptive language. The Peabody Picture Vocabulary Test (Dunn & Dunn, 1997) uses verbal instructions, but the child is required only to point to one of four pictures; this test provides a measure of receptive language. The Arthur Adaptation of the Leiter International Performance Scale (Arthur, 1952) is administered without the clinician's using spoken language and does not utilize the child's language for scoring. This scale has 54 items arranged in order of difficulty; each item requires the child to match a set of blocks with a picture.

An expressive, developmental language disorder is diagnosed when the child's vocal language is significantly delayed, but the delay is not associated with a hearing impairment, mental retardation, or infantile autism. Evidence of age-appropriate understanding of language must be present.

A mixed receptive-expressive language disorder is diagnosed when a significant delay is apparent in both the understanding *and* expression of language and when these delays are not associated with a hearing impairment, mental retardation, or infantile autism. There may also be evidence of impairment in auditory, short-term memory, auditory discrimination, and reading and spelling skills.

Etiology. The families of children with developmental language disorders have a higher-than-average incidence of these and other specific developmental disorders, suggesting the possibility of some genetic contribution to etiology. A higher incidence of specific expressive language deficits has been reported in boys with an XXY chromosome pattern (an extra X chromosome) (Graham, Bashir, Stark, Silert, & Walzer, 1988).

About one-third to one-half of children with language disorders present clear evidence of damage to the central nervous system. For example, Goldstein, Landau, and Kleffner (1958) found that 40 percent of their sample had abnormal EEG findings. Another third showed signs of minimal brain dysfunction or borderline neurological dysfunction. A study of preschool children with normal motor development and average nonverbal intelligence also found high rates of abnormal EEGs, and a significant percentage of the children with severe language disorders were born postmaturely (Maccario, Hefferen, Keblusek, & Lipinski, 1982).

Treatment. The speech therapy program for children with language disorders is usually slow and difficult. A variety of approaches to treatment have been described in case studies. They have emphasized the use of the visual sense and reading; the association of sound with visual, auditory, motor-feedback cues; the use of highly contrasted sounds; the gradual increase in the length and complexity of linguistic units; backward chaining; use of rhythm; and slower speaking rate by therapist and child (Jaffe, 1984).

Developmental language disorders sometimes do not improve with the usual forms of speech therapy. A follow-up study of children with disorders in articulation and language revealed that language problems continued through adulthood, while problems with articulation did not (Hall & Tomblin, 1978). Programs similar to that of Lovaas's for autistic children and training that emphasizes nonvocal communication (signing) appear to offer some promise for the more severely affected children (Vanderheiden & Grilley, 1975).

Phonological Disorder

Phonological or articulation disorder refers to errors in the production of speech sounds or phonemes (the smallest elements of a language). Phonemic errors are evaluated in the context of development norms; that is, the capacity to produce certain sounds varies as a function of both age and gender. During the early years, articulatory proficiency is quite variable. For example, girls tend to approximate adult-level proficiency by the age of six to seven years, while boys achieve this level of proficiency about one year later.

The articulatory errors that young children make are not a random sample of possible errors. The child's earliest words consist of sounds that can be produced with ease. These words almost always consist of nasal consonants, labial (lip) sounds, and vowels (e.g., "ma-ma," "da-da"). The production of specific sounds tends to occur in a developmental sequence (e.g., /d/ before /l/, /k/ before /t/, /m/ before /n/). This ordering may be due to several factors: the structure of the speech apparatus, ease of sound production, and relative difficulty of sound discriminability.

Assessment. Deficiencies in articulation are the most common type of speech disorder among children. Occasionally, preschool children are referred for articulation problems, but children with these problems are not usually identified until they enter school. Prior to evaluating speech and language, the speech pathologist usually requests the administration of an audiologic (hearing) test. An interview with the parents is also considered an essential part of the assessment procedure. The parental interview focuses on the child's developmental history with respect to responsiveness to sounds and words as well as verbal expression. The parents are also asked about the child's early eating behavior and whether there were problems with sucking, swallowing, or chewing.

The information provided by the parents and other professionals who have seen the child often facilitates the assessment procedure in that the focus of diagnostic testing may be sharpened. Generally, the speech pathologist's assessment includes an inspection of the interior of the mouth and an evaluation of tongue movement, since structural abnormalities of the mouth, lips, and teeth as well as limitation of tongue movement interfere with normal articulation.

The evaluation of speech itself is conducted both formally and informally. During informal assessment the pathologist attempts to engage the child in conversation about topics of interest to the child. The child's spontaneous speech is evaluated in terms of the standards for phoneme usage. A record is kept of the occurrence of sound substitutions, sound omissions, and sound distortions. Formal evaluation consists of the administration of standardized articulation tests. The goal of the speech pathologist is to determine whether there is evidence for either articulatory immaturity or articulatory dysmaturation. Articulatory *immaturity* refers to an articulatory speech pattern that is typical of children younger than the client. Such patterns frequently occur in children who are mentally retarded or of borderline intelligence. Articulatory *dysmaturation* refers to articulatory speech patterns that are not typical at any developmental stage. These patterns are usually associated with structural defects, motor problems, and neurological abnormalities.

Etiology.   Articulation problems have been associated with a variety of etiological factors. Articulation skills are highly correlated with mental age, suggesting that the factors associated with slow rates of intellectual development are also possible causes of problems with articulation. For example, a high rate of problems with communication has been associated with prematurity and neonatal respiratory distress. Hearing deficits may also account for deficits in articulation. There may be hearing loss that is confined to certain frequencies. If the impairment is limited to the lower range of frequencies, speech patterns may be markedly affected; in such cases, parents would not necessarily suspect a hearing loss because the child responds to most environmental sounds that usually consist of a broad range of frequencies. Sometimes the child is described by the parents as stubborn or preoccupied because the child's responses to their directions are minimal. Children with hearing deficits rapidly become adept at learning to lip-read and respond to gestural cues, thus often causing a postponement of referral until the articulatory speech problem is severe.

Articulatory problems may also be the product of learning experiences. If a child has as a primary speech model a person who has deficits in articulation there may be an increased probability of the child's learning the same pattern through modeling. Likewise, if a child is strongly reinforced for immature speech patterns by adults frequently imitating the child's speech, then these speech patterns may become strengthened. Fortunately, most children are exposed to a wide variety of speech models through urban living arrangements and exposure to television.

Treatment.   Historically, several approaches have been taken to treat articulatory problems remedially. During the 1920s and 1930s, emphasis was given to the phonetic-placement method in which the child was taught the "correct" position of the tongue and mouth for production of specific sounds. Subsequent research, however, has shown that in different persons a specific sound may be achieved with a variety of positions.

Since hearing is the primary sensory system for the acquisition of speech during the preschool years, many pathologists have advocated the teaching of auditory discrimination as fundamental to the correction of articulatory problems. Training auditory discrimination, including self-discrimination, makes probable generalization outside of the speech therapy sessions.

Most contemporary speech pathologists do not restrict themselves to any single approach to therapy, although among the various options, auditory stimulation is still the principal component or foundation of most therapeutic programs. The process of correcting misarticulated speech sounds must focus on these related tasks: learning to identify the sounds and discriminate among them, learning to produce the sounds in a variety of phonetic contexts, and learning to generalize the correct sounds outside of the therapy setting.

Auditory discrimination training takes up a large proportion of the initial therapy sessions and less as the sound production phase is undertaken. The pathologist introduces the sound in an interesting manner to ensure that the child will pay attention. The sound is given a name to establish its identity; for example, the /s/ sound may be called the "snake sound." To facilitate the child's learning to discriminate the stimulus sound from other sounds, the pathologist presents a series of sounds that includes the stimulus sound, and the child makes a particular response each time the stimulus sound occurs.

Initially, sounds that are easily confused with the stimulus sound are not included in the series; they are gradually included as the child becomes proficient in making the easier discriminations. After the child is able to discriminate the stimulus sound from all other speech sounds, the pathologist begins to introduce the sound as the initial sound in single words. This series of discriminations is followed by training the child to discriminate the stimulus sound when it appears in any position in the word. Training also includes the pathologist's presenting both the correct and incorrect versions of the sound and teaching the child to differentiate them. Throughout this phase of discrimination training, the pathologist may use other sense modalities to facilitate the learning process. With young school-aged children, for example, letters and words may be presented visually in conjunction with the auditory stimuli.

Relatively little research has been done on the production phase of articulation training. Webb and Siegenthaler (1957), however, in a study comparing training methods, found that verbal instructions on how to make the sound and auditory presentation of the sound followed by evaluation of the child's sound production was the most effective combination. Training in sound production proceeds from the single sound through words, phrases, and sentences to spontaneous speech. Again, the child's motivation and attention are best used by the careful choice of stimuli including visual materials and by the reinforcement of successful productions.

Generalization outside of therapy is considered by the pathologist beginning in the earlier stages of treatment. That is, the pathologist chooses words to use in therapy that are commonly said in everyday verbal interactions. The pathologist's hope is that the correct production of a word in the therapy sessions will be learned well enough to be reproduced in other environments. To facilitate such transfer the pathologist may ask the child to perform specific tasks at home or school, such as finding pictures of objects that contain a specific stimulus sound.

Speech therapy with children often involves the parents as well. Most pathologists agree that the parents should be well informed about their child's problem and about the steps that will be taken to remedy it. In addition, parents are encouraged to be supportive and positive toward the child. Pathologists disagree, however, on the extent to which parents should be directly involved in the speech therapy itself. Some research studies suggest that trained parents can be effective therapists for their own children, while other studies suggest that parental involvement may be detrimental. Future research will likely begin to delineate those factors that will predict which parents will be more effective than others.

CONCLUSIONS

Attention-deficit/hyperactivity disorder, learning disorder, and communication disorder are relatively common problems affecting preschool and school-aged children. The available research suggests that genetic, physical, and psychological risk factors are influential in their etiology. Treatment programs may involve medication, individually designed behavioral interventions, and family therapy. The most successful treatment programs are likely to be those that identify the affected children in the earliest grades.

RECOMMENDED READINGS

Barkley, R.A. (1990). *Attention-deficit hyperactivity disorder: A handbook for diagnosis and treatment.* New York: Guilford Press.

Gerber, A. (1993). *Language-related learning disabilities: Their nature and treatment.* Baltimore: Brookes.

Lyon, G.R. (Ed.). (1994). *Frames of reference for the assessment of learning disabilities: New views on measurement issues.* Baltimore: Brookes.

Rourke, B.P. (Ed.). (1995). *Symptoms of nonverbal learning disabilities: Neurodevelopmental manifestations.* New York: Guilford Press.

11

"Acting-Out": Oppositional Defiant Disorder, Conduct Disorders, Delinquency, and Substance Abuse

This chapter revised by Sharon Carmanico.

Mo, a 13-year-old boy, was referred by juvenile court because he had been caught stealing a television set. His previous contacts with the court involved truancy from school.

Mo was the third of seven children. His father deserted the home when Mo was two years old and has not been seen since that time. The younger children were fathered by a man with whom his mother currently lives. Mo does not get along with this man, who has physically abused him on several occasions while drunk. His older brothers are currently in a juvenile training school for car theft.

Mo's mother, who looked much older than her age, could not recall any problems during her pregnancy. She did not receive prenatal care, and Mo was delivered in a hospital emergency room because "he came so fast." The mother reported that Mo's problems were due to his "getting in with the wrong people."

The school reports indicated that Mo had academic problems beginning in the early grades. Although his intelligence test scores were only slightly below average, his achievement in all school subjects was poor due to "motivational" problems. The attendance record indicated sharp increases in the number of absences during the past two years.

Mo freely admitted that he hates school and is looking forward to dropping out, getting a job, and moving away from his family. When asked what kind of a job he would get, he responded that he didn't know but that "something would turn up." Mo's enjoyment of life seemed to revolve around his friends, some of whom were older than he and had already dropped out of school. He and an older boy were assigned the job of stealing a television to furnish the group's club room. Mo would not identify the other boy, who had escaped, or other members of his group.

Certain behavior disorders tend to cluster together because they are what might be termed *acting-out* or *externalizing* behaviors (Achenbach & Edelbrock, 1983). That is, the children who have these problems are doing something that violates the standards or norms set by adult society.

A large number of studies have provided evidence that different acting-out problem behaviors are intercorrelated. These disorders may vary in their impact both on the individual child and on the persons in the child's environment; some are primarily harmful to other persons, while others have their greatest negative impact on the individual displaying the disorder.

A discussion follows of Oppositional Defiant Disorder, Conduct Disorder, delinquency, and substance-related disorders. The sequence in which each syndrome is discussed corresponds approximately to a developmental trajectory, from earlier to later appearing disorders. Presence of problem behaviors at earlier ages increases the risk of problem behaviors at later ages; however, no syndrome represents a necessary or sufficient prerequisite for the occurrence of another syndrome.

OPPOSITIONAL DEFIANT DISORDER

Assessment and Risk Factors

A persistent and severe syndrome of noncompliant behavior may warrant a psychiatric diagnosis of Oppositional Defiant Disorder. DSM-IV criteria are as follows:

A. A pattern of negativistic, hostile, and defiant behavior lasting at least six months, during which four (or more) of the following are present:

    (1) often loses temper
    (2) often argues with adults
    (3) often actively defies or refuses to comply with adults' requests or rules
    (4) often deliberately annoys people
    (5) often blames others for his or her own mistakes or misbehavior
    (6) is often touchy or easily annoyed by others
    (7) is often angry and resentful
    (8) is often spiteful or vindictive

B. The disturbance in behavior causes clinically significant impairment in social, academic, or occupational functioning.

C. The behaviors do not occur exclusively during the course of a Psychotic or Mood Disorder.

D. Criteria are not met for Conduct Disorder, and if the individual is age 18 years or older, criteria are not met for Antisocial Personality Disorder (pp. 93–94).

The criteria are considered to be met when they occur considerably more often than they do in the behavior of most people of the same mental age.

The essential characteristic of Oppositional Defiant Disorder is a recurrent pattern of disobedient, negativistic, and provocative opposition to authority figures such as parents and teachers. Although the disorder may be observed as early as three years of age, it typically begins by eight years and no later than early adolescence.

Behaviors typical of Oppositional Defiant Disorder include testing limits, stubborn resistance to requests, and verbal aggression. Temper tantrums often occur following impulse frustration. Negativism, stubbornness, dawdling, procrastination, and passive resistance to authority are most frequently observed in familar settings, like home. Children with this disorder usually do not label themselves as oppositional; instead, they present their behaviors as a reasonable response to unreasonable demands by others.

Associated child problems include low self-esteem, mood swings, and substance abuse. Oppositional-defiant children are often identified as having "difficult" temperaments and negative sibling interactions during early development (Kingston & Prior, 1995). Associated family factors include high stress (Donenberg & Baker, 1993), hostile parent-child interactions, and abusive or neglectful child rearing (Lewis, Moy, & Jackson, 1985; Lewis, Pincus, & Bard, 1988). The severity of family problems and child behavioral symptoms is predictive of dysfunctional developmental outcomes (Campbell, 1995).

Oppositional Defiant Disorder may be a less severe variant or early symptomatic precursor to Conduct Disorder (Frick et al., 1991; Russo et al., 1994). Attention-Deficit/Hyperactivity Disorder is common in children with Oppositional Defiant Disorder, and parents of oppositional children frequently present histories of other conduct, mood or substance use disorders (Velez et al., 1989).

Treatment

Treatment approaches to Oppositional Defiant Disorder include individual therapy, family therapy, behavioral interventions, and parent training. Treatment models may be psychodynamic, cognitive-behavioral, or eclectic. Systematic studies of treatment efficacy have not been forthcoming; therefore, no single treatment modality has been unequivocally supported (Rey, 1993). Treatment models that integrate developmental and behavioral principles have been recommended to encourage age-appropriate, effective and adaptive behavioral improvement (Forehand & Wierson, 1993).

Parent training is the most widely accepted treatment model for Oppositional Defiant Disorder (e.g., Forehand & McMahon, 1981). This approach attempts to change dysfunctional family interaction patterns in the home. Parents are taught five skills: giving attention, giving rewards, ignoring, issuing commands, and implementing timeout. The first phase of the program teaches parents to increase social attention to reinforce appropriate behaviors and to decrease social attention to noncompliant behavior. The second phase consists of training the parents to use appropriate commands and timeout to decrease the noncompliant behavior.

Reviews of research (e.g., Wells & Forehand, 1981) and individual case studies (e.g., Richman et al., 1994; Bourn, 1993) show that training parents to change their children's behavior can be highly effective. These behavioral changes appear to be highly adaptive and durable in their effects. In a study of noncompliant children who had participated in a parent training program, these treated children were, in young adulthood, indistinguishable from matched community peers on measures of adaptive functioning (Long, Forehand, Wierson, & Morgan, 1994). However, parent training is not effective with all families. Poor outcome and high dropout rates have been linked to parent depression, low socioeconomic status, and referral by judicial agencies (Forehand & McMahon, 1981, p. 47).

CONDUCT DISORDERS

Assessment

A number of investigators have attempted to classify conduct disorders and to determine personality and behavioral characteristics of each category. As in other behavior disorders, the classification labels themselves reflect a composite of clinical/descriptive and research-based behavioral characteristics, as well as both known and inferred contributing factors.

Earlier Diagnostic Classifications. DSM-III (1980) described four types of conduct disorders: (1) undersocialized-aggressive; (2) undersocialized-nonaggressive; (3) socialized-aggressive; and (4) socialized-nonaggressive. The *undersocialized* types did not establish normal patterns of affection and close relationships with other persons, including peers. Egocentricity, superficial relationships, and manipulative behaviors predominate. Feelings of empathy or guilt are usually absent. Age of onset is usually prepubertal. The *socialized* types have some history of close attachment to others but may manipulate or aggress against "outsiders"; they are more likely to be members of gangs that promote antisocial behavior. Onset is usually during adolescence. The *aggressive* types repetitively violate the rights of others through physical violence, while the *nonaggressive* types are characterized by repeated but nonconfrontational violations of important social rules.

DSM-III-R (1987) recognized three types of conduct disorders (group type, solitary aggressive type, and undifferentiated), roughly corresponding to DSM-III diagnoses of socialized, undersocialized-aggressive, and a residual category for other conduct-disordered behaviors. DSM-III-R criteria reflected research findings that DSM-III undersocialized-nonaggressive types rarely occurred, and socialized-aggressive and socialized-nonaggressive types could not be reliably distinguished.

Current Diagnostic Classification. DSM-IV (1994) further simplifies the classification system of conduct-disordered syndromes of behavior into two types: childhood-onset and adolescent-onset. Childhood-onset is defined by the appearance of at least one of the three criterion behaviors prior to age 10; in the adolescent-onset type, criterion behaviors first occur after the age of 10. Research has indicated more chronic, severe and pervasive behavior problems in early-onset than late-onset conduct disorder. The early-onset type corresponds most closely to earlier classifications of undersocialized-aggressive and solitary-aggressive types; the late-onset type is similar to the earlier classifications of socialized and group types. Diagnostic criteria are consistent with those in previous DSM nosologies, with minor modifications that reflect research findings of prognostic features.

The first criterion for diagnosis is a persistent pattern of behavior that violates the rights of others or major social norms. The behaviors associated with Conduct Disorder include aggression toward people or animals (e.g., often initiates physical fights, has forced someone into sexual activity), destruction of property, including deliberate fire-setting, deceitfulness or theft (e.g., has broken into someone's house or car, "cons" others), and serious violations of rules (e.g., runs away from home overnight, frequent truancy from school before age 13). This criterion is met when the child or youth has engaged in at least three of the 15 possible behaviors during the last year and at least one during the last six months.

The second criterion is that the behavior problems cause significant impairment in academic, social, or occupational functioning, and the third criterion is that, if the individual is 18 years or older, the criteria for Antisocial Personality Disorder are not met.

Moffitt (1993) proposed two separate developmental pathways for antisocial behavior. The adolescent-onset subtype is viewed as arising as a transitory strategy to achieving the normative developmental goal of separation and individuation from parental authority. The child-onset subtype is seen as developing through the interaction of neuropsychological vulnerability and a criminogenic environment.

Both ADHD and academic underachievement are associated with more persistent aggression and a worse prognosis for conduct-disordered children and adolescents (Hinshaw, Lahey, & Hart, 1993).

Etiology

Early attempts to identify a single physical or environmental cause of conduct disorder have been supplanted by a general consensus that antisocial behaviors have multiple causes. Current research is being conducted on a broad spectrum of potential etiologic and developmental factors. Social learning theories and developmental approaches emphasize the role of reciprocal parent-child interactions, and transformations in this relationship across different developmental stages, in the acquisition and maintenance of antisocial behavior problems (Shaw & Bell, 1993).

Genetic and Physical Risk Factors.   Specific neurochemical anomalies at different developmental ages have been observed in controlled studies of conduct-disordered boys (Gabel, Stadler, Bjorn, Shindledecker, & Bowden, 1993, 1994). Rage reactions in children and adolescents have also been linked to neurological irregularities (Mandoki, Sumner, & Matthews-Ferrari, 1992). Antisocial tendencies may have a heritability component. Antisocial personality disorder in parents (especially fathers) has been consistently identified as a significant risk factor for conduct disorder in children. In a study of paternal and maternal risk factors, paternal antisocial personality disorder was the only significant predictor of conduct-disordered behavior in children (Frick, Lahey, Loeber, Stouthamer-Loeber, Christ, & Hanson, 1992).

Depressed levels of physiologic arousal and autonomic reactivity have been observed in adults with antisocial characteristics. Adolescents and adults in penal institutions who were diagnosed as antisocial, psychopathic, or sociopathic have been found to show less anxiety on a variety of measures in comparison with other criminals and normal controls. Antisocial adolescents and adults have significantly greater preferences for dangerous, risk-taking activities. Schmauk (1970) compared the efficiency of avoidance learning in antisocial and normal adults under three punishment conditions: physical punishment (shock), social punishment (verbal feedback of failure), loss of reinforcer (loss of a quarter). The results of this study indicate that physical punishments in the form of shock and verbal feedback for incorrect responses are not as effective in reducing incorrect responses for sociopaths as they are for normal controls. In a comparison of psychopathic and neurotic subgroups of delinquent adolescents, Moses, Silva, and Ratliff (1981) found that psychopaths outperformed neurotics under verbal reward conditions, while neurotics performed better than psychopaths under verbal punishment conditions.

Psychological and Environmental Risk Factors. Frustration-aggression hypotheses account for the occurrence of conduct-disordered behaviors as a direct result of frustration experiences (e.g., Mallick & McCandless, 1966). The social environments of a high proportion of conduct-disordered children are consistent with high frustration, for example, lack of money, poor job opportunities, and low social status. Animal research has reliably induced aggressive behaviors in animals by electric shock, separation of the young from their mothers, extinction of reinforcement, and overcrowding. Prospective research in humans has predicted conduct-disordered behaviors in childhood by earlier reports of parental stress (Berden, Althaus, & Verhulst, 1990), poor parenting skills, and maternal depression (Campbell et al., 1991). Frustration of a child's ability to reliably obtain reinforcement for normative social behaviors places the child at particular risk for persistent antisocial behaviors.

Poor parenting and dysfunctional family life may be directly or indirectly affected by the mental or physical illness of one or both parents (Dumas & Gibson, 1990). Maternal depression and paternal antisocial personality disorder appear to be strongly implicated in the development of conduct disorder. Aggressive behaviors are more common in children from stressed families with a history of mental illness (Heath & Kosky, 1992). Parents who are preoccupied with their own problems are more likely to provide inadequate supervision and to impose noncontingent punishment. Prosocial behaviors tend to be ignored or punished, while deviant behaviors are often directly or indirectly reinforced. Negative affect in maternal depression or lack of empathy in paternal antisocial personality disorder increases the likelihood of aversive interactions between children and their parents. These early psychosocial deficits typically persist, as inadequate social skills and aggressive tendencies interfere with appropriate social interactions outside the home (Patterson, DeBaryshe, & Ramsey, 1989).

Modeling and imitation have been invoked as important determinants of aggression. A number of studies have found increased aggression in children to be predicted by the amount of time spent watching television programs with aggressive content (Rubinstein, 1978). Children who observe aggressive models in person or on film subsequently exhibit increased aggression (Bandura, Ross, & Ross, 1963; Bandura, 1965). However, the child's perception of the social status of the model and the consequences to the model or to the child mediated the likelihood of an aggressive response. These findings suggest that different learning histories differentially predispose children toward aggressive reactions.

Clinical studies support the role of social learning in the development of conduct-disordered behaviors. Johnson and O'Leary (1987) concluded that conduct-disordered girls, 9 to 11 years old, may be modeling aggressive behavior patterns of their parents, particularly those of their mothers. Children who witness violence in the home are more likely to exhibit severe and persistent aggressive behaviors (Lewis, Shanok, Pincus, & Glaser, 1979; Lewis, Lovely, Yeager, & Famina, 1989). Family stressors such as parental psychopathology and environmental disadvantage may contribute to conduct-disordered behaviors through emotional unavailability, inappropriate modeling, and ineffective disciplinary strategies.

Ineffective discipline has been directly linked to both antisocial behaviors and poor academic performance in young adolescent males (DeBaryshe, Patterson, & Capaldi, 1993). The quality of discipline and the degree of preadolescents' antisocial behaviors appear reciprocally related (Vuchinich, Bank, & Patterson, 1995). The more appropriate and contingent the discipline, the less likely children are to exhibit conduct-disordered behaviors.

In a large-scale study of child aggression and family demographic and psychological variables (Eron, Walder, & Lefkowitz, 1971), parental use of punishment was generally associated with increased child aggression. However, this effect was mediated by the amount of empathy boys felt toward their fathers. Empathic boys exhibited less aggression as their fathers' punishment increased, while the nonempathic sons showed more aggression as paternal punishment increased. Mothers of conduct-disordered adolescents tended to believe that their adolescents' misbehavior was intentional, and caused by stable, global, and unsolvable problems (Baden & Howe, 1992). These findings suggest that parental understanding of the child's perspective, and the child's reciprocal understanding, play an important mediating role in disciplinary practices and outcomes. Opportunities for learned empathy likely also contribute to distinctions between more severe early-onset "antisocial" tendencies and late-onset problems of rule violation.

Observational studies of young children have suggested that aggressive behavior is often followed by reinforcing consequences, such as peer acquiescence. Developmental studies suggest that parents may tend to reinforce certain aggressive behaviors in boys but not in girls, and that boys exhibit more aggression than girls (Feshbach, 1970). Longitudinal studies have observed continuity between certain aggressive behaviors from preschool age to later ages for boys but not for girls. The impact of family stressors (such as parental psychopathology) and child factors (such as difficult temperament) demonstrated gender-specific effects on the course of aggression in toddlers (Keenan & Shaw, 1994). Gender differences in the continuity of aggressive behavior are most frequently attributed to greater parental indulgence of aggressive behavior in boys. To decrease the incidence of aggression, Eron (1980) recommended that parents be advised to socialize boys as they socialize girls.

Conduct-disordered children tend to do poorly in school despite average or better intellectual functioning. This generalized underachievement has been linked to poor motivation or lack of reinforcer effectiveness in the learning environment. Schools are generally oriented toward middle-class values in the materials used and available types of reinforcers used. Many children cannot relate to standard school materials because of wide discrepancies between their own experiences and those emphasized by the schools. In addition, many children in the schools are relatively unresponsive to their teachers as social reinforcers. In the normal course of socialization, children learn to perceive adult attention as reinforcing, based in part on a long history of adults mediating the availability of a wide range of other reinforcers. Early learning histories devoid of social reinforcement from adults impede the acquisition of normative social behaviors to attract positive attention. Teacher instructions are disregarded; academic lessons are not learned, and disruptive or truant behaviors are more likely.

Since schools have traditionally been concerned about stimulus antecedents (materials) and their relationship to learning, there has been an increased effort toward developing and utilizing materials that represent a broader spectrum of children's experiences. Much more effort, however, is needed to identify effective reinforcers of prosocial behavior and academic competence for all children.

DELINQUENCY

Assessment

Delinquency refers to illegal or age-inappropriate behaviors (e.g., drinking alcohol) that are committed by persons younger than a specified statutory age (usually between 16 and 20 years, varying from state to state). Delinquency is a legal term and has some overlap with the psychiatric syndrome of conduct disorder. Conduct disorders include a wide range of legal and illegal "acting-out" behaviors that violate social norms including physical acts of aggression against persons or property and disregard for social sanctions against stealing, lying, or running away. Conduct-disordered children and adolescents may or may not be identified by legal agencies as delinquent, but most juvenile delinquents meet diagnostic criteria for conduct disorder.

Frequency estimates of delinquency in the general community vary depending on the method of assessment. Youths identified as delinquent through arrest or other legal involvement actually represent only those delinquents who get caught. Self-reported delinquency rates are higher than those predicted by court records, and anonymous self-reports provide even higher estimates of involvement in delinquent behavior and criminal activity among adolescents. Because of this sample bias, research findings obtained from incarcerated adolescents may not generalize to delinquent adolescents in the community.

A number of factors determine whether or not a person will be caught, arrested, and convicted of a delinquent offense: the specific act (who or what it affects), background characteristics of the individual (e.g., socioeconomic status, history of previous antisocial or delinquent acts), and presence or absence of adequate parental control.

Current figures indicate that about 3 percent of children between the ages of 10 and 17 are referred to juvenile courts. Juvenile males are arrested far more often than females, and four times as many boys as girls reach juvenile court. In recent years, however, the proportion of girls involved in more serious crimes has been increasing. Delinquency occurs at a higher rate in highly populated urban areas than in rural areas. About half of the juveniles appearing in court are being charged for the first time or for minor offenses. Juvenile delinquency accounts for more theft but fewer incidents of interpersonal violence than adult crimes.

As a group, juvenile delinquents differ from nondelinquents on a wide range of characteristics and behaviors. Studies have shown that delinquents engage in more frequent, stable and severe antisocial behavior, including school truancy, lying, stealing, and fighting (e.g., Russo, Loeber, Lahey, & Keenan, 1994). They typically have more relationship difficulties, and report low self-esteem, academic failure, parental rejection, social isolation, lack of empathy, and general unhappiness. They are more likely to abuse substances, relate to deviant peers, and engage in other high-risk activities. Poor academic achievement, minimal parental supervision, and ineffective parental discipline are commonly found for delinquents (Patterson, Reid, & Dishion, 1992).

Etiology

Genetic and Physical Risk Factors.   Although genetic factors have been suggested as causes of delinquency, empirical support has been minimal. The discovery that men with XYY chromosomal configurations (an extra Y chromosome and a total of 47 chromosomes) were overrepresented in mental and penal institutions sparked renewed interest in genetic influences on antisocial behavior. However, the majority of XYY men are not incarcerated; the crimes of XYY prisoners tend to be against property rather than persons (Witkin et al., 1976), and the amount of crime accounted for by XYY typology is actually quite low. The XYY genetic pattern therefore appears to play only a small role in influencing criminal activity, and is not associated with aggressive or antisocial behaviors.

Twin studies indicate a weak but statistically significant correspondence between genetic similarity and reported criminal behaviors at different life stages. Higher concordance rates of criminal behavior were observed between identical twins than between fraternal twins (Christiansen, 1977; Crowe, 1983; Cloninger & Gottesman, 1987). However, the identical twin concordance rate explained less than 4 percent of the variance in adult crimes, and no difference in concordance rates for juvenile delinquency was observed. Court records have also been examined for similarities in criminal activity between adoptees and their biological and adoptive parents. The only significant relationship observed was between adoptee and biological parents' convictions for nonviolent property crimes (Mednick, Gabrielli, and Hutchings, 1984).

Twin studies of children and adolescents have been rare, but findings suggest different heritability patterns for males and females. On *self-report* measures of delinquency, identical twins were more alike in their antisocial behavior than fraternal twins (Rowe, 1983). Stevenson and Graham (1988) found some evidence of heritability of "antisocial deviance" for a sample of 13-year-old twins, but only for boys. Similar gender effects on heritability were observed in a study of maternal reports of externalizing behavior problem ratings for older children and adolescents (Silberg, Erickson, Eaves, & Hewitt, 1994). Heredity accounted for about 40 percent of the variance in maternal externalizing ratings for young boys, and older boys and girls, but accounted for virtually no variance in ratings of young girls.

Some of the differences found between delinquents and nondelinquents could reflect the roles of either hereditary factors or early physical trauma (prenatal, perinatal, and postnatal). Several studies have reported a high incidence of abnormal EEG patterns for delinquents; these studies were frequently flawed by the lack of adequate control groups. In controlled research, neuropsychological tests have found delinquents are more likely than nondelinquents to demonstrate neurological dysfunctions (Yeudall, Fromm-Auch, & Davies, 1982; Moffitt & Silva, 1988).

Mental retardation was once considered to be a major factor in juvenile delinquency. Earlier studies of delinquents had found their IQ scores to be lower than those of the general population. Subsequent studies with improved methodology have revealed smaller differences between the IQ scores of delinquents and nondelinquents. Several hypotheses have been suggested to account for the IQ differences. First, children with lower levels of general intellectual functioning are probably slower to learn societal standards for behavior and therefore may be more likely to become involved in delinquent behavior. Second, children who are intellectually slower are more likely to be caught while engaging in delinquent behavior and therefore more likely to be brought to court and incarcerated. Third, underprivileged individuals (who tend to have lower IQ scores) may lack the familial and financial support systems that help to keep middle-class people from going to court or being incarcerated.

The presence of learning disorders has been suggested as a possible etiological factor on the basis of findings that the majority of delinquents have at least average IQ scores but marked deficiencies in academic achievement. That is, the incidence of learning disorders appears to be substantially higher in delinquents than in the school population at large (Broden, Dunivant, Smith, & Sutton, 1981). Since learning disorders have been associated with a variety of organic factors, the inference has been that brain dysfunction may be either directly or indirectly involved in delinquent behavior. Direct causes may include problems with attention and hyperactivity. Indirect causes may include the psychological effects of poor school achievement (such as decreased levels of social approval and increased levels of extinction and social punishment by teachers, parents, and some peers) that may magnify the reinforcing effects of other peers for delinquent or other antisocial behaviors.

Psychological and Environmental Risk Factors. Environmental and psychological causes of juvenile delinquency have been emphasized in sociological theories, which focus on the development of socialized types of delinquency. Anomie theory

(Merton, 1957) proposes that lower-class people have the same values and goals as middle-class people, but they are frustrated in their attempts to achieve these goals by legitimate means and resort to illegal methods. This theory seems to be particularly relevant to American society, in which nearly every household has a television set that continually propagandizes the advantages of material goods. Lower-class culture theory (Miller, 1958) proposes that underprivileged children learn values and behaviors that are different from those taught to middle-class children. Miller suggests that lower-class children are not rewarded for obeying rules, are not taught to delay gratification, and have less moral training. The available research does not support either of these theories as a primary factor in socialized delinquency.

Delinquent and nondelinquent samples of children from the same neighborhood have been differentiated on the following variables: higher performance IQ than verbal IQ, parental physical or psychological problems, financial instability and dependence on welfare, disorganized and chaotic family life, and inadequate parental supervision (Glueck & Glueck, 1950, 1959, 1968, 1970). Although these variables are implicated in the etiology of juvenile delinquency, at present we cannot adequately predict which children will, in fact, become delinquent. Many children with such adverse conditions in their background do not become delinquent, while others from presumably good home environments do commit crimes. In a prospective study, academic problems and antisocial behavior in early childhood predicted delinquency and recidivism during adolescence and criminal behavior during adulthood (Loeber, 1988).

Family management skills appear to be negatively related to juvenile delinquency (Fischer, 1983). Lack of parental monitoring provides the opportunity for unpunished delinquent behaviors (Patterson & Stouthamer-Loeber, 1984). Larger family size is also associated with increased delinquency, probably due to the increased likelihood of exposure to sibling models of delinquent behavior (Brownfield & Sorenson, 1994).

Public schools have been criticized as one of the causes of juvenile delinquency on the basis of sociological data suggesting a strong relationship between delinquent behavior and negative school experiences. It has been suggested that educational systems are often inadvertently responsible for the occurrence of delinquent behavior because their programs do not adequately serve the needs of children.

Psychological Interventions

Psychological Therapies.   Due to the multiplicity of factors involved in the development and maintenance of conduct-disordered and delinquent behavior, treatment and rehabilitative efforts span a variety of service agencies and approaches. Psychological interventions may be provided as a recommended, optional or mandated service to incarcerated delinquent adolescents, or may be provided in the community to adolescents identified as delinquent, conduct-disordered, or otherwise in need of services.

Traditional forms of psychotherapy used with delinquents on probation or in institutions have yielded mixed but mostly negative results. Early research suggested that children with acting-out symptoms had the poorest improvement rate (Levitt, 1971). Several hypotheses have been presented to explain the negative results. First, the average conduct-disordered youth tends to be quite different from the client who typically benefits most from psychotherapy. Conduct-disordered youths have been viewed as generally less intelligent, with poor verbal skills and less motivation for treatment than successful clients. Other factors which negatively impact treatment outcome include: inflexibility of psychotherapy techniques, poor skill generalization to youths' home environment, and therapists' bias to select clients similar to themselves in cultural background and socioeconomic status. Mental health professionals from a broader spectrum of society are currently being trained to provide services for clients who might not respond optimally to the traditional psychological interventions.

The relevance of therapists' interpersonal skills to treatment outcome has been demonstrated in samples of outpatient and hospitalized delinquents. Therapists' nonpossessive warmth, genuineness, and accurate empathic understanding substantially increase the likelihood of improvement. Low levels of therapists' interpersonal skills were associated with significant deterioration in client status (Truax & Mitchell, 1971). These results suggest that the inability of therapists to relate to their clients may be a major contributing factor in poor treatment outcomes with delinquents.

The clinical relevance of these findings was supported in an innovative intervention program designed for underprivileged delinquent adolescents (Massimo & Shore, 1963; Shore et al., 1966). Treatment required the therapist's personal investment and direct participation in the acquisition of adaptive life skills, including shopping and job interviews. Dramatically reduced rates of recidivism and greater educational, vocational, and interpersonal success was observed for the treatment group, relative to a no-treatment control group. Treatment effects were maintained over several years of follow-up.

Systematic programs of behavioral intervention for aggressive youth train parents to use consistent, authoritative discipline to manage their child. Parents are taught to use positive, noncoercive control methods, to interact more appropriately as a family, to monitor their children's activities, to deal decisively with their children's unacceptable behavior, to negotiate behavioral contracts, and to develop social problem-solving skills. Research has indicated substantial and clinically meaningful reductions in deviant behavior that were maintained at least 12 months (Patterson, DeBaryshe, & Ramsey, 1989). Similar benefits were also found for the siblings of treated youth.

Operant conditioning procedures have been used to change delinquent behaviors in institutional settings. Reinforcement of appropriate social behaviors with tokens and punishment for inappropriate behaviors with timeout and loss of tokens resulted in substantial improvements in youths' behaviors (Burchard, 1967). Other institutional token systems have focused on improving academic skills to increase the opportunity for jobs after release (Cohen & Filipczak, 1971). Academic progress was reinforced with tokens that could be traded for a variety of goods and privileges (e.g., private room, weekend passes). Academic progress therefore became associated with reinforcement that allowed normalization of the youths' daily lives. Substantial increases were observed in both average IQ scores (from 93 to 105) and achievement scores (several grade levels). Of the residents who spent at least three months in the project prior to being released, the recidivism rate was 27 percent in the first year and 36 percent by the end of the second year. The previous recidivism rate for comparable youths in the same learning center was 76 percent in the first year after release.

Unfortunately, treatment interventions aimed at more discrete problems of behavior, such as sexual offending, have not been empirically supported (Lab, Shields, & Schondel, 1993) or have demonstrated only short-term effectiveness in changing target behaviors (Guevremont & Foster, 1993; Wierson, Forehand, & Frame, 1992). Gains in social problem-solving skills were not accompanied by behavioral improvement, nor were social skill gains maintained for 80 percent of the aggressive boys treated (Guevremont & Foster, 1993). Some subgroups of delinquents may be at particularly high risk for continued offending. For instance, males who committed sexual assaults during adolescence were more likely than other violent juvenile offenders to commit sexual or violent crimes in adulthood (Rubenstein, Yeager, Goodstein, & Lewis, 1993).

The last decade has produced considerable research attention to intervention programs for conduct disorders and delinquency. Many of the programs for *adolescent* offenders have produced short-term effects that are unfortunately lost. A primary reason for this loss appears to be that the youths are returned to the same environment that supported the delinquent behavior in the first place. The most successful interventions have targeted *preadolescents*, using parent-training techniques to support and maintain behavior changes (Kazdin, 1987). Increased attention is being given to the development of self-control and academic and vocational skills of institutionalized offenders. The emphasis on skill development is more likely to have long-term benefits in providing realistic alternatives to delinquent lifestyles (Little & Kendall, 1979). Literature reviews suggest that regular interventions over a period of years may be necessary for the successful treatment of antisocial behaviors (Dumas, 1989).

Research has repeatedly demonstrated that traditional approaches to punishment and treatment of conduct-disordered behavior neither prevent delinquency nor rehabilitate youths. The juvenile court system has been criticized for supporting ambiguous definitions of delinquency and assigning arbitrary penalties. Financial resources are extremely limited for juvenile treatment and rehabilitation. Professionals assigned to the juvenile's case are often overworked, underpaid, and undertrained. Community-based programs have become increasingly popular and involve parents, neighbors, and schools in the prevention of conduct-disordered behaviors and the promotion of healthy psychosocial functioning.

Parent training develops or refines parental skills in problem solving, empathic communication, and behavioral management of their conduct-disordered children. Therapeutic components include establishment of a supportive and empowering relationship with parents, practical instruction, feedback and reinterpretation, and challenging them to develop and maintain a functional level of discipline and consistency (Webster-Stratton & Herbert, 1993). The addition of a synthesis teaching component appears to improve skill generalization to the home environment and results in more consistent parenting and fewer child behavior problems (Wahler, Cartor, Fleischman, & Lambert, 1993).

Delinquency prevention programs that support at-risk youth in community-based activities have demonstrated considerable success. For example, the "Buddy System" (O'Donnell, Lydgate, & Fo, 1979) trained adult volunteers to provide friendship, companionship, and behavioral contingencies to delinquents during a one-year intervention. Two-year follow-up data showed that the recidivism rate for delinquents with "buddies" was about 25 percent lower than that for delinquents in a no-treatment control group. Improved performance and achievement at school and increased cooperation and communication at home were reported by most parents of adolescent participants in a community delinquency prevention program (Roundtree, Grenier, & Hoffman, 1993). Essential features of successful programs include street outreach, individual need assessment, supportive adult role models, peer group discussions, family interventions, neighborhood programs, and educational and vocational training (Greene, 1993).

Early childhood intervention programs which initiate child and family support in infancy or preschool years have demonstrated success at lowering juvenile delinquency rates, up to two decades later (Zigler, Taussig, & Black, 1992). A prevention program designed to reduce externalizing problems in aggressive boys with ADHD resulted in improved peer friendships and less disruptive and aggressive behavior (Vitaro & Tremblay, 1994). Treatment effects were maintained and became more prominent over a three-year period.

A number of recommendations suggest changes in those aspects of public school systems that may be fostering delinquent behavior patterns. Teachers should be provided with the training and resources to recognize the educability of all pupils and to reward a broader spectrum of achievement behaviors. Educational achievement would be best served by identification of individual patterns of strength and weakness, and grading of performance based on learning increments, rather than norm-based or arbitrary teacher rankings. Broader-based administrative and structural changes have also been suggested in order to increase the availability of materials, facilities, and programs to the large numbers of children currently excluded from educational opportunities and advancement.

The general idea behind most of the recommendations is to make all children more aware of and satisfied with their abilities and less aware of and frustrated by their disabilities. In order to effect these goals, schools need to better accommodate societal opportunities for a wide diversity of adult roles and functions. A reinforcement system based on a broader range of accomplishment may well facilitate the prevention of delinquency problems that appear to be caused by the lack of reinforcement for all but traditional academic achievements.

Recognizing the link between poor school performance and delinquent behaviors, attention is also being drawn to preschool and parental education as prevention strategies. Studies have suggested that performance during the school years is highly predicted by the child's abilities at the time of school entrance. This relationship leads to a hypothesis that preschool experiences may have a critical role in determining later school performance and thus, directly or indirectly, the probability of delinquent behaviors. It will be particularly interesting to discover in the follow-up studies of preschool intervention programs whether the incidence of delinquent behavior is reduced in proportion to the increases in learning skills.

Legal Interventions

Until this century, juveniles who committed crimes were treated in essentially the same way as adults. Around the beginning of the 1900s laws began to be changed to provide more protection for children. Juvenile courts were initially established to serve children who were neglected or delinquent. The delinquent was thus viewed as a child without adequate family or financial support. The juvenile court adopted as its goal the diagnosis and treatment of children rather than punishment, and its proceedings were considerably less formal than those of the regular courts, with judges being allowed considerably greater discretionary powers.

There are now juvenile courts in all U.S. legal jurisdictions, but the quality of these courts varies greatly. Few of the juvenile courts function ideally, however, because large numbers of cases are being handled by too few case workers, probation officers, and judges. Moreover, the courts generally do not have adequate psychological services and must either depend on other agencies for these services or process cases without them.

The process of becoming identified as a legal delinquent involves a series of decisions made by persons in the law enforcement and judicial systems. The police officer first on the scene determines whether a crime has been committed and whether the juvenile should be referred to juvenile court. Such a decision usually rests on the severity of the behavior and the officer's estimate of the likelihood of future delinquent behavior. The estimate of recurrence is based on the child's home environment and the amount of parental control. It is not uncommon for the parents to report that they cannot control the juvenile's behavior.

Police officers are not the only source of referrals to juvenile court. Any adult, including the juvenile's parents, may file a petition and require a hearing in juvenile court. In cases involving arrest, the juvenile may be released to the parents or incarcerated while awaiting the hearing. The law requires that juveniles wait no longer than five days for a hearing by a judge. During this period a juvenile court counselor or a social worker gathers information regarding the juvenile's environmental (home, school, social) background. The amount of required training or education of such court-appointed officials varies widely. Present at a typical juvenile court hearing are the presiding judge, the juvenile and the parents, the arresting officer or petitioner or both, the prosecuting attorney, the defense attorney, and the court counselor. The judge hears the evidence and recommendations and makes a decision as soon as possible.

Very few juveniles are brought to court without strong evidence of their involvement in the alleged behavior. A much greater number of juveniles who have engaged in illegal behaviors do not reach the courts. There is reason to believe that those who do appear in court are more likely to come from lower socioeconomic status families. These underprivileged youths also are more likely to be found guilty and to receive harsher penalties for delinquent behavior.

Legal interventions are imposed upon delinquent adolescents in a court of law, with the primary goals of protecting the community and minimizing recidivism, or repeat offending. The most common legal sanctions are probation or incarceration in a high-security detention facility where adolescents are imprisoned for designated sentences. Adolescents convicted of more serious crimes may be imprisoned until their 21st birthday.

Probation. After deciding that a juvenile has committed a crime, the judge has substantial latitude in determining the consequences. One alternative is to place the child on probation for a certain period of time. Probation is essentially a situation in which the court continues to monitor the child's behavior after specifying acceptable and unacceptable behaviors. The monitoring consists of periodic contacts with a probation officer. The juvenile is, of course, instructed not to engage in the criminal behavior, but judges frequently add other conditions, such as being at home by a certain hour, performing household chores, avoiding social contact with certain people, and attending school regularly. Many of the conditions set during probation are designed to help the child to avoid situations that might increase the probability of further criminal behavior. Judges sometimes require restitution through community work or paying for damages. Close monitoring of the child's activities by the parents is usually required by the court. Electronically activated ankle bracelets may also be court-ordered, so that the adolescent's exact movements and whereabouts can be tracked.

Probation with or without restitution is used frequently by the courts. It is the most likely decision for children who are appearing in court for the first time for nonserious offenses. Probation is also preferred when there is reason to believe that the parents are willing and able to monitor and report on the child's behavior. Probation may also include the stipulation that the juvenile's family receive psychological treatment. The probation officer's regular contact with a child is also designed as a therapeutic intervention; however, the lack of training and excessive caseloads for probation officers make close monitoring and personal investment difficult. There is no evidence currently that probation has an effective therapeutic function.

Incarceration. If probation is not considered to be adequate or appropriate punishment, the judge may recommend incarceration, or removal from the home setting to another environment. Incarceration usually means being sent to a detention facility that is large, impersonal, and custodial. Although some programs in the educational and vocational areas may exist, they are almost always inadequate for the needs of the inmates. Psychological treatment is available only infrequently.

Daily life in the detention facilities is highly regimented, and few decisions by the inmates are expected or allowed. Socialization is geared toward conforming to the power structure and institutional requirements rather than toward societal standards outside of the institution. There is substantial evidence that delinquents learn a great deal more in these facilities about criminal behavior and how to avoid getting caught. These factors probably contribute to the high recidivism rates found for delinquents who have been incarcerated in detention facilities. About 70 to 80 percent of youths released from detention facilities are rearrested within a few years.

Group Homes.   Due to the negative socialization experiences common in detention facilities, a strong current trend is to avoid incarceration of young offenders. Group homes provide a viable alternative, through supervised residential placement where the youths remain in their community and attend public schools. Group homes typically integrate behavior management programs, such as token economies, and traditional and vocational education opportunities in order to provide adaptive alternatives to criminal activities. Empirical research has supported the efficacy of group homes in reducing recidivism rates and increasing school continuance, at less than half the expense of incarceration (Kirigin, Wolf, & Phillips, 1979). The majority of juveniles placed in a group home successfully completed the program and did not reappear in the juvenile court system (Haghighi & Lopez, 1993).

PSYCHOACTIVE SUBSTANCE USE DISORDERS

The percentages of children and adolescents reportedly using alcohol and illicit drugs peaked in 1980, then declined during the 1980s (Newcomb & Bentler, 1989). This decrease in substance use continued into the early 1990s (Johnston, O'Malley, & Bachman, 1993; National Institute on Drug Abuse, 1991). However, substance use still presents a serious health problem among adolescents, with a majority of high school seniors reporting alcohol use within the past year and a sizable minority reporting cigarette smoking or illicit drug use during the same period.

Consumption of any psychoactive substance, including nicotine and alcohol, presents increased risk for use of cannabis, cocaine, and other illicit drugs. Adolescents who use cigarettes and alcohol are more likely to take up marijuana smoking, and those who use marijuana are more likely to try other illicit drugs (Kandel & Logan, 1984). Self-report questionnaire data indicate that drug use in adolescents is associated with high-risk-taking activities, general delinquency, sexual activity, and school misbehavior (Botvin, Schinke, & Orlandi, 1995; Hundleby, Carpenter, Rose, & Mercer, 1982).

Assessment

Under DSM-IV nosology, a substance can refer to a drug of abuse, a medication or a toxin, and includes alcohol, nicotine, hydrocarbon vapors, illicit drugs, and prescription medications. Substance use disorders are classified as dependence or abuse based on the extent of drug use and negative consequences.

The DSM-IV diagnostic criteria for *substance dependence* describe a maladaptive pattern of substance use, leading to clinically significant impairment or distress, with at least three of the seven criteria being met over a 12-month period:

> The seven criteria include (1) tolerance (e.g., a need for markedly increased amounts of the substance), (2) withdrawal symptoms, (3) substance taken in larger amounts than was intended, (4) unsuccessful efforts to control use of substance, (5) considerable time spent in attempting to obtain the substance, using the substance, or recovering from its effects, (6) important activities given up because of substance use, and (7) continued use of substance use despite knowledge of its likely being a cause of a physical or psychological problem for the user.

Substance abuse is manifested by recurrent substance use despite repeated adverse physical, legal, or social consequences. Substance abuse is diagnosed only if criteria for substance dependence have never been met. DSM-IV stipulates that the maladaptive pattern of substance use must lead to clinically significant impairment or stress as manifested by one or more of the following indicators within a 12-month period.

> The indicators are: (1) recurrent substance use that results in failure to fulfill major responsibilities at home, work, or school (e.g., frequent absences), (2) recurrent substance use in physically hazardous situations (e.g., driving "under the influence"), (3) recurrent substance-related legal problems (e.g., arrests for disorderly conduct), (4) continued substance use despite having social or interpersonal problems that are related to the effects of the substance (e.g., arguments, physical fights).

Substance-induced mental disorders may be diagnosed if specific symptoms are sufficiently severe and pervasive to warrant individual attention. Substance-induced mental disorders typically arise during an episode of substance intoxication or withdrawal and rarely persist for longer than four weeks. Symptoms of delirium, psychosis, disturbed mood, anxiety, sexual dysfunction, or sleep disturbance may be associated with acute substance use or withdrawal. In rare instances, a substance-induced disorder may manifest in persistent symptoms of dementia, amnesia, or hallucinogenic "flashbacks."

Alcohol. Reflecting their adult environment, children and adolescents use and abuse alcohol more than any other drug. Use of alcohol usually begins with peers in social contexts, but many children and adolescents use alcohol without parental permission in their own homes. Its relative accessibility and low cost encourage repeated use.

The psychoactive effects of small amounts of alcohol include reduced anxiety and greater ease in social situations. Moderate amounts impair visual-motor coordination, attention to stimuli, and judgment. Large amounts of alcohol may lead to severe drowsiness, coma, and death. Levels of intoxication are determined by blood alcohol level tests.

The chronic abuse of alcohol is associated with a variety of medical disorders affecting the intestinal organs and nervous system. It is also a leading cause of vehicular and other accidents, and a significant factor in violent crimes and adolescent suicide. Combining alcohol with other drugs can be very dangerous. When taken together, alcohol and depressants, such as barbiturates and tranquilizers, produce effects that are greater than additive and potentially lethal. Death by drowning or asphyxiation (choking on vomit) is a significant threat following loss of consciousness. Dementia, amnesia, psychosis, depressed or erratic mood, anxiety, sexual dysfunction, or sleep disturbance are symptoms associated with alcohol dependence.

Alcohol abuse usually develops within the first five years after regular drinking is established. Genetic factors appear to contribute to the development of alcoholism (Rainer, 1979). Sons of alcoholic fathers are at higher risk for developing alcoholism even when they are separated from their biological parents. Twin studies indicate that concordance rates for alcohol abuse and patterns of consumption are considerably higher for identical twins than for fraternal twins. Persons with other psychological problems and environmental stresses also appear to be at a higher-than-normal risk for developing a pattern of alcohol abuse.

Alcohol abuse continues to be a serious social problem; 14 percent of the adult U.S. population meet DSM-III-R criteria for Alcohol Dependence at some time in their lives. Long-term intervention is usually necessary following the initial detoxification. For adults, short-term hospitalization followed by outpatient treatment has been moderately successful. Community groups, such as Alcoholics Anonymous, have been most helpful by stressing abstinence in recovering alcoholics and providing social support. Similar groups provide support to children and adolescents who abuse alcohol or who have alcoholic family members.

Amphetamines.   Amphetamine and its derivatives are prescribed by physicians to treat obesity, fatigue, and depression. Students, athletes, and performers may self-administer amphetamines to enhance alertness, strength, or stamina. Mood elevation and social gregariousness are typically the desired effects from the recreational use of amphetamines. Initial stimulant effects during intoxication are replaced with depression and apathy during withdrawal. Intense substance use over a short period of time ("speed runs") is common, and is followed by severe withdrawal symptoms ("crashing").

Amphetamine abusers may have preexisting psychological problems that can be worsened by the abuse. Common adverse effects include paranoid thoughts and compulsive behaviors. Chronic use of amphetamines has been associated with the development of psychosis that is similar to paranoid schizophrenia; the psychotic symptoms usually abate within several days or weeks after the last drug dose. Other amphetamine-induced disorders include intoxication delirium, mood disorder, sexual dysfunction, and sleep disturbance.

Most adolescents who use amphetamine intermittently are at low risk for chronic or severe psychopathology, but they should be informed about the dangers of chronic use and supported in their efforts to stop taking the drug. In cases of chronic use, the individual may have to be hospitalized or confined in a supportive environment during the early phase of drug cessation. Depression and suicide have been associated with stimulant withdrawal.

Caffeine. Caffeine is consumed in a variety of food products and pharmaceuticals (e.g., weight loss aids, analgesics). The average daily caffeine consumption in the United States is about 200 mg, with the majority consumed in coffee (65–100 mg/6 oz.), soft drinks (about 45 mg/12 oz.) and tea (about 40 mg/6 oz.). Only caffeine intoxication, not dependence or abuse, is diagnosed in DSM-IV. Intoxication usually occurs after ingestion of more than 250 mg of caffeine, although effects may be observed after as little as 100 mg. Symptoms of intoxication include psychomotor agitation, restlessness, nervousness, and increased autonomic activity. Other caffeine-induced disorders include anxiety and sleep disturbance.

Cannabis. Cannabis (marijuana) is the most commonly used illegal drug in the United States; 24 percent of adolescent samples and 61 percent of adults report using it at least once. However, only 10 percent of all Americans report current use of cannabis (Kozel & Adams, 1986). Daily use of cannabis by high school seniors has also declined from a peak of 11 percent in 1978 to only 4 percent 10 years later (Soderstrom, Trifillis, Shankar, & Clark, 1988).

Cannabis may be either smoked or ingested with food. The effects are highly variable and dependent on the individual's expectations and the setting. Users frequently report enhanced perception of stimuli, a feeling of relaxation, mood changes, drowsiness, and euphoria. Short-term memory, motor agility, and reaction time are typically impaired. Anxiety, dysphoria, or social withdrawal are occasionally reported.

Minor physical effects typically develop within two hours, and may include dry mouth, reddened eyes, increased appetite, and rapid heartbeat. Long-term adverse physical effects (such as respiratory disease) have been hypothesized but not conclusively demonstrated. Nor have any substantiated deaths been attributed to the use of cannabis. Cannabis does appear to have some useful medicinal applications for the treatment of glaucoma and chemotherapy-induced nausea (Cohen, 1980). Adverse effects appear to be primarily psychological and may include acute panic reactions, paranoid thinking, and depression that lasts several hours. Anecdotal descriptions of an "amotivational syndrome" with apathy, loss of goal direction, emotional blunting, and mental dulling subsequent to chronic cannabis consumption have not been empirically supported.

Cocaine. Different preparations from the coca plant of Central and South America may be chewed, smoked, inhaled, or injected. The most commonly used form of cocaine in the United States is a powder preparation that is inhaled ("snorted") through the nostrils and enters the bloodstream through the mucous membranes. Cocaine is also combined with heroin in a "speedball" or mixed with bicarbonate soda and smoked as "crack." The introduction of crack in the mid-1980s popularized cocaine use among social sectors unable to afford more expensive powdered cocaine. The profound but fleeting "high" produced by crack often results in rapid progression from infrequent use to abuse or dependence within a few weeks or months.

Common intoxication effects include a sense of euphoria, social gregariousness, and grandiosity; however, hypervigilance, irritability, and impaired judgment also commonly occur. Intoxication is commonly followed by rebound psychological and physiological depressant effects. The severity of withdrawal symptoms increases as a function of the duration and dosage of cocaine ingested, with severe depressive symptoms and suicidal gestures possible. Other cocaine-related disorders include intoxication delirium, psychosis, mood disorder, anxiety, sexual dysfunction and sleep disturbance.

Hallucinogens.   Hallucinogens, such as LSD and mescaline, produce distortions of perception, thought, feeling, and behavior. The use of hallucinogens peaked during the 1960s and has subsequently declined, partly because of fear of adverse reactions. LSD is chemically manufactured into a liquid, sugar cubes, tablets, or capsules. Use is normally intermittent and typically takes place in a group setting.

Drug effects may be extreme, and depend largely on the expectations of the user, the setting, and the dose. Early physical effects may be experienced as nausea, restlessness, or autonomic arousal. Perceptual distortions, visual illusions, and hallucinations may follow. Sensory perceptions may be extremely distorted or magnified, sometimes to the point of the user's feeling overwhelmed. Body distortions are frequently perceived and time seems to pass slowly. Lability of mood is apparent and may range from euphoria to depression and panic. Most of the effects disappear within 12 hours.

Tolerance develops rapidly to euphoric and psychedelic effects, but not to autonomic effects such as dilated pupils and sweating. Hallucinogenics appear to remain in the body for an extended period of time, with full recovery often taking days. These factors contribute to the relative infrequency of drug intake, even among those individuals considered hallucinogen dependent.

Adverse reactions vary in their severity mostly as a function of psychological and situational factors. The most common adverse reaction is an acute panic reaction ("bad trip") that includes both hysterical and paranoid features; the user may experience fears of physical harm, paralysis, or going insane. Perceptual distortions and impaired judgement may place the hallucinogen-intoxicated individual at increased risk of harm to the self or others.

Perceptual disturbances originally experienced during an episode of hallucinogen intoxication have been reported to recur periodically over months to years. These "flashback" experiences are diagnosed in DSM-IV as hallucinogen persisting perceptual disorder. Flashbacks may occur spontaneously or may be triggered voluntarily or by environmental factors. Acute panic reactions and flashbacks are therapeutically managed by a supportive environment in which reality-testing and orientation are emphasized.

Inhalants.   Inhalants are substances whose vapors produce psychoactive effects when ingested through the mouth or nose. The most commonly abused inhalants are gasoline, glue, paint, paint thinners, and spray can propellants. Effects tend to occur immediately subsequent to "sniffing" of an inhalant, and may include visual distortions, incoordination, lethargy, euphoria, belligerence, stupor, or coma.

Because inhalants are legal, inexpensive, and readily available they are often the first recreational drug used by children, with peak use in adolescence. Patterns of dependence and withdrawal are atypical and generally less prominent than with other drugs. However, inhalants are highly toxic to the liver and kidneys, and chronic use is associated with deterioration of brain matter and dementia. Death may occur from acute respiratory failure or heart attack due to inhalants' depressive effects on the cardiovascular system.

Nicotine. The most common form of nicotine dependence occurs through cigarette smoking. Approximately 30 percent of adult Americans are nicotine dependent, with more male than female smokers. Among teenage smokers, however, gender rates are comparable. Complications of smoking include emphysema, bronchitis, circulatory problems, and a variety of cancers; these physical disorders are correlated with the amount of smoking over a period of time. Cessation of smoking in adults results in profound, successive health improvements over the next several years. Minimal psychoactive effects have been associated with nicotine.

Opioids. Opioids are synthetically produced or naturally occurring substances which interact with specific brain receptors to produce analgesic and euphoric effects. Opioids such as morphine or codeine may be medically prescribed to relieve pain. Heroin is the most commonly used recreational opioid in the United States. The drug is usually first inhaled as powder through the nose. Rapid tolerance to euphoric effects necessitates greater doses or more direct ingestion into the body, such as injection under the skin or into the veins, and larger amounts of the drug must be used more often to obtain desired effects. Compulsive drug use often develops, with activities centered around obtaining and using heroin. Illegal behavior is a common by-product to support opioid addiction.

Physical dependence to heroin develops rapidly, and withdrawal symptoms are severe and pervasive. Six to 24 hours after the last dose the first withdrawal signs occur, including drug craving, body aches, dysphoria, nausea, sweating, and irritability. Acute withdrawal symptoms continue to increase and peak at two to three days, subsiding in seven to ten days. Chronic symptoms of depression, anxiety, and insomnia may persist over weeks or months. Drug craving usually returns after withdrawal, and complete abstinence is rarely maintained once opioid dependence is established. Accidental or intentional overdose, criminal violence, and infections such as HIV contribute to the high mortality rate associated with opioid abuse (1–2 percent annual death rate).

Phencyclidines. Phencyclidines are a class of synthetic substances originally developed as surgical anesthetics, but now sold as street drugs, such as PCP and Angel Dust. Ingestion may be by mouth or intravenous injection, with peak effects occurring within hours or minutes, respectively. The most prominent effect is behavioral aggression, with belligerence, assaultiveness, impulsivity, and psychomotor agitation common. Other phencyclidine intoxication effects are largely dose-dependent. At lower doses dizziness, weakness, euphoria, and slowed reactions may occur. Moderate doses may produce disorganized thoughts, perceptual distortions, and hallucinations. High doses may result in amnesia or coma. Behavioral changes may persist for several days; phencyclidine-induced psychotic disorder may persist for weeks. Although phencyclidines are toxic to the cardiovasculature and respiratory systems, accidents, fights, and falls are the most common causes of phencyclidine-associated death.

Sedatives. Sedatives include the anxiolytics, barbiturates, tranquilizers, and hypnotics, drugs which are prescribed by physicians for relief of anxiety, tension, or insomnia. Medications are often initially obtained from a legitimate medical source or purchased as recreational street drugs. Oral administration is most common.

Sedatives produce effects that are similar to those of alcohol. At low doses, there are feelings of euphoria, relaxation, and physical incoordination. The risk of overdose increases with repeated use because larger amounts of the drugs become necessary to obtain the same psychoactive effects. After-effects of sedative use include impairment of performance and judgment, irritability, fatigue, and depression. Accidental or intentional overdoses of sedatives result in symptoms similar to those of alcohol intoxication: slurred speech, slowness of thinking and movement, and mood changes. Respiratory depression and hypotension may cause death.

The withdrawal signs are also similar to those of alcohol withdrawal, and include autonomic hyperarousal and psychomotor agitation. Severe, untreated withdrawal may produce hallucinations and grand mal seizures in up to 30 percent of dependent individuals. Acute symptoms may persist for days or weeks; more chronic malaise and depression may persist over months.

Etiology and Treatment Interventions

The etiology of substance abuse is complex. Family histories frequently indicate cross-generational effects. Most of the substances are physically addicting and provide their own immediate reinforcement in the form of an altered psychological state. In addition, persons whose lives are problematic and who have psychological problems are at considerably greater risk for using and abusing these substances. A retrospective study reported that adults who met criteria for childhood-onset ADHD had higher rates of polysubstance use than adults without a history of ADHD (Biederman et al., 1995). However, Conduct Disorder (but not attentional deficits) at age 8 years predicted substance use at age 15 in a longitudinal community-based study (Lynskey & Fergusson, 1995). Commonly associated features of substance use in these adolescents were low SES, parental substance use, and parental conflict.

Because substance dependence is so difficult to treat successfully, considerable attention is currently focused on educational prevention programs beginning in the elementary school years. School-based prevention programs targeting tobacco, alcohol, and drug abuse initially focused on providing information about negative effects. However, consistently poor outcome findings prompted a shift toward psychosocial interventions in the early 1980s (Botvin & Botvin, 1992). Psychological inoculation against peer pressure, social resistance, and self-management skills training have been found effective in deterring substance abuse in white, middle-class adolescents (Botvin, Schinke, Epstein, & Diaz, 1994). Generalization of these treatment effects to adolescents from more diverse ethnic and cultural backgrounds has not been adequately addressed.

The importance of identification of the effective components of prevention programs across a multitude of settings is illustrated by findings of negative results for certain prevention approaches. Resistance skills training to prevent alcohol use in adolescents may be ineffective or even increase the risk of alcohol use if provided in an isolated context (Donaldson, Graham, Piccinin, & Hansen, 1995). Drug prevention programs that target both active and passive social pressures through combined resistance training and normative education interventions appear most effective in discouraging substance use (Donaldson, Graham, & Hansen, 1994).

Both inpatient and outpatient treatment programs have been developed for drug-abusing children and adolescents. Recent research has begun to illuminate some of the factors associated with successful therapeutic outcomes and those aspects of intervention programs that may be ineffective or counterproductive. In a large-scale study of 5,000 adolescent outpatients treated for drug problems, improvement was associated with longer treatment, fewer prior admissions, a drug problem other than marijuana, and Caucasian race (Friedman, Glickman, & Morrissey, 1986). Twelve-step programs have had limited success in adolescent inpatient settings, with males particularly susceptible to relapse (Alford, Koehler, & Leonard, 1991). Group treatment of substance-abusing adolescents is often contraindicated, due to the strong negative impact of deviant peers upon one another, which may exacerbate problem behaviors (Dishion & Andrews, 1995). Multimodal prevention and treatment approaches that integrate family, school, and community-based interventions appear most effective in reducing the risk of substance abuse (Peters & McMahon, 1996).

CONCLUSIONS

"Acting-out" is composed of a spectrum of behaviors that violate social expectations, norms, or standards. Disobedience and ignoring parental requests for compliance are early forms of acting-out behavior. Hyperactivity and academic problems are frequent correlates of conduct disorders and juvenile delinquency. Substance abuse is prevalent among adolescents with disruptive problems of behavior. Many acting-out problems can be traced to poor parenting skills, including lack of parental monitoring of children's activities and inadequate use of contingency management. Effective intervention is most likely to be family based or to emphasize skill generalization to the home environment.

RECOMMENDED READINGS

Chesney-Lind, U., & Shelden, R.G. (1992). *Girls: Delinquency and juvenile justice.* Pacific Grove, CA: Brooks/Cole.

Goldstein, AP., Glick, B., Irwin, M.J., Pask-McCartney, C., & Rubama, I. (1989). *Reducing delinquency.* Elmsford, NY: Pergamon.

Gullotta, T.P., Adams, G.R., & Montemayor, R. (1995). *Substance misuse in adolescence.* Newbury Park, CA: Sage.

Henggeler, S.W. (1989). *Delinquency in adolescence.* Newbury Park, CA: Sage.

Horne, A.M., & Sayger, T.V. (1990). *Treating conduct and oppositional defiant disorders in children.* Elmsford, NY: Pergamon.

Kazdin, A. E. (1995). *Conduct disorders in childhood and adolescence.* Newbury Park, CA: Sage.

Patterson, G.R., Reid, J.B., & Dishion, T.J. (1992). *Antisocial boys.* Eugene, OR: Castalia.

Schinke, S.P., Botvin, G.J., & Orlandi, M. A. (1991). *Substance abuse in children and adolescents.* Beverly Hills, CA: Sage.

12

Anxiety and Depression

Maria was an attractive, dark-haired, 10-year-old girl whose parents referred her because she had developed a recurring fear that her father was going to die. She was also spending a considerable amount of time engaging in ritualistic behaviors, such as tapping objects a certain number of times and arranging her possessions in particular ways. Maria reported that she felt good only when she was completing her rituals. Although she was very intelligent and did superior work in school, Maria became upset if her performance was not the best in the

This chapter revised by Cassandra Stanton.

245

class. She spoke at length about minor problems in school and perceived herself as an inadequate student.

Although her concerns about school had been present for several years, her fear of her father's death and the ritualistic behaviors at home had a sudden onset after the accidental death of one of her uncles whose funeral she attended.

Maria's mother described herself as a perfectionist and was proud of her accomplishments as manager of the household, but she had a long history of a lack of relationships with other people and was unable to discuss her feelings. She acknowledged that her marriage was not satisfactory and that her husband did not meet her expectations either at home or in his job.

Maria's father was considerably warmer and more friendly than his wife, but he reported episodes of depression that had been increasing in frequency during the last two years and felt that they were related to his dissatisfaction with his job and his marriage. The death of his brother had further increased his family responsibilities, responsibilities with which he felt unable to cope. Concern with his own problems seemed to prevent him from acknowledging Maria's problems. His withdrawal from her difficulties was characterized by his stating that "she is just like her mother."

ANXIETY DISORDERS

Anxiety or fear is an appropriate response in a number of situations, for example, being afraid of a hot stove after being burned. Thus, appropriate anxiety can be conceptualized as a signal of impending danger. However, some psychological problems of childhood and adolescence appear to be characterized by anxiety that *does not* seem to be related to physical danger. Although the etiology of individual types of anxiety disorders is not always known, it is generally believed that they are learned in the same way that appropriate fears are learned.

Children's fears are often associated with avoidance, subjective discomfort, and somatic complaints (Silverman & Rabian, 1993). In studies examining children both in the United States and other countries, it has been found that children report more fears than adolescents, that girls report more fears than boys, and that the number of fears is comparable across nationalities (Ollendick & King, 1994). The most frequently feared stimuli relate to fears of danger, death, and physical injury. Phobias can be distinguished from fears in that phobias are more persistent, disproportionate to the demands of the situation, irrational, and cause significant interference in functioning due to avoidance of the feared stimulus. In comparison to fears and phobias, anxiety is more diffuse, lacks specificity, and tends to permeate many aspects of the child's life.

Several factors appear to be involved in the development of anxiety disorders. Sometimes, the disorder can result from an "accidental," classically conditioning pairing, such as a pairing of thunder and swimming that results in a fear of water. Some children seem to be especially sensitive, that is, constitutionally vulnerable to such situations. Some parents overestimate the child's ability to cope with potentially anxiety-producing situations and make the child more vulnerable by excessive exposure; they may also fail to teach their children ways of coping with new situations.

Anxiety disorders are not uncommon in children and adolescents. Pollock et al. (1995) reviewed epidemiological studies and reported estimates for the presence of any anxiety disorder to range from 9 percent to 15 percent. Although there is recognition of different anxiety and depression disorders, relationships among them appear to be the rule rather than the exception. Research suggests that 15.9 percent to 61.9 percent of children identified as anxious or depressed have comorbid anxiety and depressive disorders and that measures of anxiety and depression are highly correlated (Brady & Kendall, 1992). *Negative affectivity* refers to a mood state that subsumes both anxiety and depression. Children and adolescents can be anxious and depressed simultaneously.

Assessment and Diagnosis

Anxiety is a multidimensional construct that incorporates physiological, behavioral, and cognitive components. In many cases, knowing the relative influence of each of these factors will help determine the clinician's primary direction in assessment and treatment. For example, a child who is hugging her mother's leg and refusing to go to school may likely be treated very differently than a child who has a stomachache due to a test that day in school. Therefore, it is critical to gather information related to the cognitive, behavioral, and physiological symptoms that characterize the child's distress. Fearful and anxious behaviors are difficult to assess because anxiety is a subjective state, and external or behavioral correlates are not easily defined, observable, or measurable. As a result, assessment strategies must be designed with close respect for sensitivity, diversity, and applicability to the developmental stages of childhood (Eisen & Kearney, 1995).

The interview is the most widely used procedure in clinical assessment. Structured interviews, designed for quantifying data and enhancing diagnostic reliability, have been developed specifically to evaluate anxiety disorders in youth. For example, the Anxiety Disorders Interview Schedule for Children (ADIS-C; Silverman & Nelles, 1988) is a semistructured interview with both child and parent components that is widely used to assess anxiety disorders in youth (Silverman, 1991). Based on an adult version, the ADIS-C relies on DSM criteria for anxiety disorders and uses an interview-observer format that allows the clinician to gather information from the standardized interview and from clinical observations. The administration of the interview to both the parents and the child enables the clinician to obtain information from multiple sources and get different perspectives of the child's symptomatology.

Parent ratings are an important source of information on symptomatic anxiety in children and contribute to a multisource assessment that can yield a more complete picture of a child's functioning. The Child Behavior Checklist (CBCL) (Achenbach & Edelbrock, 1983) assesses the competencies and problems of children of ages 4 to 16 for both internalizing and externalizing behavior problems, with the former including items related to anxiety. The CBCL includes a teacher version (Edelbrock & Achenbach, 1984) that also encompasses internalizing and externalizing factors. Despite the importance of multiple sources of information, parent-child disagreement has been found in the clinical assessment of anxiety (e.g., Klein, 1991). Furthermore, a recent investigation of parents', children's, and teachers' reports of childhood anxiety on a structured interview showed substantial disagreement (Frick, Silverhorn, & Evans, 1994).

Because of the internal nature of anxious symptomatology, self-report measures to assess children's emotions and experiences are an integral part of assessment. Despite anxious children's tendency to underreport symptoms, questionnaires are advantageous because they are private, easy to administer, economical, and can be studied. For example, the Revised Children's Manifest Anxiety Scale (RCMAS; Reynolds & Richmond, 1978) is the most widely used self-report instrument for assessing the level and nature of anxiety in children and adolescents. The RCMAS consists of 37 yes/no items and yields subscale scores for worry/oversensitivity, physiological symptoms, concentration anxiety, and lying. It has been found to have high reliability and to discriminate between normal and disturbed children. The State–Trait Anxiety Inventory for Children (STAIC; Speilberger, 1973) is another self-report questionnaire that measures state (variable or situational) and trait (stable or chronic) anxiety. Treatment studies suggest that trait anxiety may be a key feature of Overanxious Disorder (Eisen & Silverman, 1993). Finally, the Children's Anxiety Sensitivity Scale (CASI; Silverman et al., 1991) is a self-report measure of how aversively children view different somatic forms of anxiety. A recent examination of the phenomenon of anxiety sensitivity using this measure suggested a developmental trend in which unique catastrophic interpretations of bodily sensations were more characteristic of older children (Chorptia, Albano, & Barlow, 1996).

In contrast to the RCMAS, STAIC, and CASI, all of which measure global anxiety, other rating scales measure specific subsets of anxiety. Measures specific to Social Phobia, Posttraumatic Stress Disorder, and Obsessive-Compulsive Disorder have been developed. In addition, specific self-report measures for assessing the cognitive component of anxiety have recently been developed. For example, the Children's Anxious Self-Statement Questionnaire (CASSQ; Kendall & Ronan, 1989) is a measure of negative self-focused attention and positive self-statements and expectations. Because depressed youth experience few positive self-statements, the CASSQ may be useful for discriminating anxious and depressed youth.

An increasingly popular procedure for assessing anxiety and fear is a behavioral avoidance test (BAT). During a BAT, the child is asked to gradually approach a feared stimuli, and both degree of approach and fear are recorded. Investigators can use the BAT in an arranged anxiety-provoking situation for the youth to concurrently assess the cognitive, behavioral, and physiological components of anxiety. For example, anxious youths would be asked to rate their fears and record their thoughts (cognitive); the clinicians would rate the degree of approach to the noxious stimuli (behavioral), and the children's heart rate would be measured during the test (physiological). Observations and ratings taken during behavioral avoidance tests and role plays can contribute to a multisource assessment and help clinicians identify targets for behavior change.

Reactive Attachment Disorder. Physicians have found that some infants fail to develop adequately even though they have no apparent physical problems; this condition has been called *failure to thrive.* All aspects of the infant's development appear to be affected—physical, social, and emotional. The poor physical development is manifested in low weight gain (although head circumference and usually length remain normal), immature feeding patterns, excessive sleep, and less movement than usual. The child's social and emotional behaviors are characterized by a lack of appropriate social responsiveness, such as eye contact, smiling, and reaching for the caregiver. The onset of the problem is usually before eight months of age.

Psychologically, this condition is often related to *Reactive Attachment Disorder,* because the etiology is believed to be a lack of adequate physical and/or emotional caregiving. Reactive Attachment Disorder is characterized by disturbed and developmentally inappropriate social relatedness that begins before age five years. Children with disturbed patterns of social relatedness can have two types of presentations. In the Inhibited type, the child persistently fails to initiate and respond to most social interactions in a developmentally appropriate way. For example, the child may have a highly inhibited or ambivalent response to social interactions, such as frozen watchfulness, resistance to comfort, or a mixture of approach and avoidance. In the Disinhibited type, the child exhibits indiscriminate sociability or a lack of selectivity in the choice of attachment figures. Diagnosis requires evidence that the disorder resides within the child and an assessment of the child-caregiver relationship in areas such as comfort seeking, exploratory behavior, affectionate responses, and cooperativeness.

Prevalence rates, extrapolated from the maltreatment literature, have been estimated at approximately 1 percent (Zeanah & Emde, 1994). Evidence suggests that while maltreated children are more likely to exhibit insecure and confused patterns of relatedness, they do not necessarily develop a disorder of attachment (Lynch & Cicchetti, 1991). Infants with RAD are more likely to have caregivers who are depressed, isolated, or indifferent to the child's basic physical and social needs for comfort, stimulation, and affection. Detached or neglectful caregivers or repeated changes of the primary caregiver can prevent formation of stable attachments. Maltreated children may develop various attachment styles in their attempts to cope with inconsistent and problematic parent-child relationships. Features not identified in the current criteria for RAD but shared by most of these children include unusual patterns of language and motor delays, failed acquisition of age-appropriate self-care skills, poor attention and concentration, emotional lability, aggressivity, impulsivity, and oppositionality (Richters & Volkmar, 1994).

Hospitalization with its accompanying increased personal attention frequently leads to improvement. The disorder is considered to be reversible with appropriate treatment, but some infants have died from the physical complications because diagnosis was not made soon enough. This disorder is probably an extreme example of the problems observed by Spitz (1945) and others in infants who were in orphanages and other institutions that provided only minimal physical care.

Selective Mutism. The most common feature of *Selective Mutism* is the child's failure to speak in specific social situations despite speaking in other situations. Diagnosis requires that the symptom last at least one month, be severe enough to interfere with educational achievement, and not be due to another problem (such as insufficient knowledge of the language, a communication disorder, or another disorder). Selective Mutism has been described as a rare disorder, affecting fewer than 1 percent of school-aged children. Onset is usually before age five years, and the problem is often brought to the parents' attention by a preschool teacher. Although the disturbance usually lasts for only a few months, it may sometimes persist longer and may even continue for several years.

Reports in the literature suggest that Selective Mutism may be the manifestation of a shy, inhibited temperament most likely modulated by psychodynamic and psychosocial issues and in some cases associated with neuropsychological delays (developmental delays, speech and language disabilities, or difficulty processing social cues) (Dow et al., 1995). Recently, there has been a shift in the etiological views on Selective Mutism that deemphasize psychodynamic factors and focus instead on biologically mediated temperamental and anxiety components (Black & Uhde, 1992; Leonard & Topol, 1993). Some have reported that it may develop as a reaction to trauma, such as sexual abuse or early hospitalization (MacGregor et al., 1994). Divorce, death of a loved one, and frequent moves have also been suggested as possible triggers for symptom development. Anxiety in the form of shyness, timidity, and social withdrawal has been reported as a common characteristic of children with Selective Mutism, and it has been suggested that the condition may be a variant of Social Phobia (e.g., Black & Uhde, 1995). Cognitive-behavioral treatment interventions, in addition to pharmacotherapy, have become more common than traditional psychodynamic approaches for the treatment of this disorder.

Separation Anxiety Disorder. During the early preschool years, children are likely to show signs of distress when their parents leave them temporarily. These reactions are normal, and their magnitude is probably dependent on the previous patterns established by the parents. That is, if the child's early history includes only rare instances of being left with a babysitter, for example, then the child may be expected to have a stronger reaction to mother's leaving than if the mother had established a frequent pattern of leaving the child. Children whose early years have been spent in the company of their mothers may well be very upset at being left at nursery school or kindergarten for the first time.

In Separation Anxiety Disorder, the primary feature is excessive anxiety associated with separation from family members or familiar surroundings. This disorder may be manifested by the children's refusal to stay at friends' houses or in a room by themselves or to go to school or camp. They often have problems going to sleep and may experience nightmares. When separation is anticipated, they may develop physical complaints such as headaches, stomachaches, nausea, and vomiting. They tend to have a network of fears involving danger to themselves and their families and fears of animals, monsters, accidents, burglars, and dying. When separated, they may become preoccupied with fears of something terrible happening to themselves or their parents.

Children with Separation Anxiety Disorder tend to come from close-knit, warm families, suggesting that the child may have become too attached or dependent on family members. An anxious attachment may lead to proneness to separation anxiety and a lack of confidence for exploring the world and dealing with stressful situations (Sable, 1994). In some cases, a major life stress precedes the development of the disorder. These life stresses may include moving or changing schools, illness of the child or close relative, or death of a pet or close relative.

Separation Anxiety Disorder occurs in approximately 2 percent to 4 percent of children and adolescents and accounts for approximately one-half of children seen for mental health treatment of anxiety disorders (Bell-Dolan & Brazeal, 1993). In clinical samples of children with Separation Anxiety, approximately one-half are diagnosed with another anxiety disorder (most often Generalized Anxiety Disorder or Specific Phobia) and one-third with Depression (Last et al., 1987). Without effective treatment, the disorder may continue for years and prevent the child from obtaining normal schooling.

Specific Phobias. Persistent fear of a specific object or event can lead to avoidance of that feared stimuli. If the child is exposed to the feared object or event, he or she can experience a severe anxiety reaction. *Phobias* are characterized by extreme fear of specific objects or situations that pose little or no threat in reality. Phobic adults report their recognition of the fact that the feared situation is not harmful. The subjective fear may be expressed as tremor, faintness, nausea, perspiration, and feelings of panic. Behaviorally, phobias are manifested by escape from or avoidance of the feared object or situation.

Fears and phobias are extremely common in children and are usually more frequent in girls than boys. Because these responses are so common during the developmental period, it is relatively unusual for preschool children to be referred and formally diagnosed as phobic. The most frequent childhood fears are of animals, darkness, and separation from parents. Silverman and Kearney (1992) reported that the percentage of cases referred to clinicians for fears and phobias was about 7 percent, with most of them related to school and separation.

School Phobia is one of the most common types of fear in young children. It is often the case, however, that a child's refusal to go to school is not because of a specific fear or phobia (fear related to some circumscribed stimulus), but rather because of feelings of general anxiety or depression. In many cases, School Phobia more accurately represents children who are fearful of situations involving social interaction, evaluation, or separation from a caregiver. The fear and anxiety often fall within the categories of Separation Anxiety or Social Phobia. Therefore, a more general term, school refusal behavior, is used to describe youngsters who refuse to attend school or are have difficulty remaining in classes for an entire day (Kearney & Silverman, 1990).

Social Phobia (Social Anxiety Disorder).   Children and adolescents with Social Phobia often fear and avoid school-related events such as public speaking, writing in front of others, physical education classes, extracurricular activities, and new social interactions. Situations that expose the youth to possible scrutiny of others and fears that he or she may do something or act in a way that will be embarrassing are feared and avoided. Blushing, crowds, eating in public, and using public restrooms are also particularly problematic for this population. Among adults with Social Phobia, some have been found to become anxious only when performing specific activities (sometimes referred to as the specific subtype), and others have more generalized social fears (known as the generalized subtype). Although such distinctions have yet to be made in children and adolescent populations, a substantial number of youths with Social Phobia are suggested to suffer from the generalized subtype and to fear a range of distressing situations that often refer to social distress in the school setting (Beidel & Morris, 1995).

Avoidant Disorder in DSM-III-R (1987) was generally characterized by severe and persistent withdrawal from contact with persons not well known to a youngster. Such withdrawal was thought to interfere with a child's ability to make new friends or maintain established friendships. Avoidant disorder has been subsumed under Social Phobia in the current diagnostic system, DSM-IV (1994). Avoidant Disorder and/or Social Phobia appear less common than Separation Anxiety Disorder and maintain a fairly stable prevalence pattern from early childhood to late childhood and adolescence. Children with Social Phobia have been found to have severe trait (chronic) anxiety, less confidence in their cognitive abilities, and a strong tendency toward a rigid temperamental style (Beidel, 1991).

· *Generalized Anxiety Disorder.*   In contrast to the more specific fears in Separation Anxiety Disorder and phobias, *Overanxious Disorder* involves excessive anxiety that is *not* focused on a particular situation or object. In Overanxious Disorder, the child worries about a wide variety of future events and situations. The major theme seems to be a concern about competence, particularly evaluation by others in social, academic, and athletic areas. Physical signs of anxiety, such as headache, lump in the throat, digestive problems, and nausea, are frequently present. The child seems to be unable to relax and has an excessive need for reassurance.

Overanxious Disorder is subsumed under Generalized Anxiety Disorder in DSM-IV to reflect the notion that the diagnosis involves pervasive worry and intense agitation, fatigue, difficulty concentrating, tension in various muscle groups, and sleep problems, all for at least six months. The implications of this change make the diagnosis less complex because it requires fewer physical tension symptoms, and the source of specific worry is no longer considered (Kendall et al., 1995). This disorder is common in youngsters, especially females. However, unless the child is failing in school or repeatedly seeking medical care without evidence of physical illness, referral for treatment is often not sought. Like Generalized Anxiety Disorder in adults, overanxious or generalized anxiety may predispose a youngster toward future psychiatric disturbance (Beidel, 1991).

Panic Disorder.   The key characteristic of Panic Disorder is the occurrence of unexpected and recurrent *panic attacks*. Panic attacks are discrete periods of intense fear or discomfort accompanied by physical and cognitive symptoms. Physical symptoms include increased heart rate and chest pain, sweating and trembling, choking sensations or difficulty breathing, dizziness, gastrointestinal distress, body temperature changes, and numbness or tingling. Cognitive symptoms include fear of dying, losing control, feeling as if one is in a dream, and detaching oneself from immediate sensory experiences. Symptoms of panic attacks usually appear quickly and peak after several minutes before diminishing either rapidly or gradually.

Generalized anxiety between panic attacks, worry about the future occurrence of panic attacks, and agoraphobia are complications that seem to develop in many individuals with this condition. *Agoraphobia* is characterized by fear and avoidance of places or situations where the individual fears a panic attack is likely to occur. Studies (e.g., Black, 1995) suggest that children with Separation Anxiety, particularly girls, are at risk for developing Panic Disorder and agoraphobia during childhood or as an adult. Retrospective reports of adults with Panic Disorder report the onset of the disorder most commonly to be in childhood and adolescence. For example, a recent study examining age of onset of Panic Disorder found that panic disordered adults had a significantly higher rate of childhood Separation Anxiety Disorder and higher familial risks of Panic Disorder and panic with agoraphobia and alcoholism (Battaglia et al., 1995).

While the existence of panic attacks and Panic Disorder is well established in the adult population, much interest currently exists regarding the prevalence of these phenomena in children and adolescents (Ollendick, Mattis, & King, 1994). There is little doubt that Panic Disorder, with or without agoraphobia, occurs in adolescents; however, it has been argued that younger children may not display the cognitive elements (e.g., fear of dying) that usually characterize an attack (Nelles & Barlow, 1988). As the experience of panic in young children is being investigated, clinicians are finding effective treatments for Panic Disorder in adolescence (Ollendick, 1995).

Obsessive-Compulsive Disorder.   Persons with Obsessive-Compulsive Disorder (OCD) generally show two types of clinical symptoms, obsessions and compulsions. *Obsessions* are characterized by persistent, intrusive, unwanted *thoughts* or urges that the person is unable to control. These thoughts may consist of single words or ideas, or of combinations, that often appear nonsensical to the person experiencing them. The commonly reported experience of a particular tune recurring in one's thoughts is suggestive of an obsession, but because it is relatively transient and does not significantly interfere with normal activities, it would not be classified as one.

Compulsions consist of *behaviors* that are excessively repeated to alleviate the distress associated with aversive thoughts or urges. The most common compulsions in children are washing and cleaning, followed by checking, counting, repeating, touching, and straightening (Swedo et al., 1989). Engaging in a ritualistic behavior reduces irrational fear or distress. For example, a child may touch the mirrors in a room before he or she leaves to prevent shattering and subsequent bad luck. Interference with the behavior commonly results in feelings of distress and anxiety. Anxiety is also reported when the child becomes concerned about being unable to control the compulsion.

Obsessive-Compulsive Disorder is more common than previously believed, affecting approximately .5 percent to 1 percent of children and adolescents. Since one-third to one-half of adults develop the disorder during childhood or adolescence, childhood-onset OCD is an important predictor of adult morbidity (Rasmussen & Eisen, 1990). Toro et al. (1992) examined records of 72 children and adolescents (aged 5–18 years) with OCD, and their results indicated that 77 percent had suffered some other psychiatric disorder, particularly anxiety and affective disorders. Family conflicts, social withdrawal, and poor school performance were also common features. Childhood-onset OCD has been described as chronic and debilitating and can be difficult to treat.

Posttraumatic Stress Disorder. Children who have undergone some terribly stressful event that is often, though not necessarily, outside the range of normal human experience may suffer from Posttraumatic Stress Disorder (PTSD). In many cases, the person has interacted in a situation where a direct and serious threat to one or another's body is present (e.g., being the victim of a gunshot wound, seeing someone die in an automobile accident, enduring sexual abuse). The person's reaction typically involves intense fear, helplessness, or horror. In younger children, fear may be manifested in disorganized or agitated behavior.

Children and adolescents with PTSD typically reexperience the traumatic event in distressing intrusive thoughts or memories, dreams, and, less commonly, flashbacks. Younger children often engage in traumatic play, in which they may reenact specific themes of the traumatic experience. Sleep disturbances, irritability, difficulty concentrating, hypervigilance, exaggerated startle responses, and outbursts of aggression are evidence that the child is feeling physiological arousal related to the fear and anxiety. Children with PTSD invariably avoid thoughts, feelings, or actions that might trigger recollections of the event. Child survivors of trauma may show a markedly diminished interest in usually significant activities. The loss of previously acquired skills may leave a child less verbal or regressed to behaviors such as thumb sucking or enuresis (Amaya-Jackson & March, 1995).

Kendall-Tackett et al. (1993) synthesized the findings of several studies of sexual abuse in children and adolescents and reported that one-third had PTSD and 31 percent displayed nightmares about the traumatic event. Other events that may relate to PTSD include automobile accidents, head injuries, natural disasters, wartime experiences, and exposure to parental symptoms of PTSD.

Etiology

Children with anxiety disorders have parents with a high incidence of anxiety disorders in their histories, and adults with anxiety disorders have children with a higher risk of developing anxiety disorders. A study of nearly 4,000 pairs of adult twins revealed that genetic and individual environmental factors, but not shared or familial factors, contributed to anxiety symptoms (Kendler, Heath, Martin, & Eaves, 1986). Constitutional factors have also been invoked as causal agents; the person who develops an anxiety disorder may be one who is biologically vulnerable and less able to withstand stresses. Silverman, Cerny, and Nelles (1988), reviewing results from twin, family history, and family interview studies, concluded that parental avoidance/agoraphobic behaviors are associated with child maladjustment.

The genetic transmission of anxiety disorders has received support from a classic study conducted by Torgersen (1983), who examined 32 identical and 53 fraternal twins for a variety of disorders. The concordance rate for any type of anxiety disorder (except Generalized Anxiety) was higher for identical (34 percent) than fraternal (17 percent) twins. Turner, Beidel, and Townsley (1992) reported that 43 percent of a small sample of social phobics identified at least one first degree relative who experienced social fears. There is also some evidence of higher rates of Social Phobia in the relatives of persons with Panic Disorder. In addition, family and twin studies examining the heritability of Obsessive-Compulsive Disorder have indicated some genetic influence. Leane et al. (1990) reported that 20 percent of first degree relatives of 46 pediatric OCD probands met criteria for a lifetime diagnosis of OCD. Overall, the anxiety problems that likely have the greatest genetic influence with respect to etiology are panic, obsessions, and phobias such as blood-injury (Torgersen, 1993).

Several studies have indicated a significantly higher rate of anxiety disorder diagnosis among parents of children with anxiety disorders than those with other or no problems. In addition, children whose parents have a specific phobia also tend to display a higher rate of specific phobia than normal controls (Fyer et al., 1990). Taken together, these studies strongly indicate a familial etiological factor. However, we do not know exactly what characteristics are being transmitted, including temperament, ease of habituation, and physiological vulnerability.

In an ongoing longitudinal study, Kagan et al. (1988) have identified stable temperamental styles in young children that may predict later development of anxiety disorders. Some children have been found to display *behavioral inhibition*, that is, tend to become distressed and withdrawn from novel situations. Rosenbaum et al. (1991) found higher rates of anxiety disorders in the parents of inhibited children relative to the parents of uninhibited children. In addition, children who show stable behavioral inhibition from infancy through childhood have higher rates of anxiety disorders than children who were not consistently inhibited (Hirshfeld et al., 1992). These studies raise the intriguing possibility that childhood behavioral inhibition may be a risk factor for anxiety disorders, particularly social anxiety, later in life (Herbert, 1995).

Two theories that emphasize environmental or psychological factors as causing fears and anxiety are psychoanalytic theory and learning theory. The advocates of psychoanalytic theory propose that fears and anxiety are the product of a basically disturbed personality and disturbed family interactions. For example, separation anxiety and school refusal behavior were thought to result from problematic mother-child relationships. In essence, a mother may feel incompetent in the maternal role, or even hostile toward her child. To compensate, a mother may become overprotective and enmeshed with her child, thus creating an ambivalent family environment (i.e., affectionate and rejecting) and creating separation anxiety. Due to lack of empirical evidence, psychodynamic models of anxiety etiology and treatment have fallen into disfavor and more popular etiological models of fear/anxiety have been developed that involve some combination of cognitive, behavioral, and physiological variables (Eisen & Kearney, 1995).

From a learning point of view, several behavior principles are likely to be involved in the development of fears and phobias. One principle involves classical conditioning in which the previously neutral stimuli have been paired with an aversive stimulus that elicits a strong fear or emotional response. For example, entering one's classroom following a pairing of that room and an aversive experience may produce fear and anxiety for a school-refusing child. An operant learning component is also necessary to explain the full range of behaviors that may be presented. For the school-refusing child, leaving or avoiding school itself would become strengthened by the concomitant reduction of fear. Thus, excessive aversive stimulation or even one traumatic episode could lead to the development of a phobia or anxiety. This analysis follows the paradigm used by Watson and Rayner (1920) in their famous study of conditioning Albert to fear a white rat by pairing the rat with a loud noise.

In the case of more general anxiety disorders, the operant component may become more complex. That is, parents and other relevant people in the child's environment may reinforce the child's negative statements about the feared stimuli, complaints about bad feelings, and avoidance. For example, separation anxiety is marked by a fear of leaving home and parent. Having a parent become ill while the child is away at school might result in the child's experiencing anxiety when leaving home for school. Remaining at home may be reinforced both by the avoidance or alleviation of anxiety and social reinforcement by the ill parent or others.

Individual differences in responsiveness to environmental occurrences also play a role in determining the child's susceptibility to developing school phobia, for example. A sudden, loud reprimand from a teacher, for example, will elicit a wide range of emotional responses from different pupils. Some of this variability is no doubt due to innate biological differences, while the remaining portion is dependent on the specific previous experiences of the individual children. The child who has been exposed to frequent, loud reprimands in earlier grades or at home would not be likely to respond in the same way as the child with minimal exposure to such stimuli. In fact, the latter child would be expected to experience a greater emotional response on hearing a reprimand than would the former.

The etiology of fear and anxiety disorders in youngsters continues to receive a substantial amount of research attention because of different physical, environmental, and emotional influences. The age of the child and stage of development are important factors to remember when studying anxiety in children. For younger children, associations of objects and situations with pain and negative affectivity, positively reinforced and negatively reinforced fear and anxious behavior, and observations of others likely shape fearful and anxious reactions. For adolescents, increased cognitive and emotional development will likely involve misinterpretations of physical symptoms and social events that can evolve into anxiety.

Treatment

In psychodynamic theories of anxiety in children, an understanding of the child's underlying fears is obtained through therapeutic play, drawings, and sessions with family members. Issues of treatment focus include separation, autonomy, repressed feelings, and self-esteem. The goal of contemporary psychodynamic treatment is to provide a corrective emotional experience for the child that fosters the development and expression of age-appropriate behavior.

Behavior therapists have reported a number of successful intervention programs for childhood anxiety. One of the most common behavioral techniques for treating children with fear and anxiety disorders is exposure therapy. The crux of exposure therapy is to have the child repeatedly confront a feared stimulus until the anxiety response it elicits habituates. Exposure to the feared stimulus may be conducted *in vivo*, in which the naturally occurring stimulus itself is confronted, or imaginally, in which the youngster is asked to visualize the feared object or situation. For example, children with a fear of bugs might be asked to imagine bugs with ugly detailed features or to imagine a bug crawling up their arm. The longer children are exposed to the aversive idea, the greater the likelihood that they will habituate to the aversive thoughts and that their anxiety will decrease.

These procedures have been found to be particularly effective in the treatment of specific phobias. Silverman and Rabian (1993) recommend a gradual exposure program to expose a child to a fear-provoking object or situations according to successive steps on a fear hierarchy. The *fear hierarchy* is a list of situations or interactions related to the feared stimulus that range from least to most fear provoking in nature. For example, a child who is afraid of the dark may progress along the following hierarchy: (1) sit 10 minutes with therapist in dim light, (2) sit 10 minutes with therapist in dark therapy room, (3) sit 15 minutes alone in dark therapy room, until item (10) sleep alone in bedroom. The child moves up the hierarchy with successful reduction of anxiety at each more challenging level. Exposure procedures with children are typically done gradually, although more rapid exposure (*flooding*) has been used. There is research suggesting that these procedures can successfully treat specific phobias in single sessions; however, children may become easily frightened and therefore graduated methods are recommended with this population (Albano & Chorpita, 1995).

Cognitive-behavioral therapy addresses the thoughts, feelings, and behaviors related to anxiety and seeks to change dysfunctional patterns with more adaptive responses. These therapies focus on how people respond to their environment and how their thoughts and behaviors are related. The cognitive-behavior therapist guides children through their cognitive processes before, during, and after behavioral experiences, while attending to the emotional state of the children. Anxious children are taught to build more adaptive ways of looking at things and more adaptive attitudes and actions for dealing with fearful situations. Kendall (1994) demonstrated a cognitive-behavioral intervention package to be effective in treating children with Overanxious Disorder, Separation Anxiety, and Social Anxiety. In 16 weeks, children were taught to develop realistic expectations, to develop coping self-talk and to self-evaluate performance. In addition, modeling, exposure, and relaxation training were used to reduce anxiety. Anxious children who have undergone this treatment have been found to improve significantly, and the effects were maintained over time (Kendall & Southam-Gerow, 1996).

Cognitive-behavioral approaches have been successfully used to treat various childhood anxiety disorders. Preliminary evidence suggests that cognitive-behavioral group treatment of Social Phobia in adolescence is effective. Albano et al. (1995) presented data on five adolescents treated in a group setting, and all but one were found to improve after 16 weeks of cognitive-behavioral therapy. Furthermore, Herbert et al. (1993) found a multiple component behavior therapy program that included exposure, social skills training, and cognitive-behavior therapy to be effective with 11 adolescent social phobics. A combination of muscle relaxation, exposure, and cognitive restructuring has been found to be an effective intervention for Panic Disorder in adults. Ollendick (1995) found that a similar intervention was successful in treating four adolescents with Panic Disorder and agoraphobia.

Because parents are so influential in children's lives, family-based interventions can be important. Family-based intervention techniques include communication skills training, problem-solving training, and assisting the family in designing contracts to resolve conflict or change behavior. Family-based therapy techniques have been shown to be useful for behavior problems and social skill development in children. The combination of family-based techniques with traditional cognitive-behavioral treatments may be a promising approach. Barrett, Dadds, and Rapee (1996) examined the effectiveness of a family-based cognitive-behavioral treatment compared to a traditional cognitive-behavioral treatment or no treatment at all. Seventy-nine children diagnosed with Separation Anxiety, Overanxious Disorder, and Social Phobia participated in the study. It was found that both treatment groups significantly improved with added benefits from the family-based approach. In addition, a preliminary study of Obsessive-Compulsive Disorder found that parent participation in a cognitive-behavioral program showed promise in the treatment of childhood disorders (Knox, Albano, & Barlow, 1996).

Very little is known about the effectiveness of using medications to treat childhood and adolescent anxiety disorders. As recognition has been increasingly given to a physical basis for OCD, investigators have assessed the effectiveness of medications for this disorder. Clomipramine, a tricyclic antidepressant, has been clearly demonstrated to be an effective treatment for most children and adolescents with OCD (Deveaugh-Geiss et al., 1992). There have been mixed results from studies examining the use of medications, such as the tricyclic antidepressant imipramine, for the treatment of Separation Anxiety or school refusal. Furthermore, limited trials and case studies have not established a clear basis for the use of antianxiety medication for the treatment of Generalized Anxiety

Disorder, Panic Disorder, Social Phobia, and pediatric PTSD (Allen, Leonard, & Swedo, 1995).

DEPRESSION

Only in the last 15 to 20 years has a significant amount of attention been given to depression in children. Spitz's (1945, 1946) classic studies describing the symptoms of hospitalized infants stimulated considerable interest in mother-infant separation as well as experimental research on the effects of separating infant monkeys from their mothers. Spitz observed that the hospitalized infants were retarded in intellectual, social, and motor development and called this collection of symptoms *anaclitic depression*. In addition, Spitz noted the following symptoms: apprehension, sadness, immobility, listlessness, and apathy. He believed that these symptoms were similar to those found in depressed adults.

Despite Spitz's early work, depression as a childhood psychological disorder was often omitted in textbooks on child psychopathology probably because many clinicians had serious doubts that depression or other affective disorders existed in children prior to later adolescence. Hersh (1977) suggested that our cultural mythology depicting childhood as a period without concerns may be responsible for the relative lack of attention to depression in children in contrast to the substantial attention devoted to adult depression during the last 30 years. During recent years, however, there has been an increasing acknowledgment that depression can and does occur in children.

Assessment and Diagnosis

Childhood depression is usually diagnosed by clinicians on the basis of information obtained during the interviews with the child and parents. At a conference called Depression in Childhood, sponsored by the National Institute of Mental Health in 1975, a subcommittee proposed a set of clinical criteria for the diagnosis of depression in children (Dweck, Gittleman-Klein, McKinney, & Watson, 1977). Two essential clinical features were described: (1) dysphoria or reports of feeling sad and (2) an impairment in responding to experiences that were previously rewarding. The impairment had to be apparent across settings and not confined to a specific area of functioning, and the clinical features had to be present for four weeks before the diagnosis could be made. The subcommittee also described secondary features that may be associated with the essential features: changes in self-esteem, guilt, personal and general pessimism, and blaming others. The subcommittee recognized that research was needed to determine the role of these features in children of different ages.

Most clinicians accept the DSM-IV (1994) criteria for diagnosing depression in children and adolescents as well as adults. DSM-IV (1994) describes the mood disorders as divided into Depressive Disorders ("unipolar depression") and the Bipolar Disorders. The Depressive Disorders are distinguished from the Bipolar

Disorders by the fact that there is no history of mania or periods of abnormally elevated mood in the latter.

The Depressive Disorders include Major Depression and Dysthymia. *Major Depression* refers to a combination of severe symptoms including depressed mood and/or loss of pleasure in virtually all activities and at least several other symptoms for a period of two weeks. *Dysthymia* refers to a chronic disturbance of mood for most of the day for most days for at least two years in adults and one year in children and adolescents. The Bipolar Disorders involve the presence of depressive episodes and a history of manic episodes. A *manic episode* is defined by a distinct period of at least a week during which there is an abnormally and persistent elevated, expansive, or irritable mood.

Behavior checklists and rating scales are used for screening symptoms and assessing depression in children. One of the most frequently used self-report scales is the Children's Depression Inventory (CDI; Kovacs, 1985) that was modified from the Beck Depression Inventory (Kovacs & Beck, 1977) for adults. The measure includes 27 items regarding a broad range of depressive symptoms that are rated at three levels ("not a problem" to "severe"). This measure is for children aged 7–17 years, and the items can either be read independently or be read to the youth. A parallel parent version is available, and there are published data on the correspondence of parent and child reports (e.g., Wierzbicki, 1987) and on the level of agreement with the CBCL (Jensen et al., 1988).

Other self-report measures of depression have been developed for use with children or adolescents. For example, the Mood and Feelings Questionnaire (MFQ; Angold et al., 1987) is a 32-item questionnaire that is designed to ask questions related to diagnostic assessment of depression. Wood et al. (1995) used the scale with 104 adolescent outpatients (aged 10–19) attending a psychiatric clinic and found that approximately half of the adolescents were diagnosed with Major Depression. The MFQ self-report measure was found to have acceptable reliability and was a satisfactory screening instrument for major depressive disorders diagnosed by standardized interviews with the child. There are also structured and semistructured interviews for diagnosing depression in children, and preliminary studies have established that they can be rated reliably and have promising psychometric properties (Harrington, 1993).

Epidemiological studies indicate that between 2 and 7 percent of children show signs of significant symptoms of depression; this level increases substantially during adolescence. In an epidemiological study from the Oregon Adolescent Depression Project (OADP), Lewinsohn and Rohde (1993) found the lifetime prevalence of depression for a representative sample of 1,710 high school students to be 20.4 percent. Most cases of adolescent depression (84 percent) met the criteria for Major Depression, 6 percent had Dysthymia, and 10 percent had experienced both. Only a minority of depressed teenagers (approximately 34 percent) received any treatment for their depression.

In childhood, rates of depression either do not differ between boys and girls or show a slight excess in boys. The OADP study found prevalence and incidence rates are approximately twice as great for girls than for boys between the ages of 14 and 18 years. Various models based on puberty onset and psychosocial challenges of adolescence have been developed to better understand these differences (Nolen-Hoeksma & Girguis, 1994). The prevalence, age of onset, phenomenology, and course of Bipolar Disorder in adolescents appear to be similar for both males and females (Lewinsohn et al., 1995).

Although research in the area of Bipolar Disorder in children has been slow to develop, it is currently accepted that Bipolar Disorder can be manifested in children and adolescents. Lewinsohn et al. (1995) examined 1,709 adolescents (aged 14–18 years) and reported the lifetime prevalence of Bipolar Disorders in adolescents was approximately 1 percent. An additional 5.7 percent reported having experienced a distinct period of mania. Compared with adolescents who had a history of Major Depression and adolescents without mental illness, the adolescents who had experienced bipolar or manic episodes exhibited significant functional impairment, and high rates of comorbidity (particularly with anxiety and disruptive behaviors), suicide attempts, and mental health service use.

Depression is associated with suicidal ideation and suicide attempts. Suicide is rare for children but increases sharply during adolescence. There is some concern that the rates for both children and adolescents may be increasing. Recent findings by Lewinsohn et al. (1996) from the OADP study report the prevalence rate of suicidal ideation to be fairly high, with 19 percent of the sample acknowledging ideation at some time in their lives. The rate of suicidal ideation was twice as high for persons diagnosed with depression. Suicide attempts increase dramatically in adolescence. In Lewinsohn's sample, 10 percent of girls and 4 percent of boys had made an attempt. A previous attempt remains the strongest predictor of future attempts. Other risk factors for suicide in adolescents include depression, low self-esteem, cognitive and interpersonal deficits, loss of a parent, suicidal behavior of a friend, early pubertal maturation (girls only), and access to firearms. Children who have attempted suicide perceive their family environment to be stressful and lacking in support. Asarnow (1992) found that hospitalized child suicide attempters reported their families to be less cohesive, less expressive, and more in conflict than did nonsuicidal inpatients.

Etiology

In adults, several biological etiologies have been hypothesized for Major Depression. Hereditary factors appear to be implicated because the blood relatives of severely depressed persons have a higher incidence of depression than occurs in the general population, and identical twins have a higher concordance rate than do fraternal twins. The incidence of a mood disorder in the blood relatives is high (Kutcher & Marton, 1991).

Puig-Antich et al. (1989) found that prepubertal children with Major Depression had significantly higher familial rates of psychiatric disorders in both first- and second-degree relatives, especially Major Depression, alcoholism, and anxiety disorders. Furthermore, Pfeffer et al. (1994) reported that suicidal behavior in children was associated with suicidal behavior in their first-degree and second-degree relatives, along with Antisocial Personality Disorder, assaultive behavior, and substance abuse problems.

With severely depressed adults, considerable research has focused on the role of biochemical factors. During the last two decades, increasing evidence has accumulated that depression is related to the level of catecholamines in the brain. These catecholamines regulate the transmission of neural impulses; that is, they determine the probability of information being transmitted from one neuron to another in the nervous system. Indirect evidence from the success of biological therapies (medication) in adults supports the hypothesis of biological etiologies, at least in the case of Major Depression.

Both psychoanalytic and behavioral theories have been used to conceptualize the etiology of depression. Psychoanalytic conceptualization suggests that depression is associated with grief and melancholia. Melancholia is believed to be accompanied by a loss of self-esteem through a process in which the depressed individuals convert their hostility toward a lost love object to self-hatred. Behavioral views of the etiology of depression emphasize inadequate or insufficient reinforcement. The reinforcement deficits may originate with the loss of a person who provided reinforcement, poor skills in arranging for positive reinforcement, or environmental changes that are correlated with decreases in reinforcement.

Beck's theory of depression is based primarily on cognitive factors (Kovacs & Beck, 1977). Depressed individuals view events negatively; that is, they view themselves as deficient and inadequate and attribute their bad feelings to defects within themselves. They also perceive their environment as making excessive demands on them and tend to interpret interactions in terms of failure. The negative cognitive patterns are projected to the future in the belief that the current situation and feelings will continue indefinitely. Once a pervasive attitude of self-blame is developed, other symptoms, such as indecisiveness and increased dependency, may result.

Seligman (1975) described a cognitive model of depression with a basis in learned helplessness and emphasized the individual's inability to escape or avoid aversive situations. According to Seligman, depression results from the person's *perceiving* that aversive events are going to occur whether or not a response is made. Such perceptions could be based in reality or could be derived from generalized cognition that failure is due to factors beyond one's control.

Kazdin (1990) concluded that many models of adult depression apply to children. Depressed children show Beck's negative cognition, attributional styles of helplessness and blame, and social skills deficits. Like depressed adults, depressed children make fewer friends, initiate fewer conversations, are less popular, and participate in fewer social activities than nondepressed peers. Most of these models, however, describe correlates or factors that might serve to maintain the depression rather than factors that initiate the depression. Perhaps cumulative life stresses are associated with the onset of depression; that is, genetic factors may control the level of vulnerability, while the amount of life stress may control the age of onset.

Treatment

Generally, two types of medications are used to treat depressed youth, tricyclic antidepressants and serotonin-specific reuptake inhibitors (SSRIs). Based on a review of the literature over the past 10 years, Sommers-Flanagan and Sommers-Flanagan (1996) concluded that there have been no good studies indicating that antidepressant medications are more effective than placebos in treating child and adolescent depression. Further research is needed to examine these medications. It is recommended that drug treatment be conducted with caution because side effects from these medications may be especially problematic in prepubertal children.

In general, studies have demonstrated the effectiveness of psychosocial interventions for depressed children. Cognitive-behavioral treatments often focus on social skills training, activity level increases, cognitive therapy, helplessness intervention, and self-control strategies. Poor social skills are associated with a wide variety of childhood psychological problems, and their improvement may well result in increased amounts of reinforcement and concomitant decreases in depressive symptoms. Similarly, the teaching of social skills, particularly assertiveness, may decrease the feelings of helplessness. Prescribing increases in physical activity may be intrinsically reinforcing (biologically based) or may increase the probability of reinforcement in the natural environment. Cognitive strategies would focus on improving self-esteem and problem-solving skills, while self-control strategies would focus on self-monitoring, self-instruction, and self-reinforcement.

Cognitive-behavioral models have examined correlates of depression and highlighted the importance of family factors. There is a clear relationship between parental depression and child depression suggesting that interventions not only focus on the family pattern of behavior and cognition, but on how emotions are managed in the family (Dujovne et al., 1995). Lewinsohn and Rohde (1993) developed a cognitive-behavioral intervention specifically designed for depressed adolescents that includes social skills training, positive activities, relaxation training, cognitive restructuring, communication skills, and problem-solving skills. In addition, an intervention was developed to teach the parents the skills and techniques taught in the adolescent sessions. This intervention package has been shown to be an effective, nonstigmatizing, and cost-effective treatment for adolescent depression.

CONCLUSIONS

This chapter described disorders with emotional components that either control or are highly correlated with the behavioral manifestations of the problem. The behavioral symptoms usually include avoidance of persons, places, or things. Although these disorders have environmental factors as contributors, etiological factors may also include genetic or biological vulnerability. Combinations of cognitive-behavioral treatment programs, family-based approaches, and medications appear to be effective for treating anxiety and mood disorders.

RECOMMENDED READINGS

Craig, H.D., & Dobson, K.S. (1995). *Anxiety and depression in adults and children.* Thousand Oaks, CA: Sage.

Eisen, A.E., & Kearney, C.A. (1995). *Practitioner's guide to treating fear and anxiety in children and adolescents: A cognitive-behavioral approach.* New Jersey: Jason Aronson Inc.

Harrington, R. (1993). *Depressive disorder in childhood and adolescence.* New York: John Wiley & Sons.

March, J.S. (1995). *Anxiety disorders in children and adolescents.* New York: Guilford Press.

13

Disorders Affecting

Physical Functioning

Janet was a 15-year-old emaciated girl who had been admitted to a general hospital for diagnosis and treatment of severe weight loss. She was the oldest of three daughters and had no history of significant physical or psychological problems. Her parents described her as having been easy to rear and having done well in her schoolwork. They expressed only a mild complaint

This chapter revised by Joni McKeeman, Ph.D.

265

about her being a perfectionist and placing high demands on herself. They had become increasingly concerned about her weight loss during the past year. She was not worried about the weight loss and had to be forced to go to the physician, who subsequently admitted her to the hospital.

The parents reported that she had never been overweight but that she put herself on a strict diet because she felt that she was too fat. Even after she lost weight, however, she continued to feel "too fat." At family mealtimes, she came to the table but ate only small portions of food. On a few occasions, she ate a normal amount of food but later went to the bathroom and vomited.

Examination and laboratory tests revealed no physical problems except those caused by the weight loss. Although displeased by being forced to go to a physician and being hospitalized, Janet was a model patient; she was cooperative and cheerful and spent much of her time being physically active and socializing with other patients. While in the hospital, she continued the eating pattern she had at home and continued to lose weight.

In this chapter, we examine disorders whose primary symptoms affect some aspect of physical functioning. In some instances, the disorder involves biological damage and may be life-threatening, while in other instances physical functioning is disrupted, but no long-term biological consequences are implicated. Some of these disorders can be either initiated or maintained by psychological factors. Although their etiologies are complex and not well understood, the diagnosis and optimal treatment of these disorders often require the close cooperation of several professionals.

EATING DISORDERS

Children's eating experiences have received considerable attention from both theorists and practitioners. Psychoanalytic theorists have suggested that early eating experiences and their association with the gratification of oral needs play a significant role in determining later personality characteristics. Disturbances in eating behavior itself have been traced to the inadequate gratification of oral needs. Anna Freud (1965, p. 7) has stated that psychoanalytic investigators have been responsible for the amelioration of certain eating disturbances by recommending that feeding and weaning correspond to oral needs.

In comparison with most other animals, the newborn infant is relatively helpless. All of the baby's needs must be met by another person who, in turn, must learn to understand these needs. The newborn infant has had little experience with schedules of feeding, because nutrients have been supplied continuously through the umbilical cord. Neither has the infant had more than accidental experience with sucking. Newborn infants, thus, have much to learn and much to teach their caregivers about the processes of eating and feeding.

Certain standard information about feeding the young infant is usually made available to the new mother, but infants vary greatly in terms of their frequency of eating, the amount ingested at each feeding, and reactions to formulas and milk. Very young infants spend most of their time sleeping; they awake periodically and cry until fed. The average feeding frequency for young infants is every three to four hours. The frequency of awakening tends to be lower for higher birth-weight infants, but some normal birth-weight infants may awaken as often as every hour or two. Needless to say, parents are eager for the time when they and the infant sleep through the night. Interestingly, the middle of the night feeding is usually the first one the infant "sleeps through."

During the first year of life the frequency of feeding is gradually decreased to three meals a day plus milk at naptime and bedtime. About six months after birth, solid food in the form of strained cereals, eggs, meats, fruits, and vegetables begins to be introduced into the child's diet. Foods with more solid consistencies are added toward the end of the first year when the child has several teeth and is learning to drink from a cup.

How and when to wean the infant from the bottle or breast to cup-feeding often pose problems for mothers. Psychoanalytic theory has suggested that weaning, carried out too early or too abruptly, can lead to harmful psychological consequences. Early eating behavior receives a strong contribution from the sucking reflex that is present at birth; the sucking response, however, is greatly refined through learning during the first several months of life. Thus, strong patterns of motor behavior become associated with the eating process. Other forms of ingestion, such as drinking from a cup or eating from a spoon, require a number of different motor behaviors. Transferring an infant from one mode of feeding to another should proceed in a gradual manner as the child is able to learn the new eating behaviors. Abrupt weaning before the child has acquired the new eating behaviors is likely to cause at least a temporary reduction in the ingestion of food and may be detrimental to health in extreme cases.

Pediatricians recommend that training for drinking from a cup be initiated between 8 and 12 months of age, with the bottle being eliminated at about the age of one year. Training for self-feeding with a spoon can usually be started at about one year, and within a few months most children can feed themselves with only minimal spilling. These training tasks take time and patience from the caretaker, and sometimes harried parents postpone the training, continuing to feed the child themselves, and allow bottle feeding to continue for an extended period. Children who remain on the bottle beyond the second year are often subjected to ridicule by adult family members and other children.

While the psychological importance of sucking per se has been reiterated in the clinical literature, questions have been raised as to whether its significance has not been overstated. Early studies (e.g., Davis, Sears, Miller, & Brodbeck, 1948) showed that infants who were cup-fed did not engage in more nonnutritive sucking than those who were breast- or bottle-fed. Furthermore, infants who were weaned to the cup early showed *fewer* signs of frustration than those who were weaned later (Sears & Wise, 1950). These studies suggest that the need to suck is based primarily on learning with greater sucking experience resulting in an increased sucking need.

The introduction of new foods is usually correlated with the weaning process and presents its own problems. Children tend to reject foods that vary greatly from their regular food in either taste or consistency. They push the food out of their mouths or, if forced to eat, will vomit.

One method that is likely to be successful with rejected foods is based on a fading procedure. The mother begins by mixing a small amount of the new food with the familiar food and gradually increases the proportion of new food as long as the child continues to accept the mixture. Then the familiar food is gradually faded out of the mixture until the new food is accepted by itself.

Problems related to not eating tend to occur with considerable frequency during infancy and the preschool years. The great majority of children who are brought to the attention of their physicians for refusal to eat are, however, exhibiting typical developmental patterns or are reflecting a learned pattern of behavior.

After the initial learning to suck efficiently and the adjustment of formula, infants become eager eaters, usually tripling their birth weights during the first year. During the second through fifth years of life, the rate of weight gain is decreased to about five pounds each year. It is typically during the second year that parents become concerned about the child's refusal to eat. Eating patterns become more erratic, and weight gain likewise follows an irregular pattern. The child's weight may also remain unchanged over a period of months.

During the second six months of life, when the infant begins show more autonomy, some caregivers may have difficulty negotiating the issues of autonomy versus dependency, and the "battle of the spoon" may emerge (Chatoor, Dickson, Schaefer, & Egan, 1985). Typically, infants may try to feed themselves, but the caregivers may ignore the behavioral cue and continue to insist on feeding the infants. A battle of wills may ensue, with the infants becoming angry or frustrated in their attempts at self-feeding and refusing to open their mouths. The food refusal may become generalized to other caretakers, and the concern about the child's not eating can pervade many areas of the family's life. Treatment may include behavioral strategies to give the child more autonomy during feeding and setting firm limits on maladaptive behaviors. Caretakers are also asked to be neutral during feeding and to avoid attempts at coaxing or forcing the child to eat. Meals should be offered only at regularly scheduled mealtimes with planned snacks; "grazing" throughout the day should be avoided.

It is important to keep in mind that certain other factors may also be involved with refusal of food. Illnesses of various types may cause a decrease in eating, with the rejection of food sometimes occurring before the illness is manifested. Other factors include fatigue, overstimulation, and inadequate exercise.

Rumination Disorder

Regurgitation of food is frequent in young children, especially infants. Persistent vomiting in the first days or weeks of life may be indicative of an obstruction in the digestive system. Vomiting may also be caused by an excess of swallowed air, overfeeding, allergies, or infections. If all of these factors are ruled out, then consideration is given to the possibility that the vomiting may have a psychogenic origin. Exploring the psychosocial aspects of vomiting may, in appropriate cases, provide opportunities for more effective therapy and less invasive medical or surgical treatment (Fleisher, 1994).

Children vary greatly in their proneness to vomit. Vomiting tends to occur during highly stimulating events, changes in environment, and stressful experiences associated with food. Between the ages of six and eight years, many children experience nausea and vomiting when riding in automobiles. Since vomiting may be elicited in a wide variety of situations, it is relatively easy to see how a broad range of previously neutral stimuli can become conditioned to elicit vomiting. The eating of a particular food and becoming ill while riding in a car may be classically conditioned and result in the avoidance of this food.

There is a diagnostic category for a more intense course of vomiting, *rumination disorder of infancy*. This disorder usually begins between 3 and 12 months of age. It is characterized by repeated regurgitation of food with resulting weight loss or failure to gain the expected amount of weight. To be diagnosed, the problem has to be present for at least one month and follow a period of normal eating behavior. This disorder is potentially fatal due to malnutrition.

Physicians sometimes prescribe medications, such as phenobarbital and Thorazine, to treat severe cases of psychogenic vomiting. Behavioral intervention programs have been successful in eliminating vomiting in infants and older retarded children. In one case study, Lang and Melamed (1969) treated an infant who had a normal weight of 17 pounds at six months but whose vomiting had reduced his weight to 12 pounds at nine months. The child was vomiting within 10 to 15 minutes after every meal. The behavior therapy procedures were used because other treatment approaches were ineffective and his life was endangered. Treatment consisted of a brief electric shock to the calf of the infant's leg and a loud tone when vomiting was about to occur. The response to this procedure was rapid; by the sixth session the infant was no longer vomiting. One month after discharge from the hospital he weighed 21 pounds. He continued a normal course of weight gain and social development during the year following treatment, and the procedure did not appear to have any negative consequences.

Pica

Pica refers to the persistent ingestion of a nonnutritive substance. The age of onset is usually between 12 and 24 months; pica may persist into adolescence. Most young children attempt to consume substances such as sand or grass, or during the teething period, they may chew on their crib rails or other furnishings and thereby ingest paint and wood. Normally, the child either is easily taught or spontaneously gives up these activities. Children with pica continue to seek out and eat substances that may be harmful; lead poisoning from paint and blockage of intestines are possible complications.

Pica is more common among mentally retarded and psychotic children; other predisposing factors may be dietary deficiencies, neglect, and inadequate supervision. Treatment usually consists of careful monitoring of the child and preventing the ingestion as well as providing an appropriate diet.

Obesity

A generation or two ago, a plump or overweight infant was desirable because the extra weight was viewed as a sign of health. Children then were subject to many communicable diseases and infections that today are prevented by immunization or are treated with antibiotics. During earlier sieges with disease, many children succumbed; those with extra body fat were able to survive the days or weeks with minimal nutrition (due to depressed appetite) while expending great energy to fight the infection.

Obesity is defined as a body weight that is 20 or more percent greater than the norm for height and weight. It can also be determined by skin-fold measurements that estimate subcutaneous fat. At present, being overweight is viewed as a detriment to health. Being overweight during childhood may increase the risk of cardiovascular disease in adulthood (primarily as an accumulated effect of hypertension and cholesterol), depressed growth hormone release, and higher rates of respiratory infections. Overweight infants tend to become overweight children who tend to become overweight adults. Obese adults have shorter life expectancies and a higher rate of chronic health problems.

Obesity in children is related to a number of factors. Heredity apparently plays a significant role in the probability of being overweight. Heritability for weight is as high as that for height. Studies of twins have shown that identical twins resemble one another more closely in weight than do fraternal twins, whose weight similarity is the same as that for nontwin siblings. These results do not mean that body weight is strictly determined, but rather that weight is controlled within certain limits by hereditary factors; the specific weight is still determined by activity level and food intake. Lower social class, lower levels of social support, and unmarried status of the caretaker have also been found to be risk factors for obesity (Gerald, Anderson, Johnson, Huff, & Trimm, 1994). Research has revealed some unexpected relationships among obesity, caloric intake, and activity. Several studies have found that obese persons report eating no more food than their nonobese peers; however, striking differences were found in activity level, with obese persons being much less active (see Schlundt & Johnson, 1990).

Both activity level and food intake may be affected by psychological factors. Clinicians who work with overweight children have emphasized the mother as the primary agent in the psychological contribution to obesity. Some mothers expect the child to eat unusually large amounts of food, and their children please them by cooperating. Food, in a sense, becomes a substitute for other parental behaviors, such as social attention and affection. During the preschool years the overweight child tends to maintain such a close relationship to the mother that peer relationships are only minimally developed. The mother may continue to dress and bathe the child long after it is necessary. Entering school is a traumatic experience because the child lacks many of the necessary social skills.

Disappointments and frustrations are followed by more eating, the child's principal source of comfort.

Obese children are seldom happy children. They may be characterized as dependent and immature, but simultaneously demanding. They tend to be withdrawn with peers or choose playmates who are much younger or older than themselves. Older obese children are often convinced that they are ugly and undesirable. As a group, obese children are at a higher risk for behavior disorders (Woolston & Forsyth, 1989). They may continue to show more distress in adulthood; adults who were also obese as children show higher levels of emotional distress than those who developed obesity later in life (Mills & Andrianopoulos, 1993).

Some obese children are overweight from infancy, while others develop obesity at later ages. Obesity can develop as a reaction to traumatic events, such as the death of a parent or sibling, birth of a sibling, separation of the parents, personal failures, and illnesses.

Although overeating is the behavior that most clinicians try to control with overweight adults, it appears that *underactivity* may be the more important behavior of overweight children. Research suggests that underactivity is far more prevalent among obese children than is overeating. Perhaps for some children, obesity is initiated by a decrease in activity level with no corresponding decrease in the amount of food eaten. Among the factors that may account for decreases in activity are the traumatic events mentioned earlier, the overweight condition itself, and ridicule from peers.

Treatment of obese children must take into account all of the known factors. First, an increase in exercise is usually prescribed—one hour per day during the week and three hours per day on weekends and vacations. Second, the child is given an individually planned diet high in protein and low in calories. A diet for an adolescent, for example, would have 1,200 calories. A considerable effort is made to not blame the parents or child, but rather to emphasize the positive aspects of losing weight. Sometimes, parents have to be given instructions about nutrition and the caloric value of food.

Successful treatment of obese children can be difficult to achieve. Individual psychotherapy has not proved effective, but group therapy has shown some promise of success. Group therapy capitalizes on the importance of peer social approval for most children. Behavioral approaches to the treatment of obesity in children have followed those developed for adults, including nutritional education, self-monitoring, rearranging the physical and social environments, frequent contact, response cost, and contingency contracting. Behavioral reinforcement of exercise can increase rates of exercise (De Luca & Holborn, 1992).

Epstein (1986) concluded that childhood obesity can be treated at a variety of ages. The variable that has most consistently influenced the success of treatment has been parent participation, with parents and children being seen separately rather than together. Physical exercise/activity, particularly its long-term maintenance, should be incorporated more fully into diet regimes for overweight children. Perhaps the most promising approach will be that of prevention; pediatricians are currently monitoring the weights of infants carefully and adjusting diet and caloric intake accordingly.

Anorexia Nervosa

The primary diagnostic features of *anorexia nervosa* are weight loss to at least 20 percent below height and weight standards, an intense concern about being overweight that continues during weight loss, and a body image of "fat" that continues during weight loss. This disorder usually has an onset during adolescence and affects females primarily.

The culture of the teenager, including fashion models and performers, strongly emphasizes thinness, and it should come as no surprise that more women think of themselves as overweight than are in fact overweight (Powers & Erickson, 1986). The problem usually begins with the girl's becoming very concerned about her weight and appearance and deciding to diet. The parents are usually initially supportive of the girl's dieting. However, the adolescent becomes unable to stop dieting and begins to starve herself. In addition to avoiding the ingestion of food, the anorectic frequently indulges in excessive exercise; with increasing weight loss, she stops having menstrual periods. There is a genuine risk of death by starvation with this disorder. Anorectic adolescents are without concern for their health and deny that they have a problem. They resist suggestions that they seek help and usually have to be forced by their parents to get treatment. The disorder is usually manifested in a single episode, but it may become episodic or chronic. Although the anorectic avoids eating food, she may become quite active in preparing food for the family.

The etiology of anorexia has remained elusive. A number of clinicians are convinced that the development of anorexia nervosa is indicative of pathological family relationships. Minuchin and his colleagues (1975) presented four characteristics of families that support the development of anorexia. First, the family members are intrusive and do not acknowledge each others' individuality and roles. Second, the family members are overprotective of the anorectic child. Third, the families are rigid and reinforce the adolescent's problem because they do not want anything to change. Fourth, the families seem not to have learned to resolve conflict.

Typically, when the child reaches adolescence and must negotiate the accompanying psychological challenges to separate and individuate from the family, the family is unable to make the changes needed to support this process. The adolescent, who is often a perfectionistic person who works hard to please others and minimize conflict in the family, does not "act out" to gain independence as do many adolescents faced with similar difficulties individuating. Instead, the anorectic patient strives hard to gain a sense of independence via the more "socially acceptable" but physically harmful strategy of losing weight. In families where the expression of emotions and warmth is rigid, absent, or superficial, refusal to eat can serve both to create a sense of independence and self-control and to draw family members in to emotionally support the adolescent. Although there is no question that family dynamics are involved with anorexia nervosa, it is not clear whether family factors cause rather than maintain the problem or whether they are effects. Some research findings suggest that there may be a physical predisposition toward developing the disorder, although many biological correlates of anorexia, such as amenorrhea, are clearly effects rather than causes. Experimental starvation research shows that even many of the psychological correlates of anorexia, such as irritability, depression, indecisiveness, and obsessional thinking are also seen in starved nonanorectic subjects. However, the normal starved subjects did not show intense fear of food or an ability to suppress hunger that is usually found for anorectic patients (Mitchell, 1986).

Historically, anorexia nervosa has been reported as extremely difficult to treat (Bemis, 1978). Often by the time anorectics come to the attention of a professional, they are at considerable physical risk. Perhaps a less severe criterion for weight loss should be considered; that is, for adolescents, it may be advisable to initiate intervention when a weight loss of 10 to 15 percent below height and weight standards is obtained. Variables that have been found to assist in the identification of risk groups for chronic eating problems are higher levels of psychopathology including higher rates of depression, poorer family relations, poorer body image, higher percentage of body fat, and an earlier age of menarche (Graber, Brooks-Gunn, Paikoff, & Warren, 1994).

An apparent advancement in the treatment of anorexia nervosa has been made by the application of behavior principles. The primary goal is to increase the anorectic's motivation to eat and thereby to reduce the life-threatening condition. In most instances, it is necessary for the clinician to gain complete control of the client's reinforcers before adequate progress is made. A typical procedure would include hospitalizing the client and depriving her of all privileges, such as TV, use of the phone, and visits, until weight gain is in progress. Sometimes it may be possible to implement this treatment in the home. However, anorectics are so motivated not to eat that they try to manipulate their family and cheat to avoid eating. In addition, the physical and psychological separation of the anorectic patient from the family required during hospitalization may be a crucial element of the treatment. Cognitive therapy interventions have also been specifically designed for anorectics to decrease the misconceptions that they typically have (Garner, 1986). Educational materials on starvation and its physical and psychological effects are an important component of many programs. Therapy then focuses on decreasing the faulty reasoning and erroneous beliefs about the body.

Bulimia

The primary motivation in *bulimia*, to be thin, is the same as that in anorexia. However, thinness is achieved by recurrent binges of eating followed by self-induced vomiting or purging (using laxatives). Bulimia was originally described as a component of anorexia nervosa. About half of the anorectic patients in one study indicated that they sometimes engaged in binging and vomiting (Casper, Eckert, Halmi, Goldberg, & Davis, 1980).

Bulimics tend to be older than anorectics, with an average age of onset at 19 years. Binge eating is apparently a common behavior among college students; about 3 percent (all female) of a college sample indicated that they had also induced vomiting after binging (Hawkins & Clement, 1980). Another study (Johnson, Lewis, Lore, Lewis, & Stuckey, 1984) found that 4.9 percent of female high school populations met the DSM-III criteria for diagnosis of bulimia.

The behavioral treatment of bulimia has included use of self-control, reinforcement, contingency contracting, and systematic desensitization techniques to change the abnormal eating and vomiting/purging patterns. Some success has been demonstrated in case studies, but more empirical research with larger samples is needed (Wilson, 1986).

ELIMINATION DISORDERS

After feeding, toilet training has perhaps been given the greatest attention by the traditional theoreticians and clinicians. According to psychoanalytic theory, the methods of toilet training can have long-term consequences for later personality characteristics. One assumption is that the child's body products are highly valued by the child and may be given as "gifts" to the mother or withheld as "punishment" to the mother, or they may be associated with aggression and used as weapons. The dual role of body products is viewed as consistent with the toddler's characteristic ambivalence.

Strong demands by the mother for early and rigid toilet training may result in a psychological battle between mother and child. If, on the other hand, she is able to perceive the child's needs in their ambivalent state and proceed with toilet training in a sympathetic manner, then the process should be relatively free of stress. Eventually, with or without strife, the child accepts the mother's standards of cleanliness and internalizes them. Defense mechanisms are developed to guard against the appearance of urges that are in contradiction to mother's standards. Traits such as orderliness, tidiness, punctuality, and reliability are viewed as evidence of these defense mechanisms.

Toilet training may also be viewed primarily as a learning task in which the caretaker must develop stimulus control for the elimination responses. Children vary greatly in their progress toward successful toilet training. In our society, about half of the two year olds have bladder control during the day; by the age of four years the figure is 90 percent. Night bladder control is achieved by nearly 70 percent of three year olds and 90 percent of eight year olds. Bowel control generally comes earlier; nearly 70 percent of two year olds and 95 percent of four year olds have control of their bowel movements. In general, girls are successfully toilet trained at an earlier age than boys.

During the infancy period, urination and defecation are frequent. As the child matures and the number of daily feedings decreases, there is usually a concomitant reduction in the frequency of elimination episodes. The regularity of these episodes contributes to the ease or difficulty of initiating training. The child who has a regular elimination pattern is easier to train because the caretaker is able to anticipate the elimination and place the child on the toilet at times when elimination is highly likely. The child who has an irregular pattern is usually placed on the toilet at certain (e.g., two-hour) intervals throughout the day. The probability of the child's eliminating is markedly reduced, but it is higher than zero over a number of days or weeks. In addition to regularity of pattern, the caretaker should be alert to any behavior that precedes elimination; these behaviors might include straining, irritability, or pulling at the diaper. These behaviors can serve as signals to the caretaker to place the child on the toilet.

Sometimes, the child strongly resists being seated on the toilet. This resistance seems to be due to the novelty of the situation and to conditioned fears. Many young children become fearful when the toilet is flushed or if they lose their balance while on the toilet. The latter problem can be avoided by using a potty chair.

Once the child voids or defecates in the toilet, the caretaker can use praise or other reinforcers to indicate that she is pleased with the child's performance. Since, to be most effective, reinforcement should occur immediately after the desired response, the caretaker should remain with the child in the bathroom. Pediatricians suggest that each bathroom trial last only a few minutes, with the caretaker remaining silent if there is no result. This suggestion is in contrast to leaving the child on the toilet until he or she performs. In the latter situation, toilet training may become aversive to the child, and resistance to training may develop. If the child shows strong resistance to being placed on the toilet, it is sometimes recommended that toilet training be postponed for two or three weeks. This postponement attempts to capitalize on the young child's short memory.

During the training process, the caretaker should use a specific word to signify the act of elimination. Each time the child is successful, she can use the word. After the word acquires this specific meaning, she can use the word in the form of a request outside of the bathroom environment. The child gradually learns to use the word, first to describe his or her own behavior and, second, to indicate his or her needs in an anticipatory manner. Once the child can signal his or her need to use the toilet, the caretaker can begin to train the child to become independent.

Toilet training is a long and arduous experience if the process is started when the child is too young and lacks many of the prerequisite skills. From the available research, most children have the necessary prerequisite skills to be started on a toilet-training program at about two years of age.

Functional Enuresis

Functional enuresis is defined in DSM-IV as the "repeated voiding of urine during the day or at night into bed or clothes" (p. 108). The children should have reached an age at which continence is expected (at least five years). Etiological physical disorders must be ruled out. The voiding is usually voluntary but may be intentional. For diagnosis, the child must have at least two "accidents" per week for three consecutive months. Children less than five years old (or with an equivalent developmental level) cannot be diagnosed as having functional enuresis. At age five, the prevalence of functional enuresis is 7 percent for boys and 3 percent for girls, at age 10, 3 percent for boys and 2 percent for girls, and at age 18, 1 percent for males and almost nonexistent for females.

The majority of functionally enuretic children have a close relative who has or has had the disorder (Rushton, 1989). Twin studies have shown a higher concordance in identical twins than in fraternal twins, suggesting a hereditary disposition for the disorder.

Functional enuresis can have multiple psychological effects on the child. The wetting is socially embarrassing, and the child will try to avoid situations, such as camp and overnight stays with friends, that will publicize the problem. Parents and other adults are sometimes severe in their anger and rejection and may punish the child inappropriately. The accumulation of these experiences may lead to poor self-esteem and affect behavior in other areas.

Among the factors that have been implicated in the etiology of functional enuresis are delayed development of the physical structures of the urinary system, delayed or incomplete toilet training, and psychological stress. The psychological factors may be the child's hospitalization, starting school, or the birth of a sibling. It appears that children who never have had a lengthy period of urinary continence are more likely to have delayed development or inadequate toilet training, whereas psychological stress may be a more important factor when children become enuretic after a period of urinary continence.

Three options are currently available for treating nocturnal enuresis. Two of these options are pharmacological and include treatment with imipramine or nightly bedtime treatment with a nasal spray, desmopressin acetate (DDAVP). These pharmacological treatments offer the advantage of ease of use with little effort required. Disadvantages include expense (particularly for DDAVP) and medication side effects (Williford & Bernstein, 1996; Thompson & Rey, 1995). A potential side effect of desmopressin involves hyponatremia leading to seizures, because DDAVP functions as an antidiuretic agent. Patients need to be cautioned not to drink excess fluids during the evening prior to taking the medication (Robson & Leung, 1994). In addition, treatment gains are usually maintained only while taking the medication; once the medication stops, the bed-wetting often resumes.

The third treatment option, a behavioral intervention involving the use of a bed-wetting alarm system, is both effective at treating the bed-wetting, is less expensive, and is associated with longer lasting effectiveness after the alarm is discontinued. The primary disadvantage of this system is that it requires more effort and inconvenience on the part of the caretaker and the child, as well as some guidance from professionals in implementing a behavioral program while using the alarm to gain the most benefit and to decrease relapse rates. In a chaotic household, it may be quite difficult to gain compliance from the child and caretakers. Monda and Husmann (1995) compared the effectiveness of these three approaches and found success rates of 36 percent for imipramine, 68 percent for desmopressin, and 63 percent for alarm therapy. Relapse rates six months after therapy was discontinued were quite high for imipramine (only 16 percent continent) and desmopressin (only 10 percent continent); however, 56 percent of the patients treated with alarm therapy were still dry at night.

The bed-wetting alarm system, or the "bell and pad," is based on the principles of classical conditioning. The pad, which is wired to a bell, is placed on the child's mattress. When moisture makes contact with the pad, an electrical circuit is completed, causing the bell to ring. The ringing bell awakens the child, who then uses the toilet. In this paradigm, bladder tension is the conditioned stimulus, and the bell is the unconditioned stimulus for awakening. The pairing of the two stimuli results in the child's eventually awakening in response to the bladder tension alone. Sloop (1977) reviewed studies that evaluated the bell-and-pad system and concluded that it has an 80 percent initial cure rate with a relapse of about 25 percent. Varni (1983, p. 229) concluded that while effective, the bell-and-pad method may not be practical because it takes 8 to 12 weeks, and the alarm often disrupts the sleep of other family members.

The most successful method for both day and nighttime enuresis is a procedure that involves one day or night of intensive training (followed by brief use of a urine-alarm system for the nighttime enuretics) (Azrin & Foxx, 1974). The major features of the procedure include (1) increased intake of a preferred liquid, (2) frequent practice going to the toilet with reinforcement for all successes, and (3) cleanliness training and positive practice if wetting occurs. Positive practice involved cleaning up after the accident and practicing correct toileting.

Psychotherapy was a popular treatment for enuresis when it was believed to be a symptom of an underlying psychological conflict. Psychotherapy is currently reserved for the small number of cases in which serious psychological problems are present.

Functional Encopresis

Functional encopresis is the voluntary or involuntary passage of feces in inappropriate places that is not due to a physical disorder. The child must have a chronological and mental age of at least four years before the diagnosis is made. Approximately 1 percent of five year olds have this disorder, and it is more common in males and in lower socioeconomic classes. About 25 percent of children with functional encopresis also have functional enuresis.

There are two primary types of functional encopresis: encopresis associated with constipation and overflow incontinence and encopresis without constipation. When encopresis is associated with constipation, the constipation produces fecal impaction and the intestine becomes enlarged (Walker, 1995). The walls of the intestine are stretched and lose muscle tone, decreasing the ability to move fecal material along normally. Liquid stool pools above the impaction and gradually develops sufficient pressure to leak around the impaction and produces the overflow incontinence.

A combination of factors may produce the constipation, including psychological stressors such as the birth of a sibling or parental separation or divorce. The child may withhold stools as a result of emotional factors. Other factors might include poor diet with inadequate dietary fiber or hereditary predisposition towards constipation. Some children become constipated after having experienced a large, painful bowel movement, which leads them to withhold future bowel movements for fear of more pain.

Educating the parents and child about the role of constipation and fecal impaction in the development and maintenance of the soiling is important. Most parents are surprised to learn that their child is constipated and has little voluntary control over the soiling. Some parents, believing the child has voluntary control over the soiling, have unsuccessfully used punitive measures to try to change the child's soiling patterns. Often the child is able to avoid accidents while at school and while working hard to avoid "leakage," but when the child comes home and begins to relax in front of the television or while playing computer games, the child unknowingly relaxes the anal sphincter muscle as well and the leakage occurs. Parents may mistakenly assume that the child was too lazy to go to the bathroom and deliberately soiled.

After educating the parents and child about the physiological mechanisms involved in the soiling, medical and behavioral interventions are implemented. Treatment of the encopresis and constipation is most effective when a combination of medical treatment, including stool softeners such as mineral oil and sometimes enemas, and behavioral interventions to improve toileting habits are implemented simultaneously (Cox, Sutphen, Ling, Quillian, & Borowitz, 1996). Biofeedback that focuses on teaching the child how to relax the external anal sphincter muscle is another strategy found effective in treating encopresis (Cox, Sutphen, Borowitz, Dickens, Singles, & Whitehead, 1994).

Behavioral interventions often include a "sit and produce" program, where the child is asked to sit on the toilet three times a day for 5–10 minutes, following each meal. Positive reinforcement is implemented by rewarding the child with a sticker for compliance with sitting on the toilet, and giving a second sticker if the child produces a bowel movement. A behavior chart is used to record the child's progress with these goals. Another sticker may be given for compliance with taking medication.

When encopresis is present without constipation, the etiology may involve more serious psychopathology in the child and family (Bemporad, 1978). These children have been described as "manipulative soilers" (Walker, 1978), as they soil for reasons such as passively expressing anger towards their parents. In these cases, the soiling is usually at least partially under voluntary control and is deliberate. In such instances with younger children, intervention with the parents may help the problem. Older children may require individual psychotherapy in addition to the parental intervention.

SLEEP DISORDERS

During the period immediately after birth, infants sleep virtually all of the time, waking only to eat. As they become older, the number of hours each day spent sleeping decreases. Gradually, infants' sleep schedules begin to conform to those of adults. Before the age of three or four years, most children are still taking one or two naps every day and sleeping continuously beginning soon after the evening meal until the next morning. After the naps are discontinued, the evening bedtime hour is gradually moved to later times. It is not until adolescence that the sleeping schedule approximates that of adults.

Parents may encounter problems when children recognize the discrepancy between their hour of retiring and those of other family members. Children do not want to be left out of any activities by going to sleep. Establishing a sleeping schedule and preparatory activities seems to be a satisfactory arrangement for most parents and children. The schedule must, however, conform to the child's sleeping needs; individual children vary in the amount of sleep they require for optimal functioning, just as adults do. Picking a bedtime solely on the basis of parental convenience is often not successful. Parents sometimes forget that their children's sleeping needs decrease over time and insist on their continuing to go to sleep at a time that is more appropriate for a younger child.

When children resist going to sleep at night, parents are advised to assess sleeping needs in the context of the children's past sleeping history. In addition, parents should review the stimulus events that are occurring immediately before bedtime. Children who become very activated just before bedtime may have increased difficulties falling asleep. In some families, a sleep problem may develop because the father returns home from work late in the day and plays roughhouse games with the child just before bedtime. Parents can prevent this problem by engaging in more relaxed activities, such as reading stories. Likewise, family members ought not to describe exciting events that are going to occur after the child goes to bed.

Young children typically cry when they do not want to be put to bed, but older children present a wide variety of behaviors, such as requests to use the bathroom or to get drinks of water. These behaviors are often an attempt to secure a continued interaction with other people.

Parents who remain in the room or in the same bed until the child falls asleep frequently find themselves repeating that performance weeks and months later. If a child's calls and requests for companionship at bedtime are granted, parental social contacts may serve as reinforcers, thereby strengthening these behaviors.

Sometimes, reluctance to go to sleep is accompanied by emotional responses reflecting fear on the part of the child (Dollinger, 1986). Preschool children are particularly prone to the development of fears and more often than not, going to sleep is inadvertently associated with a stimulus that elicits fear in the child. Events such as loud, sudden sounds and unfamiliar light patterns coming through the windows are sometimes sufficient for the conditioning of fear to the darkened bedroom. Fear of the dark can often be alleviated by using a night-light in the child's room.

Awakening during the night may be initiated by many different events, for example, illness, nightmares, changes in daytime routine, and wetting the bed. Once the rhythmic sleep pattern has been broken, there is a tendency for the child to continue awakening in the night in the absence of the original event.

Almost all children have occasion to wake up during the night, and almost all of them go to their parents' bedroom. Under these circumstances, the child is often taken into the parents' bed. The comfort of being taken into a warm bed has great reinforcing properties and thereby increases the probability of the child's returning to the parents' bedroom on subsequent nights. In some extreme cases, children have been known to sleep with one or both parents over a period of years. Most parents, however, are not interested in sharing their beds with a third person and realize that their children must be returned to their own beds. Occasionally, a parent accepts the child in bed as a way of preventing sexual relations with the other parent. Single parents who are feeling lonely themselves sometimes allow the child to remain for company.

Sleepwalking Disorder

The primary characteristics of a *sleepwalking disorder* are recurring episodes of behaviors that involve leaving the bed and walking without being conscious of the activity or remembering the activities. The episodes usually occur between 90 and 120 minutes after sleep has begun, during the deepest stage of sleep, Stage 4 sleep. The child typically has reduced alertness and responsiveness, a blank stare, and is relatively unresponsive to communication with others or with efforts to be awakened by others. If awakened, the child has limited recall for the events that occurred during the sleepwalking episode.

Sleepwalking disorder usually begins between the ages of 6 and 12 years and lasts several years. In the minority of cases, sleepwalking recurs during early adulthood. It has been estimated that between 1 and 6 percent of children have the disorder at some time; it is more common among males than females and usually affects more than one member of a family.

Factors related to sleepwalking include seizure disorders, central nervous system infections, and trauma. Individuals with this disorder are more likely to have an episode when they are fatigued, have experienced a stressor, or have taken a sedative before going to bed.

The most serious complication with this disorder is accidental injury. Contrary to a popular belief, sleepwalking individuals are not as careful as they would be when awake, even though they are able to see and avoid objects in their path. Parents must take special precautions to be alerted and to prevent injury if their child has this disorder.

Sleep Terror Disorder

Sleep terror disorder refers to recurrent episodes of abrupt awakening from sleep that are initiated by a scream. The individual displays the signs of intense anxiety, such as a frightened expression, rapid breathing, perspiration, and repetitive motor movements; efforts to comfort the person are not successful until the intense agitation subsides. Episodes last from 1 to 10 minutes, and there is usually no memory of the episode upon awakening in the morning.

As in the sleepwalking disorder, episodes occur between 90 and 120 minutes after sleep onset, during the deepest stage of sleep when dreaming is not usually occurring. The sleep terror disorder usually begins between the ages of 4 and 12 years and gradually disappears in early adolescence. This disorder is more common in males and affects 1 to 4 percent of children at some time. Etiology is unknown, but individuals with the disorder are more likely to have an episode if they are fatigued or under stress or have taken certain antidepressant or antipsychotic drugs. Children with sleepwalking and sleep terror disorders do not have a higher incidence of psychopathology than the general population, but sleep terror disorder may occur with increased frequency in individuals who have suffered trauma or have extremely high levels of anxiety (American Psychiatric Association, 1994, p. 584). There are no complications as far as the child is concerned, but the episodes are likely to be very stressful to the parents. Dollinger (1986) recommended that several treatment approaches be considered for optimal results: desensitization, reinforcement, and parent counseling.

MOVEMENT DISORDERS

There are a number of movement abnormalities; some of them have been related to neurological problems, while others are believed either to have a psychological origin or to be of unknown etiology.

Stuttering

Stuttering is one of the more familiar speech disorders, particularly since it is most readily identified. Stuttering may be defined as frequent interruptions of speech production by repetitions of sounds or syllables or by their prolongation, often accompanied by excessive motor behaviors. Repetitions in speech are characteristic of the young preschool child. For the great majority of children, these dysfluencies tend to decrease during the preschool years. Although there are great individual differences in the types and amounts of fluency irregularities, certain kinds of irregularities, notably syllable repetitions, are heard more frequently in children who will later be diagnosed as stutterers. The differences between potential stutterers and nonstutterers, however, are not great enough to discriminate these groups without considerable error in identification (false positives and false negatives). Perhaps future research with more refined screening techniques will lead to early identification and thus development of prevention strategies.

Because dysfluencies are so common during the preschool years, it is generally believed that speech therapy for stuttering is not indicated during this period. Some parents, however, equate developmental dysfluencies with stuttering and react in a way that exacerbates the speech irregularity. The onset of stuttering is typically between two and seven years of age with a peak onset at age five.

Stuttering affects about 5 percent of children; approximately half of the people who stutter recover spontaneously. Stuttering occurs about three times as often in males as in females. Both stuttering and other speech problems are frequently found in the families of stutterers. Speech and language delays are commonly reported for stutterers, although their intellectual functioning is usually within normal limits. Fine motor coordination is often poor, while gross motor development is within normal limits. Reading and writing difficulties are encountered by a significant number of stutterers and members of their families.

Assessment and Etiology.   Speech clinicians frequently identify forms of stuttering on the basis of observed or inferred etiological factors, but the available research literature does not provide evidence that different etiological factors produce different stuttering patterns. Thus, at the present time, it would appear more reasonable to diagnose stuttering solely on the basis of behavioral criteria and to continue the search for its causes. A diagnosis of stuttering is made by the speech clinician after careful assessment of the child's speech and language repertoire. Since stuttering is most often identified in elementary school children, both teachers and parents are primary referral sources. Speech clinicians employed by the schools provide most of the services for children who stutter. The school clinician has a certain advantage in being able to observe the child easily in the context of various school activities and in having ready access to the teacher. Thus, assessment of the child includes school observation and teacher interviews as well as the testing procedures and speech samples obtained in the office. School clinicians, however, may have difficulty obtaining parents' cooperation, thus reducing the amount of information that may be obtained with regard to the child's history and development of the problem.

As with other speech disorders, the assessment procedure includes a hearing test. Stuttering is only rarely associated with hearing loss, although it is occasionally found in conjunction with decreased levels of intellectual functioning. Other findings being equal, a child with a mental age of four years may not receive speech therapy for the same reasons that a four year old with average intelligence might not. That is, both children have a high probability of outgrowing their stuttering behavior.

It is likely that children who stutter have been subjected to numerous instances of psychological stress. Parents and teachers try to correct them, and their peers laugh at them. These reactions from important people in the child's environment are believed by most clinicians to make the problem worse. During the assessment process, the clinician attempts to evaluate the possible psychological contributions to the problem. It may be assumed that psychological factors increase in importance as the child gets older and experiences more demands and ridicule.

Both organic and psychological factors have been hypothesized to cause stuttering, but research has yet to identify whether stuttering is primarily constitutional or learned. Clinicians in the past were taught adherence to a specific, single cause for stuttering. Contemporary teaching, however, advocates an open-minded attitude toward the etiology of stuttering. This attitude has been developed on the basis of the research evidence that contradicts the notion of a single cause. That is, no single factor has been found to be involved in all cases of childhood stuttering.

Van Riper (1972, p. 252) organized the various points of view concerning the etiology of stuttering into three principal types of theories: constitutional, neurotic, and learned. Most of the available evidence supports a learned or neurotic basis for the problem, although a few studies suggest an organic basis for at least some cases. A search for possible neurological mechanisms was motivated by studies in which stuttering was produced by electrical stimulation of a certain part of the brain in an unanesthetized adult and was alleviated or eliminated following neurosurgical treatment of other conditions, such as epilepsy, brain tumors, and aneurysms.

In the past, stuttering has been linked to being left-handed or ambidextrous, suggesting a problem related to cerebral dominance. Investigations have also hypothesized an underlying neuromuscular condition that manifests itself in poorly timed nervous impulses to the speech organs. Other researchers have suggested that stutterers may have defects in auditory perception; evidence for this suggestion comes from studies in which delaying the feedback of the person's voice for a fraction of a second has produced behaviors similar to stuttering. The belief that constitutional factors are implicated in the etiology of stuttering has been strengthened by (1) behavior genetic studies showing a strong hereditary connection, (2) the substantial male-female ratio, (3) a higher than expected rate of abnormal EEG patterns, and (4) problems in fine motor coordination.

Many psychiatrists and psychologists believe that stuttering is a symptom reflecting an underlying personality disturbance. These professionals have suggested that stuttering is an extended manifestation of repressed wishes to satisfy basic oral or anal needs. The mouth movements of the stutterer have been perceived by some clinicians as a way of prolonging infantile oral activities, while other clinicians have focused on the stutterer's fear of revealing forbidden wishes. These psychoanalytic views were particularly popular during the 1940s and early 1950s and were accepted because many of the *adult* stutterers seen by psychiatrists and psychologists did present serious emotional problems.

Speech clinicians have tended to view stuttering as a learned behavior. Since so many stutterers have reported the onset of the problem during the preschool years, speech professionals have hypothesized that stuttering is a learning extension of the repetitions and dysfluencies that normally occur between the ages of two and four years. This view proposes that the developmental repetitions are inadvertently reinforced by parental attention. Most stuttering patterns are not, however, duplications of developmental speech patterns, which tend to be repetitions of whole words, rather than initial sounds. In addition, environmental stress seems to be highly correlated with stuttering patterns. It has therefore been suggested that stress or frustration is responsible for the initial stuttering pattern. At some period in the child's life, psychological pressure to communicate is strong enough to disrupt the normal flow of speech. Indeed, there are instances reported in the clinical literature of children who changed from fluent speakers to stutterers in a matter of days.

At the present time, the model that best fits most child stutterers is a two-factor learning theory, the first component consisting of the classical conditioning of the stuttering response and the second component consisting of additional strengthening through reinforcement contingencies. Other aspects of stuttering behavior, such as avoidance of certain sounds or speech in certain settings, can also be explained by the second component, operant conditioning.

Treatment.   Many types of therapy have been used for stuttering, and claims of success have been reported by their proponents. Contemporary clinicians who work with children tend to take an eclectic approach with a primary emphasis on learning principles. During the assessment process the clinician evaluates the role of environmental stimuli as potential antecedents and consequences of the stuttering behavior. In the case of young (four to eight years of age) stutterers, the clinician often discovers that the parents are reprimanding the child for stuttering and, in addition, placing substantial demands for the presence or absence of other behaviors. Under these circumstances, the clinician recommends that the parents reduce their reprimands and other demands. Occasionally, such changes in the home environment rapidly lead to a complete disappearance of the stuttering. Some children have such a low level of frustration tolerance (correlated with high rates of stuttering) that the clinician may instruct the parents in conditioning procedures whereby the child is taught to cope with gradually increasing amounts of frustration.

In some cases, the parents are not willing or able to follow the speech clinician's advice to reduce the psychological stresses in the home. If such is the case, the speech clinician may recommend supplementary psychological help for the parents or child, or both. Depending on the factors in the specific case, play therapy, role playing, or counseling for the parents may be recommended.

If the reduction of psychological stress in the home is not completely successful in eliminating the stuttering, the speech clinician embarks on a course of action that emphasizes the increase of fluent speech. One tactic involves demonstrations by the parents and the clinician of their acceptance of the child. The acceptance may be manifested in numerous ways, such as giving the child appropriate responsibilities and rewarding successful achievements. In a similar manner, parents and the clinician begin to reinforce fluent speech and eliminate attention to stuttering differentially.

Of the elementary school-aged children who receive help for stuttering, about 75 to 85 percent receive that help from speech clinicians employed by the schools. It is generally agreed that children in this age group require direct therapy. Since most school-aged stutterers have a history of stuttering lasting several years, they usually present a greater challenge to the clinician. Stutterers are probably well aware of their stuttering and have begun to react to it in several ways. The more the child tenses in order to control or prevent stuttering, the greater the difficulty and unpleasantness of speaking the child experiences. Sometimes, extensive repertoires of superfluous motor movements have developed prior to referral for therapy. Fear of speaking, virtually absent in the young stutterer, becomes more prevalent as the child experiences more and more frustration.

Several approaches to treatment of the older child who has stuttered for several years have been taken. One method is through psychotherapy alone. Even though case studies that describe the reduction and elimination of stuttering through psychotherapy have been reported in the clinical literature, speech professionals do not view psychotherapy as a useful approach for the majority of children who stutter.

A second approach for treating the older child is currently used by many speech clinicians. It includes a wide variety of techniques for teaching the stutterer to avoid or prevent the fear that precipitates the stuttering episodes. Every effort is made to convince the stutterer that it is possible to be cured. That is, the clinician uses strong suggestion to obtain the client's confidence in the successful outcome of the therapy. In addition, breathing and vocalization exercises, as well as gestures and head movements, are utilized to distract the child from the fear of stuttering. In an effort to convince stutterers that they are normal speakers, clinicians design speech situations and forms of communication that are arranged in order of difficulty or the probability of eliciting stuttering. Each level is maintained until fear and stuttering are absent. This form of treatment has resulted in numerous cures and thus has many proponents. The evidence suggests, however, that generalization to the natural environment may be poor.

The application of behavior principles has had a profound effect on therapy techniques for stuttering (Ingham, 1984). Operant conditioning approaches that reinforce fluent speech or punish dysfluent speech have been successful for some children. The greatest contribution, however, has been the introduction of behavioral methodology to evaluate the effectiveness of a variety of interventions for stuttering.

Gagnon and Ladouceur (1992) used a behavioral approach to the treatment of children who stuttered that involved multiple components: (1) awareness training that involved increasing the child's and parents' awareness of each stuttering episode; (2) modified regulated breathing, which involved instructing the child to stop speaking and take a deep breath when stuttering occurred, and the child practiced this technique with progressively lengthier sentences; (3) easy speech, involving teaching the child how to speak without tension by voluntary tensing and relaxing facial muscles; and (4) group practice, which allowed the child to generalize the newly learned skills beyond the clinic setting. The authors found that the severity of stuttering was significantly decreased following treatment.

Tic Disorders

Tics are sudden, unexpected, purposeless, stereotypic, usually brief, rapid, and frequent motor or verbal responses, occurring singly, in "bursts," or in groups of different responses. The most common are eye blinks and other facial tics, but the whole head, torso, or limbs may manifest the movement. Tics are considered to be *transient* if their intensity varies and their duration has been at least one month but not longer than one year; they are considered to be *chronic* if their intensity does not vary and they have occurred for more than a year.

The onset of transient tics is always during childhood (as early as two years) or early adolescence. Some 12 to 24 percent of school-aged children have had some history of tics; the disorder is three times more common in boys and is more common in family members of persons who have the disorder. Tics become worse with stress but may decrease when attention is focused on some activity. The individual may be able to suppress the tics temporarily. Until the mid-1970s, tics were believed to be manifestations of a neurotic process, but there has been increasing evidence that physical factors are involved in the etiology.

In the past, most of the more severely affected children were probably referred for traditional psychotherapy, but no evaluation of its effectiveness can be detemined from the available research. Behavioral therapists have used a procedure called massed practice, in which the child voluntarily performs the tic response repeatedly. This procedure has helped some children but is not uniform in its effect.

Tourette's disorder is a particular tic disorder characterized by involuntary motor tics and vocal sounds that include clicks, grunts, coughs, or words; some cases may include verbal obscenities or curse words. The onset of Tourette's disorder may be as early as two years and almost always occurs before 13; in about half of the cases, a single tic is the first symptom, and in the other half multiple tics begin to occur simultaneously. The disorder is three times more common in boys and occurs more often in family members of persons with the disorder. The disruptive effect of this disorder on home and school activities is severe. The majority of children with Tourette's disorder have learning disabilities and attentional problems (Lerer, 1987). Obsessive-compulsive symptoms, other anxiety disorders, and speech problems are also common in the children and family members of children with Tourette's disorder (Carter, Pauls, Leckman, & Cohen, 1994). It is also not unusual for children with Tourette's disorder to have sleep problems including sleep terrors and sleepwalking, and tics can be observed during their sleep.

Nothing definitive is known about etiology, but about half of the individuals have some signs of mild neurological abnormalities. The disorder can be lifelong and debilitating, and a variety of treatment approaches have been tried. From the available research, a multidisciplinary approach to treatment that includes medication, behavior therapy, and counseling is optimal (Cohen, Bruun, & Leckman, 1988; Peterson, Campise, & Azrin, 1994). Peterson and Azrin (1992) were successful in treating motor and vocal tics associated with Tourette's disorder using behavioral techniques. Tics were reduced by 55 percent using habit reversal strategies, 44 percent with self-monitoring, and 32 percent with relaxation training.

Epilepsy

Epilepsy is a collection of convulsive or seizure disorders that are caused by abnormal electrical activity in the brain. These disorders result in disruptions of consciousness or activity. Epilepsy is diagnosed on the basis of abnormal EEG brain waves and their location.

Several types of epilepsy have been described. *Grand mal* epilepsy is the best-known type and is characterized by an initial stiffening of the body followed by spasms in which the body jerks rapidly. The person is unconscious during the attack and has no memories of it. Sleep often follows the attack, and there may be headache and confusion afterwards. Attacks are often preceded by an aura, an emotional state such as depression or elation. *Petit mal* seizures are more common during childhood and involve very brief (a few seconds or less) lapses of consciousness. When they occur very frequently, the child's learning in school and behavior at home may be significantly affected by the discontinuities in the child's experiences.

The largest group of seizure disorders are those in which only a portion of the neurons in the brain develop epileptic discharges (as opposed to the more generalized grand mal and petit mal seizures) (Bernat & Vincent, 1993). They are called partial seizures and can be *simple partial seizures*, those in which consciousness is not impaired, or *complex partial seizures*, those in which consciousness is impaired. Sometimes, complex partial seizures that occur in the frontal lobe of the brain are particularly difficult to recognize, and individuals with these seizures are often misdiagnosed as having psychiatric disorders (Stores, 1992; Gedye, 1989). Individuals with these types of seizures may report complex psychological phenomena during the seizure, including a dreamlike state, fear, feelings of depersonalization, a *deja vu* sensation, and visual, auditory, or olfactory hallucinations (Bernat & Vincent, 1993).

Individual children may have one of these or other types of epilepsy or a combination of types. Children with epilepsy may have normal intelligence, but learning difficulties are common (Addy, 1987). Children with seizures have been found to be more likely to have behavior problems that include hyperactive behaviors, difficulty concentrating, confusion, impulsivity, obsessiveness, and restlessness, and dependent behaviors such as clinging to adults, frequent crying, and demanding attention than children without known health conditions (McDermott, Mani, & Krishnaswami, 1995).

Epilepsy may be due to hereditary factors or may result from head injury, tumors, poisons, anoxia, encephalitis, meningitis, and probably other factors that are related to brain damage. Transitory seizures may also occur during high fevers and in association with drug and alcohol intoxication.

Preventing seizures is the major goal of intervention because seizures are likely to cause more damage to the brain. In addition, seizures and the fear of seizures present a serious handicapping condition that can affect virtually every aspect of living. Fortunately, anticonvulsion medications such as Dilantin have been developed. They successfully control seizures in about 75 percent of cases. Some individuals with epilepsy have been successfully treated with biofeedback training (Olton & Noonberg, 1980). Ince (1976) reported a case of a 12-year-old boy with a four-year history of recurrent seizures and secondary anxiety problems. Therapy consisted of first removing the anxiety through relaxation training and then using this training whenever the onset of a seizure was anticipated. Treatment was conducted one hour a week for three months with one booster session at six months while the boy was at camp. A nine-month follow-up after therapy termination revealed that no seizures had occurred. Mostofsky (1978) reviewed the role of psychological interventions, such as psychotherapy, reinforcement, desensitization, and biofeedback, for developing a better understanding of epileptic disorders. Corbett and Besag

(1988) recommended that discussions of the problems associated with epilepsy with the affected person, family, and teachers can reduce misunderstanding, distress, and secondary psychological problems.

Cerebral Palsy

Cerebral palsy refers to a collection of disorders that primarily affect motor behavior. The earliest symptoms may be a delay in motor development and abnormal reflexes on the neurological examination. As the child grows older, other problems become apparent. The majority of children with cerebral palsy develop spasticity in one or more limbs. *Spasticity* refers to an inability to move the limb voluntarily because the muscles are contracted. Spasticity usually involves the two limbs on one side of the body (hemiplegia), the two lower limbs (paraplegia), or all four limbs (quadriplegia). Other children with cerebral palsy have abnormal movements of the limbs (dyskinesia) that may be rapid or slow. The smallest group of children with cerebral palsy develops ataxia, an inability to coordinate the muscles for maintaining posture or for walking. The motor disabilities often prevent the child from speaking or communicating in other ways.

For a long time, the severe motor disabilities of children with cerebral palsy prevented valid assessment of their cognitive functioning. In fact, it was generally assumed that all persons with these severe motor handicaps were also mentally retarded, and many were institutionalized under that assumption. Greater efforts have been under way to assess the abilities of children with motor handicaps (Cauley, Golinkoff, Hirsch-Pasek, & Gordon, 1989). It now appears that probably only one-half of the children with cerebral palsy are mentally retarded. This finding, however, does not negate the fact that many of the intellectually normal children are severely hampered in their use of that intelligence by their physical handicaps, but it has probably contributed toward a greater effort in the treatment of these physical handicaps.

Children with cerebral palsy may also benefit from the implementation of early intervention programs to maximize their cognitive development during the first several years of life when sensory and developmental stimulation is critical. The passage of Public Law 99-457 mandates special education services to children from birth to three years of age, and these educational programs have been found to be effective in improving intellectual development of children at risk for developmental delays (Blair, Ramey, & Hardin, 1995).

Psychological problems associated with brain damage occur more often in children with cerebral palsy. Other psychological problems are not as prevalent, especially in preadolescent children from middle-class environments. Parents who are able to cope successfully with the added financial and time burdens are more likely to have children whose adjustment and development are maximized. One study has reported that a group of middle-class parents rated their four- to eight-year-old cerebral-palsied children as having the same amount of self-esteem as the middle-class parents of normal children; teachers, however, gave lower self-esteem scores to the cerebral-palsied children (Teplin, Howard, & O'Connor, 1981). As physically handicapped children became aware of their limitations and the long-term implications of their handicap, they may have emotional reactions that are optimally treated with psychological intervention.

It has long been recognized that cerebral palsy is correlated with oxygen deprivation during the perinatal period. Other common factors are prematurity, maternal bleeding in the first trimester, head injury, and infections. A substantial number of children with cerebral palsy, however, have experienced no known perinatal complications, suggesting that there are prenatal and postnatal factors yet to be identified.

Treatment of the motor handicaps associated with cerebral palsy is moderately successful with some types of disorders, particularly when it is begun early in life. Kong (1969) reported that treatment begun in the first year of life is the most effective. Treatment of the motor problems is conducted primarily by physical therapists in clinic and hospital settings. Since treatment must be conducted daily, physical therapists design home therapy programs for the parents and work with the child at less frequent intervals.

Some communities provide special schools or other facilities for children with cerebral palsy. Many of these children would otherwise not receive an adequate education because their physical handicaps prevent their attending most public schools. The law now requires public buildings to provide access routes and facilities (e.g., bathrooms) for persons who need wheelchairs, braces, or crutches to ambulate. This law has greatly facilitated the effort to provide normal environments for physically handicapped persons.

Much of the treatment of the motor disabilities in cerebral palsy is an attempt to prevent further handicaps. When the muscles of the body are not used, they are highly susceptible to atrophy, a wasting or decrease in the tissues, and physical therapy can help to prevent this atrophy and related problems. If cerebral palsy is not diagnosed early enough, certain abnormalities of the muscles, and thereby the limbs, may not be corrected by physical therapy alone. In some of these instances, orthopedic surgery, which often involves the severing and/or or rearranging of muscle tissue can alleviate otherwise intractable physical handicaps.

Several studies with cerebral-palsied adults have described significant improvement with relaxation training and biofeedback, suggesting that such techniques may be applicable to children. Self-control of swallowing and positive reinforcement were demonstrated to be effective in controlling the drooling of a nonvocal spastic quadriplegic adolescent (Dunn, Cunningham, & Backman, 1987). Behavior principles are also likely to be useful in gaining both child and parental compliance for the therapeutic programs.

CONCLUSIONS

It is becoming increasingly evident that psychological factors may be involved in disorders related to physical functioning such as eating, eliminating, sleeping, and moving. In some instances, genetic and other physical etiological factors may be primary, and adverse psychological conditions serve to worsen the disorders. Even when etiology is unknown, psychological interventions may be helpful.

RECOMMENDED READINGS

Brownell, K.D., & Foreyt, J.P. (Eds.). (1986). *Handbook of eating disorders.* New York: Basic Books.

Cohen, D.J., Bruun, R.D., & Leckman, J.F. (Eds.). (1988). *Tourette's syndrome and tic disorders: Clinical understanding and treatment.* New York: Wiley.

Hardy, J.C. (1983). *Cerebral palsy.* Englewood Cliffs, NJ: Prentice Hall.

Kaplan, A.S., & Garfinkel, P.E. (Eds.). (1993). *Medical issues and the eating disorders: The interface.* Brunner-Mazel.

Peine, M. (Ed.). (1984). *Contemporary approaches in stuttering therapy.* Boston: Little, Brown.

Powers, P.S., & Fernandez, R.C. (Eds.). (1984). *Current treatment of anorexia nervosa and bulimia.* Basel: Karger.

Roberts, M.C. (1995). *Handbook of pediatric psychology* (2nd ed.). New York: Guilford.

Schlundt, D.G., & Johnson, W.G. (1990). *Eating disorders: Assessment and treatment.* Needham Heights, MA: Allyn & Bacon.

Sheldon, S., Spire, J.P., & Levy, H.B. (1992). *Pediatric sleep medicine.* Philadelphia: W.B. Saunders.

Smolak, L., Levine, M.P., & Striegel-Moore, R. (Eds.). (1966). *The developmental psychopathology of eating disorders: Implications for research, prevention, and treatment.* Hove, England: Lawrence Erlbaum Associations, Inc.

Woolston, J.L. (1991). *Eating and growth disorders in infants and children.* Newbury Park, CA: Sage.

14

Psychological Aspects of Medical

Problems and Procedures

Pediatricians and mental health clinicians have begun to recognize the importance of psychological factors in children's adjustment to medical procedures and hospitalization. As many illnesses and communicable diseases have become more easily treated or prevented, increased physician attention has been directed toward the psychological well-being of children in the medical environment. In addition, some health problems in adulthood may be the products of lifestyles that began in childhood, indicating the need for preventive measures to be initiated early in life (Melamed, Matthews, Routh, Stabler, & Schneiderman, 1988, Chapters 1–4).

This chapter revised by Anthony Spirito, Ph.D., and Emily Smith Rappold, Ph.D.

Most children in the United States are born into a medical environment, and many are continuously monitored by physicians. In contrast to a time when children were seen by physicians only when they were sick or injured, many children start their lives with a schedule of visits that include checkups and inoculations against communicable diseases. For many of us, our earliest memories of physicians are the pain and anxiety associated with being held down and given inoculations. Physicians have become aware of this association and currently have nurses or other medical personnel administer shots.

In this chapter, we examine the procedures, settings, and medical conditions that are likely to create psychological problems for children and their families. These problems are particularly important to understand because they may lead to an interruption of optimal medical care and, in some cases, may threaten the life of the child.

FEARS

A child's age or stage of development affects the child's perception of medical situations as well as the child's fears in these situations. Young children, of course, do not have the cognitive ability to understand much of what might be described to them about medical situations. However, they are capable of the classical conditioning associating pain with medical procedures and personnel.

Fears in children are likely to come from two sources: environmental novelty and classical conditioning. There is substantial research indicating that while a certain amount of novelty is enjoyable or reinforcing, stimuli that vary greatly from the familiar often engender fear responses in young children, such as crying and trying to withdraw. Thus, younger children tend to be afraid of things and situations that do not bother older children. As we become acquainted with our environment, we become less anxious or fearful in everyday situations.

However, at the same time that these fears are decreasing, other fears may be acquired. These other fears are learned on the basis of pairing or association with something that already produces fear or anxiety. As one gets older, such fears accumulate, although some of them may become extinguished.

Probably all of us have some anxiety or fears that originated in medical or dental settings during our childhood. Such fears are unfortunately responsible for many adults not receiving adequate medical and dental care; increasingly serious medical and dental problems may be developing when anxiety causes us to avoid medical and dental visits. Needless to say, many of our fears and anxieties begin with pain that accompanies either specific physical disorders or the medical procedures that are used to assess, treat, or prevent them. As you will recall, fear and anxiety are normal responses to pain, but what often happens through classical conditioning is the development of an anticipatory anxiety response that is subsequently produced by the stimulus that was present when the pain occurred or even by the thoughts and memories of the stimuli and the pain itself.

Adults, including professionals, have been relatively naive about children's fears and anxieties, particularly about those related to medical situations and procedures. Adults have tended to think of childhood as a period of blissful freedom and to deny some of its potentially negative aspects. In fact, most of the research on children's fears had until recently been based on information from parents rather than children. Given the possibility that children do not always share their fears with their parents and that children, especially males, may be punished or ignored for expressing fears, it should come as no surprise to find that children are more fearful than we previously thought they were.

When first, fourth, and seventh grade children were asked to rate specific medical fears, Aho and Erickson (1985) found that girls endorsed more fears than boys at each grade level and that the number of fears actually increased from the first through the seventh grade. In comparison to boys, girls in our society have probably been given more permission to express their fears. The increase in the number of fears as children get older probably reflects the fact that the children are experiencing an increasing number of medical procedures. In other words, having more experience with illness, accidents, and medical procedures does not necessarily reduce medical fears; it may well be that some are decreased but others are created. This study found that children who had been hospitalized had the same number and intensity of medical fears as children who had not been hospitalized.

Clinicians and researchers have become increasingly concerned about the long-term effects of children's chronic and serious illnesses on the children and their families. In a review of the research literature, Barbarin (1990) concluded that seriously ill children are at twice as much risk for psychological problems. However, not all chronically ill children experience adjustment problems. In another review of the literature (Lavigne & Faier-Routman, 1993), factors determined to affect psychosocial adjustment included medical condition parameters (e.g., severity and duration of disease), child characteristics (e.g., temperament and coping methods), and family characteristics (e.g., family functioning and parental adjustment). Barbarin (1990) recommended that families, rather than the individual ill child, be the target of intervention programs because the family unit bears much of the stress when a child becomes ill. These therapeutic interventions may include probing the meaning and impact of the illness, disease education, pain management, parent and child involvement in care, and the encouragement of familial as well as nonfamilial social-support networks. Siblings of chronically ill children may also be at risk for developing psychological problems (Lobato, Faust, & Spirito, 1988).

PAIN

Pain may come from a variety of sources, such as disease, physical injury, and medical or dental procedures; pain is also reported when the sources are unknown. There are considerable individual differences in reactivity to painful stimuli. Some of these differences may be due to physical differences among people, but it is well documented that responses to painful stimuli are greatly influenced by family and other sociocultural factors. Because such a multitude of factors influence pain behavior, a comprehensive assessment process is necessary before a treatment program for pain is initiated (Varni, 1983).

Pain is usually described as either acute or chronic. Acute pain is an effective biological warning that directs attention to injury or disease. Acute pain is intense and creates an emotional reaction of fear or anxiety. The anxiety response may in turn intensify other responses to the painful stimuli.

Chronic pain, on the other hand, appears to engender little or no anxiety response. Other compensatory behaviors, such as restricted movement or limping, may occur, and these behaviors sometimes continue after the injury has healed. Medication dependence becomes a greater problem in chronic pain patients.

Behavioral treatment for pain has been divided into two types: pain perception regulation and pain behavior regulation (Varni, 1983, p. 64). Pain perception regulation is the primary treatment approach for children's acute pain. This self-regulation includes or shares features with hypnosis, meditation, muscle relaxation, biofeedback, distraction, and guided imagery (imagining past experiences that are incompatible with pain). Pain behavior regulation, in comparison, relies on contingency management, such as giving the child social attention for "well" behaviors and ignoring "pain" behaviors. In many cases, both pain perception regulation and pain behavior regulation are used in the treatment of childhood pain complaints, especially recurrent abdominal pain and headaches.

Anywhere from 10 to 15 percent of school-aged children experience recurrent abdominal pain. In most cases, there is no definitive medical cause, and stress (at home or at school) and other psychological factors (e.g., parent modeling of pain behavior and inadvertent reinforcement of pain complaints) may play a role in the child's pain perception. In one study (Sanders et al., 1989), children with recurrent abdominal pain were treated with a multicomponent program which included instructing the parents to reinforce well behaviors rather than pay attention to the abdominal pain complaints. The children were taught to self-monitor their pain and make statements to themselves regarding their ability to control their pain. In addition, relaxation and imagery strategies were suggested to help the children distract themselves and cope better with the pain. Children who took part in this program improved more quickly and a larger proportion were completely pain-free at two-month follow-up than those in a comparison group. Fentress, Masek, Mehegan, and Benson (1986) used relaxation training and biofeedback as well as pain management guidelines for parents to reduce the frequency and intensity of headache pain in children 8 to 12 years old diagnosed with migraines.

An example of behavioral intervention for pain perception may be seen in a study by Cozzi, Tryon, and Sedlacek (1987) with sickle cell anemia patients. Sickle cell anemia patients have fairly healthy periods that are interrupted by acutely painful crises. Behavioral therapy was directed toward producing vasodilation to counteract the vasoconstriction process associated with the sickle cell crisis pain. The researchers taught the patients relaxation techniques that included guided imagery centered on a pain-free scene with suggestion of increased body warmth (vasodilation). A thermal biofeedback unit was placed on the index finger periodically to monitor body temperature. The researchers reported reductions in the frequency and intensity of the patients' pain crises, the amount of pain medication taken, and headaches.

CANCER

Cancer is a group of diverse diseases characterized by an uncontrolled growth of abnormal cells that outnumber and/or interfere with the functioning of normal cells. Cancer in young children is relatively rare with over 6,000 new cases diagnosed per year (Gotay, 1987), but as a cause of death, it is second only to accidents. Most adult cancers involve tumors of particular organs, such as the lung or liver, and glands such as the breast, while child cancers are more likely to be the leukemias. Considerable progress has been made in the medical treatment of cancer in children. For example, only a few decades ago the most common malignant disease of childhood, acute lymphoblastic leukemia, was rapidly fatal within a few months of diagnosis. Today, this disease can be controlled to the point that the majority of the affected children are alive five years after diagnosis. However, during much of this period, the children and their families are faced with psychological problems that are brought on by having to cope with the disease and its treatment.

A diagnosis of cancer is clearly a traumatic occurrence for a family. Even though great progress has been made in treating cancer and in saving lives, many people still think of cancer as an automatic death sentence. Compared to other diseases, cancer does have a high death rate. In working with the family, it is important for the clinician to determine what the child and family understand about the child's disease. Keeping the child's developmental level in mind, it is generally advised that children be told about their illness and the plan for treatment. Children who understand and openly discuss their illness are believed to be more likely to cooperate with treatment regimes (Spinetta, 1980).

Most professionals believe that it is important for children to return to school whenever they are being treated on an outpatient basis except if the cancer is directly affecting the central nervous system. Unfortunately, peer and adult reactions to the physical changes that can be caused by treatment (e.g., hair loss and scars from surgery) sometimes create anxiety and self-consciousness in the child. Children with cancer may also become anxious about the effect of their absences on their academic progress. Such problems can be treated or prevented by programs that involve the child, parents, school personnel, and when necessary, the offending peers. One such program called "The School Intervention Project," helped prepare newly diagnosed children with cancer for the return to school by having psychologists meet with the child in the hospital, setting up conferences with school personnel to discuss the child's illness, and conducting presentations to the patient's classmates to help them understand the illness, as well as a follow-up component after the child had returned to school. When compared to those who did not receive the program, this program was found to improve the reintegration and adjustment of children with cancer to their schools (Katz, Rubenstein, Hubert, & Blew, 1988).

In contrast to many forms of adult cancer, children's cancers are not associated with chronic pain, except perhaps in the final weeks during the terminal stage of the illness. One of the continuing psychological problems associated with cancer is management of the acute pain related to its treatment. Several groups of researchers have demonstrated that children's distress due to painful procedures may be reduced by behavioral approaches such as filmed modeling, relaxation training, breathing exercises, imagery, behavioral rehearsal, coaching, distraction with toys and party blowers, and incentives (see Varni, Blount, Waldron, & Smith, 1995, for a review). The researchers who have conducted these programs have also developed better ways to assess pain and distress in young children.

The most common types of side effects for the child patient that are related to the chemotherapy and radiation therapy treatments of cancer are nausea, vomiting, loss of appetite, and taste aversions. These side effects, in turn, may reduce treatment compliance and therefore threaten the child's life. Recently, more effective medicines have been developed to control chemotherapy-related nausea and vomiting. Hypnosis and other relaxation procedures are also sometimes helpful, particularly for adolescents, in relieving nausea and vomiting.

Food apparently becomes aversive because food ingestion has been accidentally paired with the nausea and vomiting that was caused by the cancer treatment (Burnstein, 1991). Such learned taste aversions are relatively common among people who get sick after eating a particular food. One pairing of the food and illness can be sufficient to cause an aversion lasting for years. Like other learned avoidance behaviors, taste aversions tend not to decrease over time but are more effectively decreased by ingesting the aversive food and finding out that illness does not follow. However, it is particularly difficult to persuade children to try the disliked food. Boeberg and Bornstein (1987) gave children with cancer strongly flavored candy (coconut or root-beer Lifesavers) after they had eaten a meal and before they received chemotherapy. Children who received the candy were twice as likely to eat some portion of the same meal on a later occasion than were children who did not eat any candy between the meal and the chemotherapy. Therefore, the researchers recommended that ingesting strongly flavored candies before chemotherapy might be a simple and effective way to avoid learned food aversions when children are receiving chemotherapy.

Other stimuli in the environment can also become paired with aversive diagnostic and treatment procedures. Particular sights, sounds, and odors, through conditioning, can cause a large number of anticipatory psychophysiological changes in heart rate, respiration, and skin temperature, as well as nausea and vomiting. Research with adults has examined the effects of distraction, hypnosis, muscle relaxation, guided imagery, meditation, and biofeedback on reducing these conditioned anticipatory responses. Distraction has been successful in controlling conditioned nausea in child cancer patients receiving chemotherapy (Redd et al., 1987).

A study of pediatric cancer survivors revealed that most of them were functioning well, and psychosocial problems were relatively rare (Fritz, Williams, &

Amylon, 1988). However, those children who receive very aggressive central nervous system treatment, particularly cranial radiation therapy, are at risk for impaired cognitive development, particularly in nonlanguage skills (Fletcher & Copeland, 1988).

SPINA BIFIDA

Spina bifida is the most common congenital central nervous defect, occurring about twice per 1,000 live births. The defect is an abnormality of the spinal cord that eliminates or reduces the neural messages below the level of the abnormality. Improved medical and surgical procedures have dramatically increased the survival rate of these children.

Children with spina bifida typically score below average on tests of intelligence. As they get older, they tend to fall behind peers, especially in visual-motor skills, suggesting that there are developmental differences between children with spina bifida and nonhandicapped children in visual-perceptual-organizational skills (Wills, Holmbeck, Dillon, & MeLone, 1990). Spina bifida is associated with delays in self-help skills, such as dressing, grooming, and hygiene; obesity; incontinence; and lack of ambulation. Some of the delays in the development of self-help skills are likely secondary to the lack of ambulation, but others can be the result of fewer expectations for skill development by caretakers and teachers. The obesity is clearly related to lack of ambulation and a decreased expenditure of calories; parents need to be informed that children with spina bifida need to consume only about half of the calories consumed by children without the problem. Obesity itself causes other problems, such as more difficulty in successful ambulation and greater potential for pressure sores.

The lack of control of urinary and bowel functioning is due primarily to the low level of innervation of that area in children with spina bifida. Incontinence creates a number of problems for the child and other family members, but perhaps its greatest negative impact is on peer social interactions (Hunt, 1981). In addition, it has often been an important factor in excluding the child from regular classes.

Fortunately, behavioral research is beginning to reveal that the problems of the child with spina bifida can be reduced. Although the lesion level obviously has an impact on the ultimate capability to ambulate, clinical research with several patients suggests that significantly greater progress can be made in helping children with spina bifida to attain functional ambulation (Manella & Varni, 1981). Similar success has been achieved for increasing the self-help skills of four children with spina bifida through a behavioral group parent training program (Feldman, Manella, Apodaca, & Varni, 1982).

CARDIOVASCULAR DISORDERS

At the present time, an American child has a one in five chance of developing signs of coronary heart disease before the age of 16 (Varni, 1983). Juvenile hypertension is estimated at between 3 and 10 percent depending on the method of measurement (Voors, Webber, & Berenson, 1978). Thus, the evidence is clear that for some persons the atherosclerotic process (obstruction of the blood vessels) begins in childhood (Voller & Strong, 1981).

Because childhood blood pressure is highly correlated with adult blood pressure and because mortality increases with the duration of hypertension, it is important that intervention and prevention programs be initiated at an early age and be maintained for long periods. Prospective studies on adults have implicated the following etiological factors in atherosclerosis, particularly in coronary heart disease: high blood cholesterol level, high blood pressure, smoking, obesity, hyperglycemia (high blood sugar level), psychosocial stress (Type A behavior), and family history of the disease. All of these factors, except family history, are modifiable; that is, they can be changed, although often not very easily.

Large-scale studies on children suggest that the same factors are predictive of later coronary heart disease. Thus, early intervention and prevention programs have focused on diet, exercise, and smoking cessation and have shown considerable promise (Coates & Masek, 1982). The dietary programs focus on increasing the consumption of complex carbohydrates and decreasing the consumption of saturated fats, cholesterol, salt (sodium), and sugar. Several school-based programs using components of dietary, smoking, and exercise education have reported success in reducing weight and other risk factors (Nader et al., 1992; Walter, Hoffman, Vaughn, & Wynder, 1988). (See the section on obesity in Chapter 13 for further information on weight control and physical exercise programs.)

A particular behavior pattern called Type A behavior and characterized by a strong drive for achievement, aggressiveness, time urgency, and competitiveness has been associated with an increased risk of coronary heart disease in adults. A measure of overt Type A behaviors in children, called the Matthews Youth Test for Health, has been devised, and there is some evidence for its stability into adulthood (Bergman & Magnusson, 1986) and validity (Murray, Matthews, Blake, Prineas, & Gillum, 1986). Like Type A adults, research with children has shown that Type A children have elevated cardiovascular reactivity to stressful laboratory tasks compared to non-Type A children (Matthews & Jennings, 1984). The aggressiveness/hostility component of Type A behavior contributes most to cardiovascular risk. Adolescents, particularly boys, who frequently direct anger outward demonstrate higher blood pressure and a greater likelihood of cigarette smoking than adolescents who do not frequently express anger in an outward manner (Siegel, 1984).

ASTHMA

Asthma is a respiratory disorder that involves intermittent obstruction of the air passages; the person has the feeling of suffocating or not getting enough air to breathe. Wheezing is a common overt symptom of asthma. A number of factors have been associated with airway obstruction: allergens, aspirin and other medications, infections, emotional stimuli, exercise, and irritants (Creer, Renne, & Chai, 1982). Perhaps any stimulus that increases metabolism either directly or indirectly through classical conditioning can be considered as having potential for initiating or prolonging an asthmatic attack. In general, there are three physical responses that may serve as the basis for an attack: contractions or spasms of the smooth muscle surrounding the airways, mucus that clogs the airways, or swelling of the lining of the bronchial tubes.

Asthma affects approximately 10 percent of children under the age of 12 years, with the occurrence being higher for boys than girls. Children from racial/ethnic minorities who are poor and live in urban areas are the highest risk population for asthma. Children who have an early age of onset and an infrequent rate of wheezing are more likely to have decreased symptoms in early adulthood. The disorder is responsible for many emergency room visits and school absences.

Medical treatment for asthma includes prescription of the bronchodilator drug, theophylline; it is absorbed slowly and therefore is useful for continuous therapy. Studies of outpatient asthmatic children have indicated that compliance is low; that is, only a small percentage of children are actually taking the drug as prescribed. Empirical research suggests that a combination of psychological adjustment, degree of family conflict, and interaction between these two variables was predictive of compliance (Christiaanse, Lavigne, & Lerner, 1989).

Biofeedback and relaxation training have not proven effective in producing clinically significant improvement in pulmonary functioning but may be helpful in reducing the conditioned anxiety and fear responses that develop secondary to asthma attacks. In at least one study (Kotses, Stout, McConnaughy, Winder, & Creer, 1996), training children to monitor their own respiratory status and to prevent and reduce their own attacks by taking appropriate preventive steps has proven effective in improving pulmonary functioning and reducing the frequency of asthma attacks.

DIABETES

Diabetes is a chronic disorder of carbohydrate, lipid, and protein metabolism and involves an inadequate production or utilization of insulin. The principal symptoms of diabetes are increased blood sugar, sugar in the urine, excessive urine production, excessive thirst, and increased eating. The long-term effects of diabetes may include kidney failure, nerve damage, blindness, and circulatory disorders. The two types of diabetes are insulin-dependent and noninsulin-dependent. The insulin-dependent diabetic produces little or no insulin and requires insulin injections. This type of diabetes tends to have its onset during a childhood growth spurt: ages 5 to 6 or 10 to 12.

Although emotional stress does not appear to have etiological significance in the onset of diabetes, stress affects diabetes control in some but not all persons with diabetes, either directly or indirectly through its effects on compliance with the diabetic regimen. Several studies have shown that everyday minor stressors and family characteristics such as conflict, poor cohesion, and low emotional expressiveness are related to poorer diabetic control (Hanson & Pichert, 1986; Marteau, Bloch, &

Baum, 1987). Stress reduction techniques may therefore be helpful in maintaining optimal intervention.

Perhaps one of the most difficult problems in the management of insulin-dependent diabetes is gaining the cooperation of the child or adolescent and parents to adhere to the long-term and time-consuming process that includes injections, collection of urine specimens, special diets, exercise, and hygiene. Since the regime is very complex, there is ample opportunity for noncompliance.

In an 18-month study of 57 children and adolescents with recent onset of insulin-dependent diabetes, compliance with the prescribed treatment deteriorated over time, with adolescents being less compliant than preadolescents (Jacobson, et al., 1987); this study also found that initial patient reports of their self-esteem, perceived competence, social functioning, behavioral symptoms, and adjustment to diabetes predicted subsequent compliance. A number of clinical researchers have found management programs that are helpful in improving compliance (Padgett, Mumford, Hynes, & Carter, 1988). These programs give considerable attention to patient and parent education as a necessary first step to improving adherence. In general, education by itself does not necessarily lead to compliance. Again, reinforcement contingencies for compliance behavior offer considerable promise for diabetic children's problems (Epstein et al., 1981; Schafer, Glasgow, & McCaul, 1982). Varni (1983) described some of these problems:

1. Insulin injections—omitting injections, giving injections at wrong or irregular time intervals, injecting the incorrect dosage, failing to alternate injection sites
2. Diet—skipping meals or prescribed snack intervals, eating too much, eating sweets
3. Urine testing—not testing at all, testing at incorrect times, reporting false results
4. Exercise—not adjusting insulin dose and diet to changes in activity level
5. Hygiene—not cleaning and checking feet, teeth, and skin on a regular basis. (p. 254)

Rainwater et al. (1988) reported the successful use of systematic desensitization for needle phobias in 25 subjects, ranging in age from 7 to 20 years, with diabetes.

SICKLE CELL DISEASE AND HEMOPHILIA

Sickle cell disease is an autosomal recessive genetic disorder that leads to the development of abnormal red blood cells. In the United States, sickle cell disease primarily affects persons of African descent. This disease is accompanied by numerous physical problems such as recurrent pain, anemia, increased susceptibility to infections, and delayed physical development as well as a decreased life expectancy. The psychosocial stressors associated with sickle cell disease are similar to those of cancer and other chronic diseases in that many aspects of the child's and the family's life are affected. Research (Fowler et al., 1988) suggests that children with sickle cell anemia may also be at risk for subtle neuropsychological deficits and decreased school performance. Active coping attempts during painful crises and pain-free periods have been shown to be related to increased social activity (Gil et al., 1993), while negative coping strategies have been related to increased symptom-reporting in children with sickle cell disease (Thompson et al., 1994).

Hemophilia is an inherited disorder in which there is an absence of a substance that facilitates blood clotting. It is a condition in males that is transmitted by females as an X chromosome-linked recessive trait. The disorder is manifested in recurrent, internal bleeding that may affect any part of the body, but the joints are most commonly affected. During the internal bleeding episodes, acute pain occurs; in addition, the repeated bleeding into the joints causes damage that is manifested in chronic arthritic pain. Thus, the hemophiliac patient often experiences chronic pain that is interspersed with acute pain episodes.

The chronic arthritic pain which often develops in persons with hemophilia poses a particular problem in that the usual response is inactivity of the joint, which causes loss of muscle capacity around the affected joint, thereby making subsequent movement more difficult and painful. After discovering that warmth decreases perception of pain in arthritic patients, Varni (1981) designed a behavioral program in which two patients were taught muscle relaxation and guided imagery that focused on blood moving to the affected joint and warm sensations. A thermal biofeedback device was used for physiological assessment. The patients were instructed to practice their relaxation exercises and guided imagery at home for a minimum of two 15-minute sessions per day. This training was effective for both patients in that it markedly reduced the number of days per week that pain was reported; the therapeutic effect continued throughout the eight months of follow-up. Moreover, stable increases in the skin temperature of the affected joints were also observed. Cognitive-behavioral techniques have also been tried to reduce the number of bleeding episodes among children with hemophilia. These techniques have had mixed success.

Another study (Woolf et al., 1989) has indicated that boys with hemophilia may be at risk for school achievement problems. Although the subjects had normal intelligence and average grades in school, one-fourth of the boys performed more than two grade levels below expected in reading and one-half performed more than two grade levels below expected in math. The authors recommended that multidisciplinary teams ensure appropriate intervention for this high-risk group.

VISUAL IMPAIRMENT

Visual impairment can range from a mild defect that interferes only minimally with everyday living to complete blindness. The legal definition of blindness is visual acuity in the better eye with correction of not more than 20/200 or a defect in the visual field so that the widest diameter of vision subtends an angle no greater than 200. The term 20/200 means that the individual has visual acuity 20 feet from a target that a normal person has 200 feet from the target. This definition was not designed for children but for adults who were being considered for welfare eligibility.

Valid assessment of children's vision is sometimes difficult or impossible. An accurate assessment of distance visual acuity, for example, can only rarely be determined before the age of three or four years. When the child has other physical or mental handicaps, diagnosis must often be delayed. Most health care professionals have had minimal or no training related to visual impairment and other chronically handicapping conditions. In addition, professionals who have not had experience working with the visually impaired may have pessimistic attitudes about their future habilitation and adjustment.

As with many other disabilities, an interdisciplinary approach to assessment of children with visual impairments is recommended. Among the professionals that would be considered for an individualized interdisciplinary team would be a pediatrician, neurologist, psychiatrist, ophthalmologist, psychologist, physical therapist, speech therapist, audiologist, and social worker.

Children with severe visual handicaps are at risk for other disabilities such as mental retardation and behavior problems (Hirshoren & Schnittjer, 1983). In addition, they are probably more likely to be adversely affected by neglectful parenting and family discord because they are so much more in need of others to arrange environmental stimulation and consistent contingencies.

Assessing the intelligence of visually impaired children is important because the risk of mental retardation is increased. Several intelligence tests have been found acceptable or adapted for assessment of children with visual handicaps. Since 1920, several adaptations of the Stanford-Binet have been offered. The latest revision, the Perkins-Binet, has been standardized on over 2,000 children between 5 and 15 years of age. The Wechsler Verbal subtests have been used with the visually impaired, but a number of items are based primarily on visual experience and would therefore seem inappropriate. At the same time, it should be recognized that loss of the visual system necessarily affects many aspects of behavior and that some facets of intelligence will be poorly developed. It is perhaps more productive to view assessment as the identification of the child's strengths and weaknesses in order to plan an intervention program that will optimize the child's future functioning.

Intervention for the blind or visually impaired child should begin as soon as possible. Beginning during infancy, parents need to be encouraged to maintain optimal levels of stimulation in which auditory, tactile, and motor experiences are provided. If the stimulation level is too low, the child is likely to become passive and disinterested and to develop self-stimulation behaviors such as rocking and eye poking. The goal is to facilitate the child's acquisition of information about the environment, including the social environment. Parents should also be encouraged to take advantage of the services that are available for handicapped children, particularly special education services for the preschool handicapped. The specially trained teacher has much to offer parents as well as the visually impaired child.

Much information can be acquired through the auditory system. Cassette tapes of books being read are one of the more recent aids for the blind. Tapes can also be used to communicate what would normally be written down (e.g., class lecture notes, homework assignments). Braille, however, continues to be the principal medium for blind persons to read the printed word. Advancement in computer science will no doubt greatly facilitate the development of materials and technology for the blind.

Although direct educational and counseling services to the visually impaired are of paramount importance, the parents of affected children continue to have needs that must be met. Parents need *information* about the child's status that is accurate and presented in a compassionate manner. They also need to know that professionals believe that they have the ability to cope with their child's problem. *Practical advice* that is tailored to the individual child's characteristics is also needed.

HEARING IMPAIRMENT

Assessment

Audition is another important sensory system that enables us to acquire information about our environment. Our ability to hear is also critical for the typical development of speech and language. Deaf children who have deaf parents who use visual communication from birth are found to develop language in a manner parallel to hearing children. The person who cannot hear not only misses out on some of life's experiences, but also must cope psychologically with an environment that is designed for the hearing person.

Exposure of the child to language early in life is related to later competence in expressive language. Deprivation of adequate visual or auditory language stimulation during the first two or three years of life prevents children from achieving their optimal language functioning. It is therefore essential that parents and professionals monitor children's hearing carefully in order to detect problems as soon as possible.

The evaluation of hearing sensitivity is described in terms of decibels and cycles per second; the decibel is a measure of sound intensity, while cycles per second designates the frequency of sound waves. In the hearing test, children listen through earphones to tones of varying decibel levels and frequencies and signal those occasions when a sound is heard. Younger children, or those who do not have clear responses for "yes" and "no," are typically conditioned to respond to sound through a learned association between visual and auditory stimuli. The frequencies presented during the hearing test are 125, 250, 500, 1,000, 2,000, 4,000, and 8,000 cycles per second, although only the testing frequencies of 500, 1,000, 2,000, and 4,000 cycles per second are necessary for screening hearing capacity related to speech sounds. Decibel levels represent the level of energy required for the average person to hear a particular frequency.

Hearing loss is expressed in terms of the number of decibels for each frequency. Decibel levels of 0 and 10 are considered to be normal, while a decibel loss level of 75 is generally agreed to be the equivalent of deafness. The decibel loss level of 15 has been set as the criterion for hearing loss in children, while the criterion for adults is 25. The reason for the difference in standards is that more acute hearing is required for the *acquisition* of language information, whereas information may be maintained or derived from the language context with fewer auditory cues. Both the amount of hearing loss and the range of frequencies affected determine the length of speech delay and the characteristics of the speech acquired.

Speech discrimination refers to the child's ability to discriminate among the various speech sounds. The sounds may be single syllables, words, or sentences, and they are presented with different backgrounds, such as quiet, noise, and competing language sounds. The assessment of the functioning of the middle ear focuses primarily on the responsiveness of the eardrum (tympanic membrane) to air pressure changes. Certain types of abnormalities are indicative of present or past ear infections and structural abnormalities.

Children with hearing disorders are at risk for a variety of cognitive and behavioral problems. Even children with intermittent ear infections during the first few years of life may show lower IQ scores and evidence of language impairment. It also appears that the achievement of children with histories of early ear infections continues to be lower than expected long after the ear infections cease.

Deaf and hard-of-hearing children without early language stimulation present a higher rate of behavioral problems. Some of these problems may have an organic basis, while others may be the result of inconsistent discipline or frustration with a confusing environment. Language is used to mediate, communicate, and discipline behavior in children. Deaf and hard-of-hearing children exhibit the same range of behavioral difficulties as hearing children, but these difficulties are compounded by the effects of early deprivation in language competence.

Etiology

About 10 percent of deafness cases may be traced to hereditary factors. At least 70 types of hereditary deafness have been identified in humans, most of which are autosomal recessive in origin; small percentages are associated with dominant transmission and sex-linked genes.

Prenatal, perinatal, and postnatal physical factors appear to account for about 55 percent of hearing disorders. Known factors include rubella during pregnancy, maternal alcoholism, difficult or premature delivery, drugs, meningitis, encephalitis, and excessive noise.

In recent years, perhaps the most attention has been given to ear infections, particularly otitis media, as an important source of hearing deficits and subsequent language deficiencies. Otitis media is an inflammation of the middle ear, the part of the ear that includes the ear drum and the small bones that transmit sound to the brain. Otitis media is most common in the first two years of life. The symptoms include earache, rubbing or tugging at the ears, drainage from the ears, and hearing impairment. Practically all children have at least one episode of otitis media by the age of six years; some children, however, are particularly vulnerable and have repeated episodes during infancy and the preschool period.

Treatment

The first intervention after a diagnosis of a hearing disorder is auditory and visual language stimulation as soon as possible. This intervention relates to optimizing the child's development and behavior given the hearing loss. To the extent that functional hearing cannot be restored, educational and speech interventions become critical. Special programs are also likely to be indicated when the hearing deficit is diagnosed and corrected even within the first year or two after birth because the child may have been deprived of important stimulation. Most speech and language intervention programs are conducted on an outpatient basis or in comprehensive programs with teachers and related services staff.

Methods of training in the schools for the deaf vary, depending on the philosophy taken in the educational approach. Although speech is more difficult to learn in comparison to the other forms of communication, most teachers of the deaf feel that the effort is worthwhile in terms of the greater positive side effects speech has in the natural environment.

Since almost all deaf children have some, albeit minimal, residual hearing, auditory training is included as part of the treatment. Deaf and hard-of-hearing children with good auditory potential are provided with information about the environment through the auditory channel. The first phase of the training involves teaching the child to listen to sounds by presenting amplified sounds and encouraging the child to play with noisemakers. The child's surroundings are arranged such that amplified sounds occur frequently and regularly. After this period of sound exposure, the child is taught to discriminate between sounds. Initially, sounds that are greatly different from one another are used; gradually, speech sounds increasing in similarity are introduced.

Speech reading is another method whereby deaf children can receive verbal communication. Prior to formal instruction, the child is taught to watch the face of the speaker. Occasionally, children with impaired hearing have learned many of the speech-reading skills before their auditory problem is diagnosed. In some cases of hard-of-hearing children, lip reading may be so efficient that the parents do not suspect a hearing impairment to be the cause of the speech delay. Deaf children have to be made aware of the potential information emanating from the mouth movements of speakers. In both auditory training and speech reading, there is a deliberate effort to emphasize pairing of words with other sensory stimuli. That is, when the word *apple* is said to a child learning speech reading, a real apple or a picture of an apple is paired with the mouth movement stimuli.

Children who are deaf or severely hearing-impaired present great therapeutic challenges. The growing professional belief is that intensive therapy is required for deaf children to acquire necessary language skills. It is also being recommended that deaf and severely hearing-impaired children begin their language training as early as possible, ideally immediately after identification. There are two main approaches to the language stimulation of deaf and severely hearing-impaired children. The first is the use of sign language as the major language stimulation. A second approach focuses on auditory and speech reading as the primary language input. Controversy exists about which of the two methods to emphasize.

The electronic hearing aid is an important invention to help children with hearing disorders. Great improvements have been made in hearing aid quality in the past decade, and they are recommended for children as soon as a hearing deficit is diagnosed. If a hearing loss involves both ears, two hearing aids are usually preferred to one.

CONCLUSIONS

Problems associated with medical conditions such as cancer, spina bifida, cardiovascular disorders, asthma, diabetes, and hemophilia, as well as visual and hearing impairment can be reduced through the use of psychological assessment and intervention procedures. These procedures include the use of tests and behavioral assessment for more accurate understanding of the patient's problems and interventions that promote compliance with medical treatment and the learning of skills that increase normal functioning as well as decrease pain and its concomitant behaviors.

RECOMMENDED READINGS

Garrison, W.T., & McQuiston, S. (1989). *Chronic illness during childhood and adolescence: Psychological aspects.* Newbury Park, CA: Sage.

Gross, A.M., & Drabman, R.S. (Eds.). (1990). *Handbook of clinical behavioral pediatrics.* New York: Plenum.

LaGreca, A.M., Siegel, L.J., Wallander, J.L., & Walker, C.E (Eds.). (1992). *Stress and coping in child health.* New York: Guilford.

Roberts, M.C. (Ed.). (1995). *Handbook of pediatric psychology* (2nd ed.) New York: Guilford.

15

Prevention

Although our understanding of children's developmental and behavior problems is far from satisfactory, it is possible to describe a number of identification and screening procedures that may lead to the prevention or early treatment of some of these problems. In some instances, the knowledge of specific etiological factors and the methodology for their assessment have been necessary prerequisites for the design of effective intervention programs; this situation is particularly true for physically based disorders. In other instances, intervention may be successful even when etiology is unknown or vaguely conceptualized. Knowledge of etiological factors, although not necessary for successful treatment, may eventually lead to more efficient and, therefore, less costly intervention programs.

Discovery of etiological factors depends, to a large extent, on assessment methods and criteria for diagnostic classification that, in turn, depend on normative information. In general, more has been learned about the etiology of behavior disorders that are precisely defined and reliably assessed than about those with definitions that allow for considerable clinical judgment.

Caplan (1964) has described three levels of prevention: (1) primary prevention refers to the reduction of new cases of behavior disorders; (2) secondary prevention involves a reduction in the duration or severity, or both aspects, of behavior disorders; and (3) tertiary prevention includes attempts to reduce long-term consequences of disability, such as institutionalization, or to prevent the disability from becoming worse. Both secondary and tertiary prevention may also be conceptualized as treatment programs because a behavior disorder has already been identified. Some behavior problems, however, do not necessarily result in later disorders but only identify the child as having a higher risk for a later disorder. Thus, in some instances, it is not clear whether a particular program is indeed primary or secondary for the individuals participating in it.

In this chapter, we review the methods and programs that have been designed to prevent children's behavior problems and developmental disabilities. Included in this review will be some of the methods and criteria for identifying children who have an above-average risk for developing behavior disorders. The focus will be on primary and secondary prevention because most of the programs described as tertiary prevention have been covered in the treatment sections of previous chapters.

PRIMARY PREVENTION

Primary prevention programs include a wide variety of medical and educational procedures. These programs may occur before and during pregnancy as well as during the child's developmental years.

Prior to Pregnancy

A number of educational programs that affect people's behavior prior to the conception of children may be described as examples of primary prevention. For example, providing schoolchildren with information about *nutrition* that improves their eating behavior can have positive effects both for them and for the children they later have. Similarly, primary prevention would include any program that improves the health status of future parents; avoidance of exposure to radiation, drugs, and other environmental substances that have adverse effects on general health or the reproductive system in particular can decrease the incidence of developmental problems in their offspring.

Immunization programs during the developmental period either eliminate or greatly reduce the probability of women's experiencing infectious diseases during pregnancy that may be harmful to the unborn child. Correcting or controlling health-related problems prior to pregnancy may also improve the physical and behavioral status of subsequently born children. Examples of such problems are hypertension and obesity.

A variety of educational programs have considerable potential for decreasing the incidence of behavior problems and developmental disabilities. Convincing adolescents to postpone pregnancy until the optimal age range and ensuring that they have the birth control information to do so is one of society's continuing challenges. Many parents of adolescents do not want to teach their children about birth control (or have them taught by others) even though it is known that contemporary adolescents have become more sexually active than those of previous generations. Prevention of adolescent pregnancy has far greater implications than those based on the age of the mother alone. Adolescent parents have greater difficulty providing adequate physical and psychological environments for their children. In many cases, their education and occupational training have been prematurely curtailed by the pregnancy and the responsibility for child care. In addition, some of their own psychological needs continue to be unmet, and feelings of intense frustration with inadequate coping skills are more likely to develop. At least some child abuse, with its physical and psychological concomitants, could be prevented if more children were planned or wanted by their parents and if more parents who were stressed had access to support from the community.

Educating young people before the occurrence of pregnancy (preparents) about the realities of rearing children may have some influence on their choices. Many adolescents have unrealistic, romantic views about parenthood; having one's own child is sometimes seen as an optimal way to ensure being loved or to have status. Although child development courses are offered in many high schools, they have generally not been designed to have the impact we are discussing here; in addition, they are taken by relatively few (usually female) students.

Effective education for preparents may need to involve all students of both sexes and may need to start before puberty. Such a program would reflect the fact that both males and females are responsible for children before as well as after birth. Furthermore, education about sexuality as well as about sexual activity and the responsibilities of parenthood may reduce the high incidence of misinformation currently given to sexually active teenagers.

Still another educational program oriented toward primary prevention is genetic counseling. Informing potential parents that they have a high probability of bearing an abnormal child can affect their decision to initiate pregnancy. Although genetic counseling is usually done after a genetically determined abnormality has already occurred in the family, it will probably be increasingly used for advising persons who have been identified as carriers through screening tests.

During Pregnancy and after Birth

Primary prevention during pregnancy includes educating the prospective parents to avoid substances and situations that may harm the fetus. Physicians usually have the primary responsibility for prescribing the best possible diet, exercise, and weight gain guidelines. They also communicate the importance of not ingesting drugs and medications without carefully monitoring and minimizing the pregnant woman's intake of alcohol and caffeine.

Primary prevention may also be considered to include abortion when it is based on the risk that the child will be born with an abnormality known to have a significant negative effect on behavior or development, or both. Induced abortion is a topic associated with much social conflict. Some people feel that all induced abortions are wrong; others feel that they are acceptable under certain circumstances, such as rape and conditions that are life threatening to the mother, and still others feel that termination of a pregnancy is a decision that should be made only by the pregnant woman. Thus, society has not yet agreed that it is preferable to prevent the birth of an abnormal child.

Technology for identifying fetuses with certain abnormalities is available. *Amniocentesis* involves the withdrawal of a small amount of amniotic fluid surrounding the fetus between the 15th and 18th weeks of pregnancy and subjecting the cells (sloughed from the fetus) in this fluid to either laboratory testing or chromosomal analysis, or both. The procedure is a reliable and accurate technique for identifying many of the known genetic abnormalities, such as Down syndrome. Because there is a small risk for miscarriage, amniocentesis is currently recommended only when the fetus is known to be at risk, such as in cases in which the mother is over 35 years old or the couple has already had a child with a genetic disorder.

Amniocentesis is also being done in the pregnancies of diabetic women. Tests on the fluid can assess the maturity of the fetus's respiratory system; therefore, physicians can now choose the best time to induce the labor of diabetic women—a time that minimizes the complications of birth due to the baby's large size and simultaneously reduces the probability of respiratory distress due to immaturity. Tests that detect carriers of certain genetic abnormalities, such as phenylketonuria, are available, but most couples currently being tested have already had an affected child or are otherwise known to be at risk. For example, it is estimated that one in 30 Ashkenazic Jews is a carrier for Tay-Sachs disease, which leads to mental retardation and an early death. Screening programs for carriers have been initiated in many communities, and if both parents are found to be carriers, each pregnancy can be monitored.

Another technique, *chorionic villus sampling* (CVS), also assesses genetic abnormalities of the fetus. Performed between the 10th and 12th weeks of pregnancy, CVS analyzes the cells that will eventually become the placenta and is considered to be safer than amniocentesis primarily because physicians have more experience doing it. In addition, a blood test, the *Alpha-Fetoprotein Test,* performed between the 16th and 18th weeks of pregnancy, is extremely accurate in diagnosing spina bifida in the fetus.

Another technological advance has been the use of *ultrasound* (sound waves) to examine the infant *in utero.* Usually performed between the 18th and 20th weeks of pregnancy, ultrasound can be used to estimate the fetus's weight and to assess the physical proportions of the fetus. Thus, parents could be informed early in the pregnancy about congenital malformations. The information obtained from the ultrasound procedure is somewhat comparable to that obtained from X-rays, but ultrasound does not have the dangers of radiation. Physicians use the information to determine whether the baby can be delivered naturally or requires a Caesarean delivery.

Public service programs on radio and television and articles in popular magazines may also be described as primary prevention; they sometimes are the only source of information that prospective parents have prior to becoming involved with a physician. These sources of information may continue to have primary prevention functions after birth as well. They may persuade parents to maintain the optimal immunization schedule and to use seat restraints in automobiles to avoid injuries due to accidents and to remove poisonous substances from the child's access.

There is enormous potential from the education of parents for the prevention of children's behavioral, emotional, and developmental problems. Teaching parents about the relationships between their behaviors and their children's behaviors and the behavior principles that govern these relationships can avoid many of the situations in which parents inadvertently strengthen behaviors that they do not want their children to have.

Sheeber and Johnson (1994) trained mothers of 3- to 5-year-olds to understand their child's temperament and to use adaptive ways of coping with difficult behavior; they found both improved behavior of the children and greater satisfaction for the mothers. A review (MacMillan, MacMillan, Offord, & Griffith, 1994) of 11 prospective studies of primary prevention of child physical abuse and neglect found that extended home vistation is effective for disadvantaged families.

Much prevention is determined by the values of parents in particular and society at large. That is, parents vary in terms of the amount of effort they are willing to contribute toward prevention of future problems. How many parents stop smoking when they are informed that their smoking increases the probability of their own child's becoming a smoker in addition to being exposed to the health hazards of living in a smoker's environment during the developmental years? How much organized social effort has there been to modify children's television programming after decades of research findings showed a relationship between watching televised aggression and the amount of aggressive behavior in children? How many parents actually monitor the television shows that their children watch? To the extent that parents are unable or unwilling to control their children's environment, their children's behavior may be adversely influenced.

For those psychological problems that are conceptualized as due to specific skill deficits, programs that develop those skills may be considered to be primary prevention. For example, Spivak and Shure (1974) developed a social problem-solving curriculum for four-year-old Head Start children that was presented to teachers who taught the children over a 10-week period (5 to 20 minutes a day). The children who received this program were superior to control children in their social problem-solving skills at the end of the program and during the kindergarten year. A reduction in maladjustment was found to be related to gains in social problem-solving skills. Similar programs for older children and other social skills have also been effective (e.g., Matson & Ollendick, 1988).

SECONDARY PREVENTION

Secondary prevention is based on our ability to identify children with behavioral and developmental problems during the early stages of their manifestation. Behavioral and developmental problems vary widely in terms of the earliest age at which they can be reliably detected. Problems that are associated with physical abnormalities tend to be identified at earlier ages. For example, the physical characteristics associated with Down syndrome are apparent at birth and are predictive of later mental retardation. We have not yet identified behavioral indicators at birth that can predict with the same level of accuracy later psychological problems. In recent years, more attention has been given to the training of professionals and the designing of screening instruments to detect the child who is likely to have significant problems. Researchers have been examining the effectiveness of intervention programs in reducing the severity of, or in some instances eventually eliminating, these problems.

Devising effective methods for predicting children's behavioral and developmental problems is an important prerequisite for prevention programs. Screening methods that identify children as high risk when they are not (false positives) or that do not identify children who have significant problems (false negatives) are wasteful of resources in the former case and inefficient in the latter case. In addition, since psychological problems become manifest continuously throughout the developmental period, screening devices must reflect changes in predictability that occur as a function of age. In general, the behavior of young children is less predictable (reliable) than that of older children.

Methods for Identifying High-Risk Children

Tests for Genetic Disorders. Inexpensive tests are available for the detection of some of the recessive genetic abnormalities, such as phenylketonuria and galactosemia; many newborn infants are currently receiving these tests with the result that the behavior disorders associated with these conditions can be largely prevented by feeding the affected children special diets. Children suspected of having a chromosomal anomaly on the basis of physical characteristics may have a chromosomal assay test performed. If an abnormality is detected, the parents can receive further testing and be advised through genetic counseling of the probability of having another affected child.

Demographic Screening. Since a number of pregnancy and labor complications have been associated with an increased risk to the child's life and development, such factors could be used to identify children who would then receive closer monitoring with physical and behavioral examinations. Early identification of children can be based on mothers' demographic characteristics and environmental conditions (Badger, Burns, & Vietze, 1981). Scurletis, Headrick-Haynes, Turnbull, and Fallon (1976) constructed from population data the following list of questions to identify women of childbearing age who have high risk for fetal, neonatal, and postnatal death:

1. What is your age?
2. How many years of education have you completed?
3. What is your marital status?
4. How many pregnancies have you had?
5. Have you had a previous fetal death?
6. Have you had a previous child born alive who is now dead?

Focusing screening only on demographic risk factors, however, would miss many at-risk children. Kemper, Osborn, Hansen, and Pascoe (1994) found that parental problems such as alcoholism and maternal depression were common in private practice and military clinics as well as in teaching clinics.

Yoshikawa (1994) proposed a "cumulative protection model" for prevention of chronic delinquency (but could also be applied to some other behavior disorders). Early risk factors (demographic and environmental) are used as a basis for offering early family support to decrease the *interactive* effects of earlier and later risk factors. Both family support for family risks and early education for child risks are proposed as necessary for optimal prevention effects.

Physical Examination. Medical care for the child after birth may also reduce risk and provide an opportunity for early intervention. Good medical care includes periodic physical examination of the child and immunization shots against diseases. Most parents are reasonably conscientious about visits to the physician for inoculations during the first year or two, but many children are not properly immunized because they have not received booster shots. Moreover, relatively few children are being examined on a regular basis when they are well. That is, physicians typically see children only when they are ill. This situation certainly diminishes the possibility of physicians' validly assessing behavioral development. Good medical care should also include assessment of the family's nutritional status, periodic vision and hearing screening tests, and alertness for possible cases of child abuse or neglect.

The value of medical care in secondary prevention depends greatly on physicians' training in normal and abnormal child development and behavior. Because family practitioners and pediatricians are the only professionals to have regular access to children before they enter school, they currently have much of the potential for providing secondary prevention programs for young children. However, research suggests that physicians identify only about half of children with developmental and behavioral problems (Glascoe & Dworklin, 1993).

Behavioral Screening Procedures. The development of reliable and valid screening tests for identifying high-risk children is in an early stage of refinement. Most of the available, valid, psychological tests for children require administration by a trained professional and an hour or more in administration time; both requirements preclude their use as screening instruments. An ideal screening instrument could be administered by a variety of professionals and paraprofessionals with minimal training in testing. Having adequate screening tests, however, will not guarantee that they will be used. Their use depends greatly on society's commitment to children in general and to children with behavior disorders in particular.

Several tests for neonates have been devised and offer some potential for identifying high-risk infants. One of the earliest tests was devised by Graham, Matarazzo, and Caldwell (1956) and revised by Rosenblith (1961). The Graham-Rosenblith test contains items that evaluate maturation, irritability, muscle tone, and vision. A longitudinal study of a large number of infants who had been administered the Graham-Rosenblith revealed that certain findings during the neonatal period were prognostic for later developmental problems (Rosenblith, 1975).

Brazelton (1974) developed a behavioral test that evaluates the neonate's organized responses to a variety of environmental events. Examples of the test items include response decrease to repeated visual stimuli; orienting response to animate visual-examiner's face; cuddlesomeness responses to being cuddled by the examiner; and self-quieting activity—attempts to console self and control state. Each of the 26 behavioral items is rated on a nine-point scale. Tronick and Brazelton (1975) reported that, while the Brazelton Scale is comparable to a standard neurological test for detecting neonates who will be classified as "suspect/abnormal" at age seven (80 percent vs. 87 percent success rate), it is superior in its lower rate of classifying as "suspect/abnormal" children who are normal at age seven. The children included in the "suspect/abnormal" category at age seven had a variety of behavior disorders (mental retardation, specific reading difficulties, speech disorders, motor disorders) as well as a number of neurological abnormalities. A number of screening tests have been devised for use with infants and preschool children. Among the available tests, the Denver Developmental Screening Test (DDST) (Frankenburg & Dodds, 1970; Frankenburg, Dandal, Sciarillo, & Burgess, 1981) has perhaps received the most research attention, and findings indicate that the DDST is reliable and valid. However, it has not yet been demonstrated as an accurate *predictor* of children's development disorders. Its high correlation with developmental and intelligence tests suggests that children who perform very poorly on DDST during the early years will have a high probability of developmental disorders at later ages.

Although we have a list of demographic factors and screening tests that can identify high-risk children, we are unable to make accurate predictions about individual children. Our screening devices appear to be inefficient in that they are not capable of identifying at an early age *all* children who will later have serious behavior disorders, and they may identify as "abnormal" a disproportionate number of children who will later have no behavior disorders. The former situation is understandable in view of the fact that certain abnormalities may not manifest themselves at the earlier ages and that certain environmental factors are cumulative and do not manifest themselves in behavior at the earliest ages. The latter situation is scientifically problematic and indicates that a significant number of infants with initially poor physical or behavioral status, or both, apparently "recover." When the variables related to their recovery are identified, the information will likely contribute toward more efficient screening devices and effective prevention programs.

In the evaluation of an intervention program, the typical study compares the behaviors of the group receiving the intervention with behaviors of a control group drawn from the same population. If both groups contain sizable portions of children who would have improved spontaneously (without intervention), the findings of the study would be diminished or, at least, obscured. Moreover, the most successful intervention programs to date have been intensive and long-term and, therefore, very expensive; it can be expected that funding for the implementation of such programs would likely be given for only those children who have a very high probability of developing behavior disorders.

The increasing interest in early identification of developmental problems has stimulated examination of the potential for using parent ratings as the initial screening procedure. Knobloch and her associates (1979) described a high validity for parental reporting of infant development on their questionnaire that was based on the Gesell Schedules. Ireton and Thwing (1974) developed the Minnesota Child Development Inventory (MCDI) that relies solely on parents' report; the MCDI has 320 items that describe behaviors of children between six months and six-and-a-half years of age. The test developers reported high reliability, and subsequent research suggests acceptable validity when MCDI results are compared with Bayley Mental Age Equivalent scores (Shoemaker, Saylor, & Erickson, 1991).

It is possible that many children of school age are not receiving treatment services simply because they have not been identified as needing such services. As mentioned in earlier chapters, most children are identified as a result of individual referrals by concerned parents, teachers, or physicians. Such a system, however, may lend itself to the underidentification of certain problems and the overidentification of other problems. The implementation of screening programs in the schools could be expected to identify a high percentage of children with behavior disorders. A screening program for schoolchildren would be likely to include tests of general intellectual functioning, school achievement, speech and language, and a behavior problem checklist. Children identified through a screening procedure could then be referred for more thorough assessment procedures. Although research has been conducted on the reliability and validity of screening tests for specific behavior disorders, few attempts have been made to design comprehensive screening instruments that could be implemented in the schools.

An exemplary screening program for children over four years of age was initiated by the Permanente Medical Group at the Kaiser Foundation Hospital in San Francisco (Allen & Shinefield, 1969). This screening program requires about $1^{1/2}$ hours and includes a wide range of physical tests and measures. The behavioral component includes tests of intellectual, visual-motor, and specific learning abilities. In addition, a behavior inventory completed by the parent evaluates sensory-motor development, communication skills, social interactions, and a variety of other behaviors. The data are computer analyzed and an interpretation of the results given to the parents within a month.

SCREENING, IDENTIFICATION, AND PREVENTION PROGRAMS

The emphasis up to the present time has been on the early identification and treatment of children at high risk for mental retardation. The development of screening devices for some of the other behavior disorders has probably been hampered by a lack of consensus on the criteria for diagnosis of the disorders and a general lack of information about which early behaviors might be precursors for the disorder. In the case of autism, for example, much of the necessary information for devising a screening test is available, but its very low rate of occurrence in the population (therefore requiring the examination of very large numbers of children in order to identify an adequate sample of children with the condition) has likely deterred investigators from conducting the requisite longitudinal studies.

Early identification of children who are at risk for or who display behavior disorders is possible with the implementation of large-scale screening programs that examine children repeatedly at specific ages beginning at birth. The particular instruments and ages of examination could be selected on the basis of current information and continuously refined as additional data are collected.

One example of a proposed age sequence would be the following: six months, 18 months, three years, five years, end of first grade (seven years), end of third grade (nine years), end of sixth grade (12 years), and end of ninth grade (15 years). These ages can be justified in terms of their representing important milestones or being optimal as far as program planning is concerned. By six months, the infant typically can sit alone, pick up small objects, and repeat syllables such as "mama" and "dada," and the infant exhibits a variety of social behaviors. By 18 months, the child should walk alone and drink from a cup, have a small vocabulary of single words, and respond to a variety of verbal requests. By this age, most children with severe problems in the motor, intellectual, language, and social areas can probably be identified.

At three years of age, the average child can jump, walk up stairs, play ball, name many common objects, combine words in sentences, and put on clothing. The five-year screening would probably shift the focus toward skills that are necessary for school performance. Given the subsequent importance of school experiences, later screenings should probably be timed on the basis of particular grades rather than chronological age. Screening near the end of the school year provides adequate time during the remaining school year and following summer for follow-up assessment and intervention program planning, if necessary.

Preschool Children

Intervention programs for high-risk children during infancy have produced beneficial effects. For example, researchers have found that infants' exploratory skills are positively influenced by the enhancement of maternal stimulation (Belsky, Goode, & Most, 1980). Premature infants given tactile and vestibular stimulation have shown improved weight gain, respiratory status, and psychomotor development (Schaeffer, Hatcher, & Barglow, 1980). Many of the detrimental effects of fetal malnutrition were shown to be reduced in a supportive caregiving environment (Zeskind & Ramey, 1981).

Prevention programs for disadvantaged children were initiated during the 1960s at about the same time that Project Head Start was begun. Virtually all of the longitudinal studies and program evaluations have focused on the preschool child. The earlier studies involved relatively brief interventions with older preschool children, while subsequent studies have focused on infant programs conducted for longer periods of time. Although there are some notable differences among the programs, they can all be described as planned "stimulation" programs. That is, the environment is arranged to provide the best possible learning opportunities for the child, who is given considerable social attention for accomplishments.

These early intervention programs have received mixed reviews. The earlier studies with older preschool children tended to report no effects or small positive effects that "washed out" within a year or two. Subsequent studies that were initiated during infancy and continued through the preschool period with structured educational programs have reported more success (e.g., Ramey & Campbell, 1984). A review of independently designed and implemented infancy and preschool programs for children from low-income families indicated that children who attended these programs were more likely to meet their school's basic requirements, to have higher IQ scores, and to feel pride for their school or work accomplishments and were less likely to be retained in grade or to be assigned to special education classes (Lazar, Darlington, Murray, Royce, & Snipper, 1982). There were indications that success was improved when the children's parents were actively involved in the programs (Goodson & Hess, 1978). Haskins (1989) concluded that model programs can produce long-term benefits that exceed the value of the original program investment, but that it is premature to argue that Head Start is cost-beneficial.

Perhaps one of the most well-known and comprehensive prevention programs, the Milwaukee Project, used mothers' IQ scores (below 75) as the risk factors for "cultural-familial" retardation in the children. In this study, intensive intervention was begun in infancy and continued during the preschool years. Garber (1988) concluded: "In each developmental period, however, subsequent to infancy (0 to 3 years), although it is possible to maintain normal IQs, it also seems that this can be accomplished only with increasing difficulty" (p. 403). Perhaps future research will help us to reduce that difficulty.

School-Aged Children

The prevention programs for school-aged children have been oriented more toward behavior problems than toward developmental problems and have included parental training, surrogate families, and school-based intervention.

Several behaviorally oriented parent-instruction programs have been implemented. Parents are generally provided with instruction on behavior management procedures through lectures and films. After there is assurance that the parents know the behavior principles and their correct application, they are supervised in their treatment of the child's behavior problem. Patterson and his colleagues

(1975) developed such a program for aggressive boys that has had demonstrated success.

The Achievement Place Model described in Chapter 11 is an example of a prevention program utilizing surrogate families. These surrogate families comprise a specially trained couple, the teaching parents, and about six youths who are at high risk for institutionalization because they have engaged in illegal behavior. This program has been implemented on a large scale and has had a positive review both in terms of lower recidivism rates and lower costs compared with institutionalization.

Several important prognostic factors have emerged from the research literature. For example, antisocial behavior as rated by teachers and peers in the first grade significantly predicts self-reported delinquency seven years later in junior high school (Tremblay, LeBlanc, & Schwartzman, 1988). In addition, low acceptance by peers is also associated with higher rates of later maladjustment (Bierman, 1987; Parker & Asher, 1987). These findings suggest that school-based prevention programs may offer considerable promise.

The Rochester Project, developed by Cowen and his associates (1979), identified first grade children as having problems or potential problems in adjustment. The prevention program included teachers' in-service education, availability of mental health consultants to teachers, after-school group meetings for the children, and parents' groups focusing on child rearing during the first three grades. Reporting on the results for 215 children, Cowen, Gesten, and Wilson (1979) found improvements on all of their measures. Comparison of the treatment group with a control group showed significantly greater improvement for the experimental group on about half of the variables measured. One methodological problem, however, was that the ratings were done by persons (teachers, aides, and professionals) who were involved with the program.

It appears that more specifically focused prevention programs may also be successful. Hops and Cobb (1973) designed a program to teach elementary school children "academic survival skills," such as attending to the teacher, volunteering answers, and looking at one's own work. Teachers are trained to implement the program, which has been found to be helpful in preventing academic underachievement.

Several school-based programs have been designed specifically for children of divorce. The results have been mixed, but Alpert-Gillis, Pedro-Carroll, and Cowen (1989) reported considerable success in preventing behavior and emotional problems in second and third grade urban children of divorce.

SOCIAL POLICY

The most advanced research knowledge about assessment, etiology, and intervention is worthless to children if society does not provide the leadership and funding for programs that apply this knowledge. Unfortunately, society has not been providing either adequate leadership or funding for programs (Peterson, Zink, & Farmer, 1992). It has been estimated that 12 percent of U.S. children and adolescents under 18 have a mental health problem severe enough to require mental health treatment (Doughery, Saxe, Cross, & Silverman, 1987). Yet, fewer than 20 percent of them receive services through traditional mental health agencies and schools (Knitzer, 1984). State mental health departments have not had the resources or leadership to design effective systems of care for children and adolescents. Many states have not had staffs assigned specifically to programs for children and adolescents. The already inadequate financial support all too often goes to the restrictive, residential, inpatient programs rather than the community-based programs.

Federal support for children and adolescents with psychological problems has been very inadequate since the mid-1970s. Children have increasingly been omitted from legislation that provides support for mental health services. Because the services for children are sparse and scattered throughout agencies, there is a tremendous need for case managers to ensure that children and their parents are successfully guided through the maze.

The lack of services and coordination of services for the chronically mentally ill led to legislation in the mid-1980s that provides grants to the states to develop organized community-based systems of care. The Child and Adolescent Service System Program (CASSP) requires that states receiving grants develop a child mental health authority and organize a coalition of state agencies that provide services to children and adolescents. CASSP focuses on providing appropriate treatment, a continuum of care, at the community level.

It has also become apparent that our knowledge based on research and practice is far greater than is reflected in the current services provided for children and adolescents. What is greatly needed now are public advocates, people who put pressure on state and federal government representatives and officials to write the legislation and provide leadership and funding on behalf of the children and adolescents who cannot do it for themselves.

CONCLUSIONS

The possibility of preventing a substantial percentage of behavioral and developmental problem cases has become increasingly feasible. Identification of etiological factors, genetic counseling, prenatal diagnosis, and early postnatal physical and behavioral assessment all contribute toward a reduction in the number of cases or the severity of children's behavior disorders, or both. Considerably more effort needs to be directed toward the prevention of behavior problems that initially manifest themselves during the school-age years. Implementation of prevention programs depends on society's placing a high priority on children and their future.

RECOMMENDED READINGS

Forman, S.G. (Ed.), (1987). *School-based affective and social interventions.* Binghamton, NY: Haworth.

Levin, G.B., Trickett, E.J., & Hess, R.E. (Eds.). (1990). *Ethical implications of primary prevention.* New York: Haworth.

Lorin, R.P. (Ed.). (1990). *Protecting the children: Strategies for optimizing emotional and behavioral development.* New York: Haworth.

McCord, J., & Tremblay, R.E. (Eds.). (1992). *Preventing antisocial behavior: Interventions from birth through adolescence.* New York: Guilford Press.

Meisels, S., & Shonkoff, J. (Eds.). (1992). *Handbook of early childhood intervention.* Cambridge: Cambridge University Press.

Peterson, L., Zink, M., & Farmer, J. (1992). Prevention of disorders in children. In C.E. Walker & M.C. Roberts (Eds.), *Handbook of clinical child psychology.* New York: Wiley.

Rickel, A.U., & Allen, L. (1987). *Preventing maladjustment from infancy through adolescence.* Newbury Park, CA: Sage.

Shaffer, D., Philips, I., & Enzer, N.B. (Eds.). (1989). *Prevention of mental disorders, alcohol, and other drug use in children and adolesents.* OSAP Prevention Monograph-2 (DHHS Publication No. ADM 89–1646). Washington, DC: U.S. Government Printing Office.

Strayhorn, J.M. (1988). *The competent child: An approach to psychotherapy and preventive mental health.* New York: Guilford.

References

Achenbach, T.M. (1986). *Child Behavior Checklist: Direct observation form* (rev. ed.). Burlington: University of Vermont.

Achenbach, T.M. (1991). *Manual for the Child Behavior Checklist/4–18.* Burlington, VT: University of Vermont Department of Psychiatry.

Achenbach, T.M. (1991). *Manual for the Teacher's Report Form & 1991 Profile.* Burlington, VT: University of Vermont Department of Psychiatry.

Achenbach, T.M., & Edelbrock, C.S. (1983). *Manual for the Child Behavior Checklist and Revised Child Behavior Profile.* Burlington: University of Vermont.

Achenbach, T.M., & Edelbrock, C.S. (1984). Psychopathology of childhood. *Annual Review of Psychology, 35,* 227–256.

Achenbach, T.M., & Edelbrock, C.S. (1986). *Manual for the Teacher's Report Form and Teacher Version of the Child Behavior Profile.* Burlington: University of Vermont, Department of Psychiatry.

Achenbach, T.M., & Edelbrock, C.S. (1989). Diagnostic, taxonomic, assessment issues. In M. Hersen & T.H. Ollendick (Eds.), *Handbook of child psychopathology* (2nd ed.) (pp. 53–69). New York: Plenum.

Achenbach, T.M., Howell, C.T., McConaughy, S.H., & Stanger, C. (1994). Six-year predictors of problems in a national sample of children and youth: I. Cross-informant syndromes. *Journal of the American Academy of Child and Adolescent Psychiatry, 34,* 336–347.

Achenbach, T.M., & McConaughy, S.H. (1996). *Empirically based assessment of child and adolescent psychopathology: Practical applications* (2nd ed.). New York: Plenum.

Ackerman, N.W. (1958). *The psychodynamics of family life.* New York: Basic Books.

Addy, D.P. (1987). Cognitive function in children with epilepsy. *Developmental Medicine and Child Neurology, 29,* 394–397.

Adler, A. (1927). *The practice and theory of individual psychology.* New York: Harcourt, Brace.

Aho, A.C., & Erickson, M.T. (1985). Effects of grade, gender, and hospitalization on children's medical fears. *Developmental and Behavioral Pediatrics, 6,* 146–153.

Albano, A.M., & Chorptia, B.F. (1995). Treatment of anxiety disorders of childhood. *Psychiatric Clinics of North America, 18,* 767–784.

Albano, A.M., Marten, P.A., Holt, C.S., & Heimebr, R.G. (1995). Cognitive behavioral group treatment for social phobia in adolescents: A preliminary study. *Journal of Nervous and Mental Disorders, 183,* 685–692.

Alford, G.S., Koehler, R.A., & Leonard, J. (1991). Alcoholics Anonymous—Narcotics Anonymous model inpatient treatment of chemically dependent adolescents: A 2-year outcome study. *Journal of Studies on Alcohol, 52,* 118–126.

Allen, A.J., Leonard, H., & Swedo, S.E. (1995). Current knowledge of medications for the treatment of childhood anxiety disorders. *Journal of the American Academy of Child & Adolescent Psychiatry, 34,* 976–986.

Allen, C.M., & Shinefield, H.R. (1969). Pediatric multiphasic program: Preliminary description. *American Journal of Diseases in Children, 142,* 161–167.

Allen, F.H. (1942). *Psychotherapy with children.* New York: Norton.

Allen, K.E., Hart, B., Buell, J.S., Harris, F.R., & Wolf, M.M. (1964). Effects of social reinforcement on isolate behavior of a nursery school child. *Child Development, 35,* 511–518.

Alpert-Gillis, L.J., Pedro-Carroll, J.L., & Cowen, E.L. (1989). The Child of Divorce Program: Development, implementation, and evaluation of a program for young urban children. *Journal of Consulting and Clinical Psychology, 57,* 583–589.

Aman, M.G., & Singh, N.N. (1991). Pharmacological intervention. In J.L. Matson & J.A. Mulick (Eds.), *Handbook of mental retardation* (2nd ed.). New York: Pergamon Press.

Amaya-Jackson, L., & March, J.S. (1995). Posttraumatic stress disorder. In J.S. March (Ed.), *Anxiety disorders in children and adolescents* (pp. 276–300). New York: Guilford Press.

American Psychiatric Association. (1968). *Diagnostic and statistical manual of mental disorders* (2nd ed.). Washington, DC: Author.

American Psychiatric Association. (1980). *DSM-III—Revised* (3rd ed.). Washington, DC: Author.

American Psychiatric Association. (1987). *DSM-III—Revised*. Washington, DC: Author.

American Psychiatric Association. (1994). *Diagnostic and statistical manual of mental disorders* (4th ed.). Washington, DC: Author.

American Psychological Association. (1985). *Standards for educational and psychological testing*. Washington, DC: Author.

American Psychological Association. (1993). *Guidelines for providers of psychological services to ethnic, linguistic, and culturally diverse populations*. Washington, DC: Author.

Anastasi, A. (1988). *Psychological testing*. New York: Macmillan.

Anastoupoulos, A.D., Guevremont, D.C., Shelton, T.L., & DuPaul, G.J. (1992). Parenting stress among families of children with attention deficit hyperactivity disorder. *Journal of Abnormal Child Psychology, 20,* 503–520.

Anastopoulos, A.D., Shelton, T.L., DuPaul, G.J., & Guevremont, D.C. (1993). Parent training for attention-deficit hyperactivity disorder: Its impact on parent functioning. *Journal of Abnormal Child Psychology, 21,* 581–596.

Anderson, C.A., Hinshaw, S.P., & Simmel, C. (1994). Mother-child interactions in ADHD and comparison boys: Relationships with overt and covert externalizing behavior. *Journal of Abnormal Behavior, 22,* 247–265.

Angold, A., Costello, E.J., Pickels, A., & Winder, F. (1987). The development of a questionnaire for use in epidemiological studies of depression in children and adolescents. Unpublished manuscript, London University.

Archer, R. (1992). *MMPI-A: Assessing adolescent psychopathology*. Hillsdale, NJ: Erlbaum.

Arffa, S., Fitzhugh-Bell, K., & Black, F.W. (1989). Neuropsychological profiles of children with learning disabilities and children with documented brain damage. *Journal of Learning Disabilities, 22,* 635–640.

Arthur, G. (1952). *The Arthur Adaptation of the Leiter International Performance Scale*. Los Angeles: Western Psychological Services.

Asarnow, J.R. (1992). Suicidal ideation and attempts during middle childhood: Associations with perceived family stress and depression among child psychiatric inpatients. *Journal of Clinical Child Psychology, 21,* 35–40.

Asarnow, J.R., Goldstein, M.J., & Ben-Meir, S. (1988). Parental communication deviance in childhood onset schizophrenia spectrum and depressive disorders. *Journal of Child Psychology and Psychiatry, 29,* 825–838.

Axline, V.M. (1947). *Play therapy*. Boston: Houghton Mifflin.

Ayllon, T., Layman, D., & Kandel, H.J. (1975). A behavioral-educational alternative to drug control of hyperactive children. *Journal of Applied Behavior Analysis, 8,* 137–146.

Ayllon, T., & Rosenbaum, M.S. (1977). The behavioral treatment of disruption and hyperactivity in school settings. In B.B. Lahey & A.E. Kazdin (Eds.), *Advances in clinical psychology* (Vol. 1, pp. 85–118). New York: Plenum.

Azrin, N.H., & Armstrong, P.M. (1973). The "mini-meal"—a method of teaching eating skills to the profoundly retarded. *Mental Retardation, 11,* 9–13.

Azrin, N.H., & Foxx, R.M. (1974). *Toilet training in less than a day*. New York: Simon & Schuster.

Babson, S.G., & Phillips, D.S. (1973). Growth and development of twins dissimilar in size at birth. *New England Journal of Medicine, 289,* 937–940.

Baden, A.D., & Howe, G.W. (1992). Mothers' attributions and expectancies regarding their conduct-disordered children. *Journal of Abnormal Child Psychology, 20,* 467–485.

Badger, E., Burns, D., & Vietze, P. (1981). Maternal risk factors as predictors of developmental outcome in early childhood. *Infant Mental Health Journal, 2,* 33–43.

Baer, D.M., & Sherman, J.A. (1964). Reinforcement control of generalized imitation in young children. *Journal of Experimental Child Psychology, 1,* 37–49.

Bandura, A. (1965). Influence of models' reinforcement contingencies on the acquisition of imitative responses. *Journal of Personality and Social Psychology, 1,* 589–595.

Bandura, A. (1969). *Principles of behavior modification*. New York: Holt, Rinehart and Winston.

Bandura, A., Ross, D., & Ross, S.A. (1961). Transmission of aggression through imitation of aggressive models. *Journal of Abnormal and Social Psychology, 63,* 575–582.

Bandura, A., Ross, D., & Ross, S.A. (1963). Imitation of film-mediated aggressive models. *Journal of Abnormal and Social Psychology, 67,* 601–607.

Barbarin, O.A. (1990). Adjustment to serious childhood illness. In B.B. Lahey & A.E. Kazdin (Eds.), *Advances in clinical child psychology* (Vol. 13, pp. 377–403). New York: Plenum.

Barkley, R.A. (1989). Hyperactive girls and boys: Stimulant drug effects on mother-child interactions. *Journal of Child Psychology and Psychiatry, 30,* 379–390.

Barkley, R.A. (1990). *Attention-deficit hyperactivity disorders: A handbook for diagnosis and treatment.* New York: Guilford.

Baroff, G.S. (1991). *Developmental disabilities: Psychosocial aspects.* Austin, TX: Pro-Ed.

Barrett, C.L., Hampe, I.E., & Miller, L.C. (1978). Research on child psychotherapy. In S.L. Garfield & A.E. Bergin (Eds.), *Handbook of psychotherapy and behavior change* (2nd ed.) (pp. 411–435). New York: Wiley.

Barrett, D.E., Radke-Yarrow, M., & Klein, R.E. (1982). Chronic malnutrition and child behavior: Effects of early calorie supplementation on social and emotional functioning at school age. *Developmental Psychology, 18,* 541–556.

Barrett, P.M., Dadds, M.R., & Rapee, R.M. (1996). Family treatment of childhood anxiety: A controlled trial. *Journal of Consulting and Clinical Psychology, 64,* 333–342.

Barton, E.S., Guess, D., Garcia, E., & Baer, D.M. (1970). Improvement of retardates' mealtime behaviors by timeout procedures using multiple baseline techniques. *Journal of Applied Behavior Analysis, 3,* 77–84.

Battaglia, M., Bertella, S., Politi, E., & Bernardeschi, L. (1995). *American Journal of Psychiatry, 152,* 1362–1364.

Bayley, N. (1969). *Bayley Scales of Infant Development manual.* New York: Psychological Corporation.

Bayley, N. (1993). *Bayley Scales of Infant Development: Second edition.* San Antonio, TX: Psychological Corporation.

Beery, K.D. (1967). *Developmental Test of Visual-Motor Integration administration and scoring manual.* Chicago: Follett Educational Corporation.

Begleiter, H., Porjesz, B., Bihari, B., & Kissen, B. (1984). Event-related brain potentials in boys at risk for alcoholism. *Science, 225,* 1493–1496.

Beidel, D.C. (1991). Social phobia and overanxious disorder in school-aged children. *Journal of the American Academy of Child & Adolescent Psychiatry, 30,* 545–552.

Beidel, D.C., & Morris, T.L. (1995). Social phobia. In J.S. March (Ed.), *Anxiety disorders in children and adolescents.* New York: Guilford Press.

Beidel, D.C., & Turner, S.M. (1988). Comorbidity of test anxiety and other anxiety disorders in children. *Journal of Abnormal Child Psychology, 16,* 275–287.

Bell, J. (1959). On rubella in pregnancy. *British Medical Journal, 1,* 686–688.

Bellak, L. (1954). *The Thematic Apperception Test and The Children's Apperception Test in clinical use* (4th ed.). New York: Grune and Stratton.

Bellak, L. (1986). *The TAT, CAT and SAT in clinical use* (4th ed.). New York: Grune and Stratton.

Bell-Dolan, D., & Brazeal, T.J. (1993). Separation anxiety disorder, overanxious disorder, and school refusal. *Child and Adolescent Psychiatric Clinics of North America, 2,* 563–580.

Belsky, J. (1988). Infant day care and socioemotional development: The United States. *Journal of Child Psychology and Psychiatry, 29,* 397–406.

Belsky, J. (1993). Etiology of child maltreatment: A developmental-ecological analysis. *Psychological Bulletin, 114,* 413–434.

Belsky, J., Goode, M.K., & Most, R.K. (1980). Maternal stimulation and infant exploratory competence: Cross-sectional, correlational, and experimental analyses. *Child Development, 51,* 1168–1178.

Belsky, J., & Steinberg, L.D. (1978). The effects of day care: A critical review. *Child Development, 49,* 929–949.

Bemis, K.M. (1978). Current approaches to the etiology and treatment of anorexia nervosa. *Psychological Bulletin, 85,* 593–617.

Bemporad, J.R. (1978). Encopresis. In B.B. Wolman, J. Egan, & A.O. Ross (Eds.), *Handbook of treatment of mental disorders in childhood and adolescence* (pp. 161–178). Englewood Cliffs, NJ: Prentice-Hall.

Bender, L. (1955). Twenty years of clinical research on schizophrenic children with special reference to those under six years of age. In G. Caplan (Ed.), *Emotional problems of early childhood* (pp. 503–515). New York: Basic Books.

Bender, L. (1960). Treatment in early schizophrenia. *Progress in psychotherapy, 5,* 177–184.

Bennett, S., & Klein, H.R. (1966). Childhood schizophrenia: 30 years later. *American Journal of Psychiatry, 122,* 1121–1124.

Benson, B.A., & Gross, A.M. (1989). The effect of a congenitally handicapped child upon the marital dyad: A review of the literature. *Clinical Psychology Review, 9,* 747–758.

Berden, G. F., Althaus, M., & Verhulst, F. C. (1990). Major life events and changes in the behavioural functioning of children. *Journal of Child Psychology, Psychiatry, and Allied Disciplines, 31,* 949–959.

Bereiter, D. (1972). An academic preschool for disadvantaged children: Conclusions from evaluation studies. In J. Stanley (Ed.), *Preschool programs for the disadvantaged* (pp. 1–21). Baltimore: Johns Hopkins University.

Bereiter, D., & Engelmann, S. (1966). *Teaching disadvantaged children in the preschool.* Englewood Cliffs, NJ: Prentice-Hall.

Bergman, L.R., & Magnusson, D. (1986). Type A behavior: A longitudinal study from childhood and adulthood. *Psychosomatic Medicine, 48,* 134–142.

Berkell, D.E. (Ed.). (1992). *Autism: Identification, education, and treatment.* Hillsdale, NJ: Erlbaum.

Bernat, J.L., & Vincent, F.M. (1993). *Neurology: Problems in primary care* (2nd ed.). Los Angeles, CA: Practice Management Information Corporation.

Bernheimer, L.P., & Keogh, B.K. (1988). Stability of cognitive performance of children with developmental delays. *American Journal on Mental Retardation, 92,* 539–542.

Bettelheim, B. (1967). *The empty fortress.* New York: Free Press.

Biederman, J., Wilens, T., Mick, E., Milberger, S., Spencer, T.J., & Faraone, S.V. (1995). Psychoactive substance use disorders in adults with attention deficit hyperactivity disorder (ADHD): Effects of ADHD and psychiatric comorbidity. *American Journal of Psychiatry, 152*, 1652–1658.

Bierman, K.L. (1987). The clinical significance and assessment of poor peer relations: Peer neglect versus peer rejection. *Developmental and Behavioral Pediatrics, 8*, 233–240.

Bijou, S.W. (1966). A functional analysis of retarded development. In N.R. Ellis (Ed.), *International Review of Research in Mental Retardation* (Vol. 1, pp. 1–19). New York: Academic Press.

Bijou, S.W., & Peterson, R.F. (1971). Functional analysis in the assessment of children. In P. McReynolds (Ed.), *Advances in psychological assessment* (Vol. 2, pp. 63–78). Palo Alto: Science and Behavior Books.

Birch, H.G., & Gussow, J.D. (1970). *Disadvantaged children: Health, nutrition, and school failure.* New York: Harcourt, Brace & World.

Birch, H.G., Richardson, S.A., Baird, D., Horobin, G., & Illsley, R. (1970). *Mental subnormality in the community: A clinical and epidemiological study.* Baltimore: Williams & Wilkins.

Birnbrauer, J.S., Wolf, M.M., Kidder, J.D., & Tague, C.E. (1965). Classroom behavior in retarded pupils with token reinforcement. *Journal of Experimental Child Psychology, 2*, 219–235.

Black, B. (1995). Separation anxiety disorder and panic disorder. In J.S. March (Ed.), *Anxiety disorders in children and adolescents.* New York: Guilford Press.

Black, B., & Uhde, T.W. (1992). Elective mutism as a variant of social phobia. *Journal of the American Academy of Child & Adolescent Psychiatry, 31*, 1090–1094.

Black, B., & Uhde, T.W. (1995). Psychiatric characteristics of children with selective mutism: A pilot study. *Journal of the American Academy of Child & Adolescent Psychiatry, 34*, 847–856.

Blair, C., Ramey, C.T., & Hardin, M.J. (1995). Early intervention for low birthweight, premature infants: Participation and intellectual development. *American Journal of Mental Retardation, 99*, 542–554.

Blau, T.H. (1979). Diagnosis of disturbed children. *American Psychologist, 34*, 969–972.

Boeberg, D., & Burnstein, I. (1987). Candy as a scapegoat in the prevention of food aversions in children receiving chemotherapy. *Cancer, 60*, 2344–2347.

Bondy, A. (1995). What parents can expect from public schools. In C. Maurice, S. Luce, & G. Green (Eds.), *Behavioral intervention for children with autism* (pp. 323–330). Austin, TX: Pro-Ed.

Bondy, A., & Erickson, M.T. (1976). Comparison of modeling and reinforcement procedures in increasing question-asking of mildly retarded children. *Journal of Applied Behavior Analysis, 9*, 108–116.

Bondy, A., & Frost, L. (1994). The Picture-Exchange Communication System. *Focus on Autistic Behavior, 9*, 1–19.

Botvin, G.J., & Botvin, E.M. (1992). Adolesent tobacco, alcohol, and drug abuse: Prevention strategies, empirical findings, and assessment issues. *Journal of Developmental and Behavioral Pediatrics, 13*, 290–301.

Botvin, G.J., Schinke, S., Epstein, J.A., & Diaz, T. (1994). The effectiveness of culturally focused and generic skills training approaches to alcohol and drug abuse prevention among minority youth. *Psychology of Addictive Behaviors, 8*, 116–127.

Botvin, G.J., Schinke, S., & Orlandi, M.A. (1995). School-based health promotion: Substance abuse and sexual behavior. *Applied and Preventive Psychology, 4*, 167–184.

Bourn, D.F. (1993). Over-chastisement, child non-compliance and parenting skills: A behavioural intervention by a family centre social worker. *British Journal of Social Work, 23*, 481–499.

Bowen, M. (1978). *Family therapy in clinical practice.* New York: Aronson.

Bowlby, J. (1952). *Maternal care and mental health.* Geneva: World Health Organization.

Brady, E.U., & Kendall, P.C. (1992). Comorbidity of anxiety and depression in children and adolescents. *Psychological Bulletin, 2*, 244–255.

Brazelton, T.B. (1974). *Neonatal behavioral assessment scale.* London: Spastics International Medical Publications.

Breen, M.J., & Barkley, R.A. (1983). The Personality Inventory for Children (PIC): Its clinical utility with hyperactive children. *Journal of Pediatric Psychology, 8*, 359–366.

Brenton, J., Bergeron, L., Valla, J., & Lepine, S. (1995). Do children aged 9 through 11 years understand the DISC Version 2.25 questions? *Journal of the American Academy of Child & Adolescent Psychiatry, 34*, 946–954.

Broden, M., Hall, R.V., & Mitts, B. (1971). The effect of self-recording on the classroom behavior of two eighth-grade students. *Journal of Applied Behavior Analysis, 4*, 191–199.

Broden, P.K., Dunivant, K., Smith, E.C., & Sutton, L.P. (1981). Further observation of the link between learning disabilities and juvenile delinquency. *Journal of Educational Psychology, 73*, 838–850.

Brodzinsky, D.M., & Schechter, D. (Eds.). (1990). *The psychology of adoption.* New York: Oxford University Press.

Broman, S., Nichols, P.L., Shaughnessy, P., & Kennedy, W. (1987). *Retardation in young children: A developmental study of cognitive deficit.* Hillsdale, NJ: Erlbaum.

Brown, D.T., & Prout, H.T. (Eds.). (1989). *Counseling and psychotherapy with children and adolescents* (2nd ed.). Brandon, VT: CPPC.

Brown, J.L. (1960). Prognosis from presenting symptoms of preschool children with atypical development. *American Journal of Orthopsychiatry, 30*, 382–390.

Brown, J.L. (1963). Follow-up of children with atypical development (infantile psychosis). *American Journal of Orthopsychiatry, 33*, 855–861.

Brownell, K.D., & Foreyt, J.P. (Eds.). (1986). *Handbook of eating disorders.* New York: Basic Books.

Brownfield, D., & Sorenson, A.M. (1994). Sibling size and sibling delinquency. *Deviant Behavior, 15,* 45–61.

Buhrmester, D., Whalen, C. K., Henker, B., & MacDonald, V. (1992). Prosocial behavior in hyperactive boys: Effects of stimulant medication and comparison with normal boys. *Journal of Abnormal Child Psychology, 20,* 103–121.

Burchard, J.D. (1967). Systematic socialization: A programmed environment for the habilitation of antisocial retardates. *Psychological Record, 17,* 461–476.

Burd, L., Fisher, W., Kerbeshian, J., & Vesely, B. (1988). A comparison of breastfeeding rates among children with pervasive developmental disorder, and controls. *Developmental and Behavioral Pediatrics, 9,* 247–251.

Burns, R.C., & Kaufman, S.H. (1970). *Kinetic Family Drawings (K-F-D): An introduction to understanding children through kinetic drawings.* New York: Brunner/Mazel.

Burns, R.C., & Kaufman, S.H. (1972). *Actions, styles, and symbols in Kinetic Family Drawings (K-F-D).* New York: Brunner/Mazel.

Burnstein, I. (1991). Aversion conditioning in response to cancer and cancer treatment. *Clinical Psychology Review, 11,* 185–191.

Buros, O.C. (published yearly). *Mental Measurements Yearbook.* Highland Park, NJ: Gryphon Press.

Butcher, J.N., Williams, C.L., Graham, J.R., Archer, R.P., Tellegen, A., Ben-Porath, Y.S., & Kaemmer, B. (1992). *MMPI-A, Minnesota Multiphasic Personality Inventory-Adolescent: Manual for administration, scoring, and interpretation.* Minneapolis, MN: University of Minnesota Press.

Butterfield, E.C. (1989). Treatment of mentally retarded people with severe behavior problems. *American Journal on Mental Retardation, 94,* 15.

Cameron, J.R. (1977). Parental treatment, children's temperament, and the risk of childhood behavioral problems. *American Journal of Orthopsychiatry, 47,* 568–576.

Campbell, S.B. (1990). *Behavior problems in preschoolers: Clinical and developmental issues.* New York: Guilford.

Campbell, S.B. (1995). Behavior problems in preschool children: A review of recent research. *Journal of Child Psychology and Psychiatry and Allied Disciplines, 36,* 113–149.

Campbell, S.B., Pierce, E.W., March, C.L., & Ewing, L.J. (1991). Noncompliant behavior, overactivity, and family stress as predictors of negative maternal control in children. *Development and Psychopathology, 3,* 175–190.

Cantor, S. (1988). *Childhood schizophrenia.* New York: Guilford.

Cantwell, D. (1975). Genetics of hyperactivity. *Journal of Child Psychology and Psychiatry, 16,* 181–197.

Cantwell, D.P., Baker, L., & Rutter, M. (1979). Families of autistic and dysphasic children. *Archives of General Psychiatry, 36,* 682–687.

Cantwell, D.P., Russell, A.T., Mattison, R., & Will, L. (1979). A comparison of DSM-II and DSM-III in the diagnosis of childhood psychiatric disorders. I. Agreement with expected diagnosis. *Archives of General Psychiatry, 36,* 1208–1213.

Caplan, B. (1964). *Principles of preventive psychiatry.* New York: Basic Books.

Cardozo, L.D., Gibb, D.M.F., Studd, J.W.W., & Cooper, D.J. (1982). Social and obstetric features associated with smoking in pregnancy. *British Journal of Obstetrics and Gynecology, 89,* 622–627.

Carlson, C.L., Lahey, B.B., Fram, C.L., Walker, J., & Hynd, G.W. (1987). Sociometric status of clinic-referred children with attention deficit disorders with and without hyperactivity. *Journal of Abnormal Child Psychology, 15,* 537–547.

Carlson, C.L., Pelham, W.E., Milich, R., & Dixon, J. (1992). Single and combined effects of methylphenidate and behavior therapy on the classroom performance of children with attention-deficit hyperactivity disorder. *Journal of Abnormal Child Psychology, 20,* 213–232.

Carr, R. (1982). Sign language. In R. Koegel, A. Rincover, & A. Egel (Eds.), *Educating and understanding children with autism* (pp. 142–157). San Diego: College-Hill Press.

Carter, A.S., Pauls, D.L., Leckman, J.F., & Cohen, D.J. (1994). A prospective longitudinal study of Gilles de la Tourette's syndrome. *Journal of the American Academy of Child and Adolescent Psychiatry, 33,* 377–385.

Casler, L. (1961). Maternal deprivation: A critical review of the literature. *Monographs of the Society for Research in Child Development, 26,* No. 2.

Casper, R.C., Eckert, E.K., Halmi, K.A., Goldberg, S.C., & Davis, J.M. (1980). Bulimia: Its incidence and clinical importance in patients with anorexia nervosa. *Archives of General Psychiatry, 37,* 1030–1035.

Cauley, K.M., Golinkoff, R.M., Hirsh-Pasek, K., & Gordon, L. (1989). Revealing hidden competencies: A new method for studying language comprehension in children with motor impairments. *American Journal on Mental Retardation, 94,* 53–63.

Cawthron, P., James, A., Dell, J., & Seagroatt, V. (1994). Adolescent onset psychosis: A clinical and outcome study. *Journal of Child Psychology and Psychiatry and Allied Disciplines, 35,* 1321–1332.

Chalfant, J.C. (1989). Learning disabilities: Policy issues and promising approaches. *American Psychologist, 44,* 392–398.

Charles, L., & Schain, R. (1981). A four-year follow-up study of the effects of methylphenidate on the behavior and academic achievement of hyperactive children. *Journal of Abnormal Child Psychology, 9,* 495–505.

Chatoor, I., Dickson, L., Schaefer, S., & Egan, J. (1985). A developmental classification of feeding disorders associated with failure to thrive: Diagnosis and treatment. In D. Drotar (Ed.), *New directions in failure to thrive: Implications for research and practice* (pp. 235–258). New York: Plenum.

Chesney-Lind, U., & Shelden, R.G. (1992). *Girls: Delinquency and juvenile justice.* Pacific Grove, CA: Brooks/Cole.

Chess, S. (1971). Autism in children with congenital rubella. *Journal of Autism and Childhood Schizophrenia, 1,* 33–47.

Chess, S., Korn, S., & Fernandez, P. (1971). *Psychiatric disorders of children with rubella.* New York: Brunner/Mazel.

Chorpita, B.F., Albano, A.M., & Barlow, D.H. (1996). Child anxiety sensitivity index: Considerations for children with anxiety disorders. *Journal of Clinical Child Psychology, 25,* 77–82.

Christiaanse, M.E., Lavigne, J.V., & Lerner, C.V. (1989). Psychosocial aspects of compliance in children and adolescents with asthma. *Developmental and Behavioral Pediatrics, 10,* 75–80.

Christiansen, K.O. (1977). A review of studies of criminality among twins. In S.S. Mednick & K.O. Christiansen (Eds.), *Biosocial basis of criminal behavior* (pp. 45–88). New York: Gardner Press.

Cicchetti, D. (Ed.). (1994). Special issue: Advances and challenges in the study of the sequelae of child maltreatment. *Development and Psychopathology, 6,* 1–247.

Cicchetti, D., & Barnett, D. (1991). Attachment organization in maltreated preschoolers. *Development and Psychopathology, 2,* 397–412.

Cicchetti, D., & Carlson, V. (Eds.). (1989). *Child maltreatment: Theory and research on the cause and consequences of child abuse and neglect.* New York: Cambridge University Press.

Clarke-Stewart, K.A. (1989). Infant day care: Maligned or malignant? *American Psychologist, 44,* 266–273.

Cloninger, C.R., & Gottesman, I.I. (1987). Genetic and environmental factors in antisocial behavior disorders. In S.A. Mednick, T.E. Moffitt, & S.A. Stack (Eds.), *Causes of crime: New biological approaches* (pp. 92–109). Cambridge: Cambridge University Press.

Coates, T.J., & Masek, B.J. (1982). In D.C. Russo & J.W. Varni (Eds.), *Behavioral pediatrics* (pp. 355–374). New York: Plenum.

Coffey, V.P., & Jessup, W.J.E. (1959). Maternal influenza and congenital deformities. *The Lancet, 2,* 935–938.

Cohen, D.J., Bruun, R.D., & Leckman, J.F. (Eds.). (1988). *Tourette's syndrome and tic disorders: Clinical understanding and treatment.* New York: Wiley.

Cohen, D.J., Donnellan, A.M., & Paul, R. (Eds.). (1987). *Handbook of autism and pervasive developmental disorders.* New York: Wiley.

Cohen, H.J. (1992). HIV infection and mental retardation. In L. Rowitz (Ed.), *Mental retardation in the year 2000.* New York: Springer-Verlag.

Cohen, H.L., & Filipczak, J. (1971). *A new learning environment.* San Francisco: Jossey-Bass.

Cohen, L.H. (Ed.). (1988). *Life events and psychological functioning.* Newbury Park, CA: Sage.

Cohen, P., Cohen, J., & Brook, J.S. (1993). An epidemiological study of disorders in late childhood and adolescence: II. Persistence of disorders. *Journal of Child Psychology & Psychiatry & Allied Disciplines, 34,* 869–877.

Cohen, R.L., & Netley, C. (1978). Cognitive deficits, learning disabilities, and WISC Verbal-Performance consistency. *Developmental Psychology, 14,* 624–634.

Cohen, S. (1980). Therapeutic aspects. In *Marijuana research findings: 1980.* Washington, DC: U.S. Government Printing Office.

Cohen, S. (1995). Biosocial factors in early infancy as predictors of competence in adolescents who were born prematurely. *Developmental and Behavioral Pediatrics, 16,* 36–41.

Cohen, S., & Przybycien, C.A. (1974). Some effects of sociometrically selected peer models on the cognitive styles of impulsive children. *Journal of Genetic Psychology, 124,* 213–220.

Conners, C.K., & Wells, K.C. (1986). *Hyperkinetic children: A neuropsychosocial approach.* Newbury Park, CA: Sage.

Copeland, A.P., & Weissbrod, C.S. (1980). Effects of modeling on behavior related to hyperactivity. *Journal of Educational Psychology, 72,* 875–883.

Corbett, J.A., & Besag, F.M.C. (1988). Epilepsy and its treatment in children. In B.B. Lahey & A.E. Kazdin (Eds.), *Advances in clinical child psychology* (Vol. 11, pp. 369–394). New York: Plenum.

Cosper, M.R., & Erickson, M.T. (1984). Relationships among observed classroom behavior and three types of teacher ratings. *Behavioral Disorders, 9,* 189–195.

Coulter, D.L. (1996). Prevention as a form of support: Implications for the new definition. *Mental Retardation, 34,* 108–116.

Cowen, E.L., Gesten, E.L., & Wilson, A.B. (1979). The Primary Mental Health Project (PMHP): Evaluation of current program effectiveness. *American Journal of Community Psychology, 7,* 293–303.

Cox, D.J., Sutphen, J., Borowitz, S., Dickens, M.N., Singles, J., & Whitehead, W.E. (1994). Simple electromyographic feedback treatment for chronic pediatric constipation/encopresis: Preliminary report. *Biofeedback and Self-Regulation, 19,* 41–50.

Cox, D.J., Sutphen, J., Ling, W., Quillian, W., & Borowitz, S. (1996). Additive benefits of laxative, toilet training, and biofeedback therapies in the treatment of pediatric encopresis. *Journal of Pediatric Psychology, 21,* 659–670.

Cozzi, L., Tryon, W.W., & Sedlacek, K. (1987). The effectiveness of biofeedback-assisted relaxation in modifying sickle cell crises. *Biofeedback and Self Regulation, 12,* 672–680.

Craig, H.D., & Dobson, K.S. (1995). *Anxiety and depression in adults and children.* Thousand Oaks, CA: Sage.

Crary, W.G., & Johnson, C.W. (1981). Mental status examination. In C. Johnson, J. Snibbe, & L. Evans (Eds.), *Basic psychopathology: A programmed text* (2nd ed.). Lancaster, England: MIP Press.

Creak, M. (1963). Childhood psychosis: A review of 100 cases. *British Journal of Psychiatry, 109,* 84–89.

Creer, T.L., Renne, C.M., & Chai, H. (1982). The application of behavioral techniques to childhood asthma. In D.C. Russo & J.W. Varni (Eds.), *Behavioral pediatrics.* New York: Plenum .

Cronbach, L.J. (1975). Five decades of public controversy over mental testing. *American Psychologist, 30,* 1–14.

Crowe, R.R. (1983). Antisocial personality disorders. In R.E. Tarter (Ed.), *The child at psychiatric risk* (pp. 214–227). Oxford: Oxford University Press.

Cummings, E.M., & Davies, P. (1994). *Children and marital conflict.* New York: Guilford.

Dahlstrom, W.G., Butcher, J.N., Graham, J.R., Tellegen, A., & Kaemmer, B. (1989). *Minnesota Multiphasic Personality Inventory—2: Manual for administration and scoring.* Minneapolis, MN: University of Minnesota Press.

Dalterio, S., Bader, F., Bartke, A., & Mayfield, D. (1982). Cannabinoids in male mice: Effects on fertility and spermatogenesis. *Science, 216,* 315–316.

Dalterio, S., & Bartke, A. (1979). Perinatal exposure of cannabinoids alters male reproductive function in mice. *Science, 205,* 1420–1422.

Darlington, R.B., Royce, J.M., Snipper, A.S., Murray, H.W., & Lazar, I. (1980). Preschool programs and later school competence of children from low-income families. *Science, 208,* 202–204.

Davids, A., DeVault, S., & Talmadge, M. (1961). Anxiety, pregnancy, and childbirth abnormalities. *Journal of Consulting Psychology, 25,* 74–77.

Davis, H.V., Sears, R.R., Miller, H.C., & Brodbeck, A.J. (1948). Effects of cup, bottle, and breast feeding on oral activities of newborn infants. *Pediatrics, 2,* 549–558.

DeBaryshe, B.D., Patterson, G.R., & Capaldi, D.M. (1993). A performance model for academic achievement in early adolescent boys. *Developmental Psychology, 29,* 795–804.

DeFries, J.C. (1989). Gender ratios in children with reading disability and their affected relatives: A commentary. *Journal of Learning Disabilities, 22,* 544–545.

DeLuca, R.V., & Holborn, S.W. (1992). Effects of a variable-ratio reinforcement schedule with changing criteria on exercise in obese and nonobese boys. *Journal of Applied Behavior Analysis, 25,* 671–679.

DeMyer, M.K. (1979). *Parents and children in autism.* Washington, DC: Winston & Sons.

DeMyer, M.K., Barton, S., Alpern, G., Kimberlin, C., Allen, J., Yang, E., & Steele, R. (1974). The measured intelligence of autistic children. *Journal of Autism and Childhood Schizophrenia, 4,* 42–60.

DeMyer, M.K., Hingtgen, J.H., & Jackson, R.K. (1981). Infantile autism reviewed: A decade of research. *Schizophrenia Bulletin, 7,* 388–451.

DeMyer, M.K., Pontius, W., Norton, J.A., Barton, S., Allen, J., & Steele, R. (1972). Parental practices and innate activity in normal, autistic, and brain-dam-aged infants. *Journal of Autism and Childhood Schizophrenia, 2,* 49–66.

de Quiros, G.B., Kinsbourne, M., Palmer, R.L., & Rufo, D.T. (1994). Attention deficit disorder in children: Three clinical variants. *Journal of Development and Behavioral Pediatrics, 15,* 311–319.

Despert, J.L. (1938). Schizophrenia in children. *Pediatric Quarterly, 12,* 366–371.

DeVeaugh-Geiss, J., Moroz, G., Biederman, J., & Cantwell, D.P. (1992). Clomipramine hydrochloride in childhood and adolescent obsessive-compulsive disorder: A multicenter trial. *Journal of the American Academy of Child and Adolescent Psychiatry, 31,* 45–49.

Diamond, G.W. (1989). Developmental problems in children with HIV infection. *Mental Retardation, 27,* 213–217.

Dishion, T.J., & Andrews, D.W. (1995). Preventing escalation in problem behaviors with high-risk young adolescents: Immediate and 1–year outcomes. *Journal of Consulting and Clinical Psychology, 63,* 538–548.

Dishion, T.J., & Patterson, G.R. (1992). Age effects in patient training outcome. *Behavior Therapy, 23,* 719–729.

Dollard, J., Doob, L.W., Miller, N.E., Mowrer, O.H., & Sears, R.R. (1939). *Frustration and aggression.* New Haven: Yale University Press.

Dollinger, S.J. (1986). Childhood sleep disturbances. In B.B. Lahey & A.E. Kazdin (Eds.), *Advances in clinical child psychology* (Vol. 9, pp. 279–332). New York: Plenum.

Donaldson, S.I., Graham, J.W., & Hansen, W.B. (1994). Testing the generalizability of intervening mechanism theories: Understanding the effects of adolescent drug use prevention interventions. *Journal of Behavioral Medicine, 17,* 195–216.

Donaldson, S.I., Graham, J.W., Piccinin, A.M., & Hansen, W.B. (1995). Resistance-skills training and onset of alcohol use: Evidence for beneficial and potentially harmful effects in private schools and in private Catholic schools. *Health Psychology, 14,* 291–300.

Donenberg, G., & Baker, B.L. (1993). The impact of young children with externalizing behaviors on their families. *Journal of Abnormal Child Psychology, 21,* 179–198.

Dougherty, D.M., Saxe, L.M., Cross, T., & Silverman, N. (1987). *Children's mental health problems and services.* Durham, NC: Duke University Press.

Dow, S.P., Sonies, B.C., Scheib, D., & Moss, S.E. (1995). *Journal of the American Academy of Child & Adolescent Psychiatry, 34* (7), 836–846.

Dubowitz, H., Hampton, R.L., Bethoney, W.G., & Newberger, E.H. (1987). Inflicted and noninflicted injuries: Differences in child and familial characteristics. *American Journal of Orthopsychiatry, 57,* 525–535.

Dujovne, V.F., Barnard, M.U., & Rapoff, M.A. (1995). Pharmacological and cognitive behavioral approaches in the treatment of childhood depression: A review and critique. *Clinical Psychology Review, 15,* 589–611.

Dumas, J.E. (1989). Treating antisocial behavior in children: Child and family approaches. *Clinical Psychology Review, 9,* 197–222.

Dumas, J.E., & Gibson, J.A. (1990). Behavioral correlates of maternal depressive symptomatology in conduct-disordered children: II. Systemic effects involving fathers and siblings. *Journal of Consulting and Clinical Psychology, 58,* 877–881.

Dunn, K.W., Cunningham, C.E., & Backman, J.E. (1987). Self-control and reinforcement in the management of a cerebral-palsied adolescent's drooling. *Developmental Medicine and Child's Neurology, 29,* 305–310.

Dunn, L.M., & Dunn, L.M. (1981). *Peabody Picture Vocabulary Test.* Circle Pines, MN: American Guidance Service.

Dunn, L.M., & Dunn, L.M. (1997). *Peabody Picture Vocabulary Test: Revised.* Circle Pines, MN: American Guidance Service.

DuPaul, G.J., & Barkley, R.A. (1993). Behavioral contributions to pharmacotherapy: The utility of behavioral methodology in medication treatment of children with attention-deficit hyperactivity disorder. *Behavior Therapy, 24,* 47–65.

du Verglas, G., Banks, S.R., & Guyer, K.E. (1988). Clinical effects of fenfluramine on children with autism: A review of the research. *Journal of Autism and Developmental Disorders, 18,* 297–308.

Dweck, C.S., Gittelman-Klein, R., McKinney, W.T., & Watson, J.S. (1977). Summary of the Subcommittee on Clinical Criteria for Diagnosis of Depression in Children. In J.G. Schulterbrandt & A. Raskin (Eds.), *Depression in childhood: Diagnosis, treatment, and conceptual models* (pp. 153–154). New York: Raven Press.

Ebbs, J.H., Tisdall, F.F., & Scott, W.A. (1942). The influence of prenatal diet on the mother and child. *The Milbank Memorial Fund Quarterly, 20,* 35–36.

Edelbrock, C.S., & Achenbach, T.M. (1983). *Manual for the Teacher Rating Form.* Burlington, VT: University of Vermont, Department of Psychiatry.

Edelbrock, C.S., & Achenbach, T.M. (1984). The teacher version of the Child Behavior Profile. I. Boys aged 6–11. *Journal of Consulting and Clinical Psychology, 52,* 207–217.

Ehlers, S., & Gillberg, C. (1993). The epidemiology of Asperger syndrome: A total population study. *Journal of Child Psychology and Psychiatry and Allied Disciplines, 34,* 1327–1350.

Einfeld, S.L., & Tonge, B.J. (1996). Population prevalence of psychopathology in children and adolescents with intellectual disability: II. Epidemiological findings. *Journal of Intellectual Disability Research, 40,* 99–109.

Eisen, A.E., & Kearney, C.A. (1995). *Practitioner's guide to treating fear and anxiety in children and adolescents: A*

cognitive-behavioral approach. New Jersey: Jason Aronson Inc.

Eisen, A.E. & Kearney, C.A. (1995). *Treating fear and anxiety in children and adolescents.* New Jersey: Jason Aronson Inc.

Eisen, A.E., & Silverman, W.K. (1993). Should I relax or change my thoughts? A preliminary examination of cognitive therapy, relaxation training, and their combination with overanxious children. *Journal of Cognitive Psychotherapy: An International Quarterly, 7,* 265–279.

Eisenberg, L. (1966). The epidemiology of reading retardation and a program for preventive intervention. In J. Money (Ed.), *The disabled reader* (pp. 3–19). Baltimore: Johns Hopkins University Press.

Elbert, J.C., & Seale, T.W. (1988). Complexity of the cognitive phenotype of an inherited form of learning disability. *Developmental Medicine and Child Neurology, 30,* 181–189.

Elliot, C.D. (1990). *Differential Abilities Scale: Administration and scoring manual.* San Antonio, TX: The Psychological Corporation.

Emery, R.E. (1994). *Renegotiating family relationships.* New York: Guilford.

Engel, E. (1977). One hundred years of cytogenetic studies in health and disease. *American Journal of Mental Deficiency, 82,* 109–117.

Epstein, L. (1986). Treatment of childhood obesity. In K.D. Brownell & J.P. Foreyt (Eds.), *Handbook of eating disorders* (pp. 159–179). New York: Basic Books.

Epstein, L.H., Beck, S., Figueroa, J., Farkas, G., Kazdin, A.E., Daneman, D., & Becker, D. (1981). The effects of targeting improvements in urine glucose on metabolic control in children with insulin dependent diabetes. *Journal of Applied Behavior Analysis, 14,* 365–375.

Erickson, M.T. (1965). Relationship between psychological attitudes during pregnancy and complications of pregnancy, labor, and delivery. *Proceedings of the American Psychological Association, 1,* 213–214.

Erickson, M.T. (1967). Prenatal and preconception environmental influences. *Science, 157,* 1210.

Erickson, M.T. (1968a). MMPI comparisons between parents of young emotionally disturbed and organically retarded children. *Journal of Consulting and Clinical Psychology, 32,* 701–706.

Erickson, M.T. (1968b). The predictive validity of the Cattell Infant Intelligence Scale for young mentally retarded children. *American Journal of Mental Deficiency, 72,* 728–733.

Erickson, M.T. (1971). Risk factors associated with complications of pregnancy, labor, and delivery. *American Journal of Obstetrics and Gynecology, 111,* 658–662.

Erikson, E.H. (1963). *Childhood and society* (2nd ed., rev.). New York: Norton.

Eron, L.D. (1980). Prescription for reduction of aggression. *American Psychologist, 35,* 244–252.

Eron, L.D., Huesmann, L.R., Lefkowitz, M.M., & Walder, L.O. (1972). Does television violence cause aggression? *American Psychologist, 27,* 253–263.

Eron, L.D., Walder, L.O., & Lefkowitz, M.M. (1971). *Learning of aggression in children.* Boston: Little, Brown.

Exner, J.E. (1986). *The Rorschach: A comprehensive system: Volume 1: Basic foundations.* New York: Wiley.

Exner, J.E. (1991). *The Rorschach: A comprehensive system: Volume 2: Interpretation* (2nd ed.). New York: Wiley.

Exner, J.E., & Weiner, I.B. (1982). *The Rorschach: Comprehensive system, Volume 3: Assessment of children and adolescents.* New York: Wiley.

Eysenck, H.J. (1950). Personality tests. In T.H. Fleming (Ed.), *Recent progress in psychology* (pp. 118–159). London: J. & A. Churchill.

Fajardo, B. (1987). Parenting a damaged child: Mourning, regression, and disappointment. *Psychoanalytic Review, 74,* 19–43.

Fantuzzo, J.N., DePaola, L.M., Lambert, L., Martino, J., Anderson, G., & Sutton, S. (1991). Effects of interpersonal violence on the psychological adjustment and competencies of young children. *Journal of Consulting and Clinical Psychology, 59,* 258–265.

Farber, B. (1959). Effects of a severely mentally retarded child on family integration. *Monographs of the Society for Research in Child Development, 24,* No. 2.

Farber, B. (1960). Family organization and crisis: Maintenance of integration in families with a severely mentally retarded child. *Monographs of the Society for Research in Child Development, 25,* No. 1.

Farmer, S., & Galavis, D. (1993). Support groups for children of divorce. *The American Journal of Family Therapy, 21* (1), pp. 40–50.

Feldman, W.S., Manella, K.J., Apodaca, L., & Varni, J.W. (1982). Behavioral group parent training in spina bifida. *Journal of Clinical Child Psychology, 11,* 144–150.

Fentress, D., Masek, B., Mehegan, J., & Benson, H. (1986). Biofeedback and relaxation-response training in the treatment of pediatric migraine. *Developmental Medicine & Child Neurology, 28,* 135–146.

Fergusson, D.H., Fergusson, J.E., Horwood, L.J., & Kinzett, N.G. (1988). A longitudinal study of dentine lead levels, intelligence, school performance and behavior. Part III. Dentine lead levels and attention/activity. *Journal of Child Psychology and Psychiatry, 29,* 811–824.

Fergusson, D.M., Horwood, L.J., & Lynskey, M.T. (1993). Early dentine lead levels and subsequent cognitive and behavioral development. *Journal of Child Psychology and Psychiatry, 34,* 215–227.

Fergusson, D.M., Horwood, L.J., & Shannon, F.T. (1989). Relationship of family life events, maternal depression, and childrearing problems. In T.W. Miller (Ed.), *Stressful life events* (pp. 609–618). Madison, CT: International Universities Press.

Ferster, C.B. (1961). Positive reinforcement and behavioral deficits of autistic children. *Child Development, 32,* 437–456.

Feshbach, S. (1970). In P.H. Mussen (Ed.), *Carmichael's manual of child psychology* (Vol. 2, pp. 159–260). New York: Wiley.

Findholt, N.E., & Emmett, C.G. (1990). Impact of interdisciplinary team review on psychotropic drug use with persons who have mental retardation. *Mental Retardation, 28,* 41–46.

Fine, S., & Johnston, C. (1993). Drug and placebo side effects in methylphenidate-placebo trial for attention deficit hyperactivity disorder. *Child Psychiatry and Human Development, 24,* 25–30.

Finster, M., Petersen, H., & Morishima, H.O. (1983). Principles of fetal exposure to drugs used in obstetric anesthesia. In B. Krauer, F. Krauer, F.E. Hythen, & E. DelPozo (Eds.), *Drugs and pregnancy.* New York: Academic Press.

Finucci, J.M., Guthrie, J.T., Childs, A.L., Abbey, H., & Childs, B. (1976). The genetics of specific reading disability. *Annals of Human Genetics, 40,* 1–23.

Firestone, P., & Prabhu, A.N. (1983). Minor physical anomalies and obstetrical complications: Their relationship to hyperactive, psychoneurotic, and normal children and their families. *Journal of Abnormal Child Psychology, 11,* 207–216.

Fischer, D.G. (1983). Parental supervision and delinquency. *Perceptual and Motor Skills, 56,* 635–640.

Fischer, M., Barkley, R. A., Fletcher, K. E., & Smallish, L. (1993). The stability of dimensions of behavior in ADHD and normal children over an 8-year follow-up. *Journal of Abnormal Child Psychology, 21,* 345–337.

Fish, B., Shapiro, T., Campbell, M., & Wile, R. (1968). A classification of schizophrenic children under five years. *American Journal of Psychiatry, 124,* 1415–1423.

Fisher, M., Barkley, R.A., Fletcher, K.E., & Smallish, L. (1993). The adolescent outcome of hyperactive children: Predictors of psychiatric, academic, social, and emotional adjustment. *Journal of the American Academy of Child and Adolescent Psychiatry, 32,* 324–332.

Fisher, P., Wicks, J., Shaffer, D., Piacentini, J., & Lapkin, J. (1992). *NIMH Diagnostic Interview Schedule for Children: User's manual.* New York: New York State Psychiatric Institute.

Fishler, K., Azen, C., Henderson, R., & Friedman, E. (1987). Psychoeducational findings among children treated for phenylketonuria. *American Journal on Mental Retardation, 92,* 65–73.

Fleisher, D.R. (1994). Functional vomiting disorders in infancy: Innocent vomiting, nervous vomiting, and infant rumination syndrome. *Journal of Pediatrics, 25,* 584–594.

Fletcher, J., & Copeland, D. (1988). Neurobehavioral effects of central nervous system prophylactic treatment of cancer in children. *Journal of Clinical and Experimental Neuropsychology, 19,* 495–538.

Folstein, S.E, & Rutter, M.L. (1977). Infantile autism: A study of 21 pairs. *Journal of Child Psychology and Psychiatry, 18,* 297–321.

Folstein, S.E., & Rutter, M.L. (1988). Autism: Familial aggregation and genetic implications. *Journal of Autism and Developmental Disorders, 18,* 3–11.

Forehand, R.L., McCombs, A., & Brody, G.H. (1987). The relationship between parental depressive mood state and child functioning. *Advances in Behavior Research and Therapy, 9,* 1–20.

Forehand, R.L., & McMahon, R.J. (1981). *Helping the noncompliant child.* New York: Guilford.

Forehand, R., & Wierson, M. (1993). The role of developmental factors in planning behavioral interventions for children: Disruptive behavioral interventions as an example. *Behavior Therapy, 24,* 117–141.

Forman, S.G. (Ed.). (1987). *School-based affective and social interventions.* Binghamton, NY: Haworth Press.

Foster-Gaitskell, D., & Pratt, C. (1989). Comparison of parent and teacher ratings of adaptive behavior of children with mental retardation. *American Journal on Mental Retardation, 94,* 177–181.

Fowler, M.G., Whitt, J.K., Lallinger, R.R., Nash, K.B., et al. (1988). Neuropsychologic and academic functioning of children with sickle cell anemia. *Developmental and Behavioral Pediatrics, 9,* 213–220.

Foxx, R.M., & Azrin, N.H. (1972). Restitution: A method of eliminating aggressive-disruptive behavior of retarded and brain damaged patients. *Behaviour Research and Therapy, 10,* 15–27.

Frankenberger, W., & Fronzaglio, K. (1991). States' definitions and procedures for identifying children with mental retardation: Comparison over nine years. *Mental Retardation, 29,* 315–321.

Frankenburg, W.K., Dandal, A.W., Sciarillo, W., & Burgess, D. (1981). The newly abbreviated and revised Denver Developmental Screening Test. *Journal of Pediatrics, 99,* 995–999.

Frankenburg, W.K., & Dodds, J.B. (1970). *Denver Developmental Screening Test.* Denver: University of Colorado Medical Center.

Freeman, B.J., Ritvo, E.R., Mason-Brothers, A., & Pingree, C. (1989). Psychometric assessment of first-degree relatives of 62 autistic probands in Utah. *American Journal of Psychiatry, 146,* 361–364.

Freud, A. (1946a). *The ego and the mechanisms of defense* (C. Baines, Trans.). New York: International Universities Press.

Freud, A. (1946b). *The psychoanalytic treatment of children.* London: Imago Publishing Company.

Freud, A. (1965). *Normality and pathology in childhood.* New York: International Universities Press.

Freud, A. (1971). The infantile neurosis: Genetic and dynamic considerations. *Psychoanalytic Study of the Child, 21,* 988–996.

Freud, S. (1905/1953). Three essays on the theory of sexuality. In *Standard edition of the complete psychological works of Sigmund Freud* (Vol. 7, pp. 125–243). London: Hogarth Press.

Freud, S. (1909/1959). Analysis of a phobia in a five-year-old boy. In *Standard edition of the complete psychological works of Sigmund Freud.* London: Hogarth.

Freud, S. (1926/1959). Inhibition, symptoms, and anxiety. In *Standard edition of the complete psychological works of Sigmund Freud* (Vol. 20, pp. 77–174). London: Hogarth.

Frick, P.J., Lahey, B.B., Applegate, B., Kerdyck, L., Ollendick, T., Hynd, G.W., Garfinkel, B., Greenhill, L., Biederman, J., Barkley, R.A., McBurnett, K., Newcorn, J., & Waldman, I. (1994). DSM-IV field trials for the disruptive behavior disorders. *Journal of the American Academy of Child and Adolescent Psychiatry, 33,* 529–539.

Frick, P.J., Lahey, B.B., Loeber, R., Stouthamer-Loeber, M., Christ, M.A., & Hanson, K. (1992). Familial risk factors to oppositional defiant disorder and conduct disorder: Parental psychopathology and maternal parenting. *Journal of Consulting and Clinical Psychology, 60,* 49–55.

Frick, P.J., Lahey, B. B., Loeber, R., Stouthamer-Loeber, M., Green, S., Hart, E. L., & Christ, A. G. (1991). Oppositional defiant disorder and conduct disorder in boys: Patterns of behavioral covariation. *Journal of Clinical Child Psychology, 20,* 202–208.

Frick, P.J., Silverthorn, P., & Evans, C. (1994). Assessment of childhood anxiety using structured interviews: Patterns of agreement among informants and associations with maternal anxiety. *Psychological Assessment, 6,* 372–379.

Friedman, A.S., Glickman, N.W., & Morrissey, M.R. (1986). Prediction of successful treatment outcome by client characteristics and retention in treatment in adolescent drug treatment programs: A large-scale cross-validation. *Journal of Drug Education, 16,* 149–165.

Frisch, R.E. (1988). Fatness and fertility. *Scientific American, 258,* 88–96.

Fritz, G.K., Williams, J.R., & Amylon, M. (1988). After treatment ends: Psychosocial sequelae in pediatric cancer survivors. *American Journal of Orthopsychiatry, 58,* 552–561.

Fuller, P.R. (1949). Operant conditioning of a vegetative human organism. *American Journal of Psychology, 62,* 587–590.

Fyer, A.J., Mannuzza, S., & Gallops, M.S. (1990). Phobias and fears: A preliminary report. *Archives of General Psychiatry, 47,* 252–256.

Gabel, S., Stadler, J., Bjorn, J., Shindledecker, R., & Bowden, C. L. (1993). Dopamine-beta-hydroxylase in behaviorally disturbed youth. *Biological Psychiatry, 34,* 434–442.

Gabel, S., Stadler, J., Bjorn, J., Shindledecker, R., & Bowden, C.L. (1994). Sensation seeking in psychiatrically disturbed youth: Relationship to biochemical parameters and behavior problems. *Journal of the American Academy of Child and Adolescent Psychiatry, 33,* 123–129.

Gadow, K.D. (1983). Effects of stimulant drugs on academic performance in hyperactive and learning disabled children. *Journal of Learning Disabilities, 16,* 290–299.

Gagnon, M., & Ladouceur, R. (1992). Behavioral treatment of child stutters: Replication and extension. *Behavior Therapy, 23,* 113–129.

Gallagher, J. (1989). A new policy initiative: Infants and toddlers with handicapping conditions. *American Psychologist, 44,* 387–391.

Galler, J.R. (Ed.). (1984). *Human nutrition: A comprehensive treatise: Nutrition and behavior* (Vol. 5). New York: Plenum.

Galton, F. (1869). *Hereditary genius.* London: Macmillan.

Garber, H.L. (1988). *The Milwaukee Project: Preventing mental retardation in children at risk.* Washington, DC: American Association on Mental Retardation.

Garber, H.L., & Heber, F.R. (1977). The Milwaukee Project. In P. Mittler (Ed.), *Research to practice in mental retardation* (Vol. 1, pp. 119–127). Baltimore: University Park Press.

Garner, D.M. (1986). Cognitive therapy for anorexia nervosa. In K.D. Browell & J.P. Foreyt (Eds.), *Handbook of eating disorders* (pp. 301–327). New York: Basic Books.

Garrison, W.T., & Earls, F.J. (1987). *Temperament and child psychopathology.* Newbury Park, CA: Sage.

Garrison, W.T., & McQuiston, S. (1989). *Chronic illness during childhood and adolescence: Psychological aspects.* Newbury Park, CA: Sage.

Gau, J.S., Silberg, J.L., Erickson, M.T., & Hewitt, J.K. (1992). Childhood behavior problems: A comparison of twin and non-twin samples. *Acta Genetica Medicae, 41,* 53–63.

Gedye, A. (1989a). Episodic rage and aggression attributed to frontal lobe seizures. *Journal of Mental Deficiency Research, 33,* 369–379.

Gedye, A. (1989b). Extreme self-injury attributed to frontal lobe seizures. *American Journal on Mental Retardation, 94,* 20–26.

Gelfand, D.M., & Hartmann, D.P. (Eds.). (1984). *Child behavior analysis and therapy* (2nd ed.). Elmsford, NY: Pergamon.

Gerald, L.B., Anderson, A., Johnson, G.D., Huff, C., & Trimm, R.F. (1994). Social class, social support and obesity risk in children. *Child: Care, Health and Development, 20,* 145–163.

Gerber, A. (1993). Language-related learning disabilities: Their nature and treatment. Baltimore: Brookes.

Gibbons, D.C. (1970). *Delinquent behavior.* Englewood Cliffs, NJ: Prentice-Hall.

Gil, K., Thompson, R., Keith, B., Tota-Faucette, M., Noll, S., & Kinney, T. (1993). Sickle cell disease pain in children and adolescents: Change in pain frequency and coping strategies over time. *Journal of Pediatric Psychology, 18,* 621–637.

Gillberg, C. (1988). The neurobiology of infantile autism. *Journal of Child Psychology and Psychiatry, 29,* 257–266.

Gillberg, C., & Gillberg, I.C. (1983). Infantile autism: A total population study of reduced optimality in the pre, peri-, and neonatal period. *Journal of Autism and Developmental Disorders, 13,* 153–166.

Gillberg, C., & Steffenburg, S. (1987). Outcome and prognostic factors in infantile autism and similar conditions: A population-based study of 46 cases followed through puberty. *Journal of Autism and Developmental Disorders, 17,* 273–281.

Gillberg, C., Steffenburg, S., & Jakobsson, G. (1987). Neurobiological findings in 20 relatively gifted children with Kanner-type autism or Asperger syndrome. *Developmental Medicine and Child Neurology, 29,* 641–649.

Gillberg, C., & Svendsen, P. (1983). Childhood psychosis and computed brain scan findings. *Journal of Autism and Developmental Disorders, 13,* 19–32.

Gillberg, I.C., Hellgren, L., & Gillberg, C. (1993). Psychotic disorders diagnosed in adolescence: Outcome at age 30 years. *Journal of Child Psychology and Psychiatry and Allied Disciplines, 34,* 1173–1185.

Gillis, J.J., Gilger, J.W., Pennington, B.F., & DeFries, J.C. (1992). Attention deficit disorder in reading-disabled twins: Evidence for genetic etiology. *Journal of Abnormal Child Psychology, 20,* 303–315.

Gittelman, R., & Feingold, I. (1983). Children with reading disorders: I. Efficacy of reading remediation. *Journal of Child Psychology and Psychiatry, 24,* 167–191.

Gittelman, R., Klein, D.F., & Feingold, I. (1983). Children with reading disorders: II. Effects of methylphenidate in combination with reading remediation. *Journal of Child Psychology and Psychiatry, 24,* 193–212.

Glascoe, F.P., & Dworklin, P.H. (1993). Obstacles to effective developmental surveillance. Errors in clinical reasoning. *Journal of Developmental and Behavioral Pediatrics, 14,* 344–349.

Glish, M.A., Erlenmeyer-Kimling, L., & Watt, N. (1982). Parental assessment of the social and emotional adaptation of children at high risk for schizophrenia. In B.B. Lahey & A.E. Kazdin (Eds.), *Advances in clinical child psychology.* New York: Plenum.

Glueck, S., & Glueck, E. (1950). *Unraveling juvenile delinquency.* New York: Commonwealth Fund.

Glueck, S., & Glueck, E. (1959). *Predicting delinquency and crime.* Cambridge, MA: Harvard University Press.

Glueck, S., & Glueck, E. (1968). *Delinquents and nondelinquents in perspective.* Cambridge, MA: Harvard University Press.

Glueck, S., & Glueck, E. (1970). *Toward a typology of juvenile offenders.* New York: Grune & Stratton.

Goldberg, D., & Wolkind, S. (1992). Patterns of psychiatric disorder in adopted girls. *Journal of Child Psychology and Psychiatry, 33,* 935–950.

Golden, C.J. (1987). *Luria-Nebraska Neuropsychological Battery: Children's revision.* Los Angeles: Western Psychological Services.

Goldenberg, I., & Goldenberg, H. (1991). *Family therapy: An overview* (3rd ed.). Pacific Grove, CA: Brooks/Cole.

Goldfarb, W. (1944). The effects of early institutional care on adolescent personality: Rorschach data. *American Journal of Orthopsychiatry*, 14, 441–447.

Goldfarb, W. (1961). *Childhood schizophrenia*. Cambridge, MA: Harvard University Press.

Goldfarb, W. (1970). Childhood psychosis. In P.H. Mussen (Ed.), *Carmichael's manual of child psychology*. (3rd ed.). (Vol. 2, pp. 765–830). New York: Wiley.

Goldfarb, W., Goldfarb, N., & Pollack, R.C. (1966). Treatment of childhood schizophrenia: A three-year comparison of day and residential treatment. *Archives of General Psychiatry*, 14, 119–128.

Goldstein, A.P., Glick, B., Irwin, M.J., Pask-McCartney, C., & Rubama, I. (1989). *Reducing delinquency*. Elmsford, NY: Pergamon.

Goldstein, D.J., & Sheaffer, C.I. (1988). Ratio developmental quotients from the Bayley are comparable to later IQs for the Stanford-Binet. *American Journal on Mental Retardation*, 92, 379–380.

Goldstein, H., Moss, J.W., & Jordan, L.J. (1965). *The efficacy of special class training on the development of mentally retarded children*. Urbana: University of Illinois.

Goldstein, R., Landau, W.M., & Kleffner, F.R. (1958). Neurological assessment of deaf and aphasic children. *Transactions of the American Otological Society*, 46, 122–136.

Goodman, R. (1988). Are complications of pregnancy and birth causes of schizophrenia? *Developmental Medicine and Child Neurology*, 30, 391–396.

Goodman, R., & Stevenson, J. (1989). A twin study of hyperactivity: II. The aetiological role of genes, family relationships and perinatal adversity. *Journal of Child Psychology and Psychiatry*, 30, 691–709.

Goodson, B.D., & Hess, R.D. (1978). The effects of parent training programs on child performance and behavior. In B. Brown (Ed.), *Found: Long-term gains from early intervention* (pp. 37–78). Boulder, CO: Westview.

Gotay, C.C. (1987). Quality of life among survivors of childhood cancer: A critical review and implications for interventions. *Journal of Psychosocial Oncology*, 5, 5–23.

Gotlib, I.H., & Avison, W.R. (1993). Children at risk for psychopathology. In Costello, C.G. (Ed.), *Basic issues in psychopathology* (pp. 271–319). New York: Guilford.

Gottesfeld, H. (1965). Professionals and delinquents evaluate professional methods with delinquents. *Social Problems*, 13, 45–59.

Gottesman, I.I. (1978). Schizophrenia and genetics. In L.C. Wynne, R.L. Cromwell, & S. Matthysse, (Eds.), *The nature of schizophrenia* (pp. 59–60). New York: Wiley.

Goyette, C.H., Conners, C.K., & Ulrich, R.F. (1978). Normative data on Revised Conners Parent and Teacher Rating Scales. *Journal of Abnormal Child Psychology*, 6, 221–236.

Graber, J.A., Brooks-Gunn, J., Palkoff, R.L., & Warren, M.P. (1994). Prediction of eating problems: An 8–year study of adolescent girls. *Developmental Psychology*, 30, 823–834.

Graham, F.K., Ernhart, C.B., Craft, M., & Berman, P.W. (1963). Brain injury in the preschool child: Some developmental considerations. *Psychological Monographs*, 77, Nos. 10 and 11.

Graham, F.K., Ernhart, C.B., Thurston, D., & Craft, M. (1962). Development three years after perinatal anoxia and other potentially damaging newborn experiences. *Psychological Monographs*, 76, No. 3.

Graham, F.K., Matarazzo, R.G., & Caldwell, B.M. (1956). Behavioral differences between normal and traumatized newborns: II. Standardization, reliability and validity. *Psychological Monographs*, 70, No. 21.

Graham, J. (1990). *MMPI-2: Assessing personality and psychopathology*. New York: Oxford University Press.

Graham, J.M., Bashir, A.S., Stark, R.E., Silbert, A., & Walzer, S. (1988). Oral and written language abilities of XXY boys: Implications for anticipatory guidance. *Pediatrics*, 81, 795–806.

Grantham-McGregor, S., Schofield, W., & Powell, C. (1987). Development of severely malnourished children who received psychosocial stimulation: Six-year follow-up. *Pediatrics*, 79, 247–254.

Gray, C.D. (1989). Opening comments on the Conference on Developmental Disabilities and HIV Infection. *Mental Retardation*, 27, 199–200.

Gray, J.W., David, B., McCoy, K., & Dean, R.S. (1992). Mothers' self-reports of perinatal information as predictors of school achievement. *Journal of School Psychology*, 30, 233–243.

Green, W.H. (1991). *Child and adolescent clinical psychopharmacology*. Baltimore: Williams & Wilkins.

Greene, M. B. (1993). Chronic exposure to violence and poverty: Interventions that work for youth. *Crime and Delinquency*, 39, 106–124.

Greenfield, S.F., Swarz, M.S., Landerman, L.R., & George, L.K. (1993). Long-term psychosocial effects of childhood exposure to parental problem drinking. *American Journal of Psychiatry*, 150, 608–613.

Grenell, M.M., Glass, C.R., & Katz, K.S. (1987). Hyperactive children and peer interaction: Knowledge and performance of social skills. *Journal of Abnormal Child Psychology*, 15, 1–13.

Groden, J., & Cautela, J. (1988). Procedures to increase social interaction among adolescents with autism: A multiple baseline analysis. *Journal of Behavioural Therapy and Experimental Psychiatry*, 19, 87–93.

Gross, A.M., & Drabman, R.S. (Eds.). (1990). *Handbook of clinical behavioral pediatrics*. New York: Plenum.

Grossman, H.J. (Ed.). (1983). *Manual on terminology and classification in mental retardation*. Washington, DC: American Association on Mental Deficiency.

Groth-Marnet, G. (1990). *Handbook of psychological assessment*. (2nd ed.). New York: Wiley.

Guess, D., Sailor, W., & Keogh, W. (1977). *Language intervention programs and procedures for handicapped children: A review of the literature*. Final Project Report, U.S. Office of Education, Division of Mental Health and Mental Retardation of the Social and

Rehabilitation Services Department of the State of Kansas.

Guevremont, D. C., & Foster, S. L. (1993). Impact of social problem-solving training on aggressive boys: Skill acquisition, behavior change, and generalization. *Journal of Abnormal Child Psychology, 21,* 13–27.

Guilford, J.P. (1959). Three faces of intellect. *American Psychologist, 14,* 469–479.

Gullotta, T. P., Adams, G. R., & Montemayor, R. (1995). *Substance misuse in adolescence.* Newbury Park, CA: Sage.

Gully, K.J., & Hosch, H.M. (1979). Adaptive Behavior Scale: Development as a diagnostic tool via discriminant analysis. *American Journal of Mental Deficiency, 83,* 518–523.

Gurman, A.S., Kniskern, D.P., & Pinsof, W.M. (1986). Research on the process and outcome of marital and family therapy. In S. Garfield & A. Bergin (Eds.), *Handbook of psychotherapy and behavior change* (3rd ed.). New York: Wiley.

Hack, M., Taylor, H.G., Klein, N., Eiben, R., Schatschneider, C., & Mercui-Minich, K. (1994). School-age outcomes in children with birth weights under 750 g. *The New England Journal of Medicine, 331,* No. 12, 753–759.

Haghighi, B., & Lopez, A. (1993). Success/failure of group home treatment programs for juveniles. *Federal Probation, 57,* 53–58.

Haley, J. (1963). *Strategies of psychotherapy.* New York: Grune & Stratton.

Hall, C.W., & Haws, D. (1989). Depressive symptomatology in learning-disabled and nonlearning-disabled students. *Psychology in the Schools, 26,* 359–364.

Hall, P.K., & Tomblin, J.B. (1978). A follow-up study of children with articulation and language disorders. *Journal of Speech and Hearing Disorders, 43,* 227–241.

Hallahan, D.P., Keller, C.E., McKinney, J.D., Lloyd, J.W., & Bryan, T. (1988). Examining the research base of the Regular Education Initiative: Efficacy studies and the adaptive learning environments model. *Journal of Learning Disabilities, 21,* 29–35.

Hallgren, B. (1950). Specific dyslexia ("congenital word-blindness"): A clinical and genetic study. *Acta Psychiatrica et Neurologica Scandinavica,* Supplement 65.

Hanson, J.W. (1983). Teratogenic agents. In A.E.H. Emery & D.L. Rimoin (Eds.), *Principles and practice of medical genetics.* New York: Churchill Livingston.

Hanson, S.L., & Pichert, J.W. (1986). Perceived stress and diabetes control in adolescents. *Health Psychology, 5,* 439–452.

Hardy, J.C. (1983). *Cerebral palsy.* Englewood Cliffs, NJ: Prentice-Hall.

Harrell, R.F., Woodyard, E., & Gates, A.I. (1955). *The effects of mothers' diets on the intelligence of offspring.* New York: Teachers College.

Harrington, R. (1993). *Depressive disorder in childhood and adolescence.* New York: John Wiley & Sons.

Harris, S.L. (1989). Training parents of childen with autism: An update on models. *Behavior Therapist, 12,* 219–221.

Harris, S., & Handleman, J. (Eds.). (1994). *Preschool education programs for children with autism.* Austin, TX: Pro-Ed.

Haskins, R. (1989). Beyond metaphor: The efficacy of early childhood education. *American Psychologist, 44,* 274–282.

Hawkins, R.C., & Clement, P.F. (1980). Development and construct validity of a self-report measure of binge eating tendencies. *Addictive Behaviors, 5,* 219–226.

Heath, E., & Kosky, R. (1992). Are children who steal different from those who are aggressive? *Child Psychiatry and Human Development, 23,* 9–18.

Heber, R., & Garber, H. (1975). The Milwaukee Project. A study in the use of family intervention to prevent cultural familial mental retardation. In B.Z. Friedlander, G.M. Sterritt, & G.E. Kirk (Eds.), *Exceptional infant: Assessment and intervention* (Vol. 3, pp. 399–433). New York: Brunner/Mazel.

Hechtman, L., Weiss, G., & Perlman, T. (1984). Young adult outcome of hyperactive children receiving long-term stimulant treatment. *Journal of the American Academy of Child Psychiatry, 23,* 261–269.

Hellmuth, J. (Ed.). (1967). *Exceptional infant* (Vol. 1). New York: Brunner/Mazel.

Henderson, H.D. (1982). Human behavior genetics. *Annual Review of Psychology, 33,* 403–440.

Henggeler, S.W. (1989). *Delinquency in adolescence.* Newbury Park, CA: Sage.

Henggeler, S., Melton, G., & Smith, L. (1992). Family preservation using multisystemic therapy: An effective alternative to incarcerating serious juvenile offenders. *Journal of Consulting and Clinical Psychology, 60* (6), 001–009.

Henker, B., & Whalen, C.K. (1989). Hyperactivity and attention deficits. *American Psychologist, 44,* 216–223.

Herbert, J.D. (1995). An overview of the current status of social phobia. *Applied & Preventive Psychology, 4,* 39–51.

Herbert, J.D., Sayers, M.D., Nishitih, P., Turk, E., Salzman, D., & Belecanech, M. (1993). Cognitive-behavioral group therapy of adolescent social phobia: A pilot study. Paper presented at the meeting of the Association for Advancement of Behavior Therapy, Atlanta.

Herjanic, B., & Reich, W. (1982). Development of a structured psychiatric interview for children: Agreement between child and parent on individual symptoms. *Journal of Child Psychology, 10,* 307–324.

Heron, W.T. (1941). The inheritance of brightness and dullness in maze learning ability in the rat. *Journal of Genetic Psychology, 59,* 49–59.

Herrenkohl, L.R. (1979). Prenatal stress reduces fertility and fecundity in female offspring. *Science, 206,* 1097–1099.

Hersh, S.P. (1977). Future considerations and directions. In J.G. Schulterbrandt & A. Raskin (Eds.),

Depression in childhood: Diagnosis, treatment, and conceptual models (pp. 147–149). New York: Raven.

Heston, L.L. (1966). Psychiatric disorders in foster home reared children of schizophrenic mothers. *British Journal of Psychiatry, 112,* 819–825.

Heston, L.L., & Denny, D. (1968). Interactions between early life experience and biological factors in schizophrenia. In D. Rosenthal & S. Kety (Eds.), *The transmission of schizophrenia* (pp. 363–376). Elmsford, NY: Pergamon.

Hetherington, E.M., Cox, M., & Cox, R. (1979). Play and social interaction in children following divorce. *Journal of Social Issues, 5,* 26–49.

Hetherington, E.M., Stanley-Hagan, M., & Anderson, E.R. (1989). Marital transitions: A child's perspective. *American Psychologist, 44,* 303–312.

Hinshaw, S.P., Henker, B., Whalen, C.K., & Erhaardt, D. (1989). Aggressive, prosocial, and nonsocial behavior in hyperactive boys: Dose effects of methylphenidate in naturalistic settings. *Journal of Consulting and Clinical Psychology, 57,* 636–643.

Hinshaw, S. P., Lahey, B. B., & Hart, E. L. (1993). Issues of taxonomy and comorbidity in the development of conduct disorder. Special issue: Toward a developmental perspective on conduct disorder. *Development and Psychopathology, 5,* 31–49.

Hirshfield, D.R., Rosenbaum, J.F., Biederman, J.S., Bolduc, E.A., Faraone, S.V., Snidman, N., Reznick, J.S., & Kagan, J. (1992). Stable behavioral inhibition and its associations with anxiety disorder. *Journal of the American Academy of Child and Adolescent Psychiatry, 31,* 103–111.

Hirshoren, A., & Schnittijer, C.J. (1983). Behavior problems in blind children and youth: A prevalence study. *Psychology in the Schools, 20,* 197–201.

Ho, H., Glahn, T.J., & Ho, J. (1988). The fragile-X syndrome. *Developmental Medicine and Child Neurology, 30,* 257–261.

Hodges, K., Kline, J., Stern, L., Cytryn, L., & McKnew, D. (1982). The development of a child assessment schedule for research and clinical use. *Journal of Abnormal Child Psychology, 10,* 173–189.

Hops, H., & Cobb, J.A. (1973). Survival behaviors in the educational setting: Their implications for research and intervention. In L.A. Hamerlynck, L.C. Handy, & Mash, E.J. (Eds.), *Behavioral change: Methodology, concepts, and practice.* Champaign, IL: Research Press.

Horne, A.M., & Sayger, T.V. (1990). *Treating conduct and oppositional defiant disorders in children.* Elmsford, NY: Pergamon.

Horney, K. (1937). *The neurotic personality of our time.* New York: Norton.

Householder, J., Hatcher, R., Burns, W., & Chasnoff, I. (1982). Infants born to narcotic-addicted mothers. *Psychological Bulletin, 92,* 453–468.

Houts, A.C., Shutty, M.S., & Emery, R.E. (1985). The impact of children on adults. In B.B. Lahey & A.E. Kazdin (Eds.), *Advances in clinical child psychology* (Vol. 8, pp. 267–297). New York: Plenum.

Huesmann, L.R., & Eron, L.D. (Eds.). (1986). *Television and the aggressive child: A cross-national comparison.* Hillsdale, NJ: Erlbaum.

Hundleby, J.D., Carpenter, R.A., Ross, R., & Mercer, G.W. (1982). Adolescent drug use and other behaviors. *Journal of Child Psychology and Psychiatry, 23,* 61–68.

Hunt, G.M. (1981). Spina bifida: Implications for 100 children at school. *Developmental Medicine and Child Neurology, 23,* 160–172.

Hurt, H., Brodsky, N.L., Betancourt, L., Braitman, L.E., Melmud, E., & Giannetta, J. (1995). Cocaine-exposed children: Follow-up through 30 months. *Developmental and Behavioral Pediatrics, 16,* 29–35.

Huschka, M. (1941). Psychopathological disorders in the mother. *Journal of Nervous and Mental Disease, 94,* 76–83.

Ince, L.P. (1976). The use of relaxation training and a conditioned stimulus in the elimination of epileptic seizures in a child: A case study. *Journal of Behavior Therapy and Experimental Psychiatry, 7,* 39–42.

Ingham, R.J. (1984). *Stuttering and behavior therapy: Current status and experimental foundations.* San Diego, CA: College Hill Press.

Inoff-Germain, G., Arnold, G.S., Nottelmann, E.D., & Susman, E.J. (1988). Relations between hormone levels and observational measures of aggressive behavior of young adolescents in family interactions. *Developmental Psychology, 24,* 129–139.

International Statistical Classification of Disease, Injuries and Causes of Death (9th rev.). (1978). Geneva: World Health Organization.

Ireton, H., & Thwing, E. (1974). *Manual for the Minnesota Child Development Inventory.* Minneapolis, MN: Behavior Science Systems.

Jacklin, C.N. (1989). Female and male: Issues of gender. *American Psychologist, 44,* 127–133.

Jacobson, A.M., Hauser, S.T., Wolfsdorf, J.I., Houlihan, J., et al. (1987). Psychologic predictors of compliance in children with recent onset of diabetes mellitus. *Journal of Pediatrics, 110,* 805–811.

Jacobson, C.B., & Berlin, C.M. (1972). Possible reproductive detriment in LSD users. *Journal of the American Medical Association, 222,* 1367–1373.

Jacobson, J.W., & Mulick, J.A. (Eds.). (1996). *Manual of diagnosis and professional practice in mental retardation.* Washington, DC: American Psychological Association.

Jaffe, M.B. (1984). Neurological impairment of speech production: Assessment and treatment. In J. Costello (Ed.), *Speech disorders in children.* San Diego, CA: College Hill Press.

Jayasekara, R., & Street, J. (1978). Parental age and parity in dyslexic boys. *Journal of Biosocial Science, 10,* 255–261.

Jensen, A.R. (1980). *Bias in mental testing.* New York: Free Press.

Jensen, J., & Armstrong, R.J. (1985). *Slosson Intelligence Test (SIT) for children and adults: Expanded norm tables, application and development.* East Aurora, NY: Slosson Educational Publications.

Jensen, P.S., Traylor, J., Xenakis, S.N., & Davis, H. (1988). Child psychopathology rating scales and interrater agreement: Parents' gender and psychiatric symptoms. *Journal of the American Academy of Child and Adolescent Psychiatry, 27,* 442–450.

Jeremy, R.J., & Bernstein, V.J. (1984). Dyads at risk: Methadone-maintained women and their four-month-old infants. *Child Development, 55,* 1141–1154.

Johnson, C., Lewis, C., Lore, S., Lewis, L., & Stuckey, M. (1984). Incidence and correlates of bulimic behavior in a female high school population. *Journal of Youth and Adolescence, 13,* 15–26.

Johnson, J.H., & Bradlyn, A.S. (1988). Life events and adjustment in childhood and adolescence. In L.H. Cohen (Ed.), *Life events and psychological functioning* (pp. 64–95). Newbury Park, CA: Sage.

Johnson, J.H., & Goldman, J. (Eds.). (1990). *Developmental assessment in clinical child psychology: A handbook.* Elmsford, NY: Pergamon.

Johnson, J.H., Rasbury, W.C., & Siegel, L.J. (1986). *Approaches to child treatment.* Elmsford, NY: Pergamon.

Johnson, P.L., & O'Leary, K.D. (1987). Parental behavior patterns and conduct disorders in girls. *Journal of Abnormal Child Psychology, 15,* 573–581.

Johnston, L., O'Malley, P. M., & Bachman, J. G. (1993). *National survey results on drug use, 1975–1992* (Volume I: Secondary school students). Rockville, MD: National Institute on Drug Abuse.

Jones, K.L. (1986). Fetal alcohol syndrome. *Pediatrics in Review, 8,* 122–126.

Jones, K.L., Smith, D.W., Ulleland, C.N., & Streissguth, A.P. (1973). Pattern of malformation in offspring of chronic alcoholic mothers. *Lancet, 1,* 1267–1271.

Jones, M.C. (1924). The elimination of children's fears. *Journal of Experimental Psychology, 7,* 383–390.

Joshi, P.T., Capozzoli, J.A., & Coyle, J.T. (1988). Low-dose neuroleptic therapy for childhood-onset pervasive developmental disorder. *American Journal of Psychiatry, 145,* 335–338.

Judd, L.L., & Mandell, A.J. (1968). Chromosome studies in early autism. *Archives of General Psychiatry, 18,* 450–457.

Kagan, J. (1966). Reflection-impulsivity: The generality and dynamics of conceptual tempo. *Journal of Abnormal Psychology, 71,* 17–24.

Kagan, J., Reznick, J.S., & Snidman, N. (1988). Biological bases of childhood shyness. *Science, 240,* 167–171.

Kagan, J., Reznick, J.S., & Snidman, S. (1990). The temperamental qualities of inhibition and lack of inhibition. In M. Lewis & S.M. Miller (Eds.), *Handbook of developmental psychopathology* (pp. 219–226). New York: Plenum Press.

Kagan, J., Rosman, B., Day, D., Albert, J., & Philips, W. (1964). Information processing in the child: Significance of analytic and reflective attitudes. *Psychological Monographs, 78,* 1, Whole No. 578.

Kalakar, H.M., Kinoshita, J.H., & Donnell, G.N. (1973). Galactosemia: Biochemistry, genetics, pathophysiology and developmental aspects. *Biology of Brain Dysfunction, 1,* 31–88.

Kallam, S.G., Ensminger, M.E., & Turner, R.J. (1977). Family structure and the mental health of children. *Archives of General Psychiatry, 34,* 1012–1022.

Kallmann, F.J., & Roth, B. (1956). Genetic aspects of preadolescent schizophrenia. *American Journal of Psychiatry, 112,* 599–606.

Kamphaus, R.W., & Frick, P.J. (1996). *Clinical assessment of child and adolescent personality and behavior.* Boston: Allyn and Bacon.

Kandel, D.B., & Logan, J.A. (1984). Patterns of drug use from adolescence to young adulthood: I. Periods of risk for initiation, continued use, and discontinuation. *American Journal of Public Health, 74,* 660–666.

Kanner, L. (1943). Autistic disturbances of affective contact. *Nervous Child, 2,* 217–250.

Kanner, L. (1954). To what extent is early infantile autism determined by constitutional inadequacies? *Proceedings, Association for Research on Nervous and Mental Diseases, 33,* 378–385.

Kaplan, A.S., & Garfinkel, P.E. (Eds.). (1993). *Medical issues and the eating disorders: The interface.* New York: Brunner-Mazel.

Katusic, S.K., Colligan, R.C., Beard, C.M., O'Fallon, W.M., Bergstrahl, E.J., Jacobsen, S.J., & Kurland, L.T. (1995). Mental retardation in a birth cohort, 1976–1980. *American Journal on Mental Retardation, 100,* 335–344.

Katz, E., Rubenstein, C., Hubert, N., & Blew, A. (1988). School and social reintegration of children with cancer. *Journal of Psychosocial Oncology, 6,* 123–140.

Katz, L.F., & Gottman, J.M. (1993). Patterns of marital conflict predict children's internalizing and externalizing behaviors. *Developmental Psychology, 29,* 940–950.

Katz, S., & Kravetz, S. (1989). Facial plastic surgery for persons with Down syndrome: Research findings and their professional and social implications. *American Journal on Mental Retardation, 94,* 101–110.

Kauffman, J.M., Gerber, M.M., & Semmel, M.I. (1988). Arguable assumptions underlying the Regular Education Initiative. *Journal of Learning Disabilities, 21,* 6–11.

Kaufman, A.S., & Kaufman, N.L. (1983). *K-ABC: Kaufman Assessment Battery for Children administration and scoring manual.* Circle Pines, MN: American Guidance Service.

Kaufman, A.S., & Kaufman, N.L. (1990). *Kaufman Brief Intelligence Test.* Circle Pines, MN: American Guidance Service.

Kaufman, I., Frank, T., Friend, J., Heims, L.W., & Weiss, R. (1962). Success and failure in the treatment of childhood schizophrenia. *American Journal of Psychiatry, 118,* 909–913.

Kaufman, K.R., & Katz-Garris, L. (1979). Epilepsy, mental retardation, and anti-convulsant therapy. *American Journal of Mental Deficiency, 84,* 256–259.

Kawi, A.A., & Pasamanick, B. (1959). Prenatal and paranatal factors in the development of childhood reading disorders. *Monographs of the Society for Research in Child Development, 24*, No. 4.

Kazdin, A.E. (1973). Methodological and assessment considerations in evaluating reinforcement programs in applied settings. *Journal of Applied Behavior Analysis, 6*, 517–531.

Kazdin, A.E. (1987a). *Conduct disorders in children and adolescents.* Newbury Park, CA: Sage.

Kazdin, A.E. (1987b). Treatment of antisocial behavior in children: Current status and future directions. *Psychological Bulletin, 102*, 187–203.

Kazdin, A.E. (1988). *Child psychotherapy: Developing and identifying effective treatments.* Elmsford, NY: Pergamon.

Kazdin, A.E. (1990). Childhood depression. *Journal of Child Psychology and Psychiatry, 31*, 121–160.

Kazdin, A. E. (1995). *Conduct disorders in childhood and adolescence.* Newbury Park, CA: Sage.

Kearney, C.A., & Silverman, W.K. (1990). A preliminary analysis of a functional model of assessment and treatment for school refusal behavior. *Behavior Modification, 14*, 340–366.

Keat, D.B. (1974). A reinforcement survey schedule for children. *Psychological Reports, 35*, 287–293.

Keat, D.B. (1979). *Multimodal therapy with children.* Elmsford, NY: Pergamon.

Keat, D.B. (1990). *Child multimodal therapy.* Norwood, NJ: Ablex.

Keenan, K., & Shaw, D. S. (1994). The development of aggression in toddlers: A study of low-income families. *Journal of Abnormal Child Psychology, 22*, 53–77.

Kellogg, C., Tervo, D., Ison, J., Parisi, T., & Miller, R.K. (1980). Prenatal exposure to diazepam alters behavioral development in rats. *Science, 207*, 205–207.

Kelly, T.E. (1986). *Clinical genetics and genetic counseling.* Chicago: Year Book Medical Publishers.

Kemper, K.J., Osborn, L.M., Hansen, D.F., & Pascoe, J.H. (1994). Family psychosocial screening: Should we focus on high-risk settings? *Journal of Developmental and Behavioral Pediatrics, 15*, 336–341.

Kendall, P.C. (1991). *Child and adolescent therapy: Cognitive-behavioral procedures.* New York: Guilford.

Kendall, P.C. (1993). Cognitive-behavioral therapies with youth: Guiding theory, current status, and emerging developments. *Journal of Consulting and Clinical Psychology, 61*, 235–247.

Kendall, P.C. (1994). Treating anxiety disorders in children. A controlled trial. *Journal of Consulting and Clinical Psychology, 62*, 100–110.

Kendall, P.C., & Finch, A.J. (1979). Developing nonimpulsive behavior in children: Cognitive behavioral strategies for self control. In P.C. Kendall & S.D. Hollon (Eds.), *Cognitive-behavioral interventions: Theory, research, and procedures* (pp. 37–79). New York: Academic Press.

Kendall, P.C., MacDonald, J.P., & Treadwell, K.R.H. (1995). The treatment of anxiety disorders in youth. In A.R. Eisen, C.A., Kearney, & C.E. Schaefer (Eds.), *Clinical handbook of anxiety disorders in children and adolescents,* Northvale, NJ: Jason Aronson.

Kendall, P.C., & Panichelli-Mindel, S.M. (1995). Cognitive-behavioral treatments. *Journal of Abnormal Child Psychology, 23*, 107–124.

Kendall, P.C., & Ronan, K.R. (1989). *The Children's Anxious Self-Statement Questionnaire (CASSQ).* Philadelphia, PA: Psychology Department, Temple University.

Kendall, P.C., & Southam-Gerow, M.A. (1996). Long-term follow-up of a cognitive-behavioral therapy for anxiety-disordered youth. *Journal of Consulting and Clinical Psychology, 64*, 724–730.

Kendall-Tackett, K.A., Williams, L.M., & Finkelhor, D. (1993). Impact of sexual abuse on children: A review and synthesis of recent empirical studies. *Psychological Bulletin, 113*, 164–180.

Kendler, K.S., Heath, A., Martin, N.G., & Eaves, L.J. (1986). Symptoms of anxiety and depression in a volunteer twin population. *Archives of General Psychiatry, 43*, 213–221.

Kessler, J. (1966). *Psychopathology of childhood.* Englewood Cliffs, NJ: Prentice-Hall.

Kestenbaum, C.J. (1978). Child psychosis: Psychotherapy. In B.B. Wolman, J. Egan, & A.O. Ross (Eds.), *Handbook of treatment of mental disorders in childhood and adolescence* (pp. 354–384). Englewood Cliffs, NJ: Prentice-Hall.

Kingston, L. M., & Prior, M. (1995). The development of patterns of stable, transient, and school-age onset aggressive behavior in young children. *Journal of the American Academy of Child and Adolescent Psychiatry, 34*, 348–358.

Kinsbourne, M., & Caplan, P.J. (1979). *Children's learning and attention problems.* Boston: Little, Brown.

Kirigin, K.A., Wolf, M.M., & Phillips, E.L. (1979). Achievement Place: A preliminary outcome evaluation. In J.S. Stumphauzer (Ed.), *Progress in behavior therapy with delinquents* (pp. 118–145). Springfield, IL: Thomas.

Kirk, S.A., & Kutchins, H. (1992). *The selling of DSM: The rhetoric of science in psychiatry.* New York: Aldine de Gruyter.

Kitchen, W., Orgill, A., Lissenden, J., Yu, V., & Campbell, N. (1987). Outcome of infants of birth weight 500 to 999 g: A continuing regional study of 5-year-old survivors. *Journal of Pediatrics, 111*, 761–766.

Klein, R.G. (1991). Parent-child agreement in clinical assessment of anxiety and other psychopathology: A review. *Journal of Anxiety Disorders, 5*, 187–198.

Knitzer, J. (1984). Mental health services to children and adolescents: A national view of public policies. *American Psychologist, 39*, 905–911.

Knobloch, H., Stevens, F., Malone, A., Ellison, P., & Risemberg, H. (1979). The validity of parental reporting of infant development. *Pediatrics, 63*, 872–878.

Knoff, H.M. (Ed.) (1986). *The assessment of child and adolescent personality.* New York: Guilford.

Knox, L.S., Albano, A.M., & Barlow, D.H. (1996). Parental involvement in the treatment of childhood obsessive-compulsive disorder: A multiple-baseline examination incorporating parents. *Behavior Therapy, 27,* 93–115.

Koegel, R.L., O'Dell, M.C., & Koegel, L.K. (1987). A natural language teaching paradigm for nonverbal autistic children. *Journal of Autism and Developmental Disorders, 17,* 187–200.

Koller, H., Richardson, S.A., Katz, M., & McLaren, J. (1983). Behavior disturbance since childhood among a 5–year birth cohort of all mentally retarded young adults in a city. *American Journal of Mental Deficiency, 87,* 386–395.

Kolvin, I., & Fundudis, T. (1981). Elective mute children: Psychological development and background factors. *Journal of Child Psychology and Psychiatry, 22,* 219–232.

Kong, E. (1969). Very early treatment of cerebral palsy. In J.M. Wolf (Ed.), *The results of treatment in cerebral palsy.* Springfield, IL: Thomas.

Korner, A.R. (1974). The effect of infants' state, level of arousal, sex, and ontogenetic stages on the caregiver. In M. Lewis & L.A. Rosenblum (Eds.), *The effect of the infant on its caregiver.* New York: Wiley.

Kotses, H., Stout, C., McConnaughy, K., Winder, J., & Creer, T. (1996). Evaluation of individualized asthma self-management programs. *Journal of Asthma, 33,* 113–118.

Kovacs, M. (1985). The Interview Schedule for Children (ISC). *Psychopharmacology Bulletin, 21,* 991–994.

Kovacs, M. (1985). The natural history and course of depressive disorders in childhood. *Psychiatric Annals, 15,* 387–389.

Kovacs, M., & Beck, A.T. (1977). An empirical-clinical approach toward a definition of childhood depression. In J.G. Schulterbrandt & A. Raskin (Eds.), *Depression in childhood: Diagnosis, treatment, and conceptual models* (pp. 1–25). New York: Raven Press.

Kozel, N.J., & Adams, E.H. (1986). Epidemiology of drug abuse: An overview. *Science, 234,* 970–974.

Kratochwill, T.R., & Morris, R.J. (Eds.). (1990). *The practice of child therapy* (2nd ed.). Elmsford, NY: Pergamon.

Kruesi, M.J.P., Rapoport, J.L., Cummings, E.M., & Berg, C.J. (1987). Effects of sugar and aspartame on aggression and activity in children. *American Journal of Psychiatry, 144,* 1487–1490.

Kupfer, A. (June 20, 1988). What to do about drugs, *Fortune,* pp. 39–41.

Kurdek, L.A., & Sinclair, R.J. (1988). Adjustment of young adolescents in two-parent nuclear, stepfather, and mother-custody families. *Journal of Consulting and Clinical Psychology, 56,* 91–96.

Kutcher, S., & Marton, P. (1991). Affective disorders in first degree relatives of adolescent onset bipolars, unipolars, and normal controls. *Journal of the American Academy of Child and Adolescent Psychiatry, 30,* 75–78.

Lab, S. P., Shields, G., & Schondel, C. (1993). Research note: An evaluation of juvenile sexual offender treatment. *Crime and Delinquency, 39,* 543–553.

LaBuda, M.C., Gottesman, I.I., & Pauls, D.L. (1993). Usefulness of twin studies for exploring the etiology of childhood and adolescent psychiatric disorders. *American Journal of Medical Genetics, 48,* 47–59.

Lachar, D., & Gruber, C.P. (1995). *The Personality Inventory for Youth.* Los Angeles: Western Psychological Services.

Lachar, D., Kline, R.B., & Boersma, D.C. (1986). The Personality Inventory for Children. In H.M. Knoff (Ed.), *The assessment of child and adolescent personality* (pp. 273–308). New York: Guilford.

LaGreca, A.M., Siegel, L.J., Wallander, J.L., & Walker, C.E. (Eds.). (1992). *Stress and coping in child health.* New York: Guilford.

LaGrow, S.J., & Repp, A.C. (1984). Stereotypic responding: A review of intervention research. *American Journal of Mental Deficiency, 88,* 595–609.

Lambert, N., Leland, H., & Nihira, K. (1992). *AAMR Adaptive Behavior Scales—School: Second Edition.* San Antonio, TX: Psychological Corporation.

Lambert, N.M., Windmiller, M., Tharinger, D., & Cole, L. (1981). *AAMD Adaptive Behavior Scale: School Edition.* New York: McGraw-Hill.

Lande, J., Scarr, S., & Gunzenhauser, N. (Eds.). (1989). *Caring for children: Challenge to America.* Hillsdale, NJ: Lawrence Erlbaum.

Landesman, S., & Ramey, C. (1989). Developmental psychology and mental retardation: Integrating scientific principles with treatment practices. *American Psychologist, 44,* 409–415.

Lang, P.J., & Melamed, B.G. (1969). Avoidance conditioning therapy of an infant with chronic ruminative vomiting: Case report. *Journal of Abnormal Psychology, 74,* 1–8.

Last, C.G., & Hersen, M. (Eds.). (1989). *Handbook of child psychiatric diagnosis.* New York: Wiley.

Last, C.G., Strauss, C.C., & Francis, G. (1987). Comorbidity among childhood anxiety disorders. *Journal of Nervous and Mental Disease, 175,* 726–730.

Lavigne, J.V., & Faier-Routman, J. (1993). Correlates of psychological adjustment to pediatric physical disorders: A meta-analytic review and comparison with existing models. *Journal of Developmental and Behavioral Pediatrics, 14,* 117–123.

Lobato, D., Faust, D., & Spirito, A. (1988). Examining the effects of chronic disease and disability in children's sibling relationships. *Journal of Pediatric Psychology, 13,* 389–407.

Lazar, I., Darlington, R., Murray, H., Royce, J., & Snipper, A. (1982). Lasting effects of early education: A report from the consortium for longitudinal studies. *Monographs of the Society for Research in Child Development, 47,* 1–151.

Lazarus, A.A. (Ed.). (1976). *Multimodal behavior therapy.* New York: Springer.

Lazarus, A.A., & Abramovitz, A. (1962). The use of "emotive imagery" in the treatment of children's phobias. *Journal of Mental Science, 108,* 191–195.

Lazarus, A.A., Davison, G.C., & Polefka, D.A. (1965). Classical and operant factors in the treatment of school phobia. *Journal of Abnormal Psychology, 70,* 225–229.

Leane, M.C., Swedo, S.E., Leonard, H.L., Pauls, D.L., Sceery, W., & Rapoport, J.L. (1990). Psychiatric disorders in first degree relatives of children and adolescents with obsessive-compulsive disorder. *Journal of the American Academy of Child and Adolescent Psychiatry, 29,* 407–412.

Lee, H., & Barratt, M.S. (1993). Cognitive development of preterm low birth weight children at 5 to 8 years old. *Journal of Developmental and Behavioral Pediatrics, 14,* 242–249.

Leigh, J. (1987). Adaptive behavior of children with learning disabilities. *Journal of Learning Disabilities, 20,* 557–562.

Lejeune, J., Gautier, M., & Turpin, R. (1959). Le monogolisme: Premier example d'aberration autosomique humaine. *Annales de Genetique, 1,* 41.

Leland, H., & Smith, D.E. (1965). *Play therapy with mentally subnormal children.* New York: Grune & Stratton.

Leonard, H.L., & Topol, D.A. (1993). Elective mutism. *Child & Adolescent Psychiatry Clinics of North America, 2,* 695–707.

Leonard, M.F., Landy, G., Ruddle, F.H., & Lubs, H.A. (1974). Early development of children with abnormalities of the sex chromosomes: A prospective study. *Pediatrics, 54,* 208–212.

Lerer, R.J. (1987). Motor tics, Tourette syndrome, and learning disabilities. *Journal of Learning Disabilities, 20,* 266–267.

Lesser, S.R. (1972). Psychoanalysis with children. In B. Wolman (Ed.), *Manual of child psychopathology* (pp. 847–864). New York: McGraw-Hill.

Levenson, H., & Pope, K.S. (1988). Behavior therapy and cognitive therapy. In H.H. Goldman (Ed.), *Review of General Psychiatry, 2,* 529–539.

Levin, G.B., Trickett, E.J., & Hess, R.E. (Eds.). (1990). *Ethical implications of primary prevention.* New York: Haworth.

Levitt, E.E. (1971). Research on psychotherapy with children. In A.E. Bergin & S.L. Garfield (Eds.), *Handbook of psychotherapy and behavior change* (pp. 474–494). New York: Wiley.

Levy, D. (1938). "Release therapy" in young children. *Psychiatry, 1,* 387–390.

Levy, S., Zoltak, B., & Saelens, T. (1988). A comparison of obstetrical records of autistic and nonautistic referrals for psychoeducational evaluations. *Journal of Autism and Developmental Disorders, 18,* 573–581.

Lewinsohn, P.M., Klein, D.N.A., & Sweeley, J.R. (1995). Bipolar disorders in a community sample of older adolescents: Prevalence, phenomenology, comorbidity, and course. *Journal of the Academy of Child and Adolescent Psychiatry, 34,* 454–463.

Lewinsohn, P.M., & Rohde, P. (1993). The cognitive-behavioral treatment of depression in adolescents: Research and suggestions. *The Clinical Psychologist, 46,* 177–183.

Lewinsohn, P.M., & Rohde, P., & Seeley, J.R. (1996). Adolescent suicidal ideation and attempts: Prevalence, risk factors, and clinical implications. *Clinical Psychology: Science and Practice, 3,* 25–46.

Lewis, D.O., Lovely, R., Yeager, C., & Femina, D. (1989). Toward a theory of the genesis of violence: A follow-up study of delinquents. *Journal of the American Academy of Child and Adolescent Psychiatry, 28,* 838–845.

Lewis, D.O., Moy, E., & Jackson, L.D. (1985). Biopsychosocial characteristics of children who later murder: A prospective study. *American Journal of Psychiatry, 142,* 1161–1167.

Lewis, D.O., Pincus, J.H., & Bard, B. (1988). Neuropsychiatric, psychoeducational, and family characteristics of 14 juveniles condemned to death in the United States. *American Journal of Psychiatry, 145,* 584–589.

Lewis, D.O., Shanok, S.S., Pincus, J.H., & Glaser, G.H. (1979). Violent juvenile delinquents: Psychiatric, neurological, psychological, and abuse factors. *American Journal of Child Psychiatry, 18,* 307–319.

Liaw, F., & Brooks-Gunn, J. (1994). Cumulative familial risks and low-birthweight in children's cognitive and behavioral development. *Journal of Clinical Child Psychology, 23,* 360–372.

Lindsley, O.R. (1960). Characteristics of the behavior of chronic psychotics as revealed by free-operant conditioning methods. *Diseases of the Nervous System, 21* (Monograph Supplement), 66–78.

Linehan, M. (1980). Content validity: Its relevance to behavioral assessment. *Behavioral Assessment, 2,* 147–159.

Lipman, R.S. (1970). The use of psychopharmacological agents in residential facilities for the retarded. In F.J. Menolascino (Ed.), *Psychiatric approaches to mental retardation* (pp. 387–398). New York: Basic Books.

Little, V.L., & Kendall, P.C. (1979). Cognitive-behavioral interventions with delinquents: Problem-solving, role-taking, and self-control. In P.C. Kendall & S.D. Hollon (Eds.), *Cognitive-behavioral interventions* (pp. 81–114). New York: Academic Press.

Loeber, R. (1988). Natural histories of conduct problems, delinquency, and associated substance abuse: Evidence for developmental progressions. In B.B. Lahey & A.E. Kazdin (Eds.), *Advances in clinical child psychology* (pp. 73–124). New York: Plenum.

Loeber, R., & Lahey, B.B. (1989). Recommendations for research on disruptive behavior disorders of childhood and adolescence. In B.B. Lahey & A.E. Kazdin (Eds.), *Advances in clinical child psychology* (Vol. 12, pp. 221–251). New York: Plenum.

Loehlin, J.C. (1992). *Genes and environment in personality development.* Newbury Park, CA: Sage.

Logue, A.W., Ophir, I., & Strauss, K.E. (1981). The acquisition of taste aversions in humans. *Behavior Research and Therapy, 19*, 319–333.

Long, N., & Forehand, R. (1987). The effects of parental divorce and parental conflict on children: An overview. *Developmental and Behavioral Pediatrics, 8*, 292–296

Long, P., Forehand, R., Wierson, M., & Morgan, A. (1994). Does parent training with young noncompliant children have long-term effects? *Behavior Research and Therapy, 32*, 101–107.

Lorenz, K. (1966). *On aggression.* New York: Harcourt Brace Jovanovich.

Lorin, R.P. (Ed.). (1990). *Protecting the children: Strategies for optimizing emotional and behavioral development.* New York: Haworth.

Lovaas, O.I. (1987). Behavioral treatment and normal educational and intellectual functioning in young autistic children. *Journal of Consulting and Clinical Psychology, 55*, 3–9.

Lovaas, O.I., Berberich, J.P., Perloff, B.F., & Schaeffer, B. (1966). Acquisition of imitative speech by schizophrenic children. *Science, 151*, 705–707.

Lovaas, O.I., Koegel, R., Simmons, J.Q., & Stevens-Long, J. (1973). Some generalization and follow-up measures on autistic children in behavior therapy. *Journal of Applied Behavior Analysis, 6*, 131–166.

Lovaas, O.I., & Smith, T. (1988). Intensive behavioral treatment for young autistic children. In B.B. Lahey & A.E. Kazdin (Eds.), *Advances in clinical child psychology* (Vol. 11, pp. 285–324). New York: Plenum.

Lovaas, O.I., Young, D.B., & Newsom, C.D. (1978). Childhood psychosis: Behavioral treatment. In B.B. Wolman, J. Egan, & A.O. Ross (Eds.), *Handbook of treatment of mental disorders in childhood and adolescence* (pp. 385–420). Englewood Cliffs, NJ: Prentice-Hall.

Lozoff, B. (1989). Nutrition and behavior. *American Psychologist, 44*, 231–236.

Lubs, H.A., & Walnowska, J. (1977). New chromosomal syndromes and mental retardation. In P. Mittler (Ed.), *Research to practice in mental retardation* (Vol. 3, pp. 55–70). Baltimore: University Park Press.

Luckasson, R., Coulter, D.L., Polloway, E.A., Reiss, S., Schalock, R.L., Snell, M.E., Spitalnik, D., & Stark, J.A. (1992). *Mental retardation: Definition, classification, and systems of supports.* Washington, DC: American Association on Mental Retardation.

Lykken, D. T. (1978). The diagnosing of zygosity in twins. *Behavior Genetics, 8*, 437–473.

Lynch, M., & Cicchetti, D. (1991). Patterns of relatedness in maltreated and nonmaltreated children: Connections among multiple representational models. *Development and Psychopathology, 3*, 207–226.

Lynskey, M. T., & Fergusson, D. M. (1995). Childhood conduct problems—attention deficit behaviors—predict adolescent substance use. *Journal of Abnormal Child Psychology, 23*, 281–302.

Lyon, G.R. (Ed.). (1994). *Frames of reference for the assessment of learning disabilities: New views on measurement issues.* Baltimore, MD: Brookes.

Lyon, J. M., Henggeler, S. W., & Hall, J. A. (1992). The family relations, peer relations, and criminal activities of Caucasian and Hispanic-American gang members. *Journal of Abnormal Child Psychology, 20*, 439–449.

Maccario, M., Hefferen, S.J., Keblusek, S.J., & Lipinski, K.A. (1982). Developmental dysphasia and electroencephalographic abnormalities. *Developmental Medicine and Child Neurology, 24*, 141–155.

Maccoby, E.E., & Jacklin, C.O. (1974). *The psychology of sex differences.* Stanford, CA: Stanford University Press.

Maccoby, E.E., & Jacklin, C.O. (1980). Sex differences in aggression: A rejoinder and reprise. *Child Development, 51*, 964–980.

Macfarlane, J.W., Allen, L., & Honzik, M.P. (1954). *A developmental study of the behavior problems of normal children between twenty-one months and fourteen years.* Berkeley, CA: University of California Press.

MacGregor, R., Pullar, A., & Cundall, D. (1994). Silent at school. Elective mutism and abuse. *Archives of Diseases of Children, 70*, 540–541.

MacLean, W.E. Jr. (Ed.). (1996). *Handbook of mental deficiency, psychological theory and research.* Mahwah, NJ: Lawrence Erlbaum

MacMillan, D.L., Jones, R.L., & Aloia, G.F. (1974). The mentally retarded label: A theoretical analysis and review of research. *American Journal of Mental Deficiency, 79*, 241–261.

MacMillan, D.L., Jones, R.L., & Meyers, C.E. (1976). Mainstreaming the mildly retarded: Some questions, cautions and guidelines. *Mental Retardation, 14*, 3–10.

MacMillan, H.L., MacMillan, J.H., Offord, D.R., & Griffith, L. et al. (1994). Primary prevention of child physical abuse and neglect: A critical review. *Journal of Child Psychology & Psychiatry & Allied Disciplines, 35*, 835–856.

Magrab, P.R., & Johnson, R.B. (1980). Mental retardation. In S. Gabel & M.T. Erickson (Eds.), *Child development and developmental disabilities* (pp. 241–257). Boston, MA: Little, Brown.

Mahoney, G., & O'Sullivan, P. (1990). Early intervention practices with families of children with handicaps. *Mental Retardation, 28*, 169–176.

Malinosky-Rummell, R., & Hansen, D.J. (1993). Long-term consequences of childhood physical abuse. *Psychological Bulletin, 114*, 68–79.

Mallick, S.K., & McCandless, B. R. (1966). A study of catharsis of aggression. *Journal of Personality and Social Psychology, 4*, 591–596.

Malone, M.A., Kershner, J.R., & Siegel, L. (1988). The effects of methylphenidate on levels of processing and laterality in children with attention deficit disorder. *Journal of Abnormal Child Psychology, 16*, 379–395.

Mandoki, M. W., Sumner, G. S., & Matthews-Ferrari, K. (1992). Evaluation and treatment of rage in children and adolescents. *Child Psychiatry and Human Development, 22,* 227–235.

Manella, K.J., & Varni, J.W. (1981). Behavior therapy in a gait-training program for a child with myelomeningocele. *Physical Therapy, 61,* 1284–1287.

Mannuzza, S., Klein, R.G., Konig, P.H., & Giampino, T.L. (1989). Hyperactive boys almost grown up. *Archives of General Psychiatry, 46,* 1073–1079.

Marc, D., & MacDonald, L. (1988). Respite care—who uses it? *Mental Retardation, 26,* 93–96.

March, J.S. (1995). *Anxiety disorders in children and adolescents.* New York: Guilford Press.

Marks, P.A., Seeman, W., & Haller, D.L. (1974). *The actuarial use of the MMPI with adolescents and adults.* Baltimore: Williams & Wilkins.

Markwardt, F.C. (1989). *Peabody Individual Achievement Test-Revised Manual.* Circle Pines, MN: American Guidance Service.

Marlowe, M., Errera, J., & Jacobs, J. (1983). Increased lead and cadmium burdens among mentally retarded children and children with borderline intelligence. *American Journal of Mental Deficiency, 87,* 477–483.

Marmar, C.R. (1988). Brief dynamic psychotherapy. In H.H. Goldman (Ed.), *Review of General Psychiatry* (pp. 515–523). Connecticut: Appleton & Lange.

Marteau, T.M., Bloch, S., & Baum, J.D. (1987). Family life and diabetic control. *Journal of Child Psychology and Psychiatry, 28,* 823–833.

Mary, N.L. (1990). Reactions of black, Hispanic, and white mothers to having a child with handicaps. *Mental Retardation, 28,* 1–5.

Mash, E.J., & Barkley, R.A. (Eds.). (1989). *Treatment of childhood disorders.* New York: Guilford.

Mash, E.J., & Terdal, L.G. (Eds.). (1997). *Behavioral assessment of childhood disorders* (3rd ed.). New York: Guilford.

Massimo, J.L., & Shore, M.F. (1963). The effectiveness of a comprehensive vocationally oriented psychotherapeutic program for adolescent delinquent boys. *American Journal of Orthopsychiatry, 33,* 634–642.

Matson, J.L., & Mulick, J.A. (Eds.). (1991). *Handbook of mental retardation* (2nd ed.). New York: Pergamon Press.

Matson, J.L., & Ollendick, T.H. (1988). *Assessing and training children's social skills.* Oxford, England: Pergamon.

Matthews, H.B., & der Brucke, M.G. (1938). "Normal expectancy" in the extremely obese pregnant woman. *Journal of the American Medical Association, 110,* 554–559.

Matthews, K.A., & Jennings, J.R. (1984). Cardiovascular responses of boys exhibiting the Type A behavior pattern. *Psychosomatic Medicine, 46,* 484–497.

Mattison, R., Cantwell, D.P., Russell, A.T., & Will, L. (1979). A comparison of DSM-II and DSM-III in the diagnosis of childhood psychiatric disorders. II.

Interrater agreement. *Archives of General Psychiatry, 36,* 1217–1223.

May, D.C., & Turnbull, N. (1992). Plastic surgeons' opinions of facial surgery for individuals with Down syndrome. *Mental Retardation, 30,* 29–33.

Mayfield, K.L., Forman, S.S., & Nagle, R.J. (1984). Reliability of the AAMD Adaptive Behavior Scale—Public School Version. *Journal of School Psychology, 22,* 53–61.

McArdle, P., O'Brien, G., & Kolvin, I. (1995). Hyperactivity: Prevalence and relationship with conduct disorder. *Journal of Child Psychology and Psychiatry, 36,* 279–303.

McArthur, D.S., & Roberts, G.F. (1982). *Roberts Apperception Test for Children.* Los Angeles: Western Psychological Services.

McCartney, J.R., & Holden, J.C. (1981). In J.R. Matson & J.R. McCartney (Eds.), *Handbook of behavior modification with the mentally retarded* (pp. 29–60). New York: Plenum.

McCord, J., & Tremblay, R.E. (Eds.). (1992). Preventing antisocial behavior: Interventions from birth through adolescence. New York: Guilford Press.

McCorkle, L.W., Elias, A., & Bixby, F.L. (1958). *The Highfields story.* New York: Holt, Rinehart, & Winston.

McCoy, J.F., & Buckholt, J.A. (1981). Language acquisition. In J.L. Matson & J.R. McCartney (Eds.), *Handbook of behavior modification with the mentally retarded* (pp. 281–330). New York: Plenum.

McDermott, S., Mani, S., & Krishnaswami, S. (1995). A population-based analysis of specific behavior problems associated with childhood seizures. *Journal of Psychology, 127,* 547–551.

McEachin, J., Smith, T., & Lovaas, O.I. (1993). Long-term outcome for children with autism who received early behavioral treatment. *American Journal on Mental Retardation, 97* (4), 359–372.

McGee, J.J., Menolascino, F.J., Hobbs, D.C., & Menousek, P.E. (1987). *Gentle teaching: A nonaversive approach for helping persons with mental retardation.* New York: Human Sciences Press.

McLaren, J., & Bryson, S.E. (1987). Review of recent epidemiological studies of mental retardation: Prevalence, associated disorders, and etiology. *American Journal on Mental Retardation, 92,* 243–254.

McLeod, J. (1979). Educational underachievement: Towards a defensible psychometric definition. *Journal of Learning Disabilities, 12,* 322–330.

Mednick, S.A., Gabrielli, W.F., & Hutchings, B. (1984). Genetic influences in criminal convictions: Evidence from an adoption cohort. *Science, 224,* 891–894.

Meichenbaum, D.H., & Goodman, J. (1971). Training impulsive children to talk to themselves. *Journal of Abnormal Psychology, 77,* 115–126.

Meisels, S., & Shonkoff, J. (Eds.). (1992). *Handbook of early childhood intervention.* Cambridge: Cambridge University Press.

Melamed, B.G., Matthews, K.A., Routh, D.K., Stabler, B., & Schneiderman, N. (Eds.). (1988). *Child health* psychology. Hillsdale, NJ: Lawrence Erlbaum Associates.

Melton, B.G. (1983). *Child advocacy.* New York: Plenum.

Menke, J.A., McClead, R.E., & Hansen, N.B. (1991). Perspectives on perinatal complication associated with mental retardation. In J.L. Matson & J.A. Mulick (Eds.), *Handbook of mental retardation* (2nd ed.). New York: Pergamon Press.

Merton, R.K. (1957). *Social theory and social structure* (pp. 131–160). New York: Free Press.

Meyers, A.F., Sampson, A.E., Weitzman, M., Rogers, B.L., & Kayne, H. (1989). School breakfast program and school performance. *American Journal of Diseases of Children, 143,* 1234–1239.

Meyers, D.I., & Goldfarb, W. (1961). Studies of perplexity in matters of schizophrenic children. *American Journal of Psychiatry, 31,* 551–564.

Middleton, H.A., Keene, R.G., & Brown, G.W. (1990). Convergent and discriminant validities of the Scales of Independent Behavior and the Revised Vineland Adaptive Behavior Scales. *American Journal on Mental Retardation, 94,* 669–673.

Mikkelsen, M., & Stene, J. (1970). Genetic counseling in Down's syndrome. *Human Heredity, 20,* 457–464.

Milkovich, L., & Van den Berg, B.J. (1974). Effects of prenatal meprobamate and chlordiazepoxide hydrochloride on human embryonic and fetal development. *New England Journal of Medicine, 291,* 1268–1271.

Miller, W.B. (1958). Lower-class culture as a generating milieu of gang delinquency. *Journal of Social Issues, 14,* 5–19.

Millman, R.B. (1978). Drug and alcohol abuse. In B.B. Wolman, J. Egan, & A.O. Ross (Eds.), *Handbook of treatment of mental disorders in childhood adolescence* (pp. 238–267). Englewood Cliffs, NJ: Prentice-Hall.

Mills, J. K., & Andrianopoulos, G. D. (1993). The relationship between childhood onset obesity and psychopathology in adulthood. *Journal of Psychology, 127,* 547–551.

Minuchin, S. (1974). *Families and family therapy.* Cambridge, MA: Harvard University Press.

Minuchin, S., Baker, L., Rosman, B.L., Liebman, R., Milman, L., & Todd, T.C. (1975). A conceptual model of psychosomatic illness in children. *Archives of General Psychiatry, 32,* 1031–1038.

Mischel, W. (1968). *Personality and assessment.* New York: Wiley.

Mischel, W. (1979). On the interface of cognition and personality. *American Psychologist, 34,* 740–754.

Mitchell, J.E. (1986). Anorexia nervosa: Medical and physiological aspects. In K.D. Brownell & J.P. Foreyt (Eds.), *Handbook of eating disorders* (pp. 247–265). New York: Basic Books.

Moffatt, M.E.K. (1989). Nocturnal enuresis: Psychologic implications of treatment and nontreatment. *Journal of Pediatrics, 114,* 697–704.

Moffit, T. E. (1993). Adolescence-limited and life-course-persistent antisocial behavior: A developmental taxonomy. *Psychological Bulletin, 100,* 674–701.

Moffitt, T.E., & Silva, P.A. (1988). Self-reported delinquency, neuropsychological deficit, and history of attention deficit disorder. *Journal of Abnormal Child Psychology, 16,* 553–569.

Monda, J.M., & Husman, D.A. (1995). Primary nocturnal enuresis: A comparison among observation, imipramine, desmopressin acetate and bed-wetting alarm systems. *Journal of Urology, 154,* 745–758.

Moore, K.L. (1982). *The developing human: Clinically oriented embryology* (3rd ed.). Philadelphia: Saunders.

Morrison, T.L., & Newcomer, B.L. (1975). Effects of directive vs. nondirective play therapy with institutionalized mentally retarded children. *American Journal of Mental Deficiency, 79,* 666–669.

Moses, J.A., Silva, J.C., & Ratliff, R.G. (1981). Discrimination learning in delinquents as a function of sex, subtype, and social reinforcement. *Journal of Genetic Psychology, 138,* 147–148.

Mostofsky, D. (1978). Epilepsy: Returning the ghost to psychology. *Professional Psychology, 9,* 87–92.

Mullins, L.L., Siegel, L.J., & Hodges, K. (1985). Cognitive problem-solving and life event correlates of depressive symptoms in children. *Journal of Abnormal Child Psychology, 13,* 305–314.

Mumpower, D. L. (1970). Sex ratios found in various types of referred exceptional children. *Exceptional Children, 36,* 621–622.

Murphy, D.A., Pelham, W.E., & Lang, A.R. (1992). Aggression in boys with attention deficit hyperactivity disorder: Methylphenidate effects on naturalistically observed aggression, response to provocation, and social information processing. *Journal of Abnormal Child Psychology, 20* (5), 451–466.

Murray, D.M., Matthews, K.A., Blake, S.M., Prineas, R.J., & Gillum, R.F. (1986). Type A behavior in children: Demographic, behavioral, and physiological correlates. *Health Psychology, 5,* 159–169.

Murray, H.A. (1943). *Thematic Apperception Test.* Cambridge, MA: Harvard University Press.

Muzyczka, M.J., & Erickson, M.T. (1976). WISC characteristics of reading disabled children identified by three objective methods. *Perceptual and Motor Skills, 43,* 595–602.

Nader, P.R., Sallis, J.F., Abramson, I.S., Broyles, S.L., Patterson, T.L., Senn, K., Rupp, J.W., & Nelson, J.A. (1992). Family-based cardiovascular risk reduction education among Mexican- and Anglo-Americans. *Family Community Health, 15,* 57–74.

National Institute on Drug Abuse (1991, Spring). Trends in drug use by high school seniors. *NIDA Notes,* p. 35.

Neal, M. (1970). The relationship between a regimen of vestibular stimulation and the developmental behavior of the premature infant. *Dissertation Abstracts International, 30,* No. 10.

Needleman, H.L., & Bellinger, D. (1984). The developmental consequences of childhood exposure to lead. In B.B. Lahey & A.E. Kazdin (Eds.), *Advances in clinical child psychology* (Vol. 7, pp. 195–220). New York: Plenum.

Nelles, W.B., & Barlow, D.H. (1988). Do children panic? *Clinical Psychology Review, 8,* 359–372.

Nelson, W.M., Finch, A.J., & Hooke, J.F. (1975). Effects of reinforcement and response cost on cognitive styles in emotionally disturbed boys. *Journal of Abnormal Psychology, 84,* 426–428.

Newcomb, M.D., & Bentler, P.M. (1989). Substance use and abuse among children and teenagers. *American Psychologist, 44,* 242–248.

Newcomber, B.L., & Morrison, T.L. (1974). Play therapy with institutionalized mentally retarded children. *American Journal of Mental Deficiency, 78,* 727–733.

Ney, P., Palvesky, E., & Markely, J. (1971). Relative effectiveness of operant conditioning and play therapy in childhood schizophrenia. *Journal of Autism and Childhood Schizophrenia, 1,* 337–349.

Nielsen, J. (1969). Klinefelter's syndrome and the XYY syndrome. *Acta Psychiatrica Scandinavica, 45,* Supplementum 209.

Nihara, K., Foster, R., Shellhaas, M., & Leland, H. (1975). *AAMD Adaptive Behavior Scale, 1975 Revision manual.* Washington, DC: American Association of Mental Deficiency.

Niswander, K.R., & Gordon, M. (1972). *The women and their pregnancies* (Vol. 1). Philadelphia: Saunders.

Nolen-Hoeksema, S., & Girgus, J.S. (1994). The emergence of gender differences in depression during adolescence. *Psychological Bulletin, 115,* 424–443.

Novello, A., Wise, P., Willoughby, A., & Pizzo, P. (1989). Final report of the United States Department of Health and Human Services Secretary's work group on pediatric human immunodeficiency virus infection and disease: Content and implications. *Pediatrics, 84,* 547–555.

O'Brian, J. D., Halperin, J.M., Newcorn, J. H., Sharma, V., Wolf, L., & Morganstein, A. (1992). Psychometric differentiation of conduct disorder and attention deficit disorder with hyperactivity. *Journal of Developmental and Behavioral Pediatrics, 13,* 274–277.

O'Brien, F. (1981). Self-stimulatory behavior. In J.L. Matson & J.R. McCartney (Eds.), *Handbook of behavior modification with the mentally retarded* (pp. 117–150). New York: Plenum.

O'Connor, M.J., Sigman, M., & Brill, N. (1987). Disorganization of attachment in relation to maternal alcohol consumption. *Journal of Consulting and Clinical Psychology, 55,* 831–836.

Odom, S.L., & Karnes, M.B. (Eds.). (1988). *Early intervention for infants and children with handicaps.* Baltimore: Paul H. Brookes.

O'Donnell, C.R., Lydgate, T., & Fo, W.S.O. (1979). The buddy system: Review and follow-up. *Child Behavior Therapy, 1,* 161–169.

O'Leary, K.D., Kaufman, K.F., Kass, R.E., & Drabman, R.S. (1970). The effects of loud and soft reprimands on the behavior of disruptive students. *Exceptional Children, 37,* 145–155.

O'Leary, K.D., & O'Leary, S.G. (1977). *Classroom management: The successful use of behavior modification* (2nd ed.). Elmsford, NY: Pergamon.

O'Leary, S.G., & Dubey, D. (1979). Applications of self-control procedures by children: A review. *Journal of Applied Behavior Analysis, 12,* 449–465.

O'Leary, S.G., & Pelham, W.E. (1978). Behavior therapy with withdrawal of stimulant medication with hyperactive children. *Pediatrics, 61,* 211–217.

Ollendick, T.H., (1995). Cognitive behavioral treatment of panic disorder with agoraphobia in adolescence: A multiple baseline design analysis. *Behavior Therapy, 26,* 517–531.

Ollendick, T.H., & King, N.J. (1994). Fears and their level of interference in adolescents. *Behavior Research and Therapy, 32,* 635–638.

Ollendick, T.H., Mattis, S.G., & King, N.J. (1994). Panic in children and adolescents: A review. *Journal of Child Psychology and Psychiatry, 35,* 113–134.

Olton, D.S., & Noonberg, A.R. (1980). *Biofeedback: Clinical applications in behavioral medicine.* Englewood Cliffs, NJ: Prentice-Hall.

Oro, A.S., & Dixon, S.D. (1987). Perinatal cocaine and methamphetamine exposure: Maternal and neonatal correlates. *Journal of Pediatrics, 111,* 571–578.

Orvaschel, H., Walsh-Allis, G., & Ye, W. (1988). Psychopathology in children of parents with recurrent depression. *Journal of Abnormal Child Psychology, 16,* 17–28.

Osterling, J., & Dawson, G. (1994). Early recognition of children with autism: A study of first birthday home videotapes. *Journal of Autism and Developmental Disorders, 24,* 247–257.

Padgett, D., Mumford, E., Hynes, M., & Carter, R. (1988). Meta-analysis of the effects of educational and psychosocial interventions on management of diabetes mellitus. *Journal of Clinical Epidemiology, 441,* 1007–1030.

Parker, J.G., & Asher, S.R. (1987). Peer relations and later personal adjustment: Are low-accepted children at risk? *Psychological Bulletin, 102,* 357–389.

Patterson, G.R. (1971). *Families: Application of social learning to family life.* Champaign, IL: Research Press.

Patterson, G.R. (1976). The aggressive child: Victim and architect of a coercive system. In E.J. Mash, L.A. Hamerlynck, & L.C. Handy (Eds.), *Behavior modification and families.* New York: Brunner/Mazel.

Patterson, G.R., DeBarsyshe, B.D., & Ramsey, E. (1989). A developmental perspective on antisocial behavior. *American Psychologist, 44,* 329–335.

Patterson, G. R., Reid, J. B., & Dishion, T. J. (1992). *Antisocial boys.* Eugene, OR: Castalia.

Patterson, G.R., Reid, J.B., Jones, R.R., & Conger, R.E. (1975). *A social learning approach to family intervention.* Eugene, OR: Castalia.

Patterson, G.R., & Stouthamer-Loeber, M. (1984). The correlation of family management practices and delinquency. *Child Development, 55,* 1299–1307.

Payne, J.S., & Patton, J.R. (1981). *Mental retardation.* Columbus, OH: Charles E. Merrill.

Pedreira, F.A., Guandolo, V.L., Feroli, E.J., Melba, G.W., & Weiss, I.P. (1985). Involuntary smoking and incidence of respiratory illness during the first year of life. *Pediatrics*, 75, 594–597.

Peine, M. (Ed.). (1984). *Contemporary approaches in stuttering therapy*. Boston: Little, Brown.

Peters, R. De V., & McMahon (1996). *Preventing childhood disorders, substance abuse, and delinquency*. Thousand Oaks, CA: Sage.

Peterson, A.L., & Azrin, N.H. (1992). An evaluation of behavioral treatments for Tourette syndrome. *Behavior Research and Therapy*, 30, 167–174.

Peterson, A.L., Campise, R.L., & Azrin, N.H. (1994). Behavioral and pharmacological treatments for tic and habit disorders: A review. *Journal of Developmental and Behavioral Pediatrics*, 15, 430–441.

Peterson, L., Zink, M., & Farmer, J. (1992). Prevention of disorders in children. In C.E. Walker & M.C. Roberts (Eds.), *Handbook of clinical child psychology*. New York: Wiley.

Pfeffer, C.R., Normandin, L., & Kakuma, T. (1994). Suicidal children grow up: Suicidal behavior and psychiatric disorders among relatives. *Journal of the American Academy of Child and Adolescent Psychiatry*, 33, 1087–1097.

Phares, V., & Compas, B.E. (1992). The role of fathers in child and adolescent psychopathology. *Psychological Bulletin*, 111, 387–412.

Phillips, E.L. (1968). Achievement Place: Token reinforcement procedures in a home-style rehabilitation setting for "pre-delinquent" boys. *Journal of Applied Behavior Analysis*, 1, 213–223.

Piacentini, J., Shaffer, D., Fisher, P., Schwab-Stone, M., Davies, M., & Gioia, P. (1993). The Diagnostic Interview Schedule for Children-Revised Version (DISC-R): III. Concurrent criterion validity. *Journal of the American Academy of Child and Adolescent Psychiatry*, 32, 658–656.

Plienis, A.J., Hansen, D.J., Ford, F., & Smith, S. (1987). Behavioral small group training to improve the social skills of emotionally-disordered adolescents. *Behavior Therapy*, 18, 17–32.

Plomin, R. (1989). Environment and genes: Determinants of behavior. *American Psychologist*, 44, 105–11.

Plomin, R. (1994a). Genetic research and identification of environmental influences. *Journal of Child Psychology & Psychiatry & Allied Disciplines*, 35, 817–834.

Plomin, R. (1994b). *Genetics and experience: The interplay between nature and nurture*. Newbury Park, CA: Sage.

Plomin, R., DeFries, J.C., & McClearn, G.E. (1990). *Behavioral genetics: A primer*. San Francisco: W.H. Freeman.

Plomin, R., & Rowe, D.C. (1977). A twin study of temperament in young children. *Journal of Psychology*, 97, 107–113.

Pollack, M., & Woerner, M.G. (1966). Pre- and perinatal complications and "childhood schizophrenia": A comparison of five controlled studies. *Journal of Child Psychology and Psychiatry*, 7, 235–242.

Pollin, W. (1971). A possible genetic factor related to psychosis. *American Journal of Psychiatry*, 128, 311–317.

Pollin, W., Stabenau, J.R., Mosher, L., & Tupin, J. (1966). Life history differences in identical twins discordant for schizophrenia. *American Journal of Orthopsychiatry*, 36, 492–509.

Pollock, R.A., Rosenbaum, J.F., Marrs, A., Miller, B.S., & Bierderman, J. (1995). Anxiety disorders of childhood. *The Psychiatric Clinics of North America*, 18, 745–766.

Polusny, M.A., & Follette, V.M. (1995). Long-term correlates of child sexual abuse: Theory and review of the empirical literature. *Applied and Preventive Psychology*, 4, 143–166.

Pope, A.W., McHale, S.M., & Craighead, W.E. (1988). *Self-esteem enhancement with children and adolescents*. Elmsford, NY: Pergamon.

Powell, J., & Rockinson, R. (1978). On the inability of interval time sampling to reflect frequency of occurrence data. *Journal of Applied Behavior Analysis*, 11, 531–532.

Powers, P., & Erickson, M.T. (1986). Body image in women and its relation to self-image and body satisfaction. *Journal of Obesity and Weight Regulation*, 5, 37–50.

Powers, P.S., & Fernandez, R.C. (Eds.). (1984). *Current treatment of anorexia nervosa and bulimia*. Basel: Karger.

Premack, D. (1965). Reinforcement theory. In D. Levine (Ed.), *Nebraska symposium on motivation* (pp. 123–180). Lincoln: University of Nebraska Press.

Prior, M. (1987). Biological and neuropsychological approaches to childhood autism. *British Journal of Psychiatry*, 150, 8–17.

Proctor, E.K., Vosler, N.R., & Murty, S. (1992). Child demographics and DSM diagnosis: A multiaxis study. *Child Psychiatry and Human Development*, 22, 165–183.

Puig-Antich, J., & Chambers, W. (1978). *The schedule for affective disorders and schizophrenia for school-aged children (Kiddie-SADS)*. New York: New York State Psychiatric Institute.

Puig-Antich, J., Goetz, D., Davies, M., Kaplan, T., et al. (1989). A controlled family history study of prepubertal major depressive disorder. *Archives of General Psychiatry*, 46, 406–418.

Quay, H.C. (1964). Dimensions of personality in delinquent boys as inferred from the factor analysis of case history data. *Child Development*, 35, 479–484.

Quay, H.C. (Ed.). (1987). *Handbook of juvenile delinquency*. New York: Wiley.

Rainer, J.D. (1979). Heredity and character disorders. *American Journal of Psychotherapy*, 33, 6–16.

Rainwater, N., Sweet, A.A., Elliot, L., Bowers, M. et al. (1988). Systematic desensitization in the treatment of needle phobias for children with diabetes. *Child and Family Therapy*, 10, 19–31.

Ramey, C.T., & Campbell, F.A. (1984). Preventive education for high-risk children: Cognitive consequences of the Carolina Abecedarian Project. *American Journal of Mental Deficiency, 88,* 515–523.

Rank, B. (1955). Intensive study and treatment of preschool children who show marked personality deviations, or "atypical development" and their parents. In G. Caplan (Ed.), *Emotional problems of early childhood* (pp. 491–501). New York: Basic Books.

Rank, O. (1952). *The trauma of birth.* New York: Brunner.

Rasmussen, S.A., & Eisen, J.L. (1990). Epidemiology of obsessive compulsive disorder. *Journal of Clinical Psychiatry, 51,* 3–10.

Reardon, S. M., & Naglieri, J. A. (1992). PASS cognitive processing characteristics of normal and ADHD males. *Journal of School Psychology, 30,* 151–163.

Redd, W.H., Jacobsen, P.B., Die-Trill, M., & Dermatis, H. (1987). Cognitive/ attentional distraction in the control of conditioned nausea in pediatric cancer patients receiving chemotherapy. *Journal of Consulting and Clinical Psychology, 55,* 391–395.

Reich, W., Herjanic, B., Welner, Z., & Gandhy, P.R. (1982). Development of a structured psychiatric interview for children: Agreement of diagnosis comparing child and parent interviews. *Journal of Abnormal Child Psychology, 10,* 325–336.

Reineke, M.A., Dattilio, F.M., & Freeman, A. (Eds.). (1996). *Cognitive therapy with children and adolescents.* New York: Guilford.

Reitan, R.M., & Davison, L.A. (1974). *Clinical neuropsychology: Current status and applications.* Washington, DC: V.H. Winston.

Reitan, R.M., & Wolfson, D. (1985). *The Halstead-Reitan Neuropsychological Test Battery.* Tucson, AZ: Neuropsychology Press.

Repp, A.C., & Brulle, A.R. (1981). Reducing aggressive behavior of mentally retarded persons. In J.L. Matson & J.R. McCartney (Eds.), *Handbook of behavior modification with the mentally retarded* (pp. 177–210). New York: Plenum.

Repp, A.C., & Singh, N.N. (Eds.) (1990). *Perspectives on the use of nonaversive and aversive interventions for persons with developmental disabilities.* Sycamore, IL: Sycamore Publishing Company.

Rey, J. M. (1993). Oppositional defiant disorder. *American Journal of Psychiatry, 150,* 1769–1778.

Reynolds, C.R., & Kamphaus, R.W. (1992). Behavior Assessment System for Children (BASC). Circle Pines, MN: American Guidance Services,

Reynolds, C.R., & Richmond, B.O. (1978). What I think and feel: A revised measure of children's manifest anxiety. *Journal of Abnormal Child Psychology, 6,* 271–280.

Rice, M.L. (1989). Children's language acquisition. *American Psychologist, 44,* 149–156.

Richman, G. S., Hagopian, L. P., Harrison, K., Birk, D., Ormerod, A., Brierley-Bowers, P., & Mann, L. (1994). Assessing parental response patterns in the treatment of noncompliance in children. *Child and Family Therapy, 16,* 29–40.

Richters, M.M., & Volkmar, F.R. (1994). Reactive attachment disorder of infancy or early childhood. *Journal of the American Academy of Child and Adolescent Psychiatry, 33*(3), 328–332.

Rickel, A.U., & Allen, L. (1987). *Preventing maladjustment from infancy through adolescence.* Newbury Park, CA: Sage.

Ricks, D.F., & Berry, J.C. (1970). Family and symptom patterns that precede schizophrenia. In M. Roff & D.F. Ricks (Eds.), *Life history research in psychopathology* (pp. 31–50). Minneapolis: University of Minnesota Press.

Rimland, B. (1964). *Infantile autism.* New York: Appleton-Century-Crofts.

Risley, T.R. (1968). The effects and side effects of punishing the autistic behaviors of a deviant child. *Journal of Applied Behavior Analysis, 1,* 21–34.

Ritvo, E., Brothers, A.M., Freeman, B.J., & Pingree, C. (1988). Eleven possibly autistic parents. Letter to the Editor. *Journal of Autism and Developmental Disorders, 18,* 139–143.

Rivers, D., & Smith, T.E.C. (1988). Traditional eligibility criteria for identifying students as specific learning disabled. *Journal of Learning Disabilities, 21,* 642–644.

Roberts, M.C. (Ed.). (1995). *Handbook of pediatric psychology* (2nd ed.). New York: Guilford.

Roberts, M.C., Carlson, C.I., Erickson, M.T., Fredman, R.M., LaGreca, A.M., Lemanek, K.L., Russ, S.W., Schroeder, C.S., Vargas, L.A., & Wohlford, P.F. (1996). A model for training psychologists to provide services for children and adolescents. Unpublished manuscript.

Roberts, M.C., Erickson, M.T., & Tuma, J.M. (1985). Addressing the needs: Guidelines for training psychologists to work with children, youth, and families. *Journal of Clinical Child Psychology, 14,* 70–79.

Robins, P.M. (1992). A comparison of behavioral and attentional functioning in children diagnosed as hyperactive or learning disabled. *Journal of Abnormal Child Psychology, 20,* 65–82.

Robinson, A., Bender, B., Borelli, J., Puck, M., & Salenblatt, J. (1983). Sex chromosomal anomalies: Prospective studies in children. *Behavior Genetics, 13,* 321–329.

Robson, W.L. & Leung, A.K. (1994). Side effects and complications of treatment with desmopressin for enuresis. *Journal of the National Medical Association, 86,* 775–778.

Roche, A.F., Lipman, R.S., Overall, J.E., & Hung, W. (1979). The effects of stimulant medication on the growth of hyperkinetic children. *Pediatrics, 63,* 847–850.

Rohn, F.J., Doherty, L.B., Waisbren, S.E., & Bailey, I.V. (1987). New England maternal PKU project: Prospective study of untreated and treated pregnancies and their outcomes. *Journal of Pediatrics, 110,* 391–398.

Roosa, M.W., Fitzgerald, H.E., & Carlson, N.A. (1982). Teenage parenting and child development: A literature review. *Infant Mental Health Journal, 3,* 4–18.

Rorschach, H. (1942). *Psychodiagnostics: A diagnostic test based on perception* (4th ed.). New York: Grune & Stratton.

Rosen, L., et al. (1988). Effects of sugar (sucrose) on children's behavior. *Journal of Consulting and Clinical Psychology, 56,* 583–589.

Rosenbaum, J.F., Biederman, J., Hirshfield, D.R., Bolduc, E.A., Faraone, V., & Kagan, J. (1991). Further evidence of an association between behavioral inhibition and anxiety disorders: Results from a family study of children from a nonclinical sample. *Journal of Psychiatric Research, 25,* 49–65.

Rosenblith, J.F. (1961). The modified Graham behavior test for neonates: Test-retest reliability, normative data and hypotheses for future work. *Biology of the Neonate, 3,* 174–192.

Rosenblith, J.F. (1975). Prognostic value of neonatal behavior tests. In B.Z. Friedlander, G.M. Sterritt, & G.E. Kirk (Eds.), *Exceptional infant: Assessment and intervention* (Vol. 3, pp. 157–172). New York: Brunner/Mazel.

Rosenthal, D. (1972). Three adoption studies of heredity in the schizophrenic disorders. *International Journal of Mental Health, 1,* 63–75.

Rosenthal, D., Wender, P.H., Kety, S.S., Welner, J., & Schulsinger, F. (1971). The adopted-away offspring of schizophrenics. *American Journal of Psychiatry, 128,* 307–311.

Ross, D.M., & Ross, S.A. (1974). *Pacemaker primary curriculum.* Belmont, CA: Fearon Publishers.

Roundtree, G. A., Grenier, C. E., & Hoffman, U. L. (1993). Parental assessment of behavioral change after children's participation in a delinquency prevention program. *Journal of Offender Rehabilitation, 19,* 113–130.

Rourke, B.P. (1978). Neuropsychological research in reading retardation: A review. In A.L. Benton & D. Pearl (Eds.), *Dyslexia* (pp. 140–171). New York: Oxford University Press.

Rourke, B.P. (1988). Socioemotional disturbances of learning disabled children. *Journal of Consulting and Clinical Psychology, 56,* 801–810.

Rourke, B.P. (Ed.). (1995). *Symptoms of nonverbal learning disabilities: Neurodevelopmental manifestations.* New York: Guilford Press.

Rourke, B.P., Fiske, J., & Strang, J. (1986). *Neuropsychological assessment of children: Treatment oriented approach.* New York: Guilford.

Rourke, B.P., Young, G.C., & Leenaars, A.A. (1989). A childhood learning disability that predisposes those afflicted to adolescent and adult depression and suicide risk. *Journal of Learning Disabilities, 22,* 169–175.

Rousey, A.B., Blacker, J.B., & Hanneman, R.A. (1990). Predictors of out-of-home placement of children with severe handicaps: A cross-sectional analysis. *American Journal on Mental Retardation, 94,* 522–531.

Routh, D.K. (Ed.). (1988). *Handbook of pediatric psychology.* New York: Guilford.

Routh, D.K., & Schroeder, C.S. (1976). Standardized playroom measures as indices of hyperactivity. *Journal of Abnormal Child Psychology, 4,* 199–207.

Rowe, D.C. (1983). Biomedical genetic models of self-reported delinquent behavior: A twin study. *Behavior Genetics, 13,* 473–489.

Rowitz, L. (Ed.). (1992). *Mental retardation in the year 2000.* New York: Springer-Verlag.

Rubinstein, E.A. (1978). Television and the young viewer. *American Scientist, 66,* 685–693.

Rubinstein, M., Yeager, C. A., Goodstein, C., & Lewis, D. O. (1993). Sexually assaultive male juveniles: A follow-up. *American Journal of Psychiatry, 150,* 262–265.

Rushton, H.G. (1989). Nocturnal enuresis: Epidemiology, evaluation, and currently available treatment options. *Journal of Pediatrics, 114,* 691–696.

Russo, M. F., Loeber, R., Lahey, B. B., & Keenan, K. (1994). Oppositional defiant and conduct disorders: Validation of the DSM-III-R and an alternative diagnostic option. *Journal of Clinical Child Psychology, 23,* 56–68.

Rutter, M., & Bartak, L. (1971). Causes of infantile autism: Some considerations from recent research. *Journal of Autism and Childhood Schizophrenia, 1,* 20–32.

Rutter, M., & Bartak, L. (1973). Special education treatment of autistic children: A comparative study. II. Follow-up findings and implications for services. *Journal of Child Psychology and Psychiatry, 14,* 241–270.

Rutter, M., Bartak, L., & Newman, S. (1971). Autism: A central disorder of cognition and language. In M. Rutter (Ed.), *Infantile autism: Concepts, characteristics and treatment.* London: Churchill-Livingstone.

Rutter, M., & Casaer, P. (Eds.). (1991). *Biological risk factors for psychosocial disorders.* Cambridge, UK: Cambridge University Press.

Sable, P. (1994). Separation anxiety, attachment, and agoraphobia. *Clinical Social Worker Journal, 22,* 369–383.

Sanders, M., Rebgetz, M., Morrison, M., Bor, W., Gordon, A., Dadds, M., & Shepherd, R. (1989). Cognitive-behavioral treatment of recurrent nonspecific abdominal pain in children: An analysis of generalization, maintenance, and side effects. *Journal of Consulting and Clinical Psychology, 57,* 294–300.

Sanders, M.R., & Dadds, M.R. (1993). *Behavioral family intervention.* Needham, MA: Allyn and Bacon.

Sandoval, J., Lambert, N.M., & Sassone, D. (1980). The identification and labeling of hyperactivity in children: An interactive model. In C.K. Whalen & B. Henker (Eds.), *Hyperactive children: The social ecology of identification and treatment.* New York: Academic Press.

Satir, V. (1964). *Conjoint family therapy: A guide to theory and technique.* Palo Alto, CA: Science & Behavior Books.

Satir, V.M., & Baldwin, M. (1983). *Satir step by step: A guide to creating change in families*. Palo Alto, CA: Science and Behavior Books.

Satir, V., Stachowiak, J., Taschman, H.A., Tiffany, D.W., Cohen, J.I., Robinson, A.M., & Ogburn, K.C. (1975). *Helping families to change*. New York: Aronson.

Sattler, J.M. (1988). *Assessment of children* (3rd ed.). San Diego: Author.

Sattler, J.M. (1992). *Assessment of children* (Revised and Updated 3rd ed.). San Diego: Author.

Scarr, S. (1981). *Race, social class, and individual differences in IQ: New studies of old issues*. Hillsdale, NJ: Lawrence Erlbaum.

Scarr-Salapatek, S. (1971). Race, social class, and I.Q. *Science, 14*, 1285–1295.

Schachar, R., Rutter, M., & Smith, A. (1981). The characteristics of situationally and pervasively hyperactive children: Implications for syndrome definition. *Journal of Child Psychology and Psychiatry, 22*, 375–392.

Schaeffer, M., Hatcher, R.P., & Barglow, P.D. (1980). Prematurity and infant stimulation: A review of research. *Child Psychiatry and Human Development, 10*, 199–212.

Schafer, L.C., Glasgow, R.E., & McCaul, K.D. (1982). Increasing the adherence of diabetic adolescents. *Journal of Behavioral Medicine, 5*, 353–362.

Scharfman, M.A. (1978). Psychoanalytic treatment. In B.B. Wolman, J. Egan, & A.O. Ross (Eds.), *Handbook of treatment of mental disorders in childhood and adolescence* (pp. 47–69). Englewood Cliffs, NJ: Prentice-Hall.

Schiffer, M. (1984). *Children's group therapy*. New York: Free Press.

Schinke, S. P., Botvin, G. J., & Orlandi, M. A. (1991). *Substance abuse in children and adolescents*. Beverly Hills, CA: Sage.

Schlundt, D.G. & Johnson, W.G. (1990). *Eating disorders: Assessment and treatment*. Needham Heights, MA: Allyn & Bacon.

Schmauk, F.J. (1970). Punishment, arousal, and avoidance learning in sociopaths. *Journal of Abnormal Psychology, 76*, 325–335.

Schneider, M.L., & Coe, C.L. (1993). Repeated social stress during pregnancy impairs neuromotor development of the primate infant. *Journal of Developmental and Behavioral Pediatrics, 14*, 81–87.

Schneider, S.G., & Asarnow, R.F. (1987). A comparison of cognitive/neuropsychological impairments of nonretarded autistic and schizophrenic children. *Journal of Abnormal Child Psychology, 15*, 29–46.

Schopler, E., & Mesibov, G.B. (Eds.). (1983). *Autism in adolescents and adults*. New York: Plenum.

Schopler, E., & Mesibov, G.B. (Eds.). (1988). *Diagnosis and assessment in autism*. New York: Plenum.

Schopler, E., & Mesibov, G. (Eds.) (1995). *Learning and cognition in autism*. New York: Plenum.

Schreibman, L. (1988). *Autism*. Newbury Park, CA: Sage.

Schroeder, S. (Ed.). (1987). *Toxic substances and mental retardation*. Washington, DC: American Association on Mental Retardation.

Schroeder, S.R. (1991). Self-injury and stereotypy. In J.L. Matson & J.A. Mulick (Eds.), *Handbook of mental retardation* (2nd ed.). New York: Pergamon Press.

Schroeder, S.R., & Schroeder, C.S. (1989). The role of the AAMR in the aversives controversy. *Mental Retardation, 27*, iii-v.

Schroeder, S.R., Schroeder, C.S., Rojahn, J., & Mulick, J.A. (1981). Self-injurious behavior. In J.L. Matson & J.R. McCartney (Eds.), *Handbook of behavior modification with the mentally retarded* (pp. 61–115). New York: Plenum.

Schwab-Stone, M. (1995). Discussion of: Do children aged 9 through 11 years understand the DISC Version 2.24 question? *Journal of the American Academy of Child and Adolescent Psychiatry, 34*, 954–956.

Schwab-Stone, M., Fisher, P., Piacentini, J., Shaffer, D., Davies, M., & Briggs, M. (1993). The Diagnostic Interview Schedule for Children: Revised Version (DISC-R): II. Test-retest reliability. *Journal of the American Academy of Child and Adolescent Psychiatry, 32*, 651–657.

Scurletis, T.D., Headrick-Haynes, M., Turnbull, C.D., & Fallon, R. (1976). Comprehensive developmental health services: A concept and a plan. In T.D. Tjossem (Ed.), *Intervention strategies for high risk infants and young children*. Baltimore: University Park Press.

Sears, R.R., & Wise, G.M. (1950). Relation of cup feeding in infancy to thumbsucking and the oral drive. *American Journal of Orthopsychiatry, 20*, 123–138.

Secord, G.J., Erickson, M.T., & Bush, J.P. (1988). Neuropsychological sequelae of otitis media in children and adolescents with learning disabilities. *Journal of Pediatric Psychology, 13*, 531–542.

Seligman, M.E.P. (1975). *Helplessness: On depression, development, and death*. San Francisco: Freeman.

Selz, M. (1981). Halstead-Reitan Neuropsychological Test Battery for Children. In G.W. Hynd & J.E. Obrzut (Eds.), *Neuropsychological assessment and the school-age child: Issues and procedures*. New York: Grune & Stratton.

Selz, M., & Reitan, R.M. (1979). Rules for neuropsychological diagnosis: Classification of brain function in older children. *Journal of Consulting and Clinical Psychology, 47*, 258–264.

Sever, J.L. (1970). Infectious agents and fetal disease. In H.A. Waisman & G.R. Kerr (Eds.), *Fetal growth and development*. New York: McGraw-Hill.

Shadish, W.R., Montgomery, L.M., Wilson, P., Wilson, M., Bright, I., & Okwumabua, T. (1993). Effects of family and marital psychotherapies: A meta-analysis. *Journal of Consulting and Clinical Psychology, 61*, 992–1002.

Shaffer, D., Philips, I., & Enzer, N.B. (Eds.). (1989). *Prevention of mental disorders, alcohol, and other drug use in children and adolesents*. OSAP Prevention

Monograph-2 (DHHS Publication No. ADM 89–1646). Washington, DC: U.S. Government Printing Office.

Shaffer, D., Schwab-Stone, M., Fisher, P., Cohen, P., Piacentini, J., Davies, M., Conners, C.K., & Regier, D. (1993). The Diagnostic Interview Schedule for Children-Revised Version (DISC-R): I. Preparation, field testing, interrater reliability, and acceptability. *Journal of the American Academy of Child and Adolescent Psychiatry, 32,* 643–650.

Shapiro, R. (1988). Family therapy. In H.H. Goldman (Ed.), *Review of General Psychiatry* (2nd ed., pp. 549–557). Norwalk, CT: Appleton & Lange.

Shaw, D. S., & Bell, R. Q. (1993). Developmental theories of parental contributors to antisocial behavior. *Journal of Abnormal Child Psychology, 21,* 493–518.

Shaw, D. S., Keenan, K., & Vondra, J. I. (1994). Developmental precursors of externalizing behavior: Ages 1 to 3. *Developmental Psychology, 30,* 355–364.

Shaywitz, B.A., Cohen, D.J., & Bowers, M.B. (1977). CSF monoamine metabolites in children with minimal brain dysfunction: Evidence for alteration of brain dopamine. *Journal of Pediatrics, 90,* 67–71.

Sheeber, L.B., & Johnson, J.H. (1994). Evaluation of a temperament-focused, parent-training program. *Journal of Clinical Child Psychology, 23,* 249–259.

Sheldon, S., Spire, J.P., & Levy, H.B. (1992). *Pediatric sleep medicine.* Philadelphia: W.B. Saunders.

Shoemaker, O.S., Erickson, M.T., & Finch, A.J. (1986). Depression and anger in third grade boys: A multimethod assessment approach. *Journal of Clinical Child Psychology, 15,* 290–296.

Shoemaker, O.S., Saylor, C.F., & Erickson, M.T. (1991). Concurrent validity of the Minnesota Child Development Inventory with high-risk infants. Unpublished manuscript.

Shore, M.F., Massimo, J.L., Kisielewski, B.A., & Moran, J.K. (1966). Object relations changes resulting from successful psychotherapy with adolescent delinquents and their relationship to academic performance. *Journal of the American Academy of Child Psychiatry, 5,* 93–104.

Short, A.B., & Schopler, E. (1988). Factors relating to age of onset in autism. *Journal of Autism and Developmental Disorders, 18,* 207–216.

Siegel, B., Pliner, C., Eschler, J., & Elliott, G.R. (1988). How children with autism are diagnosed: Difficulties in identification of children with multiple developmental delays. *Developmental and Behavioral Pediatrics, 9,* 199–204.

Siegel, J.M. (1984). Anger and cardiovascular risk in adolescents. *Health Psychology, 3,* 293–313.

Silberg, J.L., Erickson, M.T., Eaves, L.J., & Hewitt, J.K. (1994). The contribution of genetic and environmental factors to maternal ratings of behavioral and emotional problems in children and adolescents. *Journal of Consulting and Clinical Psychology, 62,* No. 3, 510–521.

Silberg, J.L., Erickson, M.T., Meyers, J.M., Eaves, L.J., Rutter, M.L., & Hewitt, J.K. (1994). The application of structural equation modeling to maternal ratings of twins' behavioral and emotional problems. *Journal of Consulting and Clinical Psychology, 62,* 510–521.

Silva, P.A., Williams, S., & McGee, R. (1987). A longitudinal study of children with developmental language delay at age three: Later intelligence, reading and behavior problems. *Developmental Medicine and Child Neurology, 29,* 630–640.

Silverman, W.K. (1991). Diagnostic reliability of anxiety disorders in children using structured interviews. *Journal of Anxiety Disorders, 5,* 105–124.

Silverman, W.K., Cerny, J.A., & Nelles, W.B. (1988). The familial influence in anxiety disorders. In B.B. Lahey & A.E. Kazdin (Eds.), *Advances in clinical child psychology* (Vol. 11, pp. 223–248). New York: Plenum.

Silverman, W.K., Fleisig, E., Rabin, B., & Peterson, R.A. (1991). The Child Anxiety Sensitivity Index. *Journal of Clinical Child Psychology, 20,* 162–168.

Silverman, W.K., & Kearney, C.A. (1992). Listening to our clinical partners: Informing researchers about children's fears and phobias. *Journal of Behavior Therapy and Experimental Psychiatry, 23,* 71–76.

Silverman, W.K., & Nelles, W.B. (1988). The anxiety disorders interview schedule for children. *Journal of the American Academy of Child and Adolescent Psychiatry, 27,* 772–778.

Silverman, W. K., & Ollendick, T.H. (Eds.). (1997). *Developmental issues in clinical treatment of children.* Needham, MA: Allyn & Bacon.

Silverman, W.K., & Rabian, B. (1993). Simple phobias. *Child and Adolescent Psychiatric Clinics of North America, 2,* 603–622.

Siperstein, G.N., & Bak, J.J. (1989). Social relationships of adolescents with moderate mental retardation. *Mental Retardation, 27,* 5–10.

Slavson, S.R. (1943). *An introduction to group therapy.* New York: The Commonwealth Fund.

Slavson, S.R., & Schiffer, M. (1975). *Group psychotherapies for children.* New York: International Universities Press.

Sleator, E.K., Ullmann, R.K., & von Neumann, A. (1982). How do hyperactive children feel about taking stimulants and will they tell the doctor? *Clinical Pediatrics, 21,* 474–479.

Sloop, E.Q. (1977). Urinary disorders. In R.B. Williams & W.D. Gentry (Eds.), *Behavioral approaches to medical treatment.* Cambridge, MA: Ballinger.

Slosson, R.L. (1983). *Slosson Intelligence Test (SIT) and Oral Reading Test (SORT) for children and adults.* East Aurora, NY: Slosson Educational Publications.

Smith, C.A. (1947). Effects of maternal undernutrition upon the newborn infant in Holland (1944–45). *Journal of Pediatrics, 30,* 229–243.

Smith, I., Beasley, M.G., Wolff, O.H., & Ades, A.E. (1988). Behavior disturbance in 8–year-old children with early treated phenylketonuria. *Journal of Pediatrics, 112,* 403–408.

Smith, S., Kimberling, W., Pennington, B., & Lubs, H. (1982). Specific reading disability: Identification of an inherited form through linkage analysis. *Science, 219,* 1345–1347.

Smolak, L., Levine, M.P., & Striegel-Moore, R. (Eds.). (1966). *The developmental psychopathology of eating disorders: Implications for research, prevention, and treatment.* Hove, England: Lawrence Erlbaum Associations, Inc.

Soderstrom, C.A., Trifillis, A.L., Shankar, B.S., & Clark, W.E. (1988). Marijuana and alcohol use among 1023 trauma patients, a prospective study. *Archives of Surgery, 123,* 733–737.

Sommers-Flanagan, J., & Sommers-Flanagan, R. (1996). Efficacy of antidepressant medication with depressed youth: What psychologists should know. *Professional Psychology: Research and Practice, 27,* 145–153.

Sontag, L.W., & Wallace, R.F. (1935). The effect of cigarette smoking during pregnancy upon the fetal heart rate. *American Journal of Obstetrics and Gynecology, 29,* 77–83.

Sparrow, S., Balla, D., & Cicchetti, D. (1984). *Vineland Adaptive Behavior Scales.* Circle Pines, MN: American Guidance Services.

Spearman, C. (1904). "General intelligence" objectivity determined and measured. *American Journal of Psychology, 15,* 201–293.

Spielberger, C.D. (1973). *Manual for the State—Trait Anxiety Inventory for Children.* Palo Alto, CA: Consulting Psychologists Press.

Spinetta, J.J. (1980). Disease related communication: How to tell. In J. Kellerman (Ed.), *Psychological aspects of childhood cancer* (pp. 257–269). Springfield, IL: Thomas.

Spitz, H.H. (1994). Fragile X syndrome is not the second leading cause of MR. *Mental Retardation, 32,* 156.

Spitz, R.A. (1945). Hospitalism: An inquiry into the genesis of psychiatric conditions in early childhood. *Psychoanalytic Study of the Child, 1,* 53–64.

Spitz, R.A. (1946). Anaclitic depression. *Psychoanalytic Study of the Child, 2,* 313–342.

Spivak, G., & Shure, M.B. (1974). *Social adjustment of young children.* San Francisco: Jossey-Bass.

Sprich-Buckminster, S., Biederman, J., Milberger, S., Faraone, S.V., & Lehman, B.K. (1993). Are perinatal complications relevant to the manifestation of ADD? Issues of comorbidity and familiality. *Journal of the American Academy of Child and Adolescent Psychiatry, 32,* 1032–1037.

Steffenburg, S., Gillberg, C., Hellgren, L., & Anderson, L. (1989). A twin study of autism in Denmark, Finland, Iceland, Norway, and Sweden. *Journal of Child Psychology and Psychiatry, 30,* 405–416.

Stein, P.A., & Hoover, J.H. (1989). Manifest anxiety in children with learning disabilities. *Journal of Learning Disabilities, 22,* 66, 71.

Stein, Z., Susser, M., Saenger, G., & Marolla, F. (1972). Nutrition and mental performance. *Science, 178,* 708–713.

Steinhausen, H.C., Williams, J., & Spohr, H.L. (1994). Long-term psychopathological and cognitive outcomes of children with fetal alcohol syndrome. *Journal of the American Academy of Child and Adolescent Psychiatry, 32,* 990–994.

Steinhausen, H.C., Williams, J., & Spohr, H.L. (1994). Correlates of psychopathology and intelligence in children with fetal alcohol syndrome. *Journal of Child Psychology & Psychiatry & Allied Disciplines, 35,* 323–331.

Steissguth, A. (1997). *Fetal alcohol syndrome.* Baltimore, MD: Brookes.

Stevens-Long, J., & Lovaas, O.I. (1974). Research and treatment with autistic children in a program of behavior therapy. In A. Davids (Ed.), *Child personality and psychopathology* (Vol. 1, pp. 169–203). New York: Wiley.

Stevenson, J., & Graham, P. (1988). Behavioral deviance in 13–year-old twins: An item analysis. *Journal of the American Academy of Child and Adolescent Psychiatry, 27,* 791–797.

Stewart, M., Pills, F., Craig, W., & Dieruf, W. (1966). The hyperactive child syndrome. *American Journal of Orthopsychiatry, 36,* 861–867.

Stipek, D., & McCroskey, J. (1989). Investing in children: Government and workplace policies for parents. *American Psychologist, 44,* 416–423.

Stoch, M.B., Smythe, P., Moodie, A.D., & Bradshaw, D. (1982). Psychosocial outcome and CT findings after gross undernourishment during infancy: A 20–year developmental study. *Developmental Medicine and Child Neurology, 24,* 419–436.

Stoneman, Z., Brody, G.H., Davis, C.H., & Crapps, J.M. (1988). Childcare responsibilities, peer relations, and sibling conflict: Older siblings of mentally retarded children. *American Journal on Mental Retardation, 93,* 174–183.

Stores, G. (1992). Types of childhood epilepsy misdiagnosed as psychiatric disorder. *European Child and Adolescent Psychiatry, 1,* 222–226.

Stott, D.H. (1973). Follow-up study from birth effects of prenatal stresses. *Developmental Medicine and Child Neurology, 15,* 770–787.

Strayhorn, J.M. (1988). *The competent child: An approach to psychotherapy and preventive mental health.* New York: Guilford.

Sudhalter, V., Cohen, I.L., Silverman, W., & Wolf-Schein, E.G. (1990). Conversational analyses of males with Fragile X, Down syndrome, and autism: Comparison of the emergence of deviant language. *American Journal on Mental Retardation, 94,* 431–441.

Sugar, M. (1984). Infants of adolescent mothers: Research perspective. In M. Sugar (Ed.), *Adolescent parenthood* (pp. 101–118). Jamaica, NY: Spectrum.

Sullivan, H.S. (1956). *Clinical studies in psychiatry.* New York: Norton.

Swedo, S.E., Rapoport, J.L., Leonard, H., Lenane, M., & Cheslow, D. (1989). Obsessive compulsive disorder in children and adolescents. *Archives of General Psychiatry, 46,* 335–341.

Taft, J. (1933). *The dynamics of therapy in a controlled relationship.* New York: Macmillan.

Tannock, R., Schachar, R.J., Carr, R.P., & Logan, G.D. (1989). Dose-response effects of methylphenidate on academic performance and overt behavior in hyperactive children. *Pediatrics, 84,* 648–657.

Task Force on Pediatric AIDS, American Psychological Association (1989). Pediatric AIDS and human immunodeficiency virus infection. *American Psychologist, 44,* 258–264.

Taylor, R.L. (1990). The Larry P. decision a decade later: Problems and future directions: *Mental Retardation, 28,* iii-vi.

Teicher, M.H. & Baldessarini, R.J. (1987). Developmental pharmacodynamics. In C. Popper (Ed.), *Psychiatricacosciences of children and adolescents* (pp. 47–80). Washington, DC: American Psychiatric Press.

Telzrow, C.F. (1987). Management of academic and educational problems in head injury. *Journal of Learning Disabilities, 20,* 536–545.

Teplin, S.W., Howard, J.A., & O'Connor, M.J. (1981). Self-concept of young children with cerebral palsy. *Developmental Medicine and Child Neurology, 23,* 730–738.

Teuber, H. (1970). Mental retardation after early trauma to the brain. In C.R. Angle & E.A. Bering (Eds.), *Physical trauma as an etiological agent in mental retardation* (pp. 7–28). Washington, DC: U.S. Government Printing Office.

Thatcher, R.W., Lester, M.L., McAlaster, R., Horst, R., & Ignatius, S.W. (1983). Intelligence and lead toxins in rural children. *Journal of Learning Disabilities, 16,* 355–359.

Thomas, A., & Chess, S. (1977). *Temperament and development.* New York: Brunner/Mazel.

Thomas, A., Chess, S., & Birch, H.G. (1968). *Temperament and behavior disorders in children.* New York: New York University Press.

Thompson, R.J., Gil, K., Keith, B.R., Gustafson, K., George, L., & Kinney, T. (1994). Psychological adjustment of children with sickle cell disease: Stability and change over a 10 month period. *Journal of Consulting and Clinical Psychology, 62,* 856–860.

Thompson, R.J., Goldstein, R.F., Oehler, J.M., Gustafson, K.E., Catlett, A.T., & Brazy, J.E. (1994). Developmental outcome of very low birth weight infants as a function of biological risk and psychosocial risk. *Journal of Developmental and Behavioral Pediatrics, 15,* 232–238.

Thompson, S., & Rey, J.M. (1995). Functional enuresis: Is desmopressin the answer? *Journal of the American Academy of Child and Adolescent Psychiatry, 34,* 266–271.

Thompson, W.R. (1957). Influence of prenatal maternal anxiety on emotionality in young rats. *Science, 125,* 698–699.

Thorndike, R.L., Hagen, E.P., & Sattler, J.M. (1986a). *Guide for administering and scoring the Stanford-Binet Intelligence Scale: Fourth edition.* Chicago: Riverside Publishing.

Thorndike, R.L., Hagen, E.P., & Sattler, J.M. (1986b). *Technical manual, Stanford-Binet Intelligence Scale: Fourth edition.* Chicago: Riverside Publishing.

Thurston, D., Graham, F.K., Ernhart, C.B., Eichman, F.L., & Craft, M. (1960). Neurologic status of three-year-old children originally studied at birth. *Neurology, 10,* 680–690.

Thurstone, L.L. (1938). *Primary mental abilities.* Chicago: University of Chicago Press.

Tijo, J., & Levan, A. (1956). The chromosome number of man. *Hereditas, 42,* 1.

Tolan, P., Guerra, N., & Kendall, P. (1995). A developmental-ecological perspective on antisocial behavior in children and adolescents: Toward a unified risk and intervention framework. *Journal of Consulting and Clinical Psychology, 63* (4), 579–584.

Tonge, B.J., Einfeld, S.L., Krupinski, J., Mackenzie, A., McLaughlin, M., Florio, T., & Nunn, R.J. (1996). The use of factor analysis for ascertaining patterns of psychopathology in children with intellectual disability. *Journal of Intellectual Disability Research, 40,* 198–207.

Torgersen, S. (1983). Genetic factors in anxiety disorders. *Archives of General Psychiatry, 40,* 1085–1089.

Torgersen, S. (1993). Relationship between adult and childhood anxiety disorders: genetic hypothesis. In C.G. Last (Ed.), *Anxiety across the lifespan.* New York: Springer.

Torgoresen, A.M. (1981). Genetic factors in temperamental individuality: A longitudinal study of same-sexed twins from two months to six years of age. *Journal of the American Academy of Child Psychiatry, 20,* 702–711.

Toro, J., Cerrva, M., Osejo, E., & Salmero, M. (1992). Obsessive-compulsive disorder in childhood and adolescence: A clinical study. *Journal of Child Psychology & Psychiatry, 33,* 1025–1037.

Touliatos, J., & Lindholm, B.W. (1981). Confluence of parents' and teachers' ratings of children's behavior problems. *Journal of Abnormal Child Psychology, 9,* 347–354.

Tremblay, R.E., LeBlanc, M., & Schwartzman, A.E. (1988). The predictive power of first-grade peer and teacher ratings of behavior: Sex differences in antisocial behavior and personality at adolescence. *Journal of Abnormal Child Psychology, 16,* 571–583.

Tronick, E., & Brazelton, T.B. (1975). Clinical uses of the Brazelton Neonatal Behavioral Assessment. In B.Z. Friedlander, G.M. Sterritt, & G.E. Kirk (Eds.), *Exceptional infant: Assessment and intervention* (Vol. 3, pp. 137–156). New York: Brunner/Mazel.

Truax, C.B., & Mitchell, K.M. (1971). Research on certain therapist interpersonal skills in relation to process and outcome. In A.E. Bergin & S.L. Garfield (Eds.), *Handbook of psychotherapy and behavior change* (pp. 299–344). New York: Wiley.

Tryon, R.C. (1940). Genetic differences in maze-learning in rats. In G.M. Whipple (Ed.), *Intelligence: Its nature and nurture, National Society for the Severely Physically Handicapped.* Baltimore: University Park Press.

Turner, S.M., Beidel, D.C., & Townsely, R.M. (1992). Behavioral treatment of social phobia. In S.M. Turner, K.S. Calhoun, & H.E. Adams (Eds.), *Handbook of clinical behavior therapy* (pp. 12–37). New York: Wiley.

U.S. Department of Education (1990). *To assure the free appropriate public education of all handicapped children: Eleventh annual report to Congress on the implementation of The Education of the Handicapped Act.* Washington, DC: U.S. Department of Education.

Vance, L.K., Bahr, C.M., Huberty, T.J., & Ewer-Jones, B. (1988). An analysis of variables that affect special education placement decisions. *Journal of Learning Disabilities, 21,* 444–447.

Vanderheiden, G., & Grilley, K. (Eds.). (1975). *Nonvocal communication techniques and aids for the severely physically handicapped.* Baltimore: University Park Press.

Van Riper, C. (1972). *Speech correction: Principles and methods.* Englewood Cliffs, NJ: Prentice-Hall.

Van Wagenen, R.K., Meyerson, L., Kerr, N.J., & Mahoney, K. (1969). Field trials of a new procedure for toilet training. *Journal of Experimental Child Psychology, 8,* 147–159.

Varley, C.K., & Trupin, R.W. (1982). Double-blind administration for methylphenidate to mentally retarded children with attention deficit disorder: A preliminary study. *American Journal of Mental Deficiency, 86,* 560–566.

Varni, J.W. (1981). Behavioral medicine in hemophilia and arthritic pain management: Two case studies. *Archives of Physical Medicine and Rehabilitation, 62,* 183–187.

Varni, J.W. (1983). *Clinical behavioral pediatrics.* Elmsford, NY: Pergamon.

Varni, J.W., Blount, R., Waldron, S., & Smith, A. (1995). Management of pain and distress. In M.C. Roberts (Ed.), *Handbook of pediatric psychology* (2nd ed.) (pp. 105–123). New York: Guilford Press.

Velez, C. N., Johnston, J., & Cohen, P. (1989). A longitudinal analysis of selected risk factors for child psychopathology. *Journal of the American Academy of Child and Adolescent Psychiatry, 28,* 861–864.

Vellutino, F.R., Steger, B.M., Meyer, S.C., Harding, C.J., & Niles, J.A. (1979). Has the perceptual deficit hypothesis led us astray? *Journal of Learning Disabilities, 10,* 375–385.

Vig, S., & Jedrysek, E. (1996). Application of the 1992 AAMR definition: Issues for preschool children. *Mental Retardation, 40,* 1989–207.

Vinnick, L., Fleiss, K., LaPadula, M., & Gonzales, M. (1996). Multimodal treatment of children with conduct disorder: psychosocial therapy manuals (unpublished manuscript).

Vitaro, F., & Tremblay, R. E. (1994). Impact of a prevention program on aggressive children's friendships and social adjustment. *Journal of Abnormal Child Psychology, 22,* 457–475.

Vohr, B.R., Coll, C.G., & Oh, W. (1988). Language development of low birthweight infants at two years. *Developmental Medicine and Child Neurology, 30,* 608–615.

Voller, R.D., & Strong, W.B. (1981). Pediatric aspects of atherosclerosis. *American Heart Journal, 101,* 815–836.

Voors, A.W., Webber, L.S., & Berenson, G.S. (1978). Epidemiology of essential hypertension in youth: Implications for clinical practice. *Pediatric Clinics of North America, 25,* 15–27.

Vuchinich, S., Bank, L., & Patterson, G. R. (1995). Parenting, peers, and the stability of antisocial behavior in preadolescent boys. *Developmental Psychology, 28,* 510–521.

Wade, J., & Kass, C.E. (1987). Component deficit and academic remediation of learning disabilities. *Journal of Learning Disabilities, 20,* 441–447.

Wahler, R.G. (1976). Deviant child behavior within the family: Developmental speculations and behavior change strategies. In H. Leitenberg (Ed.), *Handbook of behavior modification and behavior therapy.* Englewood Cliffs, NJ: Prentice-Hall.

Wahler, R. G., Cartor, P. G., Fleischman, J., & Lambert, W. (1993). The impact of synthesis teaching and parent training with mothers of conduct-disordered children. *Journal of Abnormal Child Psychology, 21,* 425–440.

Wahler, R.G., House, A.E., & Stembaugh, E.E. (1976). *Ecological assessment of child problem behavior.* Elmsford, NY: Pergamon.

Waldrop, M.F., Bell, R.Q., McLaughlin, B., & Halverson, C.F. (1978). Newborn minor physical abnormalities predict short attention span, peer aggression, and impulsivity at age 3. *Science, 199,* 563–565.

Walker, C.E. (1978). Toilet training, enuresis, and encopresis. In P. Magrab (Ed.), *Psychological management of pediatric problems* (Vol. 1, pp. 129–189). Baltimore: University Park Press.

Walker, C.E. (1995). Elimination disorders: Enuresis and encopresis. In M. C. Roberts (Ed.), *Handbook of pediatric psychology* (2nd ed.) (pp. 537–557). New York: Guilford Press.

Walker, C.E., Bonner, B.L., & Kaufman, K.L. (1988). *The physically and sexually abused child: Evaluation and treatment.* Elmsford, NY: Pergamon.

Walker, E., & Emory, E. (1983). Infants at risk for psychopathology: Offspring of schizophrenic parents. *Child Development, 54,* 1269–1285.

Walker, E.F. (Ed.). (1991). *Schizophrenia: A life course developmental perspective.* New York: Academic Press.

Walker, G.R. (1989). Gentle teaching: A behavior analytic perspective. *Behavior Therapist, 12,* 225–226.

Wallerstein, R.S. (1988). Psychoanalysis and long term dynamic psychotherapy. In H.H. Goldman (Ed.), *Review of general psychiatry* (pp. 506–523). Connecticut: Appleton-Lange.

Walter, H.J., Hoffman, A., Vaughn, R.D., & Wynder, E.L. (1988). Modification of risk factors for coronary heart disease. *New England Journal of Medicine, 318,* 1093–1099.

Walther, F.J., & Ramaekers, L.H.J. (1982). Language development at the age of 3 years of infants malnourished *in utero. Neuropediatrics, 13,* 77–81.

Waters, D.B., & Lawrence, E.C. (1993). *Competence, courage, and change: An approach to family therapy.* New York: W.W. Norton.

Watkins, J.M., Asarnow, R.F., & Tanguay, P.E. (1988). Symptom development in childhood onset schizophrenia. *Journal of Child Psychology and Psychiatry, 29,* 865–878.

Watson, J.B., & Rayner, R. (1920). Conditioned emotional reactions. *Journal of Experimental Psychology, 3,* 1–14.

Watson, J.D., & Crick, F.H.C. (1953). A structure for deoxyribose nucleic acid. *Nature, 171,* 737–738.

Watson, L.S., & Uzzell, R. (1981). Teaching self-help skills to the mentally retarded. In J.L. Matson & J.R. McCartney (Eds.), *Handbook of behavior modification with the mentally retarded* (pp. 151–175). New York: Plenum.

Webb, C.E., & Siegenthaler, B.M. (1957). Comparison of aural stimulation methods for teaching speech sounds. *Journal of Speech and Hearing Disorders, 22,* 264–270.

Weber, W.W. (1967). Survival and sex ratio in trisomy 17–18. *American Journal of Human Genetics, 19,* 369–377.

Webster-Stratton, C. (1994). Advancing videotape parent training: A comparison study. *Journal of Consulting and Clinical Psychology, 62,* 583–593.

Webster-Stratton, C., & Herbert, M. (1993). What really happens in parent training? *Behavior Modification, 17,* 407–456.

Wechsler, D. (1949). *Manual for the Wechsler Intelligence Scale for Children.* New York: Psychological Corporation.

Wechsler, D. (1974). *Manual for the Wechsler Intelligence Scale for Children—Revised.* New York: Psychological Corporation.

Wechsler, D. (1975). Intelligence defined and undefined: A relativistic appraisal. *American Psychologist, 30,* 135–139.

Wechsler, D. (1989). *Wechsler Preschool and Primary Scale of Intelligence—Revised.* San Antonio, TX: The Psychological Corporation.

Wechsler, D. (1981). *Manual for the Wechsler Adult Intelligence Scale—Revised.* New York: Psychological Corporation.

Wechsler, D. (1991). *Wechsler Intelligence Scale for Children.* (3rd ed.). San Antonio, TX: The Psychological Corporation.

Wehman, P., & Bates, P. (1978). Education curriculum for severely and profoundly handicapped persons: A review. *Rehabilitation Literature, 39,* 2–14.

Weinberg, R.A. (1989). Intelligence and IQ: Landmark issues and great debates. *American Psychologist, 44,* 98–104.

Weintraub, M., & Wolf, B.M. (1983). Effects of stress and social supports on mother-child interactions in single and two-parent families. *Child Development, 54,* 1297–1311.

Weiss, G., & Hechtman, L. (1979). The hyperactive child syndrome. *Science, 205,* 1348–1354.

Weisz, J.R., Weiss, B., Alicke, M.D., & Klotz, M.L. (1987). Effectiveness of psychotherapy with children and adolescents: A meta-analysis for clinicians. *Journal of Consulting and Clinical Psychology, 55,* 542–549.

Wells, K.C., & Forehand, R. (1981). Child behavior problems in the home. In S.M. Turner, K. Calhoun, & H.E. Adams (Eds.), *Handbook of clinical behavior therapy.* New York: Wiley.

Wenar, C., Ruttenberg, B.A., Dratman, M.L., & Wolf, E.G. (1967). Changing autistic behavior: The effectiveness of three milieus. *Archives of General Psychiatry, 17,* 26–35.

Werker, J.F. (1989). Becoming a native listener. *American Scientist, 77,* 54–59.

Werry, J.S., Methven, R.J., Fitzpatrick, J., & Dixon, H. (1983). The interrater reliability of DSM-III in children. *Journal of Abnormal Child Psychology, 11,* 341–354.

Werry, J.S., & Quay, H.C. (1969). Observing the classroom behavior of elementary school children. *Exceptional Children, 35,* 461–467.

West, M.O., & Prinz, R.J. (1987). Parental alcoholism and childhood psychopathology. *Psychological Bulletin, 102,* 204–218.

Wiener, G. (1962). Psychologic correlates of premature birth: A review. *Journal of Nervous and Mental Disease, 134,* 129–144.

Wiener, G., Rider, R.V., Oppel, W.C., Fischer, L.K., & Harper, P.A. (1965). Correlates of low birth weight: Psychological states at six to seven years of age. *Pediatrics, 35,* 434–444.

Wierson, M., Forehand, R. L., & Frame, C. L. (1992). Epidemiology and treatment of mental health problems in juvenile delinquents. *Advances in Behavior Research and Therapy, 14,* 93–120.

Wierzbicki, M. (1987). A parent form of the Children's Depression Inventory: Reliability and validity in nonclinical populations. *Journal of Clinical Psychology, 43,* 390–397.

Wilcox, J.A., & Nasrallah, H.A. (1987). Childhood head trauma and psychosis. *Psychiatry Research, 21,* 303–306.

Williams, C.D. (1959). The elimination of tantrum behavior by extinction procedures. *Journal of Abnormal and Social Psychology, 59,* 269.

Williford, S.L., & Bernstein, S.A. (1996). Intranasal desmopressin-induced hyponatremia. *Pharmacotherapy, 16,* 66–74.

Willis, D.J., & Walker, C.E. (1989). Etiology. In T.H. Ollendick & M. Hersen (Eds.), *Handbook of child psychopathology* (2nd ed.). New York: Plenum.

Willoughby, J.C., & Glidden, L.M. (1995). Fathers helping out: Shared child care and marital satisfaction of parents of children with disabilities. *American Journal on Mental Retardation, 99,* 399–406.

Wills, K., Holmbeck, G., Dillon, K., & McLone, D. (1990). Intelligence and achievement in children with myelomeningocele. *Journal of Pediatric Psychology, 15,* 161–176.

Wilson, G.T. (1986). Cognitive-behavioral and pharmacological therapies for bulimia. In K.D. Brownell & J.P. Foreyd (Eds.), *Handbook of eating disorders* (pp. 450–475). New York: Basic Books.

Wilson, J., Blacher, J., & Baker, B.L. (1989). Siblings of children with severe handicaps. *Mental Retardation, 27,* 167–173.

Wilson, R.S. (1983). The Louisville Twin Study: Developmental synchronies in behavior. *Child Development, 54,* 298–316.

Windle, W.F. (Ed.). (1958). *Neurological and psychological deficits of asphyxia neonatorium.* Springfield, IL: Thomas.

Winick, M. (Ed.). (1979). *Human nutrition: A comprehensive treatise (Volume 1: Pre- and postnatal development).* New York: Plenum.

Winick, M., & Rosso, P. (1973). Effects of malnutrition on brain development. *Biology of Brain Dysfunction, 1,* 301–317.

Wirt, R.D., Lachar, D., Klinedinst, J.K., & Seat, P.D. (1984). *Multidimensional description of child personality: A manual for the Personality Inventory for Children.* (1984 revision by D. Lachar). Los Angeles, CA: Western Psychological Services.

Witkin, H.A., Mednick, S.A., Schulsinger, F., & Bakkestrom, E. (1976). XYY and XXY men. Criminality and aggression. *Science, 193,* 547–555.

Wolfe, D.A. (1987). *Child abuse: Implications for child development and psychopathology.* Newbury Park, CA: Sage.

Wolking, W.D., Quast, W., & Lawton, J.J. (1966). MMPI profiles of parents of behaviorally disturbed children and parents from the general population. *Journal of Clinical Psychology, 22,* 39–48.

Wolraich, M.L., Siperstein, G.N., & O'Keefe, P. (1987). Pediatricians' perceptions of mentally retarded individuals. *Pediatrics, 80,* 643–649.

Wood, A., Kroll, L., Moore, A., & Harrington, R. (1995). Properties of the Mood and Feelings Questionnaire in adolescent psychiatric outpatients: A research note. *Journal of Child Psychology & Psychiatry & Allied Disciplines, 36,* 327–334.

Woodcock, R.W., & Mather, N. (1989). WJ-R Tests of Achievement: Examiner's manual. In R.W. Woodcock & M.B. Johnson, *Woodcock-Johnson Psycho-Educational Battery-Revised.* Allen, TX: DLM Teaching Resources.

Woolf, A., Rappaport, L., Reardon, P., & Ciborowski, J., et al. (1989). School functioning and disease severity in boys with hemophilia. *Developmental and Behavioral Pediatrics, 10,* 81–85.

Woolston, J.L. (1991). *Eating and growth disorders in infants and children.* Newbury Park, CA: Sage.

Woolston, J.L., & Forsyth, B. (1989). In B.B. Lahey & A.E. Kazdin (Eds.), *Advances in clinical child psychology* (Vol. 12, pp. 179–192). New York: Plenum.

World Health Organization. *Manual of the International Statistical Classification of Diseases, Injuries, and Causes of Death.* Geneva: World Health Organization.

Yarrow, L.J. (1964). Separation from parents during early childhood. In M.L. Hoffman & L.W. Hoffman (Eds.), *Review of child development research* (Vol. 1, pp. 89–136). New York: Russell Sage.

Yates, A.J. (1970). *Behavior therapy.* New York: Wiley.

Yeudall, L.T., Fromm-Auch, D., & Davies, P. (1982). Neuropsychological impairment of persistent delinquency. *Journal of Nervous and Mental Disease, 170,* 257–265.

Yoshikawa, H. (1994). Prevention as cumulative protection: Effects of early family support and education on chronic delinquency and its risks. *Psychological Bulletin, 115,* 28–54.

Zeanah, C.H., & Emde, R.N. (1994). Attachment disorders in infancy and childhood. In M. Rutter, L. Hersov, & E. Taylor (Eds.), *Child and adolescent psychiatry* (3rd ed.). London: Blackwell.

Zeskind, P.S., & Ramey, C.T. (1981). Preventing intellectual and interactional sequelae of fetal malnutrition: A longitudinal, transactional, and synergistic approach to development. *Child Development, 52,* 213–218.

Ziegler, R., & Holden, L. (1988). Family therapy for learning disabled and attention-deficit disordered children. *American Journal of Orthopsychiatry, 58,* 196–210.

Zigler, E. (1973). The retarded child as a whole person. In D.K. Routh (Ed.), *The experimental psychology of mental retardation* (pp. 231–322). Chicago: Aldine.

Zigler, E., Taussig, C., & Black, K. (1992). Early interventions to minimize delinquency. *American Psychologist, 47,* 997–1006.

Zigler, E., & Trickett, P. K. (1978). IQ, social competence, and evaluation of early childhood intervention programs. *American Psychologist, 33,* 789–798.

Zuckerman, B.S., Amaro, H., & Beardslee, W. (1987). Mental health of adolescent mothers: The implications of depression and drug use. *Developmental and Behavioral Pediatrics, 8,* 111–116.

Zussman, J.U. (1978). Relationship of demographic factors to parental discipline techniques. *Developmental Psychology, 14,* 685–686.

Author Index

Abbey, H., 203
Abramovitz, A., 121
Achenbach, T., 25, 26, 51, 220, 247, 248
Adams, E.H., 239
Adams, G.R., 239
Addy, D.P., 287
Ades, A.E., 164
Aho, A.C., 293
Albano, A.M., 248, 257, 258
Albert, J., 192
Alexander, D., 145
Alford, G.S., 243
Alicke, M.D., 130
Allen, A.J., 259
Allen, C.M., 315
Allen, F.H., 105
Allen, L., 23
Aloia, G.F., 141
Alpert-Gillis, L.J., 318
Althaus, M., 225
Aman, M.G., 163
Amaro, H., 86
Amaya-Jackson, L., 254
Amylon, M., 297
Anastasi, A., 134
Anastopoulos, A.D., 195
Anderson, E.R., 84
Anderson, G., 2
Andrews, D.W., 243
Andrianopoulos, G.D., 271
Angold, A., 260
Apodaca, L., 297
Archer, R., 40
Arffa, S., 204
Armstrong, P.M., 158
Arnold, G.S., 77
Arthur, G., 214
Asarnow, J.R., 181, 261
Asarnow, R.F., 174, 175
Asher, S.R., 318

Axline, V.M., 162
Ayllon, T., 195, 196
Azrin, N.H., 117, 158, 159, 161, 277, 286

Babson, S.G., 148
Bachman, J.G., 236
Backman, J.E., 289
Baden, A.D., 226
Bader, F., 68
Badger, E., 312
Baer, D.M., 113, 158
Bahr, C.M., 200
Baker, B.L., 153, 222
Baker, L., 178
Baldwin, M., 124
Balla, D., 140
Bandura, A., 96, 113, 225
Bank, L., 226
Banks, S.R., 185
Barbarin, O.A., 293
Bard, B., 222
Barglow, P.D., 316
Barkley, R.A., 192, 194, 195
Barlow, D.H., 248, 253, 258
Barratt, M.S., 72
Barrett, C.L., 99
Barrett, D.E., 62
Barrett, P.M., 258
Bartak, L., 176, 177, 184
Bartke, A., 68
Barton, E.S., 158
Bashir, A.S., 214
Bates, P., 156
Battaglia, M., 253
Baum, J.D., 300
Bayley, N., 32, 33
Beard, C.M., 133
Beardslee, W., 86
Beasley, M.G., 164
Beck, A.T., 260, 262

353

Subject Index